Robert Harvey is a former member [of the] Foreign Affairs Committee, was assistant editor of *The Economist*, and foreign affairs leader writer for the *Daily Telegraph*. His books include, *Global Disorder, Cochrane: The Fighting Captain, Liberators: South America's Savage War of Freedom* and *A Few Bloody Noses: The American Revolutionary Wars*. He lives in Powys, Wales.

Praise for Robert Harvey:

Liberators: South America's Savage Wars of Freedom 1810–30 (2000)

'An exhilarating and wildly enjoyable ride from start to finish.'
                                  Simon Sebag Montifiore, *Sunday Times*

'It is hard to think of any comparable attempt to come to grips with the whole vast story, and in such vivid detail.'   *London Review of Books*

'A book to applaud and a style to remember.'
                                  John Lynch, *Sunday Times*

'Harvey is at his best vividly describing what must count as one of the most daring exploits in military history.'   Raymond Carr, *Spectator*

'A riveting story, with a wealth of topographical, military and personal details, and a significant analysis of Britain's equivocal policy towards the crumbling Spanish empire.'   *Literary Review*

'What a rollicking adventure story about the heroes of Latin American independence . . . a grand history, a very readable exciting adventure story about the deeds of great men. I know of no other like it.'   *History*

Cochrane: The Life and Exploits of a Fighting Captain (2000)

'To those who are drawn to the age and especially to aficionados of [Patrick] O'Brian's work, I would recommend this book.'   *TLS*

'An entertaining and compulsive read.'   *Sunday Telegraph*

'Wonderfully readable . . . it is Cochrane's exploits that gave birth to the fictional genre of Napoleonic sea adventures.'   *Independent*

'If you combined the collected adventures of Hornblower and Jack Aubrey, you'd still be hard pressed to find as many fictional achievements so bold, brilliant and thrilling as you do in the real life of Cochrane.' *Spectator*

Global Disorder: How to Avoid a Fourth World War (2003)

'Good insights into and analysis of the growing political and economic threats that are part of a new international landscape.' *Washington Post*

'There does not appear to be a country about which he lacks detailed knowledge . . . Impressively up-to-date.' *Sunday Times*

'Harvey's views deserve to be taken seriously.' *Independent*

'Essential reading for anyone who wants to understand the world we now inhabit.' *Tablet*

A Few Bloody Noses: The American Revolutionary War (2004)

'A clear bracing narrative with enough shrewd analysis to make the overall picture full and subtle.' Dennis Judd, *BBC History*

'There is not a dry bone in this book . . . His descriptions of toe-to-toe tactics as well as the strategic consequences of each significant fight are superb. Harvey wields his pen like a sabre, slashing with gusto at cant and received wisdom.' *Daily Telegraph*

'Immensely readable and daringly even-handed.' *Spectator*

'An excellent work of history and a ripping read.' *Scotsman*

'Fascinating.' *Financial Times*

American Shogun: MacArthur, Hirohito and the American Duel with Japan (2006)

'Magnificent. Harvey never writes less than well, and he commands his material as a samurai his sword . . . Authoritative and sweeping, this is history at its best.' *The Times*

THE
WAR
OF
WARS

THE EPIC STRUGGLE BETWEEN
BRITAIN AND FRANCE 1789–1815

ROBERT HARVEY

CONSTABLE • LONDON

Constable & Robinson Ltd
3 The Lanchesters
162 Fulham Palace Road
London W6 9ER
www.constablerobinson.com

First published in hardback by Constable,
an imprint of Constable & Robinson Ltd, 2006

This paperback edition published by Constable,
an imprint of Constable & Robinson Ltd, 2007

A copy of the British Library Cataloguing in
Publication Data is available from the British Library.

ISBN: 978-1-84529-635-3

Printed and bound in the EU

1 3 5 7 9 10 8 6 4 2

minority of deputies to the original Assembly, as early as 1789: he also fought for the right of excluded classes, such as the Jews, to the vote. Remarkably, he sought to extend political rights to the blacks in the West Indies. He argued that any government decree that used the word slave would only promote French dishonour. His concept of representative government was also advanced for the time: he espoused frequent direct elections, so that the General Will could prevail over the selfish individual wills of the members, public access to parliament, and publicity for the proceedings. He was also committed to economic equality in a way that none of his contemporaries were. He advocated the subordination of the executive power to the legislature.

All of these were extraordinarily advanced ideas for the time. However, he also believed in the absolute sovereignty of parliament, as advocated by the Jacobins, and apologized for popular violence: 'If some disturbances have taken place, they should be pardoned after so many centuries of servitude and misery.' Like Rousseau, Robespierre believed that most people were good by nature – but only in a democracy. 'The people are just and in general their government . . . only strikes the guilty. When despots make revolutions against the people, their revolutionary masters, [they] are no more than instruments of cruelty and oppression; but when the people take action against despotism and the aristocracy, revolutionary measures are no more than healthy measures and acts of universal benevolence.'

He took this further. Although he defended the institution of property, he argued that the rich had taken it too far: he even argued against the bourgeoisie – by which he meant the wealthy middle-class: 'To defeat the bourgeoisie, the people must be rallied.' He favoured equality of inheritance to break down the big estates and progressive taxation. Robespierre advocated free trade, but only up to a point – he feared it could degenerate into greed and speculation under the *ancien régime*.

Most controversially, he believed that in times of revolution, terror was needed to supplant virtue: he defined terror as the application of 'proper, severe and inflexible justice'. This he inflicted through setting up the revolutionary Tribunals of March 1793. 'People,' he declared, 'do not judge like judicial courts; they do not hand down sentences.

They throw lightning bolts. Revolution is the war of freedom against its enemies. Revolutionary government gives good citizens all natural protection; it gives only death to enemies of the people.'

Robespierre was remarkable for embracing, at least a century before such views became significant, the Communist concept of the party as the embodiment of the people and the Fascist commitment to pure nationalism. If many of his ideas were also those of constitutional democracy well in advance of its time, he was also the forerunner of totalitarianism. Napoleon was at first to be closely allied with the Robespierre faction, then reject it: but the debt he owed to its extraordinarily prescient ideology cannot be doubted, both on the popular dictatorial and the nationalist score, which was to be enshrined in his concept of emperorship. Napoleon was never a profound political thinker, and it is clear that he was hugely influenced by Robespierre's political philosophy. It is doubly ironic that the 'incorruptible's' final warning was against everything that Napoleon was later to personify.

He delivered an extraordinary address in which he proposed the worship of a Supreme Being and set aside a day in every ten to worship him, honouring a different virtue each time. Robespierre staged a procession, with himself leading, dressed in a purple robe, and the people following bearing fruit and vegetables, as though in a kind of pagan ritual. It was hard not to believe that he had become quite mad. The ceremony attracted ridicule among atheists and the condemnation of Catholics.

Robespierre now issued a law giving his underlings the power to arrest virtually anyone at will and sentence them to death for spreading false news, for showing delicacy in manner and even for speaking correctly. This passed only with huge dispute in the Assembly, many of whose own members feared being so arrested. When Robespierre proposed the arrest of one of the most vigorous enforcers of the Terror, as being a sympathizer of Danton, he found himself for the first time in a minority on the Committee of Public Safety.

Robespierre descended to the Assembly and denounced the two committees, as well as a host of other institutions. This proved too much even for the usually terrorized Assembly, which erupted in a

storm of criticism – each member fearing for his life. Only Robespierre's loyal brother, Augustin, and two supporters, Saint-Just and Couthon, spoke in his favour. He then appealed to the Jacobin clubs, which volunteered to move on the two committees and arrest their members.

On 25 July a crowd tried to rescue eighty people being taken to the guillotine, but they were prevented. Robespierre sought the same day to speak to the convention, but his right-hand man Saint-Just was interrupted by Tallien. When the pale and trembling Robespierre rose he was greeted with shouts of 'Down with the tyrant.' Tallien said he would kill Robespierre if necessary. When the latter tried to speak he was shouted down. His shrill voice screaming, 'parliament of assassins, for the last time I seek the privilege of speech', was the last heard of him before his voice gave out.

Robespierre and his handful of supporters were seized and marched to the prison of Paris, where the gaolers refused to accept him, such was their terror of him. He was led to the offices of the Committee of Public Safety. A group of his supporters managed to free him and tried to take him back to the Hôtel de Ville, where 2,000 loyalists and artillerymen were waiting to acclaim him.

The Convention, learning of his release, passed a decree outlawing him and his supporters and demanded that he be immediately executed. Fighting seemed about to break out on the streets of Paris. Cannon were brought up by Convention loyalists. Augustin Robespierre tried to kill himself by jumping from a window, but survived. Saint-Just and Couthon both tried unsuccessfully to kill themselves. Robespierre fired a gun which badly wounded his lower jaw. When the besiegers broke into the dreadful scene, they seized these wretched men and carried them straight to execution. The cloth holding Robespierre's shattered jaw together was torn off on the scaffold. He issued a shout of agony, and was promptly guillotined.

It was widely assumed that he had been executed so that others nearly as badly steeped in blood, such as Tallien and Barras, who had headed the assailants at the Hôtel de Ville, could seize power for themselves. But a general outcry against the Terror was taking place, and both felt under threat, as did others. Although a handful of

Robespierre's closest supporters were seized, both Tallien and Barras refused to undertake a new wave of Terror against their own enemies – which required considerable courage, as the two could have been swept away. A general amnesty was proclaimed.

Relatives of those guillotined – the Avengers – toured the streets wearing black collars and with their hair plaited and tied up as if in preparation for the guillotine, setting upon the Jacobin bands still daring to show themselves. The Jacobin Club held a session to try and spark off a new revolution, but the Avengers broke up the sitting. A handful of Robespierre's closest associates were guillotined, including Carier, the Butcher of Nantes, and Fouquier-Tinville, the implacable public prosecutor.

On 20 May 1795 the Jacobins staged one last insurrection, breaking into the Convention and killing a deputy and being dispersed at length. Two days of rioting followed. A detachment of rural guards was sent to clear up the suburb of Faubourg St Antoine and the mob there were forced to surrender their arms. Another group of hard-line Jacobins committed mass suicide rather than be sent to the gallows. The Jacobins left only their memory – egalitarianism, revolutionary terror, escalating mass purges – to inspire future generations of murderous revolutionaries, particularly Communists in Russia, China, Kampuchea, and elsewhere.

In one key sense the French Revolution was very different to the English and American Revolutions: offshore Britain and distant America did not threaten the peace and stability of Europe. Cromwell's few interventions into continental politics were not regarded as furnishing a serious danger of infecting the continent; in any event the monarchy was restored after a decade. The American Revolution, as we have seen, had a huge impact on France but not one – to their own cost – taken seriously by the royal family and court.

The French Revolution was something else: in order to save themselves, its leaders seized on the idea of national expansion against the hostile royal powers surrounding it and sought to export its revolutionary creed, threatening to spread the contagion across Europe. When the success of Dumouriez's *levée en masse* became apparent,

there seemed no limit to the possibilities of French domination of Europe. A new weapon, the mass popular army, was sure to defeat traditional aristocratic armies with their antiquated tactics and fighting seasons. From being an egalitarian revolution, it quickly became a nationalist one as well.

Chapter 7

THE BOY FROM AJACCIO

At the time of the tumultuous events in Paris and Versailles in 1789, an obscure twenty-year-old second lieutenant, Napoleone Buonaparte, was studying and writing essays in the tiny garrison town of Valence near the French coast close to his homeland of Corsica. The young man had ambitions to become a writer and was deeply studious. He read widely: *La Chaumière Indienne*, a pastoral idyll by Bernardin de St Pierre, Buffon's *Histoire Naturelle*, Plato's *Republic*, Montigny's *History of the Arabs* and Barrow's *New and Impartial History of England*, from which he made notes approving such parliamentarians as Simon de Montfort and Pym. For Charles I and James II he expressed contempt. He noted that:

> The principal advantage of the English Constitution consists in the fact that the national spirit is always in full vitality. For a long spell of years, the King can doubtless arrogate to himself more authority than he ought to have, may even use his great power to commit injustice, but the cries of the nation soon change to thunder, and sooner or later the King yields.

More bizarrely he observed from Buffon's volume:

> Some men are born with only one testicle, others have three; they are stronger and more vigorous. It is astonishing how much this part of the body contributes to a man's strength and courage. What a difference between a bull and an ox, a ram and a sheep, a cock and a capon!

He also began a history of his native Corsica and wrote a short story in English, based on Barrow about the Earl of Essex, murdered by Charles II and the Duke of York. This somewhat lurid tale, reminiscent of the Corsican vendettas he was familiar with, was balanced by an essay on happiness, in which he conceded to feeling most satisfied meditating on the origin of nature at night and the joys of having 'a wife and children, father and mother, brothers and sisters, a friend!'

Above these joys, however, is love of country, 'that love of beauty in all its energy, the pleasure of making a whole nation happy'. The true patriot ensures 'the happiness of a hundred families', in contrast to the vain patriot devoured by ambition 'with its pale complexion, wild eyes, hurried footsteps, jerky gestures and sardonic laugh' – an almost exact description of the author in his twenties. Perhaps the most significant essay of all was a ferocious defence of Rousseau's *Social Contract* in which he argued that Christianity was possibly harmful to men: for by 'making men look forward to a later life in the next world it made them too submissive to the evils of the present'. He particularly attacked Protestantism, which by allowing freedom of thought broke up the unity of society and caused schisms and civil wars. Instead it was government that held the key to happiness: it must 'lend assistance to the feeble against the strong, and by this means allow everyone to enjoy a sweet tranquillity, the rule of happiness'. Religion was of no importance, indeed possibly harmful.

Napoleone Buonaparte had been born twenty years before the French Revolution and baptized in the Church of the Assumption of the Blessed Virgin Mary on 15 August 1769 in the small port of Ajaccio in Corsica. He was incontestably of Italian blood on both sides. The Buonapartes came from Tuscany where one ancestor, Ugo Buonaparte, had been a merchant in the service of the Duke of Swabia in 1122. The name Buonaparte derived from the good party of imperial knights who fought for the unity of Italy against the Pope. Some 350 years later a member of the clan, Francesco Buonaparte, sailed to Corsica where his descendants established themselves as lawyers working for the local government.

On Napoleon's mother's side the Ramolinos were of higher origins: they were descended from the Counts of Collalto in Lombardy and her

father, in the family tradition, was an army officer who commanded the Ajaccio garrisons and became inspector-general of roads and bridges, probably because he had been instructed in civil engineering – although there were few enough of either in Corsica. He died early and when his daughter Letizia was only five years old his wife married a Swiss naval officer, Captain Franz Fesch, who served in the Genoese navy and had been disinherited by his father for converting to Catholicism – which may account for the young Napoleon's anti-Protestant bias. Letizia was no great beauty: she had wondrously wide eyes and dark-brown hair, but she was small – a touch over five foot – and had a long, somewhat stern face as well as a prominent pointed nose and a small mouth. The combination gave her a shrewish appearance. She was uneducated but extraordinarily devout, attending mass every day.

The two families, of Italian origin, regarded themselves as among the most patrician on the island. The Ramolinos, being of superior blood but poorer means, eventually settled upon the Buonapartes for their daughter. Carlo Buonaparte, the eighteen-year-old boy, was tall with fine eyes and a prominent nose, and a pursuer of women. Carlo had studied law at Pisa University but, becoming rich on the premature death of his father when he was fourteen, had returned to Corsica to take charge of the middling family estate, a large house, two fine vineyards and some arable and grazing land.

Carlo fell in love with a beautiful girl from the Forcioli family, but family pressure induced him to marry Letizia, who was just fourteen years old – not an unusual age for a girl to wed in those days. She brought a modest dowry of thirty-one acres, a mill and a bakery. It is possible that they were not married in church but through family agreement and their consent, despite opposition from some of the Ramolinos, fearing that Carlo was too low-born and unreliable; Carlo too seems to have had his doubts.

The teenagers, after their marriage, set up house in Carlo's home, where the ground floor was occupied by his mother and a wealthy invalid uncle, Luciano, Archdeacon of Ajaccio, and the top floor by tiresome cousins. It was a crowded household. However, they had an annual income of around £10,000 from their properties, a princely

sum in those days, and Carlo's employment generated more. Letizia had two servants and a wet nurse. In poverty-ridden Corsica, the Buonapartes were considered well off; in tiny Ajaccio they were one of the richest families. They were certainly regarded as aristocracy as far as the island was concerned, and of minor noble birth as far as Italy and France were concerned, although they would be viewed as little more than middling gentry in England.

Tragedy, as so often in those days, started early: Letizia had a son, named Napoleone, who immediately died in 1765; a daughter also died. Carlo, strong-willed and amorous, then left Corsica for Rome at the age of twenty where he set up home with an older, married woman. He lived in that turbulent and beautiful capital for two years where, it was later claimed, he became Corsican emissary to the Pope, pleading for independence; this seems highly unlikely.

After seducing a virgin he had to return to Corsica under a cloud and there his good looks secured him the post of secretary to the homosexual head of the Corsican independence movement, Pasquale Paoli. Paoli, a huge man with red hair and blue eyes, who wore an embossed green uniform, lived in Corte, a fortress in the interior. An overpowering personality who had served the King of Naples, he had taken up arms against Corsica's rulers, the Genoese, since 1729, as the leader of an independence movement for this rocky backwater with its 130,000 people and the two small towns of Bastia, with 5,000 people, and Ajaccio, with 4,000. He captured the mountainous interior and drove the Genoese into the ports. Paoli secured the support of the peasantry as he fought for common pastoral land in the lowlands and primitive smallholdings in the highlands. He became admired throughout Europe, with Rousseau and James Boswell as his admirers, the former seeing him as an embodiment of the General Will, the latter as an expression of the traditional Scottish highlander.

In 1756, Corsica had been abruptly ceded by decadent Genoa to the French King, Louis XV: the Genoese had effectively lost control of the island and the newly expansionist French coveted it as a strategic point just off their coast. There was a general uprising against them not just in the mountains but in the towns. Paoli led the uprising, and Buonaparte, a young man with a good fortune from one of the best families in

Ajaccio, was an extremely useful supporter. Meanwhile Buonaparte's wife had a son, Giuseppe (Joseph), the first to survive infancy. However, the French poured in troops and crushingly defeated the Corsicans on 8 May 1769 at the battle of Ponte Nuovo.

Carlo and Letizia, as prominent independence activists, had to flee into the mountains to join Paoli at Corte: she was heavily pregnant at the time. There Paoli had to accept the inevitable, surrendered and went into exile in England along with more than 300 of his supporters. Carlo chose to stay on the island. His return to Ajaccio along precipitous mountain paths, with the pregnant Letizia cradling the infant Joseph in her arms, was to be a memory for the rest of her life. She went into labour while at mass on the Feast of the Assumption at Ajaccio Cathedral. She was attended by her sister-in-law and the baby was born, big-headed but short-limbed and weak. He was named Napoleone after a much-loved great uncle who had died recently. It was an uncommon name deriving from a Greek saint who had died in Alexandria under the Emperor Diocletian.

The little Napoleone was what today would be called a 'handful'. His elder brother Giuseppe was serious and quiet; but the infant Napoleone fought him fiercely. He was nicknamed Rabulione – the 'meddler' – and went to school at the age of five. His language was Italian. It was a mixed school run by nuns: he held hands with a girl called Giacominetta and a little verse ran: *Napoleone di mezza calzetta fa l'amore a Giacominetta*: Napoleone with his half socks makes love to Giacominetta. Maybe the boy was scruffy and wore his socks around his ankles, but in Italy *mezza calzetta* is the most common sneer towards those of a non-aristocratic background. Napoleone was extraordinarily fierce as a boy and was often in trouble for fighting. Afterwards, at the age of seven, he went to a Jesuit school.

Letizia was an extremely fierce and demanding mother. She was obsessed with cleanliness, forced him to attend mass with slaps, and would beat him with a whip on the slightest pretext, such as stealing food, bad behaviour in church or, on one occasion, laughing at a crippled grandmother. Worse, she was obsessed with outward show: 'When you grow up, you'll be poor. But it's better to have a fine room for receiving friends, a fine suit of clothes and a fine horse, so that you

put up a brave show – even if you have to live off dry bread.' She would send her children to bed without supper sometimes so that they could learn 'to bear discomfort without showing it'. Yet she lavished money on keeping the house looking smart.

She would force Napoleone to spy on his father, who liked to play cards for money with his friends in the town cafés; the boy hated the task. She believed in Corsican traditions, which were violent and based on revenge. The society was alive with vendettas, and Corsicans grew their beards – *barbe di vendetta* – until a perceived injustice was avenged. Corsican poetry was based on anguish about death from vendettas; and death was a local obsession. It was foreshadowed in folklore by owls screeching and dogs howling, a drum beating or a light shining on a house all night.

Letizia's husband Carlo was not a prepossessing character. Having been Paoli's devoted supporter, with remarkable speed he turned himself into a lackey for the French. As a lawyer he was petty-minded and ruthless, serving his own interests, seeking ownership of an estate for which his claim was dubious and then suing Letizia's impoverished grandfather, aged eighty-four, for not delivering part of her dowry. He was appointed assessor of the Royal Jurisdiction of Ajaccio by the French ruler of Corsica, the Comte de Marbeuf.

Marbeuf was an old goat: he lived with a mistress, Madame de Varennes, known as the Cleopatra of Corsica, and when she died in 1776 he pursued the strong-willed Letizia, who by now had had her third son, Lucien. The following year he secured Carlo's appointment as a deputy for the nobility representing Corsica at Versailles, and the young man spent two years away while his patron seduced his wife.

Although Letizia's next child, her first daughter, Maria Anna Alisa, born in 1777, was Carlo's, the next child, Louis, was almost certainly Marbeuf's – physically resembling him and intemperate by nature. Carlo was probably aware of the relationship and acquiesced in it as the price for advancement – not that he was anyway faithful to Letizia. Marbeuf repaid Carlo for his compliance by securing a schooling for his two sons at Autun as a preliminary to Giuseppe's being sent to a seminary at Aix and Napoleone to the military academy at Brienne in

May 1779 – the boy having evinced an early fascination for playing with toy soldiers.

Arriving there the boy had his eyes opened to a far wider world than his limited and strict Corsican childhood: travelling across the prosperous flatlands to Aix and then up the Rhône and the Saône rivers, the nine-year-old was awestruck. The château of Brienne was at the foot of a hill, and had recently been converted from a monastic seminary to a military one. It held around fifty pupils still under the control of two priests.

Napoleone was locked into a cubicle six-foot square at ten o'clock at night, to be awoken at 6 a.m. Life was tough, but Napoleone was an exemplary student, excelling in mathematics and learning French, at which he was not so good: his pronunciation was always to be Italianate. He was studious, devoting himself to the classics and to reading. Napoleone, being a Corsican whose first language was Italian, and olive-skinned by comparison with the other children as well as poorer than most, and being on a scholarship, was immediately subjected to bullying and snobbery by the mainland children; but his sheer toughness saw him through.

Four credible stories are told about his school career. When he was made to kneel in a dunce's uniform to eat his dinner as punishment for some transgression, he threw a tantrum insisting that he would kneel 'only to God'. On another occasion when fireworks exploded next to the plot Napoleone considered his own garden and other children rushed across it in alarm, he brandished a hoe at them and forced them out. He also organized a snowfight which turned serious when the boys started to coat stones with snow. At the age of eleven, he was horrified when he heard a priest proclaim that Caesar and Cicero were in hell as pagans. He recoiled from the idea that 'the most virtuous men of antiquity would burn in eternal flames for not having practised a religion they knew nothing about'. The logic was faultless, and Napoleone was showing an early admiration for great men. His Christianity was now in doubt.

A year later he decided he wanted to become a sailor. The verdict from the inspector-general of scholars was largely favourable.

M. de Bonaparte (Napoleon), born 15 August 1769. Height 5′6″. Constitution: excellent health, docile expression, mild, straightforward, thoughtful. Conduct most satisfactory; has always been distinguished for his application in mathematics. He is fairly well acquainted with history and geography. He is weak in all accomplishments – drawing, dancing, music and the like. This boy would make an excellent sailor; deserves to be admitted to the school in Paris.

Napoleone's mother Letizia opposed his naval ambitions and secured his entry into the École Royale Militaire de Paris. It was a giant step for him, and he travelled by barge along with three schoolfellows under his headmaster, Father Berton. He was astonished by the great city. He gaped 'in all directions with all the expression to catch a pickpocket'. He bought a book, *Gil Blas*, about a boy who rises from a poor provincial background to become secretary to the prime minister.

At the école, a fine building opened only thirteen years earlier, he was astonished by the luxury – the blue uniform with red collar and silver braid, the white gloves, the gold-and-blue décor of the classrooms, the lavish curtains, the pewter jug and washbasin, the excellent food and choice of puddings. He wrote: 'We were magnificently fed and served, treated in every way like officers possessed of great wealth, certainly greater than that of most of our families and far above what many of us would enjoy later on.' The number of teaching staff outnumbered the 215 cadets, and there were also 150 servants. The routine was, however, much more militaristic than in his previous school, involving drill, shooting practice and military exercises, and imprisonment with or without water for even minor infringements, although academic subjects still featured prominently in the curriculum. In winter the youths would simulate an attack on a much-fortified town, Fort Timbrune.

Napoleone was by now adept at making friends and enemies. One who had come from Brienne, Pierre François Laugier de Bellecour, had already been upbraided by Napoleone for associating with the homosexual set there; he openly did so in Paris. Napoleone, who later confessed to homosexual feelings overcome with difficulty himself, was

so angry at his friend's behaviour that he once threw him to the floor. His instructor, Alexandre de Maxis, became another firm friend and would later describe his characteristic pose at school – head bowed, with his arms crossed, that would later become a trademark.

Soon after Napoleone entered the school, his father died of cancer at the spa of Montpellier, where he had gone to seek a cure. Napoleone affected indifference – his hero was Paoli whom his father had betrayed by espousing the French invaders – but this may have been no more than a display of the self-discipline in which he was being trained. A furious rejection of his father is often cited. When later Montpellier Municipal Council sought to erect a monument to his memory he declared: 'Forget it: let us not trouble the peace of the dead. Leave their ashes in peace. I also lost my grandfather, my great-grandfather, why is nothing done for them?' But this can equally be seen as a sensible rejection of sycophantic hero-worship, and may have had little to do with his true feelings.

Napoleone was now primarily concerned for his family because the bread-winner had been lost, and it would be years before he would earn a salary. He redoubled his efforts in the school of artillery, where he showed himself to be an outstanding mathematician. When tested by the Marquis de Laplane, one of the most brilliant astronomers of the age, he secured an unimpressive forty-second place in the artillery examination out of fifty-eight, but was one of the youngest cadets to pass. At the age of sixteen he became an army officer, second lieutenant in the artillery, because there was no room in the navy.

Chapter 8

ANGRY YOUNG OFFICER

Napoleon, by now adopting the French style of his name, was appointed to the La Fère Regiment near Valence, conveniently close to Corsica, where he became convinced, regarding his older brother Joseph as too weak-minded, that he had prime responsibility to look after his mother and siblings after his father's death. Sexually, he was curiously reticent for someone with rationalist doubts about Christianity: on the way to La Fère, he did not visit a brothel in Lyon as his fellow cadets did. He had already fended off the attempts of an older woman to seduce him. When on one occasion he did try to seduce two friendly young women, he was astonished to discover that they were lesbians.

There have been innumerable studies of Napoleon's personality: one of the more curious developments in modern historiography is that at the same time as a Marxist school has obsessed itself with the impersonal, primarily economic forces that shape history, a kind of sub-Freudian view has sprung up attaching all kinds of psychological motives to the men who, according to the previous school, have little real impact upon history. Napoleon was variously said to have developed a mother complex in his youth, to have detested his father, to be a repressed homosexual, and to be a deeply embittered dwarf. There was just enough truth in these allegations for the mud to have stuck.

In fact, three more significant points about Napoleon stand out as he embraced manhood. First, he was highly intelligent and a born mathematician; second, he was highly self-disciplined and regarded himself as the natural heir of his father after his death; and, third, he

laboured under a huge burden of personal injustice (a so-called inferiority complex, or, in British terms, a 'chip on his shoulder'). This last had little to do with his height. At five foot six inches, he was on the short side, but not strikingly so: most ordinary people were little taller, and an average for a well-fed Frenchman aristocrat of the time was five foot nine. His bitterness stemmed from more understandable sources: he came from the newest acquisition of the French empire and, in spite of his schooling in France, fiercely believed in the cause of Corsican independence. He had been despised throughout his school career on account of his Corsican nationality and olive skin, an insult felt all the more strongly because he regarded himself as a high aristocrat in a way only a provincial from a tiny sea-port can.

Among the French aristocrats' sons who were his fellow pupils he was almost beneath contempt. This he reciprocated, referring to aristocrats as 'imbeciles', 'asses' and 'the curse of the nation'. He considered himself high born, with adequate reason, and yet was not treated as part of them – an explosive combination. Tough, surly and from an island background where slights were met by a vendetta and even death, he had reason enough for harbouring resentment and deep ambition. Being able and having the luck to be educated at France's most prestigious military academy, he had the perfect means to prove himself: by becoming a leader in the very nation that had annexed his homeland: that would be a triumph of vendetta indeed.

However, none of this early background explains either his rise to power or later actions: there must have been hundreds of officers in the French army with similarly complex lives and motives. He had been promoted, partly through luck, partly through ability, so that he had the potential to reach the top of French society; he had no reason to feel ungrateful to the French.

With the death of his father, he was forced to take lodgings in a noisy first floor café, next door to a billiard room and send back most of his pay to his mother, who had now lost not just a husband but a patron, the randy Comte de Marbeuf, who had married an eighteen-year-old. Yet countless other young officers were in similar financial straits. There was not much that marked out Napoleon from his peers –

except his intelligence and overweening curiosity. He was not even especially ambitious at that stage: he wanted to become a writer.

He was certainly unhappy and depressed during these penurious times. He wrote miserably:

> Life is a burden to me because I feel no pleasure and because everything is affliction to me. It is a burden to me because the men with whom I have to live, and will probably always live, have ways as different from mine as the light of the moon from that of the sun. I cannot then pursue the only manner of living which could enable me to put up with existence, whence follows a disgust for everything.

Later the same pessimism surfaced in a letter to his hero, Paoli:

> As the nation was perishing I was born. Thirty thousand Frenchmen were vomited on to our shores, drowning the throne of liberty in waves of blood. Such was the odious sight which was the first to strike me. From my birth, my cradle was surrounded by the cries of the dying, the groans of the oppressed and tears of despair. You left our island and with you went all hope of happiness. Slavery was the price of our submission. Crushed by the triple yoke of the soldier, the law-maker and the tax inspector, our compatriots live despised.

This was remarkable as an expression of his open hatred for the French. He had acquired this when, after Marbeuf's death, Corsica was ruled by spendthrift bureaucrats who had cut back payments to his mother for agricultural improvements. During this period, he was given leave to visit his home, where he was shocked to find his mother virtually unaided, and he soon procured a servant for her, Severia, who remained with her for forty years. Joseph, who was now studying law in Pisa, returned and the two old playground antagonists got on famously. Napoleon travelled to Paris to lobby for a financial grant, which failed. But at the age of eighteen he slept with a girl for the first time in his life, a Breton prostitute.

He returned to his regiment, which was now stationed at Auxonne. There he had a very relaxed work regime, needing to attend parades

just once a week, and made up for it by reading and writing. He was a furious worker, rising at 4 am and going to bed at 10 p.m., which brought on physical exhaustion. He filled no fewer than thirty-six notebooks with his thoughts in just fifteen months. He contracted malaria. During his studies he read extensively about his own specialist subject, artillery: the main contemporary exponent of this was Jean de Beaumont du Teil, who urged a sudden massing of guns in battle, rather as Pierre Bouret, another tactician, urged separating army units to help them move at speed, then massing them before a battle. Both of these ideas were to feature hugely in Napoleon's military campaigns. Du Teil's brother, Jean-Pierre, was Napoleon's commanding officer and quickly spotted his abilities.

So the historic year of 1789 dawned in France, with the nineteen-year-old officer of promise in a provincial posting. His first awareness of tumultuous change came in April, when he was ordered to join a small force to put down a grain riot in Seurre, twenty miles away. The riot was quelled before he arrived, but not before du Teil's country house had been set on fire and mutinous soldiers had seized funds. Napoleon, with his strong sense of discipline, strongly disapproved of this, although he sympathized with the burgeoning Revolution. Napoleon's studies had led him to admire Jean-Jacques Rousseau, who argued that a 'social contract' was the sole means by which monarchy could justify itself.

Although clearly reform-minded, he was horrified when in July the local mob rose up and burned the tax register as well as the offices of a provincial official. The La Fère regiment caught the contagion and mutinied against du Teil, forcing officers to submit to indignities. Napoleon and other officers restored order, but he was appalled by the indiscipline and claimed later that he was ready to fire upon the mutineers if so ordered.

Soon afterwards, as the revolt got under way in earnest, he obtained leave again to return to Corsica. It seems almost certain this was the right moment to adopt the mantle of Paoli and launch a new war of independence for his country: he saw his future as the island's leader – not unreasonably, as Paoli was ageing and his father had originally been

one of his helpers. With the outbreak of the French Revolution, the island had embraced the cause of radical reform and Paoli had been invited back to the island.

At this stage Napoleon was still torn between loyalty to his own provincial people and the French oppressor which had nevertheless recognized his talents and promoted him. Shortly after his arrival a popular uprising had taken place in Bastia, the capital. Napoleon threw himself into the political fray on the island with vigour and on 17 July – shortly after the fall of the Bastille – he met his hero face to face: Paoli stooped and white-haired at sixty-six, but still a great bull of a man, arrived in Bastia. Napoleon, who had joined the Ajaccio Jacobin Club, became a firm supporter. The local governor complained bitterly that 'this young officer was educated at the École Militaire. His sister is at St-Cyr and his mother has received countless kindnesses from the government. This officer had much better be with his regiment since he spends all his time stirring up trouble.'

Under orders, he tried to return to the mainland, but appalling weather drove him back and it was not until the end of January 1791 that he reached the mainland with his twelve-year-old brother Louis. The boy, far from being impressed by Napoleon's spartan living quarters at Auxonne, hated them and begged to return to Corsica. Meanwhile Napoleon's radical views made him deeply unpopular with many of his royalist brother officers, who threatened at one stage to throw him into the Saône. He was promoted by du Teil to first lieutenant and sent to the Fourth Artillery Regiment at Valence. There he became a member of the Society of Friends of the Constitution, and in July he openly criticized the King's attempted flight to Belgium. He was in the forefront of the sale of confiscated clerical and noble property.

Along with other members of the nobility he had lost his privileges when the new constitution came into effect, but that had no effect on his enthusiastic support for the document. He took the oath to the constitution, although thirty-two officers in his regiment refused. Napoleon has often been accused of pure opportunism. Yet at this time he could not be certain of the outcome of the revolutionary struggle in Paris, and few officers shared his views: it was clear that a

combination of his own ideals and deep resentment against the aristocracy had turned him into a genuine supporter of the Revolution.

Still confining his ambitions to Corsica, he decided to return with Louis in October. Joseph was there, as was sixteen-year-old Lucien, who resented his small brother, Jerome, the spoilt afterthought of the family, and two of his three sisters, the lovely Pauline and the musical Caroline. He was also present for the death of his miserly uncle, Archdeacon Luciano, aged seventy-six, who had kept his considerable fortune in gold coins under the bed. This proved a godsend – Napoleon suddenly, from near poverty, became quite well off.

With money at last behind him, he plunged into the arcane and insular world of Corsican politics. To avoid having to return to France, he sought election to the local National Guard militia. As lieutenant-colonel of this, he became a power in the island. In April 1792 a pro-clerical group sought to hold mass in the dissolved convent of St Francis in Ajaccio and shot one of his soldiers. Napoleon wanted to seize the citadel commanding the town from the 400 regular soldiers there, but was refused. Napoleon had the might of the law behind him, but the commanding officer dug in his heels and at length emissaries from Paris told Napoleon to calm things down by withdrawing from the town. Napoleon had to travel back to Paris to clear his name in May 1792.

There an old school friend and he would aimlessly walk across the revolution-torn city, so different from the ordered place he had known in his time at school. On 20 June they followed a large crowd pouring out of the huge market of Les Halles, joining up with two more mobs heading for the royal palace of the Tuileries. It was the occasion when the King was forced to put on the red revolutionary hat and drink the health of the people. 'The King came out of it well,' commented Napoleon, 'but it is inevitable that this is unconstitutional and a very dangerous precedent.' Napoleon was by now thoroughly disenchanted with the ordinary people. He wrote to Lucien:

> Those at the top are poor creatures. It must be admitted, when you
> see things at first hand, that the people are not worth the trouble
> taken in winning their favour. You know the history of Ajaccio;

that of Paris is exactly the same; perhaps men are here even a little smaller, nastier, more slanderous and censorious.

On 10 August the scene repeated itself as tragedy. As a large mob gathered, singing 'The Marseillaise', the new anthem of the Revolution, the King appeared, but was booed and withdrew. His lawyer advised that he, the Queen and the royal princes should take refuge in the National Assembly. National guardsmen burst into the palace, scuffling with the 2,000 Swiss Guards stationed there. Fighting broke out, and the crowd brought up cannon to shoot into the palace. The King sent orders to the guards not to resist. The crowd swarmed in and massacred them and any remaining courtiers. Some 800 were killed, their bodies savagely mutilated, the guardsmen castrated. Napoleon, now promoted to captain, was appalled.

Before reaching the Carousel I had been met in the rue de Petits Champs by a group of hideous men bearing a head at the end of a pike. Seeing that I was presentably dressed and had the appearance of a gentleman, they approached me and asked me to shout 'Long live the Republic!' which you can easily imagine I did without difficulty . . . With the palace broken into, and the King there, in the heart of the Assembly, I ventured to go into the garden. The sight of the dead Swiss Guards gave me an idea of the meaning of death such as I have never had since, on any of my battlefields. Perhaps it was that the smallness of the area made the number of corpses appear larger, or perhaps it was because this was the first time I had undergone such an experience. I saw well-dressed women committing acts of the grossest indecency on the corpses of the Swiss Guards.

Napoleon decided to accompany his sister Marie Anne (who called herself Elisa) out of the Paris charnel house and back to Corsica. There he was in for a shock: Paoli, his hero, had turned against him. The patriot leader was much more conservative than the reformist young soldier.

At this stage Napoleon was virtually a complete failure: at the age of twenty-four he was a minor player in a small revolutionary sideshow,

his own native island of Corsica, about which few Frenchmen spared a thought. All of his grandiose plans had come to nothing: he was captain in an army that had ceased to exist or respected rank, a minor nobleman in a country that abhorred the nobility. He thought of becoming a mercenary in India, a country which always seemed to grip his imagination. He was a professional soldier who had never seen active service.

Chapter 9

THE CORSICAN

By 1793, Danton and the new leaders of France, bent on territorial expansion, had decided that the soft under-belly of Europe, Italy, divided into a multitude of states and dominated in the north by the arch-enemy of the Revolution, Austria, was a fertile field for conquest. The stepping stone after Corsica was to be Sardinia; and an expedition was assembled under Admiral Truguet to take this and intimidate the mainland. Truguet arrived in Ajaccio early in 1793 with a huge flotilla and several hundred troops. Napoleon was only too eager to join the expedition, now that his local ambitions had been frustrated by Paoli. Truguet, moreover, fell in love with Napoleon's sister, Elisa, now sixteen. Napoleon saw the French as potential allies in overthrowing Paoli, whom he had come to detest with the hatred of a spurned supporter.

The latter, nominally in charge of Corsica, suggested that Truguet should attack Cagliari, the capital of Sardinia while mounting a diversionary attack on La Maddalena, an island off the coast. Napoleon was placed in charge of this operation, with 600 men in sixteen transports supported by a single warship under his command. The expedition was a disastrous failure from the start: gales forced the ships back to Ajaccio and the element of surprise was lost.

Napoleon led his men into landing on the nearby island of Santo Stefano, capturing the fort there and bombarding La Maddalena. However, having been left on the little island, he was suddenly informed that the sailors on the warship had mutinied so that the flotilla had to abandon the venture. Napoleon was very nearly stranded

ashore: he struggled down to the beach with his guns to find that only a single boat had been sent to fetch him and his men: he had to spike and abandon his guns, narrowly escaping.

On his return to Corsica at the end of February, the young lieutenant was convinced that Paoli had deliberately conspired to undermine the expedition: for Paoli, who had spent so many years in exile in Britain was, Napoleon had come to believe, a British agent. Others had come to the same conclusion: Napoleon's brother Lucien, then in France, believed it, and so did Christophe Saliceti, an old political ally of Napoleon's who was soon to head a commission of inquiry into events on the island.

In early March Napoleon was walking in the Place Doria at Bonifacio when a group of students suddenly set upon him, denouncing him as an aristocrat for his care in military dress and his insistence on cleanliness aboard the ship on the ill-fated Maddalena expedition: he was nearly lynched before being rescued by some of his volunteers. Napoleon immediately suspected Paoli of instigating this murder attempt, and demanded to see him at the Convent of Rostino. There the veteran guerrilla leader effectively confirmed that he had gone over to the British: the Revolution, he claimed, had become too extremist and he had been appalled by the King's execution. Corsican independence was his revered goal. When Napoleon disagreed, Paoli angrily left him.

Napoleon switched his support from his former hero to his rival, Saliceti, while the French authorities, alerted to Paoli's views, ordered the guerrilla chieftain to Paris on pain of being outlawed. He refused; and the French government, lacking the resources to mount an expedition to Corsica at that moment, backed down.

This infuriated Saliceti and Napoleon, who began to intrigue against him. Napoleon was arrested at Corsacci but was helped by friends, and then escaped across country to Ajaccio where, now an outlaw, he fled by sea to Bastia. There he persuaded Saliceti to launch an expedition of 400 men and two ships back to Ajaccio. But Paoli's vengeance was merciless: his supporters burnt down Napoleon's house in Ajaccio and destroyed the Bonaparte farms while Letizia and her daughters fled into hiding.

Napoleon's small expedition arrived and he jumped into the water to take his mother and her children aboard. He laid siege to Ajaccio without success and had to sail to Calvi defeated and with his entire fortune lost through his recklessness. The Bonapartes were denounced as 'traitors and enemies of the fatherland, condemned to perpetual execution and infamy' by Paoli. On 10 June 1793, the family, now destitute, set sail for Toulon in France aboard a cargo ship, narrowly escaping capture by the British. Corsica had effectively passed into Britain's hands.

To a brilliant, highly strung and imperious young man like Napoleon, the whole episode had been character-shaping. He had taken part in his first military engagement, a failure – even though his gunnery had been astonishingly accurate, destroying eighty huts and a timber yard as well as setting fire to Maddalena four times. He was quite certain he had been frustrated through the negligence of others. Had he been in charge of the expedition, he believed, it would have turned out very differently – which inspired a contempt for authority other than his own. Worse, he believed Paoli was behind his humiliation, as well as the later assassination attempt, and he was wary of others (although he was not paranoid: throughout his life he was deeply loyal to his friends).

He had now lost his family fortune and endangered his mother and sisters – a terrible setback for a man born in modest wealth, who then had had to struggle, after his father's death, and had finally emerged reasonably rich again. In addition he considered himself head of the family, and the significance of how he had lost his wealth must have weighed deeply on his young shoulders. Finally, and perhaps most significantly of all, he had cast in his lot with revolutionary France. Partly this was a furious repudiation of Paoli with his 'primitive' ideal of a peasant-led society, and partly from hurt after what he considered to be a ruthless betrayal by his hero. Quite by accident, because of his family's decision to align itself with the French, his own education there and his sympathies with the initial revolutionaries, he had been one of the leaders of the pro-French faction on the island – whereas the independence-minded Paoli preferred to align with the British as a much better guarantee of Corsica's freedom.

The Italian-descended Corsican, whose earlier intense dislike of the French was evident through jottings of the early twenties, was suddenly a genuine Frenchman whose first enemy was the British. Masson puts it with brilliant succinctness: 'Just as France had made him Corsican, so Corsica had made him a Frenchman.'

Paoli even encouraged the British to besiege the remaining French positions in Corsica, and then invited George III to become King of the island. Sir Gilbert Elliot was sent in as viceroy, and Paoli faded into retirement in England. Consequently Britain now occupied the homeland of what was to become its bitterest foe, although it did not yet know it.

It is hard to exaggerate the wretchedness of the twenty-four-year-old Napoleon in France during the terrible summer of 1793. Ruined financially, intensely guilty at having let his family down, a failure in an uncertain world, with all his academic work come to naught, and just one disastrous military engagement behind him, he was a political refugee from his own obscure island. Letizia and her daughters had to be called 'dressmakers' on their passports to ensure their safety as former 'aristos'.

Toulon was no safe haven, however. A month later there was an uprising and the British under Admiral Hood were allowed to take possession of the port. Napoleon and his family had to flee again. Much of the region of Marseilles and Lyon also rose up against the regime, along with most of the country regions of France, particularly in the west: civil war loomed. Letizia and her family moved to Marseilles where they were forced to queue for soup from a paupers' kitchen. It was a terrible fate for a proud and prosperous family, and seared a burning desire for getting even on the young Napoleon, brought up in a vendetta society.

Chapter 10

TOULON

For the moment the young officer was desperate to earn money to keep his impoverished family, and immediately rejoined his regiment in Nice. During the next few months he performed various military tasks, and was introduced by Saliceti to Augustin Robespierre, a much more amiable man than his brother, with a pretty mistress who immediately took to Napoleon. He wrote a work of Jacobin propaganda, which took a sideswipe at the hated Paoli:

> He ravaged and confiscated the property of the richer families because they were allied to the unity of the Republic, and all those who remained in our armies he declared 'enemies of the nation'. He had already caused the failure of the Sardinian expedition, yet he had the impudence to call himself the friend of France and a good republican.

Saliceti also introduced Napoleon to General Carteaux, in command of the siege of Toulon against the English and Spanish occupiers: as the artillery commander had been badly wounded, Saliceti had Napoleon appointed in his place.

It was this penniless young officer's first real break after the disastrous experience at La Maddalena. He grasped it with both hands. Toulon was defended by some 2,000 British troops as well as 7,000 Neapolitans and 6,000 Spaniards, backed up by Admiral Hood's fleet. Carteaux had 17,000 men who were blockading the city without attacking it. A former career officer of considerable vanity with a magnificent horse

and sporting a huge black moustache, Carteaux knew virtually nothing about artillery and had just two 24-pound and two 14-pound guns. Napoleon immediately set about finding more guns from Antibes and Monaco and built up parapets from which to fire them safely. Soon he had built up his arsenal to nearly 20 guns and mortars manned by 1,600 men, in an early burst of his demonic energy. He was promoted to major. Carteaux himself was meanwhile dismissed and imprisoned for incompetence. He was succeeded by Jacques Dugommier.

Dugommier immediately approved Napoleon's plan for switching the objective of the French attack from the city of Toulon to Fort Mulgrave, a fort known as Little Gibraltar, two miles to the south of the city, from which the British fleet could be fired upon at leisure. As the defending troops entirely relied on the fleet for their supplies, Napoleon reasoned that the British would have to evacuate their troops from Toulon if they were forced to withdraw the ships under fire. Napoleon brought up a battery of guns close to the fort – the 'battery of men without fear', as he called it, and for two days and nights the two sides pounded each other – with the young officer present throughout. It was an extraordinary display of bravery for an inexperienced young officer, as well as of skill in gunnery, exhibiting the deadly accuracy he had already shown at La Maddalena.

In December Dugommier, after initial hesitation which nearly resulted in his replacement by Napoleon, led the attack in heavy rain with 5,000 men, Napoleon bringing up the rearguard with 2,000. Dugommier's men were driven back three times before Napoleon attacked: his horse was shot from under him. Undaunted he led two columns and clambered over the first defences with Dugommier, passing through the gun recesses, fighting viciously with sabres and bayonets. Napoleon was cut deeply in the thigh and his leg might have been amputated, but the surgeon changed his mind.

With the guns under French command, the British evacuated 'like the herd of swine that ran furiously into the sea possessed of the devil', in Sidney Smith's phrase, after setting the arsenal and the French ships on fire. The port was reoccupied the following day. It was a huge victory for the Revolution as the previous loss of Toulon had fanned the flames of the civil war then raging throughout France.

Some 400 people were promptly executed as collaborators with the enemy. Joseph, the officer responsible, declared blood-curdlingly: 'We have only one way of celebrating this victory; this evening 213 insurgents fall under our thunderbolt. Adieu, my friend, tears of joy flood my soul . . . we are shedding much impure blood, but for humanity and for duty.'

Saliceti, the political commissioner in charge, received the credit for the victory, but Napoleon was praised by Dugommier to the skies: 'I have no words to describe Buonaparte's merit: much technical skill, an equal degree of intelligence and too much gallantry, there you have a poor sketch of this rare officer . . .'

Napoleon was promoted brigadier-general and celebrated by moving his family from the wretched digs in Marseilles to a country house near Antibes. There he relaxed with his two favourite siblings, the fifteen-year-old Louis, whom Napoleon praised for his 'warmth, good health, talent, precision in his dealings and kindness' and Pauline, both beautiful and sexually alluring already at nearly fourteen. His brother Joseph was about to marry an heiress whose father, François Clary, had been accused of royalist sympathies and died. One of her brothers had committed suicide while another was imprisoned. Joseph had intervened to get the boy freed. Napoleon seems to have fallen out with the revolutionary firebrand Lucien, and the spoilt Jerome was too young to command his older brother's attention.

Napoleon had had several promising young officers alongside him at the siege of Fort Mulgrave. Androche Junot, his aide-de-camp, was soon eying Pauline. Several other future commanders were present at Toulon, including twenty-one-year-old Geraud Duroc, soon to be Napoleon's best friend, twenty-five-year-old Louis Desaix, twenty-seven-year-old Louis Gabriel Suchet, nineteen-year-old August Marmont and twenty-nine-year-old Claude-Victor Perrin.

Napoleon was promoted to become artillery commander for the army of Italy, based at Nice, with 15,000 livres a year, impressive pay, even allowing for the rampant inflation of the time. He settled eagerly into the job, seeking to break the deadlock in the war against Piedmont, whose army was being supplied by the British through Genoa. Napoleon devised a strategy for an attack on the town of

Oneglia, although he did not take part in it himself. This proved highly successful.

He argued for an offensive to capture the western Alpine passes of Col d'Argentière, Tende and St Bernard for a major attack on northern Italy, and was supported in this by his friends in Paris, Saliceti and Augustin Robespierre. He was opposed by Lazare Carnot, the member of the Committee who was effectively war minister, who favoured an all-out attack on Spain. Napoleon argued that a concentrated attack on Piedmont would force the Austrians to divert troops from the Rhine to defend the passes there, permitting a French thrust in central Europe; but Carnot prevailed.

Napoleon also incurred the wrath of the Committee for seeking to build-up a fort overlooking Marseilles, which he considered potentially rebellious. 'I am going to position two guns in order to curb the town,' he declared. He was briefly detained under house arrest for insulting the people. This may have reflected concerns even at this stage about his overweening ambition. There may have been fears that he sought to control the city for his own or counter-revolutionary purposes.

In Paris, meanwhile, as we have seen, the fall of the Robespierres on 27 July 1794 marked the end of the Terror. With remarkable alacrity, their friends sought to distance themselves from the blood-stained and now bloodied brothers. Saliceti, who was beginning to be jealous of the successes of his protégé Napoleon, came under suspicion himself, and promptly tried to deflect the danger by accusing his friend of going off on a suspicious mission to the port of Genoa: in fact it had been a scouting mission. But Saliceti suggested Napoleon may have been depositing French gold in a Genoese bank account.

Napoleon, for his part, rushed to condemn his old friend Augustin Robespierre: 'I have been somewhat moved by the catastrophe of the Younger Robespierre whom I loved and whom I believed to be pure, but were he my brother, I would have stabbed him with my own hand had he aspired to tyranny.'

Nevertheless he was placed under house arrest for a fortnight, where he made a dignified defence of himself:

I abandoned my belongings. I lost everything for the sake of the Republic. Since then, I have served at Toulon with some distinction . . . Since Robespierre's conspiracy was discovered, my conduct has been that of a man accustomed to judge according to principles [not persons]. No one can deny me the title of patriot.

Saliceti relented and had Napoleon released. Napoleon's eagerness to save his own skin, by distancing himself from the Robespierres, does not cast him in a pleasing light, but it was understandable in the fevered climate of the time, when the merest suspicion could have brought about his execution. Besides the brothers were dead.

Although Napoleon was no egalitarian and had little time for Maximilien's more revolutionary ideas, the young officer certainly imbibed many political lessons from the ruthless Jacobins, in particular those of how a small movement, and even one man, could represent the general will of the people, as well as of the utter insignificance of human life in the balance against the general interests of the people and state. Previously reasonably humane, Napoleon's callous streak towards enormous human casualties may date from this period. Now at liberty again, the tireless young brigadier-general threw himself into military planning, pressing for his Italian campaign. Carnot continued to overrule this, but told Napoleon instead to plan for a much more limited invasion of Corsica.

The new regime, entitled the Directory, was aptly summed up by Duff Cooper as: 'The most inefficient, corrupt and contemptible [government] with which any great country has ever been cursed.' Most of them had done well out of the Revolution – black marketeers, speculators, hoarders and those who had bought up church and aristocratic lands at knockdown prices. They were hostile both to the Bourbons and the real revolutionaries: they were primarily greedy opportunists. Of these Carnot was initially by far the most substantial.

Napoleon, although not one of the new men – on his official posting he had been anything but corrupt or wealthy – stood to benefit from the new regime. Although associated with Robespierre and the Jacobins, he had quickly severed the connection. He was an officer of energy and ability at a time when France was plunging ever deeper

into war and would need both. But first he wanted to make his peace with the new regime. There was still little hint of the glittering heights to come in the career of this twenty-five-year-old brigadier; he was only one of a number of promising young officers of whom one, Lazare Hoche, was already marked out as France's greatest revolutionary commander.

Part 2

BRITAIN ASLEEP

1789–95

Chapter 11

THE APPEASERS

While France burnt and beheaded, Britain slept. Its prime minister, the thirty-two-year-old William Pitt the Younger, was six years into office when the French Revolution broke out, absurdly youthful to be the leader of a well-established power. Yet he showed none of the impetuosity of youth. As a later British prime minister, Lord Rosebery, wrote:

> While the eyes of all Europe were fixed on Paris, Pitt ostentatiously averted his gaze. He was deaf to the shrieks of rage and panic that arose from the convulsions of France. He determinedly set himself, to use the phrase of Candide, to cultivate his own garden and ignore all others. Let France settle her internal affairs as she chooses, was his unvarying principle. It is strange to read the uneventful record of the flat prosperous years as they passed in England from July 1789 to January 1793, and to contrast them with the contemporary stress and tumult in Europe.
>
> No English minister can ever wish for war. Apart from the inseparable dangers to our constitution and our commerce, his own position suffers sensible detriment. He sinks into a superior commissary; he can reap little glory from success; he is the first scapegoat of failure. He too has to face, not the heroic excitement of the field, but domestic misery and discontent; the heavy burden of taxation, and the unpopularity of sacrifice which all war entails. If this be true of every minister, with how much greater force does it apply to Pitt. The task he had set himself was to raise the nation from

the exhaustion of the American war; to repair her finance; to strengthen by reform the foundations of the constitution, and by a liberal Irish policy the bonds of Empire. At this very moment he was meditating, we are told, the broadest application of free-trade principles – the throwing open of our ports and the raising of our revenue entirely by internal taxation.

He required, moreover, fifteen years of tranquillity to realize the fullness of the benefit of his cherished Sinking Fund. His enthusiasm was all for peace, retrenchment, and reform; he had experienced the difficulty of actively intervening in the affairs of Europe; he had no particle of that strange bias which has made some eminent statesmen believe themselves to be eminent generals; but he had the consciousness of a boundless capacity for meeting the real requirements of the country. Had he been able to carry out his own policy, had France only left him alone, or even given him a loophole for abstention, he would have been by far the greatest minister that England has ever seen. As it was, he was doomed to drag out the remainder of his life in darkness and dismay, in wrecking his whole financial edifice to find funds for incapable generals and for foreign statesmen more capable than honest, in postponing and indeed repressing all his projected reforms.

To no human being, then, did war come with such a curse as to Pitt, by none was it more hated or shunned.

On the day of the storming of the Bastille, Pitt remarked: 'This scene, added to the prevailing scarcity, makes [France] an object of compassion even to a rival'. By October 1790 he was still writing:

This country means to persevere in the neutrality which it has hitherto scrupulously observed with respect to the internal dissensions of France, and from which it will never depart unless the conduct held there should make it indispensable as an act of self-defence . . . We are sincerely desirous of preserving peace and of cultivating in general a friendly intercourse and understanding between the two nations.

Three months later he declared with astonishing complacency: 'Unquestionably there never was a time in the history of this country when from the situation of Europe we might more reasonably expect fifteen years of peace than at the present moment.'

In November 1792, less than three months before the outbreak of war, his right-hand man and foreign secretary, Lord Grenville, declared:

> Portugal and Holland will do what we please. We shall do nothing . . . All my ambition is that I may at some time hereafter . . . have the inexpressible satisfaction of being able . . . to tell myself that I have contributed to keep my own country at least a little longer from sharing in all the evils of every sort that surround us. I am more and more convinced that this can only be done by keeping wholly and entirely aloof.

Pitt said a week later: 'Perhaps some opening may arise which may enable us to contribute to the termination of the war between different powers in Europe, leaving France (which I believe is the best way) to arrange its own internal affairs as it can.'

These remarkable statements preceded the French revolutionary decrees of November and December which provided assistance to all peoples who revolted against their governments and which proposed French-style revolutionary rule in such territories as Savoy and the Rhine. An assembly of British radicals was warmly welcomed in Paris with the hope that the French would soon be able to congratulate a National Assembly of England.

More extraordinary still, Pitt had actually cut back defence spending in his energetic attempts to place Britain's finances on a regular footing. In February 1792 he reduced the navy from 18,000 to 16,000 men, ended the subsidy to Hessian mercenaries, and cut back on army appropriations – although by the end of the year he was forced to raise a militia as a precautionary measure.

Not even Britain in the grip of appeasement a century and a half later bears comparison with the head-in-the-sand attitude adopted by the British towards the French Revolution. The William Pitt who was

later to become so celebrated as a war minister resembled at this time nothing more than a dormouse terrified of continental entanglement, devoid of any spark of courage or vigour. Why did Britain, under an otherwise able prime minister show such blindness?

The answer lies in a combination of circumstances. Britain's last experience of war with France, Spain and Holland joining the rebellious American colonies had ended in a defeat on points. It had also proved expensive, and Pitt was nothing if not a meticulous bookkeeper when it came to national finances (although oddly enough not his own). Both Pitt and Grenville were deeply wary of continental entanglements, and believed they could avoid them through a judicious mixture of alliances and subsidies. Britain, moreover, had undergone a colossal economic, social and demographic revolution in the second half of the eighteenth century that was dramatically altering the face of the country, and commerce was booming as never before, in part thanks to the raw materials, capital and captive markets provided by the expanding empire. Thirdly, there was a genuine apprehension about the impact of the French Revolution on Britain's increasingly frayed social and political fabric. Yet, even more significant than these political and economic factors were the character and background of Pitt himself.

Chapter 12

THE BOY-STATESMAN

William Pitt the Younger was to be Napoleon's first, most stubborn and tenacious adversary. It would be hard to think of two more completely contrasting personalities, although they were almost of the same generation. Unlike the tempestuous Napoleon, who had been born on an island fighting for national survival and by the age of twenty-five had experienced two attempts at assassination, poverty, sudden enrichment, the loss of his family fortune and had fought in one campaign and one minor engagement, Pitt had been born in an atmosphere of aristocratic security such as few men have ever experienced, his prodigious intellect and gifts cultivated with the specific aim of rising to the highest position in the land.

On 28 May 1759, one of the most glorious years in the founding of the British empire, with the triumphs of Goree and Guadeloupe, Minden, Lagos, Quiberon Bay and Quebec still reverberating in the ears of Englishmen, a second son was born to the prime minister of the day. The father was a towering intellect, orator and natural leader, William Pitt the Elder, later Earl of Chatham. Pitt's family descended from the governor of Madras in Queen Anne's reign. His grandson, Pitt's father, was a manic depressive in a family of seven children, three or four of whom were mentally unstable. The family traits were, in John Ehrman's words: 'an imperious and often quarrelsome temper, extravagant behaviour and emotion, a marked inability to understand other people, and a fundamental simplicity which sometimes gave its possessors a surprisingly sweet and winning charm.'

William's mother, Hester, was from an equally distinguished family,

the Grenvilles, a methodical, highly cultivated family which boasted George Grenville, the prime minister who first tried to introduce disinterested administration into corrupt British government and to set Britain's finances on a sound footing – and inadvertently triggered off the American War of Independence in doing so. The boy Pitt, in short, was descended from two of the greatest political dynasties of the age; and to begin with it seemed his much more stable character and penchant for administration derived from his mother. Rosebery wrote:

> He went into the House of Commons as an heir enters his home; he breathed in its his native atmosphere, he had, indeed, breathed no other; in the nursery, in the schoolroom, at the university, he lived in its temperature; it had been, so to speak, made over to him as a bequest by its unquestioned master. Throughout his life, from the cradle to the grave, he may be said to have known no wider existence. The objects and amusements, that other men seek in a thousand ways, were for him all concentrated there. It was his mistress, his stud, his dice-box, his game-preserve; it was his ambition, his library, his creed. For it, and it alone, had the consummate Chatham trained him from his birth. No young Hannibal was ever more solemnly devoted to his country than Pitt to parliament.
>
> He was destined, at one bound, to attain that supreme but isolated position, the first necessity of which is self-control; and, behind the imperious mask of power, he all but concealed the softer emotions of his earlier years. Grief for the loss of his sister and her husband are the only instances of human weakness that break the stern impressiveness of his life. Up to that last year when fate pressed pitilessly on the dying man, from the time that he went to Cambridge, as a boy of fourteen with his tutor and his nurse, he seems, with one short interval, to have left youth and gaiety behind.

The boy was brought up by tutors at home, not sent to Eton as his father had been, and went to Cambridge at the absurdly young age of fourteen. The young man was promptly given a rotten borough by a friend of his father, and entered the House of Commons at the age of

Chapter 18

THE GRAND OLD DUKE OF YORK

The British army was now reorganized on a more ordered footing, with provision for raising 175,000 regulars, 52,000 militia – some 16,000 of them in Ireland – 'fencible' (volunteer) cavalry and 34,000 hired mercenaries. A new campaign was planned, involving two pincers to close in on Paris. An army would be landed near Le Havre and move up the Seine; another would advance from the north-east: this would consist of some 300,000 men, 40,000 of them British and German soldiers which would advance from Flanders and seize the frontier fortresses.

It was the old plan again, under the old commander, the twenty-nine-year-old Duke of York whom both Pitt and Dundas privately considered incompetent, but were unable to replace: the Austrians actually preferred him because they believed they could manipulate him. The Prussians, who were to provide 100,000 men, insisted that because the war was being waged entirely in British interests they be paid £2 million. The British were understandably reluctant to pay. So too were the Austrians, who were by now deeply suspicious of their Prussian rivals. Not until April was agreement reached for a reduced Prussian force of 62,400 men at a cost of around £1 million paid largely by the British.

All now seemed well: the King of Prussia, no less, decided to command his army; the Emperor of Austria also took command of his forces, arriving in Belgium to inspect the allied armies on 9 April. This brought to an end an unseemly squabble in which the Duke of York, who had refused to serve under the Austrians' best general, General

Clairfait, because of his inferior status, agreed to serve under the Emperor. As was remarked at the time: 'one incompetent prince, who knew little about war, was thus to be commanded by another incompetent prince who knew nothing.'

Just ten days later, however, a large Polish uprising under the popular Thaddeus Kosciusko, which had broken out the previous month, moved on to capture Warsaw. This aroused intense anxiety among Britain's continental allies: the Russians wanted help to quell it; the Austrians were alarmed at the destabilization of central Europe; and the Prussians wanted to share in any possible spoils. But for the moment the campaign against France proceeded. The fortress of Landrecies was taken, partly by a brilliant British cavalry charge. It became a classic in British military history. On 24 April, two squadrons of British and two of Austrian cavalry, numbering 400 men, had come across a body of 800 French cavalry in thick woods near Montrecourt. They pursued the larger French force up a hill, where they found themselves face to face with an entire division. The British promptly charged forward, while the Austrians engaged in a flanking movement. They were taking on sixty cannon, aiming straight at them, supported by 12,000 men, ranged in six battalions. The charge of the 15th Hussars was memorably described by a young cornet, Robert Wilson:

> When we began to trot, the French cavalry made a movement to right and left from the centre, and at the same moment we saw in lieu of them, as if created by magic, an equal line of infantry, with a considerable artillery in advance, which opened a furious cannonade with grape, while the musketry poured its volleys. The surprise was great and the moment most critical; but happily the heads kept their direction, and the heels were duly applied to the 'Charge!' which order was hailed with repeated huzzas . . .
>
> The guns were quickly taken; but we then found that the chaussée, which ran through a hollow with steep banks, lay between them and the infantry. There was, however, no hesitation; every horse was true to his master, and the chaussée was passed in uninterrupted impetuous career. It was then, as we gained the crest, that the infantry poured its volley – but in vain. In vain also the

first ranks kneeled and presented a steady line of bayonets. The impulse was too rapid, and the body attacking too solid, for any infantry power formed in line to oppose, although the ranks were three deep. Even the horses struck mortally at the brow of the bank had sufficient momentum to plunge upon the enemy in their fall, and assist the destruction of his defence . . .

The French cavalry, having gained the flanks of their infantry, endeavoured to take up a position in its rear. Our squadrons, still on the gallop, closed to fill up the gaps which the French fire and bayonets had occasioned, and proceeded to the attack on the French cavalry, which, though it had suffered from the fire of part of its own infantry, seemed resolved to await the onset; but their discipline or their courage failed, and our horses' heads drove on them just as they were on the half-turn to retire.

A dreadful massacre followed. In a chase of four miles, twelve hundred horsemen were cut down, of which about five hundred were Black Hussars. One farrier of the 15th alone killed twenty two men. The French were so panic-stricken that they scarcely made any resistance, notwithstanding that our numbers were so few in comparison with the party engaged, that every individual pursuer found himself in the midst of a flock of foes.

As the British and Austrians pursued the French, they came across a baggage train carrying fifty more guns and fell upon this, spiking the guns. The pursuit continued for six miles, leaving 1,200 French casualties in its wake. There had been a couple of other considerable feats of British arms – at Vicogne, when the Coldstream Guards had crossed a narrow bridge in the face of French guns and overrun the French position, and at Lincelles when they overcame a heavily manned French redoubt – but this was the first really superb feat of arms.

The British and Austrian army now plunged on into France. Wilson again captured the intensity of the fighting at Mouveaux:

The cry of 'Charge to the right!' ran down the column, and in the same moment we were all at full speed. The enemy redoubled his

efforts, and struck at us with his bayonets fixed at the end of his muskets, as we wheeled round the dreaded and dreadful corner, already almost choked with the fallen horses and men which had perished in the attempt to pass. My little mare received here a bayonet-wound in the croup, and a musket-ball through the crest of her neck. Two balls lodged in my cloak-case behind the saddle, and another carried away part of my sash. Our surgeon and his horse were killed close at my side, and a dozen of my detachment fell at that spot under the enemy's fire. We still urged on, *ventre à terre*, pursued by bullets.

Suddenly, before the least notice could be given, the whole column of cavalry was arrested in its career, and at the same moment, of course, recoiled several yards. The confusion, the conflict for preservation, the destruction which ensued, baffles all description. Three-fourths of the horses, at one and the same moment, were thrown down with their riders under them or entangled by the bodies of others. The battling of the horses to recover themselves, the exclamations of all sorts which resounded through the air, accompanied by the volleys of the triumphing enemy, presented a picture *d'enfer* which, as one of the French then firing upon us, and afterwards taken, told me, even made his own and his comrades' hair stand on end . . . It was not till I got over the ditch that I saw the cause of our calamity. Fifty-six pieces of cannon with their tumbrels, etc, stood immovable in the road, the drivers having cut away the traces and escaped with the horses when they found the enemy's fire surrounding them. Such was the consequence of sending out as drivers the refuse of our gaols – for that was the practice of the day.

Never, never could a column be more completely surrounded and by five times its numbers; never did a body of men so circumstanced escape with such a comparatively small loss. At Pontachin a column of 1,800 French had endeavoured to force its way through some orchards. When the mass was wedged in one of them which had a very small outlet, the Austrians had opened a battery of twelve guns – 12-pounders – upon it, and with such remarkable razing precision and effect, that I myself counted 280

headless bodies. Such a beheading carnage was perhaps never paralleled.

The British and Austrians were now over-extended, partially cut off in the rear and under fire on both sides. On 8 May, the French counter-attacked at Turcoine. The British were forced to fight a rearguard action, while the Austrians remained strangely passive. The British lost nineteen guns out of twenty-eight, while eighteen Austrian battalions failed to support them. Craig, the Duke of York's adjutant-general, fulminated: 'We never saw an Austrian but by two and threes turning away. I am every day more and more convinced that they have not an officer among them.' The allies regrouped to resist the French charges at Tournai and on the Sambre.

The King of Prussia chose this moment not to join his forces in the west but in the east, on the Polish front. The Austrians, concluding pessimistically that western Flanders was lost, went on the defensive, and the Emperor decided to return to Vienna at the end of May. The Prussians now refused to do the bidding of the British, and the Austrians seemed all but out of the fight, falling back along all their lines.

On 26 June Moira landed at Ostend with some 7,000 reinforcements and marched to Ghent: one of his officers was Lieutenant-Colonel Arthur Wellesley, a novice in war. The Duke of York meanwhile wrote angrily to Prince Coburg that 'we are betrayed and sold to the enemy' by the retreating Austrians. The French crossed the Sambre again, this time under General Jourdan, with reinforcements of 70,000 men, the army of Sambre-et-Meuse, the Republic's best. They thrust between the British-Dutch forces and the Austrians to the east.

The British believed the Emperor of Austria had sold out. In fact he had left because he recognized that his brother, the Archduke Charles, was a far more gifted commander – although he suffered from epilepsy which would incapacitate him at critical moments. He was ably supported by his chief of staff, General Mack von Lieberich. But it is true that the Austrians had no great enthusiasm for the war and had long sought to disembarrass themselves of the troublesome burden of governing their far-flung Netherlands possessions.

Jourdan turned his entire army against the Austrians and they met on the battlefield of Fleurus on 26 June. The Austrians fought furiously and inflicted enormous losses on the French. The battle lasted the whole day – 'fifteen hours of the most desperate fighting I ever saw in my life', as a young officer, Soult, was later to remember, having had five horses shot from beneath him. Another soon to be famous young French officer, Bernadotte, fought beside him.

Archduke Charles boldly suggested a cavalry counter-attack to go behind the French and break their lines. But the Austrian commander, Coburg, ordered a retreat as dusk settled to a ridge called Mont St Jean above the village of Waterloo. The allied armies now fell apart, going their separate ways – the British towards Antwerp, the Dutch across the Cheldyt, and the Austrians towards the Rhine.

Brussels fell on 11 July, and Antwerp later in the month. Holland's very survival was now at stake. Nieuport fell to the French and hundreds were butchered. The Austrians were now in full flight towards the Rhine. Cologne fell in October as Jourdan's army pushed forward.

Thoroughly alarmed, Pitt, whose government had now been reinforced by the Whig faction represented by the Duke of Portland, sent two emissaries to Vienna to seek stronger Austrian support – Thomas Grenville, brother of the foreign secretary and one of the men who had brokered the end of the American War of Independence, and Lord Spencer. They were to be completely disappointed, finding in Vienna only 'weakness and inefficiency' and 'total want of vigour'.

The Austrians soon surrendered two more fortresses, Valenciennes and Condé, while demanding a subsidy of £3 million from the British for continuing the war in 1794 and a similar figure for the following year. Pitt meanwhile cut off his subsidy to the even more reluctant Prussia, which retaliated by seeking a peace treaty with France.

Faced by collapse in the Low Countries, Pitt cast desperately about, and thought he had found an ally to champion in Joseph, Comte de Puisaye, leader of the Breton resistance, who implored him for 10,000 British troops in support. But both Dundas and Moira were firmly opposed to such an 'adventure'. Pitt sought to reinforce the French émigré army along the Rhine under the Prince de Condé. In addition,

with the bloody fall of Robespierre, he sought solace in the hope of a royalist coup and peace talks to be spearheaded by a wily British envoy and effective leader of the British secret service in France, William Wickham.

Meanwhile the French invaded Holland, taking Sluys and Eindhoven and reaching Cologne. They paused only when they reached the river Waal. Pitt's talk of 'embarrassment' was now replaced by fears of a 'calamity'. The ineffectual Duke of York was recalled, along with seven regiments, leaving the British troops under the command of General Harcourt. The Dutch began to consider surrender. The British were 'hated and more dreaded than the enemy, even by the well-disposed inhabitants'.

As ice formed on the rivers, the French pressed forward across the Waal, until checked by a British and German counter-attack. At the village of Boxtel, the twenty-five-year-old Arthur Wellesley ordered his men to open their lines to allow the fleeing soldiery through, then closed his line as the French galloped forward in pursuit. He waited until they were almost upon him before giving the order to fire and, as the foremost assailants fell, the rest turned round and fled.

The situation was desperate. Supplies of transport, medical equipment – such as it was – and clothing had all broken down, although food was still plentiful. General Craig reported that the army was 'despised by our enemies, without discipline, confidence or exertions among ourselves . . . every disgrace and misfortune is to be expected'.

William Wilberforce proposed talks with France. Pitt angrily rejected this in December. Holland, however, fell to the French the following month and the principal British ally, the Stadtholder, fled to England. Amsterdam was taken on 19 January 1795, and a few days later the French cavalry galloped across the Zuyder Zee to seize the Dutch fleet, imprisoned in the ice. The British continued to retreat in a desperate shambles while the Dutch sued for peace and the French in February impounded British ships in Dutch ports.

The same month Pitt decided to withdraw the remains of the army from the continent: by April the infantry and part of the artillery were embarked at Bremen, leaving only the cavalry, some of the gunners, the Hanoverians, and what remained of the Austrians attached to the

British forces. An eyewitness described the wretched British evacuation: 'There were few who had not lost a limb; many had lost both legs and arms; numbers of them were reduced to mere skeletons.'

It had been one of the worst defeats in British military history, with casualties even higher than the previous year, around 20,000 or two thirds of the entire British expeditionary army. The French imposed strict terms on the Dutch, including taking Maastricht, part of southern Holland, and the area around Flushing. The Dutch navy and part of its army were conscripted to the war against Britain. By the end of the terrible year of 1794 it seemed game, set and match to the French: they had won twenty-seven pitched battles, killed 80,000 and taken as many prisoners. They had conquered Flanders, made Holland a puppet, crossed the Rhine, subdued the Vendée and retaken Toulon. The return of these wretched men across the Channel in defeat was a truly black day for British arms.

The Prussians now signed a peace treaty with France at Basle, and by the middle of 1795 the conclusion was inescapable that Britain's prosecution of the continental war against revolutionary France had been an utter disaster. The French had twice repulsed large combined allied armies attacking from the north, the second time crushing Holland and forcing the British to evacuate under pitiable and ignominious circumstances. France had stood alone against most of Europe, and magnificently repulsed its enemies.

After the glories of the previous century, Britain's reputation as a military power on land had descended to an all-time low: the shambles in Toulon and in Holland now eclipsed memories of the triumphs of Clive in India and Wolfe in Quebec. The British policy of trying to get its continental allies to do most of the fighting through bribery was neither very glorious nor very successful. The Hessians and the Hanoverians had proved indifferent troops; the Prussians had haggled and then deserted when the British had been unwilling to be browbeaten; and huge offers of subsidy had not yet persuaded the Austrians to take the offensive. With the Low Countries effectively in enemy hands, and Spain now lost, the only friendly country now left to Britain west of Corsica, Sardinia and parts of Italy was little Portugal.

Chapter 19

THE SPICE ISLANDS

The British land war in Europe, in conjunction with its allies, Austria, Prussia and Holland, had quickly collapsed into a shambles. At sea the overconfident French now proposed to go on the offensive against Britain, in an attempt to isolate Britain from lines of commerce and disrupt its trade routes. This had long been an objective of French government policy under the monarchy and was adopted by the revolutionaries, who were as much nationalists as radicals.

French policy towards Britain was dictated by centuries of age-old enmity, and in the half century before the Revolution, while great battles had been fought on land (in India, at Quebec, and at Yorktown, which was essentially a French rather than an American victory) the main centre of operations had been at sea. France had watched in growing anxiety and envy as the tentacles of the British empire had spread across the world. As their great rival embarked on an industrial revolution that was financed by imperial revenues, Britain moved out in front as the world's superpower. France was determined to challenge this, and above all, to do so by cutting Britain off from her economic lifelines, as she was seen to be supremely vulnerable because of her island status.

As early as January 1793, Kersaint, the Revolution's foreign affairs spokesman, had declared to the Convention: 'The credit of England rests upon fictitious wealth; the real riches of that people are scattered everywhere . . . Bounded in territory, the public future of England is found almost wholly in its Bank, and this edifice is entirely supported by the wonderful activity of their naval commerce. Asia, Portugal, and

Spain are the most advantageous markets for the productions of English industry; we should shut these markets to the English by opening them to the world.'

In October 1796, the French Republic declared that all ships of any nationality carrying British goods were subject to seizure and that only ships carrying a 'certificate of origin' to prove that the goods were not from Britain would be exempt. But the French had made a classic mistake: with the advent of an industrial and agricultural revolution in Britain, both domestic corn and textile output was increasing dramatically. Thus Britain was moving towards self-sufficiency in key areas of production. The industrial revolution permitted Britain to produce cotton, woollen and muslin goods, as well as hardwares of high value and small bulk which were ideal for smuggling past the French blockade into Europe. Steam was applied to spinning in Britain in the 1790s, taking advantage of copious supplies of coal; in France it was not used until 1812. The cost of weaving a piece of cloth in Britain while the war with France progressed fell dramatically from nearly 40 shillings in 1795 to just 15 shillings in 1810. The French under-estimated this, and believed that all they had to do was cut off trade to bring the British economy juddering to a halt. In the event, however, they found Britain only too happy to fight back.

The principal theatres of naval and colonial conflict were to be the West Indies, source of the lucrative sugar trade; the East Indies, with their spices, merchandise and bullion; and the Mediterranean, not just a trading lake in its own right, but a key to communication with the East. This global war was also played out against the Cape of Good Hope, a key staging post for trade with the East Indies; and parts of Latin America, viewed by Britain and France as a potential source of great wealth as the Spanish empire crumbled. Eventually too, for somewhat different reasons, the young United States was to be dragged into the conflict.

The West Indies' sugar trade was enormously lucrative; but the islands, with their dense foliage and high rainfall were soporifically hot, breeding grounds for disease, and increasingly prone to slave rebellions against the hugely wealthy owners of the giant and inhuman planta-tions. Pitt saw the war as an opportunity to take on France in the

colonies, always Britain's chief interest. The British had some 6,000 troops stationed in the Caribbean; and French planters on the isles of St Domingue, Martinique and Guadeloupe, deeply hostile to the revolutionary regime in France, had already appealed to the British to take their islands over.

There followed a pyrrhic campaign of an ineptitude which mirrored Pitt's disastrous conduct of the continental war against France. In February 1793 attacks were authorized on the French Windward Islands and on Tobago. In April the latter was taken in a small-scale attack, but the French garrison in Martinique drove off the British assailants in June. At the time it was learnt that the French were sending reinforcements to the West Indies but, thanks to cabinet indecision, it was not until November that a British squadron, under Sir John Jervis and Sir Charles Grey, got under way, largely because the former sensibly would wait no longer.

Meanwhile the British forces based in Jamaica had landed on Dominique, where the local planters had appealed to the British for help against a slave uprising. Mole St Nicholas promptly surrendered to the British, who now decided to block the capital, Port-au-Prince. But the British force – some 900 men at its largest – was small. Only in May 1794 was their precarious toehold on the island reinforced with the arrival of Jervis's squadron.

Jervis and Grey had already performed superbly, raiding Barbados in January with 7,000 troops, seizing Martinique in March, St Lucia in April, the Saints and Guadeloupe by the end of the month. Port-au-Prince fell in June. It was a clean sweep: it seemed that the Caribbean had become a British lake. Pitt, who by now was facing increasingly bad news in Europe, was exultant.

The West Indies were of huge commercial importance, particularly to the French, accounting for fully a third of that country's trade, mainly in sugar, cotton and coffee. Almost a fifth of the French population depended on the West Indies for their livelihoods, particularly the towns of Nantes, Bordeaux, Le Havre and Marseilles and it was no coincidence that these were some of the least enthusiastic supporters of the Revolution which imperilled that trade through war with Britain.

Then, in June, the French squadron that had escaped the British Naval blockade of Rochefort in April arrived. This landed 1,500 troops on Guadeloupe, which after fierce fighting the British had to give up, while retaining the eastern half of the island; they evacuated altogether in December. Fighting also broke out in western St Domingue. Meanwhile ferocious black uprisings occurred there and the Windward Isles, while the British forces were ravaged by tropical diseases.

The British tried to assemble a relief expedition from England and Ireland, but many of the troops were required elsewhere. By the end of the year only three regiments and a single ship from Plymouth had arrived. By then another French contingent of 1,500 French troops had reached Guadeloupe, having dodged the British blockade outside Brest. The British debated earnestly whether to counter this by raising troops from the black and mulatto populations, Pitt eventually deciding not to do so, for fear of offending local white interests.

In March, however, the black populations rose up against the British in a concerted revolt in Grenada, St Vincent and St Lucia, forcing the soldiers to retreat into their garrisons. Toussaint L'Ouverture, the legendary black leader of St Domingue, also continued to fight, and there was even an uprising in Jamaica. Reinforcements at last arrived and helped the British regain some control of Grenada and St Vincent. But thousands were lost to disease and fighting – some 2,000 in St Domingue alone.

In June 1795, a further 2,000 men were sent to the Caribbean. The following month the British took a much more serious step: a senior British commander, Sir Ralph Abercromby, was placed in charge of an army of 15,000 men with a naval squadron to retake Guadeloupe and St Lucia, to seize the Dutch settlements of Surinam, Demerara and San Eustatius (the Dutch in Europe having now made their peace with the victorious French) and completely to subdue not just Grenada and St Vincent but St Domingue and San Domingo.

The expedition was seriously delayed, and squabbles broke out as to its objectives. It was soon scaled down. Abercromby, who arrived in April 1796, retook St Lucia and then occupied St Vincent and Grenada in June. Demerara was also taken. San Domingue was reinforced, but not subdued, while Guadeloupe was left alone. These successes were

modest but they were virtually all the British government had to show as reverse followed reverse across continental Europe.

Abercromby was ordered to take Trinidad, and even Puerto Rico. For Pitt the West Indies were now the main theatre of military operations. His judgement has seriously to be questioned, perhaps even more so than over the disastrously half-hearted and ineffectual effort on the continent: for the fighting did little serious damage to French trade and did little to increase the volume of British trade. The two most important objectives of St Domingue and Guadeloupe had not been secured, with only a toehold on the one and expulsion from the other: and ultimately this costly war was to take the lives of a staggering 50,000 British soldiers and seamen, mostly through disease – nearly 40 per cent of those sent over to fight. In Pitt's defence, had he not acted, the French might have gone on the offensive against the British. But he had delivered the first blow and prioritized the campaign. He had appallingly little to show for it.

The view from London by mid-1795 was one of almost unrelieved gloom: the British had been thrown off the continent; the Dutch were now occupied and hostile; the Prussians and the Spanish had dropped out of the war, and the latter were turning hostile. Tuscany and Sardinia were already so. The Danes were potential enemies. The Russians, while now sympathetic to Britain, were too remote to offer much assistance. Britain was achieving modest successes in the West Indies, at a considerable cost of men lost through illness, for dubious long-term gains. Moreover, for more than a year there had been no spectacular fleet action, apart from several superb frigate encounters which, however, had no decisive effect on the war.

Pitt and Grenville pinned their hopes on two will-o'-the-wisps: that revolutionary France might yet collapse, of which there was little sign – they had missed their opportunity when it really was disintegrating – and that the Austrians could be tempted again to stage a major offensive against France, which seemed an unlikely course of action for the weak, serious-minded young Emperor.

An emissary was despatched to Vienna: Francis Jackson, a diplomat, left in mid-October and arrived to find the Austrian court highly

optimistic. They had launched a counter-attack and defeated the French at Mainz, then moved into the Palatinate, raising the sieges of Mannheim and Frankfurt. The Austrian chief minister, Baron Johann Thugut, was warmly welcoming, promising 200,000 men in exchange for the suggested £3 million loan, although seeking better rates of interest.

However, the rally proved to be cruelly shortlived: a combined Austro-Sardinian force was defeated at Loano, which made them pull out of the coastline west of Genoa. The Austrian commander on the Rhine, Field Marshal Francis Clairfait, sought an armistice to give rest to his exhausted men. Pitt offered peace feelers to what was seen to be a new and more moderate government in France, that of the Directory, which had just taken control. The response was a blunt rebuff. The French returned a flat no until all British conquests were returned and France was recognized as having natural frontiers extending to the Rhine, the Alps and Pyrenees. Pitt had failed to realize that the Directory, just as much as the Jacobins, required perpetual war to maintain its control, mobilizing French patriotism to distract the people from the shambles and privations at home.

Part 3

CONQUEROR OF ITALY

Chapter 15

THE APPROACH OF WAR

The second major diplomatic flurry before 1793 was to be the direct cause of the war with France. It concerned, of all countries, Holland, and two of the major continental players, pushy young Prussia and and Austria. Dominated by the latter, Holland in 1784 had come under pressure from the Austro-Hungarian Emperor, Joseph II, to open up the estuary of the Scheldt, which it controlled, and give sea access to Antwerp in the Austrian Netherlands. The Austrians had backed off, but the British had guaranteed Dutch control of the key waterway, considered essential to British continental trade, as well as engaging in a Triple Alliance with the Prussians, Austria's rival, to prevent this happening again.

Yet the Emperor had not abandoned his hopes: a tall, prepossessing man, he had levied considerable taxes from his far-flung possessions for the war with Turkey, in which he was allied with Russia, and now issued extensive liberal reforms which infuriated the conservative rulers of his many fiefdoms. There were revolts in Bohemia, Lombardy and Hungary early in 1789 and, of much more concern to the neighbouring British, in the Austrian Netherlands, when the Emperor removed the privileges of the noble estates in Brabant (most of modern Belgium).

His actions caused demonstrations by radicals who looked to France, at an early stage in its Revolution, for support, and incensed conservatives who set up a Belgic Republic looking to the Triple Alliance for protection. The Prussians were delighted by the chance to foment disorder in the Austrian empire. The problem was briefly settled with a

Triple Alliance guarantee to the Austrian Netherlands and a partial Austrian climbdown. This apparently minor nation, however, now rose dramatically to European attention with the French army's advance into Belgium and defiance of the Austrians.

With the fall of Mas, Brussels, Louvain, Liège and Antwerp in late 1792, the French threatened to pursue the Austrians into Holland and curtail freedom of navigation in the Scheldt. To add insult to injury, the French said on 3 December that they would put Louis XVI on trial. Pitt, in spite of his confident public pronouncements, was deeply anxious. Grenville had instructed Auckland, the ambassador in the Hague, to tell the Dutch government that there would be 'no hesitation' in supporting it if Holland was invaded. Dumouriez, the victorious French general, was however prepared to guarantee the neutrality of an independent Belgium so as not to offend the British, whom he rightly regarded as France's potentially most dangerous foe: but he was not in charge in France.

The mood in England was stiffening behind the uncertain Pitt. Fox launched a furious attack on the call-up of the militia. But he was roundly denounced, loyalist associations being set up in support of the government. Pitt meanwhile in December met an unofficial French envoy, Bernard Maret, and issued a virtual ultimatum: 'I . . . mentioned to him distinctly that the resolution announced respecting the Scheldt was considered as proof of an intention to proceed to a rupture with Holland; that a rupture with Holland on this ground or any other injurious to their rights, must also lead to an immediate rupture with this country . . .'

Although the French now assured Pitt they had no intention of invading Holland, Belgium had been annexed, its social system was overturned and the Scheldt agreement violated, with French warships putting in there. The British issued a dignified further declaration: 'England never will consent that France shall arrogate the power of annulling at her pleasure, and under the pretence of a . . . natural right, of which she makes herself the only judge, the political system of Europe, established by solemn treaties, and guaranteed by the consent of all the powers'. She must 'show herself disposed to renounce her views of aggression . . . and confine herself within her own territory'.

The King himself urged Pitt to take a tougher line. The French foreign minister, Pierre Lebrun, sent a letter via Maret through a British intermediary which sought to indicate a subtle French climbdown. Lebrun's letter 'authorized me to declare to Mr Pitt that the Scheldt would be as good as given up; that the Convention would do away by a revision of its law all the offensive matter contained in the decree of the 19 November [the 'fraternal' decree], and that the Executive Council had rejected the offers of Liège and some of the Belgic provinces to incorporate themselves with France.'

But Pitt was unimpressed with the offer. According to Maret: he 'went into the Cabinet with it, and in half an hour came out furious, freighted with the whole of its bile, with the addition of Mr Burke, who attended tho' not of the Cabinet; and returning me the paper, prohibited me from corresponding with the French executive council on the subject of peace or war.' Maret continued: '[he] went into the cabinet. I went away chagrined.' It seems that after all the bluster and inconsistency of the previous French approaches, the cabinet had stiffened up Pitt.

On 23 January news arrived of the execution of Louis XVI. Chauvelin was promptly ordered to leave the country. When he reached Paris on 29 January there was an outcry. An embargo was imposed on Dutch and British shipping and Dumouriez was ordered to invade Holland. On 1 February the Convention declared war on Holland and Britain and urged the British people to rise up against their masters. The news arrived in London on 7 February, and on 11 February the King declared war.

The following day Pitt announced the news to the House of Commons in what was obviously a state of inebriation. The *Morning Chronicle* compiled a verse on the prime minister at that solemn moment: 'I cannot see the Speaker, Hal, can you?/What? cannot see the Speaker? I see two.' Although Pitt was a chronic alcoholic addicted to port, he rarely lost his icy self-control: he had obviously been overcome by the enormity of the moment and the failure of his appeasement policy. The issue had been the somewhat peripheral one of Holland. To Pitt what was at stake was not just trade, but the violation of France's treaty commitment. He did not expect the

conflict to last more than a year. In the event it was to be the longest in modern British history, to convulse a continent, and to drive him to an early grave.

It is hard to reach any conclusion other than that the British government was almost wilfully blind and isolationist in the years leading up to the war, preferring to avert its gaze from the growing tumult across the Channel. The trial and execution of Louis XVI were probably the real defining moments in forcing Pitt and the British into war. The Revolution had turned seriously sour the previous August: up to then fashionable opinion, and particularly Fox and the Whigs, were prone to view it with indulgence, as a constitutionalist movement embracing civil rights and an end to French absolutism, on a par with Britain's own movement to constitutional monarchy.

The assaults on the Tuileries and the prison massacres had altered all that. The horror of what was going on across the Channel had changed the minds both of the government and the public: the cold-blooded execution of the King galvanized them, as it did George III. Navigation rights in the Scheldt and the principle of adherence to treaties were of great importance, no doubt, but not enough to propel a peace-loving nation to war. The reason was that France was seen to be a barbaric, as well as an expansionist, power.

It had, in fact, taken the British government a very long time to reach this conclusion, and if it had done so sooner – when France was at its weakest in 1791 – it might have dealt a death blow to a tottering revolution: neither the revolutionary excesses, nor Napoleon Bonaparte, nor the twenty-three-year war might ever have been. But foresight was not then – nor has it ever been – a distinguishing feature of British foreign policy. When Britain finally went to war it was with a country racked by strife, but already recovering from the first blow of attack and vigorously fighting back. Moreover, dragged reluctantly into conflict, Pitt now followed his policy of appeasement with a disastrous policy of half-hearted engagement and military blunders that were reminiscent of the initial war policy of Neville Chamberlain a century and a half later.

Chapter 16

THE PHONEY WAR

When Pitt had declared war on revolutionary France he had good reason to believe it would be a short one: the execution of the King had triggered off nearly a year and half of Terror, fratricide and bloodletting in France that did not augur well for the survival of the Revolution or the country's war effort. Meanwhile, after a long period of spectacular French military successes, her continental enemies, Prussia and Austria, at last appeared to have her on the run. Finally Pitt had an overweening confidence in the ability of British armies to bring matters to a speedy conclusion.

As soon as the war broke out, with his usual administrative efficiency Pitt embarked on four major initiatives: first, to safeguard the homeland against the remote danger of invasion from France; second, and more vigorously, under Grenville's direction, to finance Britain's friends throughout the continent; third, to put Britain's naval power in a state of readiness; fourth, to encourage the internal dissidents within France.

Pitt's first priority was defending Britain. At this stage this was not taken very seriously, because France seemed in no position to defend its own borders, let alone mount an invasion across the Channel. The government considered Hampshire, Sussex and South Kent the likeliest place for French landings. Naval squadrons were to be sent to Weymouth, Dungeness and the Dunes. Regular troops were to be raised to buttress local militia in sudden levies, and a proposal for 'driving the country' – evacuating livestock from the potential invasion areas at speed if the French came – was adopted.

Meanwhile, Grenville's diplomatic offensive was vigorous and practical. As already noted, the Russians had until recently been considered the chief danger to European peace, with the Prussians following as a close second. Catherine the Great was not quite an enemy of Britain, while the Austrians were now in an uneasy alliance with her which the British believed acted as a restraint. The double offensive of the Russians and then the Prussians against Poland had revolted public opinion in Britain, and Austrian silence suggested tacit connivance with its ally, Russia. With the coming of the French Revolution, however, relations between Russia and Britain were at last easing. Catherine detested the revolutionaries and she now at last agreed to a renewal of a commercial treaty with Britain, as well as a pact specifying co-operation in the event of war.

The Austrians, for their part, were delighted by British enmity towards France. The new chancellor, Baron Thugut, was pleased to have a counterpoise to the Prussians, whom he detested almost as much as the revolutionary French. Britain's formal allies, the Prussians, were deeply suspicious of the new British rapprochement with Austria, but the Prussians needed money from Britain and asked for it; the British were happy to oblige in return for greater military help. An agreement between the two was signed, and soon the Austrians half-heartedly joined, creating the First Coalition against France.

Grenville was also busy elsewhere. A convention was soon signed with the King of Savoy, who had lost Nice and Savoy to the French and was now threatened in Piedmont. The British held out promises of despatching a fleet to the Mediterranean to help Piedmont in its efforts to regain Nice and Savoy, and were prepared to pay money for the King to employ Swiss mercenaries. In exchange for a Savoyard army of 50,000 men, the British said they would send a fleet and provide some £200,000 a year. The promise of a British fleet was also thoroughly welcome in the Kingdom of Two Sicilies which controlled Naples in the south. The King agreed to provide 5,000 troops along with four ships of the line to help the British in exchange for British protection.

The British also sent out feelers to their old enemy Spain. The Spaniards were difficult at first, but the British offered to protect their fleets while the Spaniards helped sustain Britain's Mediterranean fleet.

Portugal, an old friend of Britain's, was also happy to join the British effort – but only after the annual convoy from Brazil had arrived safely. The Turks preferred neutrality, but were not hostile to the British. The Genoese and the Tuscans, which had strong French links, opted for neutrality. The British also looked to the German princedoms for mercenaries, as they had in the past. Hanover, linked to the British monarchy, promised to send 13,000 men to Holland. Hesse, which had provided a large mercenary army during the American War of Independence, offered some 15,000. The Swedes were also approached for support.

It was an extraordinarily ambitious and comprehensive diplomatic effort and, to begin with, it worked. Grenville was seeking to encircle revolutionary France with hostile monarchical powers. In an astonishingly short space of time he had succeeded: with British fleets projected for the Baltic and the Mediterranean, the French would truly be boxed in. The next section will look at Britain's naval offensive which in this early stage, as later, was to be Britain's major contribution to the war effort. Finally, Pitt himself took the reins of Britain's land assault, which was designed to liberate Holland and take advantage of the explosion of a series of anti-revolutionary civil wars across France.

Before looking at the British expedition, it is worth considering the nature and extent of the fighting within France itself. France's predicament looked extremely precarious at the outbreak of the war: the Austrians, soon to be joined by British and Hanoverian forces, were advancing in the north. In the east on the central front, the Prussian and Austrian armies were pressing hard. After being driven out of Mentz, they were also pushed out of the strongly fortified lines of Weissenburg by the Austrian General Wurmser.

In Piedmont, after the initial advances, the French had been edged out of their camp at Belvedere. The French had also acted rashly by attacking Spain: a Spanish army had defeated General Servan, and the Spaniards had crossed the Bidassoa, as well as taking Port Vendres and Olliolles.

Within France's own borders, the worst conflict had broken out in the Vendée, the heavily wooded and pastoral country area of hills and

streams, canals and ditches just south of the Loire, which contains an almost impassable area, known as the Thicket. There the aristocracy shared in the lives of the peasantry, who had a joint ownership of the cattle herds of the region, and took part in hunting together; nor were the nobility particularly rich. The people were also highly religious. In 1793 the region erupted into a spontaneous uprising against the revolutionaries. As a near-contemporary historian related:

Their tactics were peculiar to themselves, but of a kind so well suited to their country and their habits, that it seems impossible to devise a better and more formidable system. The Vendéan took the field with the greatest simplicity of military equipment. His scrip served as a cartridge-box, his uniform was the country short jacket and pantaloons, which he wore at his ordinary labour; a cloth knapsack contained bread and some necessaries, and thus he was ready for service. They were accustomed to move with great secrecy and silence among the thickets and inclosures by which their country is intersected, and were thus enabled to choose at pleasure the most favourable points of attack or defence.

Their army, unlike any other in the world, was not divided into companies, or regiments, but followed in bands, and at their pleasure, the chiefs to whom they were most attached. Instead of drums or military music, they used, like the ancient Swiss and Scottish soldiers, the horns of cattle for giving signals to their troops. Their officers wore, for distinction, a sort of chequered red handkerchief knotted round their head, with others of the same colour tied round their waist, by way of sash, in which they stuck their pistols.

[The Vendéans were guerrillas shooting from behind trees and bushes with whoops and shouts to alarm the enemy, then withdrawing.]

When the Republicans, galled in this manner, pressed forward to a close attack, they found no enemy on which to wreak their vengeance; for the loose array of the Vendéans gave immediate passage to the head of the charging column, while its flanks, as it advanced, were still more exposed than before to the murderous fire

of their invisible enemies. In this manner they were sometimes led on from point to point, until the regulars meeting with a barricade, or an *abbatis*, or a strong position in front, or becoming perhaps involved in a defile, the Vendéans exchanged their fatal musketry for a close and furious onset, throwing themselves with the most devoted courage among the enemy's ranks, and slaughtering them in great numbers.

The inhabitants of the Vendée traditionally carried poles with which to vault the frequent waterways, a skill the republicans lacked. For two years the war between the guerrillas' self-styled Royal and Continental Army and the republicans raged with a ferocity unparalleled elsewhere in France: the insurgents won most of the 200 recorded engagements.

Thus frustrated, the besieging republicans resorted to terror. One republican unit was labelled the Infernal for its cruelties, which included roasting women and children in an oven at Pillau. As one republican soldier noted with considerable dismay:

I did not see a single male being at the towns of Sain Hermand, Chantonnay, or Herbiers. A few women alone had escaped the sword. Country-seats, cottages, habitations of whichever kind, were burnt. The herds and flocks were wandering in terror around their usual places of shelter, now smoking in ruins. I was surprised by night, but the wavering and dismal blaze of conflagration afforded light over the country. To the bleating of the disturbed flocks, and bellowing of the terrified cattle, was joined the deep hoarse notes of carrion crows, and the yells of wild animals coming from the recesses of the woods to prey on the carcasses of the slain. At length a distant column of fire, widening and increasing as I approached, served me as a beacon. It was the town of Mortagne in flames. When I arrived there, no living creatures were to be seen, save a few wretched women who were striving to save some remnants of their property from the general conflagration.

In June 1793 the insurgents of the Vendée tried to capture the town of Nantes, some twenty-seven miles upstream from the sea, which might

have given the British a major inland base, as the river Loire was navigable up to there. But the attack was beaten off and Pitt, who had no wish at that stage to get involved in the fighting within France, refused to come to the help of the Vendée. The revolutionaries sent in a huge army of 100,000 men to subdue the region, including 15,000 crack troops. After a major defeat near Cholet, the rebels of the Vendée retreated to Brittany, which would be easier to defend, and inflicted an unexpected defeat on the republicans as they crossed the Loire near St Florent. But at Mons they were at last decisively defeated with the loss of 15,000 men.

A brilliant guerrilla commander, La Chalette, however, continued to carry out strikes against the French. The war was only finally brought to an end when another large army was despatched to Brittany and La Chalette was captured and shot in March 1796. Pitt had cynically abandoned the insurgents of the Vendée to a terrible fate: a British intervention might have proved decisive in their support.

In the south the Jacobin putsch against the Girondins caused major unrest in four key cities: Bordeaux, Marseilles, Lyon and Toulon. Bordeaux failed to unite in support of the Girondins. However, some 3,000 men took up arms against the Jacobins in Marseilles, only to be mauled at Avignon. There was an uprising in Lyon against the hated overseers in Paris, but the city was quickly surrounded by an army of 6,000 men under General Kellerman: after two months of ferocious bombardment, the city fell, although 2,000 broke out and just fifty reached the safety of the Swiss border. As an act of vengeance, all the major buildings in the city were levelled one by one and many of the rebels were rounded up and massacred. At Toulon, the key port in southern France for projecting French naval power, the insurgents led by royalist naval officers appealed for protection to the English and Spanish fleets cruising off the port, and this was promptly provided ready to give, as we have seen, Napoleon his first military triumph.

This then was the state of France when Britain joined the war at the beginning of 1793. The Jacobins, a revolutionary minority, were fighting on four fronts: in the east, in the north, in the south-west against Spain and in the south-east against Piedmont. Internally, they were facing a huge revolt in the west in the Vendée and Brittany, and

major insurrections throughout central France, as well as the defection of their main southern naval base. The revolutionaries' hold appeared precarious at best, if not desperate: all they had on their side was their new huge conscript armies, knocked into some kind of fighting shape by Dumouriez and other brilliant French officers, and the revolutionary Terror which inspired officers and men to fight as hard as possible or forfeit their lives. A decisive push by the allied forces at this stage, in particular by Britain, would have seemed enough to snuff out the revolutionary flame.

This was exactly what did not happen. The British military intervention at the outset of the war was almost unparalleled in history for its disastrous incompetence, timorousness, indecisiveness, and appalling leadership. Pitt's ministry must share the blame equally with the British commanders: this highly successful peacetime prime minister in the first years of the war turned out to be an almost wholly disastrous wartime one, and his reputation was redeemed only towards the end of the ministry. It is extraordinary that he managed to stay in office through a string of failures, but he was assisted by the support of the King, the disorganization of the opposition and the diplomatic skills of Grenville, which proved as inspired as the actual conduct of the war proved catastrophic.

Chapter 17

DUNKIRK

Pitt's first intervention was faint-hearted, despatching just 1,500 men under the command of the Duke of York, George III's favourite son, to land at Helvoetsluys in Holland to help the Dutch in February 1793. This was essentially a token gesture, and proved to be unnecessary as well, as the advancing Austrian army was already winning a series of battles – Aldenhoven, Neerwinden and Louvais – which forced the French to return to Antwerp. Other Allied forces were converging – the Prussians and the Hanoverians. The Austrian Netherlands had been recovered and Holland itself was safe.

Thus encouraged, Pitt, instead of withdrawing his redundant force, decided to take the initiative: he resolved to seize Dunkirk, once a British possession, as a bargaining counter. He believed that the war was virtually won and would be of short duration. He thought he could offer Dunkirk, once seized, as a prize to the Austrians as one of a chain of ports necessary to protect Belgium from the French, and in exchange get them to stay in the Austrian Netherlands to guarantee security (Austria had long sought to wash its hands of this distant province by handing it over to the Prussians in a territorial exchange, something the British, always uneasy at Prussian intentions, regarded with deep foreboding). The port would in any event be useful in ferrying supplies to the Austrian army, and it would be denied as a base for French privateers.

The Duke of Richmond, who was Master-General of the Ordnance and effectively minister of war, immediately tried to bring the prime minister down to earth. He had made no preparations for war, and it

would take time to train newly recruited troops. The army anyway was overstretched.

> I stated to Mr Pitt that I thought he was going on much too fast in his calculations. That men just raised upon paper were not soldiers . . . that I thought it required at least six months . . . to make them at all fit for service and that even then they would be but very young and raw soldiers . . . I particularly represented to Mr Pitt that very proper [as] his schemes and ideas were they were much too vast to be executed within anything like the time he talked of that . . . by undertaking too much he would do nothing well. That great and long preparations were necessary for all military services, and that he could not too soon fix upon the precise plan he meant to pursue, determine his force . . . appoint his commander and fix the time for his operations. [Pitt] contended strongly that the service in Flanders would not interfere with any of his other plans and talked eagerly about them as what he really had in view . . . I told him that he would find himself mistaken and he said I should find he was not, and so we parted in great good humour.

Pitt rejected Richmond's advice largely because he had no wish to get bogged down in the war within France. His objective was to guarantee Holland and seize French colonial outposts, then negotiate peace with the French. He thought he could sell the Dunkirk expedition to British public opinion as an essentially limited one designed to buttress British naval defences.

With Holland effectively cleared of the French, a conference was held in April between the British, Austrian and Prussian commanders. The three agreed to continue besieging the garrison towns along the French border, in particular Valenciennes, Condé and Mainz. These duly fell in July. The Austrian commander, the Prince of Coburg, now proposed a bold strike into France, to take Cambrai and then march on Paris itself with the aim of ending the Revolution, which was now struggling with the revolts in the south as well as the Vendée insurrection in the west.

The British objected: they preferred to stick to their limited aims and

seek a quick peace with France. This showed a disastrous psychological ignorance of the ruthless revolutionary enemy they were dealing with, which saw the prosecution of war and terror as its only means of survival: in spite of repeated British attempts a negotiated peace was never on the cards with such an enemy, which sought to bring down the old order in Europe, not engage in the kind of gentlemanly duels that had characterized previous British-French wars. Meanwhile the French began to fight back. So it was agreed to descend on Dunkirk, a town of little strategic and small tactical importance to anyone except as a useful bargaining counter for the British in peace negotiations: it was explicitly agreed that the British would have sole charge of the operation.

The British army was not, at this time, at its best. The experience of the American War of Independence, which had ended a decade before, had not been forgotten; at the same time the intervening years had dulled its edge. It was underfunded, thanks to Pitt's ill-judged parsimony. It still retained the system of purchase of commissions as a means of raising finance, with the result that too many inept, inexperienced, callow young scions of the aristocracy had bought their way to the top. It suffered too from lack of co-ordination, as each commanding officer, regarding his regiment as his personal property, managed it as he saw fit.

A story is told of a Scottish aristocratic family: when a child was heard screaming from the nursery, the nurse explained, 'it is only the major roaring for his porridge' – the infant's career was already certain. The soldiers were often middle-aged or mere boys and many were sick for much of the time. They 'swore terribly', drank furiously and were ill-disciplined and lightly clad. As for the Duke of York himself, he was plump and red-faced and certainly courageous. He was also attended by able officers such as Lord Abercromby and Sir William Erskine, but it was said of him that 'his stupidity as a man was equalled only by his ignorance as a general'.

The Duke ordered his men to march north-westward to Dunkirk on 15 August, straight into a classic military debacle. The navy shipped large amounts of supplies in secret to the port of Nieuport but these arrived late, eight days after the Duke and his 14,500 men had arrived at the outer approaches to Dunkirk. There he waited in frustration,

having lost the element of surprise. Although the town was poorly defended, the French had time to flood the marshes to the south, forcing the British to attack along the shoreline, where they were vulnerable to fire from French gunboats. While the Duke waited for his supplies, the French were able to bring up no fewer than 30,000 reinforcements.

Unaware of these developments, Pitt behaved with aristocratic hauteur in this, the first real engagement of the war. In July he went to his country home at Holmwood and then to visit his mother towards the end of August, travelling down to Walmer to walk up the partridges with his confidant, Dundas. On 3 September the ebullient Duke of York invited Pitt and Dundas to cross the Channel to witness his attack as though it were a military exercise; they declined. On 6 September he attacked – only to discover the enormous size of the army he was facing – some 45,000 men. In a huge pitched battle he suffered some 10,000 casualties and retreated rapidly.

The first battle of the war had been a complete disaster, with blame attaching to Richmond for mistakes in the supplying of the forces, the navy under the Earl of Chatham, Pitt's elder brother, for failing to furnish support in time, and the Prussians and the Austrians for failing to tie down sufficient quantities of French troops on their fronts – as well as to the hapless Duke of York. Richmond almost resigned from the government after Pitt voiced criticism. The King was furious at the humiliation of his favourite son, who took the defeat badly. Public opinion was highly critical. The British had also lost standing on the continent: they had no card to play as they had not captured Dunkirk, and their army was now redundant, with huge losses suffered in a failed and futile cause.

The Prussians immediately began to lose interest in the French war: always keen on spoils, they had anticipated an easy victory, and this was not to be had. The Prussians were anyway furious that their German-speaking rivals, the Austrians, had taken Valenciennes and Condé in the name of the Emperor, not of Louis XVI – which also infuriated French loyalist officers. The Prussians decided to switch their attentions back to Poland: Frederick William left his army on the Rhine to join his Polish forces.

The Duke of York was sent to reinforce the Austrians in besieging the town of Maubeuge. But the Austrians were beaten back and together with the British forced towards the coast. Reinforcements had to be rushed to prevent a defeat before the armies went into winter quarters. The only news that raised Pitt's spirits in 1793 had come on 13 September, when the British Mediterranean fleet and Spanish navy landed at Toulon at the request of the city, now in rebellion. This victory had come to Britain entirely by accident, without a British life being lost, where it had eluded them in north-west Europe, with a staggering loss of 18,500 men by the end of the year.

Pitt was elated and talked of the 'final success of the war' being in sight. In a flurry of activity, the government ordered ten British companies from Gibraltar as well as 10,000 Hessians from Flanders and two regiments in Ireland to be sent to reinforce Toulon, which Prussia believed would act as a bridgehead to open a new southeast front in France. The Austrians were asked to send 5,000 troops from northern Italy and the Neapolitans 5,000 more. Together with 9,000 Sardinians and 3,000 Spaniards promised for the following year, Pitt believed he could muster an army of 60,000 men in the south of France.

Yet by October there were only some 13,000 allied troops: the Austrians in particular were unimpressed by the capture of Toulon, asserting that the northern front was far more important as it threatened Paris. The Austrians, who had some 93,000 troops in the Netherlands and 38,000 on the Rhine, regarded the excitable British, with some 22,000 men including their German mercenaries (the Prussians had 46,000), as no more than minor players on the continent, and were not disposed to accept their orders.

Meanwhile the position at Toulon was turning awkward: the French pretender for the Regency after Louis's execution, his brother the Comte de Provence, wanted to land there and proclaim the restoration of the monarchy. He had to be forcibly detained at his point of departure, Genoa. The British had publicly come out in favour of monarchy in France, but only in the vaguest possible terms: 'His Majesty invites the co-operation of the people of France . . . He calls upon them to join the standard of an hereditary monarchy, not for the

purpose of deciding, in this moment of disorder, calamity, and public danger, on all the modifications of which this form of government may hereafter be susceptible, but in order to unite themselves once more under the empire of law, of morality, and of religion . . .' The aim was not to lose the support of moderate republicans. The British were also quarrelling with their Spanish allies as to who should be in command of land forces. The British naval commander, Hood, did well in the American War of Independence, but was sixty-nine and had a less sure touch on land.

However, all these ambitious plans were frustrated in mid-December when the young French artillery officer, Napoleon Bonaparte, successfully captured the heights overlooking the harbour. On the following day Hood was forced to evacuate. He gave the order to Sidney Smith to destroy the captured French fleet in a single night, that of 18 December. Smith valiantly tried to carry out his order: thirty-three French ships altogether were destroyed. One English ship was wrecked when a French powder ship nearby was blown up by the Spaniards. Eleven more were badly damaged, leaving fourteen intact. Meanwhile, there was an appalling scene, as French troops skirmished with the withdrawing British and allied forces on the outskirts of town. The inhabitants hysterically milled around the harbour, desperate to get away: some 15,000 people from Toulon were received aboard the British ships, some 4,000 aboard a single one, the *Princess Royal.*

Subsequently Hood was blamed for not having seized the entire French fleet as prizes before Toulon fell: but the Spaniards also claimed them, and a war would have broken out between the two allies had he attempted such a thing. The huge damage done to the French fleet – the first major British naval victory of the war – was however overshadowed by the utter collapse of the allied war effort in the south. The Austrians were blamed by the British but, as Chatham remarked, the situation had required either a total commitment of forces or immediate abandonment. This second appalling defeat in the 'short war' was compounded by the revenge of the Jacobins against Toulon: of Toulon's 28,000 inhabitants after the British evacuation, only 7,000 were still alive a month later.

Having failed in the north and south, the British at last turned their

attentions to the west, where the Vendée war was still in full swing. An expedition of 12,000 men, including 2,000 cavalry, prepared to descend on the Isle de Noirmoutiers opposite the mouth of the Loire, to prepare for an attack on Nantes. The commander was to be the Earl of Moira, formerly Lord Rawdon, a distinguished veteran in the American War of Independence and a protégé of Lord Cornwallis.

From the first Moira found his force being depleted by demands from other areas, particularly the West Indies. When at last he set out in December, and reached the coast of Cherbourg, he found no royalists to greet him: they had already been defeated and dispersed. By mid-January 1794, after hanging about hopelessly off the French coast, the expedition had returned to Cowes.

Still worse was to follow. Pitt tried to put the best gloss on the disaster of the first year of the war, claiming he had saved Holland and Flanders, when in fact the Austrians and Prussians had saved them, and the British had merely failed at Dunkirk and Toulon, losing nearly 20,000 men. He and Grenville resolved to embark on a new continental offensive against France with their tricky allies, Austria and Prussia.

Wroxall wrote of Pitt:

> It was not till Pitt's eye lent animation to his other features, which
> were in themselves tame, that they lighted up and became strongly
> intelligent . . . In his manners, Pitt, if not repulsive, was cold, stiff,
> and without sincerity and amenity. He never seemed to invite
> approach, or to encourage acquaintance . . . From the instant that
> Pitt entered the doorway of the House of Commons he advanced
> up the floor with a quick and firm step, his head erect and thrown
> back, looking neither to the right nor to the left; nor favouring with
> a nod or a glance any of the individuals seated on either side, among
> whom many who possessed five thousand pounds a year would have
> been gratified even by so slight a mark of attention. It was not thus
> that Lord North or Fox treated parliament.

Rosebery said his nose was turned up at all mankind. Pitt's speeches
were short and to the point. Fox remarked of him that although he
himself was never in want of words, Pitt was never without the best
words possible.

The contrast between this snooty boyish bachelor aristocrat with his
penetrating command of the House of Commons and iron self-control
and his future adversary Napoleon – an emotional, voluble, deadly
serious professional soldier with a score of lovers – could hardly have
been more pronounced. The master politician and the master gunner
had only one thing in common: cool, detached and analytical minds
capable of quick decisions and instant, practical judgements.

Pitt's first cousin, his foreign secretary William, Lord Grenville,
made an interesting contrast. Unlike the brilliant Pitt, Grenville was a
formidable, practical man of great administrative ability and domineering temperament. As Pitt's first cousin and intimate and from one of the
pre-eminent political families of the age, he regarded himself as Pitt's
equal and spoke to him as such with often brutal frankness. Being older
than Pitt, although not as talented, he perhaps harboured some
resentment at his young cousin's seamless rise to the very top. But
his indispensability to Pitt is clear from the way he remained at his side
for eighteen years after joining one of his earliest administrations.

He had first entered the government as paymaster of the forces, when most senior politicians refused to serve the 'schoolboy'; indeed Grenville's own powerful older brother, the imperious Lord Temple, who was expected to become leader of the Lords, had at the last minute refused to serve, leaving Pitt in the lurch. The young man had been deeply grateful to cousin William for providing Grenville family backing. The two cousins, along with only one other man of substance, Henry Dundas, a deeply corrupt Scottish political fixer of great ability but somewhat crude tastes, had had to face the uncertain early years of the administration together, and were bound by close friendship.

The key to Pitt's appointment at such an early age had been the support of the King. George III, an intelligent, energetic and con-scientious man, although with a callous disregard for those who served him even before his descent into madness, had come to the throne desperately seeking to establish the Crown's power as the lynch-pin of the political system in a country which since the arrival of the absentee German-speaking Hanoverians had been a republic in all but name.

For a while he had tried to rule from behind a tame prime minister, backed by a tough advocate, Lord Bute. This had failed disastrously, never more so than when Bute himself had served as prime minister, attracting the scorn of such polemicists as John Wilkes and the anonymous 'Junius'. After several further attempts, he had secured a loyal prime minister, Lord North, a brilliant man at reconciling the demands of King and parliament for twelve years: but North had presided unhappily over the failure of the American War of Indepen-dence – largely the King's fault – and had fallen.

Now the King, as his mind began to totter, was desperate for a more pliant figure and was faced instead by an attempt to take power by the man he most detested in British politics – and there were many – Charles James Fox. Pitt had been brought in as the King's puppet, allying the royal party and country squirearchy in the Commons with his famous name and his father's lingering supporters; but it was far from clear that he would survive the torrent of invective that the experienced and brilliant Fox would unleash upon this pimply youth. Temple evidently believed he would not. The young Grenville came to his help to become Pitt's indispensable right-hand man.

Modern historians have recognized the steely resolve that was sometimes needed to buttress Pitt's more petulant personality, as well as the huge grasp of foreign affairs and diplomacy that added a necessary world view to Pitt's innate provincialism. John Ehrman writes:

> [Grenville's] talents, his very appearance, were in many ways like Pitt's. Grenville had the family gift for administration and finance. He had a good mind, a strong character and his share of the family pride. He was indeed something of a caricature of his cousin – he really was as steady, as unbending, as industrious as the Prime Minister seemed to the world. Lacking any of Pitt's mercurial brilliance, his influence was perhaps the stronger. Such a character, placed in close contact with a more impressionable one, was bound to have an effect; and so it did through a succession of posts ending with that of Foreign Secretary. The influence was liberal in peacetime – the cousins studied Adam Smith together – as it was unyielding in war. Grenville was one of the most reliable agents of administrative and financial reform, and the strongest opponent of any idea of reconciliation with a republican France.

At that stage the important traits of the imperious, good-looking, unbending Grenville were his undying hostility towards the French (Pitt was much more of an 'appeaser') and his dislike of continental commitments: he saw Britain's opportunities as lying with the overseas colonies, not continental entanglements. These were to some extent contradictory views: but the evidence is that from an early stage he urged Pitt to be more resolute towards revolutionary France, against Pitt's own inclinations.

Too many historians have insisted that Pitt was cut from the same fearless cloth as his father, the 'creator of the British empire'. It is always absurd to see any son as a clone of his father. Pitt had as much of the Grenville caution, careful judgement and over-attention to detail as his father's robustness. And he had come to office after a nearly disastrous experience – the American War of Independence, which had destroyed the ministry of Lord North and very nearly wrecked the British empire as well.

Pitt came to office determined to avoid another such conflict and the King, so quick to react to foreign slights, was also chastened. This led directly to the next few years of appeasement towards France, which were certainly not Pitt's finest hour. Pitt's reputation has gone curiously unchallenged by later generations – in part owing to his longevity as prime minister, in part his own incorruptible personality. Yet while his successes were many, so too were his mistakes, one of which – his initial policy towards France – was to prove nearly fatal, and caused his cousin and foreign minister, Grenville, to despair on occasion.

Pitt was farsighted in seeking to place Britain on a firm financial footing, and providing the excellent administration needed to man the royal navy and the army, because he was seeking desperately to avoid the mistakes that had led France to become financially overstretched during the War of Independence and which were to lead to the downfall of the monarchy. In doing so, Pitt at the beginning of his ministry proved to be a brilliant domestic minister and a weak and nearly disastrous one in foreign policy – attributes which ironically were nearly to reverse themselves in his last years in office. The two main objectives Pitt set himself in his first years in office were the prosperity of the country and to maintain domestic peace. He succeeded brilliantly in the first, to begin with, and much more controversially in the second, as unrest threatened while the French Revolution got under way.

Chapter 13

PROGRESS AND REPRESSION

The Austrian Emperor, Joseph II, remarked contemptuously at the end of the American war that Britain had fallen to the status of a second-rate power. That, however, was not how it looked from Britain, now under its new young prime minister. In the late eighteenth century, in spite of the American fiasco – and a spate of brilliant British military victories under Rodney, Hood and Howe had partially redeemed that – Britain was overwhelmingly the most powerful country in Europe economically, sustained by a huge and prosperous empire and under-going a creative renaissance.

Political stability at home; imperial revenues generated from abroad; a sudden surge in agricultural income provided by land enclosures; and later, the final key ingredient, the breakthrough in innovation and technology provided by the Enlightenment and advances in science – all these conspired to create a great leap forward in British society that has had no parallels before or since. The aristocracy shared the good fortune with a new moneyed class in a field of the cloth of gold of dazzling cultural and intellectual life.

The agricultural and industrial revolutions began to transform the appearance of Britain. As the downside, however, the new urban masses that were to provide the labour pool for the world's first industrialized society were huddled into crowded, insanitary terraces. Only the need to unite against an external enemy and the comparative liberalism of Britain's political system would prevent this powder keg of misery from exploding in the early part of the following century.

In France and other eighteenth-century continental systems, while

faction struggles raged at court, these were largely in secret, neither corresponding to the real balance of forces in the country as a whole, nor providing a safety valve for discontent. Nor was debate confined to the ranks of the aristocracy and *la haute bourgeoisie*, as in France; for while the British aristocracy certainly fought to retain its influence, its real power had been diluted in the struggles of the previous century by the much larger middle class of country squires, urban merchants and professionals.

In the parliamentary maelstrom, monarch, lords and commoners battled it out, now one gaining the upper hand, now another, none succeeding in imposing his will for long. After the reign of the Whig grandees had ended with the installation of the Hanoverians, Sir Robert Walpole, bourgeois, stolid, cunning, a machine politician, and his successors Pelham and Newcastle, had ushered in the new political age.

In turn the newly ennobled Grenvilles and 'commoner' Pitt – 'issue politicians' in an almost twentieth-century mould – came to dominate the stage, vying with the remnants of the old Whig aristocracy represented by the Duke of Devonshire and the Marquess of Rockingham, and the newly assertive 'court party' of George III, represented by the cack-handed Marquess of Bute and, later and more successfully, by Lord North. The system embraced most dissent: it is scarcely surprising that it became the age of oratory, for rarely have political leaders felt so free to express their own viewpoints, unhindered by fear of official reprisal, or by the harsh disciplines of the party machine.

The vitality of parliamentary debate was but one of the lasting innovations of the eighteenth-century system. Another was the way in which general elections – although most of the seats went uncontested or were in the gift of political bosses – actually mattered. Governments could be undone and were unseated by the verdicts of limited electorates in the small number of contested seats. Public opinion, however restricted the franchise, had real influence.

A third key new feature was a massive extension in the power of the press. The vigour and vitriol of press and pamphlet attacks in the eighteenth century would shame tabloid newspapers today: rarely in human history can political issues have been aired so freely, with such crude vigour and character assassination.

The test case for press freedom was, of course, the struggle of John Wilkes in his often scurrilous attacks against not just the King's favourite, Bute, but the monarchy itself. Initially dragged off to the Tower in 1763, Wilkes was freed after middle-class and 'mob' uproar, discredited and then exiled. He returned in 1768 to secure election for Middlesex. When the government had him expelled from the Commons and fined for obscene libel, he was tumultuously re-elected while rioting spread, leading to the killing of twelve demonstrators by a company of grenadiers.

In 1769, Wilkes was again unseated, and disorder reached a crescendo, effectively bringing down the mediocre government of the Duke of Grafton, and ushering in the more pragmatic and skilful North ministry. The Wilkes agitation gradually subsided, not least because, although a gifted polemicist, he was no public speaker, nor even a real revolutionary. But his virulent journalism showed just how far the limits of press freedom now extended, and the vigour of the parliamentary debate about his own fate made it impossible for him to mobilize opinion against 'the system' – even if he had wanted to do so.

The nearest equivalent of a Danton or Robespierre in England had been, in the end, more of an Irish rogue, and not one to bring the constitution down. The Wilkes riots never posed the threat to the body politic that revolution did in France twenty years later. The system had shown that it could respond – indeed Wilkes had brought down a government – and the challenge gradually faded, after securing its greatest triumph: the right to report parliamentary debates in the press.

If Britain was politically vibrant and mature, it was also endearingly and dottily obsessed with precisely the same sorts of issues that preoccupy the British chattering classes to this day. The conduct of the royal children was a national obsession. Aristocratic scandals were highlighted by the press, from the trial of the Duchess of Kingston for bigamy, to that of Lord Baltimore for rape (he was found to have been set up by the victim's family), to the rakish life of Lord Lyttleton, and to the indiscretions of the dazzling young Duchess of Devonshire.

The fashionable woman, in 1775, was criticized by the *London Magazine* for her tendency to:

rise at ten, throw herself into a hurry, dress before she goes out, fly away to the exhibitions of painting and models and wax, and a thousand other things: take a peep at a play to encourage a poor player on his benefit night – fly to the Pantheon [the hugely fashionable new gathering place on Oxford Street] to hear Agujari sing – whisk from thence to Ranelagh, to meet dear Lord William, and adjourn with the dear creature to Vauxhall to finish the evening with a glass of burnt champagne: then, yawning on her return, assure her dreaming lord, that she cannot support it; it is too much; the human spirit will not endure it, sink dead as a flat into her bed, and rise next morning in pursuit of similar follies.

In 1787, there was a royal pronouncement against vice and immorality after a long campaign to restore family values, which inveighed against drinking, swearing and gambling. There was vigorous debate between those like the Derbyshire poet, Erasmus Darwin, who advocated bringing up children without discipline and those who urged mental control and physical punishment. Measures were enacted to improve the lot of poor children, keep them off the streets and to regulate their use as chimney sweeps (a result of the new narrow chimneys on Georgian terraced houses).

Animal and even vegetable rights were championed. Fox-hunting was criticized. Travel, and travel-writing, became middle-class obsessions. Women's fashions were characterized by plunging necklines and provocatively protruding bottoms. Debate raged over the 'masculine' roles of active women and the need to keep them attending to home and children. Sexual mores were chewed over relatively openly, and books such as *Fanny Hill* fed the public's appetite for the nascent industry of pornography. A prominent playwright, Samuel Foote, was ruined by his homosexuality.

Rich young men indulged in the 'macaroni' pursuit of foreign fashions and deriding English tastes. Capital punishment, penal reform and poverty were earnestly debated. Aristocratic decadence and irresponsibility were satirized and demonized while George III and Queen Charlotte came to represent the essence of bourgeois respectability taken to prudish extremes.

In fact, the age represented the triumph of the middle classes well before the arrival of the Victorians: if the latter have been identified with bourgeois values it is because the size of that class was much greater during the nineteenth century. If more extensive social reforms were passed later, it was because the conditions which required them had not yet materialized during the eighteenth century. But the middle classes then showed just as much sensitivity to social conditions as their descendants. The triumph of the respectable bourgeoisie had already taken place during the eighteenth century, overlaid as it was with an aristocratic veneer.

No period in British history could have been more agreeable for the well off. Scientific innovation, following in the footsteps of Newton in the previous century, abounded; intellectual and philosophical discourse raged. It was the era of a renewal of the British literary tradition – epitomized by the fashionable obsession for Shakespeare, popularized by the great actor-producer of the age, David Garrick – and such writers as Samuel Johnson, whose *Dictionary* was published in 1755; Henry Fielding, whose *Tom Jones* was published in 1749; and, later, Goldsmith, Gibbon, Sheridan and Jane Austen. Sir Watkin Williams Wynn was patron to Garrick, who was godfather to his son Charles, who in turn patronized his friend the poet Robert Southey. A member of the Dilettanti Society along with Sir Thomas Hamilton, consul at Naples and husband of the wayward Emma, Williams Wynn embodied the artistic and intellectual pursuits of the aristocracy in the late eighteenth century.

In architecture the Palladian fashion was succeeded by the neoclassical and, later, by the Gothic revival. Robert and James Adam, James Wyatt and William Chambers scattered their perfectly proportioned gems around England. In art, Hogarth's acerbic and idiosyncratic brilliance was succeeded by the finest generation of British painters – Gainsborough, Stubbs, Constable, Hudson, Kauffman, Ramsay, Zoffany, Lawrence, Turner, Hoppner and Reynolds. The Royal Academy and the British Museum were founded.

The Grand Tour to Italy became *de rigueur* for wealthy Englishmen, who called on Venice, Florence and Rome, travelled to Naples to experience eruptions of Vesuvius, and, in the case of the wealthiest, had their portraits painted by Pompeo Batoni. It was the greatest flowering of art, literature and architecture in British history.

But Britain was also on the threshold of a new, altogether more serious age. The effervescence of the eighteenth century and its light, airy, exuberant art, architecture, literature and criticism were about to be replaced by the ponderousness of administration. The huge Indian empire acquired by Clive's buccaneering adventurism in the finest tradition of the English gentleman amateur now brought searing responsibility. Above all, the new supremacy of the middle classes, based on prosperity, a flourishing entrepreneurial spirit and technical and business innovation associated with such pioneering giants as Brunel, Telford, Stephenson and Davy was about to give way to the new period of disfiguring mass urbanization and industrialization.

Major change was perceptibly creeping across the land. It was the age of speed, travel, and the end of the first generation of bright young things since the Restoration a hundred years before. The next fifty years wrought more change to the British landscape than the previous 500.

Speed astonishing by the standards of previous generations became possible. As late as 1740 it still took around six days to travel from Chester to London. By 1780 it took just two days. The time from London to Gloucester was slashed from two days to one. A journey from Bath to Oxford took only ten hours, at a miraculous speed of seven miles an hour.

By 1770 turnpike roads, which had barely linked Birmingham, Chester and Manchester with London twenty years before, criss-crossed the whole country in an intricate gridlock from Truro to Aberystwyth, Holyhead, Glasgow, Edinburgh, Berwick-upon-Tweed, Hull, Norwich and Dover. By 1765 there were an astonishing 20,000 private coaches on the road, excluding stage coaches and hackneys for public transport. The proliferation of private transport broke down rural isolation and local commercial monopolies, bringing local prices tumbling.

Another communications revolution was under way – the canals snaking across Britain. This had begun with the waterways constructed to bring cheap coal to Liverpool and Manchester in the late 1750s. By the 1780s a hugely improved canal system permitted the economic transport of bulk goods the length and breadth of England, transform-ing local economies and making possible the development of cities well

away from the coast or from ready sources of raw material. It was this colossal public investment, harnessing private capital, that permitted the industrial revolution to get seriously under way.

A revolution was under way in the countryside too: enclosures, by which individual farmers took over common land, were spreading rapidly. The land not owned by the big estates was being privatized. Nearly 4,000 enclosure acts were passed between 1750 and 1810, affecting roughly a fifth of all land in England and Wales.

The old village communes were replaced by a class of prosperous middling farmers, while the poorer rustics became seasonal labour dependent on the owners' whim. Much hardship was caused, but the employment offered by the new agricultural improvements was also considerable. 'Engrossing' permitted the amalgamation of small tenant farms into bigger units, driving many peasant smallholders off the land. Farming banks sprang up around the country, financing the new prosperous farms to stockpile their produce and drive up prices.

The novelist Frances Brooke summed up the impact of the changes in her *History of Lady Julia Mandeville*.

It is with infinite pain I see Lord T—pursuing a plan, which has drawn on him the curse of thousands, and made his estate a scene of desolation; his farms are in the hands of a few men, to whom the sons of the old tenants are either forced to be servants, or to leave the country to get their bread elsewhere. The village, large and once populous, is reduced to about eight families; a dreary silence reigns on their deserted fields; the farm houses, once the seats of cheerful smiling industry, now useless, are falling in ruins around him; his tenants are merchants and engrossers, proud, lazy, luxurious, insolent and spurning the hand which feeds them.

There was a breakdown in the old privileged relationship between landowners and farm labourers, many of the latter becoming the fodder for the new industries. It is wrong, though, to see enclosures as a cause of the industrial revolution, except in that they released some capital. Industry did not spring up to absorb surplus labour: rather the new unemployed were lucky that industry expanded at about that time to

provide them with work. Even farm workers with settled employment were attracted by the supposed comforts and wages of the new industries.

There was, too, a dramatic self-confident expansion of urban Britain. London, from around 500,000 inhabitants in 1700, had nearly doubled by 1800. Even more impressive in relative terms was the fourfold growth of Birmingham, Manchester and Leeds between 1700 and 1770. At the beginning of the century only seven towns – Newcastle, Bristol, Yarmouth, York, Exeter, Norwich and Colchester – had more than 10,000 people; by 1800 the number was more than fifty. The urban population jumped from around a fifth in 1700 to around a third in 1800, or about 2 million of England's 6 million people.

The second half of the eighteenth century also at last saw a concerted drive for urban improvement: the dingy, higgledy-piggledy, crack-paved, open-sewered streets were no more. In 1754 Westminster was paved and lighted. Drain-pipes replaced spouts. Jutting house signs were replaced by numbers. Piped water was introduced, as celebrated by George Keate in 1779: 'The good order preserved in our streets by day – the matchless utility and beauty of their illumination by night – and what is perhaps the most essential of all, the astonishing supply of water which is poured into every private house, however small, even to profusion! – the superflux of which clears all the drains and sewers, and assists greatly in preserving good air, health, and comfort.' Slums and appalling conditions continued to thrive in the approaches to London and other major cities. But the cramped industrial kennels of the Victorian era had not yet sprung up. For the most part England was a joyous combination of the best of the old with the vigour, dynamism and change of the new before the latter's ill-effects were to sink in.

With France's acceleration into revolutionary chaos after 1789, all this seemed at risk. Britain's constitutional monarchy, its well-mannered oligarchical and aristocratic system, its ordered economic revolution – all seemed suddenly endangered by the call for ordinary people to rise against their masters on the other side of the Channel. Britain's only defence was that it had evolved its own version of a Rousseau-style

social contract between governors and governed by sharply reducing the power of the monarchy, permitting free speech, and a lively and vigorously combative parliamentary system – in marked contrast to the centralized and stultified style of monarchical rule now tottering in France.

But would these defences hold, in the face of the French revolutionaries' contemptuous dismissal of parliamentary democracy as a sham? Pitt by 1790 was not at all sure. He adopted a two-pronged policy: doing as little as possible to excite the enmity of revolutionary France – a policy which was deeply unwise and unrealistic, as we shall see in a moment – and, domestically, a crackdown on the very freedoms Britain had come to cherish over the previous three-quarters of a century.

This hard domestic line was to last well beyond Pitt's lifetime and the end of the Napoleonic wars – in fact, for more than four decades all the way to the Great Reform Bill of 1832 – and may in fact have brought Britain to the verge of revolutionary upheaval. It was disastrously misconceived: the tragedy was all the greater for its being implemented by a young idealistic reformer who had worked with his great friend William Wilberforce for the abolition of the slave trade and pressed for political democracy and Catholic emancipation in Ireland. Men such as Lord Liverpool, Lord Castlereagh and the Duke of Wellington have rightly been blamed for the harsh reactionary policies of the first three decades of the nineteenth century: but the creator of these policies was none other than idealistic, enlightened young Pitt himself.

The flame of panic was lit by Burke's *Reflections on the Revolution in France* which, from a man so reformist and wedded to liberty, came as a shock in its ferocious denunciation of the revolutionaries and all their works. This precipitated Thomas Paine's counterblast, *The Rights of Man*, which secured a phenomenal readership at the time of some 200,000. Pitt's reaction was to abandon any attempts at parliamentary reform and adopt an uncharacteristic policy of repression.

In May, 1792 a royal proclamation was issued calling on the militia to act against 'evil-disposed persons acting in concert with persons in foreign parts'. A bill was introduced to prohibit revolutionary propaganda. Prosecutions were brought on trumped up charges of sedition.

A young lawyer and advocate of parliamentary reform, Thomas Muir, was sentenced to fourteen years transportation and a clergyman, Thomas Palmer, to seven years for the same offence.

Senior committees were set up in each house of parliament in 1794 which reported that traitorous conspiracies existed to foment revolution. The Habeas Corpus Act was suspended – in the event for a full six years. In 1795 the King was shot at and stoned at the opening of parliament: his coach was destroyed. A Treasonable Practices Bill and a Seditious Meetings Bill were promptly passed which forbade unauthorized meetings of more than fifty people and dispensed with the burden of proof for treason. The country's multiplicity of 'popular societies' were suppressed. Restrictions were imposed upon the freedom of the press.

In December 1792 3,000 daggers were found in a house in Birmingham, and Burke caused a sensation by throwing some of them on the floor of the House of Commons. The cabinet sat until four in the morning to discuss the implications, with Pitt declaring melodramatically: 'Possibly by this time tomorrow we may not have a head to act or a tongue to utter.' He told Wilberforce in 1795 that he would be executed in six months were the government to fall and feared that he would be murdered in his carriage. This shrill, panicking representative of the old order lashing out in all directions contrasts sharply with the image of the cool British statesman projected at the time, and is reminiscent of the attitude of some of France's pre-revolutionary aristocratic fops.

Yet some of his apprehensions seemed justified. In August 1789 there had been bread riots in North Wales. In July 1791 a 'Bastille Dinner' in Birmingham had triggered off several days of rioting and resulted in two hangings. Troops were poured into the Midlands, from Warwickshire to Oxford. The following year rioting broke out in Lancashire and Yorkshire.

The situation was exacerbated by a sudden economic downturn in the crucial year of 1792 after years of economic expansion, as a result of an inflationary explosion being fuelled by a contraction in the money supply, which put up bread prices. Indeed from around 1789 to 1802 by coincidence there were poor harvests as well, of which the worst

was in 1792. In November of that year there were more than a hundred bankruptcies – double the worst total ever recorded. By the following year there were nearly 2,000 in the year as a whole, double the figure for the previous year.

All of this contributed to a general paranoia on the issue of public security at a time of immense social and economic change. It can be argued that the government was not viciously repressive in the circumstances; but the abandonment of all impetus towards reform – which Pitt had earlier espoused – was taking place against a pressure cooker of economic grievances which were to flare up in the second and third decades of the nineteenth century.

Understandably Pitt reflected the temper of the times: his repressive measures were hugely popular and passed by enormous majorities in both houses. There was also a climate of fear that Britain was being subverted by spies and conspirators from France originally master-minded by the Revolution's last ambassador, the Marquis de Chau-velin, actually a rather inadequate and incompetent personality. Pitt's fears may have been exaggerated by the one time he had been set upon by a mob during his premiership – outside Brooks's Club in St James's Street, when his life may indeed have been endangered (but Fox, the pillar of the club, was not to blame, as was later alleged).

Touchingly Pitt displayed one further sign of his old reformist spirit. After being shown the conditions under which the working classes lived and worked in the small town of Halstead in Essex by his secretary, Joseph Smith, and remarking that he had no idea such awful conditions existed in England, he issued a bill of some 130 clauses setting up schools of charity in each parish to provide work for the destitute to be run by justices, who could build warehouses, buy materials and buy bread. Friendly societies were to be set up, child allowances were to be provided, and each person was to be allowed a loan to purchase a cow. In this remarkable version of a primordial welfare state, Pitt showed where his heart lay; but the bill was considered too progressive by some and not enough by the radicals, and was allowed to lapse. Thus one of the French Revolution's first casualties was the cause of moderate reform in Britain.

Chapter 14

THE RUSSIAN OGRE

The British Foreign Office had perhaps unrivalled powers of analysis and intelligence at the time – its detached view of the European theatre was the best anywhere on the continent. The trouble was that this calculated objectivity was always designed to lead to a single conclusion: to take any action short of war. This suited Pitt's own preoccupations with domestic affairs, and in ordinary times was probably the right policy. However, the French Revolution had entirely reshaped the map of Europe to a much greater extent than anyone was aware of at the time.

The Foreign Office analysis, shared by Grenville although his suspicion of the French was much more pronounced than that of his subordinates, was more or less as follows: continental Europe was a patchwork, and an extraordinarily complex one at that, of a kind enormously satisfying to the largely classically educated minds running the Foreign Office. What was needed was to preserve the balance of power through an alliance here, a subsidy there, a nudge somewhere else. The British empire offered scope for bold and imaginative ventures. By contrast Europe was a mass of moving diplomatic pieces and a chessboard on which there were multiple players. Before, and all the more so immediately after, the French Revolution, complacency simply oozed from the diplomatic mandarins: the Revolution had brought low Britain's greatest rival, a belated revenge for the French support of America in the War of Independence. This, in brief, was their view of the continental quilt.

Towards France, Britain's oldest antagonist and rival, there was a

scarcely disguised contempt. The country had been virtually bank-rupted by the Seven Years' War and then the American War: the events of 1789 appeared to have removed it as a player from the European stage. This was immensely agreeable to the British. Then there was another traditional enemy, Spain. This was in a state of seemingly unstoppable decline. Both of these maritime rivals were on the wane.

The real threats to European stability were at arms' length: Russia, which was growing steadily more assertive under the initially anti-British court of Catherine the Great; and the newly emergent Prussia which, however, challenged the power of an old British enemy, Austria. Austria had long vied with Britain for control of the Low Countries and traditionally tended to side with France. Finally, Poland and Sweden were two smaller but at the same time somewhat assertive powers in their own right, while the Low Countries, the German states of central Europe, the Italian states and the Balkans were prizes to be argued over. The Ottoman empire in the east was also in decline.

The trouble with this complacent traditional analysis is that it took no account of two sea-changes now occurring: the first was the French Revolution itself; the second was the modernization of the rest of Europe. For Britain and France were not alone in being affected by the new political ideas after the eighteenth-century Enlightenment. Lib-eralism and reaction were almost at war in Spain and Portugal; the Swedes, Prussians and Poles regarded themselves as newly modernizing societies. Catherine the Great and her ministers considered that they were at the forefront of an enlightened autocracy. Joseph II of Austria had just introduced sweeping reforms across his huge Habsburg possessions.

With commerce and trade spreading exponentially across the con-tinent, all Europe was convulsed – as indeed France had been through the centralizing reforms of the French monarchy and the hostility they had aroused among the nobility. The British believed all they had to do was ensure freedom of commerce for British goods and for navigation; the rest could more or less look after itself. To understand how England blundered its recalcitrant and belated way into war in 1793, a quick look is necessary at the rather modest crisis which preceded it, before

returning to continental Europe in which revolutionary France sprang up like a lion in a herd of gazelles.

Pre-revolutionary France, although always treated with a wary eye, was not seen as much of a threat to European peace immediately before the Revolution. By contrast, Russia and Prussia were the new trouble-makers, and each was to play a part in the subsequent crisis. As Rosebery pithily wrote of the former:

> If there is one point on which history repeats itself, it is this: that at certain fixed intervals the Russian Empire feels a need of expansion; that that necessity is usually gratified at the expense of the Turk; that the other Powers, or some of them, take alarm, and attempt measures for curtailing the operation, with much the same result that the process of pruning produces on a healthy young tree. One of these periods had occurred in 1791.

More than that was happening in Catherine the Great's Russia. On 6 December 1788 her chief minister, Prince Potemkin, as part of a concerted strategy of Russian advances to the south, had won the greatest victory of his life in securing the huge fortress of Ochakov which controlled the mouths of the strategically crucial Dnieper and Bug rivers. With around 15,000 men, he had attacked in the early morning and slain some 10,000 Turks. As Simon Sebag Montefiore wrote of this strategic triumph:

> The Turks were killed in such numbers and in such density that they fell in piles, over which the Comte De Damas [A French adventurer and cousin of Talleyrand who commanded one of Potemkin's armies] and his men trampled, their legs sinking into bleeding bodies. 'We found ourselves covered in gore and shattered brains' – but inside the town. The bodies were so closely packed that Damas had to advance by stepping from body to body until his left foot slipped into a heap of gore, three of four corpses deep, and straight into the mouth of a wounded Turk underneath. The jaws clamped so hard on his heel that they tore away a piece of his boot.

There was so much plunder that soldiers captured handfuls of diamonds, pearls and gold that could be bought round the camp the next day for almost nothing. No one even bothered to steal silver. Potemkin saved an emerald the size of an egg for his Empress. 'Turkish blood flowed like rivers,' Russian soldiers sang as they marched into the next century. 'And the Pasha fell to his knees before Potemkin.'

Massacres are easy to make and hard to clear up. There were so many Turkish bodies that they could not all be buried, even if the ground had been soft enough to do so. The cadavers were piled in carts and taken out to the Liman where they were dumped on the ice. Still moist with gore, they froze there into macabre blood-blackened pyramids. The Russian ladies took their sledges out on to the ice to admire them.

Over the following eleven months Potemkin captured most of the lower Danube and soon there was only the Turkish stronghold of Ismail in his way. This was assailed by 60,000 'ursomaniacs' as the Prussians described the Russians. Ismail assumed the incarnadine horror of a Dantean hell. As the:

'ursomaniacs' screamed 'Hurrah' and 'Catherine II', and the Turks fell back, they were overtaken again by the lust for havoc, a fever of blood madness to kill everything they could find. 'The most horrible carnage followed,' Damas recalled, 'the most unequalled butchery. It is no exaggeration to say that the gutters of the town were dyed with blood. Even women and children fell victims to the rage.'

These spectacular victories were not about to be abandoned by either Catherine or Potemkin easily. However, in later 1790, Pitt, flushed by a minor diplomatic success over a British ship seized by the Spanish, decided to rein in the Russian bear: this was urged upon him by Britain's unstable treaty ally, Prussia, which was deeply concerned by Russian expansion. The usually cautious Pitt took on Catherine's Russia, which had proved unco-operative over a settlement in central Germany as well as over trade. Angry at Britain's alliance with Prussia,

Catherine had established relations with the leader of the British opposition, Charles James Fox. The Russians may even have instigated Spain's seizure of the ship.

Deploying a large fleet of thirty-six big ships to the Baltic, Pitt blatantly threatened Russia, saying that unless Ochakov was restored to the Turks Britain would attack with the aid of 80,000 Prussians, as well as Turks and Poles, with which Russia was already at war. It was an extraordinary threat and one for which the British public was wholly unprepared. Virtually no one had ever heard of Ochakov and most people preferred the Russians to the heathen Turks. A huge outcry against war exploded around the country, and Fox made a withering speech denouncing the whole enterprise. Although Pitt won parliamentary majorities, they were by smaller and smaller margins: his aide Grenville was implacably opposed to the whole misconceived idea. Finally Pitt was forced to revoke the Anglo-Prussian ultimatum – not knowing that Potemkin was trying to persuade Catherine to give way. According to Sebag Montefiore:

> Catherine and Potemkin argued for days on end. Catherine wept. Potemkin raged. He bit his nails while the tumult hit Catherine in the bowels. By 22 March, Catherine was ill in bed with 'spasms and strong colic'. Even when they rowed, they still behaved like an old husband and wife: Potemkin suggested she take medicine for her bowels but she insisted on relying 'on nature'. The Prince kept up the pressure.

'How can our recruits fight Englishmen?' Potemkin asked theatrically. Then news came of the British climbdown, which intensely angered their Prussian allies. A bust of Fox was given a special place of honour in Catherine's gallery. This diplomatic crisis had nearly caused Pitt's fall after six years in office. It had been disastrously mishandled from the start.

Why had Pitt undertaken such a risk? The answer was not pressure from the Prussians, but the perception in Whitehall that Russia had become the dangerous man of Europe. Under the dazzling Potemkin and the devious Catherine, it had become a serious danger to European

peace both in its own right and as an example, if its expansion went unchecked.

Russia had secured at Ochakov a presence in the Black Sea which would permit it to trade valuable timber and naval supplies, hitherto the prerogative of the British and north Europeans, with France and Spain. Russia was now constructing a port at Kherson and one at Akhtiar, now renamed Sebastopol. Potemkin established Ekaterinoslav ('Catherine's Glory') in the empty steppe which by 1792 consisted of some 550 state buildings and just 2,500 inhabitants, and expanded Odessa.

It seemed that Potemkin's next ambition was to partition Poland, or even turn it into a satellite to quash its 'revolution' – actually the installation of a hereditary monarchy. The possibility of a war between Russia and Prussia never seemed far distant. The Russians had also recently given King Gustavus of Sweden a bloody nose during his abortive war against them.

Catherine detested the French Revolution, which she regarded as a 'poison' and 'a sickness of the mind' – although there were at this stage no thoughts of intervention against it. But with Potemkin's huge and lethal Cossack forces in the south and the substantial and militarized Russian army in the north – partly in imitation of the Prussian example – Russia was a force to be reckoned with.

The Russian army, uniquely in Europe, was made up not of mercenaries and impressed men, but of peasants recruited in huge conscription drives, often chained when they were taken away. They lived a spartan, wretched existence under sadistic aristocratic Russian officers or German and French mercenaries, but they were extremely tough, brave and devoted to their homeland. As the Comte de Langeron, a French officer who detested the beatings and forced marches from which around half the soldiers routinely died, wrote of the Russian soldier: 'He combines all the qualities which go to make a good soldier and hero. He is as abstemious as the Spaniard, as enduring as a Bohemian, as full of national pride as an Englishman and as susceptible to impulse and inspiration as French, Walloons, or Hungarians.'

Catherine herself presided over one of the most glittering, wealthy, intellectually stimulating courts in Europe and was a captivating,

benevolent ruler. She was no liberal: she drew up 500 articles or 'Great Instructions' which codified the laws of Russia according to some of the principles of Montesquieu. But she refused to abolish serfdom, for fear this would turn the aristocracy against her and upset the established order – although she convened a 500-delegate assembly to have an advisory role. It was this vibrant, aggressive country that Pitt perceived as the greater danger to European peace, not France. Napoleon much later was to conclude the same.

For my beloved Jane and Oliver

CONTENTS

ACKNOWLEDGEMENTS

The Revolutionary and Napoleonic wars were the first of the modern great conflicts dressed in the trappings of the old. On land they bore all the romance of a dying era: gaudy and colourful uniforms, cavalry charges, lances, swords and muskets; and at sea the billowing sails and magnificent, creaking, flexible structures of wooden ships. Many of the commanders on both sides were still romantic, dashing, often eccentric, gallant and chivalrous.

But they were also the first wars of mass mobilization – the French levee en masse – of rapid transportation of huge armies from one front to another – witness Napoleon's army marching in weeks from Boulogne to Ulm and Austerlitz; of colossal set piece battles involving hundreds of thousands of men and huge casualties, such as Borodino, Leipzig and Waterloo; and of the laying waste of vast territories with terrible suffering inflicted on the civilian populations of the time. Proportionately more people probably died in the Revolutionary and Napoleonic Wars than in the First or Second World Wars; and they lasted more than four times as long as either. This greatest of all wars at the time was understandably dubbed the Great War – a century before the 1914–18 war.

One of the book's central themes is that the war was a clash of national interests, not merely the whim of one man, Napoleon, much as he tried to claim the full credit. Moreover, like a Wagnerian opera, it is a story that builds up steadily to a pinnacle or climax. However dramatic the early and middle stages of the war, particularly the sea battles, they are dwarfed by the immensity of the Peninsular War,

Napoleon's invasion of Russia, the Battle of the Nations, the fall of France and then Waterloo at the end. So far as I know no one since Sir Arthur Bryant (supremely successfully, but with an understandable patriotic slant given that he was writing during the Second World War) has attempted this.

This book seeks above all to portray the intensity of the struggle between Britain and France during this period – the first between a constitutional and a modern totalitarian power – while also covering the immense continental conflict, which determined the fate of Europe and indeed of much of the world for the next century. The book also tries to evaluate the extent to which the French Revolution's and Napoleon's ideals transformed Europe, in spite of his eventual defeat. I make no apology for the length of the work: there are innumerable short histories of the Revolutionary and Napoleonic wars: but very few which seek to do justice to the whole colossal experience – perhaps the greatest conflict of all time.

I owe huge debts to the many who have helped on this venture. The bibliography contains most of the sources and books I have drawn upon. I particularly want to highlight by far the best recent biography of Napoleon by Frank McClynn, which is comprehensive, well-written and always thought-provoking – although I disagree with many of its refreshingly trenchant judgments; John Ehrman's beautifully written and exhaustive biography of William Pitt, which is surely the definitive work for decades, and is not so much a biography as a hugely comprehensive portrait of a whole age; Sir Arthur Bryant's masterly history of the war; Christopher Herrold's vivid and exciting study of Napoleon in Egypt; Charles Esdaile's brilliant account of the Peninsular War, which uniquely and importantly shows a complete appreciation of the Spanish and Portuguese points of view; and General Segur's eyewitness account and Adam Zamoyski's superb book about the Napoleonic invasion of Russia. The many other books that are as deserving are listed in the bibliography.

In more personal terms, I am immensely grateful to my teachers Michael Phillips, Peter Lawrence, John Peake and David Evans for instilling a lasting appreciation of history; to Jonathan Wright and Alan Ryan at Oxford for showing me its relevance to modern political

decision-making; to Brian Beedham and Gordon Lee of the *Economist* for sharpening my writing skills; to my father and Raleigh Trevelyan for encouraging me to write; to Marchesa Serlupi Crescenzi for information on Napoleon's Italian background; to Andrew Williams and his family, to Lawrence James and Grant MacIntyre for their encouragement; to my editors Nick Robinson, Leo Hollis, David Blomfield, Sarah Moore; to my brilliantly perceptive agent and friend Gillon Aitken; to my indefatigable and immensely painstaking and efficient assistant Jenny Thomas and to her historian husband Geoffrey for his helpful suggestions throughout; to my sister Antonella and her family; to my mother for her ideas and huge moral support; to many other good friends for distracting me; and above all as always to Jane and Oliver for supporting me and keeping me human during this immense enterprise.

ILLUSTRATIONS

The Death of Admiral Lord Nelson at the Battle of Trafalgar, 21 October 1805, after being fatally wounded by a musket ball on board the *Victory*. Colour aquatint, London (I. Hinton) 21 November 1805. © akg-images/Nimatallah.

The Battle of Austerlitz, 2 December 1805, engraving by English School, nineteenth century. Private Collection/© The Bridgeman Art Library.

Treaty of Tilsit 1807. Napoleon and Tsar Alexander agree on a Franco-Russian truce isolating Prussia. The encounter took place on the river Memel at Tilsit, 1807. Colour chalk lithograph by R. Weibezahl. © akg-images.

Charles, Archduke of Austria (1771–1847) at the Battle of Aspern–Essling, 21–22 May 1809. Napoleon was defeated by the Austrians. Steel engraving from: Bilder-Gallerie zur allgem.Weltgesch. von C.v.Rotteck, Karlsruhe and Freiburg (B.Herder) 1842. © akg-images.

Capture of Oporto (Portugal) by the French under General Nicolas Jean Soult, 29 March 1809 during the Peninsular War. Wood engraving, 1875, after drawing by Felix Philippoteaux (1815–84). © akg-images.

Death of Sir John Moore, 17 January 1809, aquatint by Thomas Sutherland after William Heath from J. Jenkins's *The Martial Achievements of Great Britain and her Allies from 1799–1815*. © Courtesy of the Council, National Army Museum, London, UK/ The Bridgeman Art Library.

The Battle of Salamanca, 22 July 1812. The British army under Wellington and the Spanish army defeat the French under Marmont. Colour aquatint by William Heath (1795–1840) and Joseph C.Stadler (1756–1827). © akg-images/British Library.

Carretadas al cementerio (Cart with corpses for the cemetery) c.1812/15 by Francisco de Goya (1746–1828). Etching and aquatint. © akg-images.

View of the Kremlin during the Moscow Fire of September 1812, colour engraving by Schmidt after Christian Johann Oldendorp (b.1772). Bibliothéque Marmottan, Boulogne-Billancourt, Paris, France. © Giraudon/The Bridgeman Art Library.

Retreat of *La Grande Armée*, November–December 1812. Colour lithograph, unsigned, c. 1890. Westfaelisches Schulmuseum, Dortmund © akg-images.

Napoleon exiled to Elba. Anonymous French artist, 1815. © Mary Evans Picture Library.

Field Marshal Prince von Blucher (1742–1819), c.1816, oil on canvas by George Dawe (1781-1829). Apsley House, The Wellington Museum, London, UK. © The Bridgeman Art Library.

Equestrian portrait of the Duke of Wellington with British Hussars on a battlefield, 1814 by Nicolas Louis Albert Delerive (1775–1818). Private Collection/ © Bonhams, London, UK/The Bridgeman Art Library.

The Battle of Waterloo, illustration for a narrative poem by Dr Syntax, published 1818, coloured aquatint after William Heath, (1795–1840). © Courtesy of the Council, National Army Museum, London, UK/The Bridgeman Art Library.

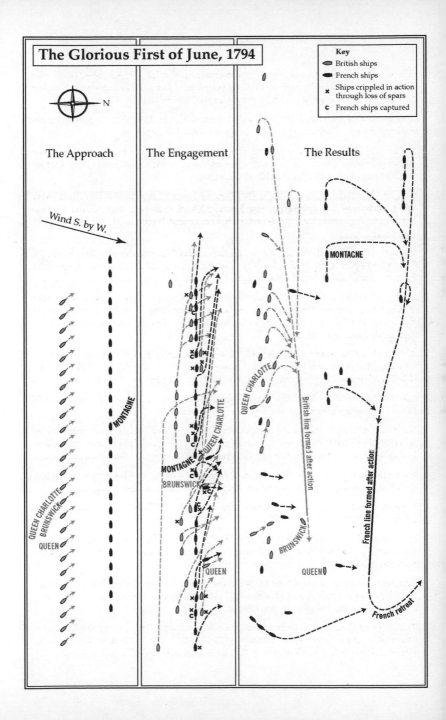

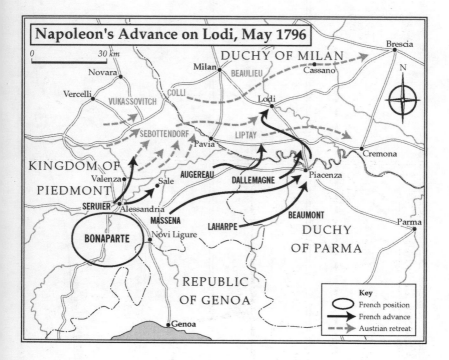

Napoleon's Advance on Lodi, May 1796

0   30 km

Brescia

DUCHY OF MILAN

Novara

Milan   BEAULIEU   Cassano

N

Vercelli

VUKASSOVITCH   COLLI

Lodi

SEBOTTENDORF

Pavia   LIPTAY

Cremona

KINGDOM OF   AUGEREAU

Valenza   Sale   DALLEMAGNE   Piacenza

PIEDMONT

SERUIER   Alessandria   MASSENA   BEAUMONT   Parma

BONAPARTE   Novi Ligure   LAHARPE   DUCHY

OF PARMA

REPUBLIC

OF GENOA   Key

French position

French advance

Genoa   Austrian retreat

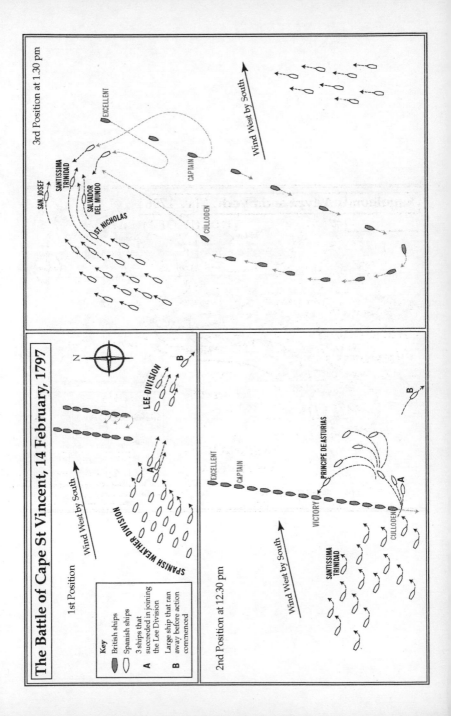

The Battle of Cape St Vincent, 14 February, 1797

Key
British ships
Spanish ships
A 3 ships that succeeded in joining the Lee Division
B Large ship that ran away before action commenced

1st Position

Wind West by South

N

SPANISH WEATHER DIVISION

LEE DIVISION

A

B

2nd Position at 12.30 pm

Wind West by South

SANTISSIMA TRINIDAD

CULLODEN

VICTORY

PRINCIPE DE ASTURIAS

CAPTAIN

EXCELLENT

A

B

3rd Position at 1.30 pm

SAN JOSEF

SANTISSIMA TRINIDAD

SALVADOR DEL MUNDO

ST. NICHOLAS

EXCELLENT

CAPTAIN

CULLODEN

Wind West by South

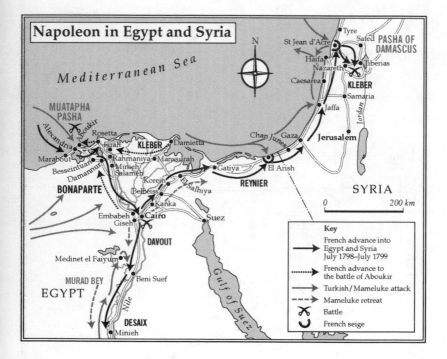

Napoleon in Egypt and Syria

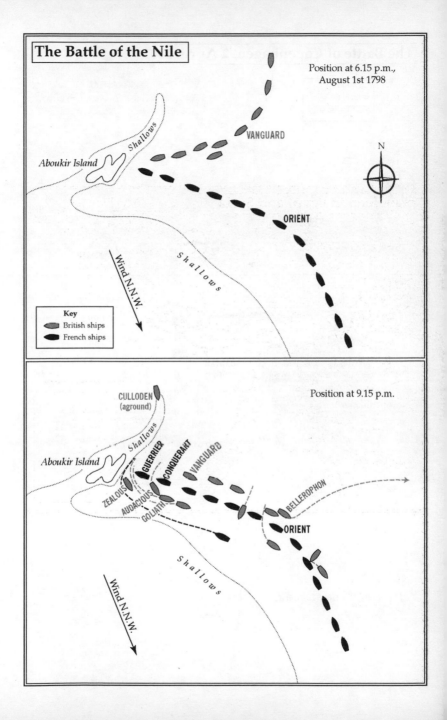

The Battle of the Nile

Position at 6.15 p.m.,
August 1st 1798

Shallows

Aboukir Island

VANGUARD

ORIENT

Shallows

N

Wind N.N.W.

Key
British ships
French ships

Position at 9.15 p.m.

CULLODEN
(aground)

Shallows

Aboukir Island

GUERRIER
CONQUERANT
VANGUARD
ZEALOUS
AUDACIOUS
GOLIATH
BELLEROPHON
ORIENT

Shallows

Wind N.N.W.

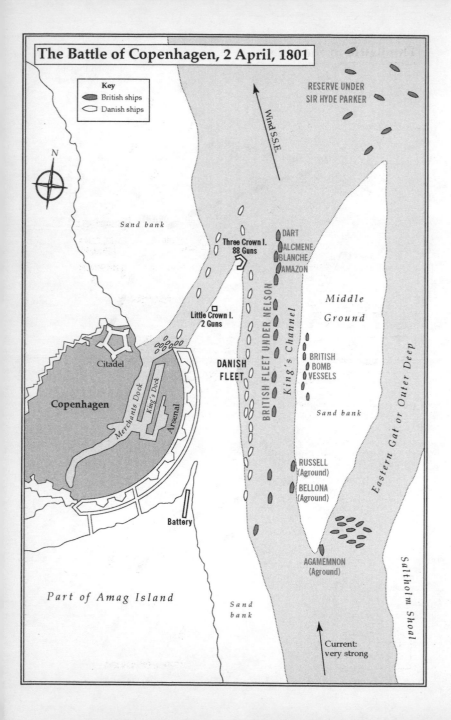

The Battle of Copenhagen, 2 April, 1801

Key
- British ships
- Danish ships

N

RESERVE UNDER
SIR HYDE PARKER

Wind S.S.E.

Sand bank

Three Crown I.
88 Guns

DART
ALCMENE
BLANCHE
AMAZON

Middle

Ground

Little Crown I.
2 Guns

BRITISH FLEET UNDER NELSON

King's Channel

BRITISH
BOMB
VESSELS

DANISH
FLEET

Citadel

Sand bank

Copenhagen

Merchants Dock
King's Dock
Arsenal

Eastern Gat or Outer Deep

RUSSELL
(Aground)

BELLONA
(Aground)

Battery

Part of Amag Island

AGAMEMNON
(Aground)

Saltholm Shoal

*Sand
bank*

Current:
very strong

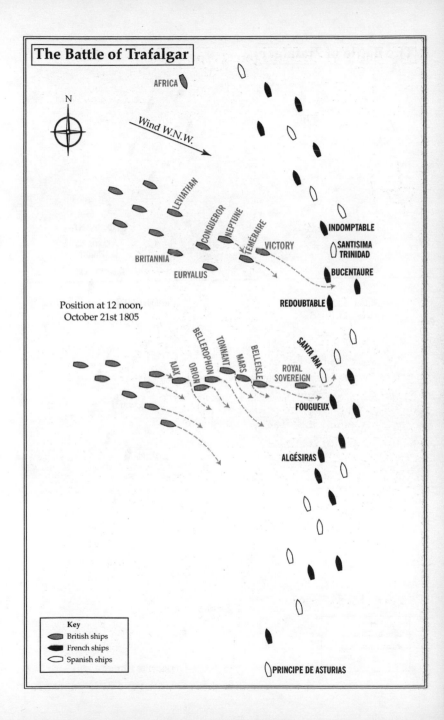

The Battle of Trafalgar

N

Wind W.N.W.

AFRICA

LEVIATHAN

CONQUEROR

NEPTUNE

TÉMÉRAIRE

VICTORY

INDOMPTABLE

SANTISIMA TRINIDAD

BRITANNIA

BUCENTAURE

EURYALUS

REDOUBTABLE

Position at 12 noon,
October 21st 1805

BELLEROPHON

TONNANT

AJAX

ORION

MARS

BELLEISLE

SANTA ANA

ROYAL SOVEREIGN

FOUGUEUX

ALGÉSIRAS

PRINCIPE DE ASTURIAS

Key
British ships
French ships
Spanish ships

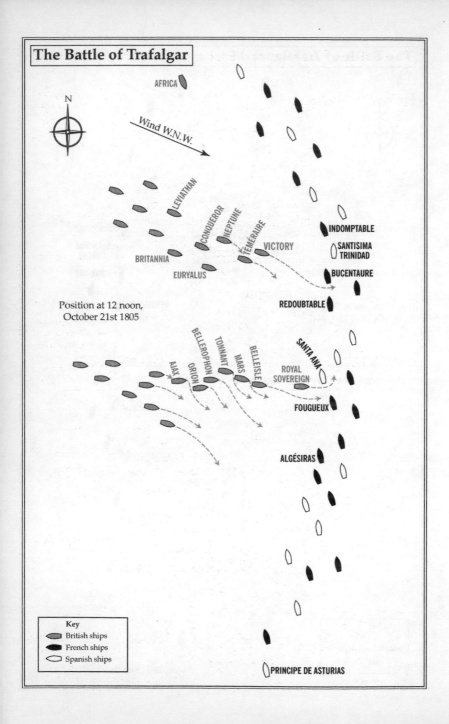

The Battle of Trafalgar

AFRICA

N

Wind W.N.W.

LEVIATHAN

CONQUEROR

NEPTUNE

TÉMÉRAIRE

VICTORY

BRITANNIA

EURYALUS

INDOMPTABLE

SANTISIMA
TRINIDAD

BUCENTAURE

REDOUBTABLE

Position at 12 noon,
October 21st 1805

BELLEROPHON

TONNANT

AJAX

ORION

MARS

BELLEISLE

SANTA ANA

ROYAL
SOVEREIGN

FOUGUEUX

ALGÉSIRAS

PRINCIPE DE ASTURIAS

Key
British ships
French ships
Spanish ships

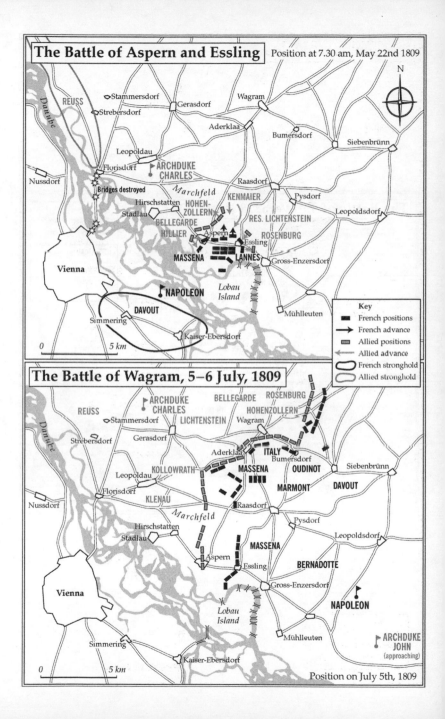

The Battle of Aspern and Essling
Position at 7.30 am, May 22nd 1809

REUSS
Stammersdorf
Streberstorf
Gerasdorf
Wagram
Aderklaa
Bumersdorf
Siebenbrünn
Leopoldau
Florisdorf
Nussdorf
Bridges destroyed
ARCHDUKE CHARLES
Marchfeld
Raasdorf
Pysdorf
Leopoldsdorf
KENMAIER
Hirschstatten
HOHEN-ZOLLERN
RES. LICHTENSTEIN
Stadlau
BELLEGARDE
HILLIER
Aspern
ROSENBURG
Essling
MASSENA
LANNES
Gross-Enzersdorf
Vienna
NAPOLEON
Lobau Island
DAVOUT
Simmering
Kaiser-Ebersdorf
Mühlleuten

N

0   5 km

Key
French positions
French advance
Allied positions
Allied advance
French stronghold
Allied stronghold

The Battle of Wagram, 5–6 July, 1809

ARCHDUKE CHARLES
REUSS
Stammersdorf
Streberstorf
Gerasdorf
BELLEGARDE
ROSENBURG
HOHENZOLLERN
LICHTENSTEIN
Wagram
Aderklaa
ITALY
Bumersdorf
Siebenbrünn
KOLLOWRATH
MASSENA
OUDINOT
Leopoldau
Florisdorf
KLENAU
MARMONT
DAVOUT
Nussdorf
Marchfeld
Raasdorf
Pysdorf
Leopoldsdorf
Hirschstatten
Stadlau
MASSENA
Aspern
Essling
BERNADOTTE
Vienna
Gross-Enzersdorf
Lobau Island
NAPOLEON
Simmering
Mühlleuten
Kaiser-Ebersdorf
ARCHDUKE JOHN (approaching)

0   5 km

Position on July 5th, 1809

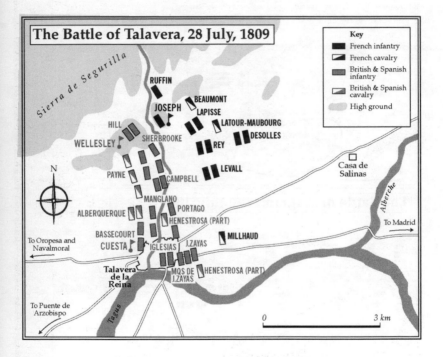

The Battle of Talavera, 28 July, 1809

Key
■ French infantry
◪ French cavalry
▨ British & Spanish infantry
◪ British & Spanish cavalry
░ High ground

Sierra de Segurilla

RUFFIN
JOSEPH
BEAUMONT
LAPISSE
LATOUR-MAUBOURG
HILL
WELLESLEY
SHERBROOKE
REY
DESOLLES
PAYNE
CAMPBELL
LEVALL
MANGLANO
ALBERQUERQUE
PORTAGO
HENESTROSA (PART)
BASSECOURT
CUESTA
IGLESIAS
J.ZAYAS
MILLHAUD
MQS DE
J.ZAYAS
HENESTROSA (PART)
Casa de
Salinas

N

To Oropesa and
Navalmoral

To Madrid

Talavera
de la
Reina

To Puente de
Arzobispo

Tagus

Alberche

0   3 km

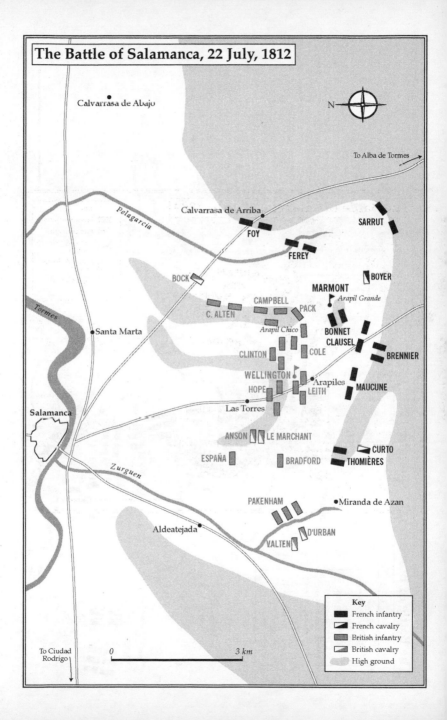

The Battle of Salamanca, 22 July, 1812

Calvarrasa de Abajo

N

To Alba de Tormes

Pelagarcia

Calvarrasa de Arriba

FOY

SARRUT

FEREY

BOYER

BOCK

MARMONT
Arapil Grande

CAMPBELL

C. ALTEN

PACK

Tormes

Santa Marta

Arapil Chico

BONNET
CLAUSEL

CLINTON

COLE

BRENNIER

WELLINGTON

Arapiles

MAUCUNE

HOPE

LEITH

Las Torres

Salamanca

ANSON   **LE MARCHANT**

ESPAÑA

BRADFORD

CURTO
THOMIÈRES

Zurguen

PAKENHAM

Miranda de Azan

Aldeatejada

D'URBAN

V.ALTEN

Key

■ French infantry
▱ French cavalry
▮ British infantry
▱ British cavalry
▒ High ground

To Ciudad
Rodrigo

0   3 km

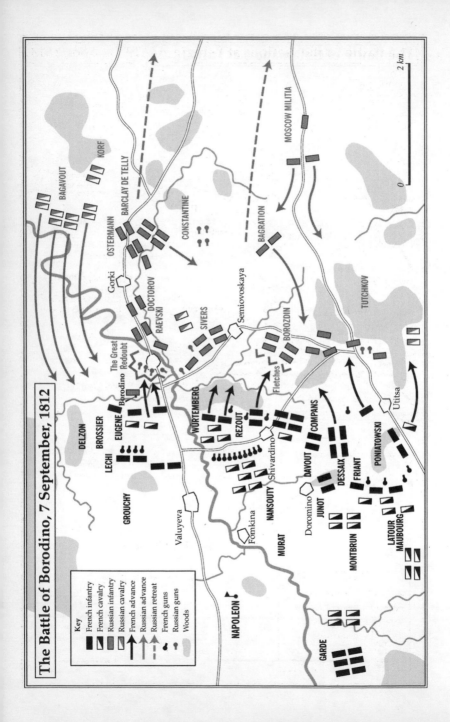

The Battle of Borodino, 7 September, 1812

Key
French infantry
French cavalry
Russian infantry
Russian cavalry
French advance
Russian advance
Russian retreat
French guns
Russian guns
Woods

BAGAVOUT

KORF

BARCLAY DE TELLY

MOSCOW MILITIA

CONSTANTINE

OSTERMANN

BAGRATION

Gorki

DOCTOROV

Semiovoskaya

RAEVSKI

SIVERS

BOROZDIN

TUTCHKOV

The Great
Redoubt

Borodino

Fletches

Utitsa

DELZON

BROSSIER

WURTEMBERG

EUGENE

REZOUT

LECHI

Shivardino

COMPANS

DAVOUT

PONIATOWSKI

GROUCHY

NANSOUTY

Doromino

DESSAIX

FRIANT

Valuyeva

Fomkina

JUNOT

MONTBRUN

LATOUR
MAUBOURG

MURAT

NAPOLEON

GARDE

2 km

0

The Battle of the Nations at Leipzig, 16–19 October, 1813

DENMARK

Copenhagen

SWEDEN

Baltic Sea

Kiel

Hamburg Lübeck

Köslin

Pomerania

Danzig
**French forces
besieged by allies** Elbing

HANOVER

Stettin

PRUSSIA

Hanover

Berlin

Magdeburg

Frankfurt

FEDERATION OF

Leipzig

THE RHINE

Dresden

Bromberg Thorn

GRAND DUCHY
OF WARSAW
(Occupied by Russia)

Posen Kalisch

Glogau

Silesia

Breslau

Bayreuth

Prague

Pilsen

Nüremberg

AUSTRIAN

EMPIRE

Key

→ French advance

-→ French retreat

→ Allied advance

-→ Allied retreat

✕ Site of battle

🏰 Major French fortress

0   100 km

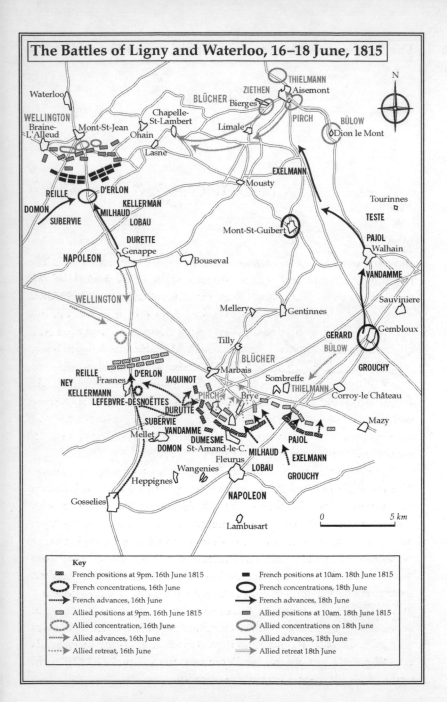

The Battles of Ligny and Waterloo, 16–18 June, 1815

Waterloo

WELLINGTON
Braine-
L'Alleud   Mont-St-Jean

Chapelle-
St-Lambert

THIELMANN
Aisemont

ZIETHEN
BLÜCHER   Bierges

PIRCH

BÜLOW
Dion le Mont

Ohain

Limale

Lasne

EXELMANN

Mousty

Tourinnes

TESTE

REILLE   D'ERLON
            KELLERMAN
DOMON   MILHAUD
SUBERVIE   LOBAU
            DURETTE

NAPOLEON   Genappe

Bouseval

Mont-St-Guibert

PAJOL
Walhain

VANDAMME

Sauviniere

WELLINGTON

Mellery   Gentinnes

Gembloux

Tilly

BLÜCHER

GÉRARD
BÜLOW

Marbais

Sombreffe

GROUCHY

REILLE   D'ERLON   JAQUINOT
NEY   Frasnes   PIRCH   Brye
KELLERMANN   THIELMANN
LEFEBVRE-DESNOËTTES   DURUTTE
            SUBERVIE   Corroy-le Château
Mellet   VANDAMME
            DUMESME
DOMON   St-Amand-le-C.   MILHAUD   Mazy
            Fleurus   LOBAU   PAJOL
Wangenies   EXELMANN
Heppignes   GROUCHY

Gosselies   NAPOLEON

                                          0   5 km

Lambusart

Key

	French positions at 9pm. 16th June 1815		French positions at 10am. 18th June 1815
French concentrations, 16th June		French concentrations, 18th June
French advances, 16th June		French advances, 18th June
Allied positions at 9pm. 16th June 1815		Allied positions at 10am. 18th June 1815
Allied concentration, 16th June		Allied concentrations on 18th June
Allied advances, 16th June		Allied advances, 18th June
Allied retreat, 16th June		Allied retreat 18th June

INTRODUCTION

Biographies of Napoleon can be weighed by the hundredweight. Yet there are curiously few recent attempts at an entire history of the revolutionary and Napoleonic wars, the colossal and protracted global struggle that convulsed all of Europe for nearly a quarter of a century. This book is an attempt to address that void: it is an unashamedly 'general' rather than scholastic work, written for a wide audience. A broad brush inevitably obscures detail, but no scholastic work could possibly do justice to that great struggle without running into a dozen volumes. My aim has been to provide a giant and vivid canvas on which to depict these globe-bestriding, world-changing events for the general reader, providing new insights and drawing on many widely neglected accounts. It is for the reader to judge whether I have succeeded.

According to Napoleon, history is a myth that men agree to believe. The revolutionary and Napoleonic wars are usually divided into two rich mythologies: the first is that of Napoleon the monster who inflicted years of suffering and slaughter across Europe, precursor to the worst tyrannies in the twentieth century; the second that of Napoleon the genius and modernizer who liberated Europe from decrepit feudal absolutism and endowed the continent with modern laws, national self-respect, and bourgeois progress. Both of these are predicated on the ultimate Napoleonic myth: his omnipotence, as powerful through the ages as the identification of Julius Caesar's power with that of ancient Rome. Both owe as much to historical propaganda as to Napoleon's vanity and his determination to write history solely in terms of his own extraordinary personality.

Napoleon's is the dominant personality in the events of this book, primarily from 1799 to 1815. But the mythology is, to say the least, extravagant with the truth. The revolutionary wars from 1792 to 1802 were as significant and dangerous to Britain and Europe as the Napoleonic phase, from 1803 to 1815. Men like Dumouriez and Carnot, now largely forgotten, first created the military machine which Napoleon later piloted. Napoleon's command over his generals, his ministers and France as a whole was more circumscribed than many people today believe. His military successes were often close-run and short-lived, and his hubris brought about defeat at Waterloo in 1815.

This book attempts to outline what really happened during the frenzied quarter of a century when Britain, having carved out a global empire and dazzled the world with its inventiveness and industrial revolution, seemed on the verge of being invaded and devastated, as so much of continental Europe had been already.

In 1788 Europe was peaceful and prosperous. There was little sign that anything would disturb the tranquility of the settled alliances between its seven great powers and the host of lesser princedoms. In Britain alone was the monarchy little more than a façade for rule by a parliament dominated by factions, commercial interests and, in the still-powerful House of Lords, the aristocracy. While the humdrum and egotistical George III had prestige and influence, he did not rule. Britain had recently suffered the grievous loss of its rebellious, although small and comparatively poor, North American colonies, but still presided over a far-flung and growing global empire.

Elsewhere in Europe, royal absolutism held sway, usually centralized around a royal court. The most powerful of these was the magnificent monarchy of France, where the tall, fair-haired, snub-nosed and acerbically intelligent King Louis XVI presided over fabulous Bourbon Versailles, with palaces so large that they bristled with whole villages of intriguing, cavorting and amorous courtiers. The King was married to a haughty Austrian princess, Marie Antoinette, cementing France's alliance of convenience with the other greatest dynasty in Europe, that of Austria's ruling Habsburgs. France was Britain's great continental rival, having just lost the Seven Years War, then outwitted the

British during the American War of Independence. Although the two nations were currently at peace, Franco-British trade, naval and military rivalry continued to be played out across the globe, from India to the West Indies.

France's greatest continental ally and rival was Austria-Hungary, a polyglot empire that dominated northern Italy, the Balkans, and most of eastern Europe. Its Emperor, presiding over a court at Vienna second only to France's in its extravagance and beauty, was soon to be the indecisive, garrulous Francis II. To the north, completing the trio of great nations that dominated the central massif of the European continent was Prussia. A newly emergent and aggressive military power under Frederick the Great, threatening the host of German principalities and buffer states between itself and France, it was now at peace with its neighbours, and ruled by the weak and vacillating Frederick William.

To the south-east lay the declining power of the Turkish Ottoman empire, still ruling a vast swathe of the Middle East but long incapable of challenging a major European nation, hundreds of years after the great Saracen offensives had petered out. The Ottomans' very weakness posed a threat to Europe simply by offering a tempting vacuum to others, in particular the quasi-barbarian power to the north, Catherine the Great's Russia, which was embarked on a policy of imperial expansion that seemed to pose the greatest threat to European stability. This strong-willed, shrewd and capricious woman had long ruled with great firmness. Now her reign was coming to an end, and the paranoid, half-insane Tsar Paul was to provide an unhappy interregnum before the accession of his strange son and probable murderer, Alexander, a young man of almost feminine beauty who alternated visionary ideas with religious fanaticism.

Finally, to the south-west was the seventh great power, now in decline but possessed of an overseas empire of fabulous wealth. Over the centuries shipments of silver to Spain had served to corrode the country's warrior ruling class. Spain was ruled by a decent but vacuous Bourbon king, Charles IV, his lascivious wife Maria Luisa and her opportunist lover, Manuel Godoy. The monarchs were to be succeeded by their brutal and reactionary son, Ferdinand VII.

These were the seven great powers of Europe, all of them absolute monarchies save one, Britain, which was a republican oligarchy in all but name. Three of them were strong and entrenched across the prosperous heartland of central Europe; the two in the south were in advanced stages of decline, while Russia in the east was regarded as primitive and potentially predatory to its Baltic neighbours in the north and the Ottoman empire in the south.

The rest of Europe was carved into a host of lesser monarchies, princelings and duchies. Sweden, Saxony, Bavaria, Portugal, the Kingdom of the Two Sicilies, Parma and Piedmont were its most significant states, most of them satellites gravitating around the orbit of the greater powers. The Pope presided as Europe's greatest spiritual prince, with his own fiefdom in central Italy, although Catholicism was under challenge from northern Protestantism. It seemed an apparently unbreakable façade of monarchical absolutism, locked in alliances, rivalries and dynastic marriages, presiding over a continent as peaceful and well ordered as at any time in its turbulent history.

In 1789 the very centrepiece of this intricate structure of peace and prosperity, Louis XVI's court at Versailles, cracked and was soon shattered into a thousand pieces. In its place there emerged first an elitist struggle for power, then an uncontrolled mob, and then the massed formations of brutally disciplined armies the like and size of which had never been seen before to pour over France's borders in a frenzy of uncontrolled warfare, initially in defence of the Revolution, then to promote its ideals, finally in torrents of outright aggression and conquest.

Within the space of a couple of years, Europe was plunged into one of the largest and longest wars of its history that was to last the best part of a quarter of a century and threaten to overturn the entire social order of monarchy and aristocratic rule and place the continent in the grip of a single militarist nation. With vast conscript armies moving at unprecedented speed and overwhelming force against the parade-ground armies of Europe with their aristocratic officers and traditional military tactics, it seemed that the militarist juggernaut would sweep all before it. The continent was plunged into a seemingly endless confrontation which ravaged whole countries from Spain and Italy in the south to

Belgium in the north-west, to Prussia and into Russia in the east, to Austria in the centre.

It was as though a volcano had erupted at the heart of Europe, belching out destruction and threatening everything in its path. It was to be perhaps the biggest bloodbath in European history, killing millions, levelling and looting, obliterating the livelihoods and homes of entire nations. This was the birth of the modern age of mass politics, revolution and total warfare, the foreshadower of the destructive wars of the twentieth century.

Although he was only a secondary player during the first phase of the revolutionary war until 1800, the carnage became associated eventually with the single man who to his friends and enemies alike seemed to incarnate the spirit of that unstoppable, relentless war machine, Napoleon Bonaparte. Throughout the war only one country stood almost continuously against him. It was the greatest challenge that the islands of Britain had faced since the Norman invasion and Spanish Armada. To the growing alarm of its leaders and people, as France's neighbours were ruthlessly cut down one after another, the struggle soon appeared to be hopeless, inviting first economic strangulation and then a murderous invasion.

Part 1

FRANCE IN TUMULT

1789–93

Chapter 1

THE COLLAPSE OF THE ANCIEN REGIME

In the beginning there was a spark. That spark was the English Revolution of 1640–60. Flaring up fiercely and briefly, it left three embers smouldering: the rhetoric and republican ideals of its main instigators, at a time when it was virtual blasphemy to challenge the divine right of kings; the proof that social and economic forces could converge to knock even the embodiment of the power of the central state off its pedestal; and, last but not least, the elemental force that was forged from the fires of revolution, so necessary to advancing it, mastering it and ultimately destroying it – that of a powerful standing army. The English Revolution of course ended with the Restoration of 1660 but the underbrush continued to burn, re-emerging in the assertion of the rights of parliament that deposed James II and the eventual establishment of a virtually powerless monarchy under the Hanoverians.

The embers of revolution, however, still smouldered to be blown by Atlantic winds across to Britain's north American colonies. There, as in Britain before the Civil War, rapid economic and demographic change in the mid-eighteenth century suddenly collided with the attempt of a centralizing state to extend its authority in 1776. The result was inevitable: the latter was swept away in a torrent: only in calmer waters further downstream, could it re-emerge in very different guise.

If the American Revolution can be described as a distant descendant of the English Revolution, the French Revolution was undoubtedly a firstborn child of the American one. It was no coincidence at all that it began when Benjamin Franklin – lecherous, egotistical, homespun, brilliant Franklin – was America's longstanding envoy to France (where

he subverted the French court by wearing shabby republican clothes amid the finery, becoming a cult figure for intellectuals), nor that Thomas Paine was to be swept up in the tumult of the French Revolution, nor that one of the first revolutionaries was the Marquis de Lafayette, one of the heroes of the American War of Independence.

Franklin, a representative of men who had rejected the authority of a monarch altogether and preached a republic was a lethal cancer in the body politic of the French monarchy, and it was almost suicidally obtuse of Louis XVI and his courtiers not to realize it, obsessed as they were with the old power struggle with Britain.

France had sought to turn the American Revolution into a dagger aimed at Britain's breast, but succeeded in striking only a glancing blow before falling on the weapon itself. For in an age of press, printing and pamphleteering the ideals of the American Revolution soon found a following among intelligent and dissatisfied men in France. The immediate catalyst for the French Revolution, however, was the French court's need to raise money – an exact echo of the cause of the English Revolution, when Charles I had had to summon parliament to raise revenue. The cost of French participation in the American war had been prohibitive, and had been met by loans. The French government afterwards ran out of ready access to lenders and in 1786 the minister of finance was forced to inform the French King that the situation could only be corrected by imposing taxes. In 1788, the *ancien régime* for the first (and last) time drew up a budget, which showed there to be a shortfall of some 20 per cent between expenses and revenues. Of the total budget, some 6 per cent was being spent on the court itself, some 20 per cent on administration, and 26 per cent on defence and foreign affairs. Nearly half was being swallowed up on debt service of some 318 million livres.

It was thought necessary to reduce the debt through taxation – not through a general increase of the taxes that already fell almost entirely on the poor classes, whose wages had risen only by 22 per cent, compared to average price increases of 65 per cent over the previous half century – but by extending taxation to the wealthy bourgeoisie and to the nobility. The cause of the French Revolution was thus not the state's attack on the poor, but on the rich!

The minister of finance, Calonne, proposed an eminently progressive taxation regime: a uniform tax on salt and tobacco across the nation, a land tax and an end to internal tariffs and freedom for the grain trade (which affected the all-important price of bread) as well as the selling off of manorial properties possessed by the church so that they would be able to pay tax. Finally tax was to be administered by provincial assemblies in which the traditional 'three estates' of France – the clergy, the nobility, and all property owners – should be represented equally.

Exactly as occurred under Charles I's exactions, and George Grenville's attempts to raise taxes in America through the Stamp Act the King's plan provoked a furious outcry from the men of property – in particular, in France, the nobility. After bitter exchanges, the King was forced to summon the Estates-General, a kind of national assembly of the three estates, which had last been convened at the beginning of the seventeenth century, to get his way. At that stage the dispute was between the modernizing centralized royal court and the reactionary nobility – not the popular image of the people against King and aristocracy.

France was in the throes of a social and economic revolution – a huge increase in population and in property: unfortunately the new prosperity was not well distributed among the expanding population. Worse, the economic boom was disrupting existing social arrangements: an urban working class had sprung up in the cities, in particular Paris, estimated at around 300,000 or around half the population of 600,000. Many of these benefited from the economic revolution, but this new concentration was also a powerful force in its own right. While the new property created a large urban bourgeoisie, the inequalities between the bourgeoisie and the workers also became obvious where they rubbed shoulders together.

In the countryside there existed a large independent peasantry which possessed few of the feudal characteristics of its English neighbours: the peasants had for centuries been emancipated from serfdom, although a few traits lingered as well as their obligation to do military service. Whereas in Britain huge landholdings and a paid agricultural workforce were, in many ways, an extension of serfdom, the French peasant was a

fiercely independent proprietor: but he was also poor, with a land-holding barely capable of supporting him. This naturally conservative class was baffled by two aspects of the economic revolution France was unleashing during the mid-eighteenth century: bread shortages caused by the archaic and corrupt system of regulation and distribution of grain, which Calonne was determined to reform, as well as by the increased appetites of the cities; and taxation at a time when purchasing power was diminishing. To the peasant it seemed that Calonne was preparing further to exacerbate their problems by levying new taxes and instituting a free for all on prices (which would actually have improved supply but lowered prices for the peasant producer). Thus another class was added to those with grievances against the *ancien régime*.

A third class of malcontents came from the lower ranks of the nobility – of which Napoleon Bonaparte was himself to be a rather atypical example. The nobility in France was very different from that in Britain where it consisted of a select group of around 1,000 hugely wealthy landowning families. There were no fewer than 400,000 'nobles' in France out of a population of some 23 million, with perhaps a fifth of the land. With the exception of the 'nobility of the robe' – high court officials of bourgeois background ennobled by the court – they were a caste.

A large part of the nobility, however was extremely poor and would lose status if they worked for a living. For these people, the King and his court were an enemy, the new moneyed classes a source of envy, and the new wealth injected into the country something of which they were not a part.

Thus France in the dying days of the *ancien régime* was a paradox – a newly enriched and developed society in which large numbers of people were alienated from the new prosperity – among them many of the squirearchy, most of the peasantry and part of the new urban working classes, as well as that part of the bourgeoisie with more or less fixed incomes. Meanwhile the newly prosperous merchant class – such as lower civil servants, professionals and lawyers – made up the overwhelming bulk of the elected members of the Third Estate in the newly convened Estates-General. The great French historian

Georges Lefebvre has brilliantly summed up the bourgeoisie on the eve of the Revolution:

> For centuries the bourgeois, envious of the aristocracy, had aimed only at thrusting himself into its ranks. More than once he had succeeded, for a great many nobles descended from ennobled bourgeois. This ambition was not extinct. The Rolands put themselves to much trouble to get themselves recognized as nobles; the Derobespierres cut their name in two; Danton spelled his as d'Anton; Brissot, son of an innkeeper of Chartres, blossomed forth as Brissot de Ouarville, or still more fashionably, de Warville. Such were the marks of gentility. Bourgeois of old stock were frankly proud of their lineage, careful not to form an improper marriage. Officeholding and the professions established among them a hierarchy of which they were exceedingly jealous . . .
>
> Since at best only a small number of bourgeois could enjoy the advantage of becoming nobles, the rest of them wound up by execrating what they envied without hope. The exclusiveness of the nobility in the eighteenth century made the ascent even more arduous than before, especially when the nobles tried to reserve the most distinguished public employments for themselves. At the same time, with increasing wealth, the numbers and the ambitions of the bourgeois continued to mount. Sacrifices willingly made for the education of their children were meeting with disappointingly little reward, as the correspondence of Sieyès with his father testifies, and still better the examples of Brissot, Desmoulins and Vergniaud. The young Barnave wrote, 'The road is blocked in every direction.' Throughout the century government administrators had expressed alarm at the spread of education, and even in the Year III (1795) Boissy d'Anglas was to fear that education would result in forming 'parasitic and ambitious minorities'.
>
> With the doors shut, the idea arose of breaking them down. From the moment when the nobility laid claims to being a caste, restricting public office to men of birth, the only recourse was to suppress the privilege of birth and to 'make way for merit'. Pure vanity played its part, we may be sure; the most insignificant would-

be noble nursed the wounds of his injured pride at the mere sight of the social distance above him. Among bourgeois of diverse kinds was forged a link that nothing could shatter – a common detestation of the aristocracy.'

The bourgeoisie put its emphasis on earthly happiness and on the dignity of man; it urged the necessity of increasing the former and elevating the latter, through the control of natural forces by science and the utilizing of them to augment the general wealth. The means, it was believed, consisted in granting entire freedom to investigation, invention and enterprise, for which the incentive was to be personal gain, or the charm of discovery, struggle and risk. The conception was dynamic, calling upon all men, without distinction of birth, to enter into a universal competition from which the progress of mankind was to follow without end. The ideas appeared in a confused way in the France of the Renaissance; subsequently Descartes inaugurated a new humanism by opening up a magnificent perspective, the domination of nature by science; finally, the writers of the eighteenth century, encouraged by English and American influences – here we must note Voltaire, the encyclopaedists, the economists – set forth with spectacular success the principles of the new order, and the practical conclusions that it seemed fitting to deduce.

The works of these writers strengthened oral propaganda in the *salons* and *cafés* which multiplied in the eighteenth century, and in the societies of all kinds which were founded in great numbers – agricultural societies, philanthropic associations, provincial academies, teaching institutions like the Museum at Paris, reading rooms, Mesmerist societies where the magnetism put in vogue by Mesmer was experimented with an, finally and above all, Masonic lodges, brought over from England in 1715.

As the Abbé Sieyès so pithily put it: 'What is the Third Estate? Everything. What has it been until now? Nothing. What does it ask? To be something.' The aristocracy, by directly challenging the reforming monarchy, had unwittingly created the instrument of its own destruction; for the Third Estate was by far the most numerous

part of the Estates-General convened through aristocratic resistance to the new taxation. The King's tax reform had thus assembled a formidable coalition of enemies, among them the aristocracy; and the aristocracy now provided the means by which those enemies could find expression not just against the King, but against the aristocracy as well.

Chapter 2

THE TENNIS COURT REVOLUTION

With the summoning of the Estates-General on 4 May 1789, and the election of members of the Third Estate at open assemblies in which the articulate bourgeoisie prevailed over the peasants, the Revolution gathered momentum with astonishing speed. The three principal leaders at this stage were an unlikely combination: the Comte de Mirabeau, an aristocrat who had deserted his class, the Abbé Sieyès, a conspiratorial priest of lower middle-class origins and the Marquis de Lafayette, a hero of the American Revolution. Mirabeau was a powerful orator and a wheeler-and-dealer of men with immense charm. Offsetting this was an absence of real principle, a quick eye for opportunity, and aristocratic indolence which had led to earlier scandals, particularly over money, of which he was chronically short. In spite of his gifts, it was believed he could be bought by the court party if they so chose; and this prevented him from becoming the natural leader of the Third Estate. Sieyès was a poor speaker and an unimpressive personality, but he was a brilliant polemical writer and he emerged as the chief theoretician of the idea that the Third Estate represented the nation, which alone possessed sovereignty, not the King. However, he was no radical, fearing rather than favouring the mob and democracy, and he was soon to be eclipsed as the Revolution took a radical turn. Lafayette was hugely rich, and as a young man he had led the French volunteers and later conscripts that fought by George Washington's side. He was an earnest and generous idealist: but he was also naïve, vain and politically inept.

Lafayette's importance in the outbreak of war between France and its neighbours can hardly be exaggerated, and it is worth looking at him

in closer detail. He had inherited his title at the age of two, when his father was killed at the Battle of Minden in the Seven Years War. Physically unimpressive, he was no athlete and was shunned at court, where his family was considered comparatively *nouveau riche*. However, he was phenomenally wealthy, with an income of around £300,000 a year by the age of twenty-one, and at the age of sixteen he had been married to the daughter of the Duc d'Ayen, head of one of the noblest families in France, who had taken the youth under his wing.

However, the Duc was not Lafayette's mentor: his military tutor was the Comte de Broglie, a former head of the French secret service, who plotted the extraordinary objective of becoming commander-in-chief of the forces in America in place of Washington, whom he and other French military leaders considered ineffectual, and then, fantastically, the elected leader of America. With an aristocratic Frenchman in charge of the colonies, he believed, the French court could be reconciled to supporting a republican revolution.

De Broglie conspired with Silas Deane, the American envoy to Paris, to persuade the wealthy but naïve Lafayette to buy his own ship and travel to America. Arriving just south of Charleston on 13 June 1778, the young aristocrat made his way across country to Philadelphia. There Congress had learned of the Broglie plot; and Lafayette, who was not a party to it, was able to save his position only by offering to serve without pay.

Washington and Lafayette had dinner together at Philadelphia's city tavern after the British evacuation of the city, and the forty-five-year-old got on famously with the twenty-year-old – Washington, who had no sons of his own, asking the youth to treat him as 'a father and friend'. While there was clearly an instant personal bond between the two, it also seems likely that, with France joining the war, Washington saw the advantage in having at his right hand a prominent Frenchman, whom he could hope to dominate because of the age disparity, and who could act as the eyes and ears of France. By the spring of 1778 he was given command of his own division. Lafayette proved a brave but poor military commander at best, but he remained closely in touch with his American 'revolutionary' friends and believed himself to be the arbiter of his country's destinies: indeed, he fancied himself as France's George Washington.

At this early stage in June, the Third Estate was moderate and timid. Then, on 20 June, the King, under pressure from the strong-willed Queen, locked the Assembly hall before it was due to meet, and the deputies responded by going to a nearby tennis court, where they took an oath to stand fast. But the King still thought he could defuse their power with a highly enlightened series of concessions such as equality of taxation, unlimited liberty and freedom of the press, as well as in effect a sitting parliament. He was proposing nothing less than an English-style constitutional monarchy. The King still felt strong enough to threaten the representatives of the people:

> If you abandon me in this great enterprise I will work alone for the welfare of my peoples . . . I will consider myself alone their true representative . . . None of your plans or proceedings can become law without my express approval . . . I command you to separate at once, and to proceed tomorrow morning each to the hall of his own order to renew your deliberations.

They took no notice. The nobility and clergy by now realized that they had to make common cause with the monarchy against more radical threats. Both decided to strike against what was now still a relatively moderate majority in parliament. In early January, the King assembled 18,000 troops from different parts of the country to enforce his claim to authority and dissolve the Estates-General. But they made no immediate move.

On 12 July the Paris mob, largely consisting of shopkeepers and craftsmen, took to the streets for the first time. The first disturbances spread with the building of barricades on the following night. The next day the crowd flocked to the barracks and seized 32,000 muskets. The mob moved into the Bastille prison, a hated symbol of authority even though it housed just three mental cases and four forgers, and was guarded by eighty retired soldiers and thirty Swiss guards. Unwisely the governor of the Bastille ordered his men to open fire on the demonstrators, killing ninety-eight and wounding seventy-three. After a time, the crowd went berserk, invaded the prison and killed six soldiers, as well as, later, the governor, whose head was carried about the city on a pole.

The mob now announced that they were forming a 'government' with its own National Guard, asking Lafayette to lead this. He gave the 'citizen soldiers' a cockade consisting of the colours of Paris, red and blue, with the colour of the King, white, in the middle. The next day the King appeared before the tennis court assembly to urge calm and then went to Paris, where he was given a cockade which he fastened to his hat. But Lafayette was not in complete control: district assemblies met around Paris and another mob attacked three prominent officials. The new Assembly decided to set up a popular revolutionary tribunal and a committee of investigation to prevent the mob taking the law into its own hands.

Uprisings broke out in towns and the country, as well as peasant riots. Châteaux and private houses were burned in a terrifying outbreak of anarchy which alarmed even the bourgeois leaders of the Revolution, who considered calling in the army, then decided to try and make concessions to the peasants and the mob by, in effect, abolishing privileges. The King arrogantly refused to sign these measures, whereupon it was asserted that 'the convention needs no royal approval, for it is anterior to the monarchy'.

On 26 August the Declaration of the Rights of Man and the Citizen was enacted: this had largely been drawn up by Lafayette in consultation with Thomas Jefferson, the American envoy to Paris, who appended a memorandum in his own hand. It bore a marked resemblance to the American Declaration of Independence. The American role in the French Revolution was considerable, spearheaded by Lafayette and Jefferson, who saw the opportunity not just to spread America's revolutionary republican ideals across the globe but to get back at their joint traditional enemy, Britain. Although a powerful and mainly moderate document, the declaration omitted the American constitution's careful prescription of checks and balances. This proved controversial, with those advancing a bicameral system, to preserve the powers of the nobility, dubbing those who sought a royal veto, to preserve the powers of the King, 'Monarchicals'. The latter's ideas were rejected, and the King in turn hardened his opposition to the new regime.

Versailles itself was a small town whose economy was dominated by the royal family. But it was intense anti-royalist sentiment that

motivated its local National Guard of several thousand; against this were some 400 Gardes de Corps, or lifeguards, of sworn loyalty to the King; and a rival force of grenadiers. At a feast for these men who sought to replace the lifeguards, the King made an unscripted appearance, giving rise to rumours he was plotting a crackdown.

The radical Jacobin tendency and the militant 'Dames des Balles' and other groups, initially of women, decided to march on Versailles with the cry of 'Bread. Bread! To Versailles.' The National Guard was called up to stop them, but instead fraternized with the mob, its commander Lafayette swept away by the tide of humanity. One of his soldiers remarked: 'Is it not strange that Lafayette attempts to control the people when it is his role to receive orders from them?' It took Lafayette some four hours after the departure of the march for Versailles to return to his post at the head of the National Guard.

The mob's allies in the former Estates-General, now the National Assembly at Versailles, were ecstatic. One of the mob declared of the nobility that 'the gentlemen wanted more light – they shall have lanterns, they may rely upon it'. He was talking of using the lines holding lanterns to hang aristocrats from the lamp-irons. A famous aristocratic retort by the Abbé Maury, was, 'My friends, when you have put me in the lantern, will you see more clearly?'

The mob broke into the Assembly, the women occupying the seat of the president and shouting at or cuddling its scandalized members. The leaders were granted a brief audience with the King, which so impressed them that they shrank back at that stage. But others were preparing to strangle members of the Assembly with their garters. During the night the extremists discovered that the few remaining soldiers were not prepared to resist, for fear of starting a bloodbath.

The King's loyalists begged him to leave: but he was prevailed upon to wait for the arrival of Lafayette and the National Guard. The mob performed a kind of drunken advance on the palace guard, then stayed there for the night, drinking, singing and firing their guns; they caught a horse, roasted it and ate it. Lafayette arrived at last with his orderly National Guard. He saw the King, guaranteed the security of the palace, persuaded the National Assembly to adjourn and then – astoundingly – went to bed.

At around three in the morning a group of extremists broke through an unlocked gate to the vast palace grounds and forced their way into the Queen's apartments before pushing aside the few guards there and killing one. They forced their way into her bedroom, from which she had escaped through a secret passage. They slashed the bed she had just been occupying with pikes and swords: allegedly she had just been in the arms of a lover, but this seems unlikely at such a trying time. The assailants' leader, Jourdain (later known as the 'head-cutter' or 'man with a beard'), was a male model from Paris armed with an axe.

At around this time Lafayette was roused from his slumbers and the grenadiers at last cleared the royal courtyard of the rabble. But a much larger mob was outside the palace itself, shouting for the 'Austrian' – Marie Antoinette – to appear. This she did with extraordinary courage on the balcony, holding the hands of her two children, who then went inside as the crowd demanded. Some jeered; but now there were shouts of '*Vive la Reine*' from the crowd.

A new cry arose: 'To Paris.' This had in fact been the objective of the Jacobin clubs who had inspired the march, and must have been their intention all along. Lafayette's National Guard, along with the 1,000 or so grenadiers, as well as the few hundred bodyguards, could certainly have resisted this: maybe he feared the National Guard would not have obeyed orders. Displaying his characteristic poor judgement – or opportunism, seeing this as a chance to bring the King under his control, for he certainly did not lack courage – he refused to defend the King and instead ordered the royal family out into that bitterly cold night.

This was the first real turning-point of the Revolution. As an anonymous account written soon afterwards, based on eye-witness description, vividly put it:

> The carriages of the royal family were placed in the middle of an immeasurable column, consisting partly of Lafayette's soldiers, partly of the revolutionary rabble whose march had preceded his, amounting to several thousand men and women of the lowest and most desperate description, intermingling in groups amongst the bands of French guards, and civic soldiers, whose discipline could not enable

them to preserve even a semblance of order. Thus they rushed along, howling their songs of triumph.

The harbingers of the march bore the two bloody heads of the murdered *Gardes de Corps* paraded on pikes, at the head of the column, as the emblems of their prowess and success. The rest of this body, worn down by fatigue, most of them despoiled of their arms, and many without hats, anxious for the fate of the royal family, and harassed with apprehensions for themselves, were dragged like captives in the midst of the mob, while the drunken females around them bore aloft in triumph their arms, their belts, and their hats. These wretches, stained with the blood in which they had bathed themselves, were now singing songs, of which the burthen bore, – 'We bring you the baker, his wife, and the little apprentice'; as if the presence of the unhappy royal family, with the little power they now possessed, had been in itself a charm against scarcity.

Some of these Amazons rode upon the cannon, which made a formidable part of the procession. Many of them were mounted on the horses of the *Gardes de Corps*, some in masculine fashion, others *en croupe*. All the muskets and pikes which attended this immense cavalcade, were garnished, as if in triumph, with oak boughs, and the women carried long poplar branches in their hands, which gave the column, so grotesquely composed in every respect, the appearance of a moving grove. Scarce a circumstance was omitted which could render this entrance into the capital more insulting to the King's feelings – more degrading to the royal dignity.

After six hours of dishonour and agony, the unfortunate Louis was brought to the Hotel de Ville, where Bailli, then mayor, complimented him upon the 'splendid day', which restored the monarch of France to his capital; assured him that order, peace, and all the gentler virtues, were about to revive in the country under his royal eye, and that the King would henceforth become powerful through the people, the people happy through the King; and 'what was truest of all', that as Henry IV had entered Paris by means of reconquering his people, Louis XVI had done so, because his people had reconquered their King. His wounds salved with this lip-comfort, the unhappy and degraded Prince was at length permitted

to retire to the Palace of the Tuileries, which, long uninhabited, and almost unfurnished, yawned upon him like the tomb where alone he at length found repose.

Louis himself remarked: 'It is wonderful that with such love of liberty on all sides, I am the only person that is deemed totally unworthy of enjoying it.'

This was the real beginning of the Revolution; for with the King virtually a prisoner in Paris it became impossible for him to become the standard around which the country could rally against the revolutionary extremists – as Charles I of England had. It is said that the Duc d'Orleans, the King's jealous cousin and rival, had in fact suborned this particular mob, and that he himself had planned the Queen's assassination and his own assumption of power as regent: he was said to have been present and watching the proceedings at Versailles, but had failed to come forward himself. Mirabeau, his supporter until then, was scathing in his denunciation of the Duc's duplicity, and the Duc was exiled to London.

Lafayette, who detested D'Orleans, was now in such control as there was and guardian of public order. The King merely bowed to the decisions of the Assembly and was surrounded in the Tuileries by 800 men placed there by Lafayette as both his protectors and his gaolers. But meanwhile two men plotted that he should escape and become a rallying point for resistance. One was Lafayette, the other Mirabeau himself. He urged the King to flee to Metz, controlled by a tough old rogue, the Marquis de Bouille, a relative of Lafayette. A first attempt to get the King to safety failed when the National Guard in April 1791 blocked him and refused Lafayette's orders to let him leave. In June the King tried again, leaving behind him a long attack on the proceedings of the Assembly, such was his confidence of success. He was arrested at Varennes, having failed to rendezvous with the forces under de Bouille, and was conveyed back exhausted and covered in dust.

The second major turning point of the Revolution now occurred; for Lafayette, fearing that matters were getting out of control, decided at last to make a stand. A meeting was held on 17 July 1791, at the

Champ de Mars, with Jacobin and republican leaders for the first time calling for the King's removal. Unfortunate bystanders were seized by the crowd and killed, their heads being put on pikes. Lafayette arrived with a detachment of National Guardsmen who were met with a hail of stones. He ordered his men at last to open fire and the mob dispersed. Order was restored and the Assembly behaved with moderation: at that stage the King should have made his escape, as many suggested; but he chose to remain.

Lafayette belatedly emerged as his defender. But in the new National Assembly, elected countrywide again by voice vote, more extreme men were preponderant: the majority were Girondins, after the southern department from which they mostly came, bourgeois lawyers determined to end the monarchy. Their leader was Brissot, who frequented the cultural salon of Madame Roland. The minority were Jacobins, more extreme men like Maximilien Robespierre, the 'sea-green incorruptible', and his corrupt but eloquent Girondin ally Danton, as well as the radical philosopher Marat, who was insatiably bloodthirsty; they controlled the Paris mob – *Les sans-culottes* (trouserless ones).

In five short months the Assembly the King had called to rein back the power of the aristocracy had ended in the overthrow of both by the middle classes, backed by the threat of mob force. Even so, the majority of the Assembly still had no intention of setting up a republic. But Louis had lost his authority, and thenceforth the real opposition to the Revolution was to come from the aristocracy. The authority of the central state, which had overreached itself in the power struggle with the nobility, had been seized by the middle classes; and although the Declaration of Rights ensured legal and property rights and did not call for economic equality, it also gave the 'nation', as enshrined in the will of the people, virtually absolute power through the National Assembly and the local assemblies, the only real holders of authority. The French central state had become, if anything, even more absolute, because the nobility was weaker before it: but power was exercised by self-appointed people's representatives, not the King.

Chapter 3

TO KILL A KING

The moderate leadership of Lafayette in the Champ de Mars in July 1791 was reinforced by a group called Les Feuillants, consisting of some 200 members of the new Assembly, constitutionalists in opposition to the Girondins and Jacobins. But they had no leader. Mirabeau had died in April 1791 and Lafayette, volatile as ever, had been bitterly criticized for his role in the Champ de Mars bloodbath. He found his supporters deserting him. As an anonymous historian wrote thirty years later, his supporters were fickle. Those who supported him:

> were Parisian citizens of substance and property, but timorous, even from the very consciousness of their wealth, and unwilling, either for the sake of La Fayette, or the Constitution which he patronized, to expose themselves to be denounced by furious demagogues, or pillaged by the hordes of robbers and assassins whom they had at their disposal. This is the natural progress in revolutions. While order continues, property has always the superior influence over those who may be desirous of infringing the public peace; but when law and order are in a great measure destroyed, the wealthy are too much disposed to seek, in submission, or change of party, the means of securing themselves and their fortunes. The property which, in ordinary times, renders its owners bold, becomes, in those of imminent danger, the cause of their selfish cowardice.

Lafayette was defeated when he stood for mayor of Paris by Petion, his radical opponent. At that stage he decided to secure his power by

urging France into war – of which more later. He also believed that command of the army would be critical to the outcome of the Revolution. With his departure, the National Guard was ruthlessly attacked by Jacobin mobs, and the Girondists tried to create their own army from among their followers. But this was subverted by the Jacobins.

Louis vetoed this proposal to set up a 'departmental' army, as well as a measure excluding parties who refused to swear an oath of loyalty to the new constitution. In thus seeking to exercise a veto when he was virtually powerless, with no real support behind him ('Think not to terrify me by threats. My resolve is fixed.') Louis showed himself to be suicidally stubborn: he had united the rival Girondists and Jacobins. One described the outcome: 'Terror, just in the name of the people, burst its way into yonder palace, whence she has so often sallied forth at the command of monarchs.'

On 20 June a carefully staged insurrection was organized involving a mob of *sans-culottes* armed with scythes, pikes and hay-forks. One flag was a pair of tattered trousers, another a pig's bloody entrails. The bourgeois citizens defended the slopes of the Palais Royale, but the mob went on to occupy and terrorize the Assembly, then moved on to the Tuileries.

Louis was trapped there, within the arch of a window with a few loyalists who erected a barricade of tables, where he was joined by the Queen and her children. Thus they faced the mob, with the King being forced to don a red cap and drink from a communal bottle – his 'Calvary'. At last Petion, mayor of Paris, called on the huge crowd of 50,000 to disperse. This humiliation led to a backlash of sympathy for the King, and Lafayette returned speedily from the war front – but without a body of supporting troops, perhaps because he feared diverting them from the fighting, more probably because he did not want to be denounced as attempting to instigate a military take-over. Lafayette made a powerful speech to the Assembly and summoned a review of the National Guard for the following day, but this had more or less disintegrated in his absence, and few dared to appear.

Lafayette, who had twice prevented the King from leaving Paris, now urged him to do so. But it was too late. Lafayette, whose

ambition, hesitations and miscalculations had done so much to create the whole crisis, and who was now responsible for France's aggressive attitude towards its neighbours, returned to the war front, while Paris descended into virtual anarchy, a band of 500 citizenry from Marseilles adding their numbers to the Girondin and Jacobin mobs.

The King had become hopelessly fatalistic: 'I have no longer anything to do with earth,' he declared. 'I must turn all my thoughts to heaven.' On 10 August the mobs again descended on the Tuileries, which were protected by a force of National Guardsmen divided in their loyalties, as well as faithful Swiss Guards and a few grenadiers who were slaughtered. The King received them not in uniform but in a violet costume, the colour of monarchy. The Queen seized a pistol and urged the King to fight: those witnesses present, as well as Napoleon afterwards, believed the National Guard would have followed him if he had given the command. But he proposed to go to the Assembly to seek its protection. The Queen was plundered of her purse by the pressing crowds. The King and his family were imprisoned in the grim and forbidding keep of the Temple.

The Jacobins set about intimidating the Assembly. Some 8,000 people were rounded up on suspicion of counter-revolution: a denunciation by a single opponent was enough, and any trace of gentility or good behaviour was damning. Marie Antoinette's friend the Princess de Lambaille was chopped to pieces and her head paraded to the Temple where the crowd called upon the King and Queen to look upon it. Priests were among the most frequent victims.

Some 4,000–6,000 died in just four days that September. The Girondins, who represented most of the countryside outside Paris, had in fact won a majority in the Assembly, but the Jacobins controlled the Paris mob, which could intimidate the Assembly. The Girondins tried to organize a 'Departmental Legion' – again a kind of army from outside Paris – but were blocked by the Jacobins. General Dumouriez, commander of the French army outside Paris, offered to bring back an army to defy the Jacobins – but the Girondins would have none of it, for fear that he would also sweep them away.

Instead they went along reluctantly with Jacobin calls for the trial and execution of the King. A committee of twenty-four was set up to

report on his misdeeds: they proved so inept at finding a reason for executing this weak but good-natured man that the National Assembly as a whole had to pronounce justice. The wily Robespierre brilliantly exploited their dilemma:

> One party must be clearly guilty; either the King, or the Convention, who have ratified the actions of the insurgent people. If you have dethroned an innocent and legal monarch, what are you but traitors? And why sit you here – why not hasten to the Temple, set Louis at liberty, install him again in the Tuilleries, and beg on your knees for a pardon you have not merited? But if you have, in the great popular act which you have ratified, only approved of the deposition of a tyrant, summon him to the bar, and demand a reckoning for his crimes.

The King and Queen were exposed to appalling conditions and indignities at the Temple, where conditions were spartan; partisan songs were sung under their windows and obscenities poured forth when they went out for the single daily walk they were permitted.

The Assembly was surrounded by the Jacobins, intimidating the delegates and jeering at the King as he arrived for his trial – where, unlike Charles I of England, he answered the charges reasonably and with saintly patience. As he said with dignity when indicted under the name Louis Capet:

> Capet is not my name – it was that of one of my ancestors. I could have wished that I had not been deprived of the society of my son during the two hours I have expected you – but it is only of a piece with the usage I have experienced for four months. I will attend you to the Convention, not as acknowledging their right to summon me, but because I yield to the superior power of my enemies.

When the motion was put to the vote, the Duc d'Orleans, who had returned from England under the name Citoyen Égalité, voted for death, to a gasp of horror, along with 387 Assembly members to 334 – a majority of 53. An historian soon after wrote:

Upon the scaffold [the King] behaved with the firmness which became a noble spirit, and the patience beseeming one who was reconciled to heaven. As one of the few marks of sympathy with which his sufferings were softened, the attendance of a confessor, who had not taken the constitutional oath, was permitted to the dethroned monarch. He who undertook the honourable but dangerous office, was a gentleman of the gifted family of Edgeworth of Edgeworths-town; and the devoted zeal with which he rendered the last duties to Louis, had like in the issue to have proved fatal to himself. As the instrument of death descended, the confessor pronounced the impressive words – 'Son of St Louis, ascend to heaven!'

The King was executed on 21 January 1793. Marie Antoinette was beheaded on 16 October, at the age of thirty-eight. The King's sister Elizabeth was executed in May 1794. The seven-year-old Dauphin was placed under the control of a shoemaker named Simon who, it is said, asked: 'What was to be done with the young wolf-whelp: Was he to be slain?' – 'No.' – 'Poisoned?' – 'No.' – 'Starved to death?' – 'No.' – 'What then?' – 'He was to be got rid of.' He died of cold, malnutrition, beating and general ill-treatment in June 1795. Only his sister, the Princess Royal, was permitted to live. It had been a massacre, to prevent a rallying point for a restoration emerging.

Chapter 4

THE REPUBLIC GOES TO WAR

For too long and far too often the wars of 1792–1815 have been dubbed the 'Napoleonic Wars' when, in fact, Napoleon was unknown at the outset and not the ruler of France until 1799. Other Frenchmen initiated the war with England and the rest of continental Europe, for elemental reasons connected with French politics and nationalism, and by the time Napoleon took control the motives, direction and even the kind of warfare involved had been established by men who are virtually unknown today. It is one of Napoleon's more remarkable feats that he is entirely associated with French expansionism at this time: yet in fact he took over a vessel already built and whose course had long been set. One of those most significant in this process was Dumouriez (the others were Hoche and Carnot), an extraordinary personality well in advance of his time who, had he not been so, might have become as celebrated as Napoleon.

Charles Dumouriez was a tough, feisty soldier who had risen to prominence during campaigns in Poland. Extremely shrewd in his political dealings, he had no firm political convictions, but was loyal to the King while being prepared to swear loyalty to the Revolution as long as the two marched in tandem. Dumouriez was the arch-rival of the political, posturing Lafayette for control of France's revolutionary army; as long as the latter was preoccupied with internal politics, the former was militarily pre-eminent.

With the outbreak of the French Revolution, the country had been immediately endangered by two of the 'big seven' countries in Europe. Absolutist Russia, while detesting everything the Revolution stood for,

took no action; nor did decadent Spain; nor, initially, did Britain. Austria, however, under Emperor Joseph II, and its rival Prussia, under King Frederick William, rose to the challenge. Joseph, a well-meaning reformer, had succeeded in stirring up dissent across his far-flung dominions by seeking to improve conditions there and overriding the local vested interests. Consequently, he had too much on his hands to fight France as well. On his death, he was succeeded by his half-brother, Leopold, a more limited but sensible man who succeeded in putting down the insurrection in Flanders and then treated the insurgents with moderation. He was alarmed by the prospect of France stirring up more trouble in Flanders and pursued a pragmatic line towards the Revolution, which had not yet tilted towards excess, partly out of concern for his sister Marie Antoinette and her husband: the correspondence between them shows that far from attempting to take advantage of the Revolution he was seeking to urge a moderate middle course upon Louis XVI. His son and successor in 1792, Francis II, pursued the same policy.

Prussia's Frederick William, however, had fewer inhibitions. The inheritor of the legacy of Frederick the Great, a superbly trained and disciplined army, he lacked both the military skill and the wisdom of his predecessor. He was out to make his mark on Europe, and his absolutist mind was appalled by the Revolution, while discerning the opportunities that he believed France's new weakness would offer him. He also wished to show up the caution of his fellow German rival, the Austrian Emperor.

A large number of French émigrés descended on these neighbouring courts and set themselves up in armed militias at Trèves and elsewhere. At the Declaration of Pilnitz in August 1791 these émigrés organized an expression of concern from Prussia and Austria for the fate of the King of France. However, Leopold had been cautious, offering to prevent the émigrés training on his territory in exchange for France reining back the activities of the Jacobins. His successor, young Francis II, was keener on joining Frederick William in threatening war on France, particularly as the circumstances of the French royal family deteriorated.

To the astonishment of both, it was the French, mired in revolutionary turmoil and with their army apparently disintegrating, having

lost many of their aristocratic officers, that declared war. The reason for this lay in internal French politics and, to begin with at least, the perverse nature of Lafayette, who sought to restore his fading political fortunes by a glorious war; he was backed in this by the constitutionalists and the Girondins, although surprisingly the Jacobins were divided. The Assembly in the autumn of 1791 passed a measure to force the King's Financial Adviser, Xavier Stanislaus, who had declared war on the country, to return to France, and pronounced a death sentence on all émigrés found in arms at the beginning of the following year. The King refused to sign this.

The French foreign minister, de Lessart, had tried to avert war by telling the Austrians that the King would soon establish his supremacy over the extreme republicans. Meanwhile an unholy combination of Lafayette and the minister of war, the Comte de Narbonne, tried to secure Assembly support for the war. Louis summarily dismissed the Comte de Narbonne. The Assembly was furious at this sudden reassertion of the royal prerogative and promptly accused de Lessart, a moderate royalist, of intriguing with the Austrian court. The unfortunate foreign minister was condemned to death and guillotined, and his successor appointed from among the Girondins: this was Charles Dumouriez.

Dumouriez was no friend of the Austrians and conceived a highly intelligent strategy of establishing a pact with Britain to keep it neutral. This was based on setting up a constitutional monarchy in France and respect for mutual trading arrangements, while detaching Belgium from Austria and setting it up as an independent state. The Austrians under their new young Emperor were incensed and demanded the return of the French King to the powers he enjoyed before 1789, the return of lands and buildings taken from the church and compensation for the German princes recently expelled by the French from Alsace and Lorraine. This was unacceptable to the French. On 29 April 1792 the French King was forced to declare war against his own brother-in-law, the Emperor, as well as against his two brothers, the Comte de Provence and the Comte d'Artois, who were leading the sputtering insurrections within France itself.

No one could have predicted that the subsequent general European

war would last twenty-three years. Who was to blame? Undoubtedly the French had acted badly in expropriating German landowners and the clergy, particularly in the historic city of Avignon, where a bloodbath had taken place. Austrian fury at the treatment of the Queen, the Emperor's aunt, was also understandable. But up to now the French had not violated other borders or pursued a policy of aggression. Such certainly was the view of the British.

Nevertheless, as Dumouriez and, before him, Lafayette had seen, there was an advantage to be had out of war – not least in strengthening the hand of the army in domestic politics. They had goaded the Austrians, and the latter and their war-hungry Prussian rivals had been all too happy to respond. However the Austrians still held aloof from any full-scale assault, although they immediately secured victories against the disorganized French army.

The Duke of Brunswick was appointed to command the joint 365,000 strong Austrian-Prussian forces: after his victories at Maastricht, Liège and Neerwinden in the Low Countries, he was a commander to be feared. However, for reasons which remain obscure, he placed a force of 15,000 French émigré cavalry, which ought to have been the elite of his force, in the rear. There were suspicions that Brunswick was waging a war of aggression: for when he captured Longwy and Verdun he did so in the name of the Emperor of Austria, not the King of France. He had a splendid army of Prussian troops and Austrian dragoons under General Clairfait; but he launched no immediate attack to disperse the raw recruits which Dumouriez, now minister of war, had raised from a levy of men from across provincial France, nor the hesitant regular army, which had lost most of its royalist officers.

Brunswick's army was blocked at the fortress of Thionville: he had too few cannon. He then moved into the Champagne region, one of the poorest in Europe, where his men fell upon a profusion of melons and grapes which immediately caused an epidemic of dysentery in the army, killing hundreds. Nevertheless the émigré cavalry scored a notable success in ambushing a column of *carmagnoles*, as the raw republican conscripts were called.

The Duke himself only took part in one action, the Battle of Valmy,

before being rebuffed by Dumouriez's forces and deciding to order a retreat. This deeply demoralized the émigrés, who had no choice but to obey the orders of their foreign commander, and the Prussians, who had obeyed the call to arms of the Emperor at great expense. The French resistance, however raw, was stiffened by the fear that any restoration of Louis XVI to his absolute powers by the émigrés would inevitably have resulted in years of revenge, bloodletting and the reimposition of feudal rule.

With the Prussian retreat, the formerly uncertain French army found new hope: they had repulsed the enemy. Recruits flowed into the surprisingly successful French armies controlled by Generals Custine in Paris, Montesquieu in Savoy and Dumouriez in the Netherlands. Montesquieu, an aristocrat of the old school but a patriot, repulsed the Savoyan army ordered into France by the King of Sardinia and took Nice and Chambery, threatening to invade Italy.

On the central front Custine struck forward against the seven German kingdoms, capturing Worms, Oppenheim and Spiree and the stronghold of Mentz. Custine had no hesitation in urging the people of central Germany to overthrow their rulers. In the north Dumouriez, ably supported by his Spanish deputy Francisco de Miranda, struck forward against Clairfait's soldiers, spectacularly winning the Battle of Jemappes on 6 November 1792. Clairfait was forced to retreat from the Austrian Netherlands with its towns undefended thanks to Joseph II's ridiculous decision to dismantle the fortifications along the frontier. The French army under Dumouriez remained firmly disciplined in its new conquests, but a shower of revolutionary officials descended on the area, pillaging the churches, plundering the land and setting up republican forms of government.

Dumouriez rushed to Paris in an effort to save the King. Bravely, and well aware that his own head was at stake if he lingered too long, he now privately proposed setting the Dauphin or the Duc d'Orleans' son – who had served under him – on the throne. But he was ordered to return to invade Holland.

At first the campaign went well: Gertruydenberg was seized and Bergenop-Zoom blockaded. But Dumouriez was blocked at William-stadt. Moreover an Austrian army had at last arrived under the Prince of

Saxe-Coburg and was threatening Belgium. Dumouriez veered about, but his army was mauled at Aix-la-Chapelle. Where before he might have been able to restore the French monarchy, his reputation was now endangered. He made a further blunder by threatening to march on Paris in a letter of 12 March 1793, in support of the King. Only six days later he was defeated in the Battle of Neerwinden. His sieges of the fortresses of Lisle, Valenciennes and Cond all failed.

He entered into serious negotiations with the Austrians and arrested four commissars sent out by the Convention to keep an eye on him, sending them to the Austrians as prisoners. He tried to persuade several commanders, including Miranda, to join him in seeking to seize control of Paris. Most refused, and the army showed no disposition to follow him as he negotiated with the enemy. He realized the game was up and fled to the Austrians, and then into exile in Britain, where he spent nearly twenty years acting as a wise counsellor to the British government during the Napoleonic war.

So ended the career of one of the most redoubtable figures of revolutionary France, a potential military dictator long before Napoleon. Far more than the feeble Lafayette before him, he had shown that revolutionary France could be great if order was restored. It was far too soon, but the lesson was not lost on the men who were later to bring Napoleon to power.

Dumouriez's early victories halted any occupation of France while it was at its most vulnerable and showed that the new popular army, with its officers promoted through merit from the ranks and its soldiers believing they were fighting for the Revolution, not merely to serve the King or the aristocracy, could be a potent force. Again, Dumouriez's successors and Napoleon were not slow to imbibe the lesson.

If the British had lent their support to the joint Austrian and Prussian forces, the Revolution might have been nipped in the bud at this early moment. However the British had absolutely no intention of intervening at this stage, and the opportunity passed. Dumouriez had certainly entertained the hope of an alliance with the British and the Austrians against the Convention, but his revolt had failed and he was forever to be damned as a traitor to France. The course of history would have been very different had he succeeded.

Chapter 5

THE LATIN ADVENTURER

Francisco de Miranda, one of Dumouriez's best generals, enjoyed a career not unlike Napoleon's early one, emerging as a potential French leader himself. The Venezuelan-born Miranda had deserted from the Spanish army and travelled extensively in the United States, Europe and Russia, where he became Catherine the Great's lover, seeking support for his goal of Latin American independence from Spain. He had previously spent three years in London pursuing this cause, but all his talk of leading South America to revolution had come to nothing. He switched his attention to the revolutionary ferment in France: a group of monarchists there had tried to get him to join a counter-revolutionary mercenary army of Russians, Swedes, Germans and Frenchmen partly backed by Catherine the Great, who had suggested Miranda's name. However, Miranda's intellectual sympathies lay with the revolutionaries.

He made a good impression on Brissot when the Girondin leader visited London, and between them they developed the idea that the Revolution in France could be spread both to mainland Spain and to Spanish America. Brissot lobbied the commander in northern France, Dumouriez, to appoint Miranda as head of an invasion force of 12,000 French infantry and 10,000 mulattos then garrisoned in Santo Domingo who, with the assistance of the French navy, might be expected to topple Spain's hold on her colonies, something France wanted almost as much as Britain.

Crossing to Paris, Miranda had found little enthusiasm for the plan there, however, and was considering a return to London when the

Austrian and Prussian armies invaded France from the east. In August 1792, as the country reeled at the prospect of defeat, Miranda, who had perhaps sold his military credentials a little too successfully, found himself offered the rank of marshal in the French army and the title of baron, as well as a fat stipend, very attractive to a man now hard pressed for the money to live in the grand style to which he had become accustomed. At the age of forty-two he was at last a real general – in the service of revolutionary France. His Russian supporters, who loathed the French revolutionaries, were appalled at the transformation, but did not sever their links with him altogether.

To his own surprise, in his first engagement, along the border between Belgium and Holland, his force of 2,000 men succeeded after seven hours of fighting in putting to flight some 6,000 Prussians led by the Graf von Kelkreuth, a capable commander. It was the first French success of the war. With uncharacteristic modesty, Miranda spoke of his 'beginner's luck in the French army'; he was promptly appointed to command a division in the front line, under Dumouriez's overall command. En route to Vaux the 10,000-strong division commanded by General Chazot suddenly encountered 1,500 Prussian hussars. The French panicked and fled; a rout seemed imminent, until the retreating forces reached Miranda's position at Wargemoulin. There, sword in hand, he stopped their flight, and reorganized the two forces into three columns to march on Valmy.

Dumouriez boldly attacked, believing that he faced a Prussian army of 50,000 men, and a major battle. Instead he was met only by covering fire; the Prussians had retreated after the French rally. Miranda's reputation soared. However, he viewed with distaste the rise of the revolutionary party in France, in particular the Jacobin faction led by Robespierre and Marat. He wrote to the American Alexander Hamilton: 'The only danger which I foresee is the introduction of extremist principles which would poison freedom in its cradle and destroy it for us.'

Miranda moved up to join Dumouriez as second-in-command of the French army in Belgium. He went to the relief of Dumouriez's army at Anderlecht, and was appointed to take over General La Bourdonnais's command of the Northern Army. As the grip of winter

intensified Miranda's forces reached the outskirts of Ambères, where he personally supervised the digging of trenches, encouraging his men while maintaining rigid discipline. Ambères was heavily fortified; on 26 November the French guns opened up and were answered from within, but not a single besieger was killed. By five in the afternoon, as plumes of smoke from the burning city curled into the sky, the Austrians were seeking terms. These took four days to negotiate and amounted to unconditional surrender, at the cost of just thirty casualties to Miranda's army.

It was another morale-boosting victory for the hard-pressed French under their inspired new general, who immediately set about reinforcing the city's defences. He arrested some of its leading citizens to exact tribute to pay for provisioning his troops, and dissolved the convents and monasteries, stripping prelates, abbots and monks of their titles. The 22,000 men under his command were soon joined by thousands belonging to the Army of the Ardennes, swelling his command to 70,000 men.

In February 1793, against his own advice, Miranda was ordered to send out 12,000 of his men to besiege Maastricht. As he expected, the 30,000 or so enemy forces proved too well entrenched. They fired some 32,000 cannon-shot in six days, but failed to inflict many casualties upon the small French besieging force. Miranda decided to withdraw, lest he lose his guns to an Austrian sortie. He was bitterly criticized for what was clearly a sensible tactical move; he was also hated by many of his own men for his draconian punishments for looting and raping.

Another much more dangerous threat now loomed. Early in March, Miranda's commander-in-chief, Dumouriez, asked his staff officers what they thought of the growing Jacobin outrages. King Louis XVI had been executed in January, the revolutionary Terror was gathering pace, and the radicals mistrusted nothing so much as the army, even though they depended upon it for the Revolution's survival against external enemies. Miranda primly replied that he disapproved of seeking the opinions of soldiers on such issues.

Soon afterwards two generals, La Hove and Stengel, were arrested on grounds of conspiracy. Dumouriez now demanded to know what

Miranda would do if the order came to arrest him, Dumouriez. Miranda said that he would have no option but to obey, adding that General Valance, as the senior general in the French army, would however be responsible for executing it. Dumouriez angrily retorted that the army would refuse to carry out any such order. A few days later Dumouriez told Miranda that he intended to march on Paris, to restore freedom: the counter-revolution was under way. To his astonishment Miranda, despite his own disapproval of the increasingly radical turn taken by the Revolution, told Dumouriez the soldiers would not obey him and that he, Miranda, might also oppose him. It was a moment of truth: from then on Dumouriez no longer trusted his subordinate.

Miranda's action is inexplicable, except in terms of self-preservation – he believed Dumouriez could not succeed. Miranda had little romantic commitment to the French Revolution and was privately highly critical of the direction it was taking. His enemies believed his ambition was to replace his superior: already the Girondin leaders had identified him as the best candidate for Dumouriez's post, should anything happen to the commander-in-chief.

Dumouriez then decided on an extraordinarily high-risk tactic, one that Miranda's partisans have always believed was an act of deliberate treachery designed to discredit their hero and lead to his downfall. Holding good defensive positions, though vastly outnumbered and out-gunned, Dumouriez determined to risk the whole French flank in an offensive against the Austrian-led forces. His motive may have been to give himself enough prestige, through victory, to march on Paris and take over the reins of power.

On 15 March Miranda had successfully repulsed an attack on Tirlemont, but with General Champmorin's forces was then ordered to attack the right flank of the enemy at Neerwinden. It was suicidal, since Miranda's 10,000 men were opposed by Austrian-led forces around 18,000-strong, well entrenched in a defensible position. The French were mown down without pity. Although he was in the thick of the fight, Miranda survived; after nightfall, he had no alternative but to sound the retreat, leaving 2,000 of his men dead. The retreat was orderly, and he handled it with great coolness.

It soon emerged that Dumouriez had known the enemy was

strongest on their right flank and weakest on their left, where his own forces were superior: the weakest part of the French force, under Miranda, had thus been ordered to attack where the enemy were strongest. From the start Miranda had opposed the plan, which he later described as 'against the rules of the art of warfare. I am astonished that Dumouriez was capable of such an error.' The suspicion must be that Dumouriez wanted Miranda to do badly by comparison with the other commanders, in a bid to discredit and remove him before the coup attempt. But he had miscalculated in believing that the centre would hold, and the whole French army was thrown back as a result of this disastrously conceived attack.

On 21 March the Austrians attacked at Pallemberg. Miranda held his positions for a day, despite severe losses, then staged another orderly night retreat. Four days later Dumouriez and Miranda met, and exchanged furious words. Dumouriez railed against the Jacobins, while Miranda criticized his commander's military ineptitude.

The Jacobins at last came to learn of Dumouriez's plotting, and of his criticism of his second-in-command. As we have seen, Dumouriez went over to the Austrians; Miranda was summoned to Paris. Arriving at the end of the month, he was immediately interrogated by Citizen Petiot, a Girondin sympathizer, who arranged for him to appear before the Committee of War and Security. At a hearing on 8 April seventy-three questions were put to him as to the conduct of the war. The questioning was barely polite. Miranda knew that his life was on the line, not just his command. He impressed his interrogators with his calm and eloquent replies, and it appeared that he would be exonerated.

But the Terror was gathering momentum. The radicals alleged that Danton had been conniving with Dumouriez – a charge which may have been true – and insisted that ordinary soldiers should testify against the actions of their superiors. The ultra radical Montagnards, with Robespierre as their new leader, attempted to incriminate Danton and his Girondin followers, the faction with which Miranda was identified. But Danton dodged the attack by himself joining the Montagnards and denouncing his former Girondin followers, among them Miranda, whose supporters Brissot and Petiot sprang to his defence against Danton and Robespierre.

On 19 April 1793 the much-feared Chief Prosecutor of the Revolution, Fouquier-Tinville, ordered Miranda's arrest, on charges of conspiring with the British government as well as with the Russians and the North Americans, and of aiding Dumouriez in his counter-revolutionary attempt to reinstate the monarchy. It now seemed all too likely that Miranda, who had led his men with brilliance, even perhaps turning the tables in the war, and who had acted with impeccable correctness in spurning Dumouriez's overtures, would be guillotined on trumped-up charges.

On 20 April he was taken before a revolutionary Tribunal presided over by Montane, with Fouquier-Tinville prosecuting. Miranda surprised those present by his calm demeanour and his eloquent and natural way of defending himself. He was also vigorously defended by Chaveau-Lagarde (who later attempted unsuccessfully to save Queen Marie Antoinette from the tumbrils): 'An irreproachable republican,' he argued, 'never fears death but cannot bear the suspicion of crime, and for a month Miranda has been suspected.'

Fouquier-Tinville rose and, in the precise, reedy voice which had condemned so many to the blade, accused Miranda of negligence in the war, and of being Dumouriez's chief co-conspirator. Meanwhile Marat's rabid newspaper, *L'Ami du Peuple*, had charged Miranda with looting Ambères after its capture. A procession of hostile witnesses was led by General La Hove and General Eustace. It was alleged that Miranda had a son and a brother-in-law in Maastricht, hence his discontinuance of the siege. A sergeant testified that the Dutch considered him 'better than a Dutchman'. The national gendarmerie, whose excesses he had tried to contain at Antwerp, accused him of a succession of crimes.

When it was Miranda's turn to speak he calmly recalled that, far from being Dumouriez's accomplice, he had been his accuser. He had withdrawn from Maastricht because he was out-numbered, and not on ground of his choosing: 'You cannot win when you don't have the advantage of the ground.' Outraged, General Eustace demanded to speak again, saying that it had been his honour 'to detest Miranda'. Remarkably, the acid, razor-sharp Fouquier-Tinville cut him down, saying he could not call an openly prejudiced witness. The defence

witnesses were called. One revealed that at the time the King's head was struck off by the guillotine Miranda had declared to his soldiers, 'This is a great blow for the politics of France.' The American revolutionary Thomas Paine himself came from London to argue with passion that Miranda would never have betrayed France, 'because the cause of the French Revolution is intimately tied to the favourite cause of his heart, the independence of Spanish America'.

Summing up, Chaveau-Lagarde claimed that no defence was necessary, because Miranda had already defended himself so eloquently; he should be 'listened to with all the dignity that became true republicans and with the full confidence the court deserves'. As the judges withdrew and the prisoners were led away, sobbing could be heard from among the crowds of onlookers. When the judges had filed back, Miranda was declared innocent. The court erupted in applause, in which even Fouquier-Tinville joined. Miranda rose to declare passionately that 'this brilliant act of justice must restore the respect of my fellow citizens for me, whose loss would have been more painful for me even than death'. On 16 May he was released and carried through crowds in the streets. He was one of the very few to stare the Terror in the face, to come under the shadow of the guillotine, and yet to escape.

Now calm and commonsense deserted him. Believing himself immune from further persecution, he withdrew triumphantly to a luxurious château in Menilmontant to rest, and to defend his reputation against the unceasing vituperation of Marat's newspaper. The Montagnards were still raining attacks upon him as 'an intriguer, a creator of faction' who, it was alleged, had bribed the jurors to let him go. His wisest course of action would have been to leave at once for England.

In 1793, Paché, former minister of war and an implacable foe, was appointed Mayor of Paris. Three days later Miranda's château was surrounded by guards, and Paché placed him under house arrest. This did not stop Miranda receiving friends and female company alike. When a large number of sealed boxes arrived, the police suspected them of containing arms and ammunition; they were crammed with books. A servant loyal to his enemies was planted in the household; Miranda knew this, but pretended otherwise.

On 9 July he was arrested again and conducted to the prison of La Force, from which very few ever emerged free. Robespierre himself now demanded the guillotine for Miranda's alleged connivance in a royalist plot. On 13 July he was brought before the Convention and again made a stirring defence, accusing his gaolers of violating the constitution 'because the body politic is oppressed when any citizen is oppressed'. He complained that he had been accused of seeking to flee the country, when he had neither horses nor a carriage and could not move two leagues out of Paris without permission from the government. He accused the dreaded Public Safety Committee of tyranny, in disregarding his previous acquittal.

Miranda had asked his doctor to prepare a dose of poison so that he could cheat the guillotine, undoubtedly a wise precaution: compared to a single major prison in Paris before the Revolution, the Bastille, there were now twenty prisons, containing about 40,000 people; 7,000 had already been guillotined; Paris was in the grip of fear.

A club-like atmosphere pervaded La Force. Miranda beautifully caught the mood when he wrote that it was as though he were 'making a long journey by boat, during which it was necessary to fill the tiresome emptiness of time with the search for useful knowledge without knowing if the journey would end in death at sea or happy arrival in port'. The Marquis du Châtelet became an inseparable companion; the two men talked at length of art, literature and travel; they played cards with packs from which, to their amusement, the court cards had been removed, and read Tacitus and Cicero. One day du Châtelet decided to swallow poison, leaving his few goods to Miranda and the other prisoners. The weeks passed slowly by.

In August Miranda appeared before the Revolution's Special Criminal Tribunal for investigation. In September he went before the National Convention again, when he asked to be allowed to go into exile in order to pursue his cause against the Spanish government. The French could not make up their minds what to do about him, but they wanted him out of the way. Miranda's frustration grew more desperate and bitter. He railed against the 'infamous' Robespierre, the 'imposter' Saint-Just, and against Danton, who had betrayed him. The police investigated the source of Miranda's funds, but found no sign that they

had been acquired illegally (his money came from his general's pay, and rich patrons). The months continued to drift slowly by, and Miranda made new friends in gaol, including the celebrated antiquarian and savant Antoine-Chrysostome Quatremère de Quincy.

In December 1794 Miranda loosed a formidable broadside against the Convention, denouncing Robespierre's 'execrable maxim that the individual's interest must be sacrificed to the public interest', an 'infernal' idea that had given tyrants from Tiberius to Philip II the justification for their misrule. His letter ended, with courageous dignity: 'I do not ask for mercy from the Convention. I demand the most rigorous justice for myself and for those who have dared . . . to compromise the dignity of the French people and poison the national image.' For a man under the shadow of revolutionary Terror and in gaol for more than a year, Miranda showed an admirably robust and indomitable spirit.

On 26 January 1795 Miranda was finally released from La Force, and promptly installed himself in a splendid *appartement* at Rue St-Florentin costing £1,400 a year − a staggering sum for those days. He was determined to make up for the deprivations of the past year and a half, of which sex − although he seems to have had access to some women in prison − was probably the most terrible. Women, the theatre and elegant parties were resumed with renewed vigour.

In prison he had met 'Delfina', the beautiful Marquise de Custine, whose husband, the famous general, was also in gaol. Miranda now embarked on a torrid affair with her − until he discovered she had also satisfied the lusts of Chateaubriand, Alexandre de Beauharnais, M. de Grouchy, Comte Louis de Ségur, Boissy d'Anglais and Dr Korev. Passionate and intelligent but undoubtedly a nymphomaniac, Delfina failed to win him back to her bed, but they continued to be seen together, and quarrelled with the intensity of lovers. Supposedly an illegitimate daughter of Louis XV, Delfina was the greatest French coquette of her time and, according to a contemporary wit, 'loved everyone, even her husband'. She showered Miranda with letters, saw him frequently, and was his last companion when he left France.

Miranda's sojourn in prison did not deter him from meddling in

revolutionary politics. Having twice escaped the guillotine he believed himself a charmed man, and now pursued his own moderate liberal agenda, which was anathema to extremists inside and outside the government. In particular, he showed an exemplary tolerance, in an anti-clerical age, of the more liberal-minded among the clergy; and (in spite of his youthful disdain of the man) he lauded the qualities of George Washington, who 'had obtained the confidence of his fellow countrymen not from his brilliance, which he cloaks, but from the calmness of his spirit and uprightness of his intentions'. Miranda's views on the direction of the French Revolution were succinctly expressed: 'I love freedom, but not a freedom based on blood and pitiless towards sex or age, like that which has been the order of the day in this country until recently.' He made no secret of the fact that he wanted to hold office in post-revolutionary France.

Miranda seems to have been sucked into an alliance between the moderates and the royalists as one of two possible leaders of a military coup. A prominent royalist remarked contemptuously that it would be astonishing if the King of France should be replaced 'by a Spanish Creole, the lieutenant of a provincial regiment of his Catholic Majesty's, and a total stranger in France where he has lived only a few years and where he has only been known since the Revolution'.

As the showdown between royalists and republicans approached, it is unclear whether Miranda sat on the fence or took part. When the government sent 1,500 troops to close down a radical 'electoral body' gathered in a French theatre at two in the morning on 4 October, revolutionary newspapers reported Miranda to have been in charge of the illicit proceedings.

Miranda went underground, was accused of being one of the principal conspirators, and then emerged to declare that he had taken no part in the parliament. Arrested and ordered out of the country, he secured a stay of execution of the order and continued to live in his usual style, but always followed by a gendarme. He managed to give him the slip one night and went into hiding, whence he bombarded the press with letters defending himself and attacking his enemies. He was eventually given official permission to stay, and continued to survive through the after-shocks of revolutionary France, always active

in half-plots, always preaching his own brand of liberal anti-monarchism and anti-extremism.

In September 1797 another alleged monarchist conspiracy was suppressed by the government, and again Miranda was named as one of the plotters. Once more he went underground, once more the police were ordered to hold the 'Peruvian' general if he had not, as was widely believed, escaped to Athens. In fact, at last wholly disillusioned with the French Revolution, fearing another long spell in prison and especially angry that France had formed an alliance with the Spain he so hated, he had resolved to go to Britain.

Passionately he kissed Delfina goodbye and, wearing a wig and green spectacles and passing as a minor businessman, took a coach to Calais, then embarked on a Danish boat, arriving in Dover in January 1798. A customs inspection there found that his case had a false bottom, filled with papers. After discussion, documents were furnished for him to travel to London, where he set about organizing his network of contacts and friends in South America and in Europe.

Chapter 6

THE TERROR

During Miranda's first arrest and trial, Paris was reeling from the battle between Girondins and Jacobins which would eventually culminate in the climax of the Revolution – an orgy of blood. The Girondins still had a majority in the Convention. When news of Dumouriez's plot leaked out, the Jacobins instantly accused the Girondins of being behind him. The Jacobins planned an ambush on the Assembly on 10 March 1793, and intended to seize many Girondin deputies by force.

Gaining intelligence of this, the Girondins launched a counter-attack, passing a motion of censure on Marat, who had urged the people to rise against the Assembly. The radical leader was forced into hiding. The Girondins were determined to take the initiative against their conspiratorial rivals, but did not summon the courage to move the Assembly from Paris, the Jacobin stronghold.

The Jacobins now assembled a small, well-organized army of around 2,000 in the Champs Elysée in central Paris, accompanied by their Paris mob: this force had guns and howitzers and surrounded the unwary deputies. The leaders of the uncommitted deputies, 'the Plain', urged the Girondins to give themselves up.

When the Girondins asked to leave the Assembly, they were stopped by soldiers: 'Return to your posts: the people denounce the traitors who are in the heart of your assembly and will not depart until their will is accomplished.' Twenty-two Girondin leaders were arrested, being convicted of 'royalism'. The Girondins were prevented from speaking in their own defence at the subsequent tribunal.

Some forty-two deputies were executed, committed suicide, or fled abroad. Brissot went wretchedly to his execution along with Vergniaud and the others, and even Velaze's corpse – he had killed himself with a dagger when sentence was pronounced – was guillotined! The wife of Robert declared memorably on her way to the scaffold, as she passed the Statue of Liberty: 'Ah, Liberty. What crimes are committed in your name.'

The Jacobins were left in undisputed control at the heart of central government, if not the country, a classic instance of a revolution devouring its children. The legal system was all but non-existent, religion outlawed, taxes uncollected and the assignat worthless currency. Revolutionary terror alone reigned, confiscating the necessary revenues, putting to death generals who did not achieve great victories, and some who did who were thought to pose a threat to the government. General Custine was condemned, remarking philosophically that 'France is a woman and my hair is going grey'.

The new government was run by the ten to twelve-man Committee of Public Safety and the slightly less powerful Committee of Public Security. Husbands were compelled to pin outside their homes the names of all those inside, in a forerunner of modern totalitarian methods of state control. Some 300,000, at a conservative estimate, were armed as stormtroopers of the Revolution, a third of them women. A revolutionary Tribunal was set up, consisting of six judges, two public assistants and, as a formality, twelve jurymen.

The two Jacobin trump cards were a promise to suppress any discontent in the army by declaring it in a state of mutiny, which would condemn opponents to the guillotine; and an exhortation to the poor to declare war on the rich. In fact any external sign of wealth was regarded as sufficient grounds for condemnation. *Egalité* had replaced *Liberté* as the keyword of the Revolution.

The Jacobins had an extensive propaganda network throughout the country, as well as an enormous spy network. A decree of terror was issued by the Committee of Public Security to its angels of death:

Let your energy awaken anew as the term of your labour approaches. The Convention charges you to complete the purification

and reorganization of the constituted authorities with the least possible delay, and to report the conclusion of these two operations before the end of the next month. A simple measure may effect the desired purification. Convoke the people in the popular societies – Let the public functionaries appear before them – Interrogate the people on the subject of their conduct, and let their judgment dictate yours.

At Nantes whole families were put aboard boats in the Loire and the craft scuttled: this was labelled 'republican baptism'. Men and women were stripped naked, bound together and killed: this was dubbed 'republican marriage'. The revolutionary army enforced order when necessary.

The assassination of Marat in his bath by Charlotte Corday, whose mind was partly unhinged in a rather different manner to his own, left just Danton and Robespierre as the Revolution's two consuls. The latter soon obtained evidence of Danton's monumental corruption and threatened to expose this to force him into retirement. Meanwhile, in his paranoia, Robespierre sought to destroy also the government of Paris, whose men had been the means by which the Jacobins had seized power.

The Jacobins also made an extraordinary attack on organized religion, forcing the bishop of Paris to denounce Christianity as priestly superstition and to deny the existence of God. 'The Goddess of Reason' – in fact a dancing girl at the Opera – was welcomed into the Assembly (where it was said she was already familiar with several deputies). The Paris commune had church bells cast into cannon and confiscated all silver and gold. Hebert, the commune leader, was the guiding force behind this. Robespierre, however, saw the excesses of the commune as an excuse further to impose his own order and in March 1794 he had the commune leaders arrested on ludicrous charges of conspiring with the British government. The revolutionary army was also disbanded as being a Parisian rather than national force.

Danton at last decided that too much blood had been shed, and spoke out in favour of clemency and the defence of property. Robespierre moved more quickly and stealthily. On 31 March he

had his great rival, the most formidable orator in the Assembly and until recently the effective ruler of France, arrested. Danton went to his trial and execution with all the contempt that that formidable but deeply flawed figure was capable of. Of Robespierre he remarked: 'The cowardly poltroon. I am the only person who could have commanded enough influence to save him.' The words were prophetic: without Danton, Robespierre was merely an ideologue and police chief, with little power base. Danton, however unattractive, had been the true leader of the Revolution; Robespierre was a brittle, sarcastic little man who was at ease only in small gatherings and had few political skills. Yet he was a political thinker of note, and his influence on both the course of the Revolution and on one of his followers, the young Napoleon Bonaparte, was to be seminal.

The government of France was now under the control of the twelve-man Committee of Public Safety, whose most powerful personality was Robespierre. Others include Louis de Saint-Just, who believed in the 'complete destruction of everything that is opposed to the committee', Herault de Sechelles, a rake, Collot d'Herbois, a psychopathic former minor playwright, as well as, later, Louis David, a superb painter and a fanatic who declared 'let us grind plenty of red'.

Robespierre, by contrast, was a brilliant political theoretician with a puritanical bent: his ideas in some ways were almost Marxist with their concept of the 'general interest'. Wisdom, he asserted, 'has disappeared in the individual and can only be found in the masses and the general interest'. For Robespierre this authoritarian view was an almost exact substitute for the old monarchical theory of personal supremacy: the People, in an abstract conception, had taken the place of the King. The movement was above the law, and was the law. The reason why the people had this power was because they had 'virtue', which equated with love of the fatherland – not obeisance to the King, as it had been up till then. For him the fatherland 'was the country of which one is a citizen and a member of the sovereign state'.

With great insight he wrote in 1784 that England was really a republic and he was not opposed to constitutional monarchy in principle. He advocated universal male suffrage, along with a tiny

But perhaps the answer is suggested by the question: by this very catholicity of affection in one who found it difficult to seek out and choose his friends. Amiable and warm, he was happy from the start to take what circumstances offered: shy and haughty, he was unable to take the initiative himself. The family combination of simplicity and pride, the power to charm or repel, must have been given a peculiar impress by his upbringing and was set hard by his early fame.

Frances Williams Wynn, a contemporary, gave this engaging account of the private man's antics:

I was about sixteen or seventeen when, at Dropmore – where I was with Lord and Lady Grenville only – Mr Pitt arrived for a visit of two days. First, I was disappointed in that turned up nose, and in that countenance, in which it was so impossible to find any indication of the mind, and in that person which was so deficient in dignity that he had hardly the air of a gentleman . . . From what I then heard and saw, I should say that mouth was made for eating; – as to speaking, there was very little, and that little was totally uninteresting to me, and I believe it had been so to everybody . . . On the second day arrived Lord Wellesley whom I thought very agreeable; partly, I fancy from his high-bred manners, and still more from his occasionally saying a few words to me, and thus making me feel treated as a reasonable creature. After we had retired for the night, I heard from the library, which was under my room, the most extraordinary noises – barking, mewing, hissing, howling, interspersed with violent shouts of laughter. I [assumed it was the servants that had come] into the room, and had got drunk and riotous; and I turned to sleep when the noise had ceased. Never can I forget my dismay (it was more than astonishment) when next day at breakfast I heard that my wise uncle and his two wise guests, whom they had left talking, as I supposed, on the fate of Europe, had spied in the room a little bird; they did not wish it to be shut out there all night: therefore, after having opened every window, these great wise men tried every variety of noise they could make to frighten out the poor bird.

twenty-one, where he made his maiden speech. Burke observed: 'It is not a chip off the old block. It is the old block itself.' He sat on the opposition benches. Appointed chancellor of the exchequer by the Earl of Shelburne at twenty-three, he was made prime minister the following year after Shelburne's administration had fallen on the terms of the peace treaty with France, Spain, and America, and the short government of Lord Portland had also fallen. The young man was greeted with universal derision. In the event, he presided over Britain for an unbroken eighteen years.

The early Pitt was an idealistic reformer, pressing for a reform bill which would widen the restricted franchise of the House of Commons, advocating the cause of Catholic emancipation in Ireland and appointing the most pro-Catholic British proconsul to date, the Earl Fitzwilliam. He also pressed for economic liberalization – he initially favoured complete free trade from Britain's ports – as well as undertaking a thoroughgoing overhaul of Britain's public finances. As a personality he was haughty, even priggish, in public, capable of a withering sarcasm towards his enemies: in private he was almost childishly affectionate towards his friends, and he loved the children he never had.

Some later suggested he was homosexual and held such feelings towards the young man later to become his protégé, George Canning; others simply that he was wedded to his job. Two formidable women acted as his hostesses – Harriet, his sister, and Jane, Duchess of Gordon, a somewhat masculine and domineering woman. John Ehrman summed up his private character:

> 'Kindness and good-humour', 'playful facetiousness'; 'playfulness, urbanity, and good-humour' – this is from one quarter. 'His laugh – love of fun – playful tricks': this is from another, less well disposed. Men who had never met him, or come across him only in public, were amazed when they caught a rare glimpse of him in private, and his friends, of whatever description, mourned him bitterly when he died . . . He was the same with all his intimates; and yet, distrustful of larger acquaintance, he seemed unconcerned who his intimates might be.

Chapter 20

THE OUTSIDER

The dismal year of 1795 was also marked by an event that went almost unnoticed in Britain. Napoleon Bonaparte, when ordered to command the artillery in the Vendée, which he regarded as tantamount to exile, under his more successful young rival Lazare Hoche, simply turned the post down. Given the importance of the revolt in the Vendée and the possibility he would make his name there, it was an extraordinary thing for him to do, and aroused suspicions that he was not really devoted to the revolutionary cause. It seems likely that he was still hoping to be sent to Italy as a theatre of operations.

Napoleon was put on leave and spent a few miserable months in Paris, where he found himself impoverished and something of a social outcast, most of his half-pay going on supporting his dispossessed family in Toulon: Napoleon was never more attractive than in his dogged support of his family in difficult times. A female contemporary remarked of him in Paris: 'I can still picture him, entering the courtyard of the Hôtel de la Tranquillité, and crossing it with an awkward, uncertain step. He wore a nasty round hat pulled down over his eyes, from which his hair, like a spaniel's ears, flopped over his frock-coat . . . an overall sickly effect was created by his thinness and his yellow complexion.'

Napoleon remarked in a letter to his older brother Joseph: 'There is only one thing to do in this world and that is to keep acquiring money and more money, power and more power. All the rest is meaningless.' Always prone to self-pity, he contemplated suicide: 'If this continues I shall end by not stepping aside when a carriage rushes past.' He

considered serving in the Russian army as a mercenary, but the Russians would not give him the rank of major, then that of Turkey, which approached him to modernize its small artillery. He agreed and prepared to leave.

Napoleon had not entirely wasted his time in Paris. He made important connections and also pursued romantic liaisons – which however his poverty and shabby and uncouth appearance did nothing to further. The truth was that after Toulon, believing himself to be the hero of the hour and free to turn down major postings at his whim, he discovered that in worldly Paris he was almost a nobody, a minor military figure, a gauche provincial whose social pretensions were sneered at.

Back in Toulon he had been attracted to the younger sister of his brother Joseph's bride, Julie Clary. The girl was only sixteen when he met her, and was known as Désirée, although Napoleon preferred her middle name, Eugénie. She was pretty, vivacious and natural, although a little plump. Napoleon treated her as a younger sister. 'Your unfailing sweetness and the gay openness which is yours alone inspire me with affection, dear Eugénie, but I am so occupied by work I don't think this affection ought to cut into my soul and leave a deeper scar.'

In April 1795 he became engaged to her. She was rich – possessed of a dowry of 100,000 francs: they became lovers. Soon afterwards Napoleon revealed his feelings in a short story, in which he called himself Clissold:

Eugénie . . . without being plain, was not a beauty, but she was good, sweet, lively and tender . . . she never looked boldly at a man. She smiled sweetly, revealing the most beautiful teeth imaginable. If you gave her your hand, she gave her's shyly, and only for a moment, almost teasingly showing the prettiest hand in the world, where the whiteness of the skin contrasted with blue veins. Amélie [the elder sister] was like a piece of French music, the chords and harmony of which everyone enjoys. Eugénie was like the nightingale's song, or a piece by Paesiello, which only sensitive people enjoy; it appears mediocre to the average listener, but its melody transports and excites to passion those who possess intense feelings.

Melodramatically Clissold is wounded in war and a friend of his father falls in love with Eugénie. Clissold decides to die in battle, and writes a letter to her:

> How many unhappy men regret being alive yet long to continue living! Only I wish to have done with life. It is Eugénie who gave me it . . . Farewell, my life's arbiter, farewell, companion of my happy days! In your arms I have tasted supreme happiness. I have drained life dry and all its good things. What remains now but satiety and boredom? At twenty-six I have exhausted the ephemeral pleasures of fame but in your love I have known how sweet it is to be alive. That memory breaks my heart. May you live happily and think no more of the unhappy Clissold! Kiss my sons.

The story is revealing for what it shows about the romantic in Napoleon, beneath the driven, chip-on-his-shoulder, self-seeking opportunist. The unromantic reality, though, was that he was on the lookout in Paris for a more advantageous match than this lively young provincial. He appears to have pursued a forty-year-old widow, and then to have been entranced by the formidable Mademoiselle de Chastenay, followed by the thirty-year-old Grace Dalrymple, a former mistress of the Prince of Wales who had been imprisoned during the Terror. In this case conversation stopped when Napoleon confessed his hatred of the English.

Napoleon was also admitted into some of Paris's most famous salons – in particular La Chaumière, the house of the president of the Convention, Jean-Lambert Tallien. His beautiful twenty-two-year-old wife, Thérésia, had already been married, divorced and nearly guillotined, and boasted a score of lovers. Thérésia sported long black hair and wore almost transparent dresses. Napoleon also met the celebrated and powerful Madame de Staël and her friend (and maybe lover) Juliette Récamier; he made friends with a sexy nineteen-year-old Creole beauty, Fortunée Hamelin. He wrote in fascination about this uninhibited society: 'Everywhere in Paris you see beautiful women. Here alone of all places on earth they appear to hold the reins of government, and the men are crazy about them, think of

nothing else and love only for and through them . . . A woman needs to come to Paris for six months to learn what is her due, and to understand her own power. Here only, they deserve to have such influence.'

In fact post-Robespierre France, as Duff Cooper writes, was shockingly decadent:

the reaction from the gloom and misery produced by the Revolution was an outburst of enjoyment which took the form of almost frenzied revelry and unbridled licence.

Dancing appeared to be the main interest of the population, and the deserted palaces of the great, the empty monasteries and convents, even some of the former churches were converted into resorts where this prevailing passion could find satisfaction. Hither, clad in transparent muslin, with bare legs, sandals, and rings upon their toes, their hair cut short and curled in what they believed to be the ancient Roman fashion, came the fair pleasure-seekers of the day to tread a measure with their cavaliers. Among the latter it was the singular mode to wear clothes which were carefully designed not to fit, to pull their hats down to their eyebrows, and to swathe their necks in vast cravats which concealed the chin and fringed the lower lip.

The outward forms of the Revolution were still observed, the new calendar and the new jargon. Toy dogs were trained to growl at the name of aristocrats, every tenth day was décadi and the excuse for a gala, at which Monsieur and Madame addressed one another with equal politeness as Citizen and Citizeness.

But society must have its leaders. The great ladies of the past had fled or perished. Their places had to be filled. Not for soldiers and politicians only had the Revolution produced 'the career open to talent'. No longer need the stern decrees of fashion be dictated by ladies of noble birth and high degree.

This is perhaps an exaggeration, based on Napoleon's later denigration of a more tolerant and less dictatorial society than his own; but it had a ring of truth. The Directory was a corrupt, liberal, almost democratic

pause between two despotisms, those of Robespierre and Napoleon himself. The young officer with his burning ambition was at once fascinated and repelled by this cosmopolitan, promiscuous society, and personally something of a wallflower rather than a participant, in his state of dishevelment and penury. Something of a prig up to now, he found his inhibitions shattered by the relaxed morals of this set, although it is unlikely he enjoyed much sexual success. He was poor, awkward and not particularly good-looking, although his strangely pale olive skin, burning eyes and hungry expression made a mark with some women, as did his slenderness – in contrast to the tubby Napoleon of later years – and formidable intelligence.

He received attention from an important source – the forty-year-old Paul Barras, the most complex member of the Directory. Barras, a corrupt and cynical man who had voted for Louis XVI's execution but was regarded as a moderate and probably had no guiding principles, seems to have taken the sallow young Corsican under his wing, possibly because he might need a skilful artillery officer for his own purposes. Napoleon also formally met Thérésia Tallien's best friend, another divorced older woman, Rose de Beauharnais, already a widow and Barras's mistress.

In September 1795, as Napoleon wallowed in self-hatred and contempt for this dissolute society, at one moment contemplating suicide, at another preparing to leave for Turkey to fight as a mercenary, he was suddenly plunged into the vortex of a political crisis. News had been received of the Comte d'Artois, the King's brother, arriving at the Isle d'Yeu on his ill-fated expedition. This enthused the royalist right, who had been asserting themselves after the fall of Robespierre. They were furious at a decree which insisted that two-thirds of the new Assembly had to be chosen from among members of the outgoing radical Convention – a clear brake on the re-emergence of the old ruling class.

On 3 October seven Parisian neighbourhoods rose in opposition to the government, supported by General Menou, commander of the Paris military garrison. Other officers responsible for the 20,000 National Guardsmen stationed in the country were hesitant. It was a right-wing coup in the making. Napoleon himself was nowhere to be

found, and almost certainly was considering joining the rebels: he confessed later that he was uncertain who to support, although he had been probably appraised of the plot beforehand.

According to the popular account, Napoleon was attending the theatre on the night of 4 October while the coup attempt was being mounted outside. From there he was summoned by Barras, who gave him three minutes to decide whether to support the constitution; if so he was offered the job of head of the artillery. Barras desperately needed a good military commander. Napoleon agreed, although whether during the three minutes or later that evening is not known. He claimed that his choice was made for idealistic reasons: almost certainly it stemmed from a cold-blooded calculation of the likely outcome. He went to work instantly, organizing the 8,000 or so loyal supporters of the Convention to face the 30,000 or so armed men, many of them soldiers or ex-soldiers preparing to attack the Tuileries.

With demonic energy, Napoleon ordered the loyal 21st Chasseurs to seize the forty guns of the National Guard's artillery at Place de Sablons. The soldiers' commander was Joachim Murat, a powerfully built born soldier and natural leader, although not an intelligent man. Murat's men seized the guns at midnight, fending off a force of National Guardsmen. Napoleon ordered the guns to be placed around the Tuileries and aimed a battery of two 8-pound guns down the Rue Neuve St-Roche, leading to the Rue St Honoré to the north-west of the royal palace, where the insurgents were expected to come. He placed some 4,000 loyal soldiers around the immense building.

There they waited until well into the following afternoon, when the rebels, armed with bayonets, broke through the barricades leading to the Rue Neuve St-Roche. They stopped at the church where they regrouped, sending snipers on to the church roof and steeple. Napoleon himself took personal command of the cannon and ordered that a murderous fire of grapeshot be poured into the rebels. Hundreds fell, and assaults from other quarters were also driven back. The rebels fled towards the Place Vendôme and the Palais Royal, pursued by Napoleon's soldiers. Another large rebel force was prevented from crossing the Seine to the south-west by guns Napoleon had set up

commanding the bridge. Several government troops had perished, but anything up to 500 rebels had been ruthlessly massacred.

The rightists left the city despairingly that night: the situation had been saved, largely by Napoleon's indiscriminate and deadly use of artillery. Compared to a major military action, it had been minor, no more than a skirmish and requiring no military skill. But the young commander had acted with decisiveness, self-confidence and, most important of all, utter ruthlessness: he had shown no qualms about mowing down scores of fellow Frenchmen with vastly superior fire-power in the streets of Paris.

It was the turning point of his life: previously a provincial officer of some military distinction, he was now a man of real power in Paris, who had saved the government by displaying a cold-blooded brutality that, had it been displayed earlier for the King of France by his supporters, might have saved the *ancien régime*. Moreover Napoleon had acted in defence of the constitutional government and against the extremists of the right, establishing himself as a true republican, not a monarchist. Barras declared gratuitously, 'The Republic has been saved!'

On assuming his appointment as a member of the Directory, Barras insisted that Napoleon take his place as commander of the Army of the Interior – although the able Carnot, France's best military chief and also a member of the Directory, strongly opposed this. 'Promote this man, or he will promote himself without you,' Barras is said to have declared. Not only was Napoleon now a considerable figure, he was given considerable personal reward by Barras for his role.

He immediately splashed out: he sent 50,000 louis to his mother, had Joseph appointed consul in Italy and gave him money to invest in Genoa. Lucien was appointed commissary of the north in the Nether-lands. Louis was promoted to lieutenant and became Napoleon's secretary. Jérôme, still only eleven, was sent to an expensive school near Paris. Like a modern gangster, Napoleon endearingly shared his good fortune with his family. A *nouveau riche*, the twenty-six-year-old hired a box at the opera, bought a magnificent carriage and gave extravagant parties at his new official residence. Behaving like a military strongman, he summoned up his 40,000 troops and militia to police

Paris and closed down the Jacobin headquarters at the Pantheon Club. Overnight he had become one of the most powerful and best known men in the capital.

Napoleon had reaped a colossal reward for this decidedly minor military effort and heartless brutality. Yet what he really sought was command of the French army in Italy, for this promised real opportunities of advancement and enrichment in place of his police role in Paris, which was already subdued. He had sought this before and presented an ambitious plan for an aggressive strike into northern Italy, which had been described by a former French commander in the Alps as 'the work of a madman such as could only be executed by a madman'. Carnot, the most powerful military figure in France, argued with Barras that he should be given the opportunity. Barras himself was hesitant, wanting his ally to remain at his side in Paris – but he was won over by Napoleon, and by his mistress, Rose de Beauharnais, who soon after the massacre had become Napoleon's lover as well.

Rose had been born in 1763 of a wealthy French family which had been based for more than 200 years on the island of Martinique, where they owned a sugar plantation and had 150 slaves. As was usual for the time, she had an arranged marriage at the age of sixteen with a dashing nineteen-year-old French aristocrat, Vicomte Alexandre de Beauharnais. He was a libertine with a violent temper, and they spent just ten months together in four years. She gave birth to two children, Eugène and Hortense, before he left to live with a mistress in Rose's own backyard of Martinique.

The two separated and Rose, who had great sexual allure although not overpowering beauty, led a promiscuous life in Paris. When her feckless husband, who had become a Jacobin, suddenly fell out of favour with Robespierre and was imprisoned, Rose loyally sought his release and was herself arrested and sent to Les Carmes prison, where both soon had second lovers – de Beauharnais the celebrated Delphine de Custine, mistress of General Miranda, and Rose General Hoche, the most promising young commander of the Revolution, whom Napoleon detested. De Beauharnais was executed on 22 July 1794, just before Robespierre's own fall, Rose being released afterwards to become Barras's mistress (Hoche rejected her with the vicious remark

that: 'such an amour can be pardoned in a prison but hardly outside . . . One may take a prostitute for a mistress but hardly for a wife.')

Napoleon dubbed her Josephine: she was kind, homely, small, brown-eyed and chestnut-haired. She had bad teeth which she concealed when she smiled. However, she exuded urban sophistication as well as sex appeal, unlike his naïve country girl, Désirée, to whom he ceased to write.

When he stopped visiting Josephine for a while, she sent him a note of reproof: 'You no longer come to see a friend who is fond of you; you have completely abandoned her. You are wrong, for she is tenderly attached to you. Come to lunch tomorrow, Septidi. I want to see you and talk to you about your affairs. Good night, my friend, I embrace you. Widow Beauharnais.'

In November 1796 they made love for the first time: he wrote her a passionate letter, which was considered very gauche of him by experienced Parisian ladies, but undoubtedly entranced her:

Seven in the morning
I have woken up full of you. Your portrait and the memory of yesterday's intoxicating evening have given my senses no rest. Sweet and incomparable Josephine, what an odd effect you have on my heart! Are you displeased? Do I see you sad? Are you worried? Then my soul is grief stricken, and your friend cannot rest . . . But I cannot rest either when I yield to the deep feeling that overpowers me and I draw from your lips and heart a flame that burns me. Ah! Last night I clearly realized that the portrait I had of you is quite different from the real you! You are leaving at noon, and in three hours I shall see you. Until then, mio dolce amore, thousands of kisses; but don't kiss me, for your kisses sear my blood.

By now the young general had fallen completely in love. (Some of his biographers were to assert that a later paramour, Marie Walewska, was Napoleon's only true love: this is quite untrue. Napoleon was utterly and embarrassingly besotted by Josephine at first, although she not by him, and only her later appalling behaviour eventually caused him to cool.)

She, at the age of thirty-two, six years his senior, was much more detached. She told a friend: 'You are going to ask, "Do I love him?" Well . . . no. "Do you feel aversion to him?" No. What I feel is tepidness: it annoys me, in fact religious people find it the most tiresome state of all.' Barras, who was growing tired of Josephine, was delighted to palm her off on his uncouth young protégé. Bona-parte's mother, Letizia, was, however, horrified at his rejection of the faithful young Désirée for this older divorced and sexually insatiable adventuress. Josephine moreover was virtually penniless, for Martini-que, where her family estates lay, was in British hands.

They were, on the face of it, an odd couple. All kind of psycho-sexual theories have been advanced for what Napoleon saw in Josephine. Yet, given their status at the time, it was not a particularly unusual match. Josephine was a hardened woman of fading charms with two dependent children. Neither of her two most recent lovers – Hoche and Barras – was prepared to marry her. She needed money and security.

Napoleon, another outsider to France, was a naïve, romantic and sexually inexperienced young man with a glittering career ahead of him which compensated for his sallow looks and lack of charm, although his intelligence and energy were obvious. Having spent most of his life in the provinces, he was captivated by this highly sophis-ticated member of Paris's most elegant set, regarding her as a passport to social acceptance. When it became clear that his patron, Barras, also favoured the match, Napoleon knew this would be useful in his career. (Joseph once accused him of merely using Josephine to get his command in Italy – which was a grotesquely unjust accusation, as Napoleon's almost embarrassing devotion to her was to reveal.) Napoleon, short and unattractive was until recently a nobody who had had little success with women. Here was one that was attractive, highly sexed, immensely assured and cosmopolitan, kind, maternal and patient with all his quirks, sudden tempers and bursts of energy and, in her own way, not unlike him – two opportunistic outsiders on the make.

It was a marriage of passion and convenience on his side, although one only of convenience on hers. They were two survivors in the

penumbra of the highly uncertain world of post-revolutionary Paris, both from dubious backgrounds, both uncertain what the future would hold. She is said to have slept with Barras on the night before her marriage on 9 March 1796. Napoleon trumped this by arriving three hours late for the wedding. Two days later Napoleon unromantically bid his wife goodbye and was on his way to take up his command of the army of Italy.

Désirée wrote to him a letter of anguish.

You have made me so unhappy, and I am weak enough to forgive you! You married! Poor Désirée must no longer love you or think of you? . . . My one consolation is that you will know how steadfast I am . . . I have nothing more to hope for but death. Life is a torment to me, since I may no longer dedicate it to you . . . You married! I cannot grasp the thought – it kills me. Never shall I belong to another . . . And I had so hoped soon to be the happiest of women, your wife! Your marriage has shattered my happiness . . . All the same I wish you the greatest joy and blessing in your marriage. May the woman you have chosen make you as happy as I had intended to make you and as happy as you deserve to be. In the midst of your present happiness do not quite forget poor Eugénie, and be sorry for her fate.

Bonaparte's new appointment owed less to Barras's favour, whether or not extracted by Josephine, than to the hard-headed military calculations of France's military chief, Carnot. Faced with the danger of a renewed Austrian attack across the Rhine which had so unsettled the French in October, he decided to launch a flanking movement. The French army was still a colossal 240,000 strong. Carnot decided to send 70,000 men under the redoubtable Jourdan to recapture the fortress of Mainz; another 70,000 would advance along the Danube valley. And Napoleon, whose old hare-brained schemes for an attack on Italy had now come of age, would be in charge of 100,000 to attack the complacent Austrian forces sheltering beneath the Alps in the Po valley.

These offensives would take the French well beyond the national borders specified by the early revolutionaries. But they were necessary

to destroy the Austrian army once and for all. They would provide enormous opportunities for plunder – particularly in the wealthy Po valley, which would provide subsistence for the expensive French army; they would allow French revolutionary ideals to be exported; they would weaken France's chief adversary, Austria; and they would also rally the French, increasingly weary of shortages and the incompetence of their government, behind the patriotic cause.

The seeds of French expansion into the non-French part of Europe were thus sown not by Napoleon but by his predecessors in the Directory. 'Greater France' was not a Napoleonic invention, however much he would later boast it was, but a matter of French national policy long before he became France's ruler: at this stage he was a mere general, doing the bidding of his political masters. In Britain his name still barely registered even in official circles.

Pitt, unusually gloomy, mused in the New Year of 1796 on the 'sad reverse of fortune, when the spirit of our allies was broken, our troops discomfited, our territories wrested from us, and all our hopes disconcerted'. The Austrians along with the Portuguese and the Neapolitan court, were Britain's last allies in the fighting in central Europe; and now the French were girding themselves up to strike a decisive blow against them. Like most observers, Pitt expected the big battle to be fought along the Rhine – as indeed did the French.

Chapter 21

ITALIAN WHIRLWIND

They had not reckoned, however, with the extraordinary military skills of the new young commander of the Army of Italy. All his qualities were now to go on display in a dazzling show of military pyrotechnics over the next few weeks that were to leave his enemies reeling and the strategic map of Europe decisively redrawn. Napoleon arrived in Antibes, where he met with his chief of staff, a great brute of a man, Louis Berthier, who was nevertheless a skilled veteran and able organizer. At Nice the slight, short, boyish-looking Napoleon with his fevered energy and torrent of words impressed his older and more sceptical principal commanders – the laconic veteran Sérurier, the ferocious adventurer Augereau, and the tall and angular André Masséna. The French Army of the South was only 37,000 strong, ill-fed, ill-clothed and mutinous.

Napoleon decided to order a probing expedition along the coast to Genoa, the obvious route from which the 52,000-strong Austrians and their Piedmontese allies could expect an attack. He asked the Genoese whether he might cross their territory, and the information was duly passed on to the Austrians. A small force under La Harpe was sent to Voltri, along the coast fifteen miles short of Genoa. The Austrian commander, General Beaulieu, promptly descended with a substantial force from his headquarters in the foothills of the Alps to give chase.

Napoleon meanwhile marched into the Cadibona-Carcara gap, a pass to the north, with his main force and ordered La Harpe to retreat. Blocking the northern end of the pass, so that the Piedmontese could not reinforce the Austrians, he lured the Austrians pursuing La Harpe

into the gap and then fell upon them with a superior force of 16,000 men on 12 April at Montenotte. The Austrians were surprised and routed, losing 1,000 casualties and 2,500 prisoners. It was the young general's first significant military victory in Italy.

He promptly wheeled about and marched his main force up the gap to face the Piedmontese. These were divided between the towns of Ceva and Millesimo. He left Sérurier to distract the force at Ceva and marched with the main army of 16,000 men to Millesimo, over-powering and capturing the 10,000 Piedmontese troops, which put up little resistance. Augereau was sent to help reinforce the French attack on Ceva, while Napoleon himself with a superior force moved quickly to overpower the 6,000 Austrians at Dego and then surprise another such force of Austrians being hurried to reinforce Ceva.

All this took place within the space of four days, with Napoleon marching and countermarching up and down the steep mountain valleys and winding roads, often at night to prevent his enemies concentrating their forces. The dispersed Austrian and Piedmontese armies scarcely knew what hit them: they were unused to such speed of attack and movement. The bemused Austrians retreated to their headquarters at Pavia, a medieval town with a spectacular *certosa* (closed monastery) while the Piedmontese retreated behind the natural barrier of the river Tanaro, to the north-west, to protect their capital of Turin.

Napoleon rested briefly before crossing the river and defeating the Piedmontese near Vico and occupying the substantial town of Mon-dovi. The Piedmontese retired to the Villa Stura near the village of Cherasco: the way was now open to the stately city of Turin, just thirty miles away. King Victor Amadeus, startled by the suddenness of the French advance and the scale of the defeats, sent envoys to meet Napoleon. Napoleon issued an ultimatum. Threatening to occupy the substantial town of Cuneo, he offered to spare Turin if his men were granted the provisions they needed. He declared that he was not despoiling the Italians, but liberating them from the Austrian yoke. He boasted:

Hannibal merely crossed the Alps, we turned their flanks . . .
Tomorrow I shall march against Beaulieu, force him to cross the

Po, cross myself immediately after and seize the whole of Lombardy: within a month I hope to be on the mountains of the Tyrol, in touch with the Army of the Rhine, and to carry the war in concert into Bavaria . . . Soldiers! In fifteen days you have gained six victories, taken twenty-one colours and 55 pieces of artillery, seized several fortresses and conquered the richest parts of Piedmont. You have taken 15,000 prisoners and killed and wounded more than 10,000 . . . The hungry soldiers are committing excesses that make one blush to be human. The capture of Ceva and Mondovi may give us the means to put this right, and I am going to make some terrible examples. I will restore order or I will give up the command of these brigands.

'Peoples of Italy!' he announced in a printed proclamation, 'The French army is come to break your chains . . . We shall respect your property, your religion and your customs. We wage war with generous hearts, and turn ourselves only against the tyrants who seek to enslave us.' The envoys agreed to his terms.

He resumed the march across very different territory to the narrow valleys of the southern Alps – the vast, almost perfectly level flatlands of the Po valley, which were hugely fertile, but also at that time riddled with swamps and the diseases and mosquitoes that infested them, although the weather at this time of year was still pleasantly temperate.

He bypassed the Austrian stronghold at Pavia, choosing to cross the river at Piacenza. There he found it to be 300 yards wide. He sent 900 men across in boats under Austrian fire to secure the opposite bank, and then ferried his army over in two days. He marched on Milan, soon reaching the bridge at Lodi, where the Austrians had a substantial force of some 12,000 men. The bridge was a rudimentary wooden structure just twelve feet wide and 200 yards long, and was overlooked by Austrian guns in a well-defended fortress.

Napoleon decided on an act of madness in such a militarily impossible situation: a frontal attack under the guns. But first he despatched his cavalry to cross lower down and attack the Austrians on their flank. Goading his infantry on with volleys of sarcasm, he

thundered down on his white horse from the town square to the bridge and, with the French drums beating 'La Marseillaise', urged his men past him as he waved his sword. They marched forward under intense enemy fire along the narrow bridge, soldiers toppling in scores into the water as they were hit, only for others to take their place.

Several jumped into the water as they approached the opposite bank to avoid the murderous Austrian shot. A few soldiers made the opposite bank, some along the bridge, some from the water. The Austrian cavalry charged to cut them down. The French were on the verge of being routed: it had all been the madness of an inexperienced young commander.

At last the French cavalry, which had spent hours finding a suitable ford, came galloping up from the flank and attacked the Austrian gunners in the fort. As the withering Austrian fire from above ceased, the French infantry surged forward along that narrow causeway of death, overwhelming the Austrian cavalry and infantry on the opposite bank. At last the Austrians gave way, leaving more than 300 dead to the 200 French lives they had taken. Some 1,700 prisoners were seized. It had been a staggering victory, owing more to sheer determination, recklessness and luck than careful planning or skill.

Milan, which dominated the fertile Po valley and all of northern Italy, was now Napoleon's for the taking. His triumphant army moved north into the city, with its imposing Sforza fortress and soaring, spiky, white gothic cathedral, and he took up residence in the old palace which the Austrian Archduke had abandoned. In the space of just three weeks he had broken across the supposedly impregnable barrier of the lower Alps and captured half of the richest region in Italy.

He had done more than that: he had proved himself as a military commander. The keys to his success as a young leader had been his feverish energy, in mustering and manoeuvring his armies with pinpoint precision across the hills and plains, deceiving, outflanking and ambushing his enemies, more a guerrilla chieftain than a conventional commander, routing the traditionalist Austrians through the sheer unexpectedness of his tactics, seizing the offensive from the beginning and placing a superior enemy army on the defensive.

He had taken advantage of the way the Austrians had divided their

forces into dominant positions at key strongpoints, while he himself would divide his forces to strike at weak points, then bring them together again to attack strong points. At Lodi he had demonstrated superb leadership and bravery in the face of seemingly impossible odds, although the attack had been reckless in the extreme and was won largely by luck. He had shown himself a fine soldier, although one yet to prove himself in a major set-piece battle.

The ease of his victories also reflects on the quality of the officers and troops opposing him. The Piedmontese were not effective fighters at that stage, while the Austrians in northern Italy had grown idle with the ease of garrisoning and were accustomed to conventional tactics of position, garrisons and lines – not to the speedy and unexpected attacks of a young energetic commander possessed of hungry republican troops who scorned the niceties and social conventions of aristocratic warfare in the eighteenth century.

Moreover Napoleon was no stickler in respect of property: one of the main incentives for his impressed men – another was the fear of execution dating back to Robespierre's day for those that failed to perform well – was plunder and the promise of being fed and clothed properly. Napoleon and his lieutenants turned a blind eye to looting. The wealth of Milan lay prostrate before Napoleon's half-starved, ragged army.

But the self-important young man now resident in the ducal palace, who had ludicrously compared his skilful but by no means epic achievement to Hannibal's crossing of the Alps, was in for a shock. To his masters in Paris he was still no more than a promising young general. They ordered him to report to the distinguished General Kellermann, the sixty-one-year-old veteran who had won the Battle of Valmy in 1792. Kellermann was to take charge of the campaigns against the Austrians in northern Italy, and Napoleon was to lead a lesser campaign against two Austrian allies further down the Italian peninsula, Tuscany and the Papal States, although ones which promised rich pickings.

Napoleon, who saw himself (as he wrote later) no longer 'as a mere general, but as a man called upon to influence the destiny of a people . . . a superior man . . . nobody has had a greater concept than mine',

had been brought brutally down to earth. He wrote furiously back: 'Kellermann would command the army as well as myself; for no one could be more convinced than I am that our victories are due to the courage and dash of the army; but I think that to give Kellermann and myself joint command in Italy would mean ruining everything.'

At this threat to resign in pique, the Directory grudgingly gave way, providing Napoleon with a valuable lesson that he could get his way by sheer self-assertion. They agreed to let him remain in command, but insisted he must not move into the Tyrol to confront the large Austrian armies there, but go south to defeat the Pope – there was a strong atheist tendency in the French government – and 'cause the tiara of the self-styled head of the universal church to totter'.

Once again, the initiative to move into central Italy came not from Napoleon but from his bosses in revolutionary France. This command could not by any stretch of the imagination be described as defensive, arising from the need to defeat the Austrian empire. The motivation was aggression and plunder, pure and simple, the first move towards the territorial acquisition of a French empire in Europe. The vast wealth and awesome artistic treasures of the Pope seemed to Paris to be there for the taking: these would ease the cost of supporting France's immense armies, serve as a further distraction for the restless French people, and enormously enrich the rulers of France themselves.

Napoleon himself, while paying lip service to revolutionary ideas and his mission in liberating Italy from Austrian rule, was equally fixated on the prospect of plunder for its own sake and, more understandably, to pay his army and thereby ensure its loyalty to himself, as French soldiers were used to being paid late if at all. Before Lodi Napoleon had already requested from Paris 'a few reputable artists to take charge of choosing and transporting all the beautiful things we shall see fit to send to Paris' – something he knew would please his masters.

To pay off his army, he levied 2 million livres from Milan – a colossal sum – and then imposed a further tax upon the citizens of northern Italy for the Directory. By July he had raised a staggering 60 million francs. Most of this came from the wealthier citizens, but these passed much of the burden on to the poorer classes. He installed a puppet

government in Milan, replacing the old aristocrats with middle-class nominees, and forced Parma and Modena to pay a large tribute in order to be spared occupation by his irresistible army. These were the tactics of the Aztecs or any other such predatory conquerors. He urged the creation of a North Italian Republic under his rule, while continuing to reiterate his promise to liberate the Milanese.

Not that the Milanese were fooled. When he departed to fight Beaulieu's remaining army, the city and neighbouring Pavia immediately rose up in insurrection against the French. Napoleon hastily returned to Pavia, crushed the uprising there, led the massacre of the 300-strong military garrison, and laid the town open to rape and pillage by his men. It was a second appalling display of his almost Asiatic ruthlessness and contempt for human life, in particular when angered – this in one of the most beautiful and historic cultural centres in Italy. The Milanese shuddered and promptly surrendered without a fight. Napoleon turned his attention to the only major city in the Po valley still holding out against him, Mantua, and laid siege to the city on 4 June.

His thoughts were also elsewhere: he was romantically besotted with his wife, to whom he wrote a letter every day, begging her to join him. But she was otherwise engaged: she had taken a lover, Hippolyte Charles, a small but dashing hussar addicted to drinking and gambling, the polar opposite to the intense, self-disciplined Napoleon. The young general ordered his two most faithful friends, Androche Junot and Joachim Murat, to bring her to him. Of the first he wrote crudely: 'You must return with Junot, do you hear, my adorable one, he will see you, he will breathe the air of your shrine. Perhaps you will even allow him the unique favour of a kiss on your cheek . . . A kiss on your heart, and then another a little lower, much *much lower*.' He also remarked that she had 'the prettiest little vagina in the world, the Three Isles of Martinique were there'. But she and the handsome Murat made love. Josephine was openly contemptuous of her absent husband. '*Q'il est drôle, Bonaparte.*'

Josephine has usually been blamed for her faithlessness: yet the marriage had been one largely of convenience for her from the beginning. Given that she did not love Napoleon in the first place,

it is hardly surprising that she drifted into the arms of other men. She told him she was seriously ill.

He responded by requesting support from Barras, her former lover and the patron of both: 'I hate all women. I am in despair. My wife has not arrived. She must be detained by some lover in Paris.' He accused her of preferring her dog to him (which may have been true). The Director ordered her to join him, and she set off with Napoleon's brother Joseph, who disliked her intensely, her lover Hippolyte, with whom she ostentatiously slept along the journey, and the faithful Junot, whom she teased by openly attempting to seduce him in front of the other travellers. When she arrived at Napoleon's sumptuous Palazzo Serpelloni, she had to endure the embraces of her husband for two days before he set off for Mantua, where Sérurier had been placed in charge of the siege.

Napoleon had also learnt that Marshal Dagobert Wurmser and a large Austrian army had left the Rhine to engage him. He fumed at the failure of the two northern French commanders to launch an expected offensive along the Rhine and keep the Austrians tied down there. But that was exactly what the Directory had calculated – that Napoleon's invasion of southern Italy would compel the Austrians to weaken their Rhine armies.

Taking advantage of the six weeks' interlude before Wurmser's armies could arrive, Napoleon embarked on his expedition to emasculate the militarily weak Papal States. Arriving in Emilia-Romagna, he easily drove off the papal army of 18,000 men, seizing Bologna, Ferrara and the rich port of Livorno (Leghorn), so denying it to the British as a base, and moved as far down as Florence to intimidate the Tuscans. He travelled 300 miles largely without opposition, helping himself to another colossal fortune, 40 million francs. To fend off an attack on the Papal States, the Pope gave him some of the greatest art treasures in the Vatican, as well as a huge tribute in gold and the port of Ancona on the Adriatic. It was a repeat of the barbarian invasion of ancient Rome, with the treasures of the Italian renaissance instead of classical antiquity as the spoils.

With news of the Austrian armies approaching northern Italy, Napoleon sped back to confront them. They had been marching

down the Brenner Pass and crossed the river Adige with 50,000 men in three columns, their objective to relieve Mantua. Napoleon moved quickly to prevent them linking up at Mantua, and fell upon the Austrian right at Lonato with a superior force of 27,000 men to the Austrians' 21,000. Wurmser tried to reunite his armies, but he was too late: Augereau led the French against him at Castiglione at the beginning of August. Some 25,000 Austrians were killed or wounded and 15,000 taken prisoner, to 5,500 French casualties and 1,400 prisoners. Once again, Napoleon had shown skill, energy and tactical brilliance as well as speed, but Wurmser was not yet defeated. He manoeuvred skilfully to attack the French and marched to relieve Mantua again.

Napoleon, who had captured Roverata and Trent in the north, set off after him and inflicted a victory on points at Bassano on 8 September. But most of the Austrian army survived intact and relieved Mantua two days later, bringing the garrison's strength up to 23,000 and rendering it virtually impregnable from Napoleon's army, which for once arrived too late, eight days afterwards. Equally, though, Wurmser's main army was now bottled up and out of commission.

The British minister in Turin, John Trevor, had written with dismay to Lord Grenville of 'the torrent of this victorious enemy'. The British watched with alarm the spectacular victories that this new French general was winning as he hurtled his way across northern Italy. This further muddied what was already a dismal strategic scene across Europe as a whole: with the occupation of Leghorn, the French had secured a powerful new Mediterranean base. Meanwhile, the court at Naples, watching the whirlwind action across Italy and seeking to avoid the same fate, was intimidated into neutrality: Britain had lost one of its oldest allies.

Worse still, as the French advance seemed unstoppable, Spain, from a position of favouring neither side, lapsed into 'hostile neutrality' against Britain in August 1796. Almost overnight, after the loss of continental Europe, the British were losing control of a second key theatre: the Mediterranean itself. Their presence there was now confined to Corsica, Malta, Minorca and Gibraltar – a handful of outposts. They were not yet at war with Spain, and desperately anxious

to avoid it if they could. But the Mediterranean was anything but a British lake.

That incorrigible pair of optimists, the cousins Pitt and Grenville, sought solace elsewhere: perhaps the Prussians would change their minds – but the British were quickly rebuffed and by June it seemed possible that the Prussians would actually join the French. Perhaps the Russians would help: but the British ambassador, Charles Whitworth, was soon grumbling about the Empress's 'scandalously evasive conduct'. Perhaps a change would come about in France: but the royalists were now on the defensive and the Directory was more firmly in control than before. The success of the French war effort had redounded to its credit: it was hardly likely to abandon the most successful of its policies, in a country still plagued by shortages and disruption. Napoleon's plundering was providing a huge and desperately needed flow of money into France.

Only Austria remained. The British poured money in to assist their ally – £100,000 in April, £150,000 in May, £300,000 for July and August, a further £150,000 a month for the rest of the year – although this was well short of Austrian demands. Still, Austria, faced with Napoleon's aggression in the south, had despatched its biggest Rhine army to meet the new threat across the Dolomites.

Disconcerted, Pitt and Grenville looked to their somewhat pyrrhic gains in the West Indies for consolation, as well as heartening news from the Cape, where the Dutch attempt to regain the Cape Colony had been beaten off; but shortages of ships and men meant the strategy for an attack on the troublesome French island of Mauritius (Île de France) – a staging post for attacks on the traffic to the British East Indies – had to be abandoned.

Pitt seemed close to despair by June 1796. He wrote to Grenville:

> I am . . . clear that (unless there happens some unexpected turn in the state of things) any idea of our enabling Austria to act with any effect beyond the present year is out of the question. In this situation it would be inexcusable not to try any chance that can be tried, honourably and safely, to set on some foot some decent plan of pacification; and I can conceive no objection in the mind of any of

our colleagues to see whether the arrangement to which you have pointed can be made acceptable both to Austria and Prussia. But though I think it should be tried, I do not flatter myself with much chance of success. On the whole my notion is that most likely, either now or a few months hence, we shall be left to sustain alone the conflict with France and Holland, probably joined by Spain, and perhaps favoured more or less openly by the Northern powers.

With Spain ever closer to joining the French, the British decided in principle to evacuate their outpost of Corsica, which would be untenable and was anyway a constant source of unrest. Britain's troublesome old ally, and Napoleon's *bête noire*, Paoli, had again to be granted safe haven in London. Pitt's spirits sank to their lowest ebb.

Two morsels of good news reached him at last. The Russian Empress, having dismembered Poland with Prussia, offered to send 60,000 Russian troops to Austria in exchange for a flat payment and a continuing subsidy of £150,000 a month. The British grasped eagerly at this straw, and even offered to hand over Corsica as a warm-water naval base for the Russians. More important, Archduke Charles won an unexpected victory in eastern Bavaria on 24 August. Generals Jourdan and Moreau had divided their armies into three columns with their flanks exposed, and had failed to bottle up Austrian forces into the strongholds of Phillippsburg and Mannheim behind their lines. The Austrians attacked on six key flanks: the French fell back down to Mainz, and Charles triumphed at Wurzburg, pushing the French back across the Rhine again in October.

Pitt exultantly looked forward to the 'annihilation' of the French across the Rhine and could see only opportunities arising from the approaching war with Spain to seize its far-flung possessions. Abercromby was despatched to seize Trinidad and Puerto Rico and even possibly send an expedition to Buenos Aires. Manila was thought to be vulnerable. Cadiz could be blockaded.

But at the same time, astonishingly, Pitt sent out peace feelers to France, despatching a senior emissary, Lord Malmesbury, in October: it was further evidence of his lack of clear commitment to the war and of his desire to appease the French, which had been apparent for years

before the declaration of war in 1793. He could hardly have chosen a worse time: the French contemptuously rebuffed Malmesbury, while both the Austrians and the Russians, who had not been consulted and had been egged on to a more robust posture towards France by the British, were furious. Grenville, who had left Pitt to be his own foreign minister while he mourned the death of a sister, was appalled and immediately stiffened the British terms.

By the end of the year, however, three further dramatic developments plunged the British into gloom again. The Empress Catherine died, to be succeeded by her suspicious, introspective son, Paul, who had hated his mother and preferred an alliance with Paris to one with London; the French attempted an invasion of Ireland; and Napoleon threw the Austrians on the defensive again.

Fortunately for Pitt the Irish invasion was as much a fiasco as the British Dunkirk expedition had been two years before. On 16 December the French fleet left Brest unopposed – the Channel fleet commander, the undistinguished Lord Bridport, was residing comfortably in Somerset. By the time its destination could be worked out, the French ships, escorting an army of some 20,000 men, had arrived in Bantry Bay. They were escorting Wolfe Tone, a young Protestant from Dublin, who had sought to unite both his own and the Catholic community in a demand for self-government. Luckily for the British, a gale blew up, preventing the French from landing and separating General Hoche, the French army commander, from the main force. The French were driven ignominiously back to Brest.

Meanwhile, Napoleon was on the move again. The Austrian victories on the Rhine made it inevitable that the Austrians would try and reassert their hold on northern Italy. While living it up in Milan amid scenes of ostentatious vulgarity, pawing at his beloved Josephine in public while she cuckolded him with Hippolyte whenever he went away, and permitting his soldiers freely to despoil northern Italy, Napoleon threw his weight around the region, occupying Modena, imposing a French garrison upon Genoa and seeking to intimidate Venice.

But the Austrians were massing again along the Brenner Pass and in November advanced in two columns – one of 28,000 men through

Vicenza towards Verona, the other of 18,000 men down the Adige valley towards Trent. The second army mauled a French force outside the city and took it. Napoleon was pushed out of Verona and with only 10,000 men – 14,000 of his men were off sick in the marshy lowlands – his position looked desperate.

On 12 November he suffered his first defeat in the Italian campaign outside Verona. He wrote nervously to the Directory: 'Perhaps we are on the verge of losing Italy. None of the expected help has arrived. I despair of being able to avoid raising the siege of Mantua, which would have been ours within a week . . . In a few days we will make a last effort. If fortune smiles, Mantua will be taken and with it Italy.' He was faced by now with no fewer than three Austrian armies, in Verona, Trent and Mantua, each bigger than his own, which might soon join up. Desperately he manoeuvred to outflank Verona and strike from the rear, staging a forced march to the Adige.

At the river crossing at Arcola he unexpectedly found an enemy force of Croats defending the bridge. As at Lodi, Napoleon gambled on a frontal assault across the bridge: to get there he needed to cross a causeway through marshes. This time he led the charge himself, clutching the French flag to give his troops courage. But, as he reported, 'we had to give up the idea of taking the village by frontal assault'. Halfway across, it seems, while cursing his troops for their cowardice, he had to retreat. He appears to have fallen into the marsh by the causeway under intense enemy fire, and been saved by his brother Louis, although the facts are disputed.

He then seems to have led his men southwards, erecting a pontoon across the marsh and eventually reached firm ground, before attacking the Austrians from the rear. The latter, taken by surprise, fell back, although they could probably have defeated the far less numerous French. Napoleon lost a large number of men – some 4,500 killed or wounded – dwarfed only by the Austrian casualties of 7,000. All of this was far from discreditable to Napoleon, although his frontal attack was probably needlessly costly. But he subsequently elevated it to the status of myth, immortalized in a famous painting by Delacroix.

Napoleon sensibly and typically kept up the pressure after this success, pushing on to encircle the second Austrian army. After a

few skirmishes, this was badly mauled at Rouco and the two main Austrian armies, although still largely intact, decided to retreat, having failed to reach Mantua. It had been a triumph more for French aggressiveness against Austrian caution than a great feat of arms or tactics. Napoleon had won by the skin of his teeth. His troops were exhausted and incapable of fighting on.

Chapter 22

KING OF NORTH ITALY

Napoleon's magnificent progress across northern Italy aroused the suspicions of the Directory: he was still only their servant, a brilliant military commander, but not a political authority in his own right. Saliceti, the Directory's representative and Napoleon's old patron and friend, became jealous and started sending unfavourable reports home; Saliceti resented being rebuked by Napoleon for openly selling plunder in the streets.

The anxious Directors sent General Henri Clarke to spy on him. This emissary found Napoleon in a foul mood 'haggard, the skin clinging to his bones, eyes bright with fever'. Clarke told him that the Directory wanted an armistice. Napoleon angrily objected. After a few encounters, Clarke's attitude changed. He wrote back to his masters:

Everyone here regards him as a man of genius . . . He is feared, loved and respected in Italy. I believe he is attached to the Republic and without any ambition save to retain the reputation he has won . . . General Bonaparte is not without defects . . . Sometimes he is hard, impatient, abrupt or imperious. Often he demands difficult things in too hasty a manner. He has not been respectful enough towards the government commissioners. When I reproved him for this, he replied that he could not possibly treat otherwise men who were universally scorned for their immorality and incapacity . . . Saliceti has the reputation of being the most shameless rogue in the army and Garrau is inefficient: neither is suitable for the Army of Italy.

After this glowing report the Directors' fears were partially assuaged. The issue of the armistice was settled by the arrival of a magnificent new Austrian army of 28,000 men under the able General Alvinzi, marching down the Adige valley, while another 17,000 under General Provera were heading for Verona. General Wurmser was determined to relieve Mantua, where 20,000 Austrians were running short of fuel in the city isolated by marshes and lakes.

With some 9,000 tied down besieging Mantua, another 9,000 sick and a further 4,000 scattered across northern Italy, Napoleon had only 20,000 men. Still, he did not wait for the superior forces of the enemy to take the offensive. Instead he marched forward to the Plateau de Rivoli, which was surrounded by hills commanding the Garda-Verona road and lying between the Adige and Tasso rivers.

At Rivoli a division of 10,000 under the tough, wily General Barthélemy Joubert was under fire between the vastly superior Austrian forces. When Napoleon arrived at one in the morning and watched the hundreds of camp fires of Alvinzi's army flickering around the plateau, he ordered an immediate attack the following morning against the superior Austrian positions, before the Austrians could descend to the plateau and organize themselves in strength.

The attack ran into serious trouble against the Austrian cavalry and guns, and soon Napoleon's flank was turned. Just as defeat seemed inevitable, General André Masséna, who had ridden his 8,000 men across snow and ice in a gruelling twenty-mile march, arrived and beat back the flank attackers. Thus reinforced, Napoleon defeated the first Austrian corps and then fell upon another weaker one. A third arrived from the rear, and Napoleon, with characteristic ferocity, turned to attack it – but would probably not have prevailed had not another French force under General Ney reached the plain just after noon.

The Austrians, after more fighting, retreated, leaving 8,000 killed and wounded or captured. After a gruelling all-day march in the open, Napoleon, who had narrowly escaped death several times and lost several horses shot beneath him, had won a classic victory largely through aggression, speed and quick responses which outmanoeuvred his opponents. It was his greatest victory yet.

Even so, he did not rest on his laurels. Knowing of the approach of

the second Austrian army under Provera marching to relieve Mantua, he ordered his exhausted, battle-scarred men on a twenty-four-hour march to assemble some thirty miles further on. On 16 January, he was at La Favoeitae. Provera was roundly beaten, losing some 7,000 men and twenty-two guns. Joubert, meanwhile, who had pursued the retreating Austrians from Rivoli with a smaller force, had taken no fewer than 7,000 prisoners.

Wurmser, whose men in Mantua were now starving and had been denied any hope of relief, sued for peace, claiming he still had twelve months' worth of provisions. Napoleon was disposed to be generous and even promised Wurmser, a renegade Frenchman whom the Directory had ordered to be shot, that he could return to Vienna. On 2 February the French marched victoriously into Mantua without a fight.

The Directory ordered Napoleon south, to punish the Pope for continuing to side with the Austrians. This proved all too easy: a series of papal towns fell without a struggle, including Bologna, Rimini and Macerata, and he was delighted to take Ancona, the second most important Adriatic port after Venice. The Pope sued for peace and under the Treaty of Tolentino ceded Bologna, Ferrara and Romagna to the French, as well as paying Napoleon 30 million francs.

One of the Directors, the atheist La Revellière, demanded that the Pope be deposed. But Napoleon realized that this sixty-nine-year-old posed no threat, and feared igniting a religious war. The Pope, he argued, stabilized central Italy and prevented its seizure by the Kingdom of Naples under Queen Maria Carolina, Marie Antoinette's sister. He assured La Revellière that the Papal States would fall to pieces by themselves, while similarly reassuring Pius VI that he had no intention of retaining them.

He then galloped back a hundred miles to the north to prepare the final blow against Austria in March. In order to achieve this, the Directory reinforced his army to 80,000 men and sent him, as counterbalances, Generals Bernadotte and Delmas. The former, a highly competent Gascon officer who had worked his way up the ranks to become a general at the age of just thirty-one, was a passionate Jacobin and close friend of St Just. Tall, good-looking, vain and

endowed with a fiery temper, he was fond of duelling at the slightest insult. Bernadotte's prickliness and vainglory had earned him a bad reputation, but he was undoubtedly a competent commander and an impressive figure. His problem was that, like Hoche, he did not owe his prominence to Napoleon, but regarded himself as a superior and rival to Napoleon, who was vastly the better soldier. He deeply resented taking orders from Napoleon: 'Over there I saw a man of twenty-six or twenty-seven who wants to appear fifty. It bodes no good for the Republic . . . I see it all. Bonaparte is jealous of me and wants to disgrace me. I have no resource left but to blow my brains out.' Worse still, Bernadotte was married to Napoleon's childhood sweetheart, Désirée, who deeply resented having been dumped for Josephine.

Napoleon's offensive against Austria with his reinforced and re-invigorated army was perfectly executed. He sent the capable Jourdan up the Brenner Pass to cut off the 15,000 Austrians still stranded in the Dolomites and to prevent a flanking attack by the Rhine Army. He personally commanded four divisions coming up from Bassano on 10 March and easily defeated a smaller force under the legendary Austrian Archduke Charles at Tagliamento before taking Klagenforth on 29 March.

The French army under Moreau along the Rhine, which was supposed to launch a simultaneous offensive, made no move, and Napoleon decided he could not take Vienna alone. He marched on Leoben, some seventy-five miles from the Austrian capital, and sent forward an advance to Semmering, just outside Vienna, to intimidate the court. He was fearful of over-extending his lines. This intimidation had the desired effect: the royal court hurriedly evacuated Vienna for Hungary. Napoleon threatened the Austrians with attack from two directions – although he had no way of ensuring that Moreau would do his part, possibly because the Directory was wary of enhancing his reputation through giving him such a project.

Napoleon drew up a peace treaty with the Austrians, although he had no authority to reach one. The treaty, like the one reached with the Pope, was relatively generous. Austria would be allowed to retain Istria, Dalmatia and Friuli, but it was to recognize that Belgium belonged to France, and to cede the Ionian Islands as well as the left

bank of the Rhine, while recognizing Napoleon's new Cisalpine Republic in Italy. Most controversially, Napoleon offered to capture Venice and deliver it up to the Austrians. This combination of threats and bribes was enough for the Austrian court, which agreed to these terms on 18 April.

Napoleon turned to the town of Verona which had risen and massacred a French garrison behind him with the connivance of the Venetians. Verona quickly surrendered, but Napoleon now had his excuse to threaten the Doge of Venice. Ignoring instructions from the Directory to leave the city state alone, he moved upon it and seized it. Napoleon followed this up by seizing the Venetian Ionian islands of Corfu, Cephalonia and Zante without any opposition. He had no authority from the Directory to do so.

He returned triumphantly to the Mombello Palace outside Milan. There he was joined by his family, upon which he lavished spoils in the style of a medieval monarch, not a republican general. Joseph was appointed ambassador to Rome with an enormous salary; and presents were lavished on Lucien, Jerome and Louis, as well as his sisters. At last the matriarch, Letizia, arrived. Napoleon embraced her on her arrival outside Milan and she told him, 'Today I am the happiest mother in the world.' But she stayed only two weeks before returning to Corsica.

Like other members of his family, she disapproved intensely of the frivolous Josephine, with her Parisian sophistication, expensive tastes, sexy clothes and barely hidden passion for Hippolyte Charles – Napoleon's young, beautiful and cheeky sister Pauline would stick out her tongue behind Josephine's back. Napoleon caught the passionate seventeen-year-old Pauline making love to one of his former officers, General Victor Emmanuel Leclerc, and insisted they get married immediately; her plain older sister Elisa similarly got married to a dull Corsican aristocrat in June. Napoleon was now in effect King of northern Italy.

Stendhal judged Napoleon's northern Italian campaigns to be his finest military actions. In fact they cannot compare with some of his later battles such as Austerlitz, which were far more complex affairs. But his achievement had by any standards been remarkable. The Directory itself reckoned that he had taken 150,000 prisoners, 540

cannon, and nine 64-gun battleships, twelve frigates and eighteen galleys. He had won eighteen major battles and sixty-seven lesser military actions.

To what extent could Napoleon himself claim the credit? With the exception of the Battle of Rivoli, the Italian campaign was a case of small-scale engagements of rapid manoeuvre, marching and counter-marching with small forces to outflank and outwit the enemy. It was somewhere between guerrilla warfare and classic eighteenth-century pitched fighting.

Napoleon's forces in Italy were not particularly brave or impressive, while the Austrian armies, although braver and more prone to defend their positions, tended to follow old-fashioned military injunctions and were overloaded with provisions. Another qualification to Napoleon's skills must be the nature of the French army. Carnot had been its creator. Thanks to the *levée en masse*, it was the most modern, efficient and above all the largest fighting force in Europe. It was a huge conscript army staffed by officers who rose to the top at this stage largely through merit and who had until recently faced the possibility that failure might be rewarded by the guillotine.

Napoleon did not create this system: he inherited it from Dumouriez and Carnot. But he added powerful incentives of his own, carrots rather than sticks. He permitted his men the freedom to feed off the land – the main advantage being that they were not encumbered by baggage trains – and saw to it that they were well fed and paid on time, usually through plunder. He also inspired them with injunctions to honour and glory and instituted the idea of awarding the Legion of Honour. To be a soldier in Napoleon's army was not to be a wretched, coerced minion destined to be cannon fodder, but a reasonably fed and clothed member of an almost invariably victorious army in the service of France and revolutionary idealism. They felt they were fighting for their country, not their feudal lords, as the Austrians did.

Yet Napoleon's greatness in this campaign lay in his energy, tactical speed and grasp of strategy. It has been said that he was not a true military innovator, and this is doubtless true, but he did apply quasi-established military doctrines with a skill and ferocity that had never occurred before. His greatest gift, of course, was as an artillery man.

France in fact was way ahead of other countries, in its modernization of artillery, a product of the *ancien régime*. As far back as 1763, Jean-Baptiste de Gribeauval, introduced lighter gun barrels of 12 or 24cm calibre which could be easily brought up and used in field battles, not just sieges, as had previously been the case. In 1793 7,000 cannon were produced in one year, a mass production of weaponry without precedent. Napoleon, as an artilleryman himself, had scorn for the ancient muskets with their propensity to jam, blow up or miss – at 200 yards only a quarter of shots hit their target, while as close as seventy-five yards only two-thirds did – and the time it took to reload, only one or two shots a minute being the average. Napoleon sensibly relied on using bayonets to frighten the enemy. But he also used artillery to devastating effect when he began any battle, and relied also on irregular snipers with lighter weapons to push forward and intimidate the enemy by shooting their officers.

Napoleon's battle tactics were usually to push his cavalry forward to attempt to defeat the enemy cavalry and force the infantry into squares, which while effective defensively had much less firepower than a general line. Then he would seek to break up the squares, with horse supporting the infantry to sow confusion. He also relied on a combination of tactics which had been used before him individually but rarely used in unison.

First, he broke with the age-old tradition of continental armies and insisted on unity of command: his generals were guided by him alone and the French were thus spared the competing commanders and armies that so plagued eighteenth-century battles – most notably and recently of course during the war in northern France and the Low Countries, where the armies of different countries got in each others' way.

Secondly, he kept his men deployed along a wide front, at a distance from the enemy. This encouraged the enemy to do the same. Then he would choose a point of attack and bring his forces together with speed to overwhelm an enemy's weakest point. Speed and concentration of force were thus beautifully choreographed. The speed with which Napoleon moved his troops displayed all the brilliance of a natural guerrilla commander. In part this derived from the high morale of the

troops, and the spoils promised them. They were not grudging peasants who had to be coerced every inch of the way but men who believed they would win and enrich themselves if they obeyed the command to move fast: time and again victories were won by men marching through the night and appearing suddenly out of the blue, surprising and demoralizing the enemy – most notably at the Battle of Rivoli.

Napoleon's other favourite tactic was the flanking movement: he rarely attacked from the front except when forced to, for example across bridges. When he did so, he always ensured that another force would materialize on a flank or to the rear to demoralize the enemy (the *mouvement sur les derrières* – which excited many a ribald comment). The trick here was to bring his army up in corps, each with its own cavalry and artillery, despatching one (usually weak) force to engage the enemy frontally, and then sending a flanking force to strike from the side or rear. Sometimes the flanking force would be quite small, or sometimes it would be the main force but it had to arrive precisely in time to rescue the frontal or so-called 'pinning' force. This required accurate timing: the enemy ideally would have committed his own reserves to battle in an effort to overwhelm the frontal force before the flanking attack.

Another favourite tactic was to drive a wedge through the 'hinge', the weakest point between enemy armies, often a hill, wood or river, and then take the separate forces on one at a time. Thus, even if Napoleon had a smaller army than the enemy overall, he would have a larger one than the particular enemy detachment he was attacking; meanwhile, he would send a smaller force to engage the second army until the first force had been overwhelmed and he could bring up reinforcements. Amusingly, in one account when Napoleon met an Austrian captain on a road and asked him about the progress of the campaign, he pretended to be an Italian – this being before the days of photography when he would be recognized. The Austrian replied: 'They've sent a young madman who attacks right and left, front and rear. It's an incredible way of waging war.'

Napoleon's tactics were not gentlemanly in the understood eighteenth-century manner. He would do anything to win. Napoleon also had a grasp of nuts and bolts maxims: never to allow his lines of

communication to be extended too far, which meant, for example, that he had to stop on the march to Vienna; like Nelson, always to attack, never wait for the enemy to do so first; always to aim for the enemy army, not cities or bases (which in fact he failed to live up to in the case of Mantua); and always to keep to a single objective.

Some of these are fairly mundane military maxims. But perhaps the key element of Napoleon's military genius (as opposed to his political philosophy where his abilities were soon to shade into megalomania) was that he combined skill, speed and imagination with the sharp mathematical brain of a skilled artilleryman. Napoleon was simultaneously supremely skilled in the most plodding arts of war and a half-insane dreamer. He said once:

> Military science consists in calculating all the chances accurately in the first place, and then in giving accident exactly, almost mathematically, its place in one's calculations. It is upon this point that one must not deceive oneself, and yet a decimal more or less may change all. Now this apportioning of accident and science cannot get into any head except that of a genius. Accident, hazard, chance, call it what you may, a mystery to ordinary minds, becomes a reality to superior men.

Yet he realized the limits of a purely mechanical approach to war:

> Tactics, evolution and the sciences of the engineer and the artillery officer may be learned from treatises, much as in the same way as geometry, but the knowledge of the higher branches of the art of war is only to be gained by experience and by studying the history of man and battles of great leaders. Can one learn in a grammar to compose a book of the Iliad, or one of Corneille's tragedies?

His secret was that he combined the two: science with improvisation. The extraordinary paradox of Napoleon's character was that he was a supremely practical military commander, and yet was later to become virtually a political lunatic in his crazed schemes for dominating the world – a unique combination. Many have tried to compare him with,

in a later generation, Hitler. But the latter was never a practical man: he was a demented, if inspired, demagogue who achieved success only at that level. Napoleon was to combine crazed vision with superb, even mathematical practicality, in an almost Einsteinian way. His feet were planted in military boots on the ground, while his head was in the higher realms of the geostrategic clouds.

This was the new King of northern Italy. His exercise of the role was the first time he showed his capacity for government – and it was deeply revealing. Two things characterized his rule: a mixture of plunder and genuine idealism. Napoleon's whole personality and success were to be defined by the fact that he combined superb military professionalism with naked and ruthless political opportunism, as well as some crazed ideas and ambitions. Again, that made him quite different from later political tyrants such as Hitler, Mussolini or Mao, who had the last two but not the first, or Stalin, who had only the second.

Napoleon's problem was that he also thought he was a ruler of genius. The worst aspect of his rule was the plundering in which, he could claim in self-defence, he was merely carrying out the orders of the Directory. Napoleon wrote to the Directory: 'We have taken almost everything fine in Italy except a few objects which are at Turin and Naples.' Lombardy paid 20 million francs and gave up all the paintings and works of art that could be seized by the French. Modena paid 10 million francs and twenty paintings. Pavia paid 2 million francs and twenty paintings. Some 6 million francs were seized from Venice, along with the four bronze horses of St Mark's, the Lion of Venice and the treasure of the Doge's Palace. From Parma he grabbed Corregio's superb 'Dawn in Naples': 'The possession of such a masterpiece at Paris will adorn that capital for ages, and give birth to similar exertions of genius.'

Galileo's manuscripts on fortifications, many of Leonardo's scientific treatises, and works of Giorgione, Rafael, Mantegna, Filippo Lippi and Andrea del Sarto were taken, while a hundred of Italy's finest carriage horses were seized as 'works of art'. The Pope was made to yield a hundred paintings, 500 manuscripts, several statues and 21 million francs in tribute. Italians were later to say that post-Napoleonic silver

was worthless, because all the antique silver had been plundered by Napoleon.

Napoleon was thought to have kept some 40 million of the 50 million francs raised for himself and his associates, including at least 3 million for himself personally. Joseph, his brother, bought a large house in Paris with his share and Letizia completely rebuilt the house at Ajaccio. Napoleon bought a house for himself on the rue de la Victoire, a large estate in Belgium and a huge house and estate on the banks of the Seine for Josephine, which cost a colossal 335,000 francs.

Napoleon's actual exercise of power was overlaid by a combination of humbug and idealism. It is hard to separate the two, but it seems clear that he resisted the Directory in its desire to promote Italy's developing republican sentiment. Napoleon explained his views on the new Cisalpine Republic:

> The republic is divided into three parties: 1) the friends of their former government, 2) the partisans of an independent but rather aristocratic constitution, 3) the partisans of the French constitution and of pure democracy. I repress the first, I support the second, and moderate the third. I do so because the second is the party of the rich landowners and priests, who in the long run will end by winning the support of the mass of the people which it is essential to rally around the French party.

He abolished the Austrian administrative system in northern Italy and set up a ruling congress of state and municipal councils. Lombardy was to be governed under a separate system. Then he tried to marry the two together in mid-1797 into a 'Cisalpine state' with a Directory of its own and an upper and lower house of Ancients and Juniors. Napoleon gravely declared:

> In order to consolidate liberty and with the sole aim of your happiness, I have carried out a task such as hitherto had been undertaken only from ambition and love of power . . . Divided and bowed under tyranny for so long, you could not have won your

own freedom; left to yourself for a few years, there will be no power on earth strong enough to take it from you.

Soon afterwards Genoa was turned into a republic. Yet only a few months later, in October, he was warning Talleyrand: 'You do not know the Italian people. They are not worth the lives of forty thousand Frenchmen. Since I came to Italy I have received no help from this nation's love of liberty and equality, or at least such help has been negligible. Here are the facts: whatever is good to say in proclamations and printed speeches is romantic fiction.' Whether this was pure cynicism or a negotiating ploy was unclear. Meanwhile negotiations with the Austrians continued for a formal peace treaty, which was eventually signed at Campo Formio in the Veneto on 17 October, with France now securing control of the Ionian Islands.

Chapter 23

THE COMING MAN

In December 1797, Napoleon returned to Paris a national hero. He declared grandiosely to the puppet French Assembly, speaking of France and Austria:

> The feudal system, and monarchy have in turn governed Europe for twenty centuries, but from the peace you have just concluded dates the era of representative governments. You have succeeded in organizing this great nation so that its territory is circumscribed by the bounds which nature herself has set. You have done even more. The two most beautiful countries in Europe, once so famous for arts, sciences and the great men whose cradle they were, behold with joyful expectation the Spirit of Liberty rise from the graves of their ancestors.

Two contemporary despatches spoke of the general whom all France was curious to see. Madame de Remusat, one of Josephine's intimates, remarked:

> Napoleon Bonaparte is of low stature and ill-made; the upper part of his body is too long in proportion to his legs. He has thin chestnut hair, his eyes are greyish-blue, and his skin, which was yellow while he was slight, has become of late years a dead white, without any colour. His eyes were ordinarily dull; when angry, his aspect became fierce and menacing . . . an habitually ill-tempered man . . . He did not know how either to enter or to leave a room, how to bow, how

to rise, or how to sit down. Whatever language he speaks, it always
sounds like a foreign tongue.

Napoleon's own private secretary confirmed that 'when excited by any
violent passion, the face of Napoleon assumed a terrible expression. A
sort of rotary movement very visibly produced itself.'

All-powerful in his own Italian republic and successful general that
he was, Napoleon was still merely a subordinate in France and one of
three top generals. The most celebrated was Lazare Hoche, the
favourite of Paul Barras, the most powerful man in the Directory.
Indeed Barras planned to make Hoche stage a military coup to end the
constant quarrels within the Directory, but even as he was preparing for
this, as well as for an invasion of Ireland, Hoche mysteriously died
before the age of thirty. The cause was variously attributed to the
impact of personal attacks, depression, tuberculosis or even that he was
murdered by poisoning. Otherwise his name today might be more
famous than Napoleon's. Bernadotte, Napoleon's other military rival,
was soon dismissed because of his publicly proclaimed left-wing
Jacobin views. But Napoleon was not above criticism, even from
his mentor, Barras, for being too hard on the Austrians. Political power
remained firmly in the hands of the Directory.

Early in 1797, while Napoleon was still in Italy, French politics had
lurched sharply to the right after an extreme left-wing plot to topple
the Directory. Two new members now joined the Directory, one
General Charles Pichegru, widely seen as favouring the restoration of
the Bourbon monarchy, the other his ally, François Barthélemy.
Carnot, the architect of France's military triumphs of the past three
years, was also believed to favour the royalists. That left Napoleon's old
patron, Barras, as head of the republican faction.

At that time too, another major figure made his appearance on the
scene, with far-reaching implications for Napoleon: the new foreign
minister, Charles Maurice de Talleyrand-Perigord. This extraordinary
émigré figure had been born in 1754 of an aristocratic family and had
been brought up by his grandmother. Against his will he had been sent
to a seminary to study for the priesthood and later promoted to become
bishop of Autun just after the Revolution. Snobbish, and with a

haughty and somewhat sardonic manner, he was a brilliant writer and talker. Barras was later to claim that he bore a remarkable physical resemblance to Robespierre, although he could not have been more different in most respects. Both supporters and detractors agreed that he had a huge intellect and sharp tongue.

A close ally of Mirabeau when the Revolution broke out, he attracted intense opprobrium from the aristocracy by ordering the seizure of church lands and then swearing allegiance to the Revolution – both of which brought about his excommunication. An American observer, Gouverneur Morris, with whom Talleyrand shared a mistress, wrote of him that 'the Bishop is partly blamed [for indulging in pleasure]: not so much for adultery, because that was common enough among the clergy of high rank, but for the variety and publicity of his amours, for gambling, and above all for stock jobbing during the ministry of M. de Calonne, with whom he was on the best of terms, and therefore had opportunities which his enemies say he made no small use of. However, I do not believe in this, and I think that, except for his gallantries and a mode of thinking rather too liberal for a churchman, the charges are unduly aggravated.'

As war with Britain approached, he departed on a mission to London to try and secure that country's neutrality. He was snubbed by the King and Queen, received coldly by Pitt and listened to by Grenville, all of whom distrusted the haughty, clever Frenchman. Although supported by Danton, as the Revolution took an ugly turn, Talleyrand fled to England and became part of a small circle of French émigrés. There he provided a remarkable statement of modern foreign policy for his own country.

We have learnt, a little late no doubt, that for states as for individuals real wealth consists not in acquiring or invading the domains of others, but in developing one's own. We have learnt that all extensions of territory, all usurpation, by force or by fraud, which have long been connected by prejudice with the idea of 'rank', of 'hegemony', of 'political stability', of 'superiority' in the order of the powers, are only the cruel jests of political lunacy, false estimates of power, and that their real effect is to increase the difficulty of

administration and to diminish the happiness and security of the governed for the passing interest or for the vanity of those who govern . . . France ought, therefore, to remain within her own boundaries, she owes it to her glory, to her sense of justice and of reason, to her own interest and to that of the other nations who will become free.

He was expelled from England in 1794, for reasons that are obscure but may have been connected to suspicions of spying, and went to America to live with the French colony in Philadelphia. In 1797, with the fall of Robespierre, he was recalled to Paris and, on the initiative of Madame de Staël, appointed minister of foreign affairs. Following an affair with the wife of his predecessor, Madame Charles Delacroix, which resulted in a child, he married a stunningly beautiful Creole wife, Madame Grand.

There followed some extremely murky politics. With an impressive election victory for the royalists, who secured a third of the members of the National Assembly, it seemed clear that the royalist Pichegru, supported by Carnot, would make an attempt to seize power, Napoleon still in Italy, whose new and large fortune had permitted the acquisition of three newspapers, launched a campaign against the royalists, almost certainly at the behest of his patron Barras, supported by Talleyrand.

Privately however, the increasingly self-confident Napoleon despised Barras almost as much as the royalists and the creator of the modern French army, Carnot, whom he saw as a rival. He told a confidant at Mombello that August: 'Do you believe that I triumph in Italy for the Carnots, Barras, etc . . . I wish to undermine the republican party, but only for my own profit and not that of the ancient dynasty . . . I have tasted authority and I will not give it up. I have decided that if I cannot be the master I will leave France. But it's too early now, the fruit is not yet ripe . . . Peace would not be in my interest right now . . . I would have to give up this power. If I leave the signing of peace treaties to another man, he would be placed higher in public opinion than I am by my victories.' Napoleon even threatened the Directory, proclaiming to his Army of Italy. 'Mountains separate us

from France: but if it were necessary to uphold the constitution, to defend liberty to protect the government and the republicans, then you would cross them with the speed of an eagle.'

He despatched his lieutenant, General Augereau, to help Barras. On the night of 3 September 1797 ('Fructidor') a coup d'état was staged: the Tuileries was surrounded and Pichegru was arrested for deportation to the West Indies – although he later escaped. Carnot escaped in his night-dress to exile in Germany, but was later brought back in 1800 as a prisoner of war. There are suggestions that Talleyrand arranged the coup in consultation with Napoleon at a distance.

The two men did not meet for the first time until December. Talleyrand gave this description: 'At first sight, his face appeared to me charming. A score of victories go so well with youth, with fine eyes, with paleness, and with an appearance of exhaustion.' Napoleon said, 'You are the nephew of the Archbishop of Rheims who is with Louis XVIII (not the Count de Lille, as it was customary to call him in Paris). – I also have an uncle, who is an archdeacon in Corsica. He brought me up. In Corsica, you know, an archdeacon is the same as a bishop in France.'

The devious and calculating Talleyrand now played an unusual role. Having been interested in securing Napoleon's military leadership to destroy the royalists, he seemed intent, possibly in deference to Barras, still the dominant figure on the Directory, on getting Napoleon out of Paris – whether because he feared him or because he believed a premature seizure of power would go wrong is unclear. Napoleon was appointed to plan the invasion of Britain in place of Hoche, who had suffered the nervous breakdown that was to lead to his early death.

Napoleon was thus the country's most prominent soldier, but not the dominant political power. He played his hand skilfully, deliberately shunning the limelight, attending discreet dinner parties, and disparaging Augereau, his fellow general, who had pretensions to become a military strongman.

Meanwhile he fretted about Josephine's continuing love affair with Hippolyte Charles, who at one stage he threatened to have executed. She was now meeting him at the house of a shady businessman who had made a fortune out of supplying poor equipment to the army of

Italy. When Napoleon confronted her, she placated him with a barrage of apologies and hysteria.

Napoleon went in February to inspect the French Channel ports from which it was proposed to invade England. There he came to the conclusion, with impeccable good sense and realism that the whole project was hopeless. He told the Directory: 'To undertake an invasion of England without being masters of the sea would be the boldest and most difficult operation ever carried out.' The invasion could only be mounted by night, to foil Britain's navy, and in winter – but the crossing would take at least six to eight hours and at that time of year would be virtually impossible

Napoleon knew that it would be folly to besmirch his reputation by embarking on a project that was doomed to failure. The directors were furious, believing this to be a tactical ploy, and that Napoleon was plotting a military coup. Tension began to mount in Paris.

Part 4

HEARTS OF OAK

Chapter 24

'TIS TO GLORY WE STEER'

There was one area where British arms immediately performed remarkable, if not unchallenged, feats: the war at sea. The British navy at the outset of the war, was, unlike the army, far from unprepared: the last major war, in which it had played a major part, the American War of Independence, had ended only a decade earlier. It had overcome the previously enormous problem of scurvy, caused by a lack of fresh vegetables; and it had learnt to copper-bottom its ships so as to keep out worms and to provide extra speed. Since then too, the Controller of the Navy, Sir Charles Middleton, later Lord Barham, had put into effect a series of major administrative reforms which had placed the navy on a much more meritocratic footing, and speeded up mobilization in the event of war.

The first major naval engagements of the war involved, appropriately enough, frigates, those glamorous, sleek, middle-sized daring raiders of the sea, not so slow, clumsy and impressive as the larger ships of the line, but equipped with the armaments to engage all but the biggest enemy ships. The job of frigates was to scour the seas in search of French privateers, non-navy ships licensed to attack merchantmen of hostile powers to intercept lines of supplies.

From the beginning of the war the success of the British frigates was astonishing. In 1793 the British captured fifty-two French men-of-war and eighty-eight privateers, compared with the French captures of just six warships – not one of them a line-of-battle ship, those ships that sailed in the traditional line to engage in fleet action, bringing all their guns to bear. The following year, with fewer French ships exposing

themselves after the disastrous first year, the British captured thirty-six French warships, seven of them being line-of-battle ships, and lost only ten, including just one ship of the line. In 1795 the British took fifteen warships to the French six. During the war as a whole, as we shall see, the British captured 570 ships altogether, with nearly 16,000 guns; they lost just fifty-nine warships, with under 1,300 guns altogether. Although the British merchant fleet suffered dreadful losses of ships, it has been estimated that less than $2\frac{1}{2}$ per cent of her annual trade was lost in this way. This was the lifeline that kept an island nation fighting.

On 13 March 1793 the brig *Scourge* captured the first prize of the war, a much larger French privateer. A month later the *Phaeton*, a 38-gun frigate, caught a heavily armed French privateer accompanying two Spanish prizes stashed with gold, one of them carrying £1 million worth: Hood, as commander-in-chief, was entitled to £50,000; the captains of the squadron accompanying the *Phaeton* received £30,000 each (around £6 million at today's values). Thus could colossal fortunes be made in a single engagement: it was a powerful incentive for captains and crews.

The first significant engagement of the war took place in May off Start Point, a spectacularly beautiful section of the Devon coast, when the 36-gun *Nymphe*, of 938 tons with 240 officers and crew under Captain Edward Pellew, soon to become a legend, spotted the *Cleopatre* of smaller size with a crew of 320. The *Nymphe* promptly gave chase and caught her up. The ships' complements saluted each other: 'Long live King George!' called Pellew's men. Captain Mallon's men responded, '*Vive la Republique!*'

After this classic gentlemanly exchange, for three-quarters of an hour they exchanged broadsides at point blank range, until the mizzen mast of the *Cleopatre* came crashing down; at around the same time her steering wheel was disabled and she swung around at right-angles to the *Nymphe*, her jib boom locked against the mainmast of the enemy ship. Pellew expected to be boarded, but the French officers had all been killed. Seeing the confusion, he ordered his men aboard the *Cleopatre*.

In just a few minutes the British had seized control of the ship from the disorganized French crew and pulled down her colours. Captain Mallon, mortally wounded, attempted valiantly to destroy his signal codes by eating them, but chewed up his own commission instead. Of

the 320 aboard, sixty-three had been killed and wounded, while the *Nymphe* had suffered fifty casualties. It was hardly the greatest of victories, achieved against a smaller ship in a strictly conventional manner, but it was the first of the war. King George III came down in person to Portsmouth to congratulate Captain Pellew.

The principal fleet was the Channel Fleet (also known as the Western Squadron and the Atlantic Fleet). By 1795 the Channel Fleet had twenty-six ships of the line, including seven giant three-deckers, seventeen frigates, a hospital ship and two fireships. By 1805 this had increased to thirty-five ships of the line and seventeen frigates. Its main job was to blockade the French fleets at Brest, Rochefort, L'Orient and Cherbourg and the Spanish port of Ferrol.

To the west, the sixteen-ship Irish Squadron consisted principally of one ship of the line and ten frigates, its task primarily to protect Ireland from invasion. The Channel Islands Squadron, which was based at Guernsey, had eleven ships, including three frigates: its main purpose was to use its proximity to the French coast to spy on shipping movements.

Much more substantial was the North Sea Squadron, which consisted of fifty-six ships, including twenty ships of the line. There was also a small Downs Squadron, with just one ship of the line, to patrol inshore in the Channel, and a force at Leith. A Baltic Fleet was also intermittently formed.

The Mediterranean Fleet was the second most important in the navy. It had sixty-two warships in 1797, including twenty-three ships of the line and twenty-four frigates. (By 1812 this had risen to a staggering ninety ships, twenty-nine of the line and twenty-one frigates – the biggest fleet.)

In the West Indies there were the Jamaica and Windward Island Squadrons: the Jamaica Squadron had seven ships of the line and fifteen frigates by 1797. The Leeward Islands Squadron had twelve ships of the line and sixteen frigates. There were also two small squadrons to the north based at Halifax in Nova Scotia and Newfoundland. The substantial East India Squadron consisted of thirty-two ships, including ten of the line and seventeen frigates in 1797.

These formidable fleets and the 120,000 seamen that manned them faced a French fleet of some 241 ships, including eighty-three of the

line and seventy-seven frigates, and some 60,000 seamen, based principally at Brest, Rochefort, L'Orient and Toulon. The British merchant marine was colossal in size, consisting of some 16,000 ships, employing nearly 120,000 men.

For a young midshipman joining a British navy schooner, for example, it proved an exciting world of professionalism, occasional cruelty, and self-contained claustrophobia amid the almost familial intimacy of a ship's company. It could be hard going at first, although the navy was hardly the sink of institutionalized brutality that is popularly conceived. The sloop was a small, fast ship. It had two masts, each rigged with fore and aft sails. Its twenty-eight 9-pound guns were assembled on a single deck. The quarters for the midshipmen were damp and dark, below the gun-deck, though more spacious than for the seamen, and were only dimly illuminated by candles and the few cracks of light that showed from the decks above. The lonely midshipman, on his first few nights aboard, would have found the quarters stiflingly close, hunched in a 'cot' – a hammock of canvas stretched across a frame – with only a shelf for his possessions. In port the seamen's cots actually touched each other. At sea there was much more room, as men took turns to take the watch.

About half of the crew would have been 'impressed' – most of them merchant seamen. More than four-fifths of ordinary seamen, and half of able seamen, were aged under twenty-five. Only about a fifth were married. Boys of between six and eighteen were to be found aboard ship, many of them engaged simply in playing as well as learning the ropes. There were also plenty of animals aboard, including the inevitable rats, but also such livestock as cattle, sheep, pigs and goats, for food. British ships were however, kept rigorously clean.

The damp below the decks could be pervasive, depending on the condition of the timbers. In summer, especially in the tropics, the heat and stench could be overpowering, although in winter the cramped conditions meant that men rarely suffered from the cold. As a midshipman became accustomed to being awoken at 6 a.m. to hurry about his new duties, he would quickly have understood the no-nonsense approach to naval discipline, although its harshness varied enormously from ship to ship. Such discipline and inflexible routines were con-

sidered essential to keeping order among so many men at such close quarters.

In less well-ordered ships, young midshipmen were at the mercy of 'oldsters' – men passed over for preferment who would probably have to spend the rest of their lives in their jobs. Even young midshipmen could be venomous. As one seaman observed:

> We had a midshipman on board of a wickedly mischievous disposition, whose sole delight was to insult the feelings of seamen and furnish pretexts to get them punished . . . He was a youth of not more than twelve or thirteen years of age; I have often seen him get on to the carriage of a gun, call a man to him, and kick him about the thighs and body, and with his feet would beat him about the head; and these, though prime seamen, at the same time dared not murmur.

'Cobbing' – being beaten by a stockingful of wet sand – was a frequent form of physical abuse. The men's routine sexual needs were usually accommodated in port by allowing prostitutes on board, a practice the vast majority of captains turned a blind eye to, and even regulated to reward the deserving. The cry 'show a leg' in the morning derives from the need to check whether a man or a woman was in a cot, the latter being allowed to sleep on undisturbed. The 'cockpit' of a ship derived its name from the place where the all-too-frequent brawls between the working girls or 'port wives' occurred.

As for the quality of the food aboard ships, much depended on the climate, whether the ship was close to port, and whether the food was properly stored. Without refrigeration or canning the possibilities for deterioration were much greater. The purser, whose job it was to provide the food, was one of the ship's company, and he too was liable to be judged by his peers.

The rations were the subject of strict written regulations: a packet of biscuits each day for every seaman, which in practice was often sodden and weevil-ridden; and a gallon of small beer, a very weak version of the real drink, no more really than water flavoured with hops. The beer ration was often changed to a pint of wine or half a pint of rum, the latter usually being mixed with water and called grog, the seaman's

favourite drink. Each seaman was also entitled to 4 pounds of salt beef, 2 pounds of salt pork, two pints of peas, 3 pounds of oatmeal, 6 ounces of butter and 12 ounces of cheese a week. Flour, suet, currants and raisins were also issued. Where possible cabbage and greens were provided, along with the lime and lemon juice that had largely conquered the most dreaded disease, scurvy.

Although in practice particular items often went short and food often went bad, these were substantial enough rations – as they had to be to keep the crew strong and able-bodied. The threats to food were legion, according to one purser. Biscuit was endangered:

> by its breaking and turning to dust; of butter, by that part next to the firkin being not fit to be issued; of cheese, by its decaying with mould and rottenness and being eaten with mites and other insects; of peas, oatmeal and flour, by their being eaten by cockroaches, weevils and other vermin, and by that part at the top, bottom and sides of the cask being so often damaged, as not being fit to be issued; besides the general loss sustained in all these provisions by rats, which is very great . . .

Punishment was a fact of life, but flogging was not all that frequent, except on a minority of ships. A typical average was some fifteen floggings per ship in nine months, usually of between twelve and twenty-four lashes, although occasionally far more. This made severe punishment a significant part of navy life, but hardly a daily occurrence. Captain Frederic Chamier describes the first flogging he witnessed as a young midshipman:

> The Captain gave the order 'Give him a dozen.' There was an awful stillness; I felt the flesh creep upon my bones, and I shivered and shook like a dog in a wet sack. All eyes were directed towards the prisoner, who looked over his shoulder at the preparations of the boatswain's mate to inflict the dozen: the latter drew his fingers through the tails of the cat, ultimately holding the nine ends in his left hand, as the right was raised to inflict the lash. They fell with a whizzing sound as they passed through the air, and left behind the reddened mark of sudden inflammation . . .

At the conclusion of the dozen I heard the unwilling order. 'Another boatswain's mate!' The fresh executioner pulled off his coat. The prisoner had said nothing during the first dozen, but on the first cut of his new and merciless punisher, he writhed his back in acknowledgement of the pain; the second stripe was followed by a sigh; the third by an ejaculation; and the fourth produced an expression of a hope of pardon. At the conclusion of the dozen, this was granted, and the prisoner released.

Another observer remarked that after two dozen lashes: 'the lacerated back looks inhuman; it resembles roasted meat burnt nearly black before a scorching fire.' This was undoubtedly very harsh, but not more so than many punishments ordinary people could expect on land. Provided punishment was meted out fairly, and not excessively, it was probably supported or at least accepted by the majority of the men, who disliked their fellows getting away with serious offences, particularly major theft, for which the cat-o'-nine tails was prescribed, or less serious ones, such as malingering.

There were lesser forms of beating for more minor offences – such as minor stealing, always deeply unpopular on board ship, for which a man could be made to walk a gauntlet with his shipmates hitting him with knittles or small ropes. Liars were publicly humiliated by being made to clean the heads (latrines) for several days. Other punishments included ducking or a public scrubbing – usually for a dirty man – or wearing the cangue, a wooden collar with a cannonball attached, for several hours.

The terrifying ordeal of being flogged around the fleet, applied only in the most serious cases of mutiny, was extremely rare, although performed with sadistic precision to ensure the victim did not die – for example 200 lashes would be applied at a time on three successive fortnights. Keel-hauling – being dragged under the length of the ship – is believed to have died out in the seventeenth century, when it was also extremely rare. Only desertion at sea, murder, sodomy, and extreme cases of theft were punishable by death. Mutiny was often not punished at all if non-violent and the purpose was the removal of a hated officer.

Chapter 25

THE FLOATING WORLD

The ships of the British Navy ranged in size from the minuscule gunboat to the magnificent first-rated three-deckers that provided admirals and their officers the space to live in state. In 1808 a first 120-gun three-decker was built. There were also 90-gun second-rate three-deckers, whose hulls were tall and short, and therefore sailed badly; these were being phased out, as were the still more unwieldy 80-gun three-deckers (although 80-gun two-deckers were more manoeuvrable). The bulk of the line-of-battle ships were, however, 74-gun two-deckers; 65-gun two-deckers were a cheaper version of these, and regarded as very poor quality; they were being phased out. Smaller 50-gun two-deckers were short, but of slightly better sailing quality.

Frigates, with their speed, manoeuvrability and gunpower, were the real stars, acting in flotillas or single-ship actions. The 38-gun frigate was the most popular of these, with some eighty in service, compared with the increasingly obsolete 44-gun frigates, the still popular 40-gun frigates and the smaller 28-gun ships. The cheap, quickly built and even more nimble sloops (of which there were about 200 in 1801) also performed a major role. Bomb vessels had been created to act as mortars capable of firing explosive shells at enemy ports. Brigs (with fourteen 24-pound carronades), schooners (with four to six guns), cutters (with ten 18-pound carronades), and gunboats with a single gun made up the complement.

On some ships there were only two masts but on a larger ship three. The sails on the latter were divided into the jibs at the front of the ship, the foresails on the foremast, the staysails also on the foremast but

behind them, the mainsails on the mainmast, the staysails also on the mainmast but behind them, and the mizzen sails on the mizzen (rear) mast, with the spanker billowing out behind. In turn, the sails were on three horizontal levels, main, topmast and topgallant. The topmen, whose work was the most dangerous and skilled, were the strongest and bravest of the men, and respected as such aboard ship. Their main job was to loose sail or furl it or, more commonly, 'reef' it, that is shorten it by gathering a section up to the 'yard' and tying it with lengths of ropes sewn into the sail called reef points or let out reefs. The yard was the spar or the crossbeam to which the sail was secured.

Next in the pecking order came the fo'c's'lemen, who were usually older, often former topmen who had lost their agility. They had charge of the jib sails at the front of the ship as well as the anchor there and the guns. The third group of seamen, also usually older, were the afterguard, handling the spanker, the guns at the stern and, most importantly, the braces, the ropes to which all the sails in the ship were attached. The waisters were usually the dullest-minded in the middle of the ship, handling the foresail and mainsail, as well as pumping the bilges. Lowest in the hierarchy were the idlers, not because they were idle but because they did menial tasks. They included the carpenter and his mates, the cook and the officers' servants, usually ship's boys. In addition each ship usually had around fifty marines, to fight on land and enforce order.

The men were divided into two watches for each side of the ship, the larboard (the left or, in today's term, port) and starboard (the right). There were inflexible routines aboard ship – the 4 a.m. call with the idlers being called to scrub the decks and prepare the galley, the off-watchmen being woken at around 6 a.m., the stowing of cots and tidying of quarters. Breakfast was at 8 a.m., divisions at 9.30, when the men went on parade, followed by the various ships' tasks and drilling at 10.00. At 11.30 there was a break to 'up spirits' – have a ration of beer or grog – with lunch at noon. After the afternoon work, the day ended at 4 p.m. with another up spirits and evening meal. The two main drills were gun practice and setting sail, which most well-ordered ships could do all at once in from four to six minutes, a remarkable achievement for around 15,000 square foot of sail in a medium-sized 31-gun frigate.

Ships would practise zigzagging into the wind or away from it, tacking from one side to the other because they could not sail directly into it, no more in fact than 67.5 degrees on either side of the wind direction. Tacking was a skilful and difficult manoeuvre, which involved briefly facing the wind and risked missing stays and falling astern on the original tack or being unable to catch the wind on either side. The equivalent manoeuvre away from the wind – wearing – was much easier and faster, although more dangerous in heavy seas or before a strong wind because of the speed of the ship. A ship tacking into the wind travelled, of course, much more slowly than one wearing away from it.

Ships would average a speed of around 6 knots, but they could go as fast as 14 knots for short stretches, which was essential when a smaller ship was being chased. James Gardner, a lieutenant aboard ship, described sailing in a gale and under chase from two French battleships:

> We should have been captured for a certainty if the Frenchman had possessed more patience. And so it happened: for a little before six, when he was within gunshot, the greedy fellow let another reef out of his topsails, and just as he had them hoisted, away went his foreyard, jib-boom, foretopmast, and maintopgallant mast . . . We immediately let two reefs out of the topsails, set topgallant sails and hauled the main tack on board, with a jib a third and the spanker. It was neck or nothing. For my part I expected we should be upset and it was with uncommon alacrity in making and shortening sails between the squalls that we escaped upsetting or being taken.

The ship had covered 120 miles in twelve hours before getting away. By such superb seamanship as this were ships won or lost.

In gun drill powder and shot was rarely used because captains were anxious to conserve this as they were responsible for its costs as a contemporary naval officer observed: 'It is customary in many ships in a general exercise to go through the motions without loading or firing once in a year, and in others to exercise a few guns every day, and seldom to have a general exercise or to fire the guns.'

The twenty-eight guns of most sloops were on a single deck, and the

crew was trained to clear for action in five minutes (fifteen minutes on a ship-of-the-line because the lower deck had to be stripped of more cumbersome material) and fire three broadsides in ninety seconds, although this varied according to the pitch of the sea, because the cannon had to be rolled forward from the recoil. The guns were the smallest large ones, 9-pounders (that is they fired cannonballs (shot) weighing 9 pounds). These went up to 12-, 18-, 24-, 32- (the most common, $9\frac{1}{2}$ feet long) and 42-pounders (then almost obsolete). Carronades were increasingly in fashion as both shorter and with a larger ball.

The heaviest guns on a battleship were mounted on the lower deck. Doors covered the gun ports when not in use, to keep out spray. The guns could be moved slightly to right or left and raised or depressed, but could not be aimed, except by judging the roll or pitch of the sea in relation to the enemy ship. The first broadside of all the guns on one side of the ship was usually fired together: then firing was at will, depending on the speed and skill of the gun crews, usually at least eight men.

Round shot was the most common type, and was used by the guns on the lower deck against the enemy's hull. Double-headed or chain shot was used against the enemy's rigging. Grapeshot from the upper deck was used against the men on the enemy's deck. Roundshot was extremely effective at close range. A 24-pounder was capable of penetrating a wooden hull 2 foot 6 inches thick. But the ranges fell away sharply. Such a gun had a range of 200 yards, or 2,200 yards if elevated before falling to the ground; at these distances it would do little damage. A carronade had a range of around 340 yards. The ship thus had to get in close to fire effectively, and sometimes collided with the enemy.

Accuracy was, of course, extremely limited, rendered more so by the smoke of battle and the effect of reloading under fire. The British were traditionally believed to aim during the downroll of the ship at the enemy's hull, to kill their gunners. The French traditionally fired high, to disable the masts and rigging, which would inhibit the enemy's manoeuvring and allow them to move in for the kill, or get away. In practice these decisions were taken on the spur of the moment, as

circumstance dictated. The British were certainly much more effective, the number of ships they captured or disabled being vastly higher than the French score.

After each shot the hot gun had to be sponged out to remove debris. A cartridge of powder in cloth was then rammed down, followed by the shot, and then a wad of ripe yarn to fix it. A priming iron was then inserted into the touch-hole on top of the gun along with a quill of powder which was lit by a flammable wick.

There were two standard types of small arms – long-barrelled muskets used to fire across at enemy ships, and pistols used in hand-to-hand combat when the ship was boarded. Boarders would be issued with cutlasses. An officer wrote: 'According to the custom prevailing from the earliest period of naval history to the present day, in boarding or opposing boarders, the pistol is held in the right hand, and in the attempt to board is fired and thrown away to enable the boarder to draw his cutlass, which yet remains in the scabbard or left hand.'

According to another officer: 'Eagerness and heat in action, especially in a first onslaught, ought never to be the cause of a man putting himself so much off his guard . . . as to lift his arm to make a blow with his cutlass . . . But on the contrary, by rushing sword in hand straight out and thereby the guard maintained, and watching his opportunity of making the thrust, the slightest touch of the point is death to his enemy.' Pikes and tomahawks were also used, as were hand grenades, smoke bombs and 'stink pots', largely to confuse the enemy.

Most ships had a marine complement. This dated back to 1664, when they had the role of forming boarding parties as a sea-going infantry. However it was later realized that sailors made more skilled boarders. Instead the marines fulfilled two functions: as a kind of military police, separated from the sailors and used to suppress mutinies and be at hand during punishments; and in amphibious operations, when they usually took the lead.

Navigation was done by compass and the use of seamarks to estimate the position of a ship off the land, as well as the use of log lines – dragged behind the ship – to estimate the ship's speed, and lead lines to work out the depth of the water in dangerous inshore navigation. Although courses were meticulously plotted, navigation was at best

more of an art than a science, as Captain Basil Hall commented: 'The ship's place each day, as estimated from the log-board, is noted on the chart; and also the place, as deduced from chronometers and lunar observations. The first is called the place by dead reckoning, the other the true place. The line joining the true places at noon, is called the true track; and that joining the others is called the track or course by dead reckoning. As it happens, invariably, that these two tracks separate very early in the voyage, and never afterwards come together, unless by accident.'

Life at sea was confined, essentially, to four variables for most of the time: the sea; the wind and the sky; the ship; and the crew. The sea was the most unpredictable, and the one that took most getting used to. The disrespect for the sea manifested by those who travel aboard large ships today, or even humble ferries, was never displayed by those in sailing vessels. It was their potential killer at all times, except in extremely fair weather, and a sailor had to grow accustomed to subdue his own initial fear of it and to understand it in all of its moods – gently swelling, growing, mountainous, calming. The construction of these vessels, with their relatively shallow draughts and rounded hulls, which were designed to make them more manageable and manoeuvrable under sail, meant that they were much more sensitive to the movements of the sea than a large ship of today, and finding one's sea-legs took a considerable time for a newcomer aboard. The sea in all its moods provided, day after day, the only scenery for those aboard, always changing, yet always the same. Similarly, the wind and the sky, of relatively little importance to those on dry land, were a real menacing presence to those aboard ship. Experienced sailors could tell what slight changes in the direction or strength of the wind, or in the height, shape and speed of the clouds overhead, or even in the light, portended.

The ship itself – confined, cramped, creaking, leaking, smelling, uncomfortable, crowded and in constant sickening motion, yet simultaneously home and the very daily means of survival to the crew – loomed much larger in the lives of those aboard. Although most aboard regarded their tasks as a matter of routine, the furling and unfurling of the sails, the handling of the ship, the navigation with only primitive

compasses and leads for sounding depths, the judgement of the winds and sea, the techniques of sailing and tacking all required the constant exercise of skills and seamanship.

The strains of living so closely to other men in that confined space, far closer for most than the most crowded of schools or factories, were intense. It mattered hugely whether one's immediate superior or subordinate or crewmates were pleasant or harsh, fair-minded or vindictive, friends or bullies, cheerful or resentful. To a great extent the intensely formal, layered and disciplined structure of life aboard had evolved to make sure the human parts worked smoothly alongside each other. The little community would have been utterly strange and alien at first, at times even alarming and depressing. But it could be exhilarating: for the challenge was the freedom of roaming the whole world, with strange ports and alien cultures as destinations. A sailor was simultaneously a confined prisoner aboard ship and had the freedom of the entire globe.

There were six principal tasks for the British navy in the war that began in 1793. The first was to blockade the French by watching their principal ports for any sign of movement and giving chase if they emerged and bring them to battle: that the French did not blockade Britain's ports was a sign of the British fleet's acknowledged superiority – a curious feature of the war; for French crews were their equals as seamen, and the French ships were actually better built and faster. There seemed to be some curious British mystique both of flair and the sheer courage to engage aggressively in fighting that caused even the French to avoid fighting them wherever possible, break off engagements at the earliest opportunity, and adopt defensive rather than aggressive tactics.

The second task of the British fleets was to deter French invasion; the third to enforce the economic embargo against the French empire; the fourth to provide escorts to convoys bringing vital supplies to Britain and generally to protect Britain's huge and life-supporting maritime trade; the fifth, to attack the enemy's trade; and the sixth to transport British military forces and supply them when these engaged in overseas expeditions. Of these tasks, blockade duty was wearying and relentless, while convoy duty was equally tiresome. Raiding enemy ships and

coastal ports was glamorous and exciting, if dangerous, and offered the opportunity for advancement and prize money.

The principal admirals of the time have not come down in history as attractive figures. They are usually portrayed as crabby old men with a disciplinary streak, reining back the talents of the dashing young captains of the age – apart from Nelson, of course, who somehow brought the glamour of youth to his admiral's epaulettes. Yet they had far greater responsibilities, for the safety of whole fleets, and a more difficult task: that of preserving a semblance of tactics and order in battle when winds and seas, the strong personalities of the individual captains, and the sheer difficulty of receiving and reading signals, sometimes at a distance of a few miles, all conspired against order.

The First Lord of the Admiralty was the head of the Admiralty board. During the decades of war with France there were eight of these. At the outset of war the First Lord was the Earl of Chatham, Pitt's older brother, who showed no great ability in the job and was soon replaced by the competent Earl Spencer. Other politicians who held the post were Viscount Melville, a capable but corrupt Scottish political boss; Thomas Grenville, the able brother of the foreign secretary; Earl Grey, later to become a reforming prime minister; and the competent Charles Yorke.

The two most prominent naval figures were Barham, the extremely skilful organizer of the British navy before the war and, much more controversially, Earl St Vincent, whose abilities as a seaman were among the foremost of his age, but whose crustiness had a knack of making enemies. The commander of the prestigious Channel Fleet at the outset of war was the sixty-eight-year-old Earl Howe, 'Black Dick', one of the heroes of the American War. He was succeeded in 1799 by Lord Bridport and then by St Vincent himself the following year. Admiral Cornwallis followed in 1804, and then St Vincent again succeeded after an interval, being followed by the bold and capable George Elphinstone, Viscount Keith.

Admiral Lord Gardner was the most notable commander of the Irish Squadron, and Sir James Saumarez of the Channel Isles Squadron. Keith was a distinguished commander of the North Sea Fleet, while Sir Hyde Parker and the disastrous Lord Gambier commanded the Baltic Fleet.

The hugely important Mediterranean Fleet was variously commanded by the capable but elderly Viscount Hood, another American war veteran, Admiral Hotham, St Vincent, Keith and in 1803 by Nelson himself. He was succeeded by Collingwood, another brilliant sailor, Sir Charles Cotton, and the remarkable sea-captain Sir Edward Pellew in 1811. St Vincent (as Sir John Jervis) had also briefly commanded the West Indies Squadron. The East Indies Squadron was at one stage commanded by Keith.

Of this handful of men, Howe, St Vincent, Keith, Saumarez, Hood, Pellew and Collingwood have come down in history as great commanders, with the genius of Nelson at their head. In spite of their crusty reputation, Britain was well served by her admirals during more than two decades of war. Most of these had reached their positions through ability and were not of aristocratic or moneyed origin, unlike the army commanders; only the system of seniority, which made it difficult for younger men to be promoted because of the large number of longer-serving men with a better claim to the few senior positions available, served to block promotion by ability.

It was the captains, however, who were the glamorous stars of the navy. The two most celebrated were, of course, Nelson and later Thomas, Lord Cochrane. Others included Saumarez, Sir John Warren, Sir Sidney Smith, Sir Richard Keats, Sir Robert Barlow, Eliab Harvey, Sir John Murray, Commander John Wright, Samuel Sutton, Manvers Sutton, Commander Nathaniel Dance, Sir William Hoste, Sir Charles Brisbane, Sir Philip Broke, James Bowen, Edward Pellew, Sir Robert Calder, Charles Stirling, Commodore Sir Home Popham and John Hayes. These men were to be in the front line of the British war against revolutionary France.

Chapter 26

THE GLORIOUS FIRST OF JUNE

The war at sea got off to a slow start, damping down the widespread expectation in Britain of instant victories in the country's natural medium of war. Lord Howe, commander of the Channel Fleet, picked a cautious course, protecting cargo vessels – some fifty in the first four months of the war – with not a single ship thus accompanied being lost, cruising about to deter French attack, keeping trading lines open and seeking to confine the enemy to port without engaging them aggressively.

This phoney war no doubt fitted in well with Pitt's refusal to pursue the war with any great enthusiasm in the hope that the French would soon conclude peace. Howe remained at Spithead or at the fleet's anchorage in the spectacular Tor Bay off the coast of Devon. When he set sail in May, he was forced back twice by gales, although he sighted but did not catch a French squadron. The navy was partly blamed by public opinion for the Dunkirk fiasco.

By the beginning of 1794 there was much greater pressure on Howe to achieve a substantial naval victory. Parliament increased spending on the navy by £4 million to £5.5 million. The total fleet was now 279 vessels manned by around 85,000 men. Howe was bitterly attacked for his tactic of 'open blockade' – waiting for the French to emerge from Brest and Rochefort from the safety of British waters, which it was feared, might permit French fleets to escape. However, the old man with the hangdog expression was more astute than he appeared. Nelson himself was to call Howe 'the finest and greatest sea officer the world has ever produced'.

The reason for Nelson's tribute was the revolution in naval tactics invented by Howe, which was radically to transform the nature of maritime warfare. Before then British fleet actions were rigorously confined to respecting the line-of-battle. Article 20 of the Permanent Instructions stated insistently that 'none of the ships of the fleet shall pursue any small number of enemy ships till the main body be disabled or retreat'. The British would traditionally attack aggressively 'from the weather gauge' – that is the side the wind was blowing from – because the smoke of battle would therefore drift on to the enemy and because the attacker had the advantage of deciding the timing and length of the action. However, this also meant that lower-deck guns would sometimes fire into the sea, because the wind would tilt the ship, and the men on the upper decks were exposed to enemy musket shot. Moreover, the French, who preferred to defend and conserve their ships, could easily break away from the action, which the British could not do without crossing the enemy fleet.

British commanders during the American War of Independence chafed under the Permanent Instructions and tried to stretch them. But it was Howe who finally issued a new set, giving much greater flexibility to commanders: If the fleet was larger than that of the enemy and some ships found themselves without an opponent, they were 'to distress the enemy, or assist the ships of the fleet, in the best manner that the circumstances will allow'. In certain circumstances, ships were allowed to pursue their beaten opponents out of the line and, above all, provision was made for breaking the enemy's line, in a highly effective manner, on the orders of the commander-in-chief. Howe was to put his innovation to devastating effect, in the first great naval engagement of the revolutionary war with France.

Howe's objection to close blockades was that they placed too much wear and tear on ships and men as well as being expensive. He was certainly wrong: as the later blockades were to show, they were not just effective in bottling up the enemy, but in steeling the officers and men for war at sea.

On 2 April 1794 a huge convoy of grain worth £5 million departed Virginia for France (the Americans were taking commercial advantage of the war to supply both sides). Some 117 merchantmen were bearing

deeply needed food supplies to relieve the French people, who were suffering from the collapse of agricultural production following the Revolution. The French squadrons – one from Brest and one from Rochefort – gave the apparently drowsy Howe the slip and escaped to sea. Their commander, Admiral Villaret-Joyeuse, sailed out into the open Atlantic, to meet the convoy and escort it into Brest.

When the two French fleets had escaped, Howe made the second mistake of splitting his forces into one under Admiral Montagu to intercept the colossal convoy while he pursued Villaret-Joyeuse. In fact he should have kept his fleet united and simply gone in pursuit of the French admiral, who was sure to meet the convoy. In his defence he reasoned that the convoy might slip away while the French engaged his fleet – which is in fact what happened anyway.

On 28 May Howe spotted the distant French fleet ten miles away to the south-east on the horizon. He immediately ordered his fleet in pursuit, but could not catch it up. He ordered four of the fastest British ships – the *Bellerophon*, the *Thunderer*, the *Marlborough* and the *Russell* – in pursuit. They soon caught up with the stragglers of the French fleet, a small two-decker and a massive three-decker, the *Revolutionnaire*.

The four British ships in turn engaged this giant, disabling its mizzen mast and forcing it to wear and tack before the wind into a pursuing British ship, the *Audacious*, which although only half its size and gunpower, engaged it closely as night fell. The battle continued to blaze in the darkness, with the smaller British ship fighting with lethal accuracy, losing just three men to the French ship's 400. The French battleship was almost dismasted, while the British ship was also badly damaged. The fury ceased at about midnight as the two ships drifted slowly apart.

By dawn a fog had descended. When this rose the *Audacious* observed that two other French ships were coming to the crippled *Revolutionnaire*'s help, and the British ship sped to Plymouth to escape. The French ship was towed back to Rochefort. It was a good start for the British.

To the south-west, the British fleet of twenty-five ships continued to pursue the evenly matched French fleet of twenty-six on a parallel course, trying to narrow the distance between them. By noon they

were exchanging fire, hopelessly out of range of one another. Howe now ordered his ships to tack and make directly for the French line – in complete contravention of classical naval tactics, setting a precedent for Nelson years later. As the naval historian Brian Lavery has observed:

> Breaking the enemy line could be a very risky manoeuvre. A ship had to turn towards the opposing line, so that her guns would be largely ineffective while the enemy was at full strength. The structure of her bows was weaker than that of her sides, and she could suffer much damage on the approach. However, once she was passing between two ships of the enemy line, she could use both her broadsides, and the enemy could use none. Having passed through, she could engage the enemy on the other side, which was probably unprepared. If she had started with the weather gage she would now have the lee gage, and thus cut off the enemy's retreat. Breaking the line was a tactic which could win battles, and it did at the Saintes, St Vincent and Trafalgar. Perhaps it would have been too risky if the gunnery of other fleets had been as good as that of the British fleet; but in the given circumstances it was highly successful.

Howe's flagship, the *Queen Charlotte*, broke through under heavy fire, followed by two others, cutting off the rearguard of six French ships behind. Villaret-Joyeuse promptly wore his own flagship, the *Montagne*, around (a hugely difficult naval task, not like reversing a car) and came to the rescue. Meanwhile the clumsy *Queen Charlotte* took too long to turn back to engage the enemy. They escaped, but now the three British ships were to windward and thus held the initiative to attack.

Night descended again, and then a further fog that lasted twenty-six hours. Lieutenant Codrington, peering into the eerie gloom, remarked to Howe that 'God knows whether we are steering into our own fleet or that of the enemy.' British lookouts occasionally glimpsed the tops of sails across the ocean of fog, an alarming and sinister scene. Only on the morning of 1 June did the murk clear – to reveal that the French had drifted some six miles to leeward, and had been reinforced by four more line-of-battle ships, giving them a slight edge over the British. As

thousands of British sailors for the first time contemplated battle in this floating world of rival fleets, it must have seemed an awesome moment: the British had retained the all-important weather gauge.

Howe resorted to controversial battle tactics – with a difference: he mustered his fleet in a perfect line, each ship to engage a French opponent – so far, so conventional – but ordered each to cut through behind his adversary and engage to leeward, so that the British guns, firing upwards into the French hulls, could be used to maximum effect while most of the French shot fell into the sea. Breaking the line in this way was a complete revolution, and an amazing idea for an old man – although perhaps one he had bottled up all his life until command should fall to him. When the two fleets were four miles apart, he gave the order for the fleet to advance.

The leading British ship, the *Caesar*, advanced until within 500 yards of the leading French ship, but then it suddenly hesitated and opened fire, throwing the rest of the British fleet into confusion. Angrily Howe ordered the *Queen Charlotte* to perform the planned manoeuvre as an example to the fleet, and ran up under French fire to behind Villaret-Joyeuse's flagship, the *Montagne*. Guessing his intention, the *Montagne* slackened its sail, while the next French ship, the *Jacobin*, tried to close the gap. 'There won't be any more room to get through,' exclaimed Howe. 'My lord, the *Queen Charlotte* will make room for itself,' replied the ship's master, Bowen. A terrifying spectacle now presented itself, which caused the French revolutionary commissar to flee to the safety of his cabin: the three huge ships were hurtling towards collision.

It was the *Jacobin*'s captain who broke first: fearing he was about to collide with his own flagship in front, his helmsman turned to leeward in the nick of time, just as Howe's own flagship reached the stern of the *Montagne*. Codrington, who was a commander on the lower deck, described what happened next:

> the ports were lowered to prevent the sea washing in. On going through the smoke, I hauled up a port, and could just see it was a French ship we were passing. I successively hauled up the ports and myself fired the whole of my seven weather guns into her, then ran to leeward and fired the lee guns into the other ship. The weather

guns bore first as we went through on the slant, therefore I had time for the lee guns . . . In passing under the *Montagne*'s stern I myself waited at the bow port till I saw the Frenchman's rudder (guns 32-pounders, double-shotted), and then I pulled the trigger, the same sea splashing us both, and the fly of her ensing brushed our shrouds. I pulled the trigger of the whole seven guns in the same way, as I saw the rudder just about the gunroom ports.

On going on deck, Bowen, in answer to my asking if I had done wrong in firing without any immediate orders, said, 'I could have kissed you for it!' Bowen explained, 'In going through, the helm was hard up, and we were thinking we should not clear her, and we quite forgot to send you any orders.'

Some 300 Frenchmen were killed on the *Montagne* and a gaping hole made in the stern through which large numbers of people were seen to fall from the admiral's cabin. Bowen sharply turned the ship's helm about, and with a brilliant manoeuvre the *Queen Charlotte* slipped in between the *Montagne* and the *Jacobin*, its guns blazing on both sides – which in theory exposed it to a combined firepower of 200 guns. But the *Jacobin*, after two broadsides, had had enough and veered away. The *Montagne* was crippled, barely replying as the British thundered broadside after broadside into her, and eventually it drifted out of action. But two more French ships, the *Juste* and the *Republicain*, came up to attack, and the former was put out of action. The *Queen Charlotte* was by now also virtually inoperative.

Just behind the *Queen Charlotte* the 74-gun *Brunswick* under the command of Captain Eliab Harvey had similarly sought to break the French line. The *Vengeur*, of similar proportions but a much taller ship, aimed to cut him off: to attack the French ship, Harvey brought his helm up hard, and the two ships collided with a sickening grinding of timbers which threw most of the two ships' companies to the decks. 'We got her and we'll keep her,' declared Harvey.

The French, however, now used their 36-pound carronades in their towering poop to rake the deck of the *Brunswick* with withering fire, while down below, the British guns, whose portholes were actually locked into place by the proximity of the French ships, simply fired

through the wood into the French hull. Through the jagged holes on both ships, the gunners could actually see one another as they reached to reload. An officer described one incident: 'Our men, by shouting and gestures, endeavoured to scare the Frenchmen from their object, but without effect, for a man was on the point of putting the cartridge into the gun, when the second captain of our gun, who had been worming the gun, suddenly reversed his rammer, reached over, and twisting the worm into the Frenchman's clothes, hauled him overboard; this decided the business in our favour!'

With a heavy swell rolling, the two ships fired alternately upwards and downwards into each other for three hours before the French gunners abandoned their posts. Another French ship, the 80-gun *Achille* came to the *Vengeur's* assistance, but fire from the *Brunswick's* rear guns succeeded in dismasting it, and it surrendered, though the *Brunswick* had no boats to board her with. Meanwhile, the *Vengeur's* crew attempted to board the devastated upper decks of the *Brunswick* below it, but men swarmed up from the lower decks and drove the assailants back. When the hat of the *Brunswick's* wooden figurehead was shot off, Harvey lent his own which the carpenter nailed solemnly on as shot poured from all sides. Harvey soon afterwards had his right arm completely shattered but refused assistance. Another British ship also tried to help, but dared not fire for fear of doing damage to the *Brunswick*, so closely was it locked together with the French.

At last, after five appalling hours, it became clear that the *Vengeur* was sinking: it struck its colours and called for help. As the *Brunswick* had no boats, two other British ships came up and took off 400 men, including the captain; many others, some of whom had broken into the spirit room and got drunk, went down with her. The *Brunswick* had lost a third of its men and guns and was dismasted, but limped back into Portsmouth.

These two engagements were the most celebrated in a furious battle all along the line: the overall result was six prizes taken by the English and another six French ships dismasted, which the French admiral skilfully rescued. Howe's timid flag captain advised the admiral, who wanted to attack again, not to do so for fear 'they will turn the tables upon us'. The crippled French fleet limped back to Brest. The

exhausted sixty-nine-year-old was helped from his chair on the quarterdeck. 'We all got round him,' said Codrington; 'he was so weak that from a roll of the ship he was nearly falling into the waist.' 'Why, you hold me as if I were a child,' observed Howe. Meanwhile the huge merchant convoy sailed right across the scene of the battle through the wreckage. Admiral Villaret-Joyeuse blustered: 'What did I care, for half-a-dozen rotten old hulks which you took? While your admiral amused himself with refitting these, I saved my convoy, and I saved my own head!'

He was putting a gloss on what was the first significant French defeat in the whole revolutionary war. 'Black Dick' was the first real British hero of the war, revolutionizing naval tactics, breaking with precedent in almost the same way as Napoleon was to do on land. The old man seemed an unlikely figure to have been the most unconventional commander for a century.

It was a desperately needed victory after all the setbacks in continental Europe. When news reached home, 'Rule Britannia' and the National Anthem were sung at the opera, bells pealed and London was illuminated. The 'Glorious First of June' preceded the King's own birthday by three days, and the King and Queen in person received the victorious fleet at Portsmouth.

The victory disguised Howe's failure to intercept the convoy and later the following December to stop the Brest fleet escaping again to rendezvous with the Toulon fleet – although fortunately it was turned back by a gale. Two other squadrons got away, one for the West Indies, thanks to the lax policy of distant blockade. But Howe on the Glorious First of June had won a first, famous victory at sea, a harbinger of things to come.

There were other, smaller triumphs in 1794. 'Flying squads' composed of a few ships based in Falmouth were also policing the Channel. The foremost among these was commanded by Sir John Warren, whose captains included Pellew, as well as Richard Goodwin, considered the finest seaman of the age, Sir John Saumarez and Sir Andrew Snape Douglas, a brilliant prize captain. In April Warren's squadron had spectacularly chased a French squadron off the Breton coast and

captured three prizes, inflicting 120 casualties for losses of ten killed and twenty-four wounded. In June Saumarez, who had earlier made his name by capturing a French ship, the *Réunion*, without losing a single casualty, attacked a much larger French ship than his own, the *Crescent*, which had 132 guns to his own thirty-six, to allow the rest of his squadron to escape, before running down the strait between Sark and Guernsey, where the French did not dare follow.

Soon afterwards Warren and Pellew destroyed three small French ships just off Brest, under French noses. The same squadron then captured the 48-gun *Revolutionnaire*. But French captains could also prove impressive. Zacharie-Jacques Theodore-Allemand, commander of the 50-gun *Expérience* and a squadron of four other ships, wrought havoc in September along the west coast of Africa, burning down Freetown, Sierra Leone, and other British outposts, taking 210 unarmed ships and merchantmen, as well as a 12-gun schooner.

An expedition under Elphinstone allied with the efficient Major-General Craig had, however, arrived at the Cape of Good Hope to wrest control of this strategically vital staging post to the East Indies from the new Dutch 'Batavian Republic', a puppet of France. It was entirely successful, a triumph both at sea and on land. Another force under Admiral Rainier succeeded in conquering Trincomalee in Ceylon from the Dutch, and by the following February it had gained complete control of the island. Two other limited naval actions also took place: Lord Bridport, the new Channel Fleet commander, captured three 74-gun ships, although the main French fleet escaped. Admiral Hotham, the new Mediterranean Fleet commander, captured two French ships of the line and, in another action, blew up another. These were far from decisive engagements; but they helped to boost fraying British morale.

Chapter 27

THE IRISH FLANK

Britain had one glaringly weak point as it faced revolutionary France. This was not across the Channel on its eastern and southern coasts, nor in Scotland and Wales, both bound by acts of union, but in Ireland, a seething hotbed of misgovernment and discontent, with hundreds of years of bitter hatred and vendettas – against the British, between peasants and squirearchy, between Catholics and Protestants.

Ireland was the one part of Britain that contained some of the conditions that had fomented the French Revolution. While the more excitable French revolutionary leaders dreamed about a direct invasion of England, the more sober among them saw a much more realistic possibility of an insurrection that would spread across all Ireland, tie down and then overwhelm tens of thousands of British troops, when successful, and provide a staging point for an invasion of England from the west, as well as a base from which to destroy its naval supremacy and intercept trade to Britain from America and the colonies. To some it seemed that only a spark was needed to ignite an Irish insurrection. The French attempt to take Ireland has been taken much less seriously than it deserves: for no fewer than six such invasions were attempted between the end of 1796 and 1798. Some were the stuff of comic opera; others were far more dangerous.

The French Revolution had occurred when resentments in Ireland were running high. The country, with a population of 7 million, consisted, as one contemporary observer, Lord Hutchinson, put it, of 'a corrupt aristocracy, a ferocious commonalty, a distracted government, a divided people'. Another contemporary remarked: 'The mass of the

people require no organisation, being perfectly ready to join any force that may land.' The country had obtained a measure of self-government towards the end of the American War of Independence under the formidable Irish Whig Protestant leader, Sir Henry Grattan, himself an able and moderate man. But, as one later historian wrote:

> It would be difficult to find in history a more corrupt and absurd legislature. It was a parliament of eloquent speeches and of shameful jobs. It was itself the symbol of the supremacy of a class. Ireland under Grattan's parliament, it is customary to say, enjoyed its independence; but its 'independence', to quote Green, 'was a mere name for the unchecked rule of a cluster of great families'; an oligarchy as narrow, and as despotic, as anything Venice ever knew. It had almost every vice a parliament could possess. It was the parliament of a minority and of a class; it represented all the worst ideas of Protestant 'ascendancy'. No Catholic could sit in it or vote for it. In the short eighteen years of its existence it passed some fifty Coercion Acts and inspired at least one bloody rebellion.

A great Irish leader of the time, the Protestant Wolfe Tone, now became the guiding advocate of outright independence – unusually, though, he sought common cause between Ulster Protestants and the Catholic peasantry, the overwhelming majority: he established in 1791 the Society of United Irishmen, conspiratorially made up of eighteen-man cells grouped together into district and provincial committees, with a select executive Directory of five. It was Tone who was to give the French their main opening.

The British government was by no means insensitive to Irish demands: the decision in the 1760s to give Dublin its own parliament was part of this. Pitt then attempted to give Ireland free trade with Britain – a proposal which to his astonishment the Irish parliament rejected in 1795. In 1792 and 1793 he passed laws giving Catholic peasants limited rights to vote, sit on juries and own property – a policy bitterly resisted by a parliament dominated by Protestant gentry, although the oligarchy's control was still safeguarded, as Catholics could not be elected to parliament.

The following year Lord Portland, the head of the Whig grandees in England, joined Pitt's government. The most influential figure in this, apart from Portland, was Earl Fitzwilliam, owner of the largest house in Britain, Wentworth Fitzwilliam. He was another of the Whig grandees, guided by lordly principles of paternalism, in particular towards his extensive estates in Ireland. He was described as lacking in brilliance, but his advocacy was 'sound and direct, his principles most honourable and his intentions excellent'.

Fitzwilliam was appointed Lord-Lieutenant of Ireland – effectively viceroy – and, believing he had Pitt's agreement to far-reaching reform, landed in January 1795. Less than six weeks later he was recalled. During that short sojourn he ignited the country's powder keg: for he gave Ireland what had hitherto been lacking – hope. First, he dismissed most of the corrupt officials running Ireland. Then, saying 'no time is to be lost', he declared that the Catholic gentry must be eligible to sit in parliament to diminish the tension in the country: 'Not to grant cheerfully on the part of government all the Catholics wish will not only be exceedingly impolitic, but perhaps dangerous.' He said he would press ahead with his reforms unless he was issued instructions to the contrary.

His despatch to London was delayed by bad weather, and then pigeonholed for eleven days. When it was read, King George III had the political equivalent of a seizure, declaring it would 'overturn the fabric' of the Glorious Revolution. Pitt promptly instructed Fitzwilliam to put the reforms on ice. The latter furiously dared Pitt to recall him: 'These are not the times for the fate of the empire to be trifled with.' He was dismissed, and Dublin was draped in mourning. Fitzwilliam Square stands to this day as a tribute to an honourable and enlightened patrician whose reforms might have prevented the ensuing two centuries of strife.

Ardent patriots now made up their minds that political change in Ireland could only come from France or from an appeal to arms. Wolfe Tone, agitating for full independence, travelled to Basle to persuade the French to invade Ireland. Tone insisted that 200,000 Irishmen would rise up in support, three-quarters of them armed, to oppose the 10,000 ill-equipped British troops there. The Directory in France was per-

suaded, and in the early winter assembled a formidable force under Lazare Hoche.

A fleet of sixteen ships of the line and twenty frigates and lesser ships was assembled to convey transports carrying 18,000 troops. The fleet was delayed waiting for the Spanish fleet to accompany it, and put to sea without the latter on 15 December 1796, from Brest on its way to Bantry Bay. At first, Hoche's expedition was favoured by luck. Two British squadrons had been assigned to intercept it. One, under Admiral Colpoys off Brest, had been blown fifty miles to the west by gales and entirely missed the French fleet's departure, eventually returning to Spithead. Another, under Lord Bridport, failed to leave Spithead at all for a fortnight.

Not a single French ship was to be captured by the British during the whole expedition – although the redoubtable Pellew, in the *Indefatigable*, managed alone to instil panic in the fleet as it negotiated a treacherous channel, the Raz de Sein, driving a huge 74-gun battleship on to a reef and causing the French fleet to divide into two separate flotillas. When the two rejoined, to Wolfe Tone's dismay, the ship carrying Hoche and the French Admiral Morard de Galles was missing. 'I believe,' wrote Tone, in a wrath too deep even for expletives, 'it was the first instance of an admiral in a clean frigate, with moderate weather and moonlit nights, parting company with his fleet.'

On 22 December the reunited fleet of thirty-seven ships – still without Hoche and Morard de Galles – was some twelve miles off Bantry Bay, but the wind proved too much in the narrow strait leading to the bay. Tone remarked angrily: 'I believe that we have made 300 tacks, and have not gained 100 yards in a straight line.' Just twelve ships actually reached the bay, while twenty-five others were blown away out of sight. The weather worsened further, and five days later only six battleships with four transports carrying 4,000 men remained under General Grouchy, Hoche's second-in-command. He decided against landing and sailed for Brest, arriving on 12 January, long after the rest of the fleet and a day before Hoche and Morard de Galles in the frigate *Fraternité*.

Four French ships had been wrecked and seven stragglers captured by the British during this sorry expedition which had ended without

any landing at all. Hoche's reputation was besmirched and from then on the French were to be much more careful about further Irish expeditions, although they did try, on a smaller scale, which itself was counter-productive.

The Directory now decided to try to sow terror along the English mainland itself. A pirate expedition was organized under an American officer, a Colonel Tate, consisting of 1,800 men recruited from prisons and among the vagabonds and beggars of France. They were dressed in black uniforms and dubbed the Black Legion. Their destination was Bristol, Britain's great port in the west of England, which was to be looted and burnt to the ground. The expedition, on which Tate was accompanied by his mistress, set sail in February 1797 escorted by two French frigates, a corvette and a lugger. They arrived at Ilfracombe in north Devon and landed a couple of boats ashore, breaking into several houses and carrying away valuables before scuttling some of the fishing boats in the harbour. Many went barefoot or wore wooden clogs, and most got drunk on local beer and refused to obey orders. Hearing of the approach of a regiment of angry local volunteers, the little liberating force departed.

They sailed to the coast of Pembrokeshire, where once again they engaged in plundering and burning buildings. At the approach of the militia and Welsh volunteers they withdrew. Seeing a group of Welsh women spectators in their colourful red shawls, they are said to have mistaken them for a force of British regular troops, whereupon they surrendered. Tate's mistress beat him about the head in fury. The few ships that had brought them were taken by British vessels without a fight. The experience of these two disastrous expeditions convinced the French to lay off invading the British Isles for a while.

Early in 1798, Ulster erupted in an orgy of violence. The uprising, consisting of discontented but also warring Protestants and Catholics alike, calling themselves 'citizens' and supporting a French-style Directory, sought self-rule from the British. People were burnt alive and lynched, houses razed. As the rebellion threatened to spread, the British forces swelled to some 60,000 men under the able and immensely

experienced veteran of the American wars, General Cornwallis. In May insurrections also broke out in the counties of Dublin, Meath and Kildare. The French insisted that the time was ripe to hasten to the aid of the Irish. Tone believed his moment had at last arrived.

Even so, after their earlier experience, the French despatched only a small force, Tone arguing that it was but necessary for the French to land for the population to rise in revolt against the English. A force of 1,200 infantry and four cannon set sail accompanied by three 40-gun frigates in August. Humbert, their commander, was a tough and experienced soldier and his men were veterans from Italy and the Rhine. They reached Killala Bay in calm waters on 22 August and went ashore that evening unopposed. Humbert displayed considerable skill and determination. He defeated a small company of volunteers and occupied Killala. There at last local people began to join him. Advancing on Castlebar, some twenty miles to the south, these French professionals encountered a much larger force of militia and routed them, capturing 14 guns and taking 3,000 prisoners: about 100 British soldiers were killed.

However, four columns of British regular troops, some 4,000 men, were now on the way and Humbert soon found himself being pursued. He eluded his hunters for ten days before being surrounded at Ballinamuck, where he surrendered. Two factors had caused Humbert's debacle: the Irish had failed to rally to him in anything like sufficient quantities, and those that had rallied were untrained and without arms; and the British had responded with the customary overwhelming force that they had used against Irish insurgents in the past.

On 16 September 1798 the French mounted a further attack from Brest, with the 74-gun *Hoche*, accompanied by eight 40-gun frigates and an invasion force of 3,000 with a huge amount of stores and considerable artillery, destined this time for Lough Swilly. Tone, under the alias of Smith, went along for a second time. The leader of the expedition was the experienced Commodore Bompart. Reaching Tory Island on the Irish coast on 11 October, the invading force was for once detected by British ships – a flotilla under Sir John Warren

of three 74-gun ships and five frigates. The French made a run for it, and the British gave chase into a furious storm which dismasted the French flagship and so battered one of the frigates that it began to sink. One of the pursuing British ships, the *Anson*, was also dismasted.

Ruthlessly Bompart ordered the stricken French ship to wreck itself upon the shore, sending up rockets to distract the British and lure them to their doom on the rocks. The crippled ship disobeyed and by dawn the British flagships had caught up with the ailing *Hoche*. The furious firefight that ensued lasted three hours, leaving half of *Hoche*'s crew dead and most of its guns destroyed. Bompart struck his colours, as did three of the French frigates. A further three were captured two days later and only two made it back to port. It was a calamitous defeat for an expedition that had not even been able to land. Wolfe Tone himself was captured and later committed suicide in prison, knowing that his fate otherwise would be the gallows.

There were two other minor expeditions. Another Irish freedom fighter, Napper Tandy, had set sail for Donegal on 5 September in a French brig accompanied by forty-five French soldiers and a huge volume of leaflets calling upon 30,000 men to rise up when he landed. They reached Rutland Island off Donegal ten days later and landed. But they soon heard of Humbert's defeat and hastily re-embarked, returning unscathed a week later. On 26 October a relief expedition for Humbert arrived at last and, also learning of his failure, sailed back to Brest. They were spotted by British ships and pursued, but escaped by ditching most of their guns and equipment.

Of the three major expeditions, involving some 9,000 troops altogether, one had been beaten by the weather, another defeated on land, and another routed at sea. The promised Irish uprising had not materialized, largely because the population was too cowed, the French had arrived in too small numbers and the British were present in unexpected strength. The French had grossly underestimated the size of the task: had a much bigger army landed, the Irish might have risen up, believing they would not be left to their fate against British retribution. It was a case of too little, too late. Moreover, the French never had command of the sea and only luck had allowed five

expeditions to reach Ireland unintercepted. Even a huge expedition would have faced the hazard of Atlantic gales.

Pitt believed the immediate danger was past, but that it was essential to follow up such an event by immediate steps for a union: only by guaranteeing the Irish the same government, franchise and trading privileges as England possessed would that country be freed from French subversion. It was a noble ideal, but it required full Catholic emancipation – and the King was dead set against it. Ironically, this was the issue that was to bring Pitt's ministry to an end and topple France's greatest enemy from power.

Chapter 28

CAPE ST VINCENT

At the beginning of 1797, the French revolutionary leaders of the Directory were formulating a far more ambitious plan for striking at England than the flanking attack through Ireland. With both the powerful Dutch and Spanish fleets now on their side, they resolved to make a rendezvous of all three fleets to create a grand armada to sweep British seapower from the Channel, inflict a crippling blow at British trade and permit an invasion force to cross. With overwhelming naval power this should not have proved too difficult. All that the three fleets had to do was to evade the British blockade, and avoid an engagement before they met up.

Britain's predicament was therefore truly appalling. Napoleon was on his final mopping-up operation in Italy and about to inflict the blow that would knock Austria out of the war. That would leave Britain with just one ally on the entire European continent – small, loyal Portugal, which was militarily insignificant. At sea Britain had held her own, but had won no decisive triumph. The Glorious First of June had proved a huge boost to morale and badly damaged the French fleet, but that was soon repaired. The frigate captains were performing daring raids and keeping the shipping lanes open, but that was all. Meanwhile the British had been all but expelled from the Mediterranean with the fall of Corsica: only the troops that had been taken from the island to Elba remained, along with the outposts of Malta, Minorca and Gibraltar.

The fate of the British was now to rest decisively in the hands of two very different men. The first was a small man with an elfin, sardonic,

bitter expression, a cunning squashed rodent face at once harsh, determined and slightly humorous: Sir John Jervis, 'Black Jack', was one of the most detested commanders in the navy, known equally for his unbending love of discipline as for his tongue-lashing of subordinates. He seemed to possess a cruel, even sadistic streak: he would make junior officers bow low before him – 'lower, sir, lower' – for his own amusement. He resorted frequently to the lash and the death sentence. Yet he was an excellent naval strategist – the originator of the 'close blockade', and was enormously tough and determined, inspiring respect as well as dislike in his men. He cared nothing for the opinion of others. He was personally incorruptible, in a service full of malpractices, and his determination to stamp them out was later to prove his undoing. At that moment he was commanding the British fleet off Spain's western coast, bottling up the Spanish fleet at Cadiz.

The second man, utterly unlike this stern, acerbic old sea salt, was at the same time given a dangerous duty to perform within the Mediterranean: to evacuate the British troops on Elba with just two frigates, the *Minerve* and the *Blanche*. His name was Horatio Nelson. As he set off on 19 December 1796, he ran into Spanish frigates at nearly midnight. He called out, 'This is an English frigate', and told the captain of one to surrender. A voice shouted back with a Scottish accent, 'This is a Spanish frigate, and you may begin as soon as you please.' The captain was a descendant of the Stuart dynasty. A furious gunbattle ensued. Nelson three times offered a ceasefire in exchange for surrender, and received the answer, 'Not while I can fire a gun.' After some ninety minutes the two Spanish ships struck their colours, but by then another Spanish frigate had heard the noise of the cannon and was upon Nelson. He had to cast off his prize and engage this, until with dawn he saw two huge Spanish battleships approaching. Heavily outgunned, he had no choice but to run before them for a whole day.

On eventually reaching Elba, he performed his task of taking off the island garrison, and then returned to Gibraltar on 9 January, where he learned that the Spanish fleet had slipped the blockade and was heading out into the Atlantic. He set off to join the main fleet on 11 January, but was soon pursued by two Spanish ships of the line.

At that moment one of the *Minerve*'s sailors fell overboard, and a boat

commanded by Lieutenant Hardy was lowered to go to the rescue. The boat was quickly swept away by the tide, and Nelson had to decide whether to go to their rescue and risk coming within range of the huge ships chasing him or abandon the boat. He decided to pick up his men. The Spanish ships, seeing to their amazement the British ship backtracking ('backing its mizzen topsail' in the jargon) was confused, wondering whether a trap was being sprung with some as yet unseen British ships lurking over the horizon: why else would a tiny ship sail directly towards two huge ones? In turn they took in their sails and held back, while the *Minerve*, having picked up the little boat, returned to its former course.

Then the chase was on again. When night fell, Nelson ordered all the lights to be hidden and changed course suddenly: he thus threw off his pursuers. He was congratulating himself on the coup as the ship rolled in a gentle swell beneath the stars. Then it became apparent that the stars were rather too low – in fact on almost every side: he was in the middle of the thirty-ship Spanish fleet. He was astonished to observe it sailing south and decided it was heading for the West Indies; so he tagged along during the night to sense its direction, taking the colossal risk of detection and annihilation or capture.

Abruptly, it changed course west after Nelson had watched a barrage of signal lights being exchanged in the gloom. The *Minerve* skilfully, still pretending to be part of the fleet, drifted away, its lights hidden, to report on the Spanish fleet's direction to Jervis, who was stationed off Cape St Vincent (São Vicente), on the barren south-western extremity of Portugal.

Nelson reported directly to the acerbic Jervis, and then assumed command of his own ship, the *Captain*. That night the signal guns of the Spanish fleet were sounding eerily off to the south-west. In the morning a thick mist blocked the view of both fleets. It was a tense moment, one that would be crucial to the war. If Britain lost, the way would be open for the enemy to command the Channel and prepare for the invasion of Britain.

The lookouts strained in the eerie murk covering the Atlantic roll. The mist suddenly lifted to reveal one of the most awesome and picturesque fleets ever assembled, a floating township of thousands of

men inhabiting edifices taller than any buildings yet constructed on land. There were no fewer than twenty-seven battleships; these included the biggest ever made, the four-decker *Santissima Trinidad*, with no fewer than 212-guns, six three-deckers with 112 guns each, two 80-gun vessels and seventeen 74-gun ships. In terms of firepower it was perhaps the greatest armada ever hitherto assembled.

With a low swell that morning, the sight of these baroque castles gently bobbing in the western Atlantic left the British sailors that saw them speechless with awe. Nelson described the ships as 'the finest in the world [but] the Spaniards, thank God, cannot build men'. There was a deathly calm about the whole scene, while Jervis's fleet observed strict silence. It was as though the British had spotted an enormous and beautiful city of palaces at sea.

On paper, the strength of the Spanish fleet was overwhelming: it had a total of 2,292 guns compared with the 1,332 guns of the fifteen-strong British fleet. Yet, compared to the extremely tight formation of the latter – Nelson remarked, in a rare tribute, 'of all the fleets I ever saw I never beheld one in point of officers and men equal to Sir John Jervis's' – the Spanish lines were straggly and ill-ordered, perhaps because they had never expected the British to be so near, a consequence of Nelson's night-time feat of detection.

Jervis immediately spotted a weakness in the Spanish defence: the six ships at the rear were several hundred yards away from the main fleet. If he could cut through the gap, the six would be at his mercy. In an instant he signalled from his flagship, the *Victory*. The two perfectly ordered British lines – each ship at an equal distance from the other – quickly formed a single line with a precision of sailing and navigation remarkable in such huge vessels.

With Thomas Troubridge in the *Culloden* leading, they made at full canvas for the gap; the *Victory* was in seventh place, and Nelson's *Captain* in thirteenth, nearly at the rear, a position held by Collingwood on the *Excellent*. The six isolated Spanish ships sought desperately to tack against the wind, to rejoin the main fleet. At about the time *Culloden* reached the gap, the Spanish vice-admiral's ship, the 113-gun *Principe de Asturias*, had veered round into a position where it faced the seventh ship in the British line – Jervis's own *Victory* – which like a

spear was severing the Spanish fleet in two. A tremendous broadside from the British ship raked the Spanish one, which withdrew hastily to leeward.

Just ahead three ships from the main Spanish fleet had succeeded in slipping past the point of the British spearhead: but these nine Spanish ships, now isolated from the main fleet, were to leeward of the British and were reluctant to do battle with a far superior force: they were effectively out of the fight, and now sailed off in headlong flight. The odds between the main fleets were now much more even: eighteen Spanish ships to fifteen British ones.

As the Spanish fleet turned with the wind to try and escape past the tail of the British line, Troubridge, leading it, tacked skilfully from his south-westerly course to a northerly one, being followed by the rest of the line, describing a v-shape. Nelson in one of the two rearmost ships, spotted the Spanish manoeuvre, which would permit the whole fleet to escape, slipping past the back of the British line before Troubridge could lead it back up. The *Captain* threw the rulebook to the winds, steering in a reverse course around the ships immediately behind and crossing the front of Collingwood's *Excellent* to try and intercept the fleeing Spanish fleet. He was set on engaging the biggest ships leading the entire Spanish fleet in an attempt to delay them while the British fleet could come up to attack. The *Excellent* followed his example by breaking the line.

The flag captain of Jervis's *Victory*, seeing this blatant flouting of orders, was outraged and insisted that a signal be sent to recall them: but Jervis, usually the most punctilious and disciplinarian of men, had realized what they were doing and refused. The little *Captain* now found the main body of the entire Spanish fleet bearing down upon itself, headed by the four-decker *Santissima Trinidad*, more of a moving skyscraper of the seas than a ship, flanked by two 112-gun ships, the *San Josef* and the *Salvador del Mundo*, each larger than Jervis's own flagship, with three 80-gun ships immediately following them: the *Captain* seemed destined to become matchwood before these behemoths.

Undaunted, Nelson made straight for the *Santissima Trinidad*, all guns blazing. For nearly an hour the plucky little ship endured the simultaneous fire of six much bigger Spanish ships, but many of the

Spanish shots went wide and hit other Spanish ships. Soon the *Captain* was reduced to a floating hulk, but Collingwood furiously engaged one of its tormentors and compelled it to surrender before moving upon the next, the *San Nicholas*. The Spanish fleet began to veer away, perhaps out of astonishment at the boldness of the attack by just two small ships. At that moment Troubridge's *Culloden*, leading the British line on its new north-west course, reached the scene of the fighting and the battle swept past Nelson's disabled *Captain*.

Even in this condition Nelson renewed the attack on the nearest ship, the 84-gun *San Nicholas*, which had also been dismasted. The British sailors swarmed up the remaining masts and spars of the *Captain* in order to drop aboard the *San Nicholas*'s deck, which towered above the smaller British ship; others grabbed the Spanish ship's cable. Nelson himself broke through a window on the lower deck. The leader of the British boarders on the upper deck furiously cut down the Spaniards facing him and then enterprisingly hauled down the Spanish colours, as officers began to surrender to him.

Down below, the Spanish guns were still firing at a nearby British ship, the *Prince George*, while another Spanish giant, the *San Josef* on the other side of the *San Nicholas*, was crammed with marines firing with their muskets at the British boarders. Nelson ordered his men to stand by the hatchways with their muskets, to prevent the still fighting Spaniards below from pouring on to the deck, then summoned a boarding party to attack the *San Josef*, which was passing just six feet away and was in turn being raked by the muskets of the British marines.

Nelson climbed up the ropes on this side and was astonished to encounter a Spanish officer announcing surrender – the admiral had been hit and was dying. The British captain made the officers hand over their swords. As Collingwood later wrote: 'On the deck of the Spanish first-rate *San Josef* he received the swords of the officers of the two ships, while a Johnny, one of the sailors, bundled them up with the same composure he would have made a faggot, and twenty-two of their line still within gunshot!'

Nelson had captured a 112-gun enemy three-decker across the deck of an 80-gun Spanish three-decker from his own much smaller two-decker: the feat became known as 'Nelson's patent bridge for boarding

first-rates'. Meanwhile the missing lee flotilla of eight Spanish ships had veered round to attempt to rejoin the main Spanish fleet. Jervis formed a line to prevent the junction and protect the four Spanish ships he had taken as prizes, as well as the disabled *Captain*. At this stage the Spanish fleet had had enough. Headed by the limping *Santissima Trinidad*, it made for Cadiz.

Nelson now had to face a foe every bit as dangerous as the Spanish: the wrath of the disciplinarian Jervis for so blatantly flouting the fleet's orders. As he climbed wearily and apprehensively aboard the *Victory*, part of his hat blown away by shot, he was astonished to find the usually unemotional Jervis rush forward to embrace him. The disapproving flag-captain reminded the admiral that Nelson had disobeyed orders. 'He certainly did,' exclaimed Jervis, 'and if you ever commit such a break of orders I will forgive you also.'

Jervis thus established his immortality, as a man who recognized boldness and genius when he saw it, even though the rules were flouted. Later it was said that Nelson alone had saved the day, or the Spanish fleet might have escaped, and that Jervis had been largely out of the battle. This was untrue. The latter had headed straight for the fight and had initiated the first engagement with a Spanish ship; and he also had shown speed in veering his ships around when the Spaniards nearly outmanoeuvred him to return to the battle. Above all, he had displayed the boldness to engage a far superior fleet, while traditionally admirals would decline battle unless the odds were much more even. Nelson was later to turn this in to an art form, but Jervis had shown the way. Finally, for all his severity, Jervis's obsession with order had ensured a perfect formation and clockwork manoeuvring by his fleet – unlike the indiscipline that had so nearly cost Howe victory on the Glorious First of June.

In terms of prizes the victory was not overwhelming – just four Spanish ships taken, with twenty-three others escaping, leaving the fleet largely intact, although with several badly damaged, including the mighty *Santissima Trinidad*. But Jervis and Nelson had confounded the plan to unite the French, Spanish and Dutch fleets. They had also established a ferocious reputation for the British fleet which the Spanish now sought to avoid engaging at all costs, and which prevented the

French from venturing out to seek battle against the close blockade of enemy ports that Jervis now rigorously enforced. Above all, as with the Glorious First of June, the Battle of Cape St Vincent was a tremendous boost to British morale at a time when the nation's plight seemed truly desperate – akin to the Battle of Britain in the Second World War a century and a half later.

Nelson's actions in taking on the cream of the Spanish fleet veering down upon him in a single ship, fighting the flagship, then capturing two large ships, had now created a legend – and Jervis was far too generous a man to be jealous: instead he promoted his subordinate mightily. As Nelson himself wrote, 'The more I think of my late action the more I am astonished. It absolutely appears a dream.' But he was disgusted not to have captured the *Santissima Trinidad* itself. 'Had not my ship been so cut up, I would have had her!' Yet alongside the soaring fame of young Nelson deserves to be placed the figure of Jervis, now to be elevated to Earl St Vincent. Like Howe before him, he had shown boldness, a readiness to grasp opportunities, impeccable seamanship and disregard for conventional tactics in striking contrast to his deeply conventional reputation.

Chapter 29

MUTINY

Scarcely had Pitt, his ministers and the country ceased celebrating the great triumph at Cape St Vincent when a blow came which shook Britain to its very foundations. It marked the closest moment that France came to defeating Britain in the entire period of the revolutionary and Napoleonic wars. It was all the more bizarre in that the French played no part whatsoever in inflicting this blow – indeed, had no idea it was taking place at all. For a month Britain virtually lost its ability to fight in the only theatre in which it had been successful so far – at sea. Britain was suddenly left unguarded, at the mercy of its enemies. Worse still, it seemed on the brink of precisely the kind of insurrection that the revolutionaries of France had so long dreamt of. What occurred was a genuine outburst of authentic working-class dissent, and it came from within the very service that had become the shield of Britain against foreign invasion – the navy, the thin wooden line of magnificent ships that were all that stood between the country and French domination.

On 15 April 1797, the pride of the British fleet rode at anchor at Spithead; this was the Channel Fleet, and it was preparing to weigh anchor to pursue the French fleet, which had left Brest. As dawn broke, a signal was given by the flagship, the *Queen Charlotte*. Then, instead of the billowing of sails from the ship as it set out to sea, an extraordinary sight was observed – the foreshrouds of the flagship were thick with sailors, and they burst out into three cheers. In an instant, the same happened in the foreshrouds of all the other ships, each cheering group answering the other. Below, the officers of the fleet could only look on bewildered,

some incandescent with fury, others bemused and frustrated: every one of the men above them was technically liable to flogging or even death for that most heinous of naval crimes, not just disobeying orders but mutiny. The entire Channel Fleet had gone on strike.

There was nothing any of the officers could do. The marines were supposed to enforce order, but could not do so against every ship's company, even if the men with guns could get the upper hand. It was a naked insurrection, and for a moment Pitt's government feared that revolution was indeed what was on the sailors' minds: nothing like this had ever happened in the history of the navy, or indeed in British history. Two days later the First Lord of the Admiralty, Lord Spencer, rushed down to Portsmouth and the following day three admirals – Gardner, Colpoys and Pole – were rowed aboard the *Queen Charlotte* to negotiate. The admirals were old men bewildered by this entirely new situation, having to talk as equals to common sailors instead of giving them peremptory orders.

The mutineers, in fact, had excellent cause for their actions, which were arrears of pay and bad food. Their demands were extraordinarily modest by any standards: first, 'that our provisions be raised to the rate of sixteen ounces to the pound, and of a better quality'. The purser deducted two ounces out of every pound of meat and of flour in his ration as his perquisite. The purser of the period had no fixed salary; he was paid by gains of this character, and, naturally, as his perquisites expanded the rations of the sailors shrank.

Second, 'your petitioners request that your honours will be pleased to observe that there shall be no flour served while we are in harbour'. That is, they wanted fresh bread while in port, instead of weevily biscuits. Also, 'that it might be granted that there be a sufficient quantity of vegetables of such kinds as may be most plentiful in the ports to which we go'.

Third, that there be 'better care of the sick, and that the necessaries for the sick be not on any account embezzled'.

Fourth, 'that we may be looked upon as a number of men standing in defence of our country, and that we may in some wise have grant and opportunity to taste the sweets of liberty on shore when in any harbour, and we have completed the duty of our ship after our return from sea'.

They concluded 'that we should suffer double the hardships we have hitherto experienced before we would suffer the crown of England to be in the least imposed upon by that of any other power in the world,' but they were obdurate that they would not weigh anchor unless the enemy's fleet put to sea and threatened Britain.

The strike had been carefully planned. Lord Howe, the highly popular former First Lord of the Admiralty, had for several weeks been receiving round robins and anonymous letters of complaint from Portsmouth, and had inquired of the admiral there whether there were real grievances. The captains there had put the whole business down to a few agitators. On 12 April, however, the port admiral learnt that there was a definite plot to take control of the ships on 16 April, so he rushed forward the date for departure of the fleet to the 15th, hoping to forestall it, but failed.

The seamen's leaders were highly organized. They imposed their own discipline which was enforced through floggings. Each ship had its own 'seamen's captain' to see that watches were kept and order observed, reflecting the high professionalism on which the seamen prided themselves. Every morning the crew was to man the fore-shroud bars at eight o'clock and give three cheers as a sign of solidarity. A rope was hung at the end of the yardarm of each ship as a deterrent to indiscipline, although most miscreants were punished by being dunked in the sea three times to the intense amusement of crew members. Respect was to be shown to the officers, although they were not to be obeyed. The mutineers' 'delegates' – their leaders – were piped aboard like officers and met in the admiral's state cabin of the *Queen Charlotte*.

There the mutineers received the emissaries of the Admiralty. It was decided that Spencer, as First Lord, should not go aboard for fear he would be seized as hostage. So Gardner, Colpoys and Pole went across, where the first, an old martinet, started railing at the sailors as 'skulking fellows who know the French are getting ready for sea and are afraid of meeting them'. The strikers' leaders, quite reasonably, had asked for Pitt himself to guarantee their demands, and for a royal pardon: this was their only guarantee against terrible retribution. But after Gardner's outburst the meeting broke up.

The mutineers now raised the red standard of rebellion on the ships and loaded their guns to repel an expected attack. Then news arrived that the government had bowed to their demands: these were to be met, and the King had signed a royal pardon on 22 April, after just a week of tense stand off. Cheering broke out across the fleet and the red flag was lowered. The fleet sailed for St Helen's Bay. But arriving there the seamen learned, first, that the Admiralty had issued orders to the marines to be ready for a fight and suppress any further mutiny and, second, that an outburst of anger in the House of Commons had erupted against the Admiralty's concessions. In an instant the mutiny was reignited and by 7 May all the St Helen's ships were defiant once again.

Meanwhile Admiral Colpoys, who had reoccupied his old ship, the *London*, at Spithead, ordered his men to fire on the mutineers' boat when they arrived to seek support: three 'delegates' were killed and five wounded. As the shots rang out, Colpoys' own seamen revolted: one group tried to bring a gun round to fire on the marines. In the tense confrontation the first lieutenant of the ship shot a sailor's leader dead before being seized by mutineers and taken to the noose on the yardarm to be hanged. Colpoys rushed forward into the angry cluster of seamen and told them that he had acted on orders from the Admiralty, which he had issued to the lieutenant, and that he if anyone was to blame and should be hanged. The lynch-mob read the orders, or pretended to do so, very few being able to read, and the lieutenant was set free. The other officers were also set free, but the mutineers decided that full publicity should be given to the Admiralty's 'concessions'. Guns were trained on the ships from the shore, while the ships' guns were trained back at them.

The dispute dragged on for another tense week. At last the most popular admiral, 'Black Dick', Lord Howe, arrived at Portsmouth on 14 May. The hero of the Glorious First of June was received aboard with much fanfare, where he proceeded to defuse the situation and agreed to the sailors' new demand that the most hated officers be transferred to other ships: this list makes interesting reading:

> 1 admiral, 4 captains, 29 lieutenants, 5 captains of marines, 3 lieutenants of marines, 3 masters, 4 surgeons, 1 chaplain, 17 masters'

mates, 25 midshipmen, 7 gunners, boatswains, and carpenters, 3
sergeants, 3 sergeants of marines, 2 corporals of marines, 3 masters-
at-arms.

The dispute had at last been settled, and to music the seamen rowed
around the bay in procession in honour of 'Black Dick'. On Monday
16 May the fleet set sail at last, a month late, to blockade Brest. The
French were either entirely ignorant of the whole affair, or had failed to
take advantage of the precipitous collapse of Britain's defences.

Yet the crisis was far from over. Just four days earlier, at Sheerness,
the North Sea Fleet staged an exact replica of the original mutiny with
the men climbing into the forespars and cheering. Again the mutineers
demanded that 'no disrespect be shown to any officer whatsoever' and
even that swearing be banned. They were equally punctilious about
discipline, but it was an altogether uglier revolt. The seamen's leader,
Parker, set up a blockade of the Thames and would only allow ships to
go through to London with permits signed 'L. Parker, Admiral'. This
turned the ordinary people of London against the mutineers. Pitt
ordered a flotilla of gunboats to be prepared for use against the strikers.
Communications to the ships were cut off. Pardons were offered to all
those who gave up the strike, and those who persisted were told they
would be branded as rebels.

Troops poured into Sheerness and the inhabitants were expelled.
The buoys and beacons at the mouth of the Thames were moved, so
that any attempt by mutinous ships to escape would be endangered. All
trade to London was now blocked by the mutineers, and it was feared
that they would move upriver to shell the capital with their twenty-
four warships. It was only when it became apparent that news of the
royal pardon had been suppressed by Parker and the other strikers'
leaders that the seamen began to waver. In addition, they were running
out of supplies: although they were blockading London, they themselves were being blockaded from the shore. Finally, on 31 May, after
two weeks, they parleyed, offering to return to sea in exchange for two
months' pay and clothing, and a pardon.

However, the government's mood had hardened since the Portsmouth mutiny had been settled, partly because Britain was no longer

completely undefended against the French and partly because of the fear that strikes would soon become endemic: the much less important North Sea Fleet was to be made an example of. Their demands were refused and two ships left the strike. This was offset by the arrival of four other mutinous ships from the squadron blockading the Dutch coast, which gave the increasingly desperate seamen's leaders some respite. Parker and his associates were now considering escaping to Ireland or America (although patriotically they never contemplated France).

When on 9 June Parker ordered the fleet to flee to sea, none of the other 'captains' obeyed: they went on strike against their own strikers' leader. Two more ships suddenly bolted from the mutinous fleet, and were fired upon by the others. Meanwhile fights broke out within the remaining ships: several sailors were killed. On 13 June five more ships broke away, leaving just fourteen. The following day these hauled down the red flag and the *Sandwich* hauled up a white flag and made for port.

Parker was seized, along with 300 other ringleaders. The revolt's leader, who came of a respectable lower-middle-class family with a small estate, was aged thirty, dark and good-looking with a prominent nose. He made an impression with his dignified calm at the trial, and was hanged at the yardarm after dropping his own handkerchief as a signal to the executioner. His parting words were: 'I wish only to declare that I acknowledge the justice of the sentence under which I suffer, and hope my death may be considered a sufficient atonement.' Other seamen's delegates were also executed or, in that most cruel of ritual punishments, flogged around the fleet. Henceforth any further such mutinies were ferociously repressed.

St Vincent himself led the way when a mutiny broke out in his fleet off Cadiz; that ferocious old disciplinarian ordered the execution of a mutineer in 1798 aboard the *Marlborough*, a ship seething with discontent, and surrounded the ship with the rest of the fleet, threatening to sink it unless the execution was carried out by the seaman's shipmates. Three other ships which had nearly joined the uprising were also threatened, and St Vincent ordered armed boats to row around one of them, the *Prince*, threatening to attack her if she went to the aid of the *Marlborough*.

A month later there was another attempted mutiny in St Vincent's fleet, this time from the most disaffected element among the seamen, the United Irishmen, many of whom, after Wolfe Tone's failure, had been impressed aboard the Royal Navy. (Some 25,000 Irish, most of them completely loyal, served aboard British ships at the time.) The leader of the rebels was a man named Bott, one of Tone's senior lieutenants who sought the support of 200 men aboard the *Princess Royal*. Along with conspirators aboard a number of ships, Bott intended to seize the ships, murder the officers and hijack the whole fleet to Ireland.

St Vincent himself was in no doubt about the depth and danger of this audacious conspiracy, which would have dealt a death blow to British naval strength in the Atlantic and Mediterranean. Bott, however, was by chance ordered to go on a routine boat mission just when he was supposed to lead the insurrection. He decided not to attract suspicion by refusing; and the other mutineers, panicking when the time set for the uprising had passed, revealed the plot. With St Vincent's customary savagery, the ringleaders were arrested and hanged.

There were several other such plots discovered at the same time, although not on so large a scale, aboard the *Caesar* (in which six men were condemned to death for planning murder), the *Defiance* and the *Captain*, ten of whose crew were flogged through the fleet. But the spark had gone out of naval rebellion. In retrospect, what was remarkable was the way in which the first great mutiny, that at Spithead, had not been met with the brutality meted out to the later outbreaks.

The answer lay partly in Howe's gentle and conciliatory character; but primarily in the very real fear on the part of Pitt's government that revolution might spread through the fleet which was Britain's only real protection at the time: had the French taken advantage of the mutiniest – (there are suggestions but no real evidence, that they instigated the Sheerness mutiny, as well as the one against St Vincent) Britain would have been left defenceless.

Chapter 30

THE BATTLE OF CAMPERDOWN

The most remarkable episode in the mutiny of the North Sea Fleet led directly to Britain's third, and perhaps least known, great naval triumph after the Glorious First of June and the Battle of Cape St Vincent. The improbable protagonist was a giant of a man, a colossal six foot four inches in height, with a craggy weathered face, a huge chest and an even bigger belly who towered over every scene in which he appeared, so that young people would follow him through the streets of Chatham simply to look upon so powerful and impressive a man.

Admiral Lord Duncan, commander of the North Sea Fleet, in spite of his enormous physique and cliff-face features, was no fool: his penetrating eyes with their thoughtful, even intellectual expression revealed him to be more than a blunt old sailor. He was not brilliant, but he was practical and intelligent, as well as being utterly fearless. He had distinguished himself most famously at the attack on Moro Castle in the West Indies, where he had led his men through a gap in the walls armed only with a walking stick.

When mutiny broke out aboard his flagship, the *Venerable*, Duncan showed no hesitation: he simply strode down among the mutineers and challenged them: they went back to work. He spoke directly and plainly to them, displaying a deep Scottish religious streak in telling them off for swearing: 'If there is a God,' he told them, 'and everything round us shows it – we ought to pay Him more respect. In the day of trouble the most abandoned are generally the first to cry for assistance and relief from that God whose name they have daily taken in vain.' His somewhat awed men replied in a letter apologizing for the mutiny:

'No one knows what unforeseen deamon possess our minds to act as we did; theirfore we pray and put our trust in the Almighty God that our future conduct may be acceptable to you and suficent to convince you of our fully repenting of our past mis-conduct.'

He proceeded to travel by boat from ship to ship through his fleet to suppress the mutiny, and on one ship grabbed a mutineer by the collar and dangled him over the side of the ship, declaring, 'My lads, look at this fellow who dares to deprive me of command of the fleet.' The mutiny sputtered to a halt in his North Sea Fleet. When mutiny broke out at Sheerness he immediately ordered his fleet to sea from Yarmouth – to find only one ship, the *Adamant*, following his own *Venerable*, as he sailed on 29 May.

He reached the Texel three days later with his lonely companion ship, to find the Dutch fleet preparing for combat. 'I looked into the Texel last evening and saw in the roads fourteen sail of the line and eight frigates, with a number of other vessels, amounting in the whole to ninety-five.' These were formidable odds for a single flagship and another small one, but Duncan told them with grim Scottish humour that 'the soundings were so shallow that his flag would still fly above the shoal water after the ship and company had disappeared'.

The biggest expeditionary force yet for the invasion of Ireland, some 35,000 men under the most redoubtable of all French generals, Lazare Hoche, had been preparing to embark at Texel for the invasion of Ireland. Wolfe Tone was there too, complaining as ever about adverse winds which were delaying sailing. Some 4,000 Dutch troops had actually embarked, although shortly before Duncan's arrival, Hoche died suddenly: he was the only French military commander then with greater prestige than Napoleon and might indeed have been preferred over him as France's military dictator had he lived.

Duncan's ships set about blockading the Texel on their own. They policed the narrowest part of the Channel outside the Dutch port, through which only one ship could move at a time and for three days and nights kept the crew on full alert while waiting for the Dutch to emerge. When the wind turned, he was forced to withdraw, and in one of the most ingenious naval deceptions of the time, feigned signals to an imaginary fleet just over the horizon, to give the Dutch the

impression that a huge force awaited them. Thus the mighty Dutch fleet was kept in port for nearly a fortnight by just two ships until, after the collapse of the Sheerness mutiny, on 17 June the rest of the fleet joined Duncan.

Rather more convincingly, the blockade then resumed for nearly four months, until the Dutch fleet decided to try and break out under Admiral de Winter with twenty-one ships manned by 7,000 seamen while Duncan was refitting the bulk of his fleet at Yarmouth. A small watchdog cutter sailed at speed for Yarmouth, firing its guns excitedly to alert Duncan, who promptly put to sea and intercepted the Dutch fleet on 11 October.

De Winter organized his fleet in a disciplined line parallel to the shore some five miles out. Duncan did not hesitate: he chose to attack frontally, in two groups, passing through the enemy lines and engaging them on the lee side, with the advantage of being able to fire up into the enemy ships while their shot would often fire overhead into the sea. It was a gamble, because it would place the British ships between the Dutch fleet and a potentially dangerous shore, especially if the wind got up.

The religious Duncan prayed with his officers on the quarter-deck as the two fleets closed. Captain Onslow of the *Monarch*, in charge of the second group, reached the enemy line first, aiming for a narrow gap with such determination that the ship behind had to slow its course. He pulled through, firing broadsides in both directions, then swinging around alongside the *Jupiter*, the Dutch vice-admiral's ship. The *Venerable*, leading the second group to the north, broke the line behind the Dutch flagship, the *Vreheid*.

The Dutch broadsides were equally lethal, but much slower – one to every three British. The battle was brutal and straightforward, ship against ship, and lasted three long hours with immense courage being displayed on both sides until, under the superior British rate of fire, the Dutch ships one after another began to surrender. Duncan observed: 'The pilot and myself were the only two unhurt on the quarter-deck, and De Winter, who is as tall and as big as I am, was the only one on his quarter-deck left alive.' At last the *Vreheid* also lowered her colours and de Winter, as was the Dutch custom, proposed to escape in a small

boat. To his astonishment he found a British officer had crossed a huge raft of wreckage to make him prisoner.

De Winter, with his officers about him openly crying, crossed the wreckage, fell into the sea, and was rescued. His second-in-command escaped with a handful of ships. Only seven of the twenty-one ships that had been the pride of the Dutch navy escaped. Duncan gathered with his men in the presence of the captured de Winter to offer thanks for victory. De Winter told Duncan: 'Your not waiting to form a line ruined me. If I had got nearer to the shore before your attack, I should probably have drawn both fleets on it, and it would have been a victory to me, being on my own coast.'

It was not an elegant victory, simply a slogging match, ship for ship. Once again traditional tactics had been abandoned in favour of a frontal attack, but this time a disorganized one. However, by his direct and immediate attack, as de Winter realized, Duncan had prevented the Dutch getting into position closer to their own shore, and the superiority, speed and skill of the British gunners had done the rest.

It was a huge relief for the British nation, worrying almost daily for an invasion that never came: it completely destroyed the Dutch fleet, which although smaller than the Spanish, was much more feared for the courage of its seamen. *The Times* remarked that the amount of money spent toasting the health of Admiral Duncan would increase the revenue's duty by £5,000. A third great naval victory had been won, in a fight in which the British navy had very nearly been deprived of its fleet: and the sixty-six-year-old Duncan joined Howe and St Vincent (at the times of their respective victories), as sexagenarian toasts of their country. With the victory of Camperdown, the threat of invasion had momentarily passed.

Part 5

THE INVASION OF EGYPT

Chapter 31

THE LURE OF THE SPHINX

The tension in Paris that followed Napoleon's return from Italy was defused by an extraordinary decision, whose midwife was Talleyrand – to despatch Napoleon at the head of a huge expedition to Egypt. It was certain that Talleyrand inspired the idea: nearly a year before, in January 1797, he had argued that Egypt would make the perfect colony for France, being much closer than the West Indies. A month later Napoleon, clearly in contact with Talleyrand, whom at that stage he had not met, made a similar argument: 'The time is not far distant when we shall feel that, in order to destroy England once and for all we must occupy Egypt. The approaching death of the vast Ottoman empire forces us to think ahead about our trade in the Levant.' Napoleon suggested occupying Malta, then administered by the Knights of St John, as a first stage. In January and February 1798 Talleyrand, as foreign minister, delivered two impressive presentations for this course to the Directory.

French statesmen had long toyed with the idea. It might seem crackpot, but it had huge attractions for Napoleon: like Italy, and unlike Britain, Egypt was likely to be a walkover: the country was a distant fiefdom of the decaying Ottoman empire but in fact was virtually independent under an ancient and ruling caste, the Mamelukes: he could not believe it would put up any stiffer resistance than the Italians had. It appealed to Napoleon's innate sense of mysticism and romanticism, as a new Alexander the Great forging a great empire for France in the east.

It made some logistical sense too: with Britain's conquest of the

Cape Colony, Britain's Indian empire seemed secure; but if French ideas for digging a canal across Suez to the Red Sea could be realized, the French would have a far faster route to India to attack the British and join up with their enemy Tippoo Sultan. Napoleon believed he could more effectively strike at Britain through Egypt than by leading a doomed invasion of the British Isles. Napoleon and Talleyrand also believed that seizing Egypt would give a final push to the tottering Ottoman empire which would then lie at France's feet. Talleyrand, as part of the scheme, was to become ambassador in Constantinople to await Napoleon's victory. Napoleon thought the time was not yet ripe to seize power in Paris – indeed he feared he was in personal danger from his enemies there: by taking Egypt he could return covered in glory. He remarked of the Directory: 'The Parisian lawyers who have been put in the Directory understand nothing of government. They are mean-minded men . . . I doubt that we can stay friends much longer. They are jealous of me. I can no longer obey. I have tasted command and I would not know how to give it up.'

The evidence seems overwhelming that Talleyrand was playing a double game: on the one hand, by indulging in Napoleon's eastern fantasies, he appeared to be his closest friend and supporter; on the other he was removing from Paris the most dangerous player there, which would permit the wily foreign minister to dominate the intrigues in the capital. For their part the Directors were only too glad to be rid of the threatening Bonaparte.

However to guarantee success to the scheme for invading Egypt, Napoleon's demands were heavy: he had little doubt he could cross the Mediterranean, which had been abandoned by the British. But he had to overawe the Egyptians with overwhelming force. Accordingly he demanded 24,000 men – which he proposed to double with recruits from Egypt – the money for 10,000 horses and 5,000 camels and 150 field batteries. He would use the Toulon fleet for the crossing – some 400 transports to be convoyed by fifteen battleships, fifteen frigates and thirty-seven lesser craft.

To pay for the expedition, Napoleon proposed barefaced looting: he despatched a henchman to occupy helpless Switzerland and extract from the mountain state no less than 16 million francs in gold and as

much again in art and supplies. Meanwhile, General Louis Berthier was sent to pick a quarrel with the ageing Pope and plundered a huge quantity of gold.

Napoleon himself recruited the flower of the French army: General Louis Charles Desaix, a tough young ex-aristocrat to whom Napoleon had taken a rare personal liking; the veteran Jean-Baptiste Kléber, an old enemy of Napoleon but a superb general; Alexandre Dumas as cavalry commander, the father of the famous novelist to-be; Louis Caffareli as chief engineer; Berthier as his chief of staff; Androche Junot as his closest aide; and the young Joachim Murat.

Napoleon chose to dress up this nakedly imperialist venture with an appeal to France's highest sensibilities. He was going to educate the people of Egypt and embark on a great enterprise of scientific discovery; some 150 men of science, art and letters were also recruited for this fabulous *folie de grandeur*. These included the inventor of geometry, Gaspard Monge, along with another brilliant mathematician, Jean-Baptiste Fourier, who specialized in studying heat (which would be useful in Egypt); Gratet de Dolomieu, the mineralogist after whom the Dolomites are named; Nicolas Conté, a famous balloonist; Matthieu de Lesseps, (whose son was to build the Suez Canal, inspired by his father after the expedition); and two brilliant artists, Vivant Denon and Pierre-Joseph Redouté, as well as the poet Parseval-Grandmaison.

Napoleon's most brilliant coup was to keep the whole colossal enterprise completely secret: the British, watching the massed troops across the Channel, suspected nothing and with no presence in the Mediterranean failed to detect the build-up. Nor would it have made any sense to them. At the last moment Napoleon was nearly foiled when war threatened to break out with Austria after troops attacked the French embassy in Vienna when Napoleon's old rival, Bernadotte, who had gone there as ambassador, provoked them by raising the Tricolor on his embassy. Napoleon dissuaded the Directory from declaring war.

By the time of his departure on 19 May the Army of Egypt had swollen to 38,000 men. Napoleon left Josephine behind for her own safety, inviting her to join him later: she never did, as she was badly injured in an accident when a balcony she was standing on collapsed.

So began the most harebrained, pointless and vainglorious adventure in Napoleon's entire career before his invasions of Spain and Russia, which in some respects it resembled, and foreshadowed, revealing him to be a brilliant tactician and hopeless strategist.

On 17 May 1798 the vast expeditionary force of warships and troops set sail from Toulon. For fully eight hours 180 craft sailed past the flagship *L'Orient*. There were thirteen three-masted ships of the line with billowing sails and a combined firepower of 1,026 cannon; forty-two frigates and other smaller warships; and 130 transports bearing 17,000 troops, some 16,000 sailors and 700 horse. There were 1,000 artillery pieces, 100,000 rounds of ammunition and nearly 600 supply wagons.

This colossal armada sailed to rendezvous with three smaller fleets from Genoa, Civitavecchia and Ajaccio in Corsica, which would double the number of ships and bring the total manpower to 55,000. This was no on-the-cheap British-style imperial adventure, but empire-building on a colossal, overwhelming scale. The horizon of canvas stretched some four square miles. Napoleon Bonaparte, still only thirty-one years old, stood watching, his breast surging at the huge force he commanded.

The day before he had addressed his troops with a speech full of bluster and reckless promises that reflected his growing sense of absolute self-confidence and destiny:

Officers and soldiers, two years ago, I came to take command of you. At that time, you were on the Ligurian coast, in the greatest want, lacking everything, having sold even your watches to provide for your needs. I promised to put an end to your privations. I led you into Italy. There all was given you in abundance. Have I not kept my word?

['Yes!']

Well, let me tell you that you have not done enough yet for the motherland, nor the motherland for you. I shall now lead you into a country where by your future deeds you will surpass even those that now are astonishing your admirers, and you will render to the Republic such services as she has a right to expect from an invincible

army. I promise every soldier that upon his return to France, he shall have enough to buy himself six acres of land.

Years later one of his intimates, his secretary Fauvelet de la Bourienne, suggested that Napoleon's megalomania was already well advanced by this time. He quoted Napoleon: 'Europe is a molehill. Everything here wears out: my glory is already past; this tiny Europe does not offer enough of it. We must go to the Orient; all great glory has always been acquired there.'

In around 1800 he remarked to Madame de Rémusat:

In Egypt, I found myself freed from the obstacles of an irksome civilization. I was full of dreams . . . I saw myself founding a religion, marching into Asia, riding an elephant, a turban on my head and in my hand the new Koran that I would have composed to suit my needs. In my undertakings I would have combined the experiences of the two worlds, exploiting for my own profit the theatre of all history, attacking the power of England in India and, by means of that conquest, renewing contact with the old Europe. The time I spent in Egypt was the most beautiful in my life, because it was the most ideal.

Napoleon was always a combination of dreamer and practical man of action, and the sheer immensity and imagination of the task ahead must have gone to the young man's head and seriously warped his judgement, making him severely misjudge the terrain and the enemies facing him. Even his later invasions of Spain and Russia showed more careful planning, more limited objectives and a greater grasp of reality, although they too ended in disaster. The expedition to Egypt was to be an awesome foreshadowing of both, exposing the dangers of penetrating hundreds of miles into hostile, unknown territory in ignorance of the dangers, the enemy, the terrain and the climate – in this case intense heat and shortage of water. It was mounted as though the French army could expect to live off the land and move as easily across desert as across fertile Europe.

★   ★   ★

Napoleon's first objective was the island of Malta. He had a strange, almost upstart contempt for the ancient order that governed the island, a key staging post in the Mediterranean, which he accused of exploiting and starving the local population. They were certainly a decadent lot, a rotten fruit waiting to be picked off the tree by the modernizing Napoleon. The Order of the Knights Hospitalier of St John of Jerusalem had come into existence during the First Crusade and had been recognized as a religious order by the Pope in 1113. They had been evicted from Jerusalem in 1187 and then from Acre, their last castle in the Holy Land, in 1291 before settling on Rhodes from which they staged raids against Moslem shipping. Not until 1522 were they evicted from Rhodes, finally settling in Malta in 1530. There they had defended the island heroically in 1565 for five months against the Saracen navy and army of Suleiman the Magnificent, which lost 30,000 men.

For the next century they continued to harass the Ottoman navy before turning to trade in an increasingly peaceful Mediterranean lake. Then the warlike chivalric order declined into an ineffectual customs force protecting a lucrative trading network. Although most of the Knights were French, they were deeply hostile to the Revolution and in 1797 the French government was alarmed to learn that both Russia and Austria were considering seizing the strategically placed island. Napoleon was instructed to get there first as a strategic way station on his path to Egypt.

On 9 June the Maltese awoke to witness a truly terrifying spectacle: the entire French fleet and invasion force stretching across the horizon. The newly elected German Grand Master of the Order, Baron von Hompesch, surveyed with dismay his own forces: 332 Knights, of whom fifty were too old to fight (many instantly deserted): a garrison of just 1,500 men manning 1,000 guns, many of which had not been fired for nearly half a century, whose powder was mostly rotten; and a local ill-armed militia of some 10,000.

Napoleon delivered an ultimatum and a little sporadic resistance broke out, mainly in Gozo. Three Frenchmen were killed. Two days later Hompesch sued for an armistice – he could do little else – on condition that he receive a principality and a generous pension from the French, with the other Knights also getting pensions. The French

joyously descended on to what was to be their last slice of paradise before the hell for which they little knew they were destined.

Malta's huge population of prostitutes and its luxurious orange groves and fruit were enjoyed to the full. As Lieutenant Desvernois observed: 'They showered us with a thousand attentions and civilities. It is not surprising that they bear so easily the state of celibacy to which the rules of their Order condemn them. Most of them have mistresses who are ravishingly beautiful and charming and of whom they are not the least bit jealous.'

Thus the greatest chivalric order in Europe had been bullied into surrendering without a fight. They were rewarded with ashes, for Napoleon immediately reneged on the armistice agreement and ordered the summary destruction of all traces of the order's rule, while also spurring his men into a characteristic frenzy of plunder. Napoleon ordered the Knights to leave within three days without their pensions or possessions, carrying just 40 francs each. The mint and the church of St John were plundered, yielding a booty of 5 million francs of gold, 1 million of silver and 1 million of gems. As consolation, the Knights were allowed to keep a cherished splinter of the True Cross. It is hard to explain this callous ruthlessness except as an attempt to endear him to the Moslems of Egypt, as a belated act of vengeance against their old Christian foe; he was shortly to display the astonishing lengths he would go to to win over Islamic support.

After just a week of frenzied orders issued to stamp out Malta's separate existence and incorporate it as a French protectorate, he departed with his troops and ships on 18 and 19 June. It took a further fortnight to reach Alexandria. During that time a remarkable comedy of errors was played out in the eastern Mediterranean. Napoleon's officers and men were ignorant of their destination, as elaborate precautions had been taken to conceal it, except from senior officers, to the extent that Napoleon had failed to equip his troops with water-containers for the Egyptian desert – a shocking omission which was to cost innumerable French lives – or training in landing ashore or desert survival and warfare.

Nor was Napoleon aware that his fleet's nemesis was approaching in the shape of a British fleet under Admiral Horatio Nelson; the French

commander knew only that a squadron of three British ships was believed to be in the Mediterranean, which his hugely superior naval forces could make short work of. Nelson himself, however, was equally unaware of the position of the immense French fleet and, by a series of fantastic coincidences, utterly failed to find them on their sea crossing, which might have spelt the end of the French expedition and a watery grave for some 50,000 Frenchmen, mostly aboard defenceless transports. Instead there followed one of the most remarkable duets in the history of naval warfare – a cat and mouse game in which each adversary was blind and only vaguely aware of the existence of the other.

Chapter 32

STRANGE YOUNG MAN

Horatio Nelson, Napoleon's adversary in the Mediterranean, was one of the most extraordinary military fighters these islands have ever produced, a man whose temperament resembled none more so than that of Napoleon himself, although his motivations were very different.

Nelson was born on 29 September 1758, a year before William Pitt, who was to be his war leader, and more than a decade before Napoleon Bonaparte, who was to be his mortal enemy. Like the latter, and unlike Pitt, he was born in provincial obscurity, in the tiny Norfolk village of Burnham Thorpe, the son of a well-to-do parson, Edmund Nelson, whose wife had aristocratic connections – her great-great grandfather had been son to Sir Robert Walpole, the British first minister throughout the reigns of George I and George II. His son, Horace Walpole, fop, dilettante and creator of Strawberry Hill Gothic, was Nelson's godfather, which was a powerful connection indeed.

His father's clerical 'livings' – one of them awarded by Eton College – were prosperous, affording him four servants and allowing his wife to bear eleven children, of which eight survived, which even in those days was a large family. Horatio was the fourth surviving son, preceded by two elder brothers, Maurice and William, and a sister, Susannah. His two younger brothers died young, as did a sister; a much younger sister, Horatio's favourite, Catherine, survived. Nelson's mother, perhaps worn out by childbirth, died at the age of only forty-two in 1767, when Horatio was at the impressionable age of nine. In 1770, the boy Horatio, by common consent a forceful personality even in childhood, asked his uncle, Captain Maurice Suckling, whether he could serve on

his ship which was due to see service against Spain in the dispute over the remote Falklands Islands in the South Atlantic. Aged just twelve, he was appointed midshipman – not an unusual age to start in those days. When the international crisis eased, he was posted under Suckling aboard a guard-ship in the Medway, the 74-gun *Triumph*.

As a middling son in a gentry family Horatio would be expected to make his own way in life, and the navy presented an attractive career for a resourceful boy. In academic studies at the respectable Royal Grammar School in Norwich, Horatio had shown little aptitude for academic work, except in his written English, which was to show later in his despatches. As a midshipman aboard a formidably large two-deck ship of the line, he pursued a simple, spartan and unexceptional life of mundane duties, acquiring the skills of seamanship from the bottom; he also served aboard a merchantman to acquire sailing experience.

At the age of fifteen he was granted his first adventure. The *Carcass* was due to sail to seek the fabled North-West Passage across the top of America to the East Indies. The young midshipman begged his uncle, Captain Suckling, to be allowed to go on the expedition. Its Captain Lutwidge was a friend of Suckling's; Horatio got his way. The journey took four months and brought Nelson within ten degrees of the North Pole. Another midshipman vividly described the twenty-four-foot ice wall which threatened to destroy the ship and the walrus to which they harnessed it to try and tow it to safety. The North-West Passage went undiscovered. Horatio was proud enough of being given command of a cutter with twelve men and boasted of his navigational abilities. Later writers embroidered it with a supposed encounter between Horatio and a bear on an ice floe which he was supposed to have fought off with the butt of a musket.

On his return he was promoted to a frigate, the *Seahorse*, bound for the East Indies. He was blown back by the trade winds to the Cape of Good Hope – he was later to scorn Cape Town, which he evidently disliked on this occasion. He won £300 at cards in one port but vowed to give up gambling. He formed a favourable impression of Trincomalee in Ceylon, visited the magnificent British settlements at Calcutta and Bombay and even sailed up the Persian Gulf to the foetid port of Basra. Virtually no record survives of his adventures there, perhaps

because he wrote few letters or his family destroyed them later as not reflecting on his glory in later life. He may indeed, like that other young man seeking his fortune in the Indies half a century before, Robert Clive, father of Britain's Indian empire, have been unhappy on his travels.

He contracted malaria, which was to recur all his life, and was despatched on the six-month journey home, ailing and seemingly condemned to obscurity in his profession, even voicing thoughts of suicide by throwing himself overboard (malaria is a notoriously depressive illness). He had already acquired the frail and delicate appearance that made others want to mother him, and which seemed so implausible in a hero. In his fevered state he experienced a curious conversion, believing that he would become 'a hero and confiding in Providence that I will brave every danger'. Intriguingly, Clive had experienced a similar call of destiny on his own failure as a young clerk to commit suicide with a pistol: the gun did not go off. Horatio may have felt that having escaped death, yet felt its closeness, he was unafraid in future to brave it.

On his arrival in Britain in the summer of 1776, as the American colonies raised the banner of independence, at the age of eighteen he found his fortunes had changed dramatically for the better. Captain Suckling had been appointed to the key post of Controller of the Navy. His young protégé was promptly appointed acting lieutenant aboard the 64-gun *Worcester*, which sailed to Cadiz.

The keen young man evidently made a good impression and the following year he took his lieutenant's examination before three captains – the chairman of which, in a not uncommon display of nepotism in the supposedly egalitarian navy, was none other than Captain Suckling. He passed with flying colours and unlike so many of his more frustrated peers, almost certainly under Suckling's patronage, was immediately appointed second lieutenant aboard the 32-gun frigate *Lowestoffe*, under Captain William Locker.

By the age of nineteen the young man had thus travelled twice halfway around the world, to its coldest northern reaches and its most tropical equatorial climates, experienced a dozen of the world's ports, and now, under the close patronage of a very senior naval figure, seemed embarked on a solid if unexceptional career.

Locker, as was his custom with his younger officers, commissioned the first known portrait of the young Horatio. He emerges as slim, fresh-faced, with a delicate, almost feminine complexion and an expression of a sensitivity. The keen alert brow and eyes and the dominant nose are offset by the gentle lips and chin: at that tender age Horatio exuded a curious mixture of determination, intelligence and grace. He looked more like a foppish, art-loving young nobleman than a naval warrior.

Horatio tended to get on with his superiors and he and Locker hit it off right from the start. The young lieutenant admired Locker for his dictum: 'Lay a Frenchman close and you will beat him' which was reminiscent of his own advice to the young Thomas Cochrane years later: 'Always go at 'em'. He was fearless from the start, his courage belying his slight frame. He was appointed to the Jamaica station, notorious for its tropical diseases, where he boarded a French privateer in a gale in his first real naval action; afterwards he admitted to his enjoyment of the danger. Admiral Sir Peter Parker, the fleet commander there, was an old friend of Horatio's uncle and took him aboard his flagship as third lieutenant, soon promoted to first. When Suckling died, Parker took over as Horatio's mentor.

The war between Britain and France and its rebellious American allies was now under way. Horatio soon showed his mettle, taking part in the capture of three prizes, of which he was entitled to a thirty-second share, securing his first modest financial capital. In 1779 he was made master and commander of his first ship, the *Badger*, a small two-masted brig. With this he rescued the crew of a sloop accidentally set on fire. Under Parker's patronage Horatio continued his effortless rise, being appointed to the coveted position of post-captain of the *Hinchinbrook* in June 1779. Still only twenty, he was one of the youngest ever to be so appointed – a faster rise than either Hood or Jervis.

He had risen through family connection and patronage – first from Suckling, then Locker, then Parker. Being respectful, loyal, disciplined and a fine sailor, he clearly had an uncanny ability to impress his superiors. As promotion to admiral was merely a matter of seniority among post-captains, Nelson was now clearly in the fast stream to the

top. Yet extraordinarily he was largely untested, except as a promising seaman: he had never been in a significant engagement.

It was not that the young captain showed any reluctance to put himself in the line of fire. In February 1780 the governor of Jamaica, General John Dalling, conceived a madcap scheme for invading the Spanish province of Nicaragua, securing the towns of the north during the American War of Independence. He assembled 2,000 regular troops and a hundred 'volunteers' from the backstreets of Kingston to stage a landing at the mouth of the San Juan river.

Nelson was ordered by a reluctant Parker to escort this force to the mouth of the river. On arrival, the intrepid young officer ignored his orders to return and took command of the land force, which had to drag canoes along the bank of the river to avoid its strong downstream currents, plunging deep into the rainforest which was infested with snakes and alligators. By early April they reached the fortress of the Immaculate Conception, near the huge freshwater inland sea of Lake Nicaragua. Nelson urged immediate attack, but fell seriously ill and was evacuated downstream in a canoe to take up a new appointment as captain of the 44-gun frigate *Janus*. The castle meanwhile surrendered, but the hopeless expedition fizzled out as the little British invading force succumbed to tropical diseases.

Nelson himself only just survived his illness, and was unable to take up his new command, to his bitter disappointment. He was shipped back to England and sent to convalesce at Bath, where he spent months recovering. It had been another terrible career setback for a man with an apparently golden staircase to the top. He still had seen no significant action.

In the autumn of 1791 he was given a new command: the 32-gun *Albemarle*, a French prize of unprepossessing appearance. Still less promising was his mission: dull escort duty for convoys of merchantmen in the Baltic, the North Sea and the Atlantic. There at last he ran into the enemy: he was pursued by five French ships of the line and a frigate for ten hours before, in a first superb display of seamanship, eluding them in fog and then sailing across the shoals of Newfoundland's St George's Bay, and on to where the larger ships could not follow.

In Quebec he fell in love with the daughter of the provost marshal of the garrison, the sixteen-year-old Mary Simpson. When ordered to New York – perhaps because her father disapproved – he displayed his romantic streak by threatening to disobey orders in order to stay with her. When he arrived in New York, his old talent for ingratiating himself with his superiors had not deserted him, and Admiral Hood, another old friend of Suckling, took an immediate shine to him, although he turned down the twenty-four-year-old's extraordinarily ambitious request to command a ship of the line.

Nelson made friends with the King's younger son, Prince William, who was serving as a midshipman aboard Hood's flagship. The Prince later gave this impression of the strange, ambitious, slight young man:

> He appeared to be the merest boy of a captain I ever beheld; and his dress was worthy of attention. He had on a full-laced uniform: his lank unpowdered hair was tied in a stiff Hessian tail, of an extra-ordinary length; the old-fashioned flaps of his waistcoat added to the general quaintness of his figure, and produced an appearance which particularly attracted my notice; for I had never seen anything like it before . . . My doubts were, however, removed when Lord Hood introduced me to him. There was something irresistibly pleasing in his address and conversation; and an enthusiasm, when speaking on professional subjects, that showed he was no common being . . . I found him warmly attached to my father . . .

Thus Nelson first displayed the romantic – or perhaps merely snobbish and self-interested – attachment to royalty which was later to do him so much harm.

Nelson learnt that Turks Island in the West Indies had been taken by the French. He assembled a force of four small ships, bombarded the town and landed some 170 seamen, before being forced to retire with eight men wounded. It was a small attack and, with peace soon concluded, Nelson returned to England where his ship was laid up. He continued to cultivate his grand friends, however, being introduced by Hood to the King and visiting his friend Prince William at Windsor as well as Admiral Parker at his country seat. He paid a visit to France

and nearly became engaged to Elizabeth Andrews, a minor heiress he met there. Nelson dabbled in politics, enthusiastically supporting Pitt who, just a year younger than he, had been asked to form a government. He even considered standing for parliament himself.

Hood gave him command of the small 28-gun frigate *Boreas* newly returned from the West Indies. Arriving in Barbados in the summer of 1784, just after the conclusion of the final peace with France, he fell into the parochial bitchiness of expatriate military duty at peace. He took an instant dislike, for once, to his superior, Admiral Sir Richard Hughes, and to his wife's 'eternal clack', flirted openly with the governor of Antigua's pretty young wife, Mary Moutray, and admirably led a one-man crusade against local merchants illegally trading with the now independent American colonies. In the latter, at least, he showed integrity and courage.

After thus offending almost everyone he could, clearly bored by serving in this peaceful small-town backwater and treating others as his inferiors, he met Fanny Nisbet, a young widow with a five-year-old son, the daughter of a prominent judge on the island. One of Fanny's friends had vividly described the young Horatio Nelson in a letter to her:

> He came up just before dinner, much heated and was very silent: yet seemed, according to the old adage, to think the more. He declined drinking any wine: but after dinner, when the resident, as usual, gave the three following toasts, the king, the queen and royal family, and Lord Hood, this strange man regularly filled his glass, and observed, that these were always bumper toasts with him: which having drank, he uniformly passed the bottle, and relapsed into his former taciturnity. It was impossible, during this visit, for any of us to make out his real character; there was such a reserve and sternness in his behaviour, with occasional sallies, though very transient, of a superior mind. Being placed by him, I endeavoured to rouse his attention by showing him all the civilities in my power; but I drew out of him little more than yes and no. If you, Fanny, had been there, we think you would have made something of him; for you have been in the habit of attending to these odd sort of people.

Fanny certainly 'made something of him'; for, the summer of 1785 Nelson was plainly infatuated, declaring that to live in a cottage with her would be like living in a palace with anyone else. She was a petite, dark-haired, nervous young woman, graceful and good-looking, but her shyness and reticence were unfairly to gain her a reputation for coldness. At the time she was housekeeper to her mother's brother, John Herbert, the wealthy president of the island council, descended from the distinguished Herberts of Powys and Pembroke.

Nelson was soon writing passionate letters to her: 'As you begin to know something about sailors, have you not often heard that salt water and absence always wash away love? Now I am such a heretic as not to believe that faith: for behold every morning since my arrival [at Antigua], I have had six pails of water at day-light poured upon my head, and instead of finding what the seamen say to be true, I perceive the contrary effect . . .'

He begged Herbert for her hand, but the rich old man counselled delay. Nelson was a highly promising, if rather odd, young man, yet in poor health and someone who had upset the local establishment. It was unsurprising that Herbert thought this impecunious captain something of a comedown for his beloved niece who belonged to the most prominent family on the island (and islanders are nothing if not snobs) and would one day inherit his fortune.

Nelson found himself with the task of escorting Prince William, who had been appointed captain of the frigate *Pegasus* at the age of twenty-one. William was soon at odds with his ship's officers and regarded Nelson as his best friend as he careered around the Leeward Islands in search of amusement. As Nelson complained: 'How vain are human hopes. I was in hopes to have been quiet all this week. Today we dine with Sir Thomas [Shirley], tomorrow the prince has a party, on Wednesday he gives a dinner in St John's to the regiment, in the evening is a mulatto ball, on Thursday a cock fight, dine at Col Crosbie's brother's and a ball, and on Friday somewhere but I forget, on Saturday at Mr Byam's the president [of Antigua] . . . Some are born for attendants on great men, I rather think that is not my particular province.'

Prince William acted as best man at Nelson's wedding which was held in considerable style on 11 March 1787. The wedding, held at Herbert's extensive house, Montpelier, was celebrated with an enormous banquet and ball attended by 200 people.

Nelson, who was suffering from one of his periodic bouts of ill-health, had at this time turned into something of a disciplinarian, flogging three of his men with two dozen lashes for using mutinous language – a very severe punishment. He then sentenced another man to death for desertion, but the sentence was not carried out. On his return to England he had another fourteen crewmen flogged. By the time he had paid off the men on his ship, the *Boreas*, he had had sixty-one of its 142 crew flogged – a huge proportion for the time. Nelson went on fawning to Prince William in England: 'I am interested only that Your Royal Highness should be the greatest and best man this country ever produced . . . When I go to town, I shall take care to be presented to His Majesty [the King] and the Prince of Wales, that I may be in the way of answering any question they may think proper to ask me. Nothing is wanting to make you the darling of the English nation, but truth.' Nelson's friendship with the Prince, with whom the Admiralty was profoundly dissatisfied, won him no favours. Together with his brothers, the Prince of Wales and the Duke of York, William was seen to be opposing Pitt's government more or less openly, much to the irritation of their father, the King.

Nelson constantly badgered his superiors for a ship but obtained none: this was peacetime and few were available. Moreover, he was regarded for the first time with disfavour as an undiplomatic young man who had offended just about every vested interest in the West Indies, associated too closely with Prince William and had risen above his station. He had seen little action, been promoted largely through connection, and apart from a few minor skirmishes and a few acts of seamanship, he was anything but a hero. There were many others with far better claims. No doubt his disciplinarian streak did not go unnoticed: it was regarded with approval by some, disapproval by others. Both Lords Howe and Hood of the Admiralty were pestered with demands for a ship for Nelson, which annoyed them. Angrily Nelson contemplated entering the service of the Tsar of Russia as a mercenary.

Meanwhile he introduced his wife to his father, Edward, who got on famously with his modest, charming and beautiful young bride. Seven-year-old Josiah, her son, went to school in Norfolk. Nelson was to spend another three years in Norfolk, bombarding the Admiralty with demands for a ship – even control of a cockleboat, he remarked caustically. He was a young man in a hurry who had greased his way quickly up the slippery pole and now had attracted the ire of his superiors through his arrogance.

Chapter 33

THE ACTION HERO

There are striking parallels between Nelson's and Napoleon's careers. That self-important young man had also married a widow from the West Indies – had also experienced brilliant early success, been disappointed, his career stranded in the doldrums leaving him contemplating serving Russia or Turkey. Napoleon secured his next big break at the age of twenty-six. Nelson had to wait until the beginning of 1793, when he was aged thirty-four, for another chance to prove himself. In his case it was command of a ship – but a fine one, the *Agamemnon*, a 64-gun ship of the line, the smallest, as war with France inexorably approached. Moreover Nelson had succeeded to modest wealth, having inherited £4,000 from an uncle. Josiah, his stepson, was appointed a midshipman aboard the *Agamemnon*. He left Fanny in order to captain his new ship to Cadiz and then sailed to the French port of Toulon.

There the people of the city had rebelled against the Revolution and Hood, Nelson's commander, offered them his protection. Nelson was despatched to seek troops from the court of Naples, which was allied to Britain. Here he made the acquaintance of the boorish King Ferdinand IV and his formidable Queen. The young British captain was received in state, dining with the King who lent him the 4,000 soldiers he sought.

The burly, ugly King's wife was the real power in the land: Maria Carolina was Austrian, sister of Marie Antoinette of France, and her prime minister was John Acton, descended from a prominent English family. The British Ambassador, Sir William Hamilton, was a noted

collector, and a former member of the fashionable Dilettante Society in London. Nelson was entranced to meet Hamilton's wife, Emma, a celebrated beauty. Nelson wrote to his wife: 'She is a young woman of amiable manners who does honour to the station to which she is raised.' Possibly this is a reference to her humble origins as a black-smith's daughter who had mothered an illegitimate child at sixteen and had been mistress to several men of importance, including the painter George Romney, who painted her fresh sensuousness frequently, before she took up with Hamilton, who married her in 1791. It was rare in those days for marriage with a member of the lower orders not to attract social opprobrium; possibly she had succeeded because of her beauty and charm, and the ease with which she fitted into upper-class society. She danced beautifully, spoke Italian and French and became Queen Maria Carolina's best friend.

Nelson was enchanted, but left after only six days. Returning to Toulon, he was despatched to establish a British naval base on the island of Corsica where he learnt soon afterwards, to his dismay, that Toulon had been regained by the French, thanks to the enterprise of a daring young French artillery officer, Napoleon Bonaparte, although the name would have scarcely registered at the time with the British officer. Nelson was expected to establish an alternative British naval base on Corsica, where Paoli was in open insurrection against the French. Furious with the army, which advised against laying siege to Calvi, Nelson ordered his sailors to disembark and set up guns outside the port of Bastia, which was bombarded and blockaded by sea. Towards the end of May 1794 the town surrendered.

Nelson now repeated the feat with Calvi, but was twice wounded by enemy fire; his right eye was blinded by splinters in the second attack. Some consider his early fearlessness under fire reflected a morbid death wish; in fact Nelson and many other officers considered that exposing oneself to the dangers experienced by the men was an essential part of leadership; if there was any unusual psychological element it is that Nelson, unlike most men, felt entirely calm under fire and possibly even relished the heat of battle, as have so many natural warriors.

Calvi surrendered in August. The army commander, Colonel John Moore, an extremely able officer, claimed later that both ports could

have been taken by simple blockade – possibly an excuse for his own caution. Nelson and Hood claimed the credit. The former by his ceaselessly activity and reckless bravery had at last had the chance to demonstrate what a leader of men he could be under fire. Nelson had somewhat redeemed the setback suffered with the loss of Toulon. He travelled in style to Genoa and Leghorn, where he acquired a girlfriend – his 'dolly', as one fellow captain put it – although he corresponded eagerly with Fanny: it was by no means uncommon for officers away from their wives for long periods to have dalliances in foreign ports.

In March 1795 near Genoa he had experience of fleet action, pursuing the French two-decker *Ça Ira* along with fifteen French lesser warships. The *Agamemnon*, the fastest ship in the fourteen-strong British fleet under the Mediterranean command of Admiral William Hotham, caught up with the *Ça Ira*, which was already being fired upon by a small British frigate, the *Inconstant*, and skilfully manoeuvred to stay out of range before coming up to deliver a full broadside, thus disabling the French ship.

Nelson continued to fire upon her until other French ships came to the rescue, while the rest of the British fleet in the meantime hurried up to reinforce Nelson. Soon both the *Ça Ira* and another French ship struck their colours, some 350 men having been killed or wounded aboard the French ships, compared to just thirteen aboard Nelson's own.

The impetuous young captain quarrelled with the cautious Hotham and was dismayed when the fearless veteran Hood, with whom he got on much better, was pensioned off, possibly because of his failure to hold Toulon. Hotham was replaced in 1795 by Admiral Sir John Jervis, with whom Nelson immediately got on. Jervis appointed Nelson to command the 74-gun *Captain*, in which he later joined Jervis at the Battle of Cape St Vincent which scattered the Spanish fleet and in which he performed a decisive role (see page 232). Nelson described the battle amusingly in a letter to Fanny:

> There is a saying in the fleet, too flattering for me to omit telling – viz. 'Nelson's Patent Bridge for boarding first rates', alluding to my passing over an enemy's 80-gun ship . . . Nelson's recipe for

cooking Spaniards was: 'Take a Spanish first rate and an 80-gun ship and after well battering and basting them for an hour keep throwing in your force balls, and be sure to let these be well seasoned . . . then skip into her quarter gallery window sword in hand and let the rest of your boarders follow as they can . . . then you will only have to take a hop skip and jump from your stepping stone and you will find yourself in the middle of a first rate quarter-deck with all the dons at your feet. Your olla podrida may now be considered as completely dished and fit to set before His Majesty.'

Rear-Admiral Sir William Parker suggested that his own ship, the *Prince George*, had been responsible for the surrender of the *San Josef*, but Nelson's account was the more widely accepted. Nelson was promoted to rear-admiral and made a Knight of the Bath for his heroic part in the battle.

He was at last, at the age of thirty-nine, the popular hero he craved to be. There was no doubt of his courage, dash and naval genius, but he had had to work extremely hard at success, having twice been frustrated by severe illness and once by his own tactlessness. He also met Britain's growing need for a hero. The thirst for one stemmed from two features of the age: the growing influence of the press, which sought a figure of daring and glamour to excite the reading public; and the need for the government and the Admiralty to bolster its own popularity through a hero's exploits. Elderly admirals like Howe, and crabby ones like St Vincent, did not fulfil this need. In fearless, handsome young Nelson a figure was at last found which could fit the role: like Robert Clive before him, Nelson was to become a celebrity far exceeding that of film or pop superstars of our own age.

Following Calvi, Genoa and Cape St Vincent, Nelson plunged again headlong into enemy fire – this time with much less justification. After another month of blockade off Cadiz, during which Nelson enthusiastically and unattractively supported Jervis's draconian actions against mutineers in the fleet, it was learnt that treasure ships from Latin America carrying some £6million worth of bullion were expected to

dock at Tenerife. Nelson promptly suggested that the island should be seized.

This was no easy task. The historian, W.H. Fitchett has eloquently described the daunting nature of the island:

> Santa Cruz does not offer many facilities for attack from the sea. The shores are so high that a ship is very apt to be becalmed beneath them: they are pierced by sudden valleys, through which, as through so many funnels, the wind drives; so that a ship, becalmed at one moment, may heel over to a furious gust at the next. The beach is a steep slope of loose rocks and water-worn stones, made slippery with seaweed. On this a great sea breaks almost incessantly, and the loose mass grinds and shifts under its stroke. The shore, it may be added, dips so sharply that the water, at a distance of only half a mile, has a sounding of forty-five fathoms. A ship, in a word, can find no anchorage except close under the overwhelming fire of the forts.

On 21 July 1797 Nelson set out with a force of around 1,000 sailors and marines and launched a surprise night attack on the capital, Santa Cruz, under the command of his friend Thomas Troubridge. But a gale arose when they were still a mile from shore and as dawn broke they were compelled to return. On the following day they succeeded in landing and climbed a hill opposite the citadel but again retired without achievement.

On 24 July Nelson himself led the attack – which as a rear-admiral and flag officer broke with precedent and placed his life in danger. But it is easy to see why he was so impatient after previous failures. He later wrote: 'The honour of our country called for the attack, and that I should command it. I never expected to return, and am thankful.'

With the enemy now alerted and possessed of some 8,000 troops on the island, instead of the few hundred or so the British believed, and in command of a heavily fortified citadel, the enterprise was doomed from the start. The boats containing Nelson and his 600 men missed the pier in the night darkness and most were smashed into splinters by the surge. Nelson commanded one of the two boats that succeeded in finding the pier – only to discover that it lay directly beneath the

citadel, which opened up with a withering burst of fire. Grapeshot
shattered Nelson's right arm as he stepped ashore. Josiah, his stepson,
improvised a tourniquet and he was rowed out to the *Theseus* where it
was amputated. Meanwhile Captain Samuel Hood cannonaded the
town until the island's governor offered to help evacuate the remainder
of the force and to provide supplies to the ships.

Nelson bore his terrible wound and the failure of the expedition
bravely, although he feared it would be the end of his career: no one,
he believed, would have any use for a left-handed admiral. St Vincent
responded with gruff and uncharacteristic generosity: 'Mortals cannot
command success. You and your company have certainly deserved it.'
Josiah was promoted master and commander by St Vincent for his
heroic role in the affair.

Nelson was allowed to return home after more than four years at sea
and was reunited with his wife and father at Bath. He had changed
hugely: with his missing arm, white hair, frail frame and blind eye, he
was almost unrecognizable. The face was no longer pampered and
immature. While his good eye continued to blaze forth determination
and stern impatience, his cheekbones were more prominent and his
nose had become the rudder of a thinner, hungrier visage. His mouth
was now pursed and tight-lipped in determination and the familiar
slight curl of arrogance, even cruelty, of the later portraits had made its
appearance, which made him all the more attractive to women.

If his daring success at Cape St Vincent had made him a name familiar
across England, the disaster at Tenerife, which should have destroyed his
career for its recklessness and inadequate preparation, cemented his
reputation as a great national hero. The romantic image of the dashing
fearless seaman who had led his men into battle under murderous fire, and
was now armless, his sleeve pinned to his uniform, with a patch piratically
slung over one eye (he never in fact wore one) had come to stay.

He still suffered great pain, as his arm remained septic. He was
awarded his Knighthood of the Bath and given the Freedom of the
City of London. He was received by the First Lord of the Admiralty,
Lord Spencer. His wife Lavinia penned this portrait of him and his
devotion to Fanny:

The first time I ever saw Nelson was in the drawing room at the Admiralty; and a most uncouth creature I thought him. He was just returned from Tenerife, after having lost his arm. He looked so sickly, it was painful to see him: and his general appearance was that of an idiot; so much so, that when he spoke, and his wonderful mind broke forth, it was a sort of surprise that riveted my whole attention . . . He told me that his wife had dressed his wounds, and that her care alone had saved his life. In short, he pressed me to see her, with an earnestness of which Nelson alone was capable. In these circumstances, I begged that he would bring her with him that day to dinner. He did so, and his attentions to her were those of a lover. He handed her to dinner, and sat by her; apologising to me, by saying that he was so little with her, that he would not, voluntarily, lose an instant of her company.

This time, as soon as Nelson was fit for service again, he was given a ship, the *Vanguard*, with Edward Berry as his flag captain. He sailed to rejoin St Vincent, who assigned him command of a Mediterranean squadron to discover why the French were assembling a huge fleet in great secrecy at Toulon.

On the way the *Vanguard* nearly foundered in a storm. And the three fast frigates accompanying Nelson, which were crucial to his scouting out the French fleet, were lost. 'Were I to die at this moment, want of frigates would have been stamped on my heart,' he remarked. He was given orders to do virtually as he pleased in order to destroy the French Mediterranean Fleet. But all he had was three battleships, now that he had lost the frigates.

Still off Toulon, he was joined at last by a further eleven ships of the line despatched by St Vincent. In a remarkable part of deception, St Vincent met reinforcements which had been sent from England, a long way off Cadiz, had them painted the same colour as his blockading fleet, then swapped them for most of his own fleet, leaving the Spanish unaware that another fleet had been sent to join Nelson.

British intelligence was lamentably defective as to the destination of the huge fleet being prepared at Toulon which the French had dubbed, to confuse the British, the Left Wing of the Army of England. A French

newspaper had deliberately hinted that the force was being prepared for an attack on England or Ireland, and it seemed likely that the idea was to link up with the Brest fleet to attack either. *The Times* considered Portugal or Ireland the most likely targets. Pitt himself opined on 31 May that the destination was Ireland. Accordingly he requested a 'report on the arrangements which were made, for the internal defence of these kingdoms, when Spain, by its Armada, projected the invasion and conquest of England; and application of the wise proceedings of our ancestors, to the present crisis of public safety.'

This involved all the usual paraphernalia of national defence: the building of blockhouses in each of London's squares and the placing of barricades, alarm bells and a supply of hand grenades in each street. 'All obnoxious foreigners [were] to be sent out of the country . . . no foreign servants, male or female [were] to be allowed' and prisoners of war were to be put into prison ships 'so that they may be destroyed in cases necessary for the defence of the country'. The Aliens Bill was revived and habeas corpus suspended. Fortunately, very few of these preparations were put into effect. However, the suspicion was now beginning to dawn on Nelson that the French were destined for Egypt. By 17 June, discovering that the French had given him the slip from Toulon, he had travelled down to Naples, where the ever-welcoming Sir William Hamilton had intelligence that the French had gone to Malta. Nelson wrote, with his usual insight: 'I shall believe that they are going on their scheme of possessing Alexandria, and getting troops to India – a plan concerted with Tippoo Sahib, by no means so difficult as might at first view be imagined.'

Having at last divined the French intention, Nelson turned to attack. Believing the French fleet to be no more than six days' sailing time ahead, he crowded on the canvas. On 20 June he pushed through the Strait of Messina between Italy and Sicily: the French armada was about 160 miles away. Napoleon to his consternation also learnt of the presence of a new, reinforced British fleet moving towards the eastern Mediterranean and set off towards Crete to baffle his pursuers:

On nearly parallel eastward courses, the two fleets, one immense, the other compact, came within a few tantalizing miles of each other on

the night of 22–23 June, which was shrouded in dense fog. The smaller British fleet, under as much sail as it could, simply cruised past the cumbersome slow-moving French armada with its vulnerable troop transports.

Nelson sent the *Mutine*, commanded by Captain Harvey, as his advance ship to Alexandria. There Harvey was dismayed to discover nothing except a few local craft at anchor. Once again the speed of the British was to blame: he had arrived ahead of Napoleon. The highly-strung Nelson was disconsolate. It seemed he had been in error after all: the French must have sailed west.

The following day, in a state of nervous exhaustion, he at last gave the order to sail west, back to Sicily. As he told Troubridge later: 'My return to Syracuse in 1798 broke my heart . . . On the 18th I had near died with the swelling of some of the vessels of the heart.' He wrote to Fanny: 'I have not been able to find the French fleet, to my great mortification . . . I yet live in hopes of meeting these fellows, but it would have been my delight to have tried Bonaparte on a wind; for he commands the fleet as well as the army . . . We have gone a round of 600 leagues, with an expedition incredible, and I am as yet as ignorant of the situation of the enemy as I was twenty-seven days ago.'

The very same evening that he had set sail away from the direction of Alexandria the French arrived off the port. Napoleon, well aware of the danger to his expedition every day his army stayed aboard ship with a hostile British fleet cruising around the area, ordered its disembarkation with characteristic speed on 1 July.

Chapter 34

BATTLE OF THE PYRAMIDS

Only two days earlier Napoleon had at last revealed his destination to his cramped, surly troops in a declaration that was as eloquent as it was avowedly humane:

Soldiers!

You are about to undertake a conquest whose effects on the world's civilization and trade are incalculable.

You will inflict upon England a blow which is certain to wound her in her most sensitive spot, while waiting for the day when you can deal her the death blow.

We shall make some wearisome marches; we shall fight a few battles; we shall succeed in all our enterprises; destiny is for us.

The Mameluke beys, who exclusively favour English trade, who have oppressed our merchants with vexations, and who are tyrannising over the unhappy people of the Nile valley, will cease to exist a few days after our landing.

The people with whom we shall live are Mohammedans. Their chief creed is this: 'There is no God but God, and Mohammed is His prophet.'

Do not contradict them. Act toward them as in the past you have acted toward the Jews and the Italians. Respect their muftis and imams, as you have respected the rabbis and the bishops.

Show the same tolerance toward the ceremonies prescribed by the Koran and toward the mosques as you have shown toward convents and synagogues, toward the religions of Moses and of Jesus Christ.

The Roman legions used to protect all religions. You will find here customs quite different from those of Europe; you must become used to them.

The people of the countries where we are going treat their women differently from the way we do: but, in all countries, the man who rapes a woman is a monster.

Looting enriches but a few. It dishonours us, it destroys our resources, and it turns the people whom we want to befriend into our enemies.

The first city we shall see was built by Alexander. At every step we shall find tales of deeds worthy of being emulated by the French.

Napoleon ordered the disembarkation to proceed at once at Marabur Beach, some eight miles west of Alexandria, overruling the protestations of Admiral Brueys that the area was unsafe and that the gale was increasing in vehemence. The landing was a nightmare, with many boats filled with troops capsizing as darkness enveloped them.

Napoleon had little concern for casualties among his own men. He was certain of the rightness of his decision to get the majority ashore immediately. He had landed earlier and reviewed soaked troops under the full moon, ordering them to proceed onwards immediately to take Alexandria. The men, many of whom had taken eight hours to land across the three miles of rough sea and shoals that separated the shore from the ships, had no supplies, no artillery, no appropriate clothes, no food and no drinking water.

Napoleon led the way on foot. Lieutenant Thurman described the army's ordeal: 'I can assure you that it was thirst which inspired our soldiers in the capture of Alexandria. At the point the army had reached, we had no choice between finding water and perishing.' This was bad enough at night; but when the sun rose the exhausted men found themselves parched. Meanwhile Bedouin horsemen gathered in increasing numbers, rounding up stragglers, including many women.

Arriving outside Alexandria at about 8 a.m., Napoleon sat exhausted beneath Pompey's Pillar outside the city, while its governor frantically sought reinforcements from Cairo. He had just one barrel of gunpowder and a few horsemen to defend ancient walls riddled with

breaches. Then the French marched forward in disciplined lines to attack while the defenders loosed off a volley of gunshots, stones and screams. Both Generals Kleber and Menou were injured, but the assault was quickly accomplished. The defenders retired to the inner citadel, where occasional snipers fired on the French. Private Millet described what happened next:

> We already thought that the city had surrendered and were quite surprised when a volley of musketry was fired at us as we were passing by a mosque . . . A general who happened to be there ordered us to force the gate and to spare no one we found inside. Men, women, and children . . . perished under our bayonets. However, since human feelings are stronger than vengeance, the massacre ceased when they cried for mercy: about one third of them were spared.

A large delegation of inhabitants surrendered to the French and Napoleon soon made his entrance. A sniper opened fire upon him, narrowly missing his foot. Napoleon issued a remarkable proclamation promising Egyptians their liberty:

> In the name of God, the clement and the merciful. There is no divinity save Allah; He has no son and shares His power with no one.
>
> In the name of the French Republic, founded on liberty and equality, the commander-in-chief of the French armies, Bonaparte [lets it be known that] the beys who govern Egypt have insulted the French nation and oppressed French merchants long enough: the hour of their punishment has come.
>
> For too many years that gang of slaves, purchased in Georgia and the Caucasus, has tyrannized over the most beautiful region of the world. But Almighty God, who rules the universe, has decreed that their reign shall come to an end.
>
> Peoples of Egypt, you will be told that I have come to destroy your religion. This is an obvious lie. Do not believe it! Answer back to those impostors that I have come to restore to you your rights and to punish the usurpers; that I worship God more than the Mame-

lukes do; and that I respect His prophet Mohammed and the admirable Koran.

Tell them that all men are equal before God. Intelligence, virtue, and knowledge alone differentiate them from one another.

Now tell us, by what intelligence, virtues, or knowledge have the Mamelukes distinguished themselves to possess an exclusive right to everything that makes life agreeable and sweet?

Is there a beautiful estate? It belongs to the Mamelukes. Is there a beautiful slave, horse, or house? All this belongs to the Mamelukes.

If Egypt be their farm, then let them produce the deed by which God gave it to them in fee. But God is righteous and merciful to the people. Henceforth, with His help, no Egyptian shall be excluded from high office, and all shall be able to reach the highest positions; those who are the most intelligent, educated, and virtuous shall govern, and thus the people shall be happy.

Once you had great cities, large canals, a prosperous trade. What has destroyed all this, if not the greed, the iniquity, and the tyranny of the Mamelukes?

Kadis, sheiks, imams, tchorbadjis and notables of the country, tell the people that the French also are true Moslems. The proof is that they have been to Rome the great and have destroyed the throne of the Pope, who always incited the Christians to make war on the Moslems, and that they went to the island of Malta and expelled the Knights, who fancied that God wanted them to make war on the Moslems. Besides, the French have shown at all times that they are the particular friends of His Majesty the Ottoman Sultan (may God perpetuate his rule!) and the enemies of his enemies. The Mamelukes, on the contrary, always have refused to obey him; they never comply with his orders and follow only their whims.

Happy, thrice happy are those Egyptians who side with us. They shall prosper in fortune and rank. Happy are those who stay in their dwellings without taking sides with either of the parties now at war. When they know us better, they will hasten to join us in all sincerity.

But woe, woe to those who side with the Mamelukes and help them to make war on us. There shall be no salvation for them, and their memory shall be wiped out.

Napoleon saw himself not as a colonial conquistador but as a civilising force seeking to free the oppressed of Egypt from their existing colonial masters, but this was a spectacular misreading of the history of Egypt. Egypt was indeed something of a suppliant nation under the yoke of foreign oppressors; but it did not follow that the French were any more welcome.

The government of Egypt when Napoleon arrived was one of the most unusual in the world. The country was technically a province of the Ottoman empire, France's traditional ally, which had been captured by Suleiman the Magnificent's father in 1517, who accepted the title of Caliph, or spiritual ruler. But he left in place a state of twenty-four provinces ruled by Mameluke beys, or governors, who together formed a ruling council, the diwan, presided over by the Turkish proconsul, the Pasha. In practice the only real power exercised by the Caliph and the Pasha was that of raising tribute from the Egyptians, which was all indeed that the Ottomans were really interested in.

Real power lay in the hands of the Mamelukes, a warrior caste dating back to 1230 who, astonishingly, hailed from the Caucasus, being mostly Georgians and Circassians. There were some 12,000 of these, brought in as a private army by the early sultans. They married only among their own race, although they kept Egyptian harems; they did not have children by their wives or concubines, because the women preferred to abort themselves rather than lose their looks. Instead boys of between eight and ten years old were brought from the Caucasus and trained as warriors.

This caste was entirely parasitic, living off the Egyptians, oppressing the local population and fighting among themselves. They were reputed to be the best horsemen in the world, superb fighters and savagely cruel towards those they oppressed. As a near contemporary account states: 'The youthful slave, purchased with a heedful reference to his strength and personal appearance, was carefully trained to arms in the family of his master. When created a Mameluke, he was received into the troop of the Bey, and rendered capable of succeeding to him at his death; for these chiefs despised the ordinary connections of blood, and their authority was, upon military principles, transferred at their death to him amongst the band who was accounted the best soldier.'

The French calculated that the Bedouin tribes who roamed the desert with their nomadic flocks and sheep and herds of cattle, and the fellahs, the farmers of the fertile land around the Nile, would welcome the enlightened French in freeing them from the savage yoke of this alien white caste. This proved a sadly mistaken assumption. But Napoleon's second belief, that a disciplined French army equipped with modern arms and tactics could overcome more traditional warriors, however fearless, proved correct.

Napoleon's initial tactics were brutally simple and probably justified: to press forward as fast as possible and overawe and overwhelm the enemy before it had a chance to gather its forces. This, however, required a characteristic indifference towards the suffering of his own men. Having captured Alexandria, Napoleon secured the release of the prisoners taken on the night's march from the beach. It turned out that the men, whose pale skins were attractive to the tribesmen, had been repeatedly raped while the women were merely beaten. This proved a powerful deterrent to stragglers from the main force and frequently French soldiers who fell behind in the heat or had fallen ill preferred to shoot themselves rather than fall into enemy hands.

Napoleon ordered his army forward to Damanhur and Rosetta, at the Nile delta, and then forward to join up at El Rahmaniyah further up the river – altogether a march of sixty miles. The routes were across semi-desert, and the troops had only dried husks to eat and nothing with which to carry water. At the first stop, there were only two nearly empty wells to provide water for 4,600 men. Lieutenant Vertray described the scene: 'It was a pity to see men stretched on their bellies around that fetid hole, dying of thirst, panting and unable to satisfy their craving. I have seen, with my own eyes, dying men beg and implore their comrades for pity, while those comrades were fighting among themselves over a little dirty water. I saw some of them die in torture.'

When they reached Damanhur, an impoverished town, a cavalry commander, General Mireur, berated Napoleon for leading the army into a hopeless and irresponsible war, and then walked out into the desert, where he may have been robbed and killed, or may have shot himself.

At El Rahmaniyah the troops went delirious with joy to see the Nile. As Lieutenant Desvernois reported: 'The soldiers broke ranks to throw themselves into it. Some kept their clothes, even their weapons. Others took the time to undress, then ran to the water, dived into it, and stayed in it for several hours. Many found their death by drinking too greedily.' There were large fields covered with water-melons (about the only thing that grew at that season); the soldiers gorged themselves on them, and they continued to eat water-melons, and practically nothing but water-melons, all the way to the site of the Battle of the Pyramids, which itself was a water-melon field.

Napoleon meanwhile received intelligence that Murad Bey, the Emir al-Hadj, leader of the annual pilgrimage to Mecca and virtual ruler of Cairo, was assembling an army. Murad Bey was a huge, pale-skinned man sporting a shaggy golden beard. He had married the enormously wealthy widow of a former ruler of Egypt, Napiss, and ruled through the distribution of spoils and his own mixture of cruelty and courage. He lived in a huge palace at Giza with an enormous harem.

Napoleon ordered the army to march overnight on 12 July and instructed it to observe the strictest discipline as the only means of defeating the enemy. The following morning the French saw the Mameluke cavalry drawn up in formation westwards from the Nile, barring their path. Desvernois recalled:

In the background, the desert under the blue sky; before us, the beautiful Arabian horses, richly harnessed, snorting, neighing, prancing gracefully and lightly under their martial riders, who are covered with dazzling arms, inlaid with gold and precious stones. Their costumes are brilliantly colourful; their turbans are surmounted by aigret feathers, and some wear gilded helmets. They are armed with sabres, lances, maces, spears, rifles, battle axes, and daggers, and each has three pairs of pistols . . . This spectacle produced a vivid impression on our soldiers by its novelty and richness. From that moment on, their thoughts were set on booty.

The Mamelukes had trained their horses to perfection to canter and stop at a moment's notice. They carried carbines which, once fired,

would be slid under their shoulders; they then fired their pistols. They threw javelins and for hand-to-hand fighting wielded scimitars which could split a man's head in half. They were large, handsome Caucasians. They attacked magnificently, but found themselves faced by French infantry squares which sent forth deafening, disciplined volleys of shot as they approached. The French drove the Mameluke horsemen off with no losses of their own.

On the Nile itself, two rival flotillas exchanged 1,500 rounds of artillery in a fierce firefight and the seven Mameluke Greek-manned gunboats were winning until four French gunboats succeeded in blowing up the Mameluke flagship. The victorious French troops now resumed their march towards Cairo, looting mud villages and slaughtering their inhabitants as they went. In one village alone, 900 men, women and children are believed to have perished. The officers could do nothing: the men were crazed with thirst, weariness and bloodlust.

On 21 July the French found that the main Mameluke army was drawn up waiting for them in front of Cairo, with the Great Pyramids in the distance. Napoleon ordered his men to draw up into the familiar squares and declared theatrically: 'Soldiers, forty centuries look down on you!' The Battle of the Pyramids has been described as one of Napoleon's greatest victories. It was hardly that, although the Mamelukes did have the advantage of fighting on their own chosen terrain.

The French had overwhelming superiority of firepower and numbers – some 25,000 men compared to 6,000 Mameluke cavalry and perhaps 15,000 infantry. (Napoleon himself wildly exaggerated the Mameluke numbers at 78,000 men, which exceeded the total known to be in all of Egypt.) The Mameluke warrior style was, as before, no match for modern French tactics and arms. Lieutenant Vertray described the scene:

> General Reynier gave the order, 'Form your ranks' and, in an instant, we had formed our square, ten men deep, to absorb the shock. This manoeuvre was executed with truly extraordinary precision and sang-froid . . . The soldiers fired with such coolness

that not a single cartridge was wasted, waiting until the very instant
when the horsemen were about to break our square. The number of
corpses surrounding our square soon was considerable, and the
clothes of the dead and wounded Mamelukes were burning like
tinder . . . The blazing wads of our muskets penetrated at the same
time as our bullets through their rich uniforms, which were
embroidered with gold and silver and floated as lightly as gauze.
Nevertheless the Mamelukes fought bravely and hopelessly with
unbelievable ferocity for an hour.

Meanwhile French artillery was shelling the Mameluke infantry with
howitzers in their rear. Seeing this, Murad Bey ordered a retreat
towards the Pyramids. Their defensive fortifications were then taken
amidst much carnage, the defenders fleeing to the Nile, where
hundreds were drowned. It was a biblical scene. Another force of
Mamelukes on the east bank of the Nile managed to reach Cairo and
gather up some of their possessions before fleeing into the Sinai desert.
Around 1,200 had been killed against French losses of 250 dead and
seventy wounded.

It had been little short of a massacre, and only the Mamelukes'
extraordinary courage had preserved their honour and inflicted significant losses on the French. Napoleon had seized his chance with
characteristically brutal efficiency. It was certainly no great feat of arms,
simply a typical colonial victory of superior European weaponry.

That night some 300 Mameluke sailing vessels, set alight by their
own owners to stop them falling into French hands, lent the desert a
vivid glow, while French soldiers frantically tried to put the flames out
from the riverbank to salvage the valuables aboard. Desvernois found
on one cavalryman he had killed on land rich booty – a 'canary-yellow
turban made of cashmere . . . more than five hundred gold pieces sewn
into his skull cap . . . a magnificent sabre, its sheath and pommel inlaid
with gold; its handle was a rhinoceros horn, and the blade was black
Damascus steel.'

On 22 July Napoleon entered Cairo, contemptuously remarking
that the 300,000 inhabitants were 'the world's ugliest rabble'. He was
not alone in being unimpressed. Major Detroye commented viciously:

Once you enter Cairo, what do you find? Narrow, unpaved, and dirty streets, dark houses that are falling to pieces, public buildings that look like dungeons, shops that look like stables, an atmosphere redolent of dust and garbage, blind men, half-blind men, bearded men, people dressed in rags, pressed together in the streets or squatting, smoking their pipes, like monkeys at the entrance of their cave; a few women of the people . . . hideous, disgusting, hiding their fleshless faces under stinking rags and displaying their pendulous breasts through their torn gowns; yellow, skinny children covered with suppuration, devoured by flies; an unbearable stench, due to the dirt in the houses, the dust in the air, and the smell of food being fried in bad oil in the unventilated bazaars.

When you have finished sight-seeing, you return to your house. No comfort, not a single convenience. Flies, mosquitoes, a thousand insects are waiting to take possession of you during the night. Bathed in sweat, exhausted, you spend the hours devoted to rest itching and breaking out in boils. You rise in the morning, unutterably sick, bleary-eyed, queasy in the stomach, with a bad taste in your mouth, your body covered with pimples, or rather ulcers. Another day begins, the exact copy of the preceding one.

Napoleon occupied a superb, well-equipped palace but was keenly aware of the need to provide for his force of colonialists. He sent off a letter to France demanding: 'a troupe of actors; a troupe of ballerinas; at least three or four puppeteers, for the common people; about a hundred French-women; the wives of all those serving in this country; twenty surgeons, thirty pharmacists, ten physicians; foundry workers; liqueur manufacturers and distillers; about fifty gardeners and their families, and seeds of every variety of vegetable; . . . 300,000 reels of blue and scarlet cloth; soap and oil.' Nothing ever arrived, for soon he was to be entirely cut off from the mother country. Napoleon could have little inkling that he was about to experience the greatest disaster of his life so far, and the third most humiliating experience of his entire career.

Chapter 35

BATTLE OF THE NILE

At first it seemed that Horatio Nelson was the one who had been made to look a fool: his roller-coaster career appeared about to plunge again as it became apparent that the French fleet had completely eluded him at the beginning of July – hence his condition of manic nervous exhaustion. Would his triumph at St Vincent and bravery at Tenerife outweigh the blow to his reputation as the man who let the French fleet slip through his fingers?

The British press, fickle as ever, was beginning to turn. *The Times* commented that it was extraordinary that a fleet of 200 vessels should have eluded Nelson for so long. The *Morning Chronicle* said that a more experienced commander should have been chosen, perhaps St Vincent himself. The *Herald* agreed: 'Perhaps it may not be amiss to employ the gallantry of Admiral Nelson under the good fortune of others, until his turn comes around.'

Nelson himself, after his frenzied chase, now lapsed into inexplicable inertia while his ships were revictualled at Syracuse. It was surely his duty to resume the chase as quickly as possible, to find out whether the French fleet had indeed gone west or remained in the eastern Mediterranean rather than dawdle for three weeks at anchor. His newly acquired golden touch seemed to have faded. Nelson did not leave Syracuse until 23 July to resume his search, travelling eastwards again, directly towards the Peloponnese. Five days later he at last heard reliable news that the French fleet was at Alexandria and sailed south.

Just over three days later, at a quarter to three on the fateful afternoon of 1 August, a lookout from the masthead of the *Zealous*

shouted that he had spotted a huge line of topmasts against the sky. Captain Howard signalled the news to Nelson in his flagship, the *Vanguard*. Instantly he threw off his depression. He summoned his officers to dinner and declared that the following morning he would either be in the House of Lords or Westminster Abbey.

He ordered his captains to proceed under full sail with a favourable following wind to attack the French fleet. He later recalled:

> When I saw them [the French ships] I could not help popping my head every now and then out of the window (although I had a damned toothache) and once, as I was observing their position, I heard two seamen, quartered at a gun near me, talking, and one said to the other, 'Damn them, look at them. There they are, Jack, if we don't beat them, they will beat us.' I knew what stuff I had under me so I went into the attack with a few ships only, perfectly sure that the others would follow me, although it was nearly dark and they might have had every cause for not doing it, yet they all in the course of two hours found a hole to poke in at.

Nelson had long discussed with his captains the tactics they should follow if they found the French fleet at anchor and therefore unable to flee: to attack if possible on both sides and engage only half the enemy line first, so as to bring overwhelming firepower to bear against each ship. It was a variation on Admiral Howe's tactics on the Glorious First of June, to attack when least expected, engage only part of the enemy, cut that part off and attack. The old dignified tactic of drawing up a parallel line-of-battle and engaging the enemy ship by ship was for Nelson as outdated as the frontal engagement in land war was for Napoleon. Nelson's second brilliant improvisation was simply that of going on the attack as soon as the French fleet had been spotted, even though this would inevitably mean fighting most of the battle at night. What followed was one of the most overwhelming and decisive naval victories in history, and also one of the bloodiest, with immediate and huge repercussions for the war as a whole.

★   ★   ★

There is a case for saying Napoleon was not primarily responsible for the impending debacle. Once the Directory had made up their minds to send the expedition to Egypt, it was inevitable that French ships and transports would be exposed to the possibility of sea attack by the British. This was surely a risk inherent in the whole project, and nothing Napoleon could have done would have entirely guaranteed its safety. But he also explicitly failed to give the French Admiral Brueys orders to sail for the safe port of Corfu. Instead he asked the admiral to decide which of two anchorages was safer – the port of Alexandria or Aboukir Bay to the east. Brueys was reluctant to be trapped in Alexandria harbour which could be blockaded and whose entrance was hard to navigate, and preferred Aboukir Bay, where he had a good anchorage and room to manoeuvre.

Admiral Brueys had had three weeks at Aboukir Bay to prepare his fleet for an attack. He had planned to link his ships together by cables and to keep them inshore so that the enemy could not slip between them and the coastline. He also intended to keep them close enough to the battery of mortars he had installed on Aboukir Island to make it suicidal for any ship to run the gauntlet between his fleet and the shore. Aboukir Island was a small outcrop just off Fort Aboukir, at the point of the crescent-shaped bay that ended with the mouth of the Nile. Both the island and the shore were protected by shoals and waters deemed too shallow for men of war to pass.

However Brueys had neglected to put the cables in place; nor had he bunched his ships close together, but spread them out over more than a mile; and in order to give them space to swing at anchor – traditionally about 200 yards was allowed between ship and anchor – had allowed for a narrow channel of deep water on the shore side of the ships. Worse, the ships' guns were all trained out to sea; most of the ones on the shore side were not even in place and the presence of stores there made it difficult to reposition them quickly.

Many of the crewmen, perhaps a third, were ashore, digging wells and gathering provisions when the British fleet was sighted. For this at least Brueys cannot be faulted: he promptly signalled for them to return aboard, but only a fraction did. Brueys, a cautious man, expected the British attack to be mounted the following day, when Nelson's fleet

had had time to rest and get into position and Brueys could make his own dispositions at leisure.

The French comforted themselves in the knowledge that they enjoyed considerable superiority (Brueys underestimated the size of the British fleet). They had a 120-gun flagship, *L'Orient*, three 80-gun ships of the line, nine 74-gunners, four frigates and several gunboats. The British had twelve 74-gun ships of the line and a 50-gunner. The French disposed of some 200 more guns than the British. There were some 11,200 sailors aboard the French ships compared to 7,400 British.

Only at around four o'clock in the afternoon, as the British fleet approached under full sail, did the astonished French admiral realize Nelson's intention to attack at once. Brueys summoned his three senior admirals to discuss whether to meet the British at sea or at anchor. The arguments for staying at anchor prevailed: the French crews were inexperienced and could not be expected to sail and fight at the same time; the ships had only provisions for a day and could not escape into the Mediterranean; and three of the French battleships were anyway in poor condition.

The two foremost British ships, the *Zealous* under Captain Hood and the *Goliath* under Captain Foley, were in a race to be the first to engage. The *Goliath* ran up its staysails and suddenly pushed forward, taking the lead. Foley had a captured although inaccurate French chart and did not pause to make soundings as he aimed for the narrow gap between Aboukir Island and the foremost French ship, *Le Guerrier*.

Subsequently Foley claimed he had acted on his own initiative, and in a sense he had; but all the captains were aware of Nelson's tactics of engaging the enemy at anchor on both sides and Nelson had already told Hood to see if there was enough deep water between the island and the French. 'Where there was room for a French ship to swing [at anchor] there was room for an English ship to pass,' Nelson had been fond of saying.

George Elliot (later Sir George), then a midshipman aboard Foley's ship, took up the story:

When we were nearly within gunshot, standing close to Captain Foley I heard him say to the master that he wished he could get

inside the leading ship of the enemy's line. I immediately looked for the buoy on her anchor, and saw it apparently at the usual distance of a cable's length (200 yards), which I reported. They both looked at it and agreed there was room to pass between the ship and her anchor . . . the master then had orders to go forward and drop the anchor the moment it was a ship's breadth inside the French ship, so that we should not exactly swing on board of her. All this was exactly executed.

The mortars on the island opened up, but their range fell short. The sun was just beginning to set spectacularly fast off the Egyptian coast, the giant red ball visibly inching towards the horizon at around 6.30, when Foley gave the order to fire as he arched around *Le Guerrier* and a full broadside rocked the French ship. Foley put out his anchor to stop the *Goliath*'s momentum, but it failed to 'bite' into the sea floor and the *Goliath* shot past to stop opposite *Le Conquerant*, the second ship in the French line, in time to fire a second broadside.

The French admiral in charge of the van, still on his way back from his meeting with Brueys, waved frantically at his captains to open fire – which they were reluctant to do without orders. By the time they did, the second ship, the *Zealous*, was in place to rake the unfortunate *Le Guerrier* with another broadside. The French response was lamentable: they had not even run out most of their guns.

The *Orion* followed the other two ships, dangerously close to the shoals, and slipped in to engage the third French ship on the inside. A French frigate had the temerity to open fire on it, and was destroyed with a single broadside from the *Orion*, which had also raked *Le Guerrier* a third time, bringing down its remaining mast and leaving it a wreck. The *Orion* engaged two ships simultaneously.

The *Theseus* came next, once again pouring shot into *Le Guerrier*, and then navigated the small channel between the British and French ships between broadsides, exchanging fire with the latter, before curving around the *Orion* to engage another French ship; all of this was flawless seamanship of the highest order. The French guns' elevation was aimed at the other British ships; so the *Theseus* took advantage to run under the arch of the shot. Another British ship

followed on the inside. The British ships could be distinguished in the darkness by the four horizontal lights on the mizzen peak.

Nelson, in his flagship the *Vanguard*, was next and led the way down the outside of the French line, engaging its third ship, the *Spartiate*, which was already under attack from the *Theseus*, between two fires. Pounded by a combined total of 148-guns, the ship quickly surrendered. The *Bellerophon*, behind the *Vanguard*, found itself in the already fallen darkness engaging the huge French flagship, *L'Orient*, with its 120-guns. Two of the *Bellerophon*'s masts fell under the intense fire from *L'Orient*, which set her on fire three times and killed a third of the crew before she drifted off to port crippled. Immediately three more British ships took up the fight against the deadly three-decker.

The brave but devastated *Le Guerrier* had by now struck her colours, as had two other French ships, the *Conquerant* and the *Spartiate*, attacked by Nelson. But he had once again been seriously wounded, an inch of skin falling from his brow over his good eye, with blood pouring down his face. 'I am killed,' he said, 'Remember me to my wife.' He was carried below for treatment. The French admiral, Brueys, likewise had no sooner dismasted the *Bellerophon* when he was hit, nearly cut in two by a cannonball at 7.30. He refused to go to the infirmary so that he might die on the bridge.

Meanwhile disaster had struck a British ship, the *Culloden*, commanded by Sir Thomas Troubridge, regarded as second only to Nelson in the British fleet. He had sailed too close to Aboukir Island and run aground. With two British ships out of action compared to three French, the battle was far from won.

Then, under fire from three much smaller ships, it became apparent that the giant *L'Orient* was ablaze. Some historians allege, based on a second-hand story from the poet Samuel Taylor Coleridge, that phosphorous firecrackers had been thrown on to the deck by the British: but this would have been very difficult to achieve with the three-decker French ship towering over the British ships and it was the French rather than the British that carried firecrackers. The French believed oil cans left behind by painters started the fire.

Ensign Lachenede described the crisis on *L'Orient*:

Everything at that moment contributed to increase the confusion. The pump, it was found, was broken; the hatches were hidden under mounds of debris; the buckets which we kept on the forecastle were scattered all over the place; we had to have some brought up from the holds; five ships had surrounded us and were firing at us with double intensity. After incredible but futile efforts, we left the bridge deck, which was covered with flaming corpses. The mainmast and the mizzen crashed toward port . . . The ship was burning fore and aft, and already the flames were reaching the 24-pounder battery. And yet in the 36-pounder battery, the men seemed to be unaware of the danger, and they continued to fire vigorously.

At about ten o'clock, after well over an hour fighting the fire, Admiral Ganteaume, who had succeeded Brueys, gave the order to abandon ship. A nine-year-old boy who refused to leave his injured father, Captain Casabianca, was immortalized as the boy who 'stood on the burning deck whence all but he had fled'. The colossal ship blew up a few minutes later, at about 10.15, with a blast that was felt some twenty-five miles away, lighting up Alexandria and Rosetta, sending blazing timbers and bodies far into the air.

After the awesome explosion, there was a ten-minute silence, as all the gunners on both sides, subdued by the spectacle, stopped firing. Out of 1,000 men aboard *L'Orient*, only seventy survived, including a lieutenant who was picked up by a British ship naked except for his hat, which he had saved, he explained, to prove he was an officer. With *L'Orient* sank some £600,000 (around £120 million in today's values) in gold coins, ingots and diamonds – the treasure looted from the Knights of Malta, which was supposed to finance Napoleon's expedition.

The French ship *Franklin* was the first to recommence firing after the deathly lull, although two-thirds of that ship's company had been killed or wounded. She surrendered at 11.30. Another French ship, *Le Peuple Souverain*, was a wreck by 11 p.m. *L'Artemise* drifted ashore and was set on fire by her crew; it blew up in the morning. By then the flagship was no more, six of the French ships had struck their colours, three ships

had gone ashore and the *Tonnant* was a floating wreck, although it ultimately surrendered with 120 men killed and 150 wounded. Only two French ships remained and made good their escape.

An inexplicable element of the whole battle was the failure of the commander of the rear, Admiral Villeneuve, to order his ships to come to the help of those in the van under attack. Napoleon was later scathing: 'It was only at 2 p.m. the following afternoon that Admiral Villeneuve seemed to take notice of the fact that there had been a battle going on for the past 18 hours . . . it was in Villeneuve's power to turn the battle into a French victory even as late as daybreak.' This is clearly unfair, but Villeneuve gave no satisfactory explanation. Still more inexplicable is that Napoleon, who was so frightened of being caught at anchorage by Nelson that he had disembarked his army on the very evening of their arrival, should have left the fleet exposed to British attack for a full month. Perhaps both Napoleon and Brueys genuinely did believe the anchorage at Aboukir Bay was impregnable: if so it was a huge risk to take, for the French navy rarely so exposed itself to the British. It was a colossal and unforgivable mistake on the part of both men.

Napoleon later accused Brueys of ignoring an explicit order to leave for Corfu. This account was directly contradicted by Vice-Admiral Ganteaume, in a subsequent despatch to the minister of war: 'Perhaps it may be said that it would have been advisable to have quitted the coast as soon as the disembarkation had taken place. But considering the orders of the commander-in-chief, and the incalculable force afforded to the land-army by the presence of the squadron, the admiral thought it was his duty not to quit these seas.' Brueys was killed in the battle, so was unable to defend himself. But probably, if granted permission, he would have sailed his ships to safety on Corfu. Almost certainly Napoleon's calumny against Brueys was a lie to protect his own reputation.

It was a famous victory indeed. The French fleet had been virtually annihilated. The French had lost eleven of their thirteen battleships and some 4,000 men to two British ships and some 900 men. More than 3,000 French prisoners had been taken, most of whom were later set loose ashore, as the British could not care for them. At a stroke the

British were masters of the Mediterranean, although a considerable French fleet still remained in the Atlantic. Napoleon's army in Egypt was stranded. True, the troop transports remained at Alexandria, but without the protection of the French fleet they could be picked off at will by the British.

Nelson, in the aftermath of the battle, despatched Sir James Saumarez with six French prizes to Gibraltar and himself left with three ships for Naples, leaving behind three battleships and three frigates to blockade the coast of Egypt. All communications between Napoleon's army and France had been severed. Nelson decided against an attack on Alexandria itself because he believed the French defences there to be stronger than they actually were: Generals Kléber and Menou were fearful that he would attempt an attack.

Napoleon, when he learnt of the disaster on 13 August, feigned indifference. He told his officers: 'Well, gentlemen, now we are obliged to accomplish great things: we shall accomplish them. We must found a great empire, and we shall found it. The sea, of which we are no longer master, separates us from our homeland, but no sea separates us from either Africa or Asia.'

Yet the impression further afield of the most unqualified naval victory in the whole conflict was immense. It was felt in Russia, where the new Tsar Paul – the pro-British Catherine had died in 1796 – now began to end his francophile policy and move towards hostility towards France. It was felt in Austria, which was emboldened to re-enter the war against revolutionary France. It was felt in Constantinople, where the Ottoman Emperor had watched aghast Napoleon's invasion of one of his great provinces. Above all it was felt in Britain, which was desperately in need of good news. A joyous mob gathered in Whitehall, forcing all those who wore hats to doff them in tribute, in an early display of crowd power. Hood said Nelson had saved Europe from anarchy and misery, while Lady Spencer exulted: 'Joy, joy, joy to you, brave gallant, immortal Nelson! May that great God, whose cause you so valiantly support, protect and bless you to the end of your brilliant career. Such a race surely never was won. My heart is absolutely bursting with different sensations of joy, of gratitude, of pride, of every

emotion that ever warmed the bosom of a British woman – and all produced by you, my dear, my good friend.' Lady Hamilton wrote to him: 'If I was King of England, I would make you the most noble, puissant Duke Nelson, Marquis Nile, Earl Alexandria, Viscount Pyramid, Baron Crocodile and Prince Victory, that posterity might have you in all forms.'

When Nelson arrived in Naples after the Battle of the Nile, Queen Maria Carolina exclaimed, 'Oh brave Nelson! Oh God bless you and protect our brave deliverer.' The simple-minded King Ferdinand called him his 'deliverer and preserver'. Suddenly it seemed for the first time that French domination of Europe was not inevitable after all and that those few places such as Naples which still held out could survive. Nelson was made a baron – Lord Nelson of the Nile. Pitt had wanted to confer a viscountcy, but the King was reluctant to confer even a peerage, perhaps disapproving of his support of Prince William. There was a small outcry that he had not been granted a greater title. Pitt ordained that a pension of £20,000 a year be set up for Nelson and his two male heirs (£4 million at today's values). Fanny Nelson was received by the Queen.

Nelson himself suffered nausea and splitting headaches from his new wound, and was also plagued again by malaria. He increasingly felt himself to be a child of destiny, writing that 'Almighty God has made me the happy instrument in destroying the enemy's fleet'. His mood was understandable. After his career had once more teetered with his failure to find the French fleet, its destruction had conferred greatness beyond any expectation. He had served God, the King and his country to the very summit of duty and glory. Moreover he felt himself increasingly under divine protection, for he always sensed he was close to the next world. He had nearly died in the Indies of disease; he had nearly died in Nicaragua of illness; in Cape St Vincent he had risked his life in open combat; he had nearly been killed in Tenerife; now again he had escaped death by the narrowest of margins.

Yet as so often with this strange, attractive, romantic, severe, duty-driven genius of a naval commander, pride came before a fall, hubris was followed by nemesis. Sailing to Naples to have his crippled flagship refitted, he was greeted by the kind of welcome only the Neapolitans

can give. When the *Vanguard* arrived on 22 September, it was surrounded by a flotilla of boats and music. Nelson was lodged in the splendid palazzo of Sir William and Lady Hamilton, who bathed his wounds in ass's milk. On his fortieth birthday, some 1,700 people were invited to a ball, eighty of them supping with the Hamiltons. The Sultan of the Ottoman empire sent him an aigrette, a superbly embossed if bizarre clockwork jewel.

Hamilton persuaded Nelson that he had an even greater role to play: to help expel the French, who he suggested were seeking to annex Naples, from Italy. Nelson agreed with him and Queen Maria Carolina that unless the King took action he would be deposed by the French. In November the King was persuaded to send a force northwards under the Austrian General Mack, while Troubridge was despatched to help the Duke of Tuscany in Leghorn to outflank the French rear. A week later Ferdinand was in Rome taking up residence in the Farnese Palace.

The triumph was shortlived. A week later a formidable French army marched on Rome, taking 10,000 Neapolitans prisoner and most of the rest hastily abandoned their baggage. On the King's return, the Queen became fearful of a French-inspired uprising by Jacobins and recalled the fate of her sister, Marie Antoinette. Nelson summoned Troubridge's squadrons from Leghorn and agreed to carry the royal family and their court to the safety of Palermo in Sicily. This infuriated the Neapolitan naval commander, Count Caracciolo.

Emma Hamilton is said to have led the royal family through a secret passage from the royal palace to the harbour. The *Vanguard* was piled high with royal Neapolitan treasures – around £2½ million worth (£500 million in today's currency). Bad weather kept the ship in harbour for a day in deadly peril of discovery, and the passage across to Sicily was, according to Nelson, the worst weather he had ever experienced. The royal family were in the depths of despair and their youngest child, Prince Albert, died on the voyage in Emma Hamilton's arms.

The royal family was however greeted with rapture in Palermo, and Ferdinand was soon engaged in his favourite pastime, hunting. Meanwhile the French took Naples and proclaimed it a republic on

Christmas Eve. It was a small compensation for the loss of their fleet at the Battle of the Nile. What exactly the victor of that battle – whose job it was to harass the French throughout the Mediterranean – was doing as an aide to this corrupt Bourbon court was a question that increasingly exercised the minds of his British superiors.

Chapter 36

THE UPPER NILE

Napoleon, his boats now literally burnt behind him by his enemy, had no alternative but to press on with his surreal adventure into Egypt. For all his triumphalism, it was soon apparent that he controlled only three cities – Cairo, Alexandria and Rosetta – and was confronted by the sullen hostility of the population. At El Mansura, for example, a local French garrison was massacred by the inhabitants. The only survivor, Private Mourchon, gave this vivid description:

General Vial, when passing through El Mansura, left a detachment of 120 men . . . The day after General Vial left with his battalion, three soldiers of the garrison were assassinated by the inhabitants, one being stoned while standing guard duty, another while bringing soup to a sentry, the third while returning from his post . . .

From then on, we barricaded ourselves in the house we used for a barracks . . . [About two days later] at approximately 8 am, the barracks was surrounded by a large number of Moslems, carrying various weapons. One of them tried to set the house on fire . . . but was killed by one of our dragoons: they then tried to tear the house down. In short, the fighting . . . lasted until 4 pm. We then marched out of the house, in which we had lost eight men . . . As we marched through the streets to leave the town, we were shot at continuously from the windows; we returned the fire as best we could. When we reached the open country, the same individuals pursued us and kept firing. Some of them ran to nearby villages to look for reinforcements.

. . . During the retreat, a bullet traversed my left thigh . . . At daybreak, there were twenty-five or thirty of us left, and we were still pursued by the enemy . . . Having run out of cartridges, we defended ourselves with steel. The wounded, of whom there were ten, preferred drowning themselves to falling into the enemy's hands. When only fifteen of us were left, a multitude of infuriated peasants threw themselves upon us, stripped us of our clothes, and massacred us, my comrades and me, with clubs; I threw myself into the Nile all naked with the intention of drowning myself, but since I can swim, instinct proved the stronger and I reached the opposite shore . . . I began to walk without any fixed purpose.

I saw seven Moslem horsemen approaching and threw myself into the Nile again. Having noticed that two of them were beckoning to me, I returned on shore; one of them fired at me pointblank, but his carbine jammed; the other said something to the effect that I should be spared and handed me over to two armed peasants . . . who tied my hands and led me to a village along a thorny path on which I suffered much, being barefoot and wounded. At the village, the inhabitants unbound me, took care of me, fed me, and showed me much kindness. I remained thus . . . until today, when the villagers came . . . to tell me that a barge loaded with French soldiers was passing by . . . I cannot omit mentioning that the person who took care of me most was a child about eight years old who secretly brought me boiled eggs and bread.

Outside Rosetta, General Menou's party was set upon by armed peasants, and the painter Joly was murdered. Most of the passengers of a French ship that reached Marabut were massacred by Bedouins.

Napoleon's response to the loss of his entire fleet and the precariousness of his grip upon Egypt was entirely characteristic: he pushed ahead with his make-believe attempt to turn the country into a colony and persuade the inhabitants of his benevolence. Meanwhile he continued with his military effort to subdue the rest of the country: for Napoleon, attack was always the best form of defence.

Napoleon attempted at first to woo the tribal chiefs, with limited

success; his efforts at making friends with his defeated enemy, Murad
Bey, were rebuffed, as were his peace feelers to the governor of Acre,
Ahmad Pasha, known as Djezzar (the Butcher), the Pasha of Damascus
and the Bey of Tripoli. Unknown to him, Talleyrand had broken his
promise to go to Constantinople and seek the Turkish government's
consent to the takeover of Egypt. Instead Talleyrand informed the
luckless French envoy there of France's intervention in Egypt in
brutally frank terms:

> All trade in the Mediterranean must . . . pass into French hands.
> This is the secret wish of the Directory, and, moreover, it will be the
> inevitable result of our position in that sea . . . Egypt, a country
> France always has desired, belongs of necessity to the Republic.
> Fortunately the consistently insolent and atrocious attitude of the
> beys toward us and the Porte's powerlessness to give us satisfaction
> have allowed us to introduce ourselves into Egypt and to fix
> ourselves there without exposing ourselves to the charges of law-
> lessness and ambition . . . The Directory is determined to maintain
> itself in Egypt by all possible means.

Following the news of the Battle of the Nile, the Turks steeled
themselves to declare war on France, locking up the unfortunate
envoy in a notorious dungeon, the Seven Towers. By thus swooping
on Ottoman Egypt, the French had antagonized the Russians, who
regarded themselves as the natural predators of the Ottoman empire,
and set themselves up in rivalry for its carcass. The result was foresee-
able: the Russians and the Turks, traditional enemies, now became
allies against the French. The people of Malta also rose up against the
French, who were confined to the towns there.

Napoleon blithely refused to believe the Turks had issued a firman
that the Egyptians should rise up against the French. He seemed to
believe that the Turks should welcome the French for seizing one of
their provinces. Instead he issued detailed orders for purifying water
and setting up windmills and water mills. He even on one occasion
dressed up in a turban and kaftan – until his appalled staff officers talked
him out of it.

Meanwhile he encouraged his scientists and scholars in the 'Institute' to pursue researches into Egypt. If there was to be one positive aspect of France's Egyptian experience, it was the extraordinary work of the French Egyptologists, scientists, scholars and experts on that ill-fated expedition. A detailed map of Egypt was drawn up by his cartographers. Napoleon's Egyptologists were transfixed when Captain Bouchard discovered the 'Rosetta stone', which proved much later to be the key to the ancient hieroglyphic Egyptian language. Napoleon meanwhile even offered to convert to Islam, provided he and his men were permitted to drink and were not subject to circumcision.

General Kléber, a more experienced general who was to succeed him in his command of Egypt, was bitterly critical of his methods:

> Never a fixed plan. Everything goes by fits and starts. Each day's business is transacted according to the needs of the day. He claims to believe in fate. He is incapable of organizing or administering anything; and yet, since he wants to do everything, he organizes and administers. Hence, chaos and waste everywhere. Hence our want of everything, and poverty in the midst of plenty. Is he loved? How could he be? He loves nobody. But he thinks he can make up for this by promotions and by gifts.

Many of Napoleon's edicts were deeply unpopular – in particular the taxes to pay for his army. He also took measures to regulate, for sanitary reasons, the slaughter of lambs, which often took place in the streets of Cairo. This incensed many people, as did his removal of the gates separating the many parts of the city and the imposition of a tax on property. Ordinary Egyptians were shocked by the way Frenchwomen refused to wear veils and disported themselves in public: they were afraid that Egyptian women would be similarly corrupted.

Finally, on 21 October, the explosion occurred. Nicholas the Turk, the main Islamic chronicler of the French occupation, wrote:

> One fine day some sheikh or other of El Azhar started to run through the streets, shouting, 'Let all those who believe that there is but one God take themselves to the Mosque El Azhar! For today is

the day to fight the Infidel.' Now, although most of the population was informed [of what was about to happen], the French were living in utter unconcern. In an instant, the city was boiling over, and news of it came to General Dupuy [the commandant of Cairo]. He was a very hard man. He leapt to his feet. 'What is going on?' – 'An uprising of the beggars of the city, who are gathered in the quarters of Khan Khalili and Nahhasin.' He left instantly, followed by only five horsemen . . . He rode to Khan Khalili and saw the populace and some workingmen erecting barricades. A Janissary suddenly appeared from around a street corner and hit him over the back with a police stick. The general fell from his horse. His men carried him off . . . but he died on the way.

The mob ran wild, attacking the French quarter and sacking the house of General Cafarelli which contained many of the most cherished French scientific instruments.

Napoleon, in a towering rage, ordered artillery to be directed at the El Azhar mosque, the centre of the insurrection, and then sent three infantry battalions and 300 horse to attack it, under General Dumas. They forced their way through the narrow, chaotic streets. An Egyptian chronicler, El-Djabarti, wrote: 'They entered the Mosque El Azhar with their horses and they tied them to the *kiblah*. They broke the lamps, the candles, and the desks of the students; they looted everything they could find in the closets; they threw on the ground the books and the Koran and trampled upon them with their boots. They urinated and spat in the mosque; they drank wine in it, and they broke the bottles and scattered the pieces in all the corners. They stripped everybody inside the mosque and took their clothes away.'

By the end of the following day, the insurrection was over, leaving some 3,000 Egyptians killed and 300 French dead. All those found carrying arms were executed, as were the members of the council of rebel leaders. 'Every night,' Napoleon boasted, 'we have about thirty heads chopped off.' It was a crowning display of ruthlessness, although he took no reprisals against ordinary people. Napoleon issued another megalomaniac pro-Islamic proclamation:

Sherifs, ulemas, preachers in the mosques, be sure to tell the people that those who, with a light heart, take sides against us shall find no refuge in either this world or the next. Is there a man so blind as not to see that destiny itself guides all my operations? . . . Let the people know that, from the creation of the world, it is written that after destroying the enemies of Islam and beating down the cross, I was to come from the confines of the Occident to accomplish my appointed task. Show the people that in more than twenty passages of the holy Koran what has happened has been foretold and what shall happen has been explained . . . If I chose, I could call each of you to account for the most hidden feelings of his heart, for I know everything, even what you have told to no one. But the day will come when all men shall see beyond all doubt that I am guided by orders from above and that all human efforts avail nought against me. Blessed are they who, in good faith, are the first to choose my side!

Napoleon seemed to win no local supporters through his loudly proclaimed tilt to Islam. Instead he merely witnessed the decline of his own forces. The Egyptian resistance had been emboldened by the destruction of the French fleet. As Nicholas the Turk put it: '[the people] knew for certain that the French had lost all hope of receiving aid from their own country . . . All we have to do is to resist them, to hold out against them, and we'll be rid of them in the end, for whatever does not grow must diminish.'

Meanwhile a plague broke out: thanks to Napoleon's own insistence upon hygiene, only 2,000 or so French troops were affected. Napoleon's methods were characteristically thorough for his men: 'Have them strip as naked as they were born and take a good sea bath. Make them rub themselves from head to foot, and make them wash their clothes . . . In consequence of the advice of the medical officers I ordered that all the buboes which did not appear likely to suppurate should be opened.' To encourage hospital staff, he decreed: 'Every day you will have a superior officer make the rounds of the hospitals . . . visit all the patients, and have all attendants and employees who refuse to give the required care and food to the patients shot on the spot in the courtyard of the hospital.'

With plague, killings by the locals and suicides decimating his troops, Napoleon decided to try and recruit locally. He set up a Mameluke Corps in his army. He also tried to recruit 'Black Mamelukes' – '2,000 black slaves over sixteen years old'. These ideas suggested that Napoleon was trying to create his own Egyptian empire, manned by his supporters, virtually independent from France: his ideas of racial integration were, at least, reasonably advanced.

At this stage six of Napoleon's generals – veterans who viewed him with some scepticism – wanted to return to France: they included Kléber, Menou, Berthier and Dumas. Kléber, Menou and Berthier were persuaded to stay, while Dumas left. Berthier, who was to serve as Napoleon's loyal and unbelievably efficient chief of staff for sixteen years, was an extraordinary figure, devoted to Napoleon and passionately in love with the faraway Madame Visconti. Napoleon later observed wonderingly:

I never saw a passion like that of Berthier for Madame Visconti. In Egypt, he would watch the moon at the same time that she was supposed to look at it herself. In the middle of the desert, he put up a tent for her cult: he put Madame Visconti's portrait inside it and burned incense there. Three mules were used to transport this tent and his baggage. Often I would enter and lie down on the sofa with my boots on. It made Berthier furious; he thought it was a profanation of the sanctuary. He loved her so much that he provoked me into talking about her, although I always spoke ill of her. He didn't care; he was delighted if one talked about her at all. He even wanted to leave the army to go back to her. I had my despatches all ready, received his parting wishes, assigned him an *aviso* [a courier ship] – when he came back to me with tears in his eyes.

Talleyrand, in a despatch that did not reach Napoleon until much later, bluntly told him that he was on his own:

Since we cannot send you any help, the Executive Directory knows better than to give you any orders or even instructions. You will

determine your line of conduct according to your own position and to the means you dispose of in Egypt . . . Since it would be difficult, at the present moment, to make possible your (i.e. your army's) return to France, there are three choices open to you: either to remain in Egypt and to establish yourself in such a manner as to be safe from a Turkish attack (but you are aware that for part of the year the country is extremely unhealthy for Europeans, especially if they receive no assistance from the homeland); or to march to India, where, if you get there, you will no doubt find men ready to join you to fight English domination; or, finally, to march on Constantinople and to meet the enemy who is threatening you. The choice is up to you and to the brave and distinguished men who surround you.

As early as the end of August, Napoleon had displayed his resilience in the face of adversity by sending General Desaix with just under 3,000 men to chase Murad Bey, the former ruler of Egypt and now its rebel leader. Desaix, a year older than Napoleon, hailed from a family of country squires in the Auvergne. He had risen to fame as one of General Moreau's subordinates in the Army of the Rhine. Bright and ambitious, Desaix decided to link his fortunes to Napoleon when in Italy, but he had few illusions about his new master whom he considered 'extremely addicted to intrigue. He is very rich, as well he might be, since he draws on a whole country's revenues . . . He believes neither in probity nor in decency; he says all this is foolishness; he claims that it is useless and doesn't exist in this world.'

Desaix was described by Napoleon as 'a little black-looking man', ugly in appearance and 'always badly dressed, sometimes even ragged'. But he was extraordinarily brave, driven by glory and duty, 'intended by nature to be a great general'. Although he had a mistress in France, he was accompanied on his travels by, among others, 'Sarah, a madcap Abyssinian, fifteen years old'.

Desaix's expedition against Murad Bey was to prove an epic of adventure and endurance. They left on the night of 25 August on a flotilla of boats, some of them armed with cannon, travelling some

hundred miles up the Nile before marching inland to try and ambush the Mamelukes at Bahnasa, only to find they had left. They sailed a further 150 miles up to Asyut, where again they found the bird had flown, then turned back towards Cairo.

Desaix's troops went back down the Nile, branching out to travel up Joseph's Canal, an ancient waterway, reaching Bahnasa again, where they disembarked and finally caught up with Murad at El Lahun. There the old pattern of the French forming infantry squares to repel attacks by the Mameluke cavalry repeated itself. The fighting was brutal. An eyewitness reported: 'One of our men, stretched out on the ground, crawled toward a dying Mameluke and slit his throat. An officer asked him, "How can you do such a thing in the state you're in?" "It's easy for you to talk," the soldier answered, "but me, I've only a few more minutes to live, and I want to have fun while I may." ' Desaix had won with 150 casualties to the Mamelukes' 400. Desaix attempted to pursue Murad and his horsemen, but they proved too fast.

After resting, Desaix returned up the Nile to Asyut, where he captured Murad's boats, although he and his men had fled again. Desaix travelled further up the valley which narrows between two mountains to Girga, which Murad had once again just left. There Desaix halted, waiting for supplies to come upriver. Meanwhile Murad Bey was building up a huge array of 7,000 cavalry, 5,000 foot soldiers and his own 2,000 Mamelukes to take on Desaix's 1,000-strong cavalry and 3,000 infantry. When the two met, the French formed into two infantry squares with the cavalry in the middle and the artillery on either side. This efficient formation repelled Murad's attacks and once again he and his Mamelukes fled into the desert.

Desaix's men resumed their chase, encountering their first crocodiles at Dandara. They were awestruck by the temples of Luxor and Karnak, on seeing which they broke out in applause and then presented arms while their bands struck up. The painter Denon, who was with them, sketched the scene before they proceeded up to Aswan, Murad again having left it forty-eight hours earlier. 'Toward the west, the eye discovers a huge desert; to the south, the awesome sight of the steep rocks forming the cataract. They seem to signify that here are the limits of the civilized world. Here nature seems to bar our route and to say to

Louis XVI is seized by the mob, 1792

The Royal Palace in Paris under siege, 1792

Young man about to change
the world: Napoleon at 16

Conqueror of northern Italy: Napoleon's most glorious campaign, 1797

The Battle of Cape St Vincent: Britain's first decisive naval victory, 1797

French Pharaoh and the Sphinx: Napoleon in Egypt, 1798

Battle of the Nile: Nelson strands the French in Egypt, 1798

Brumaire: Napoleon seizes power, 1799

Battle of Copenhagen: Nelson dares, and wins, 1801

France prepares to invade Britain: boats, balloons and tunnels, in an imaginative contemporary engraving, 1804

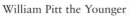

William Pitt the Younger

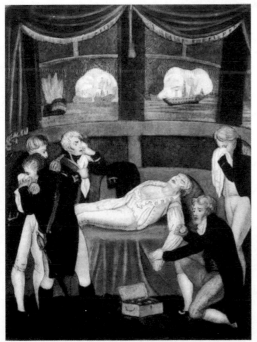

Nelson dies as he learns of
triumph at Trafalgar, 1805

Austerlitz: Napoleon's greatest victory

us, stop, go no further. To the east is Elephantine Island, its verdure and palm groves contrasting with the arid mountains that surround it.'

The French captured an island. There one of Desaix's officers observed:

> Men, women, and children, everybody threw themselves into the river. Faithful to their ferocious character, mothers could be seen drowning the children they could not take with them and mutilating their daughters in order to protect them from being raped by the victors . . . I found a girl seven to eight years old who had been sewn up . . . in a manner that prevented her from satisfying her most pressing needs and caused her horrible convulsions. Only after a counter-operation and a bath was I able to save the life of that unfortunate little creature, who was as pretty as could be.

General Belliard, the commander of the forces at Aswan, ruthlessly ordered the destruction of all the wheat in a nearby village, so that the Mamelukes could not live off the land. 'The poor inhabitants could watch, within an hour, the destruction of the fruit of three months' labour . . . I gave the peasants who had stayed behind a few coins and told them that, if they should starve, they ought to send for some durrah at Aswan.' He also ordered his men to rape for their amusement and to terrorize the population.

The inhabitants soon had their revenge. The flotilla remained behind while the French departed downriver. In April the Arabs arrived and *L'Italie*, a French gunboat was boarded and the band aboard was captured and forced to play ashore while the rest of the prisoners were first raped and then chopped up; the band was then subjected to the same fate.

Some 7,000 Arabs now joined in the fight – mostly warriors from Mecca come to resist the infidels. Belliard's 1,000 men retreated hastily into a firefight with another column of Arabs downstream, at the village of Abnod, where several hundred Meccans were killed. Desaix decided he had gone far enough. Crossing the Nile he returned to Asyut. The objective was to impress upon the locals the French control of the territory. At Asyut he nearly caught up with Murad Bey who,

however, had induced the local people to rebellion. The French mowed down some 1,000 of them.

Desaix spelt out the reality of the situation in a despatch to Napoleon:

> If you leave this country without troops for just an instant, it will revert immediately to its former masters . . . I shall not bore you with a recital of our hardships. They would not interest you . . . I have addressed to you, General, several urgent requests for munitions. I knew how desperately they were needed; as a matter of fact, my situation is critical. People who ask for something always sound as if they felt sorry for themselves. Nevertheless, consider what we are up against. My soldiers have no cartridges except those they are carrying in their kits. The least you can do, General, is take notice of what is being asked of you. There are 1,800 Mamelukes in Upper Egypt. I shall go and fight them.

Desaix ordered Belliard to march to the Red Sea port of Kossier, some 150 miles of desert away, to stop the flow of Arab volunteers. Amazingly Belliard succeeded, crossing this desolate and mountainous expanse in just three days to capture Kossier. He returned just as quickly.

Now that the supply of Arab recruits had been choked off, Murad Bey and the Mamelukes kept away from the French force, Murad himself travelling down to bivouac near the Great Pyramids. Desaix had momentarily conquered Upper Egypt in an astonishing feat of endurance and bravery for the French. Nicholas the Turk wrote: 'From that moment on General Desaix devoted himself to the pacification and organization of Upper Egypt, with an intelligence, an administrative knowledge, a tactfulness, a courage, a zeal, and a magnanimity that were admirable; so that Upper Egypt was better governed than was the Delta.'

Napoleon Bonaparte himself travelled to Suez to take formal possession of the Red Sea port, in a carriage accompanied by three servants. There he met dignitaries from the Hejaz, Yemen and Muscat and forded the Red Sea to visit the 'Fountains of Moses' – famous

springs. The party nearly perished in the fast-flowing tides as they returned. Napoleon also followed the bed of the ancient canal which linked the Red Sea to the Bitter Lakes and appointed surveyors to investigate the possibility of building a new canal – anticipating Ferdinand de Lesseps's construction of the Suez Canal two generations later.

On his return Napoleon continued his proconsulship with a volley of peremptory orders and reforms, encouragement of his scholars and scientists and a rare – for him – plunge into debauchery. The latter was understandable. He had long been aware that Josephine, with whom he remained besottedly in love, had been cuckolding him. At the end of January, Androche Junot, one of his confidants, had brutally and abruptly informed Napoleon of Josephine's unfaithfulness, providing letters and details, in the presence of two other officers. Napoleon was utterly humiliated by Junot's crass exposition and declared: 'Divorce, yes, divorce – I want a public and sensational divorce! I don't want to be the laughing-stock of Paris. I shall write to Joseph and have the divorce pronounced . . . I love that woman so much I would give anything if only what Junot told was not true.'

He wrote despairingly to his brother Joseph: 'The veil has been horribly torn asunder. You are the only person remaining to me; I treasure your friendship . . . Arrange for me to have a country house when I return, either near Paris or in Burgundy . . . I am weary of human nature. I need to be alone and isolated. Great deeds leave me cold. All feeling is dried up. Fame is insipid.' It was one thing for Josephine to pursue her amours; quite another for Napoleon to be humiliated as a cuckold in public.

It was hardly the life-changing moment that some of his biographers have suggested. Napoleon's ruthlessness and cynicism were in evidence long before this event and he behaved no differently afterwards. But he now felt utterly free to be unfaithful himself, after a surprisingly sexually continent life for so unscrupulous a man in other regards. Possibly he even felt he had an obligation to do so as a display of manhood and of revenge against Josephine: in sexual matters, as in

everything else, Napoleon was calculating and governed by the impression his behaviour would make upon the outside world.

His affections turned to Zevah, the sixteen-year-old daughter of a prominent sheikh. She became known as 'the General's Egyptian'. She suffered sadly afterwards: when the French departed, according to El-Djabarti: 'The daughter of the sheikh El-Bekri was arrested. She had been debauched by the French. The pasha's emissaries presented themselves after sundown at her mother's house . . . and made her appear [before court] with her father. She was interrogated regarding her conduct, and made reply that she repented it. Her father's opinion was solicited. He answered that he disavowed his daughter's conduct. Then the unfortunate girl's head was cut off.'

A few months later he met Pauline Foure, a twenty-year-old French girl with striking long black hair, nicknamed Ballilote. Her husband was immediately given leave from the French army but was intercepted by the British and was returned, by way of making mischief, to Egypt. She was dubbed Cleopatra and became Napoleon's official consort, riding with him in his carriage, although his stepson by Josephine, Eugène de Beauharnais, understandably refused to attend on her. Napoleon was angered by her failure to produce a child – to which she allegedly retorted, 'It is not my fault'.

Chapter 37

INTO THE HOLY LAND

It soon became apparent that the Turks were preparing for action against the French army of occupation in Egypt. This was to consist of a double offensive: Djezzar at Acre was preparing a huge army to march by land; and the Turkish 'army of Rhodes' was to be ferried across the Aegean by the British maverick commander Sir Sidney Smith, who had been given command of a flotilla in the eastern Mediterranean – much to Nelson's irritation. Napoleon, his power base and army in Egypt shrinking by the day, decided to pre-empt the land attack by assembling an army of 13,000 infantry and about 800 cavalry equipped with fifty guns. Only 5,000 French soldiers would be left in Cairo.

Napoleon was not in fact headed just for what today is called Syria, but for modern Israel and Palestine, the classical Holy Land. Syria was a region of the Turkish empire divided into five pashaliks – Aleppo, Damascus, Tripoli, Acre and Jerusalem. Napoleon was still apparently dreaming of a far-flung empire, despite his setbacks in Egypt, and sent a message to Tippoo Sahib, the great enemy of the British in India, hoping that 'the Mamelukes and the Arabs of Egypt . . . would join his forces; that by June he would be master of Aleppo and Damascus, with his outposts in the Taurus Mountains and having under his immediate command 26,000 French troops, 6,000 Mamelukes and Arabic horsemen from Egypt, 18,000 Druses, Maronites, and other Syrian troops; and that Desaix would be in Egypt, ready to assist him with 20,000 men, 10,000 of them Frenchmen and 10,000 Negroes with French cadres. In these circumstances, he would have been in a position to force the Porte to make peace and to secure its consent to his march on

India. If fortune favoured his projects, he could reach the Indus by March 1800 with 40,000 men, despite the loss of his fleet.' Unfortunately for him, Tippoo was soon to be killed in the British assault at Seringapatam.

Napoleon's immediate aims were more practical: to pre-empt an Anglo-Turkish attack; to force the Turks to the negotiating table; and to deprive Smith's naval squadron of its supply bases in Syria. While these aims seemed practical, in fact Napoleon had grossly underestimated the difficulties in his path. Believing always that advancing French troops were irresistible, he seemed to regard this as a merely punitive raid, without realizing the colossal difficulties of the terrain he was to cross and the hostility of the populations there.

Napoleon sent General Lagrange on ahead to establish a fort at Katia, and then on to the town of El Arish where Djezzar was concentrating his forward troops. At the last moment it was decided to send the artillery by sea, because of the difficulties involved in crossing the desert. The march across Sinai, even in winter, was certainly a huge ordeal: the desert was empty and arid, while the cold and the rain penetrated the inadequate French clothing (based on the supposition that the desert was always hot), and food was soon in short supply, many mules and camels being slaughtered for food.

When General Reynier, in the vanguard, reached El Arish he found it was defended by 1,200 infantry and some 600 horsemen who had been sent to reinforce the 1,500 garrison. Reynier first massacred the inhabitants of the village, then attacked the Turkish encampment at night, bayoneting the sleeping soldiers: some 500 were killed and 900 taken prisoner, for a French loss of three. The French then besieged the fortress, and were astonished to lose some 400 men on the first day, as the defenders fired back undaunted. A breach was at last made in the wall and the following day its 800 remaining defenders surrendered. The French were delighted to find plenty of food – but dismayed to find a roomful of victims of the plague.

The French marched on to Gaza across even more arid desert and there they found more supplies. They moved on to Jaffa, a town with a wall and a citadel on top of a hill. On 7 March their attack began. Within a few hours the town itself had been taken and the troops went

on a rampage over the next several hours, killing anyone they found, some 2,000 altogether, men, women and children – 'anyone with a human face', as a French witness remarked. Napoleon and his officers did nothing to stop the slaughter.

There were still some 2,500 Turkish soldiers in the citadel. Napoleon sent two aides to parley with them. They offered to surrender provided they were spared – an assurance the aides readily gave. The Turks filed out and gave up their arms. There followed one of the most cold-blooded atrocities ever committed by Europeans in a modern war, a forerunner of Nazi atrocities in the Second World War. It was personally ordered by Napoleon. Peyrusse, the army paymaster, recounts the chilling deed:

> That, in a city taken by storm, the infuriated troops should loot, burn, and kill whatever comes their way, is something demanded by the laws of war, and humanity covers these horrors with a veil. But that, two or three days after the attack, when passions have calmed down, one should order, in cold-blooded savagery, the murder of 3,000 men who have surrendered to us in good faith! Posterity no doubt will pass judgment on this atrocity, and those who ordered it will find their place among the butchers of humanity.
>
> About 3,000 men put down their arms and were instantly led to our camp. By order of the commander-in-chief, the Egyptians, Moroccans, and Turks were separated.
>
> The next morning, all the Moroccans were taken to the seashore, and two battalions began to shoot them down. Their only hope of saving their lives was to throw themselves into the sea; they did not hesitate, and all tried to escape by swimming. They were shot at leisure, and in an instant, the sea was red with blood and covered with corpses. A few were lucky enough to reach some rocks. Soldiers were ordered to follow them in boats and to finish them off. . . Once this execution was over, we fondly hoped that it would not be repeated and that the other prisoners would be spared.
>
> Our hopes were soon disappointed, when, the next day, 1,200 Turkish artillerymen, who for two days had been kept without food in front of General Bonaparte's tent, were taken to be executed.

The soldiers had been carefully instructed not to waste ammunition, and they were ferocious enough to stab them with their bayonets. Among the victims, we found many children who, in the act of death, had clung to their fathers. This example will teach our enemies that they cannot count on French good faith, and sooner or later, the blood of these 3,000 victims will be upon us.

Major Detroye coolly kept a tally of the killings – 2,000 during the attack, then 800 massacred on 8 March, 600 on 9 March and 1,041 on 10 March – to yield a grand total of 4,441. On 9 March, in a surely conscious act of hypocrisy, Napoleon issued a proclamation to the people of Palestine: 'Remain quietly at your homes . . . I guarantee everybody's safety and protection . . . Religion especially shall be protected and respected . . . for it is from God that all good things come: it is He who gives victory.'

Why was this act of bestiality carried out by Napoleon, a ruthless man certainly, but not one who usually indulged in slaughter for its own sake? None of the justifications ring true. He said he could not spare men to take the prisoners back to Egypt, that he could not guard them or feed them and that if he released them they would merely have departed to reinforce Djezzar at his stronghold at Acre, just as, he claimed, 900 of the garrison at El Arish had made for Jaffa. (The true figure could not have been more than 450.)

Yet a couple of hundred Frenchmen could have guarded the disarmed Turks and the French now had plentiful food and supplies – seized from the garrison at Jaffa. If they had reinforced Djezzar, they would have had to be armed and fed by the Turks; it seems more likely that most would have deserted. The likeliest explanation was that Napoleon wanted to make a grisly example for Djezzar's benefit – he himself had an awesome reputation for cruelty – if he failed to abandon his garrison and flee before Napoleon.

Napoleon was in a sense showing that he could be as cruel as Djezzar or the Turks, known for massacring whole villages to subdue the population. He may also have had a white man's contempt for the lives of another race. If so, whatever had happened to Napoleon's civilizing mission in the Middle East? In a career which throughout was marred

by the inflicting of colossal bloodshed and suffering, Napoleon's cold-blooded murder of the 4,000-plus in Jaffa ranks as one of his worst and least defensible atrocities.

For a European, the occasion was unpardonable and a violation of the normal practices of war: however much suffering had been inflicted already during the French revolutionary wars, the cold-blooded massacre of thousands of prisoners by the regular French army was unprecedented. Napoleon had, in the English phrase, 'gone native'. He had succumbed to the barbaric practices of the people he was fighting against in the name of civilization. Just as his commanders in Upper Egypt, knowing the fate that would befall them if they were captured, thought nothing of putting whole villages to the sword, burning them down and raping the women, Napoleon had similarly acquired a cheap and contemptuous view of human life.

All of Napoleon's worst defects were to surface during this extraordinary expedition across the Holy Land: his utter conviction in his own invincibility – that a few thousand disciplined Frenchmen under his command were all that were required to make the rotten façade of Ottoman rule collapse, just as Mameluke rule had crumbled before him; his restless impatience and improvisation, which made him embark on an expedition with virtually no preparation and no knowledge of the terrain, climate or enemy that he would encounter; his belief that he could rout his enemies merely through aggression; his psychopathic contempt for his troops, whom he could sacrifice without the slightest compunction and whose sole purpose was to serve for his own greater glory; his utter indifference to the loss of human life; and his ruthlessness as a general, which time and again wrongfooted his enemies – for he refused to play by any known rules. Tactics considered contrary to the rule of war, or simply unlikely to succeed, were Napoleon's secret weapon. No one would expect him to resort to them.

As so many commented at the time, it seemed that the massacre at Jaffa had at last incurred divine wrath. No doubt infected by the sick at El Arish, Napoleon's troops suddenly started going down with the plague. One patient described the illness: 'This illness begins with a hot fever, followed by a severe headache and the formation of a bubo or

gland, in the groin or in any other joint, about the size of an egg. Once the bubo appears, the patient may be reckoned as dead. If he survives four days, there is considerable hope for him, but this rarely happens.' Some thirty men were dying a day – only one in twelve of those infected surviving. Soon some 300 soldiers had the plague.

Napoleon then showed another side of his extraordinary nature: his almost inhuman lack of fear. He went to visit his dying soldiers in the makeshift hospital at Jaffa. One of his doctors described the visit:

> On March 11, 1799, General Bonaparte, followed by his general staff, felt it incumbent upon himself to visit the hospital . . . The General walked through the hospital and its annex, spoke to almost all the soldiers who were conscious enough to hear him, and, for one hour and a half, with the greatest calm, busied himself with the details of the administration. While in a very small and crowded ward, he helped to lift, or rather to carry, the hideous corpse of a soldier whose torn uniform was soiled by the spontaneous bursting of an enormous abscessed bubo.

Napoleon did not catch the disease and his visit did much to reassure his soldiers, as well as to convince them of his quasi-supernatural powers. This was not a visit of compassion: it was simply a morale-boosting expedient to try and reassure his men on the eve of yet another gruelling march up the coast of the eastern Mediterranean.

Chapter 38

THE SIEGE OF ACRE

Napoleon was now about to face his most formidable Middle Eastern enemy. Djezzar came from Moslem Bosnia and had become a Mameluke servant to Pasha Ahmed, then ruler of Egypt, who had employed him as an assassin against rival beys. After quarrelling with his patron, he had set himself up as Pasha of Acre where, according to a French victor, 'he had immured alive a great number of Greek Christians when he rebuilt the walls of Beirut, to defend it from the invasion of the Russians. The heads of these miserable victims, which the Butcher had left out, in order to enjoy their tortures, are still to be seen.' Napoleon was counting on the support of the Druzes and Christians, who had suffered badly under Djezzar's rule.

Djezzar's stronghold was the ancient crusader castle of Acre, built on a promontory which jutted out to sea, only a quarter of it vulnerable to assault from the land. Although the walls seemed to be crumbling, they were immensely thick and reinforced by several towers, including one dominant one and a castle just within. Djezzar possessed some 250 guns and there were some 10,000 civilians within the small fortified town's walls.

Djezzar had initially considered the stronghold to be indefensible, and favoured withdrawing. But he had been reinforced by two remarkable men – Sir Sidney Smith and Louis-Edmond le Picard de Phélipaux. Smith was an adventurer who had fought with the Swedes against the Russian navy and then had appeared in Toulon when that port was briefly in the hands of the English, being put in charge of burning the French fleet, which he did only half successfully.

In 1796 he had been captured by the French after leading a series of raids against French shipping and imprisoned in the dreaded Temple prison in Paris under the shadow of the guillotine.

He was rescued early in 1798 by the aristocratic Phélipaux, a figure on whom Baroness Orczy may have modelled the Scarlet Pimpernel. Remarkably Phélipaux had been in the same class as Napoleon Bonaparte. They had shared a desk and frequently fought each other, with Phélipaux establishing himself as Bonaparte's academic superior. From the outset of the Revolution, Phélipaux took the royalist side, trying to start a revolt in 1795 before being arrested, escaping and then being rearrested in 1797. The following year he planned the daring escape of Sir Sidney Smith by seducing his gaoler's daughter and then arriving with four friends disguised as policemen at the main gate of the prison.

When Smith escaped, he was given command of a ship of the line, the 80-gun *Tigre*, and Phélipaux sailed with him. Acting independently of Nelson, to the latter's intense irritation, he was appointed commander of the Alexandria Squadron in place of Hood. Hearing of Napoleon's expedition to the Holy Land, he sent Phélipaux off in the *Theseus* to Acre. There the renegade French royalist persuaded Djezzar to remain in the stronghold and strengthened his fortifications. Smith in his ship and two smaller vessels soon followed him there with several gunboats.

When Napoleon took the port of Haifa and established his headquarters at Mount Carmel, which overlooked the Bay of Acre, to his dismay he spied British ships already there. The French flotilla carrying Napoleon's siege artillery arrived in the bay that foggy day and ran straight into the British squadron: six of the French vessels were captured, although three escaped. It was a bitter blow to the French.

Napoleon nevertheless ordered a siege, positioning his camp beyond the range of Acre's guns and digging trenches in a zigzag towards the walls in classical fashion to protect the besiegers from the fire of the fortress. The French had few guns, having lost most of their siege artillery, and only a slightly larger force than that within the castle – some 13,000 men. Worse, Smith was able to use the captured French guns against Napoleon's army. Smith's ships were also able to bombard

the French assailants from the sea. The British had control of the waters which surrounded two-thirds of the fortress and were able constantly to resupply their forces from the sea, while Napoleon had more limited supplies.

The impetuous Napoleon attacked the fortress during the early hours of 28 March with the aim of making a breach in the walls which could be scaled. The fortress and the British ships opened up with a retaliatory fire that killed forty French gunners and knocked out all but seven of their guns. Then the French infantry attacked en masse and the Turks momentarily began to withdraw from the ramparts only to be beaten back to their posts by Djezzar in person. The French proved unable to mount ladders up to the next level, which was thirty feet above the walls, and fled.

Napoleon sought to blow up the main tower with a mine and attacked again three days later. The French were beaten back and Napoleon's stepson, the eighteen-year-old Eugène de Beauharnais, was wounded. To celebrate the repulse of the French, Djezzar had several hundred prisoners he held within the fort massacred. Smith made a futile attempt to stop this.

Napoleon now had to turn to face another enemy: a convergence of Turkish-led armies in his rear mustering to help Djezzar. Characteristically, the French commander chose to attack. Some 4,500 men were marching from the region of Galilee. General Kléber, with a force of 1,500 men, was ordered to rout it near Cana, scene of the miraculous conversion of water to wine. Another force was moving east from near Lake Tiberias. General Murat, with two infantry battalions, marched to meet them and launched an immediate attack down a slope on the Turkish troops: some 5,000 Turks fled and Murat's men fell upon the spoils.

Kléber now found himself facing the Pasha of Damascus's huge army beneath Mount Tabor – some 25,000 cavalry and 10,000 infantry. The French, intimidated by this vastly superior force, were attacked, and for ten desperate hours fought from within their infantry squares. As Private Millet wrote: 'We would gladly have given up the little bread we had for some bullets and gunpowder. We had not had time to eat, and even if we had had time, we could not have taken advantage of it,

because we were so worn out with thirst and fatigue that we could not even speak. At a short distance there was a lake, which the division was unable to reach, so that there was no way of refreshing ourselves.'

It seemed only a matter of time before they were overrun and slaughtered in a potentially fatal blow to the surreal expedition. Fortunately Napoleon had learnt of their plight. Reaching a hill above the battlefield in the nick of time, he ordered two cannon to be fired. The effect was instantaneous: 'The Ottomans panicked and turned to flight. Seeing this, the commander had another cannon shot fired, and the rout became general. The Ottomans scattered in all directions, toward the mountains and into the valleys. The French who watched this from a distance rejoiced at the spectacle and broke into peals of laughter.'

The Battle of Mount Tabor had been won with only a score of casualties among the French. Kléber's men marched forward. Millet remembered: 'Here we were, wading up to our waists in the water of that same lake of which, only a short while ago, we craved to drink a cup. But we no longer thought of drinking but only of killing and of dyeing the lake red with the blood of those barbarians, who only a moment before had hoped to cut off our heads and drown our bodies in that very same lake, where they themselves were drowned and which was filled with their corpses.'

Napoleon spent two nights at Nazareth, where that convert to Islam and his atheist-indoctrinated men rediscovered their childhood Christianity and celebrated a *Te Deum* and a christening. The monks at the nearby monastery tended the French wounded.

On his return to Acre, an exultant Napoleon learnt that his old rival Phélipaux had died, probably of the plague. The French commander ordered another mine to be placed at the base of the main tower prior to a further assault. Peyrusse wrote:

> Its only effect was to blow up a corner of the tower . . . The grenadiers boldly charged the breach, although it was clear that it was impossible to penetrate it. The enemy, installed at the top of the tower and hidden behind the battlements, flattened our troops with

rocks, shells, and hand grenades. However, since nothing could turn back our troops, the Turks resorted to two or three powder kegs which they threw on them. All our men were suffocated, although a few managed to run away half-burned.

Another attack the following day yielded much the same result. Smith recalled: 'I am here amusing myself very well in my favourite way, harassing the heroes of the great nation, and making them feel that the very best thing that can happen to them is to become my prisoners, for by this means they will get their bellies full and go home to their families.' However, he experienced a serious mishap. Captain Miller of the *Theseus* had collected some seventy shells which had failed to explode with the intention of packing them with British gunpowder. A midshipman was appointed to do this but accidentally exploded one of the shells, which set off the rest. Miller and forty others were killed, while fifty were wounded and the *Theseus* was reduced to a wreck.

Reinforced at last by the arrival of siege artillery overland, Napoleon staged another attack on 6 May, which was repulsed, and then another, before at last the seventh assault took the tower. Then the assailants swarmed into Djezzar's gardens, where they were mown down from the inner line of defences. Meanwhile the Turks too had received reinforcements of artillery; but they were deeply apprehensive that Napoleon, who had made a huge breach in the walls and now held the main tower, would win after all.

On 10 May, when a Turkish fleet carrying an army of 7,000 could be seen approaching but became becalmed, Napoleon ordered his men into a frenzied last assault over the half-burnt and putrefying bodies of Frenchmen killed in earlier attacks. Kléber himself played a huge part. A French contemporary wrote: 'Kléber, with the gait of a giant, and his thick head of hair, had taken his post, sword in hand, on the bank of the breach, and animated the assailants. The noise of the cannon, the shouts, the rage of our soldiers, the yells of the Turks, mingled themselves with the bursts of his thundering voice.' Amid appalling carnage, the assault was beaten off.

It had been Napoleon's last throw. He had lost so many men he could continue no longer: some 1,200 had been killed in the fighting,

some 1,000 had died of the plague and more than 2,000 were wounded or ill. Smith wrote triumphantly: 'Could you have thought that a poor prisoner in a cell of the Temple prison – an unfortunate for whom you refused, for a single moment, to give yourself any concern, being at the same time able to render him a signal service, since you were then all-powerful – could you have thought, I say, that this same man would have become your antagonist, and have compelled you, in the midst of the sands of Syria, to raise the siege of a miserable, almost defenceless town?' Napoleon's hatred of Smith was such that his name could not be mentioned in his presence for decades.

Napoleon decided to retreat having lost a third of his men – a decision up to now unparalleled throughout his career. He ruthlessly told his chief doctor: 'If I were in your place, I should put an end to the sufferings of our plague patients and, at the same time, to the danger they represent for us, by giving them opium.' This the doctor refused to do; so the ministering angel suddenly turned murderer of his own men. He had the fifty plague victims in the hospital poisoned so as not to hold up his retreat. Although some of his later supporters have denied the truth of this episode, virtually all French witnesses confirmes it and Napoleon himself said he had left laudanum beside the plague victims so that they could administer it themselves. He may also have feared further infecting his troops. Smith volunteered to take all the wounded and sick aboard his ships, but Napoleon out of pride refused.

Napoleon now resorted to propaganda. He spent four days looting the town of Acre to inflict revenge, to disguise his preparations for retreat and to be able to claim victory. He wrote to Menou in Cairo:

> I shall bring many prisoners and captured flags with me. I have razed Djezzar's palace and the ramparts of Acre, and I have bombarded that city in such a manner that no one stone remains in its place . . . Djezzar is seriously wounded. I am anxious to see you and to get back to Cairo, all the more so since I see that, despite your zeal, a great number of wicked men are trying to disturb the public peace. All this will vanish as soon as I arrive just as the clouds yield to the first ray of the sun.

Napoleon wrote to the Directory brazen lies to excuse his lifting the siege of Acre: 'The occasion seemed to favour the capture of Acre, but our spies, deserters, and our prisoners all reported that the plague was ravaging the city and that every day more than sixty persons were dying of it . . . If the soldiers had entered the city . . . they would have brought back into camp the germs of that horrible evil, which is more to be feared than all the armies in the world.'

Peyrusse, the army paymaster, reported the dismal state of his army on the subsequent retreat:

> We had no means of transportation whatsoever and we had a thousand or twelve hundred wounded and sick to carry with us, besides about forty pieces of artillery . . . All the rest, guns of every calibre, mortars, shells, bombs, muskets, bullets – that is, virtually the entire ordance – had to be buried in the fields and on the beach. We blew up the gunpowder we had left; all the caissons were piled up and burned in the plain . . . Everything was ready for our departure . . . when, on May 20, the enemy made a lively sortie; it lasted almost all day. The fire was terrible. The enemy kept on throwing himself into our trenches, but Reynier's division . . . kept pushing him back with heavy losses.

Bearing more than 2,000 sick and having picked up a further 1,000 or so along the way, in a gruelling foreshadowing of the retreat from Moscow, they moved under enemy harassment, laying waste to what settlements there were, so as to deny provisions to their pursuers. Bourienne wrote:

> I saw with my own eyes officers who had limbs amputated being thrown out of their litters [by their bearers] . . . I have seen amputated men, wounded men, plague-stricken men, or people merely suspected of having the plague, being abandoned in the fields. Our march was lit up by torches with which we set fire to the towns, the villages, the hamlets, and the rich harvests that covered the land. The entire countryside was on fire . . . We were surrounded by nothing but dying men, looters, and arsonists. The

dying, by the roadside, were saying in a barely audible voice, 'I am only wounded, I haven't got the plague.'

On 30 May the defeated force reached Gaza. It took ten days to cross the Sinai desert amidst appalling suffering. Only 5,000 troops survived, yet on 14 June Napoleon was back in Cairo, parading his gruesome defeat as a great triumph. Back in Egypt he found that two rebellions had broken out against French rule: one in Alexandria and one in Cairo. In Alexandria, a self-styled Mahdi or Moslem holy man had led several thousand followers into seizing Damanhur and had slaughtered the French garrison before being dispersed by a larger French force which massacred some 1,000 of these zealots in the small town. In Cairo, where Napoleon's returning force joined the remaining garrison of 15,000, 3,000 of whom were sick, he began the mass execution of the Moslem protestors. General Dugua, who had to carry this out, proposed 'Since executions are becoming frequent at the Citadel, I intend to substitute a head-chopper *(un coupeur de têtes)* for the firing squad. This will save us ammunition and make less noise'. 'Agreed,' Bonaparte wrote in the margin.

On 15 January Napoleon learnt of the arrival of a Turkish fleet – which he had claimed he had destroyed – off the coast of Alexandria. There were five battleships, three frigates and fifty troop transports, supported by the British squadron of Sir Sidney Smith. The Turks soon captured Aboukir Fort: they had around 7,000 men. (Napoleon claimed the figure to be 18,000.)

With singular efficiency, Napoleon marched a force of some 10,000 men and 1,000 cavalry under Kléber to Alexandria. On 24 July the French attacked the three Turkish lines of defence which put up fierce resistance. Then Murat's cavalry arrived at noon and with extraordinary ferocity broke through all three lines towards the fort itself. The Turks panicked and 1,000 escaped to the fort, while another 2,000 were massacred when the infantry followed up the attack. Some 4,000 fled into the sea, where most drowned and many others were shot from the shore.

Khedive Mehemet Ali was one of the swimmers to survive: he was later to create the dynasty of Egyptian kings that ended in Farouk in the

1950s. Murat himself captured the Turkish commander, Mustafa Pasha, an old man with a white beard who fired at the French commander, wounding him in the jaw, before the latter's sword took off two of his fingers. Some 2,500 Turks were still barricaded in the fort. They refused their pasha's pleas to surrender and 1,000 of them died of thirst and hunger – they even drank salt water – before they gave up. Instead of being executed as they expected, they were given food and water, but some 400 more died.

About 1,000 Frenchmen had been killed or wounded in the battle, compared with 6,000 Turks. It was sweet revenge for Acre, albeit not a particularly glorious French triumph; still it permitted Napoleon to rehabilitate himself somewhat, not that he had ever admitted defeat at Acre. 'This beautiful battle', as Napoleon described it, allowed the master of propaganda to portray the whole appalling Middle Eastern adventure as culminating in a glorious victory and defeat for the Turks.

In fact, with the exception of the occupation of Cairo against primitive if colourful troops and the spectacular nature of Desaix's expedition up the Nile, it had been disaster. Napoleon had lost one third of his men against an inferior and primitive enemy. Egypt remained seething with opposition to French rule; and his expedition to take Constantinople had ended in defeat before a crumbling crusader fortress commanded by a brigand and an English adventurer, while his advance and retreat had taken place in horrific circumstances for his own forces as well as the enemy.

The effect of the enterprise upon Napoleon himself was considerable, removing any inhibitions he previously felt about risking his men or destroying the enemy. He had also acquired a colonialist's contempt for old laws and customs, as well as the belief that if he acted boldly enough, he could conquer and rule almost anything, including his own country. Now he planned to return to Paris to do exactly that.

After the fall of Aboukir, Napoleon returned to Cairo for only a week and, ignoring reports that a large combined Franco-Spanish fleet was in the Mediterranean to evacuate or reinforce his men, secretly fled as soon as he believed the departure of the Anglo-Turkish fleet would allow him safe passage. He left instructions to 'strike hard at the first sign of trouble . . . chop off six heads per day but always keep smiling'.

He took with him a nineteen-year-old Armenian Mameluke as bodyguard; Roustam Raza was not to leave his side until almost the end of his career. His faithful Berthier came too, as did the superb cavalry commander Murat and Eugène de Beauharnais, his young stepson, who had more than proved himself. Only when he was already on the road to Alexandria did he tell General Menou that he was going. He left instructions to the capable Kléber, who was to be his successor and had come utterly to despise Napoleon. Then, after waiting all night for a favourable wind, he left aboard ship at around 8 am. The journey back was long and hazardous: Napoleon's ship, *Le Muidon*, twice caught sight of British ships off the North African coast but was not spotted. In appalling weather they reached Corsica on 30 September and Napoleon spent a few nights at his old home with his mother Letizia. Sailing from Corsica, the ship ran into a severe gale and again spied British ships in the distance. On 9 October he was back in France at last.

Kléber's fury at being abandoned by Napoleon knew no bounds: the preening, vain incompetent, bumptious young man who had got France into this mess – for Kléber himself had opposed the whole invasion of Egypt – had now fled as the situation deteriorated, and had been so embarrassed that he had not even informed Kléber he was doing so. Perhaps he feared being arrested if Kléber had learnt of his desertion.

Kléber was the polar opposite of the small bundle of manic energy he replaced: six foot tall, of stern and striking appearance, with flowing curly hair and a stentorian voice, Kléber was a soldier's soldier. He did not believe the French occupation of Egypt would last long, and saw no need to colonize the country or win over the people by pretending he was a Moslem. He poured scorn on Napoleon to his brother officers as 'the hero' or 'the Almighty' and accused him of stealing some 2 million francs from the treasury and leaving a deficit of 10 million francs, 4 million of which was in soldiers' pay.

With a Turkish army on the way from Gaza and opposition increasing to French rule, Kléber talked directly to the Turks, offering to restore Egypt to them and return to the old Franco-Turkish alliance.

Sidney Smith interceded on his behalf to the Grand Vizier of the Ottoman empire, who at first proved reluctant to forgive.

Meanwhile the French suffered another humiliation. The Turkish army of 40,000, after taking Gaza, moved on El Arish and massacred some hundred Frenchmen who had already surrendered. Even so, Kléber and the Grand Vizier reached an agreement there, under which the Turks would provide transports to evacuate the French army, and the Ottomans would withdraw from their alliance with Russia and Britain, in exchange for a French withdrawal from Egypt. Kléber's reasoning was brutally realistic:

> an exact mathematical calculation: we must not fight but we must compromise with those barbarians while we are still strong enough to enforce the faithful execution of the terms agreed upon . . . Since Bonaparte's return to France, there has been time enough to send us not one but ten courier ships. None was sent, because the government had nothing to promise me . . . If I win a victory, all I gain is a three-month respite . . . If I am beaten, I am responsible toward the Republic for 20,000 citizens, who will be unable to escape being massacred by a lawless and infuriated soldiery . . . since, in this respect, we have set a fatal example for them to follow.

However Smith now learned that the British government, believing the French in Egypt to be on the brink of total defeat, had disavowed the agreement at El Arish. (In fact the British government had changed its mind, but neglected to inform Smith in time.) By then the Turks, under the terms of the agreement, had arrived in Cairo. Kléber, appalled by the British disavowal, promptly ordered his men into the field and in a spectacular battle near the ancient Heliopolis routed a Turkish army four times as large and within a week had chased them out of Egypt altogether. Napoleon had never won such a victory.

Even so, Kléber sought desperately to reach agreement with the Turks: he told General Menou, who had congratulated him:

> My stupidity is so enormous that even today I do not believe that the Convention of El Arish was a political mistake or that there is

any reason to lose one's head over the victory I have won with my army. Even today, I am profoundly convinced that, by means of that treaty, I had succeeded in putting a reasonable end to an insane enterprise. Even today I remain convinced that we shall receive no help from France and that we shall never . . . found any colonies in Egypt unless the cotton plants and palm trees should soon produce soldiers and bullets . . .

One Turkish contingent bypassed the French after Heliopolis and reached Cairo, which had been left unprotected. Thus encouraged, mobs took to the streets, causing a few weeks of looting, rape and anarchy. Kléber was forced to bombard the city, eventually regaining control and expelling the Turks. Soon afterwards Kléber was assassinated by an Arab fanatic, who had his hand cut off and was then impaled alive in a French reprisal more akin to the methods of their 'barbarian' enemies. It was long alleged, possibly rightly, that the assassination was a British plot: certainly France thus lost one of its best, most far-seeing and humane generals.

Menou took over. His zest for turning Egypt into a French colony had been second only to Napoleon's. Menou, a capable but small-minded administrator, immediately repudiated the treaty of El Arish. The British, giving up all hope of peace after this catalogue of misunderstandings, sent Sir Ralph Abercromby of West Indies fame at the head of an army which landed in Aboukir Bay early in 1801 under heavy fire, which cost them 600 men. At the Battle of Canopus a fortnight later, Menou lost around 4,000 men to British losses of around 1,500, but Abercromby himself was mortally wounded.

The British succeeded in cutting off Menou in Alexandria from the garrison in Cairo and secured the support of Murad Bey, who had long been harassing the French, although that old rogue died soon afterwards. The Turks also re-entered Egypt from the east. General Balliard, in charge of Cairo, decided to capitulate rather than fight for a lost cause. Some 13,000 French troops were permitted to evacuate Cairo bearing arms, under the supervision of Sir John Moore, and embarked at Rosetta, arriving in France in October. Menou's forces held out for some weeks at Alexandria but sought terms at the end of August. The

British insisted on keeping the Rosetta Stone which provided the key to Egyptian hieroglyphics.

Of more than 50,000 French soldiers and civilians who had come over with Napoleon on that surreal adventure into Egypt, fewer than half – some 23,000 – returned. Napoleon's objectives in conquering Egypt were almost entirely frustrated except in two regards: he had broken the power of the Mamelukes who were soon to be seen off by Mehemet Ali, the founder of modern Egypt. French archaeological and scientific interest in Egypt was also to continue for several decades, resulting eventually in the building of the Suez Canal by de Lesseps. But the Saharan sands swallowed up Napoleon's imperial foray there as surely as they had for centuries the great temples of ancient Egypt. All that was left was the loss of a large army and a huge fleet.

Part 6

THE SHORT PEACE

Chapter 39

COUP D'ÉTAT

Napoleon returned to Europe gratifyingly preceded by news of his victory at Alexandria. In spite of the appalling disaster of the Egyptian campaign as a whole, he behaved from the first like a conquering hero, presenting the campaign as his greatest military triumph to date. Arriving on 9 October, he ignored the requirements of quarantine and set out immediately on the week-long journey to Paris. On the way, he was greeted by fair-sized crowds, especially in Avignon, and arrived in the capital on 11 October.

There he discovered that, although he was regarded as a victorious general, he was only one of many. Moreover, the tide in the fast-moving war in Europe had turned again. The Russians, who had entered the war on Austria's side partly out of anger at France's intervention in Ottoman Egypt – Russia regarded Turkey as its own rightful prey – had succeeded in reversing the Napoleonic conquests in northern Italy, taken Turin, and forced the French out of Rome. Generals Moreau, Schérer and MacDonald had all been defeated. By the end of June only Genoa and part of Liguria remained in French hands. The Austrian commander, Archduke Charles, had defeated Jourdan on the central front and even the hapless Duke of York in alliance with the Russians had managed to capture most of Holland. All of this had earlier encouraged Napoleon to pose, bogusly, as France's only successful military commander, the man who could yet save his country.

By October, however, things looked rather different: Masséna had defeated the Archduke Charles at Zurich two months before and the

Russians and the Austrians were beginning to quarrel bitterly. Ney meanwhile defeated the Austrians on the Rhine. In the same month as Napoleon arrived, General Bruce had soundly beaten the wretched Duke of York in Holland and forced the British to evacuate once again. All of these men were skilful generals at least on a par with Napoleon. The difference was that they lacked his overweening ambition and scheming political mind.

On his arrival in Paris, he decided to have it out with the errant Josephine who had so embarrassed him. Both his welcoming brothers, Joseph and Lucien, confirmed that Hippolyte Charles had lived with her for months at a time, and that the two of them were enjoying huge kickbacks from military contracts secured in his name. When Napoleon arrived at her house, he found her away – in fact she had travelled to Lyon to meet him, but he had taken a different route. When she returned exhausted from the futile journey at eleven o'clock at night, she found that Napoleon had locked her out of the house.

She spent the night on the doorstep begging to be let in – until she was joined by her daughter Hortense and the brave young Eugène, who eventually persuaded their stepfather to yield. After a further burst of anger he calmed down and soon they were making love with all the passion of newlyweds. Josephine remarked of Napoleon: 'He is a man who has never loved anyone but himself; he is the most ingrained and ferocious egotist the Earth has ever seen. He has never known anything but his own interest and ambition.' But Napoleon must have been besottedly in love with her, or he would never have forgiven her for her liaison with Charles and her holding him up to ridicule.

She, for her part, was now increasingly committed to him, not just for his successes but to maintain her ever more expensive tastes. Moreover Josephine was an intriguer herself, and a valuable political ally for him. She told Napoleon that his old flame, Désirée, Joseph's sister-in-law, had married Jean Bernadotte, one of Napoleon's most dangerous political rivals who had briefly served as minister of war before antagonizing the most powerful man in the Directory, the Abbé Emmanuel Sieyès. Bernadotte was of humble Gascon origin, but was tall, with thick, curly black hair, an imposing nose and the adopted manner of a grand aristocrat. He has received a bad press, partly because

of his arrogance and largely because of Napoleon's intense dislike. But he was particularly dangerous as the most powerful leader in the army of the then Jacobin faction, the left-wing descendants of Robespierre (which did not prevent him accepting a royal crown when offered it, as so often is this way with revolutionaries). Bernadotte was one of the senior generals not afraid of standing up to Napoleon. He refused to call upon Napoleon on his return and suggested that he be court-martialled for abandoning his army in Egypt and refusing to be quarantined. He also refused to attend an official dinner in Napoleon's honour, on the grounds that the latter might be carrying the plague. Napoleon, however, was the more cunning: instead of rising to his provocations he sought to neutralize him by dragging him into his orbit. Désirée would report on her husband to Napoleon's family circle.

Josephine remained close to Paul Barras, still a member of the Directory, but no longer its dominant figure. Barras, formerly Josephine's lover, regarded Napoleon almost paternally as his protégé. But Barras was widely identified as the most corrupt member of a ruling elite famous for its venality: with a reputation for reckless affairs with members of both sexes, for gambling and for selling government jobs, his reputation was not enhanced by his being a cousin of the now notorious Marquis de Sade. Moreover, the unprincipled Barras had secretly gone over to the royalists, who were working for the restoration of Louis XVIII and were now perhaps the most powerful faction in France. Barras had allegedly been bribed some 12 million francs to do so.

Napoleon had no time for the royalists: he wanted to rule himself, not restore the monarchy. So he turned to Louis Gohier, ostensibly the most powerful of the Directors and yet another lover of the astonishing Josephine, who had a remarkable ability to attract men of power. Gohier represented the interests of the Thermidoreans, the majority on the legislative council under the 1795 constitution, the Council of Elders (a kind of senate) and the Council of Five Hundred (a kind of lower chamber), who broadly favoured the status quo and opposed a return to the monarchy or a move to the left under the Jacobins. But Gohier was tainted as one of the corrupt circle around Barras and was

besides deeply suspicious of Napoleon's ambition. At a cordial meeting
he turned down Napoleon's request to be made a Director, pointing
out that he was only thirty and that the minimum age for a director was
forty.

Napoleon turned back to Barras as a possible ally and bluntly asked
him what he thought about ousting the Directory with a coup. Barras
professed himself horrified at the idea, partly because he feared
Napoleon would soon take power should such a coup take place,
even with himself, Barras, leading it, and partly because of his secret
new support for the monarchy.

The other two Directors being minor figures in the pay of the Abbé
Sieyès, Napoleon was forced to look to this divine to further his
political ambitions. Privately Napoleon detested the abbé. This sinister
intellectual cleric with a bald head, long nose and reedy voice, living
alone with only books by Voltaire for company, had some claim to be
the instigator of the French Revolution itself, with his famous pamphlet *We are the Third Estate* and his early prominence alongside Mirabeau
and Lafayette. Although a liberal by inclination, he had outlasted the
tyrannies of Danton and Robespierre, and replied, when asked what he
did in the Revolution, 'I survived': he had manoeuvred sufficiently
skilfully and treacherously to avoid the guillotine.

Now at fifty-one he had ambitions to become dictator of France,
and wanted to dissolve the Directory and the cumbersome existing
constitution. What he needed, he confessed to friends, was 'a sword',
by which he meant a general willing to carry out a coup and install him,
Sieyès, in power. He first approached Joubert, but the general was
killed in Italy. Both MacDonald and Moreau refused to take part in any
such plot.

Sieyès then turned to Napoleon: the savant was sufficiently intellectually arrogant to believe he could dominate the energetic but
supposedly less intelligent soldier – although he paid him a rare
compliment: 'I intend to work with General Bonaparte because of
all soldiers he is nearest to being a civilian.' Sieyès also had a cadre of
impressive conspirators around him, including the devious and ruthless
chief of police, Fouché, the subtle but duplicitous foreign minister,
Talleyrand, and Napoleon's own brother Lucien, who was a promi-

nent member of the Council of Five Hundred. Lucien began putting it about that Barras had sent Napoleon to Egypt to perish, along with the best men in the army, because he regarded them as a threat.

Sieyès approached Napoleon to ask him if he would act as the 'sword' in a coup. Napoleon, deeply distrustful of this intellectual-politician, nevertheless agreed. The plotters refused to let the unreliable Bernadotte in on the conspiracy, instead seeking to neutralize him; but he had the backing of a large section of the army, its Jacobin meritocrats, including generals Jourdan and Augereau. The next step was to get Barras to support the plotters, along with his protégé Roger Ducos, which would have furnished them with a majority on the Directory to legitimize their seizure of power. Barras refused.

The conspirators carefully drew up a plan: the Directors would be asked to resign and the Councils of Elders and of the five hundred would be required to appoint a committee to draw up a new constitution. The key point was that the sitting of the councillors would take place outside Paris, at the Palace of St Cloud, to prevent the Paris mob, thought to be loyal either to the Jacobins or the monarchy, staging demonstrations and intimidating the Assembly. Both Barras and Gohier, separately suspecting Napoleon, suggested he be given control of an overseas army. He refused, pretending he was ill. Barras himself approached Napoleon to ask him to join in his own plot to install the King. Napoleon said no.

At this point, the venal collective leadership of the five Directors, jostling for power, hardly gave the impression of a firm hand. Yet France was not in the throes of national disintegration: its political system was perfectly adequate, although imperfect. In place of absolute monarchy, the incompetence and disturbances of the initial liberal Revolution and the monstrous tyranny of Danton, Marat and Robespierre which had created a bloodbath, government by the Directory had been moderate, had curbed revolutionary excesses and had supervised the war effort brilliantly under the gifted Carnot, then less ably after his eclipse.

True, the Directory was deeply corrupt. But corruption under the monarchy had been institutional on a completely different scale; and successive governments had been incompetent as well as corrupt – with

the exception of the 'sea-green incorruptible' Robespierre's rule by
mass murder. Napoleon himself was certainly no sea-green incorruptible. The Napoleon of Italy and Egypt had looted on a par with the
ancients, and distributed patronage lavishly to his family and friends,
with Josephine in the forefront; he had no scruples about helping
himself and amassing fortunes. Corruption was simply part of the
politics of rulers of the day across Europe – Napoleon helping himself
on a bigger scale than anyone else.

A further charge brought against the Directory was that of economic
incompetence; and it is true that France at the time was in dire
economic straits, although not so serious as had existed under the
Jacobins, when much of the population was on the brink of starvation.
In 1794 the gold franc was worth 75 paper francs; four years later the
exchange rate was 80,000 – hyper-inflation. Coffee cost around a franc
a grain, a plank of wood some 7,000 francs while sugar was rationed
and bread and cheese were almost out of the reach of the ordinary
person. The Directory had addressed the problem by raising taxes,
levying 100 million francs from France's most powerful political class,
the new rich. Progressive taxation and improved administration only
made more enemies, as, less defensibly, did its violent anticlericalism.

But it is instructive to look at the real cause of France's inflation,
which can be summarized in two words: military expenditure. The
French Revolution had spawned a monster with a seemingly inex-
haustible appetite – the French army. This huge institution simply
absorbed money like a sponge, much of it expended in bribing officers
to stay loyal to governments. The cost of foreign wars was enormous,
and required further conquests to generate the spoils needed to provide
the money to further finance the occupying forces. The problem with
the Directory was that it was too weak to rein in the army: if it had
been stronger it might have been able to conclude peace with its
neighbours, now that most of France's territorial demands and the
concerns for its security were satisfied.

Napoleon's solution to France's economic problems was relentless
continued expansion and plunder to pay for France's needs and to
finance yet more foreign wars. France was becoming a perpetual war
machine, financing itself by gobbling up yet more territory, which in

turn required yet more war and finance. The establishment of a military dictatorship was not only no solution, but a further ratcheting up of the problem. Ultimately there was a call for a strong leader in France, as there always is in times of economic discontent.

The prime reason for Napoleon's plotting was ambition, pure and simple. He wanted to become dictator of an expansionary France. His problem at this stage was that he was only one of several senior generals who qualified for this role, and he had to find some sort of constitutional figleaf for his putsch: this was provided by the over-clever Abbé Sieyès. Through the use of naked force, the abbé sought to use Napoleon to bring himself to power unconstitutionally. Little did the wily ex-priest realize the contempt in which the crude little general held him, or that within a matter of weeks he would be discarded by Napoleon as so much surplus civilian baggage.

Napoleon's hagiographers, and even his detractors, have always portrayed the coup itself – known as 17 Brumaire (19 November) under the Revolution's absurd calendar – as a masterpiece of skill and political planning. In fact by the standards of an effective Latin American coup, for example, it was no more than a half-botched affair that very nearly went spectacularly wrong. First, Napoleon abruptly cancelled a meeting with Barras the night before on the grounds that he had a headache. Barras guessed exactly what was afoot: 'I see that Bonaparte has tricked me . . . and yet he owes me everything.'

Napoleon rose early the following morning and sent a letter to the Council of Elders summoning them to an urgent meeting. Then he invited all the top generals to secure their support or at least their neutrality. Bernadotte alone came in civilian clothes and told him he wanted no part in the conspiracy. The military governor of Paris, General Lefevre, who had the key control of the army units stationed in the capital, asked whether Barras was part of the coup; Napoleon lied that he was. Gohier however refused to be summoned by Napoleon, who intended to place him under arrest.

At the Council of Elders, Sieyès persuaded the majority to move to the Palace of St Cloud, which he knew could be surrounded and intimidated by Napoleon's soldiers. Napoleon himself went to the

Council of Elders and solemnly swore to uphold the Republic: he was appointed commander-in-chief of all units in the Paris area. He immediately went to address the troops and furiously attacked the Directory for undermining the army.

Gohier, the leader of the Directory and Jean Moulin, the fifth member, who was loyal to him, went to the Tuileries to confront Napoleon. The general bluntly told them that Sieyès and Ducos had resigned, as well as Barras, another lie, so that the Directory had been dissolved. When Gohier refused to resign he ordered both men placed under house arrest. Meanwhile two other conspirators, Talleyrand and Admiral Bruix, arrived at Barras's house to inform him that all the other members of the Directory had resigned, and demanded his own resignation. Talleyrand had been given 2 million francs to bribe Barras to resign. There are conflicting accounts as to whether the money was paid, or whether Talleyrand simply pocketed it (or paid Barras half a million and took the rest, as some suggested). Barras resigned without a fuss.

So far the conspiracy had worked like clockwork. But on the following day Napoleon travelled to St Cloud to find the palace still being prepared for the crucial sitting of the Assembly. Desperately worried, he paced up and down in an upstairs room. Outside, a handful of veterans formed a palace guard to protect the parliamentary sitting. Before them, Murat had drawn up 6,000 men loyal to Napoleon.

The Elders did not meet until 3.30, when the resignation of the Directors was announced. It was proposed that a new Directory be elected. Napoleon was appalled: he had been counting on the Elders to set up a committee to draw up a new constitution. It seemed the representatives were beginning to understand that a coup was in the making – and that it was being organized by their supposed saviour, Napoleon himself. Napoleon could stand their prevarications no longer, and illegally broke into the sitting. He declared: 'You are at the edge of a volcano. Let us save at all costs the two things for which we have sacrificed so much, liberty and equality.'

'What about the constitution?' heckled one of the Elders.

The constitution, Napoleon told them, was no longer required. Conspiracies were being hatched in its name. 'I know all about the

dangers that threaten you.' 'Name the conspirators,' shouted another delegate. Napoleon blurted out another falsehood, that Barras and Moulin had been inviting him to place himself at the head of their conspiracy. He was now thrashing around, red-faced with the effort of lying as the parliamentarians interrupted him: he was no orator, except to obediently silent troops.

He began to bluster angrily and almost incoherently: 'I shall preserve you from dangers surrounded by my comrades in arms. Grenadiers, I see your bearskins and bayonets . . . With them I have founded republics . . . If some orator in the pay of a foreign power should propose to outlaw me, may the lightning of war instantly crush him! If he proposed to outlaw me, I should call on you, my brave companions in arms! Remember, that I march accompanied by the god of victory and the god of fortune.' An angry murmur of dissent spread through the room and Napoleon strode out, having made a fool of himself and endangered his coup.

He strode over to the chamber in which the popular assembly, the Five Hundred, were sitting. As soon as he arrived his arm was grabbed by a Jacobin member. 'How dare you. Leave at once. You are violating the sanctuary of the law.' There were shouts of 'Kill him' and 'Get out'. Then a general cry arose, '*Hors la loi!*' – 'Outlaw' – a charge which if it stuck would condemn Napoleon to death. The two guards accompanying Napoleon were seized and held and Napoleon himself shaken as the deputies surged towards him. It was a scene that recalled the fall of Robespierre.

Pale and trembling with shock, Napoleon was rescued by five guards who broke into the chamber. When he emerged his face was streaked with blood, allegedly from the attacks of his assailants, although it seems more likely that Napoleon himself scratched his face, which was pockmarked with acne sores, for dramatic effect. Lucien Napoleon as president of the Assembly succeeded at last in getting the Five Hundred to quieten down. Meanwhile Napoleon, frustrated in his attempt to secure a constitutional coup, had now decided that brute force was his only solution. He mounted his horse and rode to Murat's troops, the blood still on his face, and ordered a detachment to bring Lucien to him.

When his brother arrived he addressed Murat's forces. The majority of the Assembly, Lucien declared, being as accomplished a liar as his brother, were being terrorized by a minority armed with knives in the pay of England, and had tried to kill Napoleon. Then he urged the palace guards outside to break in and remove them. Brandishing a sword, Lucien pointed at Napoleon theatrically and swore that he would kill him 'if he ever interferes with the freedom of Frenchmen'. The men could see deputies hanging out of the window of the chamber calling for Napoleon to be arrested as an outlaw.

What persuaded the guards more than Lucien's rhetoric was fear of Murat's 6,000 troops outside, who could overwhelm them in an instant. There Generals Augereau and Jourdan had been urging the troops in vain to have nothing to do with the coup. The ordinary soldiers disarmed the largely honorific Assembly guard and filed into the chamber, ordering the deputies out. When they refused, their commander ordered his men to clear them out by force and the deputies at last got the message: most escaped by the windows.

Soon afterwards Lucien rounded up eighty deputies drinking in nearby taverns, a quorum, and at 2 a.m. they formally dissolved the Directory and set up a triumvirate of consuls to govern France consisting of Napoleon, Sieyès and his henchman Ducos. Committees were set up to draft a new constitution. Napoleon went to swear an oath of loyalty to the Republic before the Elders. No one was fooled: it was a military coup d'état secured by force, with only the thinnest veneer of constitutionalism. True, Napoleon had to share his power with Sieyès. But what the wily abbé failed to understand was that his authority depended entirely on force, and Napoleon provided the force: Sieyès in reality was the junior member of the two.

Still, Napoleon had to go through the necessary formalities of entrenching his power. He agreed to settle down with Sieyès, Ducos merely acting as an observer, to draw up a new constitution to replace the one just overthrown. So it was that France's youngest general, a thirty-year-old with a distinguished military record in Italy and a largely disastrous one in Egypt and Syria, a man who had abandoned his army and his countrymen to certain defeat and presided over the annihilation of his fleet, seized power in France by force on 9

November 1799, a dramatic day that was to change the world. He had proved himself a skilled general, although not by any means France's best. He had become adept, however, in taking advantage of the divisions within France's government to suit his own purposes, and in seizing the opportunity that his concentration of military force outside the Assembly had allowed him.

Even so, it had been a shabby seizure of power by armed men from the constitutional representatives of the nation. None observing that crude putsch could have believed that the future of Europe was now radically to change. For up to then, France seemed to be gradually settling down to constitutional rule, and the expensive revolutionary war might even have been winding down. By contrast Napoleon, as a military strongman, was committed to an expansionist continuation of the war with a ferocity, determination and ambition few who had not witnessed his Egyptian and Syrian campaigns could have foreseen.

It is possible that the great European war might at last have fizzled out around the turn of the century had the Directory or some kind of constitutional successor remained in power. Napoleon's seizure of power was to prolong it for a further sixteen years, with two deceptive pauses – more than twice as long as it had already lasted – and cause immeasurable suffering to the peoples of Europe.

The final step in Napoleon's accession to supreme power had yet to be taken. Napoleon appointed his closest associates to senior posts: Talleyrand became minister for foreign affairs, Fouché minister of police, Berthier minister of war and Murat commander of the constitutional guard – Napoleon's own personal force. Masséna was appointed commander of the army in Italy and MacDonald commander of the Army of the Reserve. All of these men were allies of Napoleon, but they were also substantial figures in their own right and to some extent were a check on his absolutism: at this stage Napoleon was merely first among equals. Moreover he was forced to retain the highly professional General Moreau, whom he deeply distrusted.

Napoleon's immediate priority was to be rid of the Abbé Sieyès, who considered himself the real ruler of France. After weeks of fruitless discussion on the shape of the new constitution, led by Sieyès who

favoured a system of checks and balances and powerful assemblies, Napoleon urged Sieyès to resign. He stood down as a consul, and was then out-argued by the tireless Napoleon in the committee at the beginning of December. Napoleon cunningly adopted the form of the Sieyès plan, setting up no fewer than four assemblies – a legislature of 300 members, a senate of sixty, a tribunate of a hundred and a council of state with some thirty to forty members. In fact these more or less nullified each other: the ministers were to be responsible to the consul, not to these talking shops.

On 12 December the constitution was finally approved. Sieyès, supported by his partner, was given the honorific job of proposing Napoleon as First Consul. Jean-Jacques Cambacérès, a forty-six-year-old Napoleonic loyalist who in theory represented the Jacobin interest, was fellow consul: he was an imposing looking and verbose lawyer, a carefully groomed bachelor whose saying was 'a country is governed by good dinner parties', of which his own were among the best in Paris. Charles Lebrun, a sixty-year-old economist who had served under Louis XVI in the finance ministry, was chosen as a sop to the royalists, thus balancing the two major political factions. In fact Lebrun turned out to be a brilliant financier and Napoleon came to depend on him as his chief economic adviser.

Napoleon submitted the constitution to a plebiscite – perhaps the first dictator in history to wield this traditional prop of absolutism, so that he could claim that his authority derived not from divine right, or nomination by the oligarchy, or the use of force, but from the people – and this could not be overturned by his political rivals. The result would have brought a flush of envy to the cheeks of many a twentieth-century dictator: 3,011,007 votes were cast in favour to just 1,562 votes against – 97 per cent of the vote to 3 per cent. In Paris the result was 12,440 votes to just 10 against. Half a million votes had been cast by the army en masse without the formality of a ballot, while up and down the country votes were registered by show of hands at public meetings. This was responsible for around half the votes cast in favour. Nevertheless a colossal 6 million Frenchmen did not vote at all: the First Consul thus secured only 17 per cent of the real vote. Napoleon was now a one-man ruler under the constitution, through the wielding of

force, through nomination by the oligarchy and now – in theory at least – through popular plebiscite. It was a formidable combination.

Napoleon's assumption of power represented the end of the revolutionary process that had begun in 1789 and had lasted exactly a decade. France had undergone a brief period of constitutional monarchy, followed by mob rule, Jacobin terror, collective leadership and now dictatorship. The Revolution had turned full circle. France was now under the control again of a one-man ruler – although unlike the hereditary Bourbons he represented a new moneyed class that had emerged from the ashes of the Revolution. The revolutionary ideals of the Jacobins were to be trampled into the ground, along with virtually all the principles so vigorously asserted during the Revolution.

Equality also was to go by the board: for Napoleon began almost immediately to acquire the trappings of a monarch and a court, in contravention of his professed beliefs in meritocracy. It seemed that the founding of a new dynasty was not far away either. For all his revolutionary pretensions, as soon as he had absolute power, he began to re-establish absolutism – with him as the monarch. Ironically his most dangerous opponents during the early years of the regime were not to be the Jacobins and radicals but the supporters of the previous dynasty, to whom Napoleon was a mere usurper. Napoleon's response to those who were to accuse him merely of installing another absolutism was that he had modernized the system. It will be seen to what extent that claim was justified.

Napoleon's first priority, as befitted a man whose entire career had been a military one, was to turn the tide of war. This was crucial to establishing his legitimacy. He had been chosen as a strongman to end the corruption, muddle and alleged maladministration of the Directory; but if he could not guide France to victory in war, the choice of a general to lead France would be fatally undermined.

Chapter 40

MARENGO

In Britain, Pitt and Grenville, those most intractable of France's enemies, had enjoyed a year of respite. The threat of invasion had been lifted from Britain's shores with Nelson's victory at the Battle of the Nile and Napoleon's invasion of Egypt. His failures there had coincided with Russia's entry into the war in alliance with Britain. The Austrian chancellor, Baron Johann Thugut, had advised Emperor Francis to approve a Russian expeditionary force commanded by the legendary Marshal Alexander Souvorov. With skill and speed Souvorov soon expelled France from almost all of northern Italy – which helped to put Napoleon's much vaunted Italian campaign in perspective. Conquering Italy was not as hard as it looked. Others were capable of similar feats. Archduke Charles, Austria's best general, had driven the French back in southern Germany and northern Switzerland. Then, as we have seen, the pendulum swung back: the capable Masséna turned the tables at Zurich. By the end of the year the 'mad Tsar', Paul, had decided to abandon the coalition.

Napoleon meanwhile began frantically to train his men for an offensive against the Austrians: to fund the expedition he resorted to robber-baron tactics, arresting the fabulously wealthy banker Gabriel Ourard for treason, then pardoning him when he paid ransom money in the shape of a colossal loan. Napoleon's immediate goal was to defeat the two Austrian armies of General Kray in Germany and General Mélas in Italy. Each of these was around 100,000-men strong; after that he intended to occupy Vienna.

Napoleon engaged in a new initiative – mobilizing, equipping

artillery corps and restoring the National Guard under Junot. He also created the army corps – virtually independent armies consisting of two infantry divisions, a division of light cavalry, artillery batteries and a corps of engineers that could act almost self-sufficiently and autonomously. The First Consul assembled part of the Army of the Reserve under Berthier around Dijon which would reinforce each of France's two main armies – Moreau's 120,000-strong Army of the Rhine and Masséna's smaller Army of Italy, with 36,000 men, which was operating between the Alps and the coast.

Napoleon concocted a fantastically complex and ambitious strategy, the result of his over-promotion from commanding relatively small armies in Italy and Egypt to command of all France's armies: he brought Moreau's army together into a single corps to engage Kray, while the Army of the Rhine and part of the Reserve would make a dash through Switzerland on the southern flank and then veer north to capture Vienna. If Mélas's army tried to obstruct the latter, the Army of the Rhine would attack. Napoleon's strategy was, however, dangerously over-elaborate.

Moreau, who regarded himself as Napoleon's equal as a commander, refused and insisted that he should command the whole army in an offensive against the central front; he guessed rightly that Napoleon was trying to cut him down to size. That discomfited Napoleon, who decided to attack principally across northern Italy. Unfortunately, the Austrians had come to precisely the same conclusion: fearing that any offensive along the Rhine would run into stiff French resistance, they decided to go for a southern strategy: a surprise attack under Mélas was staged against Masséna's forces.

The Austrian general succeeded in splitting the French army. Masséna was left stranded in Genoa with just four weeks' rations for his 10,000 men. The other 18,000 men were pushed beyond the Var river. The British fleet, meanwhile, blockaded Genoa. Masséna's days looked numbered. Mélas now intended to invade France through Provence. Meanwhile Moreau was holding back from launching his long-expected northern offensive.

At that stage, with his armies in trouble in Italy to the south and apparently blocked in the north, Napoleon himself decided to take

charge of the Army of the Reserve which had moved to Geneva and, which Berthier had shown little skill in commanding. On 6 May 1800, Napoleon travelled to Geneva to take charge of 50,000 troops. Desaix, the hero of the Egyptian campaign, had just arrived and was ordered to join the First Consul. Napoleon's new strategy was both simple and brilliant: to launch an unexpected assault over the Alpine passes into Italy and attack the Austrians where they least expected it – in the rear.

To the north, Moreau had at last staged an offensive in late April, defeating Kray at Moskirch and forcing him into Ulm. Masséna was still holding out on half rations, which permitted Napoleon to launch what was to become his trademark manoeuvre *'sur les derrières'* – a descent on the Austrians through the Alps. On 15 May he launched his attack across the Brenner Pass. Although this was no Hannibal-style achievement, it was difficult enough, and Napoleon skilfully sent armies through smaller passes to deceive the Austrians.

On 22 May Napoleon's army of 50,000 crossed the forty-kilometre pass with its guns dismantled and packed in pieces on sledges. For the time of year, the weather was poor, and snow blocked some of the pass. On learning that Fort Bard, an Austrian outpost at the end of the pass, threatened his army, Napoleon hastily decided to travel with his troops on a mule on a slippery and dangerous descent, where he was almost thrown several times. Napoleon managed to slip his remaining artillery pieces past Fort Bard in a snowstorm; but he lost almost all his other equipment.

On arriving at Ivrea, astonishingly, Napoleon decided not to come to the relief of the beleaguered Masséna at Genoa but instead retreated eastwards to Milan. This was in accordance with his previously thought-out strategy, but condemned Masséna's army, which was forced to surrender on 4 June, incidentally harming the reputation of one of Napoleon's chief rivals. Mélas occupied the city and then marched to Alessandria to counter Napoleon's movement on his rear. Napoleon tried to intercept him, and Mélas managed to avoid such an encounter for several days. As this chase ended, Napoleon decided to spend the night at the village of Marengo. The following morning – 14 June – Napoleon's 22,000 men and 20 guns were surprised by around 32,000 Austrian troops and some hundred cannon. Napoleon despe-

rately called for support from Desaix, leading one of the smallest French forces across the passes, as well as another splinter army.

The battle began at nine in the morning and after hours of fierce fighting, with the reserve of 800 Consular Guard being thrown in at three o'clock, the French were in retreat and the battle seemed over. At that moment Desaix and his small force and 18 guns arrived in support. At four o'clock Napoleon staged his last throw, initiating a small artillery barrage with Desaix's guns and his few remaining ones, and blowing up an ammunition wagon.

The Austrians in the plain below, pursuing him, were caught by surprise: their right began to give way and then they fled in disarray at 9 p.m. Napoleon remarked: 'The fate of a battle depends on a single moment.' But the heroic Desaix had been mortally wounded: of all Napoleon's generals before or since he was one of the greatest and most attractive. Napoleon was devastated. He spoke of his 'deep anguish for the death of the man I loved and esteemed more than anyone'. Some 6,000 Austrians were killed and 8,000 taken prisoner, and 40 guns were captured. The French lost about 6,000 men.

Napoleon had won by the skin of his teeth, having made several disastrous mistakes, primarily in dispersing his men. His decision not to relieve Masséna was perhaps his greatest error: if he had, Mélas might not have been able to force him to surrender and been diverted. Although he had shown his usual flair for reacting quickly under pressure, Napoleon's career had very nearly been cut short at Marengo; for if he had lost the battle his enemies in Paris would have closed in upon him. The battle was not particularly big or skilfully fought by the French, but its repercussions were far greater than its size. It was a turning point.

In a double stroke of luck for the French, Mélas decided to negotiate the next day, even though the blow to his army was far from mortal. At the Convention of Alessandria, all Austrian armies were withdrawn east of the Ticino river and all strongholds were given up west of Milan. Yet behind the Mincio the Austrians still had 55,000 men and 300 guns. Napoleon followed up his success by sending Murat to occupy the Papal States and sent a small army to take Tuscany.

To the north, however, Francis decided to appoint his young

brother, the eighteen-year-old Archduke John, in place of Charles, who had fallen ill, in a push across the central European front. John attacked across the river Inn against Moreau's army and, more by accident than design, confronted it at Hohenlinden. General Ney, Moreau's most brilliant subordinate, pulverized him: a colossal 18,000 Austrians were killed or taken prisoner. This was a far more decisive battle than any of Napoleon's up to then.

Marengo and Hohenlinden came as bitter blows to the Austrians. At the delightful summer palace of the Habsburgs at Schönbrunn, resplendent yet with the lightness of a Viennese waltz, the Austrian royal family would play hide and seek, row on the lake, and chase their favourite dog, Tisbe. The Emperor Francis was to be seen carrying his son around in a wheelbarrow. A delightful family man, Francis was weak and entirely lacked the intelligence of his father, Emperor Leopold II, who had sought to avoid war with France at all costs. Shallow, verbose, with a paranoid predilection for his secret services, he had dismissed the octogenarian chancellor, Wenzel von Aunitz, who had arranged the dynastic marriage of Marie Antoinette, Leopold's sister, to Louis XVI of France and instead relied on the advice of Baron Thugut and his former tutor, Count von Colloredo, an able man although a curiously affected dandy. Thugut was bent on war with France, while Colloredo was more pragmatic. After the disaster of Hohenlinden, the capable Archduke Charles and Colloredo assumed power.

Charles was ordered to come to the rescue: but in just a fortnight Moreau's forces had advanced nearly 200 miles and just before Christmas they were only fifty miles from Vienna. At this stage Archduke Charles wisely pressed for an armistice, which was signed on Christmas Day. Thugut was dismissed. In February 1801, the Treaty of Luneville was signed, which was similar to that of Campo Formio, with three key differences: the King of Naples was to be allowed to return from Sicily; Parma was ceded to the French, but its Duke was allowed to become ruler of Tuscany; and Austria had to agree to accept the Rhine as the natural frontier of France.

It seemed a relatively fair basis for a European settlement, one that might provide a foundation for a lasting European peace; and Moreau,

not Napoleon, was clearly the French general who had made it possible, winning the decisive victory. But Napoleon held the strings in Paris: Marengo, in spite of the narrow margin and small scale of victory, was hugely inflated as his triumph (it was largely that of the slain Desaix), cementing his hold on France.

During the two months he had been away, Carnot, the army minister, Bernadotte, his perennial Jacobin rival, and even Lafayette, still active, had variously plotted to seize power. But the news of Marengo was used by Napoleon's supporters to provoke an explosion of popular celebration in Paris which consolidated the First Consul's position. Followed as it was by Austria's suing for peace, the French could at last believe that peace was at hand: ironically, Napoleon was being hailed not as a victor but as a man of peace.

As the Austrian armistice coincided with the decision of the erratic Tsar Paul to withdraw from the war against Napoleon, Britain was left again as France's sole opponent. Napoleon had been making overtures for peace. 'Frenchmen,' he proclaimed. 'You want peace. Your government wants it even more than you.' Why did Napoleon want peace? He had just won two victories, one great one under Moreau and a smaller one under himself, and he was not disposed to risk defeat until his rule was much more firmly entrenched in France. The country's borders were now re-established as far as the Rhine, and Napoleon's old gains in Italy had largely been restored. He wanted to extinguish the remaining royalists in western France. The country's finances were exhausted. Above all, he knew the French people were yearning for peace after more than a decade of internal bloodletting and fighting outside wars for survival. With both Austrian and Russia out of the war, it was time to do a deal with Britain.

Napoleon is widely considered by historians to have been duplicitous in seeking peace: he was thought to be after a respite so that he could resume the war rearmed and more aggressively; the British too are said to have considered the peace no more than a lull. Yet this is not how it seemed at the time. Napoleon may have genuinely believed that peace was possible now that France's continental enemies were neutralized, and that France needed to settle down behind defensible borders after nearly a decade of war.

At first, though, neither Pitt nor the King would consider ending the war. Pitt had desperately tried to keep Austria in the war, offering further bribes. Meanwhile the British captured Malta in September 1800, as well as inflicting a decisive defeat on France's allies in India. Napoleon tried to outflank the stubborn British by seeking an alliance with the Tsar – until recently France's bitter enemy. Paul took the bait and formed a League of Neutral Nations which included Sweden, Denmark and Prussia to close the Baltic to British trade, a further ratcheting up of Napoleon's Continental System. Paul also suggested an alliance with France to destroy Russia's oldest enemy, Turkey, and a joint expedition to take India from the British. Some 35,000 Russians on the Volga were to join up with 35,000 French troops to further these ambitious aims. Napoleon, reverting to his reckless dreamer mode, seems to have been captivated by the idea: an alliance of two madmen for huge and distant empires.

In a dramatic development in March 1801 Tsar Paul was found strangled, an act widely attributed to the British secret service. It is impossible to establish the truth of this mysterious event, other than that the principal plotters were General Benigsen, a Hanoverian officer of great ability who was pro-British and anti-French and who had been stripped of his rank by Tsar Paul; Prince Zoublow and his brother, from a major noble family, supported by much of the aristocracy; and a part of the imperial family that hated Paul and, in particular, the upstart French government.

Benigsen was certainly the chief executor of the conspiracy: the British ambassador in St Petersburg, Lord St Helens, provided this little-known but gripping account of the plot, and his intimate knowledge suggests at least British passive complicity. On the night of 23 March, according to St Helens:

> Benigsen at the head of a group of armed officers in the plot, approached the new palace of St Michael, under the show of a relief from the Palace Guard. They passed the drawbridge and the first sentinels without interruption, but some alarm spreading from their arriving at so unusual an hour, it reached a private hussar, who usually slept in the Emperor's ante-chamber. This man had time to

make himself heard through the door, which was, however, immediately burst open by the assailants, who found the Emperor attempting to make his escape through a private door which led to the Empress's apartments; but which was instantly secured by General Benigsen, who cried out, '*Sire, vous êtes arrêtéz*'. The Emperor then lost all presence of mind, and while he was endeavouring to vent some unintelligible efforts of reproach, he was struck to the ground by some of the inferior conspirators, who afterwards strangled him with his sash. It is added that when a surgeon who lived in the palace examined the body and declared that he was not absolutely without some chance of recovery, some further and more violent means were immediately used to render it impossible.

Though the event in itself occasioned a general sensation of joy, both in the capital and throughout the empire, it appears that if the object of the Zoublow family was to acquire a large share of power under the new reign, that design has been entirely defeated, as they are looked upon with an eye of mistrust by the present Emperor, and are become universally unpopular, even with the soldiery.

Whatever the truth, the assassination dramatically altered the drift of events in Europe, as Napoleon was forced to shelve his eastern ambitions. Yet he was still riding high: by bullying he secured from the declining Spanish empire, always afraid of French attack and formally allied to France, the huge prize of Louisiana in North America for a pittance (the 'Louisiana purchase') and he reached an agreement of co-operation with the United States which barely bothered to conceal its hostility to Britain. Elba, which could not be defended, was also ceded to France by Naples. Talleyrand, the wily foreign minister, argued vociferously for peace with Britain; but as the French seemed to be doing well until the assassination of the Tsar, Napoleon was at first less enthusiastic. Another major setback however soon convinced him that even alone Britain was still a power to be reckoned with. Once again it was delivered by Horatio Nelson.

Chapter 41

COPENHAGEN

Nelson's career had by now resumed its familiar pattern of a dizzying plunge after a soaring achievement. After the Battle of the Nile, his greatest triumph to date, he moored at Palermo, where he endured a bout of morbid depression. He wrote to Lady Parker, Sir Peter's wife: 'A few weeks will send me to that bourne from whence none return: but God's will be done . . . You who remember me always laughing and gay, would hardly believe the change . . . Soon, very soon, we must all be content with a plantation of six feet by two, and I probably shall possess this estate much sooner than is generally thought.'

After the King and court had fled Naples, the working-class lazzaroni ran riot in the city, killing their enemies, releasing prisoners from the gaols and occupying the city's castles. The French forces outside the city decided to intervene to install a middle-class French-style Jacobin republic, but in the bitter fighting that ensued 1,000 French soldiers were killed to some 4,000 lazzaroni. The French installed what they called a Parthenopean Republic after Naples' name in classical times, which Nelson derided as a 'Vesuvian Republic'. He despatched Troubridge to blockade the city and seized the offshore islands of Capri, Ischia and Procida.

Troubridge executed his orders with his customary vigour and ruthlessness. He mocked the softness of a judge towards his victims: 'He talks of it being necessary to have a bishop to degrade the priests, before he can execute them. I told him to hang them first, and if he did not think the degradation of hanging sufficient, I would piss on their damned Jacobin carcasses, and recommended him to punish the

principal traitors the moment he passed sentence, no Mass, no confession, but immediate death, hell was the proper place for them.' He apologized for not sending on the head of a leading republican to Nelson, as the weather was too hot. Nelson displayed a similar authoritarian streak. He wrote to one of his captains: 'Your news of the hanging of thirteen Jacobins (at Procida) gave us great pleasure: and the three priests (sent to Palermo) I hope return in the Aurora, to dangle on the tree best adapted to the weight of their sins.'

Meanwhile the King had given his backing to Cardinal Fabrizio Ruffo, a former papal official, who had assembled a self-styled Christian Army of the Holy Faith in Calabria. This fought its way to the gates of Naples, where the French had left just 500 defenders in the Fort of St Elmo, while the republicans occupied the castles dominating the port, Nuovo and Uovo.

At this stage Nelson decided to sail to Naples with the Hamiltons. Arriving off the great port, he found that Ruffo had granted the French and their allies an armistice, which the infuriated British admiral considered tantamount to a capitulation. Nelson summoned Ruffo aboard his flagship – his fleet now consisted of nine warships, a formidable sight in the Bay of Naples – and insisted that the treaty be scrapped, which Ruffo refused to do.

The other British allies in Naples – Achmet on behalf of the Turks and the Russians – insisted that Nelson respect the treaty on the grounds that it 'was useful, necessary, and honourable . . . seeing that the deadly civil and national war was ended by that treaty without further bloodshed, and that it facilitated the expulsion of the common alien enemy from the kingdom. That as it had been formally entered into by the representatives of the said powers, an abominable outrage would be committed against public honour if it were to be violated . . .' At last the British admiral relented and peacefully occupied the castles of Nuovo and Uovo, the strongholds of the pro-French forces.

Nelson now turned on an old acquaintance, Count Caracciolo, who had deserted to the French. Nelson ordered the count to be tried by six Neapolitan officers. The court narrowly decided that he should be executed, a sentence Nelson enacted with indecent speed, refusing any

appeal and Caracciolo's request to be shot instead. Sir William Hamilton wrote:

> Caracciolo and twelve of the most infamous rebels are this day to be sent to Lord Nelson. If my opinion is relished they should be sent directly to be tried by the judge at Procida . . . Caracciolo will probably be seen hanging at the yardarm of the *Minerva*, a Neapolitan frigate, from daybreak to sunset, for such an example is necessary . . . Such a sight we have seen this morning! Caracciolo with a long beard, pale and half dead, and never looking up, brought bound on board this ship, where he now is with . . . other villainous traitors . . . It is shocking to be sure, but I that knew their ingratitude and crimes, felt less than many of the spectators. I have just time to add that Caracciolo has been condemned by a majority of the court-martial, and Lord Nelson has ordered him for execution this afternoon at five o'clock at the foremast yardarm of the *Minerva*, and his body thrown into the sea.

The decision shocked many people, for Caracciolo had been a personal friend of Nelson and had accused the King of deserting and plundering Naples – charges with a firm foundation. Nelson's mean streak was never more in evidence.

He turned his attention to the sole French holdout, the castle, while he did nothing as anti-Jacobin mobs ran riot in the city, killing and burning two Jacobins and eating their flesh. Jacobins were executed, many apparently on the instructions of the Queen acting through her friend and interpreter Lady Hamilton, who both of them encouraged Nelson in his severity. The fort eventually surrendered.

The republicans seem to have been given assurances that they would be landed at Toulon and were held aboard polaccas in the bay under the watchful eye of British ships. Then Nelson offered up the prisoners aboard the polaccas to summary Neapolitan justice, violating the surrender armistice: ninety-nine out of some 180 were executed, some of them quartered and burned. This atrocity was to besmirch Nelson's reputation almost as much as Napoleon's atrocities in the Holy Land: although Nelson was not directly

responsible, he could have prevented it. Meanwhile King Ferdinand arrived on 10 July.

On the first anniversary of the Battle of the Nile, Nelson, acting more like an oriental potentate than a British admiral, described how he was feted in a letter to his wife:

> A large vessel was fitted out like a Roman galley. On the oars were fixed lamps and in the centre was erected a rostra column with my name, at the stern elevated were two angels supporting my picture. More than 2,000 variegated lamps were fixed round the vessel, an orchestra was fitted up and filled with the very best musicians and singers. The piece of music was in great measure my praises, describing their distress, but Nelson comes, the invincible Nelson, and we are safe and happy again.

Nelson accepted a dukedom from King Ferdinand of Naples, that of Brontë (the Greek word for thunder) and an estate on the fertile volcanic slopes of Mount Etna, which in fact was largely uncultivated and yielded no income at all in his lifetime. The East India Company had granted him £10,000 in recognition of his actions on the Nile, which he generously shared with his father and brothers and sisters. But Nelson was now suffering from hubris after the Nile and three times ignored the direct orders of the new commander of the Mediterranean Fleet, Lord Keith, to send ships to protect Minorca; in the end he sent off four under-armed sloops. He wrote sarcastically to the First Lord of the Admiralty, Lord Spencer, alluding to Keith's failure to prevent the combined French and Spanish fleet from escaping from the Straits of Gibraltar to Cadiz. The Admiralty wrote back congratulating him on rescuing Naples but chiding him for disobeying Keith. Nelson replied: 'I only wish that I could have been placed in Lord Keith's situation . . . I would have broke the orders like a piece of glass: in that case, the whole marine of the French would have been annihilated . . . although I regret to say it, I do not believe any sea officer knows the sea and land business of the Mediterranean better than myself.'

The admiral was by now virtually out of London's control. Their lordships could not easily act against the British hero they had built up

in the public's mind. To Keith's alarm, in his absence from the Mediterranean, Nelson was appointed commander-in-chief of the Mediterranean Fleet. Nelson's *folie de grandeur* was on painful display in his reply to an unjustified accusation of his profiteering from contracts for beer and wine for his fleet. 'I defy any insinuations against me or my honour. Nelson is as far above doing a scandalous or mean action as the heavens are above the earth.' More accurately, he was sharply criticized for the appalling conditions in which Naples's 10,000 rebel prisoners were held. In September Troubridge was sent to take the port of Civita Vecchia near Rome and accepted the eternal city's surrender – thus fulfilling a prophecy, claimed Nelson, that he would take Rome one day with his ships. Nelson's actions began to be criticized in England. Fox launched a ferocious attack on Britain's greatest hero in parliament, without actually naming him:

I wish that the atrocities of which we hear so much, and which I abhor as much as any man, were indeed unexampled. I fear that they do not belong exclusively to the French . . . Naples for instance has been what is called 'delivered', and yet, if I am rightly informed, it has been stained and polluted by murders so ferocious, and by cruelties of every kind so abhorrent, that the heart shudders at the recital. It has been said not only that the miserable victims of the rage and brutality of the fanatics were savagely murdered, but that in many instances their flesh was eaten and devoured by the cannibals who are the advocates and the instruments of social order. Nay, England is not totally exempt from reproach if the rumours which are circulated be true.

I will mention a fact, to give ministers the opportunity, if it be false, of wiping away the stain that must otherwise fix upon the British name. It is said that a party of the republican inhabitants of Naples took shelter in the fortress of the Castle de Uovo. They were besieged by a detachment from the royal army, to whom they refused to surrender, but demanded that a British officer should be brought forward, and to him they capitulated. They made terms with him under the sanction of the British name. It was agreed that their persons and property should be safe, and that they should be

conveyed to Toulon. They were accordingly put aboard a vessel, but before they sailed their property was confiscated, numbers of them were taken out, thrown into dungeons, and some of them, I understand, notwithstanding the British guarantee, actually executed.

Meanwhile Nelson's increasingly flagrant affair with Lady Hamilton, which may not have started until the return of the court to Naples, was also beginning to scandalize opinion in Britain, as was Sir William's seeming acquiescence in his own cuckoldry. After Nelson, who seemed simultaneously to be 'vainglorious' and in wretched health, went to sleep with her, she would rise to gamble away his money at £500 a night at the gaming tables. *The Times* wrote slyly: 'Heroes and conquerors are subdued in their turn. Mark Antony followed Cleopatra into the Nile, when he should have fought with Octavius! And laid down his laurels and power, to sail down the Cydnus with her in the dress, the character, and the attitudes of Venus.'

Nelson's wife Fanny, separated from him for two years, wrote seeking to join him, but Nelson said he could not guarantee her safety. When summoned briefly to visit Keith at Leghorn and leave his beloved Emma, he wrote adoringly to her:

Separated from all I hold dear in this world what is the use of living if indeed such an existence can be called so . . . no separation no time my only beloved Emma can alter my love and affection for you, it is founded on the truest principles of honor, and it only remains for us to regret which I do with the bitterest anguish that there are any obstacles to our being united in the closest ties of this world's rigid rules, as we are in those of real love. Continue only to love your faithful Nelson as he loves his Emma, you are my guide I submit to you, let me find all my fond heart hopes and wishes with the risk of my life as I have been faithful to my word never to partake of any amusement or to sleep on shore . . . my only hope is to find you have equally kept your promises to me, for I never made you a promise that I did not as strictly keep as if made in the presence of heaven, but I rest perfectly confident of the reality of your love and

that you would die sooner than be false in the smallest thing to your own faithful Nelson who lives only for his Emma.

Nelson neglected his duties to set off on a five-week pleasure cruise aboard his flagship with the Hamiltons, visiting Syracuse's Roman ruins and then Malta. During one of his 'nights of pleasure' on the trip, Emma conceived a child by Nelson. Sir William continued to turn a blind eye.

Nelson conveyed the Queen and her daughters to Leghorn, where he refused to join Keith but travelled instead to Vienna with his lover. They journeyed by land to Trieste in four carriages with three luggage wagons. They reached Vienna, where the Queen's daughter was Empress. Nelson, now emaciated and prematurely old, made an odd contrast with the by now vast Lady Hamilton. They were feted like royalty. Nelson and the Hamiltons then travelled overland across Europe before sailing down the Elbe to catch a ship to Yarmouth. Nelson spent some £3,500 on the journey – some £700,000 at today's prices. At Yarmouth the crowds detached the horses from his carriage and pulled it themselves.

He stayed with Fanny on his first night home, where she underwent the ordeal of entertaining the Hamiltons to dinner. He was mobbed in the Strand and was given a ceremonial sword by a grateful City of London. But the newspapers were full of ribaldry: Cruikshank depicted the *ménage à trois* smoking pipes, with Lady Hamilton commenting, 'The old man's pipe was always out, but yours burns with full vigour.' Nelson replies: 'Yes, I'll give you smoke, I'll pour a whole broadside into you.' The unhappy Fanny had to endure fraternizing in public with Nelson and his mistress. At the theatre on Drury Lane she uttered a cry and fainted.

Nelson began to quarrel with his old mentor St Vincent. The crusty old disciplinarian had always enjoyed an unusually cordial relationship with Nelson, in spite of the latter's repeated insubordination, owing to his spectacular naval victories and also the ruthless streak in the younger man, which St Vincent admired. The quarrel was mundane, about prize money. As Nelson was commander of the Mediterranean Fleet,

he claimed the prize money due to the senior admiral – one-eighth from three frigates which had been taken at Finisterre. St Vincent, who was the senior admiral, insisted that Nelson's command did not extend that far.

One of Nelson's virtues was his generosity – some would say recklessness – with money and, for someone so illustrious who had been in so many battles, he had secured little in prize money, preferring glory to the mere lucre acquired in capturing defenceless merchantmen. His share of the four frigates would have amounted to £13,000, which would have been a very useful sum at a time when Nelson was deeply over-extended, partly owing to his generosity towards the Hamiltons (which had helped to secure Sir William's acquiescence in the undignified arrangement), partly because he had taken an expensive house off Piccadilly, so as to live in a manner suitable to one of his fame.

St Vincent appears to have softened when he met Nelson in Torquay and the two old friends reminisced and planned together:

Nelson was very low . . . appeared and acted as if he had done me an injury, and felt apprehensive that I was acquainted with it. Poor man, he is devoured with vanity, weakness, and folly; was strung with ribbons, medals, etc, and yet pretended that he wished to avoid the honour and ceremonies he everywhere met with upon the road . . . I could discover by the manner of Lord Nelson, when he was here, that he felt he had injured me, but we parted good friends, and as he owes all the fame, titles, badges, and distinctions he wears [to] my patronage and protection, and I still continue kind to him in the extreme, I hardly think it possible he can break with me.

As the next adventure approached, Nelson's infatuation with Emma grew to manic proportions: he wrote to her three times a day on occasion. Emma, for her part, dazzled London with her extraordinary sex appeal, although she was hugely overweight, which was attested to by almost everyone who met her. She also displayed a shrewish intelligence tainted by mean-spiritedness. She portrayed Fanny in these terms, in one of her very few letters:

The apoticarys widow, the Creole with her heart black as her feind like looking face was never destined for a Nelson for so noble minded a creature. She never loved him for himself. She loved her poor dirty escalopes [Aesculapius, Fanny's first husband, Dr Nisbet] if she had love, and the 2 dirty negatives made that dirty affirmative that is a disgrace to the human species [Josiah]. She then starving took in an evil hour our hero she made him unhappy she disunited him from his family she wanted to raise up her own vile spue at the expence and total abolation of the family which shall be immortalized for having given birth to the saviour of his country. When he came home maimed lame and covered with glory she put in derision his honnerable wounds She raised a clamour against him because he had seen a more lovely a more virtuous woman who had served with him in a foreign country and who had her heart and senses open to his glory to his greatness and his virtues.

This can be excused as an illiterate outburst of jealousy. Yet many of Nelson's family, his father excepted, took her side against Fanny, who was whispered about behind her back as cold and prim. Fanny felt utterly humiliated as her husband's infatuation with Emma became more obvious, yet she still wrote to him with tenderness and sought to reconstruct the marriage. Sir William himself made no complaint to the man who had made him a figure of ridicule, whom he considered a close friend, perhaps because he recognized that at his age his own physical flame had gone out.

As for Nelson, he was like a selfish, greedy child, besotted with Emma, a man who spent all his spare time in an adolescent infatuation. Yet in spite of his appalling treatment of Fanny, at this stage he still behaved with some decorum, giving her half his income and still trying to recommend her son Josiah for promotion. With the birth of a daughter, Horatia, to Emma – Fanny (like Josephine with Napoleon) had failed to provide him with a child – his passion redoubled. Love is not governed by reason, or commonsense, and has no sense of ridicule.

The middle-aged admiral was deeply in love, and perhaps his passion was sharpened by his constant presentiment that he would die soon, owing to his frail health, or would be killed in action. In turn his obsession with the closeness of death meant that he remained prepared

to take absurd risks – for dying presented few fears for a man who believed he was anyway doomed to an early grave. Nelson was beginning to thirst for an action to maintain the reputation which was sagging under the twin weights of the atrocities in Naples and his dalliance with Lady Hamilton.

Britain now had to face a new and unexpected threat, a deadly combination of the two most aggressive powers in Europe: Napoleon's France and Tsar Paul's Russia. The mentally unbalanced Paul had been incensed by Britain's occupation of Malta, which had cunningly been promised him at the last moment by Napoleon. The Russians were also chafing under the British system of searching their ships, and those of other Baltic states, to prevent supplies reaching France. In December 1800 Paul ordered all British ships in Russian ports to be seized and their crews made prisoner. Then he pressured Sweden into signing a 'treaty of armed neutrality', which Denmark and Prussia, adroitly changing sides, soon joined. Russia, Denmark and Sweden together had some forty warships at their immediate disposal and could probably raise as many again at short notice. It was tantamount to a declaration of war by the Baltic powers against Britain. The British decided to respond decisively and with speed: as soon as the freezing weather of the Baltic winter permitted, a fleet of eighteen ships of the line was despatched on 12 March 1801 under Sir Hyde Parker and Nelson to 'negotiate' Denmark's withdrawal from the league – although war was not formally declared. In the British view, the League had to be smashed before it had even begun to assemble its forces.

When the fleet arrived off Copenhagen Parker attempted to negotiate with the Danish government, but was rebuffed. The scene was set for a battle unlike any other of Nelson's major engagements – not a fight in the open between fleets but a brutal war of attrition between the British fleet and the shore defences of the city.

Parker had placed Nelson in command of ten ships of the line, two 50-gunners, seven frigates, and nine small craft. The senior admiral remained in command of eight more ships of the line some three miles away. Nelson was presented with his trickiest challenge yet, to attack down a narrow Channel between a huge shoal – the Middle Ground –

and the shoals along the coast of Copenhagen. Along the latter a
gauntlet of eighteen Danish men of war; some of them already unsafe
and in poor condition, many of them no more than grounded gun
batteries, mounted guard. In addition, to the north of the Channel
there were two forts. It was a formidable defence.

Nelson was at his most nervously aggressive at the council of war on
31 March. According to Colonel Stewart: 'Lord Nelson kept pacing
the cabin, mortified at everything which savoured either of alarm or of
irresolution. The council was told of the strength of the Swedish
squadron, whereupon Nelson sharply interjected, "The more numerous the better." As for the Russians, "I wish they were twice as many.
The easier the victory, depend on it!" ' Nelson was given a further two
ships, then hoisted his flag aboard the *Elephant* on 1 April. He sent the
intrepid Captain Hardy to take soundings at night in a muffled boat
right under the nose of the Danish ships.

On the morning of 2 April, the wind was favourable for him to sail
up the Channel between the Middle Ground and the coastal shoal.
The local pilots refused to serve for fear of causing the fleet to be
grounded. Captain Murray in the *Edgar* led the way. According to the
log of another ship:

> A more beautiful and solemn sight I never witnessed. The *Edgar* led
> the van . . . A man-of-war is at all times a beautiful sight, but at such
> a time the spectacle is overwhelming. We saw her passing on
> through the enemy's fire, and moving in the midst of it to gain
> her station. Our minds were seized with a sort of awe. Not a word
> was spoken through the ship save by the pilot and helmsmen, and
> their commands, being chanted very much in the same manner as
> the responses in a cathedral service, added to the solemnity.

The plan was meticulous: the *Edgar* was to pass the first four ships firing
broadsides, then anchor beside the fifth ship, the two ships behind her
overtaking to engage the next two ships, and then the following ships
to pass on ahead to engage one by one the ships farther forward. The
idea was for all the ships to rake the first four Danish ships with repeated
broadsides, but without stopping, and then engage the rest.

Disaster struck almost immediately: the *Agamemnon* went aground on the southern tip of Middle Ground, while the *Bellona* and the *Russell* also went ashore a little way farther up. Nelson himself was in the next ship, the *Elephant*, and saw that only if he passed to the west of the stranded ships was he likely to find the elusive deep-water channel. As his ships sailed down the Danish line, now just 700 feet away, the two sides exchanged murderous broadsides. The exchange lasted four terrible hours, with dreadful carnage being inflicted on both sides. On the *Edgar* 142 crew members were killed; on the *Monarch*, 218 lost their lives. Nelson, deprived of three of his main ships, had sent the frigates led by Captain Riou to exchange fire with the powerful 90-gun batteries on Three Crown Island at the northern tip of the Channel.

Parker was watching helplessly more than a mile away to the northeast of the Middle Ground, entirely uncertain how the fighting was going as smoke enveloped the ferocious battle. Captain Otway, his flag captain, went in a boat to discover what was happening, and while he was away Parker ran signal 39 from the mast of his flagship, the *London*: this meant 'discontinue the action'. The frigates, exchanging a terrible pounding with the shore batteries, obeyed, although Riou, already wounded, was deeply upset: 'What will Nelson think of us?' he exclaimed, and then was almost cut in two by fire from the Danish shore battery.

So arose one of the most celebrated incidents in Nelson's career: according to Colonel Stewart, who was beside him, Nelson saw the signal and made no comment but continued pacing the deck. His signal-lieutenant asked whether he should raise the same signal over the *Elephant*, so as to pass the message down the fleet. 'No, acknowledge it,' said Nelson. Then he asked, 'Is my signal – number 16 [for close action] flying?' 'Yes, my lord.' 'Mind you keep it so.' Nelson turned to his flag captain, Foley, and remarked, 'You know, Foley, I only have one eye. I have a right to be blind sometimes.' He raised his telescope to his blind eye and said, 'I really do not see the signal. Damn the signal. Keep mine for close action flying.'

This version was first given in Clarke and M'Arthur's extensive *Life of Nelson*. Southey's classic *Life of Nelson*, written in 1813, repeated the same story, as well as that of the ship's surgeon – that he ordered his

own signal for close battle to be nailed to the mast – which must have been hearsay, for surely the surgeon would have been down below tending the wounded.

Colonel Stewart himself wrote three versions of the story, and the 'blind eye' gesture only emerged in the last. Terry Coleman, in his excellent revisionist biography of Nelson, points out that 'Stewart did not mention the story in the first two versions, or in a six-page letter he wrote after the battle, and a journal', and concluded that the story was a later piece of embroidery. He may be right, although it would have been unusual for such a senior officer to fabricate such a story. Just possibly Stewart had considered the story an unimportant detail at the time, not realizing the high colour it added to the scene.

It served also to obscure the more important aspects of the battle. For Nelson undoubtedly did the right thing in disregarding an order from an admiral far from the scene of the battle. To continue the action was the only thing that he safely could do, for to discontinue it and withdraw would have exposed all his ships to withering and destructive broadsides as they ran the gauntlet to get out of the channel – not to mention the danger of running aground on the treacherous shoals. Vice-Admiral William Young of the Admiralty said as much to Lord Keith, both of them usually sticklers for discipline.

Nelson was absolutely right in his act of insubordination. He was facing one of the trickiest situations of his career: unlike at Cape St Vincent he did not confront the enemy fleet in open seas; unlike the Nile he could not send his ships inshore to attack the Danes on both flanks. He was committed to a straightforward exchange of fire against an enemy with superior firepower, between shoals that trapped his fleet. There was no room for imagination or dramatic manoeuvring. It was more like a land battle than a naval one.

Soon his position began to look critical, and it looked as if Nelson was facing his first defeat in a major fleet action. The *Elephant*, and the *Defiance* at the northern end of the line were under intense fire and seemed likely to be destroyed, while the *Monarch*, which was also in the vanguard under the guns of the fort, had sustained huge casualties. But then the *Dannebrog*, the Danish flagship, spectacularly caught fire and, with its cables cut, drifted down the Danish line sowing alarm. At half

past three it blew up. Other floating batteries had also cut their cables and some had sunk; but still Nelson could not lead his ships to safety under the intense fire of the Three Crown Island shore batteries.

Coolly, with his ship continuing to fire, he resorted to a brutal threat. He addressed a letter to the Danes: 'Lord Nelson has directions to spare Denmark when no longer resisting but if the firing is continued on the part of Denmark Lord Nelson will be obliged to set on fire the floating batteries he has taken, without having the power of saving the brave Danes who have defended them.' He insisted on sealing the letter with wax, and did so with great care while Stewart asked him why he was taking so long. Nelson replied that he did not want the Danes to believe he was acting in a hurry. This missive was received by the Danish Prince Regent, Frederick.

The young prince was less concerned by the fate of the men aboard the now helpless hulks than the possibility that the British, in this desperate situation, might bombard his capital. The Danes, who had no real quarrel with the British and were already regretting their alliance with Russia, acquiesced, to Nelson's intense relief.

He was able to extricate his ships from that channel of death. Even then two ships collided, the *Ganges* and *Monarch*, and, three ran aground including his own *Elephant*. They would have been helpless if the Danish batteries had still been firing. The following day he was able to reflect on his three beached ships at the south end of the mudbank. He had salvaged all of his ships with the loss of around 350 men killed and 600 wounded: the Danes had lost some 1,800 men and 3,500 were taken prisoner in the captured ships. It was a victory on points – the least decisive of Nelson's greatest battles.

By a threat and a trick he had got out of an extremely dangerous situation. Stewart wrote: 'Lord Nelson then commanded a cessation of hostilities, and by prolonging it under one pretext or another, in four and twenty hours after got our crippled ships off the shoals, and from under the guns of the enemy's batteries . . .'

After the battle Nelson said apprehensively to Foley: 'Well I have fought contrary to orders and I shall perhaps be hanged. Never mind. Let them.' Meanwhile he pressed for a more permanent truce. 'Bomb ships' were brought up to threaten to bombard Copenhagen. He told

the Danes: 'We are ready. Ready to bombard this night.' Looking at the palace and wooden houses of the beautiful old city he remarked: 'Although I have only one eye, I see that this will burn very well.' The Danes replied that they feared the Russians would bombard them if they pulled out of their alliance, and Nelson offered to protect them with a British fleet. He personally conducted the negotiations on shore. At last agreement was reached. An exultant Nelson wrote:

1st We had beat the Danes. 2nd We wish to make them feel that we are their real friends, therefore have spared their town, which we can always set on fire; and I do not think if we burnt Copenhagen it would have the effect of attaching them to us; on the contrary they would hate us. 3rd They understand perfectly that we are at war with them for their treaty of armed neutrality made last year. 4th We have made them suspend the operations of that treaty. 5th It has given our fleet free scope to act against Russia and Sweden.

His fleet now moved up the Baltic towards its real target, the Russian fleets at Revel and Kronstadt. But then the news arrived that the Tsar had been assassinated before the battle of Copenhagen. Nelson argued that it was by no means certain the new Russian government would be any better disposed towards Britain and, with the overwhelming strength of eighteen ships, urged an attack on each of the dispersed Russian fleets at Carlscrona, Kronstadt and Revel. They could be destroyed in turn. But Parker insisted on taking the fleet back to Kioge Bay.

On 5 May, however Parker was recalled and Nelson appointed to command the fleet. By 12 May Nelson had led it back to Revel only to fund that the Russian fleet there had gone and joined the one at Kronstadt. The new Tsar, Alexander I, meanwhile reversed policy, releasing British merchant ships which had been seized and signing an agreement with Britain under which British goods were again allowed to sail in Baltic waters. Thus the threat to Britain's trade with the north had been decisively dispelled – partly thanks to Nelson's skill and daring, partly to luck.

Chapter 42

PEACE IN OUR TIME

After his success at Copenhagen, Nelson's career plunged again in what had become for him a familiar pattern. Up to now, except at the Nile, he had been a subordinate commander because of his youth. Not that that made much difference; as one of his captains said, to his irritation, as far back as 1797: 'You did just as you pleased in Lord Hood's time, the same in Admiral Hotham's, and now again with Sir John Jervis. It makes no difference to you who is commander-in-chief.' He was now to gain a command of his own – but one he did not want. On his return to England in July 1801 he was promptly appointed to command the Channel Fleet in case of French invasion.

Nelson was deeply sceptical that any such possibility existed, and justifiably so, but he took to his new duties, compiling a memorandum to the Admiralty about the threat. Unable to stay passive for long, on 4 August Nelson despatched a flotilla of gunboats and bomb vessels, as well as a ship of the line, to bombard Boulogne where there were 2,000 French soldiers. Thousands of spectators lined the cliffs of Dover and Deal to watch the action with telescopes. The attack did minimum damage, but served to warn the French to be on their guard. It was said that Nelson had been 'speaking to the French'.

Nelson was in an irritable mood, a celebrity increasingly unhappy with the expectations and admirers he had aroused. 'Oh how I hate to be stared at,' he complained moodily aboard his flagship. 'Fifty boats, I am told, are rowing about her this moment to have a look at the one-armed man.'

Nelson summoned some of his youngest captains to plan for a frontal attack on Boulogne: five squadrons would be involved. The aim was to

attack the ships moored across the harbour with boarding parties supported by mortar ships at night, when the French ships could not be expected to fire back for fear of hitting their own. It was a 'cutting-out' expedition on a grand scale.

Nelson was confident. He wrote to Emma: 'It is one thing to order and arrange an attack and another to execute it. But I assure you, I have taken much more precaution for others than if I was to go myself . . . After they have fired their guns, if one half of the French do not jump overboard and swim on shore, I will venture to be hanged . . . If our people behave as I expect, our loss cannot be much. My fingers itch to be at them.'

His adversary was France's greatest naval commander, Admiral Louis-René Latouche-Tréville, and he was prepared: netting had been strung down from the upper rigging to the ships' sides to repel attack. The ships were attached to one another by chains with strong cables securely anchored to the seabed. The French commander observed the British making preparations during the day of 15 August. That same night boatloads of British sailors were dropped off the coast wearing white armbands for identification at night and carrying cutlasses, pikes, tomahawks, pistols, muskets and knives. It was to be a daring inshore raid – except that the French were fully alert to them.

Taking advantage of the incoming tide, the British boats swept silently in – and two of the foremost were carried past the French fleet by the swirling, racing waters. The French tossed a cannonball into another, which sank her. The fourth crew attempted to board the *Etna*. As a junior British officer abroad wrote: 'But a very strong netting, triced up to her lower yards, baffled all our endeavours and an instantaneous discharge of her guns and small arms from about 200 soldiers on her gunwale knocked myself, Mr Kirby, the master of the *Medusa*, and Mr Gore, a midshipman, with two-thirds of the crew upon our backs in the boat, all either killed or wounded.'

As the men tried to clamber across the unexpected netting they encountered, they were shot at by the French on deck. One ship was captured. But as the commanding officer of the raid reported later to Nelson: 'I was prevented from towing her out by her being secured by

a chain and, in consequence of a very heavy fire of musketry and grapeshot that was directed at us from the shore, three luggers and another brig within half a pistol-shot, and not seeing the least prospect of being able to get her off, I was obliged to abandon her.'

By about 4 a.m. the boats were returning, having utterly failed in their task, while Nelson stood off the French coast, in a frigate, watching. At midday the British sailed back to Deal, with forty-four men killed and 128 wounded and not a single prize: only ten Frenchmen had been killed and thirty-four wounded. The raid had been a complete, if relatively minor, fiasco. The French sang joyfully: 'Off Boulogne, Nelson poured hell-fire! But on that day, many a drunk/ Instead of wine, drank salt water/off Boulogne!' Nelson wrote disconsolately: 'I am sorry to tell you that I have not succeeded in bringing out, or destroying the enemy's flotilla moored in the mouth of the harbour of Boulogne. The most astonishing bravery was evinced by many of our officers and men.'

Later he sank into deep melancholy. He wrote to the Admiralty Secretary: 'A diabolical spirit is still at work. Every means, even to posting up papers in the streets of Deal, has been used to set the seamen against being sent by Lord Nelson to be butchered and that at Margate it was the same thing, whenever any boats went on shore. "What, are you going to be slaughtered again?" Even this might be got over but the subject has been fully discussed in the wardrooms, midshipmen's berths, etc . . . as I must probably be, from all the circumstances I have stated, not much liked by either officers or men, I really think it would be better to take me from this command.' He wrote to St Vincent: 'I own I shall never bring myself again to allow any attack to go forward, where I am not personally concerned; my mind suffers much more than if I had a leg shot off in this later business.' At the funeral of two young midshipmen killed in the action he wept and was even more distraught when a young protégé, Captain Edward Peake, who had been wounded, subsequently died.

Nelson had regularized his affair with Emma, and acquired a property, Merton Place in Surrey, where she could play his hostess. He was disappointed by his father's intense disapproval of his dalliance. The

elderly churchman was not in thrall to the hero-worship which surrounded his son and which legitimized his ostentatious, in some eyes, flaunting of his mistress and humiliation of his wife. Nelson defended his conduct towards Fanny, whom his father adored, in a letter: 'My dear father – I have received your letter and of which you must be sensible I cannot like for as you seem by your conduct to put me in the wrong it is no wonder that they who do not know me and my disposition should. But Nelson soars above them all and time will do that justice to my private character which she has to my public one. I that have given her [Fanny], with her falsity . . . £2,000 a year and £4,000 in money and which she calls a poor pittance . . . I could say much more but will not out of respect to you, my dear father, but you know her, therefore I finish.'

In December 1801 Fanny wrote imploringly: 'Do, my dear husband, let us live together. I can never be happy until such an event takes place. I assure you again I have one wish in the world, to please you. Let everything be buried in oblivion, it will pass away like a dream. I can now only entreat you to believe I am most sincerely and affectionately your wife Frances H Nelson.' Brutally Nelson had a secretary write back: 'Opened by mistake by Lord Nelson, but not read.'

Nelson blamed Fanny for turning the old man against him. Nelson's behaviour towards Fanny was reprehensible, and his obsession with the gross and spiteful Emma distasteful, but the truth was that he had fallen out of love with the former and in love with the latter; and love is ungovernable, particularly in a man who believes he can do as he likes and fears he may have only a short time left to live. When his father's doctor wrote to his son that the parson was dying, Nelson replied: 'I have no hopes that he can recover. God's will be done. Had my father expressed a wish to see me, unwell as I am, I should have flown to Bath but I believe that it would be too late; however should it be otherwise and he wishes to see me, no consideration shall detain me a minute.' The old man died the same day. Nelson did not attend the funeral.

The superstar admiral also fell out with one of his oldest friends and comrades in arms. Thomas Troubridge had been with Nelson at Cape

St Vincent, Tenerife, the Nile and in Sicily. Troubridge was a brilliant and valiant sailor, but an even harsher disciplinarian than Nelson. However, when Nelson and Emma left Naples in 1799, he made the cardinal error of criticizing the Queen of Naples, technically the island's sovereign, for not providing food for the starving people there:

> I am not very tender hearted, but really the distress here would even move a Neapolitan . . . I have this day saved 30,000 people from dying; but with this day my ability ceases. As the King of Naples, or rather the Queen and her party, are bent on starving us, I see no alternative, but to leave these poor unhappy people to starve, without being witnesses to their distress. I curse the day I ever served the King of Naples . . . We have characters, my lord, to lose; these people have none. Do not suffer their infamous conduct to fall on us.

Troubridge also criticized Nelson for going with Emma to Leghorn. Nelson was furious and wrote a bitter letter to his old friend. Troubridge replied: 'It really has so unhinged me, that I am quite unmanned and crying. I would sooner forfeit my life, my everything, than be deemed ungrateful to an officer and friend I feel I owe so much to . . . I [pray] your lordship not to harbour the smallest idea that I am not the same Troubridge you have known me.'

When Nelson fell out with St Vincent over the issue of prize money and the latter's own disdain for Emma, Troubridge was chosen by the First Lord to serve on the Admiralty board. This further angered Nelson. Yet he soon returned to confiding in him in his letters, calling him his 'old faithful friend'. But on his return to England, Nelson had begun to suspect that Troubridge was responsible for his unwanted command of the Channel Fleet – which he believed was deliberately intended to keep him apart from Emma.

He was livid when St Vincent pointedly compared Troubridge's 'magic' to his own. He complained about the 'beasts' of the Admiralty keeping him at sea. He was furious with Troubridge:

> Tomorrow week all is over – no thanks to Sir Thomas. I believe the fault is all his, and he ought to have recollected that I got him the medal

of the Nile. Who upheld him when he would have sunk under grief
and mortification? Who placed him in such a situation in the kingdom
of Naples that he got by my public letters, titles, the colonelcy of
marines, diamond boxes from the King of Naples, 1,000 ounces in
money for no expenses that I know of? Who got him £500 a year
from the King of Naples? . . . Who brought his character into notice?
Look at my public letters. Nelson, that Nelson he now lords it over. So
much for gratitude. I forgive him but by God I shall never forget it. He
enjoys showing his powers over me. Never mind, although it will
shorten my days . . . I have been rebuffed so that my spirits are gone,
and the great Troubridge has what we call cowed the spirits of Nelson,
but I shall never forget it . . .

Even the long-suffering Sir William Hamilton was now at breaking
point. He wrote:

I have passed the last 40 years of my life in the hustle and bustle that
must necessarily be attendant on a public character. I am arrived at
the age when some repose is really necessary, and I promised myself
a quiet home, although I was sensible, and said so when I married,
that I should be superannuated when my wife would be in her full
beauty and vigour of youth. That time is arrived, and we must make
the best of it for the comfort of both parties.

Unfortunately our tastes as to the manner of living are very
different. I by no means wish to live in a solitary retreat, but to have
seldom less than 12 or 14 at table, and those varying continually, is
coming back to what was become so irksome to me in Italy during
the latter years of our residence in that country . . . I have no
complaint to make, but I feel that the whole attention of my wife is
given to Lord N and his interest at Merton. I well know the purity
of Lord N's friendship for Emma and me, and I know how very
uncomfortable it would make his lordship, our best friend, if a
separation should take place, and am therefore determined to do all
in my power to prevent such an extremity, which would be
essentially detrimental to all parties, but would be more sensibly
felt by our dear friend than by us.

In March 1803 the tolerant old man died. By that time Nelson's reputation was in tatters again. It was ever thus. His undistinguished early career and oblivion in the West Indies had been followed by the glory of Cape St Vincent, which had been succeeded by the glorious failure at Tenerife, then by the triumph at the Nile, then by the squalid comedy of excess and cruelty at Naples, then the triumph at Copenhagen, then by failure at Boulogne and the cruelty of his treatment of his wife, father and Sir William Hamilton all for Emma's sake. By that time too peace had broken out; and Napoleon's formidable British foe, his reputation savagely compromised, was contemplating the prospect of a quiet life for the first time.

The Treaty of Amiens reflected Britain's long weariness with war, as well as the inadequacy of Britain's new prime minister, Addington, appointed after King George III fell out with Pitt over the issue of Catholic emancipation. Negotiations began on 1 October 1801, but it was not concluded until 27 March 1802. Its terms were some of the most shameful in British history. Britain surrendered virtually every outpost in the Mediterranean, including Elba, Minorca and the key outpost of Malta, which was to be evacuated in three months and occupied by Neapolitan troops guaranteed by the six major powers. Of the territories she had gained in the war, only Ceylon and Trinidad were to remain in British hands, while the latter was to remain her only significant outpost in the West Indies. France retained all her continental possessions except for Naples and the Papal States. Piedmont, Elba and Liguria effectively became French satellites. Holland was also effectively annexed, and Napoleon soon made it clear that Switzerland would be also.

The Peace of Amiens brought an atmosphere of eerie unreality to the European scene. After nearly nine years of non-stop fighting, the parties had drifted into the eye of the hurricane although some mistook it for escaping the storm altogether. After just a year of calm, they were to re-enter the storm and not emerge for another twelve years. In that brief interlude the combatants had time to reflect and peer at each other: to discover whether peace really was possible. For France's new ruler had decided that the Revolution, which had unleashed the

tempest, was at an end. Was Napoleon a pragmatic leader of France that the rest of Europe could live with?

The amiable, pompous Lord Addington plainly thought so, as he had conceded almost every demand that France had asked for. Napoleon thought so too, for he had secured much of what he wanted from Britain without a fight. If his adversary would leave him as the undisputed power in Europe, why should not the world's greatest maritime and greatest continental powers live alongside one another?

For the moment the war party in Britain was smothered by the overwhelming relief of the population at the prospect of peace. Grenville remarked caustically that the treaty was secured on the principle of England giving up all she had taken and France keeping all she had acquired during the war. William Windham, the former secretary of war, head of Britain's spy network and Norfolk magnate, was equally opposed to the peace. A sympathizer, Charles Burney wrote to him: 'I had always seen the danger of making peace with France under her present rulers . . . With all Europe at her feet, except this country; in actual possession of half Germany, the Netherlands, Switzerland, Savoy, Piedmont, Lombardy, Genoa, the Ecclesiastical States . . . as are Naples, Spain and Portugal as well as Holland: and all this territory and its inhabitants under the direction of such miscreants, regicides, assassins, plunderers, Jacobins, atheists and anarchists! – what had we to expect?' Sheridan observed that Amiens was a peace of which everybody is glad and nobody is proud.

These, however, were lone voices. British nobility flocked to Paris to see Napoleon's brilliant foreign minister, Talleyrand. Lady Bessborough gushed at a dinner party at the foreign ministry: 'I never saw anything so magnificent – the apartments beautiful, all perfumed with frankincense and as soon as seventy-eight people (of which the company consisted) sat down, an immense glass at the end of the room slid away by degrees, and soft and beautiful music began to play in the midst of the jingle of glasses and vaisselle. The dinner was, I believe, excellent but from some awkwardness in the arrangement it was very difficult to get anything to eat.'

Talleyrand did not impress everyone. Many considered him pom-

pous and affected, with a diseased white face gazing out over his extravagant clothes – 'the most barefaced teller of untruths I had ever met with,' commented one British visitor. Fouché, the ruthless chief of police, was described as 'foxy' and unnaturally pale, a small man in a resplendent blue uniform and the boots of a hussar.

The British visitors were most curious of all to meet France's new ruler, the man who had ended the Revolution, welcomed back the émigrés, restored the church, and concluded peace. This was surely someone Britain could live at peace with. Power always hypnotizes the gullible and even the shrewd Fanny Burney was impressed.

> The door of the audience chamber was thrown open with a commanding crash, a vivacious officer-sentinel . . . nimbly descended the three steps into our apartment and, placing himself at the side of the door, with one hand spread as high as possible and the other extended horizontally, called out in a loud and authoritative voice, 'Le Premier Consul!' You will easily believe nothing more was necessary to obtain attention; not a soul spoke, or stirred, as he and his suite passed along.
>
> [I had] . . . a view so near, though so brief, of his face as to be very much struck by it. It is of a deeply impressive cast, pale even to sallowness, while not only in the eye but in every feature, care, thought, melancholy and meditation are strongly marked with so much of character, nay, genius and so penetrating a seriousness – or, rather, sadness, as powerfully to sink into an observer's mind . . . He has by no means the look to be expected from Bonaparte, but rather that of a profoundly studious and contemplative man.

Less exalted visitors that flocked across the Channel during that phoney peace found Paris pleasing, although smaller than expected.

English visitors were shocked by the nearly transparent and low cut dresses of French women. A British officer observed: 'The Bishop of Durham would expire at seeing the dresses . . . The ladies are almost quite naked . . . There cannot be anything so profligate, so debauched, or so immoral as the ideas or manners of all ranks of people, particularly the higher class.' It was generally agreed that the most beautiful and

cultivated young woman in Paris was the young Madame Rémusat. Fox's secretary, John Trotter, described her as 'a lovely phantom, breathing a thousand delicious charms . . . and so ingenuous and unaffected! Shunning the ardent gaze and, if conscious of her dazzling beauty, unassuming and devoid of pride; rich in the first of female virtues – a kind and noble heart!'

Not everyone was overwhelmed. One visitor considered France 'the completest military despotism'. Charles Williams Wynn wrote of 'the almost Asiatic pomp, splendour and luxury of the government. [Napoleon] rules with a rod of iron without the smallest attention to popularity.' Lord Aberdeen observed that 'a martial air reigns through the town, soldiers parade most of the principal streets and keep the peace; the utmost respect is paid to everything military.' Another English visitor remarked that 'the civilian power is not distinguishable in Paris. It is the musket and the bayonet that settle all differences.' Wordsworth, who returned to France after more than a decade's absence, was shocked by what he saw and quickly returned, after hearing that Napoleon had been made Consul for life, to sing the praises of English liberty:

> Here, on our native soil, we breathe once more.
> The cock that crows, the smoke that curls, that sound
> Of bells; – those boys who in yon meadow-ground
> In white-sleeved shirts are playing; and the roar
> Of the waves breaking on the chalky shore; –
> All, all are English. Oft have I looked round
> With joy in Kent's green vales; but never found
> Myself so satisfied in heart before.
> Europe is yet in bonds; but let that pass,
> Thought for another moment. Thou art free,
> My Country! And 'tis joy enough and pride
> For one hour's perfect bliss, to tread the grass
> Of England once again.

The English people were on the whole delighted to be at peace. Addington incautiously abolished income tax, halved the size of the

British army, disbanded the volunteer regiments, reduced the fleet of warships from a hundred to forty, broke up the Grand Fleet at Torbay and discharged 40,000 sailors. Lord St Vincent was summoned with his enormous prestige to launch an attack on corruption in the dockyards, which brought them to a near standstill. It was peace in our time.

The peace was used by Napoleon to gain time for a programme of further expansion southward. As this dawned even on Addington's addled government, the British dragged their feet in leaving Malta. This angered Napoleon, who demanded they leave the island forthwith. The British refused. He needed more time to rearm, so he proposed that the Russians take over the island on a ten-year lease. This was refused. Napoleon was furious and overplayed his hand.

The able British ambassador in Paris, Charles, Lord Whitworth, along with his wife, the haughty Duchess of Dorset now came into play. With his beaky nose, self-assurance and switch-on – switch-off charm, he was perfectly suited for his role. In March 1803 he enraged Napoleon by treating him with particular disdain. The Emperor, accustomed to complete deference, buttonholed Whitworth with very considerable agitation: 'We are too sensible of the advantages of peace. But now you mean to force me to fight for fifteen years more! . . . If you arm, I shall arm, too! If you fight, I shall fight also! You think to destroy France; you will never intimidate her! . . . You should respect treaties! Bad luck to those who cannot respect treaties!'

A British witness reported graphically:

Bonaparte either was, or pretended to be, in a rage. Never, throughout his life, a gentleman in his feelings or conduct, he now outraged a ceremony and a time of courtesy, coming up to Lord Whitworth and addressing him in the loudest tones of anger and even with gestures which suggested the possibility of an assault. Lord Whitworth was a tall, handsome man with great dignity of manner. He stood perfectly unmoved whilst the Little Corporal raged and fumed beneath him – now and then saying a few conciliatory words as to the desire of his government to secure an honourable peace. Yet so violent was the demeanour of Bonaparte that Lord Whitworth was compelled to think what he ought

to do with his sword if, in his person, the Majesty of England was to
be publicly insulted by an actual assault.

On 12 May Whitworth resolved to leave Paris, and by 18 May the war
had been renewed. Napoleon thereupon issued an order unprecedented in European diplomacy to arrest all Englishmen in Paris
between the ages of eighteen and sixty: some 700 of them were
rounded up, 400 of them businessmen. There were fears that they
would be used as hostages and even executed.

The British, under their inept prime minister, immediately went on
the defensive against Napoleon's bombast and assembly of an invasion
force. There was only one man, everyone knew, with the stature to
rally the nation.

At his country house in Walmer, William Pitt was enjoying the first
real free time he had ever had in his life. Prime minister at twenty-four,
after more than seventeen unbroken years in office, he enjoyed laying
out the gardens of his small estate, shooting and seeing a handful of old
friends. Yet with the declaration of war, in his notional office of Lord
Warden of the Cinque Ports, he endeared himself to the British people
by throwing himself into the general defence of Britain: he raised and
drilled a volunteer corps of 3,000 men.

After more than a year of refusing to attend the House of Commons, he
made his first appearance like a ghost. On 20 May 1803, Thomas Creevey
wrote of him that his old-port-ruddied complexion was sallow, his face
downcast, his speech interrupted occasionally by coughing. There was 'a
universal sentiment in those around him that he was done'. George
Canning, Pitt's faithful young disciple, had written on his birthday:

> And O! if again the rude whirlwind should rise,
> The dawning of peace should fresh darkness deform,
> The regrets of the good and the fears of the wise
> Shall turn to the pilot that weathered the storm

Yet Pitt would not move against Addington, his old friend, whom he
had agreed to support loyally when he had left office. The diehard

opponents of the government were led by Pitt's old friend and intimate, William, Lord Grenville, his first cousin and former foreign secretary, a steely and principled Whig grandee responsible for the superb execution of foreign policy during the preceding years, and Charles James Fox, the perennial and mercurial opposition leader who, however, had long opposed war with France and even now refused to take the threat of invasion seriously.

But these two political giants, alongside Canning, continued to stay outside a government of mediocrities whose only able figure was a young Ulsterman, Lord Castlereagh, who was trying to prod Addington towards war. Creevey wrote: 'Upon my soul! It is too shocking to think of the wretched destiny of mankind in being placed in the hands of such pitiful, squirting politicians as this accursed apothecary and his family and friends.'

Britain's enfeebled government was now buffeted by another misfortune: in February 1804 King George III caught a chill reviewing volunteers, and his old insanity returned with a rush. He opened parliament with the words 'My Lords and Peacocks'. With his equilibrium apparently in danger, the hideous prospect of a regency under the future George IV during a time of acute national crisis loomed: Pitt viewed the prospect of a rudderless Britain under an indebted, usually drunk, bigamously married voluptuary and a feeble prime minister with mounting horror.

Pitt had suffered from the legacy of his own slow response to the problem posed by revolutionary France. While many British politicians had been calling for war after the execution of Louis XVI, Pitt still hoped for peace – leaving the French Convention to declare war on 1 February 1793. As Rosebery summed it up:

> It is, then, abundantly manifest from every source of evidence that war was forced on the English ministry; that Pitt carried to an extreme his anxiety to avoid it; that his resignation could not have averted it; and that in any case it was impossible for him as a man of honour, or a serious statesman, to resign. We shall see, when war had begun, his constant endeavours to put an end to it. Whether he was a great war-minister, as he is generally considered, or an

incapable war-minister, as he is called by Macaulay, he is certainly the most strenuous peace-minister that ever held office in this country.

Pitt had also formed a deeply hostile view of Napoleon as a devotee of war.

all centred and condensed into one man, who was reared and nursed in its bosom, whose celebrity was gained under its auspices, who was at once the child and champion of all its atrocities and horrors. Our security in negotiation is to be this Bonaparte, who is now the sole organ of all that was formerly dangerous and pestiferous in the Revolution.

He paid the colossal price of discarding his principled support for Catholic emancipation in order to resume the reins of government. Pouring sarcasm upon the government, he brought it down in a debate on the army. Pitt was a coldly calculating man, accustomed to being in power virtually all his adult life. It must be considered possible that he had installed the luckless Addington precisely because he knew he would fall flat on his face, while the former leader bided his time, engaged upon patriotic duties likely to make him even more popular as a war leader. A couple of days later he issued his call to arms. Creevey described it: 'The great fiend bewitching a breathless House, the elevation of his tone of mind and composition, the infinite energy of his style, the miraculous perspicuity and fluency of his periods . . . Never, to be sure, was there such an exhibition, its effect was dreadful. He spoke nearly two hours – and all for war, and for war without end!'

Fox's own view of Napoleon, while at one stage almost treasonable, had changed drastically after meeting the man of power during the peace. At first he was adulatory and fascinated, his secretary describing Napoleon as 'a small and by no means commanding figure, dressed plainly, though richly, in the embroidered consular coat – without powder in his hair, [he] looked at the first view like a private gentleman, indifferent as to dress and devoid of all haughtiness.'
Napoleon spoke to Fox:

Ah! Mr Fox! I have heard with pleasure of your arrival. I have desired much to see you. I have long admired in you the orator and friend of this country, who, in constantly raising his voice for peace, consulted that country's best interests, those of Europe and of the human race. The two great nations of Europe require peace; they have nothing to fear; they ought to understand and value one another. In you, Mr Fox, I see with much satisfaction, that great statesman who recommended peace because there was no just object for war; who saw Europe desolated to no purpose and who struggled for its relief.

Fox observed of Napoleon that he was 'easy and desirous to please without effort . . . In one particular only he noticed the manner of a man who acts as a superior, which was that he sometimes put questions and did not wait for the answers before he proposes other questions. It has been observed that he smiles with his mouth but that his eyes never have a corresponding expression.' But he was later appalled when Bonaparte grimly accused the war secretary, William Windham, and Pitt.

Bonaparte went on saying he would have forgiven open enemies in the cabinet, or the field but not cowardly attempts to destroy him, such as . . . setting on foot the infernal machine [a bomb attempt on his life]. Mr F. again with great warmth assured him he was deceived, that Mr Pitt and Mr Windham, like every other Englishman, would shrink with horror from the idea of secret assassination. 'You do not know Pitt,' said Bonaparte. 'Yes, I do know him,' replied Mr F. 'and well enough to believe him incapable of such an action. I would risk my head in that belief.' Bonaparte, after a moment, walked away in silence.

Chapter 43

THE CONSUL'S PEACE

Napoleon needed this respite to impose his own stamp on French politics. Peace was as popular among ordinary Frenchmen as among the English. Many considered Napoleon's greatest achievement to have been his decisive administration after the years of bloodshed and the years of alleged corruption and division under the Directory – although the comparative prosperity that so struck the British visitors in 1802 was in fact a legacy of the Directory.

Napoleon's first priority was to build-up France's finances through his highly competent economic adviser, Lebrun. He promptly raised some 5 million francs through a forced loan and raised another 9 million in a lottery. A corps of tax collectors was created: 840 senior officials sent to every department in the land: This increased the tax take by nearly 100 per cent. Indirect taxes were levied on wine, luxuries, salt and tobacco. He also sought to curb government waste and introduced an audit office.

The economy began to boom, particularly as banks and the moneyed classes began to reinvest in France in the belief that stability had been attained under Napoleon. A fall in the price of bread added to his popularity. Borrowing from Pitt's experience in England, he set up a sinking fund to try and reduce national debt. More radically, he created the Bank of France, which controlled the money supply as well as issuing its own credit.

At the beginning of his rule, Napoleon also raised money by selling off state assets previously confiscated from the aristocracy as well as plunder from his Marengo campaign. He openly subsidized key

industries and offered loans to manufacturers who provided jobs. He strictly controlled politically sensitive grain prices and when bread prices suddenly rose again in 1802 he took every conceivable measure to dampen popular anger, buying huge quantities of bread abroad and flooding France with it. Napoleon was an unashamed state interventionist or *dirigiste* – what would be called a corporatist today – meddling in every aspect of his country's economic life to secure his political ends.

Napoleon's second priority was to reform France's labyrinthine legal system with its hundreds of different courts adjudicating different statutes in different areas – a legacy of feudalism. Since 1789 alone 14,000 decrees had been passed. Napoleon remarked: 'We are a nation with 300 books of law yet without laws.' His solution was to cut the Gordian knot with a stroke of his military blade. He produced a single 'Code Napoleon', a compromise between the common law practised in the north and the Roman law in the south. More than 2,000 articles were drafted. On the whole the Code was enlightened and liberal for its time, ensuring equality before the law, an end to feudal duties, freedom of employment and the rights of private property and civil marriage.

However, there were no workers' rights enshrined in the law, and the employers' decisions were always to be upheld. Workers were placed under police supervision and obliged to carry identity cards, while strikes and associations of workers were prohibited, and the police had the authority to settle disputes. The Code certainly represented the interests of the new moneyed business classes. Napoleon has often been congratulated for his liberal attitude to divorce. In fact he toughened up the Revolution's approach, which had permitted fully a third of French couples to divorce in its first years, insisting that divorce by consent take place only if both sets of parents agreed, after two years' separation and before twenty years of married life had passed. Under his new rules only sixty couples a year in Paris met the necessary requirements.

Napoleon also reflected his strong Mediterranean bias in his attitude to women. He once declared: 'Women these days require restraint. They go where they like, they do what they like. It is not French to

give women the upper hand. They have too much of it already.' He upheld the principle of wifely obedience in marriage. Women convicted of adultery could be gaoled for up to two years; men were merely fined. Fathers were given the right to imprison rebellious children.

Napoleon was more enlightened in establishing a system of independent circuit judges, freed from political control, and he tried to defend the jury system, which had been brought over from England under the Revolution, against widespread criticism. In practice the system of investigating magistrates gave the state legal authorities much greater power than their counterparts in Britain and there was virtually no presumption of innocence for those suspected of an offence. They were assumed to be guilty unless they could prove otherwise.

If justice was now perhaps less arbitrary than under the *ancien régime*, when it was largely administered in the interests of the local aristocracy and the central state, it was almost entirely centralized. The Code Napoleon, which was to ripple out to many other countries soon to be brought under French rule, also had the advantage for Napoleon of stripping the aristocracy of other lands of much of their power over their peoples, permitting the French to rule unhindered.

A third major reform lay in the field of education: Napoleon reopened the clerical primary schools and set up 300 secondary schools across France, with early specialization and the principal of universal entry. He also created elite lycées, in which pupils wore blue military-style uniforms and were drilled and learnt musketry, as well as Latin and mathematics as principal subjects, much as he had when a boy. In education as elsewhere, Napoleon's prime purpose was subordination to the central state. He set up the University, a supervisory body to ensure that all schools turned out citizens 'attached to their religion, their ruler, their native land and their family'. All teachers had to swear an oath to these principles. Another innovation was the Légion d'Honneur, to be awarded for distinction in every field, eventually encompassing 30,000 people.

Napoleon also splashed out on great public works projects: he lavished money on road-building – which was useful for moving his armies quickly across France – and built three great roads across the

Alpine passes of the Great St Bernard, the Little St Bernard and the Col de Tend whose main purpose, again, was to make easier Italy's absorption into France.

He constructed three great ports – Cherbourg, Antwerp and Brest – to extend French naval power; and he built the canals connecting the Rhine to the Rhone, the 160-mile Nantes-Brest Canal and the San Quentin. These permitted the passage of goods and vessels across France rather than by sea, where they would be vulnerable to British attack, and facilitated the country's industrial revolution later on.

Finally, Napoleon centralized France's own internal administration. Each department was given its 'prefect'. In theory they were nearly as powerful as the 'intendants' under the old regime, and in fact they were more powerful, as they were not countered by the power of the provincial nobility. The prefects were personally appointed by Napoleon, and their word in the departments was law. Beneath the ninety-eight prefects there were 420 sub-prefects in the *arondissements* and these controlled the 30,000 municipal councils and their mayors. The system was far more centralized than under Louis XVI, although in practice the strong local character of provincial France provided a considerable degree of autonomy.

Behind the power of the state stood Napoleon's militaristic form of government. 'It is the soldier who founds a Republic and it is the soldier who maintains it.' Napoleon had little time for the talking shops he had set up under the new constitution. The senate was largely a rubber stamp and Napoleon further diluted this by increasing its membership from sixty to 100. The 300-member legislative body and the hundred-strong tribunate, which sometimes opposed him, were reduced in size and his principal critics removed from both. Decrees and orders in council were constantly issued to bypass the feeble legislature.

In reality it was military dictatorship, Napoleon ruthlessly cracked down on potential opponents. Madame de Staël, whose salon became the focus of opposition to Napoleon, whom she considered a crude and dangerous boor, was exiled from Paris after she had published *Delphine*, which criticized the new constitution. The hapless Abbé Sieyès was kept under virtual house arrest on his estate, while Barras

was exiled from France altogether. When the senate proposed that the
dictator be given a further ten-year term, Napoleon called for his
consulate to become one for life. This was subjected to a referendum in
1802: the figures were only marginally different from those in the
previous referendum, with some 3,600,000 in favour, some 8,000
against. Again the result reflected the endorsement of only one-sixth of
the electorate. A soldier reported the method used to secure his vote:
'One of our generals summoned the soldiers in his command and said
to them: "Comrades, it is a matter of nominating General Bonaparte
consul for life. You are free to hold your own opinion; nevertheless, I
must warn you that the first man not to vote for the Consulate for life
will be shot in front of the regiment."'

Napoleon certainly enjoyed widespread support. He had brought
order and stability, and economic confidence was increasing. Moreover
he had brought peace after long years of suffering on terms favourable
to France. He embodied the power of the wealthy, the new provincial
bourgeoisie who had inherited the prestige of the old pre-revolutionary nobility, and the large class of prosperous peasants that now
owned much of the land.

Napoleon was also happy to surround himself with old families, to
create his own private court and endow it with a distinctly monarchical
flavour. In 1801 he even revived court dress for men, including knee
breeches. His own constumes became more fantastic as the years passed.
He sported embossed ermine capes, fur-lined jackets and suspenders
with white stockings. Josephine was given her own ladies-in-waiting
from among France's noblest families, and white was deemed the
appropriate female attire in court. Napoleon was preparing to ascend
a further rung on the ladder from military dictator to monarch. Before
then, however, he had to subdue two dangerous nests of opposition: the
royalists themselves, who regarded him as a usurper and an upstart, and
the left-wing Jacobin opposition, many of them paradoxically concentrated in the meritocratic army. Both were minorities. The royalists were
too small in numbers and too repressed to mount a serious popular
challenge. However, the Jacobins, though equally small in numbers, did
present a threat; for just as Napoleon was essentially a general who had
come to power by force, so another general could depose him by force.

His response was to impose a vigorous police state and spying network under Fouché. Fouché, however, privately sympathized with the Jacobins. If Napoleon was paranoid, he had much to be paranoid about; for at the very heart of his system of absolute control there were challengers who wanted to seize the reins. Nor were they slow to show their hand. He was equally quick to respond, with the ruthlessness that had marked his ascent to power.

Napoleon was extremely careful to nurture his own power bases – the wealthier peasantry and the *haute bourgeoisie* represented by Talleyrand; the secret state represented by Fouché; and, above all, the army, which he treated as a privileged elite. Although he ran a dictatorship, he could not crush opposition with ruthless purges of a Stalinist kind without antagonizing these power bases. He was therefore forced to tolerate dangerous rivals about him, such as Talleyrand and Fouché, until they overplayed their hand. Even then he was cautious about cutting them down for fear of stimulating a far more general opposition. Thus there were limits to his absolutism and he felt himself continually under threat from internal opposition.

During 1800 a series of plots were hatched to murder or oust Napoleon. In October there was a plot to stab him with a stiletto in his box at the Opera – a forerunner of Lincoln's assassination – spearheaded by the adjutant-general and reflecting dissent among senior military officers. He and his fellow conspirators were rounded up and executed. There followed the assassination plot that came nearest to succeeding. On 24 December 1800, a royalist conspirator disguised as a peddler, François Carbon, led an old carthorse and its wagon carrying a large wine cask to rue St Nicaise, just north of the Tuileries. There he asked a fourteen-year-old girl to hold the bridle for a few minutes and disappeared around the corner to watch. The barrel was full of gunpowder and he held a fuse that he was to light at a signal from an accomplice when Napoleon's coach was on the way to Haydn's *Creation* at the Opera. Inside the Tuileries, Josephine had persuaded a sleepy Napoleon to accompany her to the performance. He left with three aides in an advance carriage, preceded as usual by a troop of mounted grenadiers. Josephine had lingered to have her

shawl arranged, and her carriage followed some three minutes behind.

Napoleon's coachman was drunk, it being Christmas Eve – a piece of luck that was to save the First Consul's life. Rounding a corner, he saw the way ahead was blocked by the cart, but instead of slowing down, he urged his horses after the grenadiers, who had veered to avoid it. The man supposed to tip off Carbon lost his nerve, so the assassin lit the fuse a split-second too late. The combination of the delay and the coachman's drunken urgency rushed Napoleon's carriage safely past the cart.

When the bomb went off – the world's first example, perhaps, of a cart bomb – it blew the street to bits: nine people were killed, including the unfortunate little girl, and twenty-six were injured. The guards riding behind Napoleon's carriage were thrown from their saddles, but the First Consul was uninjured. Josephine's carriage was much further behind than usual. The occupants of this were shocked and she fainted, but none of them was hurt.

Suspicion fell on Napoleon's military aides. Why, for example, did the troop of grenadiers not stop to clear the obstructing cart out of the Emperor's way, instead of rushing past? Even Josephine was not above suspicion. For it was Josephine who had wheedled the reluctant Napoleon into going to the Opera, which he had not wished to do. Then Josephine had dawdled – which put her well to the rear of the blast. Only its late detonation had almost turned her into the victim.

Napoleon was incensed at the attempt on his life. 'For such an atrocious crime we must have vengeance like a thunderbolt; blood must flow; we must shoot as many guilty men as there have been victories,' he ranted. We might think it would have been history's most celebrated assassination, eclipsing even that of Archduke Franz Ferdinand at Sarajevo that triggered the First World War in its consequences and certainly those of Lincoln and the Kennedys. Ironically however, it would not have been recognized as such, for Napoleon by 1800 was a successful dictator and general, but not the fearsome conqueror of Europe he was to become.

Josephine was herself an intriguer with close links to many of

Napoleon's rivals. Even so, it is hard to believe she would have gained any advantage from his death – although she was acutely conscious of the precariousness of her position until she provided him with his longed-for son and heir. More likely military insiders were in on the plot with the aim of installing one of Napoleon's rivals in the army high command. Napoleon took advantage of the plot to launch a preemptive attack on his Jacobin enemies, who were not involved: 130 of their leaders were arrested and imprisoned or sent to Devil's Island, the notorious prison in the Caribbean.

In fact the ostensible ringleaders were in England – their chief being Georges Cadoudal, a Breton who trained royalist guerrillas and had received financial support from Windham, head of the British secret service. Cadoudal was a strong, ugly man, who was planning to put the Comte d'Artois, the energetic younger brother of the pretender, the Comte de Provence on the throne. He was to try a second time, once more in close co-operation with two of the most powerful and exotic figures in British intelligence, Sir Sidney Smith and Captain John Wright, Smith's former cellmate in the Temple prison in Paris.

Wright had been brought up in Minorca and spent most of his early career in the Vendée, liaising with French royalist rebels. Two years later, in 1803 he commanded a small squadron of brigs and cutters to smuggle French royalists in and out of the country. One of these landed the royalist General Cadoudal in 1803, along with the celebrated General Charles Pichegru, now a royalist but who had nevertheless served under Robespierre and been president of the lower house of parliament under the Directory.

Cadoudal and Pichegru travelled in closed carriages to the house of one of their sympathizers and finally to Paris in January 1804. There they met up with the third conspirator, General Jean Victor Moreau, the former commander of the Army of the Rhine, and victor of the spectacular battle of Hohenlinden. The plan was extensive. Cadoudal was to arrange the assassination of Napoleon, Moreau's troops were to seize the capital and Pichegru to instal a new Bourbon King.

Cadoudal's plan was to dress up sixty of his plotters as hussars to take part in a parade in the Place du Carrousel, where Napoleon was to pass on inspection, and then strike him down with knives. If this bore some

resemblance to the murder of Caesar, it also had distinct overtones of the recent assassination of the Tsar Paul, in which British intelligence may have played a part: it is possible that the same British minds worked on both conspiracies.

Moreau was far more representative of the mainstream French army than Napoleon who was junior to him as an officer and had a smaller following in the army (quite apart from being a Corsican compared to Moreau's well-established mainland background). Moreau saw himself as a potential dictator in place of Napoleon, rather than as a stalking horse for a new King. When he let this be known, the royalists Pichegru and Cadoudal were horrified.

At the end of January 1804 a double agent tipped off Napoleon's supporters as to the arrival of the conspirators in Paris. A suspected conspirator, Dr Querelle, was arrested, tortured and threatened with execution; he broke down and revealed the addresses of the safe houses where Cadoudal had stayed, as well as confirming the existence of the plot. A servant of Cadoudal was captured at one of the safe houses and tortured, revealing his master's current whereabouts, but the bird had flown before the police arrived.

Finally Moreau was arrested in early February, which proved easy enough as his movements were public knowledge. Pichegru was then captured in his hideout at the end of the same month, after a fierce struggle. Cadoudal himself, after a spectacular chase in a coach, shot the two policemen following him and then tried to mingle with the crowd that assembled at the spot, only to be recognized and arrested.

Oddly, however, there was a mystery over the Bourbon prince they had planned to put on the throne. Cadoudal had been visited by a mysterious figure. According to Fouché he was '. . . an important personage . . . extremely well dressed . . . when he was in the room . . . everybody . . . rose and did not sit down until he had retired.' This description corresponded neither with the age of the Comte d'Artois, nor the person of the Duc de Berri . . . The Duc d'Angoulême was at Mittau . . . the Duc de Bourbon was known to be in London. Attention was therefore directed at the Duc d'Enghien. D'Enghien, aged just thirty-one, was the only son of the Duc de Bourbon, the grandson of the Prince of Condé. Fouché was certain of his complicity.

Talleyrand wrote on 8 March recommending the arrest of the young Duc, of whom Napoleon had never even heard.

On the night of 15 March a force of 300 armed men was despatched across the French border to Baden and seized the Duc in bed; his faithful dog jumped into the carriage into which he was bundled. The kidnappers reached Strasbourg, where they waited four days before being ordered to the Forest of Vincennes outside Paris. There the alleged young pretender ate a hearty meal, asking his captors what they intended to do with him. After supper he was taken to a room where a general and six colonels were waiting. There he admitted receiving 4,200 guns a year from the British who had told him to wait on the Rhine 'where I would have a part to play immediately'. He demanded to see Napoleon. 'My name, my rank, my manner of thinking and the horror of my situation induce me to hope he will not refuse my request.'

The following day he was summoned at six o'clock and led down a stone staircase. He asked where he was being taken and, receiving no answer, assumed he was in no danger. Instead he was led out to the dry moat of the castle, where a hole had been dug and a captain and six soldiers were waiting. 'I gave the word to fire,' said the quartermaster. 'The man fell and, after the execution, I learned that we had shot the Duc d'Enghien.' The dog was led away howling.

It had been one of Napoleon's most characteristically brutal and decisive acts. He was determined to show he would be pitiless towards any further conspiracies and to remove the most promising pretender (the others being the bloated and idle Comte de Provence and his younger brother, the scheming and vindictive Comte d'Artois). The illegal abduction of a senior prince of the royal blood across national borders was a scandalous act of international piracy, and the royal courts of Europe reacted as though they had been struck in the chest, having lost one of their own.

Possibly Napoleon underestimated the reaction to the murder of this hitherto obscure prince. The new Tsar of Russia was appalled: Baden was ruled by his father-in-law, Joseph, who had tried to dissuade Napoleon from the act and called it a 'barbarity'. Even Fouché was said to be aghast. The next horror was the discovery of the veteran

Pichegru's body in his gaol cell. He had been garrotted with a neckcloth attached to a sharp stick. It was announced that he had committed suicide – something almost impossible to do with a garrotte.

In June the other conspirators were tried and sentenced. Napoleon had taken a considerable risk in arresting the popular hero Moreau, which could have set off a revolt in the army or a popular uprising. In the event, Moreau's courage at his trial was applauded by the crowd. He 'was as calm as his conscience; and, as he sat on the bench, he had the appearance of one led by curiosity to be present at this interesting trial, rather than of an accused person, to whom the proceedings might end in condemnation and death . . . The result, clear as day to all present, was that Moreau was a total stranger to all their plots, all the intrigues, which had been set on foot in London.' The popular general was sentenced to just two years in prison because of the paucity of evidence against him and Napoleon's fear that his condemnation might spark an uprising. Soon afterwards he was exiled to the United States.

Cadoudal and thirteen others were sentenced to death. Cadoudal was executed on 25 June, telling the gaoler, 'We have achieved more than we intended. We came to give France a King; we have given her an Emperor.' It was an ironic jest, as his conspiracy was indeed directly responsible for Napoleon's decision to become Emperor. He asked to be the first to be executed.

Wright, the British liaison officer for the conspiracy, was captured on his ship off the French coast soon afterwards. He made a fight of it and was wounded in the leg. His surgeon reported: 'Our firing almost ceased, three of the guns being dismounted and the rest encumbered with lumber from falling booms, the supporters having been shot away and the vessel nearly sinking, Captain Wright was forced to hail that he had struck [surrendered] just in time to save the lives of the few that could keep the deck, as the gunboats were rowing up alongside with numerous troops to board.'

Wright was denounced as 'a most artful and dangerous adventurer' and imprisoned in the Temple. He languished there as a spy, demanding to be treated as a prisoner of war, for more than a year; then just a

week after the Battle of Trafalgar he was found with his throat slit. According to the French, he had cut his throat with a razor.

The Times wrote: 'We fear there is no doubt of the fact of Captain Wright's decease but we cannot believe that a gallant officer, who has so often looked death in the face and was proverbial for courting danger, fell in the manner mentioned. Those, who ordered and perpetrated the midnight murders of Pichegru and the Duke d'Enghien, can, no doubt, explain the nature of Captain Wright's death.'

Years later in St Helena Napoleon was furious at the accusation that he was responsible. One who spoke to him then remembered:

He asked me to my great surprise if I remembered the history of Captain Wright. I answered, 'Perfectly well and it is a prevailing opinion in England that you ordered him to be murdered in the Temple.' With the utmost rapidity of speech, he replied, 'For what object? Of all men, he was the person whom I could have most desired to live. Whence could I have procured so valuable evidence as he would have provided on the conspirators in and about Paris? . . . If I had acted properly, I should have ordered Wright to be tried by a military commission as a spy and shot within twenty-four hours, which by the laws of war I was entitled to do. What would your ministers, or even your parliament, have done to a French captain that was discovered landing assassins in England to murder King George? . . . They would not have been so lenient as I was with Wright. They would have had him tried and executed *sur le champ*'

Chapter 44

THE EMPEROR'S WAR

The plot had one unintended consequence, alluded to by Cadoudal. Napoleon resolved to make himself Emperor as fast as possible so as to create a dynasty, he said, which would survive in the event of his death. He had already hinted as much: 'If I die in four or five years, the clock will be wound up and will run. If I die before then, I don't know what will happen . . . These fanatics will end by killing me and putting angry Jacobins in power. It is I who embody the French Revolution.'

One of his backers said: 'They want to kill Bonaparte; we must defend him and make him immortal.' A motion was introduced in the tribunate to make Napoleon Emperor of the French: 'The imperial destiny should be hereditary in his family.' The honest Carnot opposed it. To establish his throne in the popular will, Napoleon held yet another referendum. This time 3,570,000 votes were counted in his favour against some 2,500 votes. The pattern by now had been established.

Napoleon's elevation to Emperor is too often glossed over as simply a reaction to the assassination threat. In fact it was a turning point. Napoleon's real reasons for seeking the title were many. Indeed, he could reconcile it with the notion of being a republican – as had briefly been the case in ancient Rome. It was quite distinct, in his opinion, from the crown of the Bourbon monarchy: to have called himself King would truly have been a repudiation of the Revolution, unacceptable to his remaining Jacobin supporters. By securing a mandate from the people, he could mysteriously anchor his rule in the will of the French nation, making it distinct from a King ordained by divine right from above.

All of these were coherent reasons. Yet Napoleon was no fool: the title as he well knew was a throwback to the Roman Empire originally, and more recently to the Holy Roman Empire. It was generally attached to a ruler with much wider domains than his native country: and by becoming Emperor, Napoleon was signalling France's pre-eminence among nations, with a great many vassal states. But the title signalled both an expansionary power and, in Napoleon's case, a man determined to establish a dynasty as lasting as any that had sat on the French throne, though one rooted in the popular will rather than ordained by God. It was also an end to Napoleon's republican pretensions. Abroad, the few remaining admirers of the French Revolution were heartbroken: Wordsworth, as we have seen, returned disillusioned to his native land; Fox's eyes were opened; Beethoven in Vienna tore up the dedication of his Third Symphony to Napoleon; Simon Bolivar, a young man visiting Spain and France at the time, was horrified by the decision.

It also marked an inner change within Napoleon's own volatile and explosive personality. Napoleon had all his life been a combination of the practical man of action and the egomaniac dreamer. In Egypt the latter trait had won and had led him to disaster. The practical man had then reasserted himself and had seized power in France. Now again he was exhibiting a self-belief that was to prove his undoing: for as an Emperor he had to continue to maintain France's paramountcy in Europe.

He could argue that he was doing no more than emulate the Emperor Joseph of Austria; but the latter was the heir to an ancient title, carried on now by the fiction of the Holy Roman throne and ruling over a vast and varied collection of peoples. Napoleon could not have signalled more clearly his intention to do likewise, to add to France's dominions under his control. To those that had plotted against him in France, he was responding that he was no mere general, no mere military dictator, but the aspiring ruler of all Europe, endorsed by popular plebiscite, and legitimized by force of arms not just in France but outside. That he was no longer 'freeing' the countries he conquered in the name of progressive revolutionary ideals did not matter: progress was synonymous with France's national interest and his own

rule. He was not just the foremost citizen of France but of the world. Both he and France were now committed to incorporating new territories into the empire.

His immediate *folie de grandeur* displayed itself most clearly with the decision to insist that the Pope come to Paris for the coronation. This, Napoleon argued, would secure the support of all Catholics as well as impress foreign countries with his legitimacy. In fact it was merely a supreme vanity, designed to impress the world with his special status.

Napoleon meticulously organized his own coronation, choosing the eagle as the emblem of France, adopting a sixth-century Gallic motif as his own, equipping himself with a sword which was supposedly that of Charlemagne, and designing a crown of gold laurel. On 2 December 1804, Napoleon walked with his brother Joseph into Notre Dame. 'Joseph, if only our father could see us,' said Napoleon to his brother.

The Pope said mass and at the appropriate moment anointed Napoleon in the style of a French monarch. Then Napoleon crowned himself so, as he said, to avoid a dispute between the Pope and the Archbishop of Rheims, who traditionally crowned the monarch. The real reason was to establish the supremacy of state represented by Napoleon, over the church; the archbishop would surely have given way to the Pope, who would not normally have stirred from Rome for the occasion.

Napoleon then crowned Josephine Empress. To the last moment she feared she would not be given this accolade. After the Pope had discreetly withdrawn, Napoleon intoned the coronation oath: 'I swear to uphold the integrity of the Republic's territory, to respect and impose the laws of the Concordat and religious freedom, to respect and impose the respect of equal rights, political and civil liberties, the irrevocability of the sale of national property, to raise no duty and to establish no tax except through the law, to uphold the institution of the Legion of Honour, to rule only in the interests of the happiness and glory of the French people.'

Napoleon immediately afterwards insisted that he had not changed. Mostly he poked fun at those intimates who called him 'Sire' or 'Your Majesty'. Yet he was quick to put into place the full flummery of an imperial court, exceeding that of even Louis XIV in its pretension. In

the front rank was his own family – as quarrelsome a group of competing nepotists as was to be found anywhere. Josephine, the Empress, was universally despised by the Bonaparte clan, and Napoleon's sisters deeply resented having to bear her train. Letizia had been furious to be given the patronizing and inadequate title of '*Madame Mère de son Majesté l'Empereur*' and refused to attend the coronation altogether.

Napoleon's amiable but incompetent older brother Joseph caused him little trouble, and his marriage to Bernadotte's sister-in-law gave Napoleon a valuable link with a potentially troublesome military Jacobin challenger.

Lucien, his younger brother, however, was a greater problem. Good-looking, eloquent and a natural politician, Lucien was intensely disliked by Napoleon, although he shared Napoleon's political interests. After his bravura performance in helping to stage Napoleon's military coup, he was rewarded with the powerful ministry of the interior but then embarrassed Napoleon by comparing him to Cromwell and was sent off as ambassador to Spain.

Later he returned to Paris as a businessman. Napoleon wanted him to marry the widowed Queen of Etruria; instead Lucien married a businessman's widow, Madame Alexandrine Joubertoun, in secret. Napoleon furiously attacked his young brother for marrying a 'whore'. 'At least my whore is pretty,' was the rejoinder, for which Napoleon never forgave him. Lucien was supported by Letizia and went off in a sulk, accusing Napoleon of having slept with his stepdaughter Hortense who had married Louis, Napoleon's next brother.

Louis was an idler, a neurotic, a dreamer and a homosexual; the marriage was forced upon both parties by Napoleon and Josephine. There was speculation that Napoleon had indeed fathered Hortense's son, because his own wife Josephine could bear no children, as a means of producing an heir from a surrogate mother; Napoleon was certainly distraught when tragedy struck and the five-year-old boy died. But Napoleon personally got on well with Louis, who posed no challenge to him.

Jerome, the youngest sibling, was good-looking but spoilt, boastful and disagreeable; he enraged Napoleon by marrying a beauty in

America after deserting the ship he was serving on. However Napoleon was later to admire his pretty wife.

Napoleon's sisters were hardly easier personalities. They demanded the right to be called princess, as his brother's wives were, and Napoleon relented. The plain but intelligent Caroline was intensely ambitious and cold. She had married General Joachim Murat, one of Napoleon's oldest lieutenants, the beefy, dashing, courageous cavalry commander who had been beside him at the massacre in rue St Raul, and then served with him in Italy and Egypt as well as acting as his principal lieutenant during the military coup. He was good-looking, curly-haired, blue-eyed and thick-lipped, the most romantic-looking of Napoleon's generals. Of humble origins – he was an innkeeper's son – he was the hero of his countrymen and very attractive to women. Murat, reflecting Caroline's views, detested Josephine and had reported to Napoleon the evidence of her infidelity.

Brave and attractive though he was, Murat was also stupid and Caroline had incomparably the better brain, often turning him against his old friend, her brother, whom she understood better than he did. After the successful Marengo campaign, Napoleon had rewarded Murat by making him head of the elite Army of Observation and the commander-in-chief in Italy, where he settled down to looting on a grand scale. He and Caroline ruled in great splendour in Milan and both enjoyed countless affairs.

Elisa, the second sister, was the intellectual of the family, but so ugly as to be almost deformed. She ran a fashionable salon from her home in Paris, which was frequented by the vicious revolutionary painter, David, and a circle of literary women. Her husband, a Corsican soldier, was more or less estranged from her.

The favourite of Napoleon's sisters was Pauline, who was not just stunningly beautiful and sexually irresistible, but a nymphomaniac. At seventeen she had married a pompous young general, Emmanuel Leclerc, who had stood alongside Napoleon at Toulon. She was vague, somewhat neurotic and given to laughing for no reason: and she adored men. At a tender age she had been the lover of three much older generals at once – including Moreau. Another of them was General MacDonald. In 1801 Napoleon suddenly appointed Leclerc

commander-in-chief of an expedition to the large Caribbean island of St Domingue, which was divided between Haiti and Santo Domingo. Many believed the intention was to remove Pauline from Paris, where her love life was scandalizing society. She was said to have taken part in an orgy with five men before departing, and taken three lovers with her aboard ship.

This was the 'imperial family' that Napoleon installed at the pinnacle of French society – a Corsican clan which had suddenly ascended to supreme power, and behaved with the inner jealousies and abandon of those suddenly elevated to status and wealth. Beneath them were Napoleon's ministers, of which Talleyrand and Fouché, bitter rivals, were the most prominent.

Beneath them Napoleon created a whole new imperial 'nobility' which was largely drawn from the ranks of his low-born army. These were made marshals, and given huge incomes. In May 1804 Napoleon appointed eighteen marshals (in later years he appointed as many again). They included his closest military cronies: Murat, inevitably, the ever-loyal chief of staff Berthier, Lannes, Masséna and Augereau. To these were added able commanders not personally loyal to him, including Jourdan, Soult, Ney and the thirty-four-year-old Davout, already a brilliant soldier. It was a superb stratagem which bought off those most likely to pose a challenge to his rule. Such men were later rewarded with grand titles. Massena became Duke of Rivoli and Prince of Essling. Ney became Duke of Elchirgen and Prince of Moskva. Only two of Napoleon's closest cronies, Junot and Suchet, were at this stage left out.

Below this inner circle of 'aristocracy', Napoleon created no fewer than twenty-three dukes, (swollen to thirty-one by the end of the reign), 193 counts (450), 648 barons (1,500) and 117 knights (1,500). Napoleon said with breath-taking hypocrisy: 'The institution of a national nobility is not contrary to the idea of equality, and is necessary to the maintenance of social order.' It was a colossal system of honours, spoils and patronage designed to ensure loyalty to the upstart Empire. His senior 800 generals were awarded some 16 million francs in subsidies.

The French Revolution had turned full circle. A man who still professed himself to be a republican had created an upper class based on

cronyism and military power that far surpassed that of Louis XVI. What was even more remarkable was that Napoleon was still a comparatively young man of thirty-five and possessed by no means the most distinguished record in the French army. His first campaign in Italy had been brilliant but small-scale, his second in Egypt had been disastrous after two initial one-sided victories, and he had only narrowly won the middle-sized battle of Marengo.

Napoleon's greatest military achievement to date had been in a putsch. Yet within four years he had established himself as Emperor, created a dynasty, a new aristocracy and a formidably centralized and overwhelmingly powerful system of control, which would have been totalitarian had he possessed twentieth-century means of mass manipulation. He had set himself up as a great military leader only to himself and to a few of his cronies, yet he laid claim to be the greatest man in Europe and to be the pinnacle of his entire country's social structure. He regarded himself as master of Europe – with Britain having bowed to his peace terms, with Austria accepting subordinate status, with Prussia an ally and Russia cowed.

Yet beneath the strutting, chest-puffing vanity, was he in fact a realist, a man with whom Britain could live at peace? Addington certainly thought so when he concluded the Treaty of Amiens in 1802. In an astonishingly short space of time, however, the British were to change their opinion. Who was to blame? On the face of it, the British, who by the spring of 1803 seemed intent on renewing hostilities. A surprising number of scholars share this view. Yet the year of phoney peace deserves close examination – as do Napoleon's own motives.

Napoleon in 1803, shortly before the conspiracy that was to provide the pretext for his assuming the imperial mantle, viewed the world with a characteristic mixture of ambition, confidence and insecurity. His greatest enemy, Britain, had just made peace on humiliating terms. To the French leader this seemed a great victory: the British were apparently exhausted by war and were fearful of having to fight alone against the French. The victory against Nelson at Boulogne confirmed the view of France's new ruler that he now had his adversary beaten, even that their fabled sea-power was now held in check.

Looking to the east, France had regained control of most of the

Italian peninsula. Looking to the north, Russia, the most dangerous power fifteen years before, no longer posed an immediate threat, while Austria, repeatedly though not decisively defeated, was intent on peace. Prussia, once a threat, was governed by the indecisive Frederick William who had not made up his mind whether France or Russia posed the greater threat. (He was to change his mind six times between 1803 and 1806.) France, therefore, was the undisputed master of the continent.

In some respects this was frustrating. France had control of the Low Countries (although under the treaty France had proceeded to dismember Holland), its borders were secure on the Pyrenees, up to the Rhine and across the Alps. There was nowhere else to go. This presented problems; for France's army required territory it could live off. France alone could not sustain it, and the army was the backbone of Napoleon's power. He hardly had the option of reducing it to normal levels.

For Napoleon to remain unchallenged and imperial, he had to be more than just the ruler of a greater France. The way in Europe was blocked unless he occupied the territory of other great powers and precipitated a new general war. There were two alternative arenas for the projection of military power: one was to found an empire in the west; and the other was to expand in the east. Either of them entailed rivalry, friction and even war with Britain. For Albion was not a continental power, but a mercantile one with empires in both directions. Napoleon had briefly flirted with the idea of a joint expedition with Russia across Persia and into India — an idea aborted with the assassination of the friendly Tsar Paul.

Napoleon had also toyed with the idea of establishing an empire in the Americas. In a sense this was decided for him. Following the slave uprisings which had caused such appalling suffering to the British, Toussaint l'Ouverture shared out Haiti with the French commander, Rigaud. When the latter was recalled to France by Napoleon, Toussaint became increasingly assertive and in 1801 declared the island's independence — which threatened the interests of the French planters there. Napoleon could not assent to this, and despatched Leclerc, along with Pauline, and an army of 25,000, supported by the Rochefort

Squadron under Admiral Latouche-Tréville. The squadron arrived at Cap Haitien in February 1802 to find the island in the hands of Toussaint's designated successor, the rabidly anti-French Christophe. When the French landed farther down the coast and advanced on the town, it was burnt by Christophe, leaving only a hundred houses intact. Leclerc, installing Pauline in one of them, engaged Toussaint's army the following month and captured the legendary black leader, sending him in chains to France, where he died miserably soon afterwards in prison.

In the summer months the French, like the British before them, succumbed to yellow fever. Pauline, to her great credit, visited the sick and bravely held receptions and concerts in the governor's mansion, the band playing on even as one of its members collapsed with the dreaded disease. Within a year 12,000 French soldiers were infected and 2,000 had died of yellow fever. Leclerc's garrison was reduced to 2,000 men.

Christophe led a growing insurgency. Leclerc ordered Pauline aboard ship while he set off to fight, and won. But within a week of his victory he too was dead from yellow fever and in November 1802, the widowed Pauline, still aged only twenty-two, set sail for home with her small son. The United States had vigorously protested when, under pressure from the French, the Spanish had closed off the lower Mississippi to American shipping. Faced by the wipeout of his forces in the West Indies, Napoleon's hopes of imperial expansion in the Americas were at an end.

He looked with renewed longing towards the east for expansion. In Europe that meant consolidating his hold upon Italy, which he calculated the Austrians were not strong enough to defend; and further afield that meant reviving his oriental dream of chasing the British out of India. The former was a short-term objective, the second based in the long run on expanding French power to a point where the British would inevitably have to acknowledge French supremacy. So for Napoleon the peace was just a lull before the next leap forward in French power, as much to consolidate his own domestic regime as to advance France's interests abroad. Accordingly he began a ship-building programme intended to construct twenty-five ships of the line a

year, to give him a fleet of some 200. He also appointed General Decaen as captain-general in India, with instructions to negotiate with the Indian princes to launch a general war on the British. On his voyage to India, Decaen stopped to consult with the French-controlled Dutch authorities who had taken over the Cape Colony so recently abandoned by the British.

French emissaries were despatched to Algeria and to the Ionian Islands to look for possible bases. The British ambassador in Naples observed that the French were surveying the Italian coast from Ancona to Taranto. 'This may be very useful to them and facilitate their progress eastwards, the idea of which they have never abandoned any more than they have forgotten for a moment their views upon Italy.' Lord Keith in the Mediterranean warned of a possible French occupation of Corfu and Sardinia. In Constantinople and Alexandria there were rumours that Napoleon was seeking to partition the Ottoman empire with Russia. The British consul in Baghdad reported the passage of French envoys to Persia and Afghanistan.

Sheridan summed up the situation in a brilliant speech in parliament: 'I see in the physical situation and composition of the power of Bonaparte a physical necessity for him to go on in this barter with his subjects and to promise to make them the masters of the world if they will consent to be his slaves. [Conquering England] . . . is the first vision that breaks upon him through the gleam of morning; that is his last prayer at night, to whatever deity he may address it, whether to Jupiter or to Mahomet, to the Goddess of Battles or to the Goddess of Reason.' All of these French aspirations in the east were for the moment vague and evanescent, but one thing was essential to French ambitions there: the British evacuation of Malta, which otherwise would threaten French domination of the Mediterranean and any expansion to the east, and which had been agreed upon in the peace treaty.

It was not Malta, however, which was the first bone of contention between the two old enemies. The British were galvanized by two places which were quite outside their sphere of interest – to Napoleon's great bewilderment and irritation – for Britain was about to pass through one of its periodic fits of moral indignation.

The first issue was Napoleon's cavalier treatment of Italy. Breaking his promise to recognize the autonomy of the Cisalpine Republic, he first attempted to secure the election of his brother Joseph as president; the latter, however, refused, because he sought to become Napoleon's heir, something Napoleon hesitated to make him because Joseph had no heirs himself. So Napoleon browbeat the Republic's deputies to elect him president of the state. He used this as a precedent for seeking to make the other Italian states overturn their rulers and set up puppet states. Piedmont and Elba were incorporated as French dependencies, followed swiftly by Liguria and Parma. Colonel Dyott, visiting Bologna and Turin, found 'everything Frenchified, including the guillotines and the trees of liberty in the squares, the inns packed with French officers, the ballroom an obscene, bawdy display of naked women', the palaces, gardens and convents destroyed and looted.

This was distressing enough, but the French occupation of Switzerland aroused even greater indignation. Here Napoleon had seized a canton so that he could control the Great St Bernard and Simplon Passes (by taking Piedmont he had secured the Mont Cenis Pass). His defence was that this was not specifically prohibited by the Treaties of Luneville and Amiens. The treaty did however specify that he withdraw his garrison from Switzerland. When the main towns rose up in opposition Napoleon sent in Marshal Ney to take over the country, claiming that the Swiss were incapable of running their own affairs, although they had peacefully and liberally done so for a millennium.

The Swiss appealed to the British for help, and Addington offered arms and money. Furiously Napoleon insisted that the British had no part to play in continental affairs and were not adhering to the Treaty of Amiens. As no continental power went to the help of the British, Addington had to abandon his efforts and look ridiculous, while the mountain state was annexed and the Swiss leader imprisoned in the Castle of Chillon.

Meanwhile French troops still remained in possession of Holland, which under the Treaty of Amiens they had agreed to evacuate, threatening British ports. This had been the prime cause of the war of 1792. Another serious British complaint arose from the discovery of an edict issued by the French to seize every vessel under 100 tons in

weight carrying British goods which came within four leagues of the French coast, even ships seeking shelter from bad weather. One ship in the Charent estuary was seized because its cargo was of British manufacture: in effect, the blockade was still in force.

On a more emotional level, Napoleon was incensed by the lampoons against him in the British press, and demanded that they be suppressed, refusing to accept the government's embarrassed explanation that it had no power to do so. Lady Bessborough remarked: 'If Bonaparte chooses to go to war for the newspapers à *son loisir*, we must fight through thick and thin; but do not let us imitate *Le Moniteur* and begin a war because the French newspapers are impertinent.'

The inert government of Addington, although strengthened by the addition of the young Lord Castlereagh, who harboured few illusions about Napoleon, came under increasing ridicule. It was bitterly opposed by the Grenville and Buckingham factions and by Windham, Pitt's former protégé. Now George Canning applied his mordant wit and gift for verse to the 'wretched pusillanimous toadying administration':

> 'Tis thro' Addington's Peace that fair plenty is ours;
> Peace brightens the sunshine, Peace softens the showers;
> What yellow'd the cornfields? What ripen'd the hay?
> But the Peace that was settled last Michaelmas Day?

> And shall not such statues to Addington rise
> For service most timely – for warning most wise
> For a treaty which snatch'd us from ruin away,
> When sign'd with a quill from the Bird of To-day.

> Long may Addington live to keep peace thro' our borders –
> May each House still be true to its forms and its orders –
> So shall Britain, tho' destined by Gaul for her prey
> Be saved as old Rome by the Bird of To-day!

Misreading Addington's vacillations as a sign of terminal British weakness, Napoleon nevertheless wanted to avoid war at all costs

while his programme of ship-construction was under way and while he built the French army into an overpowering force. He decided to use threats to prevent Britain going to war. He declared at the end of January 1803 in his most bullying manner that he would sacrifice 100,000 men rather than allow the British to interfere in Swiss affairs.

He also published a report by Colonel Sebastiani, one of his spies, suggesting that the departing British troops at Alexandria had performed feebly and that as soon as the British had gone France should reoccupy Egypt. The British, by now thoroughly alarmed, decided it would be unwise to evacuate Malta, as Napoleon appeared to be considering another Egyptian expedition.

The British ambassador in Paris, Lord Whitworth, after receiving Napoleon's frontal blast, told him that the British withdrawal from Egypt would proceed as agreed. The evacuation from Malta would also proceed if Napoleon promised not to attack the Turkish empire, in particular Egypt, paid compensation for his unauthorized annexation of Switzerland and Piedmont, and if he would guarantee Malta's independence, which would also have to be underwritten by other great powers. Meanwhile the British raised 10,000 men to reverse cuts in their navy after Amiens and protested at the invasion by French agents, supposedly commercial, who provided Napoleon with details of British harbours and defences.

If Addington thought he could appease Napoleon through sweet reasonableness, he was sorely mistaken. Napoleon, accustomed to getting his own way through fearsome displays of childish pique, was astonished when the British showed no sign of conceding Malta and even raised the stakes by demanding a speedy French withdrawal from Holland, as they were obliged to do under the Peace of Amiens, as well as from Switzerland. In exchange the British offered to recognize the new Etrurian kingdom and even the Italian and Ligurian Republics. Talleyrand tried to flannel: he proffered a guarantee of Malta's neutrality. The British responded by demanding a ten-year lease of the island.

The nation's mood had enormously changed in the space of six months since the halcyon summer of 1802. Napoleon's casual annexation of Switzerland and much of Italy, his continuing preparations for

war, and his expedition to the West Indies followed by a renewal of his threat to the east had convinced most British policymakers of his insincerity. Thomas Campbell captured the mood: 'The very front and picture of society would grow haggard if that angry little savage, Bonaparte, should obtain his wishes. I think I see our countrymen trampled under by his military like the blacks of San Domingo on their own fields! – our very language abolished for that of the conqueror, America and all the world lost for want of our protection, and the fine spirit of our political economy changed into the politics of a drill sergeant.'

Lord Auckland remarked laconically, 'Had he amused us a year or two, our disarming would have been complete and we should not have had a chance of effectual resistance.' It has been widely asserted that both sides viewed the Treaty of Amiens as no more than an interlude in the war. This is mistaken: the British had earnestly believed and hoped that it was the beginning of a lasting peace, while Napoleon intended to use it to build-up his forces in an attempt to intimidate the British out of any further war or, if necessary, to defeat them. Now the British had belatedly awoken to the prospect that Napoleon did not envisage a settlement of Europe except under his total domination. He had overplayed his hand and had aroused his enemy long before he intended to, while his plans for rebuilding his navy were in their infancy.

He now sought desperately to stave off the British declaration of war at least until his fleet had returned from the West Indies. When at the last moment the Russians agreed to mediate over Malta, the British took no notice. Lord Malmesbury, one of the most emollient of British diplomats, merely interpreted this as Napoleon seducing the Russians: 'It appears that Russia has been gained over – won by France by corruption and flattery – lost by us by indolence, incapacity and ignorance. It is the manner in which Russia has declared herself favourable to France that has terminated the discussion on war. Had Russia been neutral or passive Bonaparte would have given way.'

The British declared war on 16 May. As a French writer, Lanfrey, puts it:

In order to satisfy a petty rancour against obscure writers, whom the noble hospitality of the English nation protected, he alone had enkindled [the war], in contempt of the advice of his counsellors, in contempt of the remembrance of all the evils that were not yet retrieved, in contempt of the will of the nation that was hungering for the benefits of peace. And in order to avenge this miserable affront, millions of men were going to fight for more than ten years, to tear each other to pieces, to die all kinds of deaths, upon all the continents, upon all the seas, at every hour of day and night, in the deserts, upon the mountains, in the snow, in flaming cities as in obscurest villages, from the Tagus to the Neva, from the Baltic to the Gulf of Taranto, in Spain, in Russia, and as far off as India!

Napoleon's vicious and petty act of revenge was to ignore the convention of expelling foreign nationals when going to war, and instead imprisoning the 10,000 or so British civilians in France for the full duration of the war – in most cases a numbing ten years.

Part 7

SAILOR SUPERSTAR

Chapter 45

BRITAIN UNDER SIEGE

It looked more like a water-beetle than any kind of seafaring vessel seen before. It was bulbous, flat-bottomed, with a big 18- or 20-pound cannon-like proboscis peering from its prow. This ungainly vessel was the unlikely prototype of the largest invasion force ever assembled to attack the British Isles, in prosaic contrast to the picturesque galleons of the Spanish armada in 1588, but through sheer force of numbers the much greater threat. For three years, and in particular during the summers of 1803, 1804 and 1805, the British were held in thrall.

The extraordinary invasion craft, like fledgling sea-saucers from another planet, could each contain sixty to eighty troops and were sailed by five to six seamen. They bore rudimentary sail-sloops and were rigged like a Schweling fishing boat, but had only a three- or four-foot draw of water. The troops slept on two inclined platforms which ran the length of the vessel, while the officers had a little cockpit of their own at the stern. Such was the first account given to an incredulous British Admiralty of the extraordinary invasion craft being hammered out in record time by boatbuilders all over France to be marshalled at Boulogne, from which Napoleon's invasion of England was to be launched.

In January 1804 a much more detailed description had arrived, written by an English spy in Paris, a Mr Sullivan, who asserted that 400–500 of the extraordinary craft were being prepared:

> The above boats it is supposed will draw from 2 feet 9 inches to 3
> feet 9 inches when the detachments are therein. The number of

such according to report are from 130 to 150 rank and file. The
boats are of course of two sizes. The one apparently about 36 feet
long by 14 or 15 feet wide, the other 46 feet long by 16 or 18 feet
wide, and they are to be provided with 12 or more paddles, one half
forward, the other aft, for the purpose of a general dash under the
guns of the several batteries of the intended places of invasion, or to
advance or retreat as occasion may require. The small boats are
intended for this object and the large for the disembarkation.

The boats are about 3/5ths of the length flat, they then swell out
into a curve rising from the keel about 8 feet, within which are rows
of seats across for the purposes of seating the men; to prevent them
being seen; and to protect them from distant small shot, they rising
from two benches at a time to fire as occasion may require, viz.
either front, rear, obliquely right or left, and also two deep the
whole length of the boats' larboard and starboard sides, in short the
whole forms one solid column, and they seat themselves to reload.
Please to observe that from the seat upwards the sides of the boat are
only of inch deal boards nailed to the ribs, and that the height from
the seat is about 3 feet 10 inches. The invading army are to be
provided with six days' provisions of bread and wine, some of the
boats are to carry light artillery to be disembarked and drawn by
men. . . .

There were other craft as well: *prames*, 100-foot long sailing vessels
armed with 24-pound cannon and capable of carrying 150 men;
chaloupes canonnières armed with howitzers to act as escorts; and *guilots*
to transport horses, ammunition and artillery. The invading force
resembled nothing so much as a wood-and-sail version of the huge
craft that less than 150 years later were to carry out the landings at
Normandy on D-Day.

The beetle boats attracted instant derision. The design had been that
of Pierre Forfait, the inspector-general of the fleet, a mathematician
and scientist previously known for designing shallow-draught cargo
barges for use on the Seine. One prominent French academician, Denis
Decrès, called them 'monstrous ideas . . . which are as wrong as they
will prove to be disastrous . . . a heap of monstrous baubles'.

General Charles Dumouriez, the most prominent French exile in Britain, observed contemptuously; 'so far as the hope of even a third of these 1,200 boats navigating in battle order – they are poorly built, heavy, overloaded – across the heavy seas currents and winds of the Channel, it's an absurdity which reveals the greatest ignorance of the elements in which this tactical march would be carried out.' A British admiral who captured one of the landing craft called it a 'contemptible and ridiculous craft' which would be dispersed by any storm down the Channel 'like so many chips down a millrace' or would be picked off one by one, as swimmers are by sharks.

Napoleon, it was asserted, was a gunnery officer who believed such gunboats could hold off the elements as well as the British fleet and overcome Britain's defences. He considered the Channel little larger an obstacle than some of the big continental rivers his armies had crossed. Indeed, he had considered fantastic plans for the invasion, including a kind of pontoon bridge of 'floating forts' (another idea of Forfait), an early version of the Channel Tunnel which would permit troops to be suddenly projected one night into Kent, and even a huge balloon capable of carrying 3,000 men.

Yet it was always a mistake to ridicule or underestimate Napoleon. The sheer size of Napoleon's forces were awesome: he had some 1,400 craft altogether at his disposal, as well as 115,000 men, including 77,000 infantry, 12,000 cavalry, 4,000 guns and 4,000 wagons, as well as 17,000 support troops and 7,000 horses. These were concentrated largely at Boulogne, but also dispersed across a wider area of the French coast. Some 60,000 men manned the French defences.

One of Napoleon's purposes in creating the landing craft was so that they could be easily transported overland, evading the predatory British naval missions mounted along the coast. (Canal transport had been rendered tricky by a brilliant British inland raid to sink canal craft and block the waterways.) Like modern landing craft, the French ones were designed to convey many men. Like them too they could beach to disembark the men along the sandy shores of England, aided by their shallow draught. All Napoleon needed was a day of dead calm across the Channel, and to protect these valuable troop-carriers from the British fleet, which had either to be engaged or diverted safely away.

Napoleon at least was in earnest. He had built a pavilion on the cliffs
above Boulogne, a wooden edifice 100 foot long, consisting of three
rooms, including a meeting room, and a rotunda overlooking the
harbour. The meeting room had only one chair, for the Emperor
himself: his officers had to stand. In 1803 he had already staged a
triumphal review of his troops outside Boulogne. *The Times* reported:

> He rode on a small iron-grey horse of great beauty. He was
> preceded by about three hundred infantry and about thirty Ma-
> melukes formed a kind of semi-circle about him . . . As soon as he
> and his attendants had passed through the gates, he ordered them to
> be shut to prevent their being incommoded by the populace. The
> execution of this order very much dampened the ardour of the
> Corsican's admirers, who remained entirely silent, although the
> moment before the whole place resounded with *Vive Bonaparte!*

Now on the day after his thirty-fifth birthday he reinspected them.
To an explosion of salutes from naval batteries and the roll of 2,000
drums, the Emperor mounted a dais on a small hill between which
the bands of the Imperial Guard had been drawn up: on the
surrounding slopes of this natural amphitheatre were 80,000 men
drawn up in sixty infantry regiments and twenty cavalry squadrons.
Some 20,000 civilian spectators watched. In the afternoon a flotilla of
some 1,000 arrived, converging from different points, safely braving
the possibility of British attack. It was a magnificent display. Their
successful arrival was, however, spoiled a little as Madame Junot
reported:

> the officer who commanded the first division of the flotilla had run
> foul of some works newly erected along the coast. The shock
> swamped some of the boats and several of the men jumped over-
> board . . . The accident was exceedingly mortifying, happening as it
> did, in the full gaze of our enemies, whose telescopes were pointed
> towards us and it threw the Emperor into a violent rage. He
> descended from the throne and proceeded with Berthier [his chief
> of staff] to a sort of terrace, which was formed along the water's

edge. He paced to and fro very rapidly and we could occasionally hear him utter some energetic expression indicative of his vexation.

The following day a spectacular fireworks display took place, involving 15,000 Roman candles; a ball followed. However, Napoleon was soon to learn, that just two days previously, his best admiral, Louis René de Latouche-Tréville, had died of an infection caught in Santo Domingo, to be replaced by a painfully inept successor, Comte Pierre de Villeneuve.

That Napoleon was deadly serious in his intention of invading was much later confirmed by his doctor in his diary of St Helena. Barry O'Meara was told that Napoleon planned to lure the British fleet away from the Channel:

> Before they could return, I would have had the command of the Channel for two months, as I should have had about seventy sail of the line, besides frigates. I would have hastened over my flotilla with two hundred thousand men, landed as near Chatham to arrive in four days from the time of my landing. I would have proclaimed a republic and the abolition of the nobility and the House of Peers, the distribution of the property of such of the latter as opposed me amongst my partisans, liberty, equality and the sovereignty of the people.

The imminent threat of invasion galvanized the ordinary person in Britain far faster than the languid ministry's feeble calls for mobilization. The arrests of the British citizens in France electrified the country. As Romilly said: 'If it had been Bonaparte's object to give strength to the British ministry, and to make the war universally popular in England, he could not have devised a better expedient.'

The new government went on a propaganda offensive. An *Invasion Sketch* declared:

> There are some labouring people so deluded, as to think they have nothing to lose if the French should conquer this island. Money, they say, they have none: their goods are not worth an enemy's

taking; work must be had whoever is master; ploughing, sowing, harvesting, threshing must go on; there must be carpenters, masons, smiths, tailors, and shoemakers in villages, manufacturers in towns; so that their case will be the same as heretofore; and the wisest thing they can do is to keep in a whole skin, and leave the rich to fight it out, if they will, in defence of their property . . .

If there be one person so lost to all love of his country and the British constitution as to suppose that his person, his property, and his rights and his freedom would be respected, let him contemplate the following pictures – not overcharged, but drawn from scenes afforded by every country – Italy, Holland, Switzerland, Germany, Spain, Hanover, which has been exposed to the miseries of a French invasion.

Bonaparte's Confession of the Massacre at Jaffa was widely distributed. A picture book of *The Corsican Assassin's Progress* was made available at places of public entertainment. Hardy's Trumpet Major describes:

a hieroglyphic picture of Napoleon. The hat represented a maimed French eagle; the face was ingeniously made up of human carcasses, knotted and writhing together in such directions as to form a human physiognomy; a band or stock shaped to represent the English Channel encircled his throat, and seemed to choke him; his epaulette was a hand tearing a cobweb that represented the treaty of peace with England; and his car was a woman crouching over a dying child.

Napoleon was described variously as a pervert and seducer of his sisters; a dwarf with a squint and jaundice; and the grandson of a butcher and son of a traitor and a whore. A favourite children's nursery rhyme ran:

> Baby, baby, naughty baby,
> Hush, you squalling thing, I say;
> Hush your squalling, or it may be,
> Bonaparte may pass this way.

Baby, baby, he's a giant,
Tall and black as Rouen steeple;
And he dines and sups, rely on't,
Every day on naughty people.

Baby, baby, he will hear you
As he passes by the house,
And he, limb from limb will tear you,
Just as pussy tears a mouse.

Harriet Martineau provided a cheerful antidote to the hysterical
jingoism of the times:

One day at dessert when my father was talking anxiously to my
mother about the expected invasion, for which preparations were
made all along the Norfolk coast, I saw them exchange a glance,
because I was standing staring, twitching my pinafore with terror.
My father called me to him, and took me on his knee, and I said:
'But, papa, what will you do if Boney comes?' 'What will I do?' said
he, cheerfully. 'Why, I will ask him to take a glass of port with me,'
helping himself to a glass as he spoke. That reply was of immense
service to me. From the moment I knew that Boney was a creature
who would take a glass of wine I dreaded him no more.

This outpouring of hatred against the potential invader was matched by a
patriotic call to bear arms. Never before had Britain mobilized on such a
scale. By the autumn of 1803, 342,000 men had joined voluntary
organizations, swamping the government's ability to provide appropriate clothing and weaponry. William Wilberforce believed fully 1
million would have joined if permitted to – a tenth of the population.
They were paid for eighty-five days' training a year. Ordinary farm
labourers in smocks were drilled by dashing young men in expensively
bought uniforms. One description might have come straight from *Dad's
Army* nearly a century and a half later: 'The Wimborne Volunteers have
been ordered to march to Poole and their Captain, Doctor Pickford, a fat
little man, was strutting up and down the town with a fussy step and

important mien, which diverted us extremely but spread terror in the hearts of many of the inhabitants of Wimborne.'

Uniforms were all the rage. Lady Hester Stanhope, Pitt's high-spirited niece, inspected the colonel of the Berkshire militia.

> Somebody asked me . . . what I thought of them and I said they looked like so many tinned harlequins. One day, soon after, I was riding through Walmer village when who should pop out upon me but the colonel, dressed entirely in new regimentals . . . 'Pray, pardon me, Lady Hester,' said the colonel, 'but I wish to know if you approve of our new uniform.' Of course I made him turn about, till I inspected him round and round – pointed with my whip, as I sat on horseback, first here and then there – told him the waist was too short and wanted half a button more – the collar was a little too high – and so on; and, in a short time, the whole regiment turned out with new clothes.

George Cruikshank, later to become the famous caricaturist, wrote graphically:

> In one place you might hear the 'tattoo' of some youth learning to beat the drum, at another place some march, or national air being practised upon the fife and, every morning at five o'clock, the bugle horn was sounded through the streets to call the Volunteers to a two hours' drill, from six to eight, and the same again in the evening and then you heard the pop, pop, pop of the single musket, or the heavy sound of the volley, the distant thunder of the artillery and then sometimes you heard the Park and the Tower guns firing to celebrate some advantage gained over the enemy.

Robert Harvey, later to be one of Wellington's commanders in the Peninsular War, mustered the Norfolk Volunteer Regiment, one of no fewer than sixty in the county. Professional men would rise at four and do three hours' drill before going to work, some returning for more in the evening. Walter Scott found the drilling 'a very poignant and pleasing sensation'.

The commander-in-chief was needless to say, the Duke of York, a plump caricaturable figure who was an able administrator although a hopeless military commander. He concentrated his forces in the southeast, the strongpoints being Chelmsford, north of the Thames, and Chatham to the south. If these were overrun, a second line of defences was envisaged running from Blackheath to Battersea and Wandsworth, extending to the Sussex Downs in the south. Admiral Lord Keith believed the most vulnerable points to be Weymouth Bay, the stretches between Brighton and Folkestone, Dungeness and East Anglia. Oddly, he dismissed the threats to the Downs and Kent – which were in fact Napoleon's favoured targets.

Along the coast, Deal, Walmer and Dover had strong fortifications and guns, but Dungeness was exposed, so defences were hurriedly constructed. A network of Martello towers – edifices with guns on top and thirteen-foot-thick walls – were built in Sussex, Kent, Suffolk and Essex. A huge military camp was built at Weedon in Northamptonshire on the Grand Union Canal which included a small palace for the King and houses for the government in the event of London being captured. A popular ditty called 'The Bellman and little Boney' reflected the confused feelings of the time:

> This little Boney says he'll come
> At merry Christmas time,
> But that I say is all a hum
> Or I no more will rhyme.

> Some say in wooden house he'll glide
> Some say in air balloon,
> E'en those who airy schemes deride
> Agree his coming soon.

> Now honest people list to me,
> Though income is but small,
> I'll bet my wig to one Pen-ney
> He does not come at all.

A system of beacons covered the coastline: there were frequent alarms when the beacons were set ablaze by sparks. Grenville and other opponents of the government grew increasingly derisory about the government's defensive tactics. When blockhouses were proposed to defend the Thames, Canning wrote caustically:

> If blocks can a nation deliver,
> Two places are safe from the French:
> The one is the mouth of the river,
> The other the Treasury Bench!

Pitt on coming to office had proposed at once to go on the offensive. As he made his preparations and another glorious summer descended, the prospect of invasion seemed unreal.

Pitt embarked on a two-pronged offensive: the government courted allies, most notably the Russians; and decided to stage an attack on the French coastal defences. He even toyed with the ideas of a remarkable American inventor, Robert Fulton, who had imaginatively tried to pioneer steam-driven paddleships for Napoleon, as well as a crude submarine and torpedoes, *Nautilus*, with a 21-foot long hull and hand-driven propeller worked by its crew of three, which could descend some 25 feet below the surface and stay submerged for three-quarters of an hour.

Fulton's ideas were referred to a secret committee, which described the submarine as impractical, but further investigated torpedoes, which were dubbed 'hogsheads' or 'carcasses'. These were primitive in the extreme:

> made of copper and . . . spherical in form; hollow to receive their charge of powder, which, by means of machinery that worked interiorly, and so secured to be perfectly watertight, exploded at the precise moment that you chose to set it to. The mode of managing them was in this wise: two, attached together by means of a line coiled carefully clear, were placed in the boat ready to be roped overboard. The line was buoyed by corks, like the topping of a sein [net], so as to allow the carcasses to sink to a certain depth and no further.

When you had approached near enough to the vessel against which you meant to direct the carcass and saw clearly that you were in a position that the line could not fail to strike her cable, one carcass was dropped overboard and, when that had extended the full length of the line from the boat, then the other, both having been carefully primed and set to the time, which would allow of their floating to their destined object before they exploded. Of course, it is presumed that wind and tide set in the direction, so as to ensure their not deviating from their course . . .

That was the biggest catch of all – and in this they more resembled mines than submarines. The project was quietly shelved.

Spurred by Pitt, Lord Keith had decided to stage a morale-boosting attack on Boulogne at the end of the summer of 1804. In October a serious assault was staged with four 'explosion vessels' packed with gunpowder as well as Fulton's torpedoes. The attack resulted only in the destruction of a French pinnace with around thirty men. Still the British tried: there were two more attacks in November. Other plans included a joint torpedo-rocket attack – the latter were supposed to divert French attentions from the approaching torpedoes – and a catamaran joined by a platform with a ramp which could be used for landing a field gun and fifty soldiers to stage commando raids. The truth was that 'the coast of iron and bronze' built by Napoleon, comprising batteries and stone defences, while not impregnable, was very strong. 'One field gun to every league of coast is the least allowance', Napoleon had ordered, and the British could make little impression. Their raids at least demonstrated that the government was no longer passively defensive, as Addington's had been.

Still, though, Napoleon made no move. This was largely because of the delays involved in constructing his invasion fleet and bringing it to anchorage. Napoleon also began to understand that his huge force – which he fondly imagined could cross on a cloudy night under cover of fog (but what about collisions?) would need a covering fleet. 'Eight hours of night in favourable weather will decide the fate of the universe,' he declared. But the practicalities were that the armada might be overwhelmed by an unexpected squall, or suddenly be-

calmed, and would anyway take at least three tides to float. He had to postpone the attempt. But he did not give up, claiming that 'nearly 120,000 men and 3,000 boats . . . only await a favourable wind to plant the imperial eagle on the Tower of London'.

With characteristic ruthlessness he declared that it did not matter if 20,000 men were drowned on the way. 'One loses that in battle every day.' On 20 June he insisted on holding a naval review in appalling weather. Several ships were wrecked and 20,000 men lost. But the greater danger was losing his entire invasion force.

At last, by January 1805 he had accepted that the crossing was impossible without the French fleet either protecting the huge flotilla or diverting the British fleet. Armed with this brilliant new intuition, there followed three extraordinary attempts to use France's fleets in the Atlantic and the Mediterranean to achieve just this, in elaborate and intricate battle plans that sought to imitate at sea the precise movements of bodies of men Napoleon so successfully commanded on land. It seemed that Napoleon had at last discovered the formula for success.

In the summer of 1805, with the British guard at home now lowered, although more men had received training in arms than ever before, it seemed likely that at last the years of French preparation would pay off and a huge landing would be staged on the English coast, which would probably force the British back at least to their second lines of defence around London and possibly even result in the loss of the capital. It was the most desperate moment of the war for Britain. Pitt, now seriously ill, presided over a faltering government. At last the reckoning had arrived. Britain was at the mercy of the largest invasion force ever used against her; and with Britain subdued, Napoleon and France would be the unchallenged masters of 'Europe from the Atlantic to the Rhine, from the Netherlands to Naples, the greatest empire in the continent's history since Roman times, Charlemagne included'.

As his own private secretary, Méneval, remarked: 'Napoleon expected the overthrow of England to be a mere three months' business. The first victory would have opened the road to London. Communications established in Ireland and Scotland, and a general uprising against the

privileged classes of the English lords would have done the rest.' Later Napoleon was famously to declare that: 'England is naturally meant to be an appendage to France. Nature made her just as much one of her islands as Corsica and Oleron.' No doubt he had the Norman invasion of 1066 in mind as well.

Part of the reason why Napoleon's seriousness is doubted in 1804 was because of the experience in 1795, when he was the general in charge of the earlier threatened invasion of England and immediately decided the feat was impossible, remaining on the French Channel coast only to divert attention from the planned invasion of Egypt. During the summer of 1804, a war with Austria in the east was not an immediate prospect and one he believed he could avoid.

If the preparations for invading England were indeed a feint, they were to be among the most expensive in the history of warfare. The establishment of huge army camps, the building of artificial harbours, the colossal costs of constructing landing craft – all of these would have been deliberately wasted if the projected invasion was all along intended to be a bluff. The idea, in retrospect, seems absurd. It seems all the more so in view of the deadly seriousness of Napoleon's naval preparations, based on his understanding that massed ship protection was necessary for an invasion to be successfully mounted. These were to involve the bulk of his fleet, consisting of some seventy ships, which he summoned back from the West Indies.

In London Earl St Vincent, the First Lord, who had so rashly launched an attack on corruption in naval dockyards during the short year of peace, so that half his ships were left unrepaired, had come to exactly the same conclusion. With the declaration of war his policy was to blockade the French ports closely so that their warships would never obtain even momentary control of the Channel and be able to escort the invasion fleet across. As Nelson put it, 'Our first line of defence is close to the enemy ports.'

'Let us,' declared Napoleon, 'be master of the Straits [of Dover] for six hours and we shall be masters of the world.' As usual, this was hyperbole: if the British regained control of the Straits and cut off the cross-Channel supply line to an invading French army, it would have been in desperate trouble. However, it contained a grain of truth. The

British fleet was divided in three – Cornwallis and Collingwood blockading Brest, L'Orient and Rochefort, Keith blockading the Texel and Nelson in the Mediterranean watching Toulon. The returning fleet from the West Indies took shelter in Spanish ports, where they were blockaded, first by Sir Alexander Cochrane and later by Sir Edward Pellew. British frigates acted as watchdogs keeping an eye on the French fleets' movements.

Blockade duty was grim and thankless as ships sought to maintain their stations. Gales and shifting tides threatened to batter them on to shoals if they came too close to the shore, while if they stood too far off the enemy might give them the slip in bad weather. The log book of the *Impetueux* in the gale of December 1803 gives some idea of the conditions.

> At four strong gales, with heavy squalls. At half-past six strong gales, with heavy squalls; carried away the starboard main brace and larboard main topsail sheet; sail blew to pieces; mizzen and fore staysail blew to pieces, and mainsail blew from the yard. At eight obliged to scuttle the lower deck; ship labouring very much, and gained six inches on the pumps. At quarter-past eight the carpenter reported the mizzen mast was sprung, in consequence of the vangs of the gaff giving way. At half-past eight was struck with a sea on the larboard quarter, stove in eleven of the main-deck ports, half-filled the maindeck, and carried away the chain-plate of the foremost main shroud. Bore up under a reefed foresail. Saw a line-of-battle ship lying to, with her head to the southward, and her sails split and blowing from the yards.

In the Mediterranean, weather conditions were a little easier, although violent gales could blow up suddenly, and Nelson was hundreds of miles away from friends, his only bases being Malta and Gibraltar. Nelson's tactic was not to blockade too closely, but to seek to lure the French out and do battle: he kept just a watching frigate offshore and his main ships out to sea. These were scattered all the way from the Balearic Islands off Spain, to Sardinia and Corsica, each ship patrolling sections of the sea with a frigate accompanying Nelson's flagship, the

Victory, to herd all the ships together if the French fleet broke out: 'Every opportunity,' said Nelson, 'must be offered to the enemy to put to sea, for it is there we hope to realize the hopes and expectations of our country.'

Latouche-Tréville, in command of twelve line-of-battle ships, accused Nelson of 'running before him', much to the latter's amusement. From May 1803 to August 1805 Nelson left his ship just three times, for less than an hour on each occasion; small wonder the admiral's gait was far more accustomed to the rolling of his ship than to the firmness of dry land. The blockades vastly tested and improved British seamanship, as well as lowering the quality of French sailing, for their ships were kept bottled up in port for months at a time. When the French fleet tried to slip away from Toulon in a gale, they were immediately driven back into port. Nelson commented wryly: 'These gentlemen are not accustomed to a Gulf of Lyon gale, which we have buffeted for twenty-one months and not carried away a spar.'

While Britain anxiously anticipated an invasion, Napoleon had changed his mind several times as to how to stage this. During the autumn he had declared confidently that all he wanted was a calm Channel and winter fog – until it was pointed out to him that his force might get lost in a fog. Calm waters were anyway unlikely to last for long during the winter. The sheer size of the invading fleet would require as many as three tides to carry it from French ports, which raised the prospect of part of the force wallowing at the mercy of the British ships and the weather as it waited for the rest to come out. Reluctantly Napoleon abandoned his idea of staging an invasion in winter.

He conceived a new plan: luring the British fleet to go in chase of one of his fleets, so that another fleet might accompany the invasion force in the spring or summer. He also had 20,000 troops on hand in Brest ready to invade Ireland. Cornwallis was forced to stay off Brest or further out in the Atlantic, anticipating an attack on Ireland. Meanwhile Latouche-Tréville's ships in Toulon would escape Nelson's blockade, move eastwards to lure Nelson in pursuit, then veer west and escape through the Straits of Gibraltar, defeating the British squadron blockading Brest and, reinforced from that port, acting as an escort for the attacking armada.

Like so many of Napoleon's naval plans, it had all the mathematical precision of a land manoeuvre, but failed to allow for the unpredictability of naval warfare – the surprise movement of enemy fleets, the difficulty in locating them, the changes in the weather and tides that could throw the best laid ideas into disarray. This plan was drafted in January 1804, but it was soon overtaken by unpredictable events.

But the very capable French Admiral Latouche-Tréville suddenly fell dead from a heart attack, as he walked up to the observation point at Toulon, as he did nearly every day, to look out for the British fleet. Admiral Villeneuve, of whom Napoleon rightly had a far lower opinion, took his place. A new variant of the strategy evolved: the Brest Squadron under Admiral Ganteaume was to emerge, sail far out into the Atlantic and then sweep back to land 18,000 men in Northern Ireland, which was believed to be ripe for insurrection.

Meanwhile the Toulon and Rochefort fleets were also to break out, liaise in the West Indies and attack the British there. Napoleon believed that the British would despatch thirty ships of the line to defend their West Indian possessions in pursuit of the twenty French ships. Meanwhile Admiral Ganteaume's fleet was to curve back around northern Scotland to convoy the invasion landing craft to England, while the British fleet was still messing about in the West Indies.

This fantastic scheme was ingenious and over-complex. It required far too many variables to go according to plan. Napoleon hesitated and, as the summer passed, he assembled no more than three-quarters of the 130,000 troops he needed, along with 1,100 invasion barges. He decided the opportunity had passed that year, and resolved to try again the following summer. Pitt emerged from retirement to the House of Commons, where he gave a stirring call to arms:

> We are come to a new era in the history of nations; we are called to struggle for the destiny, not of this country alone but of the civilized world. We must remember that it is not only for ourselves that we submit to unexampled privations. We have for ourselves the great duty of self-preservation to perform; but the duty of the people of England now is of a nobler and higher order . . . Amid the wreck and the misery of nations it is our just exultation that we have

continued superior to all that ambition or that despotism could effect; and our still higher exultation ought to be that we provide not only for our own safety but hold out a prospect for nations now bending under the iron yoke of tyranny of what the exertions of a free people can effect.

The hapless Addington resigned the following day. The King sent for Pitt and it seemed at last that a coalition government, a ministry of all the talents, was to be formed under Britain's most resolute political leader. A 'large comprehensive administration' was drawn up which would include Fox and Fitzwilliam, as well as Grenville as Lord President of the Council and Grey as secretary of war. But inexplicably Pitt, although he held a strong hand and should have been able to dictate to the erratic old King, hinted that he would not insist on Fox and Grenville, whom the monarch detested, joining the government. He suggested that the King should 'understand distinctly that if after considering the subject, he resolved to exclude the friends both of Mr Fox and Lord Grenville, but wished to call upon me to form a government without them, I should be ready to do so, as well as I could, from among my own immediate friends, united with the most capable and unexceptionable persons of the present Government; but of course excluding many of them, and above all, Addington himself, and Lord St Vincent.'

Thus Pitt, no longer himself the bold figure of old and visibly ailing, gave the sometimes mad King latitude to dictate the shape of his ministry: and he biliously refused to admit Fox, saying he would prefer civil war. Grenville, now in honour bound to his fellow Whig, Fox, refused to join in sympathy. Pitt was bitter towards his cousin: 'I will teach that proud man that in the service and with the confidence of the King I can do without him, though I think my health such that it may cost me my life.' He was deprived not only of Britain's greatest orator but of his invaluable foreign secretary and closest counsel in government at the time when Britain most needed both.

The new cabinet was so weak, apart from Canning and Castlereagh, that it was dubbed 'the administration of William and Pitt'. Pitt resumed the office of prime minister on the same day, 18 May

1804, that Napoleon was proclaimed Emperor. The scene was thus set for a duel to the death between the staunchest opponent of revolutionary France and the new dictator that had throttled the Revolution and channelled its energies into French overseas expansion.

Pitt appointed Dundas, now Lord Melville, his able but corrupt party manager, as First Lord of the Admiralty. He immediately took steps to reverse St Vincent's anti-corruption policy, but he was soon censured for corruption himself in the House of Commons and Pitt lost one of his closest lieutenants.

The huge burden of defending Britain's shores against Napoleon's colossal war machine was now in the hands of a sick man. Pitt rose to the task magnificently. He resolved to take the war to France. In October and November of 1804 Boulogne was bombarded with rockets. Pitt also took the war to Spain, whose neutrality was a cover for an alliance with France. Spain had already paid some £3 million towards French naval costs and offered fifteen line-of-battle ships and 40,000 troops in support. The British demanded that Spain close her dockyards to French shipping. Then in September four British frigates intercepted four Spanish treasure ships returning from the Spanish colonies off Cape Santa Maria. The Spanish resisted: one ship blew up and the other three were captured with £1 million aboard. On 12 December Spain declared war upon Britain and committed twenty-five ships of the line and eleven frigates to the fight against Britain. On paper this enormously strengthened Napoleon's position; but Pitt had been right in regarding the Spanish as effectively already part of the enemy war effort.

Pitt's third offensive was to try and renew the land war against Napoleon. Once again he trawled the European continent for allies. First in his sights was Russia under its new young Tsar, Alexander. By November the latter, appalled by the murder of the Duc d'Enghien, was moving towards an alliance, and was tempted further by Pitt's offer of £1.25 million for every 100,000 troops Russia put into the field. An Anglo-Russian alliance was formally signed at St Petersburg in April 1805.

Alexander, the grandson of Catherine the Great, had as his main aim a revival of the policy of expansionism. He wanted Russia to be in the

front rank of Europe. Both Britain and France before 1792 had viewed Russian expansionism as the main threat to European peace, but now Pitt judged it could be well employed defeating the more immediately aggressive French expansionism.

The next target for Pitt's proactive diplomacy was Austria. Both the Emperor Francis and his best soldier, his younger brother the Archduke Charles, favoured peace, partly to reinvigorate the Austrian army. Public opinion in Vienna was favourable to peace. But in February 1803 the French had imposed terms on Germany's western statelets, which Austria had long regarded as being within its sphere of influence. Forty-one historic free cities and sixty-six ecclesiastical principalities were done away with and replaced by a handful of bigger entities loyal to France. Austria was fobbed off with three small prince-bishoprics along the Tyrol. The Prussians were given a majority in the electoral college that chose the Holy Roman Emperor, which would have the effect of excluding the Habsburgs from that honorific title. Austrian irritation turned to outright anger when Piedmont and Elba were seized.

This was followed by Napoleon's coronation, which outraged the Austrian court as presuming to give the Corsican upstart the same rank as their Emperor. As already noted, Beethoven, who had so admired Napoleon's progressive credentials that he had dedicated his Third Symphony to him, struck out the dedication, calling it the Eroica instead. Austria became increasingly irritated as Napoleon appropriated the sword of Charlemagne, as well as a crown with the Charlemagne circlet, and secured the Pope's attendance at the coronation. Austrian diplomats, horrified at this upstaging of their Emperor, with Napoleon by now claiming Charlemagne as King of the French rather than the Germans, responded with derision that at the coronation 'one sister [of Napoleon] sulked, another held smelling salts under her nose and a third let the mantle drop; and this made things worse because it then had to be picked up.'

Napoleon them went a stage further. He travelled to Milan to become King of Italy on 26 May. For this occasion he wore Charlemagne's 800-year-old crown, taken from Monza. This was effectively an annexation of much of Italy and contrary to the Treaty of Luneville.

It is hard to see Napoleon's behaviour in any other light than that he was spoiling for a fight. He took pleasure in bullying Austria and did not care if the Austrians were finally provoked into standing up for their interests because he was sure he would win. By now even Austria's feeble court party was fuming with impatience and had decided this was the right time to strike, with Napoleon's main army encamped outside Boulogne in preparation for the invasion of Britain. The news that Alexander's Russia was preparing to join Britain in war against Napoleon finally tilted the balance.

On 8 August 1805, all Pitt's frenzied diplomatic efforts bore fruit: the Third Coalition was formed. Sweden and Naples also decided to join. Prussia hinted it might do so at a later date. This time it seemed the French had taken on too much. By provocation they had turned Britain against them. By abducting and murdering the Duc d'Enghien, they had aroused the ire of the Tsar. By crowning himself King of Italy, Napoleon had finally pushed the Austrians to breaking point.

This time the allied forces seemed overwhelming. The Austrian army was 250,000 strong and had never been completely defeated by the French in battle. The Russians had 200,000 at their disposal, while the other allies could assemble another 50,000 between them. Britain would continue to contribute its naval forces.

France faced war on several fronts: a Russo-Swedish attack from Pomerania; a Russian force of 40,000 to support the Prussians – if they chose to join the coalition – moving along the northern frontier towards Hanover and Hall; an Austrian thrust under Archduke Frederick with 90,000 men into Bavaria, where it would be reinforced by a Russian army of some 50,000. Further south Archduke Charles was to command 100,000 men to secure northern Italy; he would then join up with a smaller force of 20,000 men under Archduke John in the Tyrol. By the summer of 1805 Pitt had thus assembled the mightiest coalition ever to face France on land. It had been a remarkable achievement for a sick man, assembled in little more than a year.

Elsewhere round the globe, the tide also seemed to be turning Britain's way. The withdrawal of the French fleet from the Caribbean enabled Samuel Hood and General Grinfield to reoccupy St Lucia and Tobago and, later, Demerara, Berbice and Essequibo – the Dutch

settlements which had been restored to Holland at the Peace of Amiens. Surinam was soon taken too. The French army in Haiti submitted to the British, so as not to be slaughtered by Christophe's slave army. Only the large islands of Martinique and Guadelupe remained French, along with Curaçao which succeeded in beating off a British attack.

Meanwhile General Decaen, reaching India, had demanded the fort and enclave of Pondicherry under the terms of the Peace of Amiens. The British governor-general, Lord Wellesley, refused, even before news of the outbreak of hostilities between Britain and France reached him. Wellesley promptly struck out at the Marathas, the central Indian rulers whom the French had been courting in the autumn of 1803. After two spectacular campaigns in different regions he secured the ancient Moghul capital of Delhi, along with Hindustan and the Deccan. Meanwhile, his thirty-four-year-old younger brother Arthur Wellesley won a triumph at Assaye in September 1803.

Chapter 46

TO THE WEST INDIES

Within barely more than a year Napoleon's dreams of an empire in the West Indies had been completely dashed; the same had now happened in India; he had been deterred from reinvading Egypt; and he faced encirclement by the great powers of Europe. Pitt's waning but tough statecraft seemed more than a match for Napoleon's military skills. Yet, entirely undaunted, the new Emperor proceeded with his intention of destroying his most dangerous foe.

In January 1805 the French at last got their break. Admiral Missiessy, with four ships of the line and 3,500 troops, escaped from Rochefort in a snowstorm, evading the blockading fleet, which was sheltering in Quiberon Bay; and a week later Villeneuve escaped with nine ships of the line from Toulon while Nelson was loading supplies in Maddalena Bay in Sardinia. Nelson immediately sailed to Cagliari and to Palermo to defend these ports. He then proceeded all the way to Alexandria and found nothing. To Napoleon's fury, the cautious Villeneuve had returned to Toulon in a storm. However, Missiessy's fleet and army was soon wreaking havoc in the West Indies.

Now Napoleon unveiled his grand design for landing in Ireland and stirring up a rebellion there, attacking the West Indies and staging his invasion from across the Channel. He ordered Ganteaume to sea on 26 March to carry out the first stage. The French admiral's twenty-one ships found their way blocked by fifteen British ships. He asked for permission to engage. Napoleon refused; so he remained bottled up.

Villeneuve, spurred on by the wrath of the Emperor, slipped out of Toulon again at dead of night on 30 March. There now began the

greatest naval chase in history. Villeneuve's objective was to fulfil his assigned role in Napoleon's latest plan, which at least had the merit of simplicity. Villeneuve's fleet was to rendezvous with that of Ganteaume at Martinique as well as the troops in the West Indies. The aim was to lure the British fleets after them; the joint French fleet would then return across the Atlantic, pick up more French ships and at last defeat what remained of the British fleet in the Channel so that the French invasion force could cross.

Villeneuve did not yet know that Ganteaume's fleet had been blockaded. Villeneuve steered south, believing Nelson's fleet to be off Barcelona. In fact Nelson had deliberately appeared off the great Spanish port to lull Villeneuve into a sense of false security and then sailed eastwards to the Gulf of Rhodes, still believing that Napoleon's navy might be headed towards Egypt. But Villeneuve learnt of Nelson's eccentric course from a merchantman and steered north of the Balearics, for concealment, and then escaped south and west through the Straits of Gibraltar.

Nelson cruised anxiously back to Sicily, unsure of the enemy's intentions. Reaching Cartagena, Villeneuve signalled to the single French and fifteen Spanish battleships there to join him. Vice-Admiral Sir John Orde, who was supposed to be blockading Cadiz, decided that discretion was the better part of valour and withdrew his five battleships. The French ship and six Spanish battleships joined Villeneuve, who disappeared over the western horizon.

There was considerable shock in England that Villeneuve had escaped: on the London Stock Exchange consoles fell to 57. The French 'can get out when they choose' declared a fashionable lady. Nelson was blamed. The British admiral, having gone in entirely the wrong direction, now had to battle against unfavourable winds across to the western Mediterranean. His progress was slow, averaging ninety miles a day in the end.

Napoleon was delighted by news of Villeneuve's escape. Never convinced by Nelson's reputation, he had watched the British commander repulsed off Boulogne in 1801 and now outwitted by Villeneuve. The Emperor instructed Ganteaume to stay where he was while Villeneuve was to arch round the north coast of Scotland and then

convoy the invasion fleet from the Texel, as in the original plan. He was then to overwhelm the British blockading fleets at Ferrol and Brest and with an impregnable armada of sixty battleships guarantee the safe crossing of the invasion transport.

The new First Lord was Admiral Sir Charles Middleton, now Lord Barham, the genius who as Controller of the Navy had revived the senior service after the American war. Now seventy-eight, but still in full possession of his faculties, he had ordered Sir Alexander Cochrane to reinforce the five British warships in the West Indies with his own. He ordered a flying squadron of seven more warships under Collingwood to reinforce Cochrane.

Pitt meanwhile had assembled a 'secret expedition' of several thousand soldiers under Sir Eyre Coote, a British Indian veteran, and Sir James Cruz to sail for the Mediterranean where they were to liaise with a Russian force from Corfu. Pitt feared that Villeneuve had sailed to intercept it and Nelson, who was supposed to be protecting the Mediterranean, had disappeared. Barham ordered Collingwood to go to the rescue of the secret expedition, stripping the western approaches of the Channel of ships so as to bring his force up to eighteen warships.

To the astonishment of both Barham and Napoleon, Missiessy suddenly turned up with his four battleships off Rochefort. The reports had been false: he had not fled to Dominica or Tobago but had returned across the Atlantic. Meanwhile Nelson, who had at last reached Gibraltar, learnt of the secret expedition which had then arrived at the mouth of the Tagus in Portugal and had occupied the forts there in anticipation of the arrived of Villeneuve's fleet. The expedition's commanders in turn learnt that Nelson was nearby, and they sailed in delight to meet him. There, escorted by two battleships, they made their way eastwards towards Gibraltar. Pitt's expedition was safe.

After this wholly unnecessary diversion, Nelson decided to leave in pursuit of Villeneuve to the West Indies. He remarked: 'I was in a thousand fears for Jamaica, that is a blow which Buonaparte would be happy to give us. I flew to the West Indies without any orders, but I think the ministry cannot be displeased . . . I was bred, as you know, in

the good old school, and taught to appreciate the value of our West India possessions.' This was very nearly a colossal misjudgement.

He had left twenty of his twenty-three cruisers behind in the Mediterranean; so he now had ten ships of the line and three frigates to pursue a fleet twice as large. Soon after he departed, Collingwood arrived to escort the secret expedition; he despatched two further battleships across the Atlantic to reinforce Nelson.

News arrived that Villeneuve had reached Martinique on 16 May. Barham immediately feared that when Nelson arrived in the West Indies, Villeneuve would sail straight back to Europe where the Straits of Dover had been stripped of most of their defences. Cornwallis, blocking Brest, was ordered to send ten of his battleships to reinforce Collingwood's small Channel flotilla. The remainder of the scrappy Channel fleets – Cornwallis's twelve ships, the five still off Rochefort and several more in British ports – were to join together if Villeneuve suddenly materialized in British waters.

Nelson's fleet crossed the 3,200 miles from Gibraltar to Barbados in just three weeks – an average of 135 miles a day, an extraordinary feat, as his slowest ship, the *Superb*, was barely seaworthy. Nelson could not be certain of finding Villeneuve, and was ready to sail back immediately if he did not. On 4 June the British fleet reached Barbados where they learned that the French had indeed arrived, and had left. Nelson was exultant, believing he had caught his man. He made the signal, 'Prepare for battle'.

On the advice of General Brereton he sailed for Trinidad in pursuit, where he found no sign of the Franco-Spanish fleet. Nelson was furious: 'But for General Brereton's d—d information Nelson would have been, living or dead, the greatest man in his profession England ever saw. Now, alas! I am nothing . . .'

Nelson immediately made for Grenada to the north. There he learnt that Villeneuve had been sighted at Martinique on the 5th – the two fleets had passed within a hundred miles of each other. The unsuspecting Villeneuve, who had lost 3,000 of his men through sickness, had orders to remain in the West Indies until joined by Ganteaume and to capture as many British islands as possible. He had sailed to Guadeloupe to pick up troops, and to his shock had learned that Nelson had been

anchored off Barbados just days before. In spite of his overwhelming naval superiority, that was enough for Villeneuve: he set sail immediately back across the Atlantic to Ferrol.

Nelson had succeeded in his first object without a fight. The West Indies had been saved for Britain. When Nelson reached Antigua, he discovered that he was four days behind Villeneuve, but he had no idea where the French fleet had gone. He had a difficult decision to make: had Villeneuve set off to attack Jamaica, or had he sailed for Europe? He was relieved at last to hear from a young captain that Villeneuve's thirty-two-ship fleet had been sighted making for the north-east. On 13 June Nelson set sail for Gibraltar.

Villeneuve arched back across the Atlantic to the north. He had the choice of liaising with the Rochefort or Ferrol Squadrons and assembling a mighty fleet in the Channel of more than forty ships of the line to crush the few British ships still there. Nelson sent the *Curieux*, his fastest ship, on ahead to warn Barham of Villeneuve's return, and this overtook the French fleet to arrive at Plymouth on 7 July.

Hearing the news, Barham acted with a speed that belied his age and ordered ten ships from the Channel Fleet and five from the Rochefort blockade to stand in Villeneuve's path. The unimaginative Sir Robin Calder was put in charge. On 22 July, after a delay of three days, Calder's squadron was cruising off Ferrol in thick fog as Villeneuve's twenty ships of the line arrived, neither fleet seeing the other. At noon the fog lifted. Calder was daunted by the size of the enemy fleet, but after five hours of hesitation he ordered his ships to engage as fog descended again. The fighting was inconclusive and confused, lasting several hours before two Spanish ships surrendered.

The following day dawned with the two fleets having drifted seventeen miles apart, again separated by fog. Neither of these cautious commanders chose to attack. It was a deeply unimpressive dress rehearsal for a much larger battle. Nelson would have shown no such hesitation. On 20 July Villeneuve reached the safety of Ferrol, which Calder had been seeking to blockade. Calder withdrew to join Cornwallis's blockading squadron at Brest.

There Nelson had already arrived, left his ships and sailed back to England for long-deserved leave – for the first time in more than two

years. He was bitterly disappointed and neurotically ill again. The great chase had failed. The French fleet had escaped. He had travelled nearly 7,000 miles in vain. The histrionic, highly-strung seeker after glory was plunged into despair.

Yet he need not have felt such disappointment. The West Indies were safe and he and Barham had between them frustrated Napoleon's latest attempt at an invasion. Nelson's pursuit of Villeneuve back to Europe at such speed – Napoleon believed Nelson's fleet would tarry behind in the West Indies – and Barham ordering the interception of Villeneuve's fleet had prevented the junction of the French fleets that would have secured mastery of the Channel before Nelson's return.

Napoleon for once explained his objective in simple terms two months later:

> My plan [had been] to concentrate 40 or 50 battleships at Martinique by movements concerted from Toulon, Cadiz, Ferrol, and Brest; then have them return suddenly to Boulogne; get control of the straits for fifteen days; have 150,000 men and 10,000 horses ready; disembark in England, seize London and the Thames. This plan almost succeeded. Had Admiral Villeneuve, instead of going into Ferrol, merely effected his junction with the Spanish squadron, and made sail for Brest to join Admiral Ganteaume, my army was over, and there was an end to England. To carry out this plan, it was necessary to collect 150,000 men at Boulogne, a flotilla of 4,000 boats, and immense stores, get all this on board ship, and yet prevent the enemy from guessing my intentions: this seemed impossible.
>
> If I was to succeed it was by doing the reverse of what seemed obvious. If 50 ships of the line were going to cover the passage of the army to England, all that we needed at Boulogne were transports; and the immense display of gunboats and floating batteries of various kinds was absolutely useless. Collecting 4,000 vessels of this sort was opposing cannon to cannon, ship of war to ship of war; and the enemy were taken in. They believed I intended to force the passage by means of the flotilla, and never realized my actual plan. When, after my fleet had failed to carry out its manoeuvre, they perceived the

danger they had run, fear seized on the cabinet of London, and every thinking man admitted that England had never been so near disaster.

He was beside himself with rage when Villeneuve sought the safety of Ferrol.

> I believe that Villeneuve hasn't enough in him to command a frigate. He has no decision and no moral courage. Two Spanish ships have been in collision, a few men are sick on his own ships, add to that two days of unfavourable winds, an enemy's ship reconnoitring, a report that Nelson has joined Calder: and his plans are changed, when, taking these facts one by one, they amount to nothing. He has not the experience of war, nor the instinct for it.

The French had missed their chance for good. In fact the invasion of England had been averted by the West Indies chase. Napoleon had abandoned it in principle long before the Battle of Trafalgar was fought more than three months later. By then, the Emperor, waiting and watching from the cliffs above Boulogne, was already beginning to worry about news of the great armies assembling in the east. For that he had his own actions entirely to blame. As Seeley wrote:

> At the very same time, when his grand stroke against England was in suspense, Napoleon extended his power so recklessly in Italy, behaved with such insolence to the German Powers, and shocked public feeling by acts so Jacobinical, that he brought upon himself a new European coalition. It was the great mistake of his life. He was not, in the long run, a match for England and the Continent together; and he made, at starting, the irremediable mistake of not dividing these two enemies. He seems, indeed, to have set out with a monstrous miscalculation, which might have ruined him very speedily, for he had his plans for an invasion of England and a war in Europe at the same time.

The Emperor was now at last diverted that fateful summer from peering hungrily at England. On 3 August he wrote to General Daru:

You will read in the *Moniteur* some articles that will make you think war with Austria is coming. The fact is that this power is arming. I want her to disarm; if she won't, I shall pay her a little visit with 200,000 men which she will not soon forget. However, if any one asks you, and in your speeches, say that you don't believe in it, because I have had ample warning. For it would obviously be sheer folly to make war on me. There is certainly not in all Europe a finer army than the one I command today . . . I have made up my mind: I will either attack Austria and reach Vienna before November – to face the Russians, should they put in an appearance; or else my will, and that is the word, is that there should be but one Austrian regiment in the Tyrol. I want to be left to conduct my war against England in quiet.

On 13 August he declared:

My fleet sailed from Ferrol on the 17th with 34 ships of the line; there was no enemy in sight. If my instructions are followed, if it joins the Brest fleet and enters the Channel, there is still time; I am master of England. If, on the contrary, my admirals hesitate, manoeuvre badly, and don't carry out my plans, all I can do is to await winter and then cross with the flotilla; it's a risky operation. Such being the state of things, I must attend to the more urgent matter. I can place 200,000 men in Germany, and 25,000 in the kingdom of Naples. I march on Vienna, and do not lay down my arms until Naples and Venice are mine, and I have so increased the electorate of Bavaria that I have nothing further to fear from Austria. I can certainly pacify Austria after this fashion during the course of the winter. I shall not return to Paris until I have touched my goal. My plan is to gain two weeks. I want to get into the heart of Germany with 300,000 men before any one suspects it.

The following day he signalled Villeneuve anxiously: 'I hope you have reached Brest. Start; lose not a minute and, with my combined fleets, sail up the Channel. England is ours. We are all ready, everything is embarked. Appear here for twenty-four hours, and all is over.' But to

his anger and astonishment, he learnt that Villeneuve had made for Cadiz, instead of Brest, because he was running short of supplies, and evidently feared running into the British fleet. But Napoleon's focus of attention had shifted to the east. His huge invasion force for Britain was left stranded like a beached whale.

On 25 August he wrote to Talleyrand:

> My movement is begun. You can say that, as my frontiers are exposed I am moving 25,000 men to protect them. Don't show boldness, but absolute cowardice. It's a matter of gaining twenty days and of preventing the Austrians from crossing the Inn while I am marching on the Rhine. I did not suppose the Austrians would be so active, but I have made so many mistakes in my life, that I am past blushing for them.

He also raged furiously:

> How small England will become when France gets two or three admirals who are willing to face death! . . . Admiral Villeneuve has touched the limit! The thing is unthinkable! Send me a report covering the whole expedition. Villeneuve is a low rascal who must be ignominiously cashiered. Without plans, without courage, he would sacrifice everything to save his skin!

It was almost possible to feel sorry for the Emperor. In those few days the fate of Europe and of Britain was decided. The siege of Britain was lifted. Napoleon's revenge on Villeneuve was to be the quite unnecessary sacrifice of the French fleet at a time when all hope of invading Britain had ended and it had no need to expose itself to risk.

Nelson, quite unaware of the great victory he had achieved without firing a shot, sought solace with Lady Hamilton. Horatia's governess spoke of him: 'Thank God he is safe and well. Cold water has been trickling down my back ever since I heard he had arrived.' Then he travelled to Piccadilly to another riotous reception by the people. He was a hero such as Britain had never known before.

It was then in the waiting room of the war office that an historic encounter occurred – the only one of its kind. Sir Arthur Wellesley, a young officer recently returned from India with a growing reputation, recounted:

> He could not know who I was but he entered at once into conversation with me, if I can call it conversation, for it was almost all on his side and all about himself and, in reality, a style so vain and so silly as to surprise and almost disgust me.
>
> I suppose something that I happened to say may have made him guess that I was somebody and he went out of the room for a moment, I have no doubt to ask the office-keeper who I was, for when he came back he was altogether a different man both in manner and matter. All that I had thought a charlatan style had vanished and he talked of the state of the country and of the aspect and probabilities of affairs on the continent with a good sense and knowledge of subjects both at home and abroad that surprised me equally and more agreeably than the first part of our interview had done; in fact, he talked like an officer and a statesman.

Chapter 47

TRAFALGAR

On 2 September the peace of Nelson's domestic household in the country was disrupted by an official arrival: a messenger bearing the news that Villeneuve had moved to Cadiz. What could it mean? Nelson hurried to see Pitt. Neither man could know that Napoleon had already abandoned the whole invasion enterprise.

Pitt's orders this time were for Nelson to assume the Mediterranean and Atlantic commands and destroy the French fleet. Nelson immediately drew up his battle plan, as usual a departure from convention, to attack in three lines. One of his subordinates recounted:

> Nelson explained that to reach a quick decision he would divide his own fleet into three divisions: one, composed of the fastest ships, would be held in reserve; the other two would steer for the enemy line at right angles and in line ahead, although that would render them vulnerable in the final approach. 'I would go at them at once, if I can, about one-third of their line from their leading ship,' he went on. 'What do you think of it? I think it will surprise and confound the enemy. They won't know what I am about. I will bring forward a pell-mell battle and that is what I want.'

He had a fraught meeting with Emma, 'who could not eat and hardly drank and was swooning at the table'. She was broken-hearted at his departure 'as our dear Nelson is immediately going. It seems as though I have had a fortnight's dream, and am awoke to all the misery of this cruel separation. But what can I do? His powerful arm is of so much

consequence to his country.' He ordered a coffin already made out of the broken timbers of the French flagship *L'Orient* at the Nile to be prepared for him. He hugged his little daughter Horatia five times before leaving on the night of 13 September.

Nelson's fatalism and obsession with death were such that he certainly anticipated dying, although he had expected to die many times before. He embarked before a large crowd. Many were in tears, many kneeling and blessing him. His flagship was the *Victory* again, after a twenty-five-day absence. Arriving to join the fleet blockading Cadiz, he showed compassion towards Admiral Calder, who had been relieved, giving him the dignity of a 90-gun ship of the line to take him home, which he could ill-afford to spare.

He received a rapturous welcome from the fleet which he described in his curiously naïve, boyish manner: 'I believe my arrival was most welcome not only to the commander of the fleet [Collingwood] but also to every individual in it.' He summoned his captains aboard and set out his plan of action in great detail: its virtue was its simplicity. 'When I came to explain to them the Nelson touch it was like an electric shock, some shed tears, all approved, it was new, it was singular, it was simple and from admirals downwards it was repeated it must succeed if ever they will allow us to get at them.'

He had decided to attack in two columns, not three as originally intended. The columns would sail in parallel to each other to the centre of and rear of the enemy line and break through, the first column about twelve ships from the rear, the second ten ships from the van. This would effectively cut the French van off from the action, leaving it struggling to go about and come to the aid of those behind: the British would thus have eliminated the French superiority in ships and guns. It was a variation on Howe's breakthrough in naval tactics on the Glorious First of June and Nelson's own strategy at the Battle of the Nile.

The captains crowded into the low-ceilinged wood-panelled cabin of the *Victory* were famous names in themselves. Nelson's second-in-command, Collingwood, was a bluff, uncomplicated man and an unimaginative fighter, but an excellent sailor; there was Nelson's flag captain Hardy, the legendary Pellew, as well as Fremantle, Blackwood,

Codrington, Duff, Louis and others, all towered over by the giant Captain Hallowell, a striking contrast to the slight, delicate figure before them, towards whom they felt almost protective.

Now there was nothing to do but settle down to the tedious business of blockade, waiting for the French to make their move. If they had any sense, they would make none. For the time being the timorous Villeneuve and his admirals were determined to stay in safety in Cadiz, but the huge thirty-five-strong combined Franco-Spanish fleet was running short of supplies.

For once in his life Nelson seemed calmly resigned to waiting. He watched his sailors perform a play for the amusement of the officers and crew, ordered all his ships to be painted yellow with black stripes like giant wasps, for easy identification in battle and insisted that better provisions were served to his men.

With characteristic skill he kept his fleet well out of sight of Cadiz, some fifty miles to the west, communicating through a small line of signalling ships with a frigate squadron watching the port. With a westerly wind blowing, he knew he would be able to close quickly on Cadiz. If an easterly blew he could take refuge on the African side of the Straits of Gibraltar, which would allow him to remain within striking distance of Cadiz.

Villeneuve received a letter from the Emperor. It proposed to replace him with Admiral Rosally, in the event that his 'excessive pusillanimity' kept him at Cadiz. The Emperor 'counts the loss of his vessels for nothing if he loses them with honour,' Napoleon declared. This accusation of cowardice was too much for any man of honour to bear. On 19 October Villeneuve decided to take advantage of a light wind from the north-east to carry the fleet south and escape through the Straits of Gibraltar.

The French, after being bottled up in harbour for so long, made their exit clumsily – only twelve ships emerging by nightfall. Ville-neuve had ordered a third of his fleet to remain behind, to form a reserve French fleet to come to the aid of the main fleet if attacked. This further complicated the departure and only on 20 October did the remainder emerge, to form five straggling columns nine miles long. The fleet consisted of eighteen French and fifteen Spanish ships,

mostly of 74 guns, although four possessed more than a 100. The great and sinister red-and-black Spanish *Santissima Trinidad*, the four-deck veteran of the Battle of Cape St Vincent, towered above them all with its 150 guns. The colossal *Santa Anna* was entirely draped in funereal black. To those crowding along the shore of the Spanish mainland to watch, it was a mighty armada of magnificent ships rolling in the high sea like a stately procession of ducks, colourful in plumage, stately in bearing, ragged in line.

On receiving the news from his signal frigates that the French had broken out, Nelson wrote to Emma: 'My dearest, beloved Emma, dear friend of my bosom, the signal has been made that the enemy's combined fleet are coming out of port. We have very little wind, so that I have no hopes of seeing them before tomorrow. May the God of Battles crown my endeavours with success . . .'

He sailed slowly towards the shore to cut off the French. The wind changed direction twice, and he twice altered his course accordingly. When Villeneuve saw the British fleet in an orderly line on the horizon on the morning of Monday, 21 October, he realized to his horror that it consisted of twenty-seven ships, not eighteen as he had expected. He considered making a bolt for the Straits and escaping to Toulon, but then decided to go north and make a run back to Cadiz. He abandoned his tactical dispositions and ordered his captains to form a single uneven line.

He issued his last instruction: 'There is nothing to alarm us in the sight of an English fleet. Their 64-gun ships have not 500 men on board; they are not more brave than we are, they are harassed by a two years' cruise; they have fewer motives to fight well.' He then watched through the night as the British frigates signalled the whereabouts of the French fleet to Nelson's ships, which were waiting like predators on the horizon, with rockets and gunfire.

The day dawned pleasantly, with a soft breeze. Nelson to the west was at ease, touring the gun-decks of his ship where he was cheered by his 1,000 men. He knew he could catch up with the French and put his plans into action at leisure. The prospect of action always seemed to induce in him an unnatural calm.

He sat down to prepare a prayer of moving simplicity:

May the great God, whom I worship, grant to my country and for the benefit of Europe in general a great and glorious victory, and may no misconduct in anyone tarnish it, and may humanity after victory be the predominant feature in the British Fleet. For myself individually, I commit my life to Him who made me and may his blessing light upon my endeavours for serving my country faithfully. To Him I resign myself and the just cause which is entrusted me to defend. Amen, amen, amen.

He then issued his famous signal: 'England expects that every man will do his duty.' This irritated Collingwood, who believed signals should be reserved for practical instructions.

At the last moment, Nelson seems to have decided to attack at right-angles straight into the French fleet, rather than closing at a more oblique angle, perhaps to present a smaller front to the fire of French ships as his column approached, perhaps out of impatience, although Villeneuve had no prospect of escaping to Cadiz, still some twenty miles away. He had decided to lead the first column himself, Collingwood leading the second. Captain Blackwood who had been ordered aboard the *Victory* to be at his side, urged Nelson to shift his flag to the *Euryalus*, where he could direct the battle from safety. Nelson brusquely refused, and rejected another suggestion that the *Téméraire* under Captain Harvey should lead the attack.

The two fleets were now in a slow motion drama impelled by the slightest of breezes, the French and the Spanish extending in a great crescent about four miles long, the British in two columns, which had in fact broken up into bunches with every ship trying to be first into the action heading for the centre and rear like two slow-moving spears.

As picturesque as these elegant sailing craft with their sleek wooden hulls and their billowing sails might appear, they were colossal engines of war, packed with explosives, approaching each other with the purpose of inflicting as much damage and killing as many people as possible. It seemed improbable to the spectators on shore that the beauty and peace of this slow-moving scene, the stately procession of magnificent, gaudy and multicoloured ships with their bosomy sails billowing almost as far as the eye could see, from north to south and

across to the western horizon, would engage soon in horrific and destructive conflict.

The fleets were not evenly matched; the French had some 400 more guns than the British and double the number of men. But Nelson had compensated for this by his tactics, and his guns also fired twice as fast as the French and Spanish ones. The British were also vastly more experienced sailors than their enemies, who had for many months been cooped up in port. Slowly, elegantly, unhurriedly, the spears moved towards their targets in the centre of the great arc of the Franco-Spanish fleet.

It was Collingwood's glory that he arrived first beneath the sinister black hull of the *Santa Anna*. This was the moment of greatest danger. The huge ship and its neighbours were able to concentrate their fire on the British ship, which could not return it as its guns were not broadside to the enemy. The *Fougueux* behind the *Santa Anna* attempted to block Collingwood's *Royal Sovereign,* which steered straight for it, as though to ram it. The *Fougueux* took evasive action to avoid collision.

The *Royal Sovereign* broke the line between the stern of the *Santa Anna* and the bow of the *Fougueux*. Collingwood raked both ships broadside as he passed. 'What would Nelson give to be here!,' he exclaimed triumphantly. 'How I envy him,' said Nelson, observing from the head of his slower-moving line. That first British broadside disabled some fourteen guns and killed some 300 of the *Santa Anna*'s crew. Swinging her helm round, the *Royal Sovereign* came alongside the towering Spanish ship on the lee side; the Spanish captain replied with his own broadsides.

Five ships were soon firing at the *Royal Sovereign*. For fifteen more minutes 'that noble fellow Collingwood', as Nelson dubbed him, was entirely alone in the action, and it was extraordinary that his ship was not destroyed. Then he was joined at last by the *Belleisle*, the *Mars*, the *Tonnant*, the *Bellerophon* and the *Ajax* coming up behind him in his column.

Nelson's column was now at last approaching the Franco-Spanish line. He had intended to attack the enemy flagship, the *Bucentaure*, but there was nothing to identify it, so he made for his old foe, the

Santissima Trinidad. As the *Victory* approached, the French fired single shots to test whether she was within range. The seventh blew a hole in the *Victory*'s topsail. The British held their breath for two minutes more, and then a pandemonium of fire broke out from the enemy fleet as she approached.

For nearly forty minutes more the *Victory* ploughed on, unable to return fire, under this hail of shot. At 500 yards' distance the mizzen topmast came down. The ship's wheel was disabled and its sails were shredded. A single shot killed eight marines in the poop and another struck a launch, showering splinters on Nelson and Hardy, who were standing on the quarter-deck. Another cannonball ripped Scott, Nelson's secretary who was standing beside them, in two. 'This is too warm work, Hardy, to last long,' declared Nelson without emotion. Some fifty officers and men were killed in those first volleys.

As they approached the French line they spotted Villeneuve's flag flying aboard the *Bucentaure*, but the *Victory* could not veer towards it without exposing her side to fire from the *Redoutable* and the *Neptune*. 'Take your choice,' Nelson instructed Hardy. The *Victory* steered past the stern of the French flagship, and at last opened fire with a 50-gun broadside directly into the *Bucentaure*'s bow at point-blank range. Some twenty guns were disabled and 400 men killed.

The *Victory* turned alongside the *Redoutable*, which closed her lower deck gun ports to avoid being boarded, the two ships becoming entangled. Meanwhile the *Neptune*, the *Bucentaure*, the *Redoutable* and the *Santissima Trinidad* were pouring fire into the *Victory*. But she was soon supported by the *Téméraire*, the next in line, then the British *Neptune*, the *Leviathan*, the *Conqueror*, the *Africa* and the *Agamemnon*. The van of the Franco-Spanish fleet meanwhile had sailed ahead, leaving two clusters of ships fighting about half a mile apart from each other, where Nelson's and Collingwood's squadrons had penetrated the French line.

The *Victory* raked the *Redoutable* with broadsides, but its Captain Lucas was a formidable fighter. Although his ship was crippled, the sharp-shooters he had placed in the tops were still firing lethally down on to the deck of the *Victory*. A French mariner called Guillemand, who was one of Lucas's best marksmen, took up the story:

The two decks were covered with dead bodies, which they had not time to throw overboard. I perceived Captain Lucas [his own captain] motionless at his post, and several wounded officers still giving orders. On the poop of the English vessel was an officer covered with orders, and with only one arm. From what I had heard of Nelson, I had no doubt that it was he. He was surrounded by several officers, to whom he seemed to be giving orders. I saw him quite exposed and close to me. I could even have taken aim at the men I saw, but I fired at hazard among the groups I saw of sailors and officers. All at once I saw great confusion on board the *Victory*; the men crowded round the officer whom I had taken for Nelson. He had just fallen, and was taken below, covered with a cloak.

If this is accurate, and Guillemand indeed fired the fatal shot, he was not aiming specifically at Nelson but at a group of Englishmen, even though he had recognized the admiral.

This is understandable. The sharpshooter was aiming at a distance of fifty yards in the heat of battle from one swaying ship on to the deck of another. Even an excellent marksman could not have been sure of his target. Nelson has been much faulted for so exposing himself to danger and wearing his decorations in battle. Yet his uniform was dusty and the decorations were stars sewn into it, not his usual glittering metal ones. The Frenchman claimed he recognized him from his single arm as well, something Nelson could not cover up. It is hard to believe that Nelson had a death wish, as some have alleged, or that he actually sought death on the field of battle. He was a man who loved glory and the acclaim of his countrymen: in destroying the enemy fleet as he intended to, he would already have acquired glory and a place in the affection of Britons to the end of his days, which he wanted to share with his beloved Emma and Horatia.

Much more likely, for a man accustomed to leading his men by example, by exposing himself to their risks, by being in the thick of the action, by showing cool detachment in the face of great odds which allowed him to direct the course of the battle, he believed he could cheat death as he had so many times before. He knew the risks, but it was his style of leadership to seek to defy them. His place was at the

head of his men, in undress uniform and decorations, so that he could be recognized by them and show that he did not fear the enemy nor should they.

It was meaningless to talk of his staying out of battle and directing operations from afar. As had been shown in Parker's case at Copenhagen, no admiral could direct operations where he could neither comprehend the course of the action nor expect to be obeyed by the captains in the thick of it. Once battle was joined it had to be carried through to the end in ship-to-ship engagements until one side or the other broke it off. This was not a land battle that could be directed from a hill with orders to various units to advance, retreat or redeploy.

The very basis of Nelson's extraordinary career and the esteem in which he was held by his fellow countrymen was that he exposed himself fearlessly to risk. Other naval commanders had done just the same – Howe at the Glorious First of June, Jervis at St Vincent, Duncan at Camperdown. History has not been kind to those who stayed at a safe distance. Young Blackwood was later to lament: 'I wish to God he had yielded to my entreaties to come on board my ship. We should all have preserved a friend, and the country the greatest admiral that ever was, but he would not listen to it.' But Nelson had no other choice than to lead his men and expose himself to risk.

The bullet passed through his left shoulder, was deflected into his chest, ruptured an artery and shattered his spine. It could hardly have been more damaging. 'They have done for me at last, Hardy,' he said as he fell slowly. 'My backbone is shot through.' He covered his face with a handkerchief so as not to be recognized and dishearten his men. A marine and two sailors carried him down to the cockpit. His crew had little chance to observe what had happened. The fighting was as fierce as ever.

With the deadly fire of the marksmen having all but cleared the top deck of the *Victory*, and much of the *Redoutable* itself wrecked and on the point of surrendering, the latter's sailors tried desperately to board the British flagship without success. The French crew had fought with unbelievable tenacity and ferocity: of its complement of 643 men, 522

were killed or wounded, an extraordinarily high casualty rate, particularly for a smaller ship attacking a larger. Nearby the *Temeraire* had
also attacked the *Redoutable*, coming under fire from the *Fougueux* and
the French *Neptune*.

However the French flagship proved less formidable. Badly damaged
by the fire from the *Victory* and under attack from the *Conqueror*,
Villeneuve surrendered, once its last mast fell. A marine officer, three
marines and two sailors came aboard and found 'a very tranquil,
English-looking Frenchman, wearing a long-tailed uniform coat
and green corduroy pantaloons'. The marine took Villeneuve and
his two companions aboard his little launch, and tried to return to the
Conqueror. He could not find it in the bedlam of fighting around him,
so he escorted his eminent prisoner aboard the nearest English ship, the
Mars.

The *Conqueror* had taken on another giant ship, the *Santissima
Trinidad* itself, which was also under fire from several others. The
behemoth's mainmast came crashing down, like a huge skyscraper at
sea. A British officer recorded: 'This tremendous fabric gave a deep roll,
with a swell to leeward, then back to windward, and on her return
every mast went by the board, leaving her an unmanageable hulk on
the water. Her immense topsails had every reef out, her royals were
sheeted home but lowered, and the falling of this majestic mass of spars,
sails, and rigging plunging into the water at the muzzles of our guns was
one of the most magnificent sights I ever beheld.'

The giant Spanish ship threw a Union Jack over its side in surrender,
but the *Conqueror* was off in search of new prey. So no one arrived to
take possession until the *Africa* despatched a lieutenant who found a
solitary Spanish survivor on the main deck. At that moment several
ships of the Spanish van, which had at last tacked about, seemed to be
coming to the rescue. So the Spaniard replied that the ship was still
fighting, and the lieutenant hastily retreated to his boat unmolested. In
the end the *Santissima Trinidad* was not rescued but was captured by
another British ship, the *Prince*.

In Collingwood's battle cluster, his flagship was pounding away at
the other giant Spanish ship, the *Santa Anna*, and beat it into submission. After an hour and a half, though, the *Royal Sovereign* was almost in

as bad a state, with just its foremast left standing, and had to be taken in tow. Around Collingwood, the battle raged: the *Belleisle* took on three ships one after the other, including the *Fougueux*. The *Belleisle* was soon dismasted. The *Mars* came to her rescue, drawing off one of the attackers, but another French ship joined in. Undaunted, the *Belleisle* continued to pour shot into the nearest Frenchman, which struck its colours.

Then the *Leviathan* and *Polyphemus* arrived, followed by the *Swiftsure*. The *Mars* went on to engage four ships simultaneously, a Frenchman on each side with a Spaniard behind reinforced by a Frenchman. The last's broadside killed her captain, Duff. Codrington's *Orion* closed silently into battle, under orders not to fire, until it was alongside a French ship; then bringing down all three of its masts in a devastating broadside, the *Orion* forced it to strike its colours. The *Orion* proceeded to attack *L'Intrepide*, which it also quickly forced to surrender. The *Tonnant* was engaged with the *Algeciras*, which attempted to board it; a single Frenchman succeeded in getting aboard and was captured. The *Tonnant* went on to capture two prizes.

Perhaps the most desperate fight by a British ship was that of the *Bellerophon*, which, after breaking the enemy line, found herself under fire from a ship on either side, and three from behind. The ship was entirely dismasted and as her sails fell they caught fire. The captain and some 115 men were killed. But the wreck still fought on, and forced the *Monarca* to surrender. The *Bellerophon* then pounded the *Aigle* into submission; but as all her launches were out of action, an officer dived overboard, swam to the *Aigle* and climbed up her rudder chains to claim the prize. The *Bellerophon* – dubbed the 'Billy Ruffian' by her unclassically minded men – was later to play an even more fateful part in the Napoleonic saga.

Aboard the *Victory*, the long, heroic, pathetic and tragic tableau of Nelson's death was unfolding. When the ship's surgeon reached his side, Nelson told him, 'I am mortally wounded. You can do nothing for me, Beatty. I have but a short time to live.' Beatty prodded the wound with his finger and realized his admiral was right. He was running a high temperature and desperately thirsty. 'Drink, drink, fire,

fire' he kept repeating and was given lemonade, water and wine. He asked repeatedly for Hardy. The captain came after an hour during a lull in the fighting. 'Well, Hardy, how goes the day with us?' Nelson asked. Hardy replied that twelve or fourteen ships had surrendered. 'I hope none of our ships have struck, Hardy?'

'No, my Lord, there is no fear of that.'

'I am a dead man, Hardy,' the admiral replied. Hardy returned to his duties and Nelson turned back to the doctor: 'All pain and motion behind my breast is gone and you know I am gone.' Beatty concurred. 'God be praised. I have done my duty,' breathed Nelson. Meanwhile the counter-attack by the returning French van had been blunted by the *Victory* and other ships: three more prizes were taken. Hardy returned to inform Nelson that it was now certain that fourteen or fifteen prizes had been taken. 'That is well. But I had bargained for twenty,' was the grudging reply.

Nelson's seamanship and prescience remained to the last. The fleet, having comprehensively defeated its enemies, was now facing a more dangerous one still: catastrophe from the weather, a threat Collingwood, in the thick of battle, seemed to be neglecting. Nelson gave his last order. The growing swell, in spite of the fine weather, had alerted the great man that seriously bad weather was on the way: catastrophe threatened partially disabled British ships and wholly disabled prizes, which could be driven by the wind on to a lee shore. With all his energy Nelson suddenly called out, 'Anchor, Hardy, anchor!' Hardy remarked that Collingwood was now in charge. 'Not while I live, I hope, Hardy. No, do you anchor, Hardy.' After a while he said, 'Don't throw me overboard. You know what to do.'

With the poignancy of a child facing an unknown threshold about to be crossed, Nelson called out for human comfort. 'Kiss me, Hardy.' The burly captain kissed his cheek. 'Now I am satisfied. Thank God I have done my duty.' Hardy leaned over to kiss him again on the forehead. 'Who is that?' 'It is Hardy.' 'God bless you, Hardy.'

After Hardy had left again for the quarter-deck, Nelson told the ship's chaplain, who was rubbing his chest to ease his pain, 'Remember that I leave Lady Hamilton and my daughter Horatia as a legacy to my country.' He added a moment later, 'I have not been a great sinner,

doctor.' He wept, repeating, 'Thank God I have done my duty.' His last words were 'God and my country'. He died at about four o'clock.

The battle raged on a little longer before Admiral Dumanoir called off the last four French ships still fighting. Fifteen minutes later the Spanish commander, Admiral Gravina, ordered his crippled remaining ten ships back to Cadiz. After about another half hour, the fighting ended. The 'grim and awful scene', as Codrington was later to describe it, was over. The fact that it had taken place at sea in those huge floating wooden stately homes that were the great ships of the time could not conceal the fearsome toll of the battle. More than 7,000 men had been killed or badly wounded altogether, the casualty levels of a major land battle. The decks were covered in blood, with bodies and limbs lying everywhere. The swelling sea itself was reddened and packed with floating corpses as the hulks of great and crippled vessels milled about directionless.

Alongside the horror of the scene, awareness of a colossal British victory began to dawn on the men. Seventeen French and Spanish ships had been taken in all, and one had blown up spectacularly in battle. The remaining fifteen had escaped. The British had not lost a single ship, although several were badly mauled. The British had lost some 450 killed and 1,400 wounded, compared to 3,400 French dead and 1,200 wounded, and 1,000 Spaniards killed and 1,400 wounded. Some 4,000 prisoners had been taken.

Of the remaining French and Spanish ships, eleven escaped to Cadiz while four were attacked a fortnight later by a British squadron off Cape Ortegal under Captain Richard Strachan, and were captured without a fight. Of the eleven, five attempted a breakout two days after Trafalgar, recapturing two of the British prizes, but three were lost in the gale. The remainder were virtual prisoners in port, and the French ships were eventually to be seized by the Spanish. The colossal fleet of thirty-three warships had been effectively annihilated. Although not quite as complete as the Battle of the Nile, it had been an over-whelming victory.

The significance of Trafalgar went even further, although no one realized it at the time, for the French consoled themselves with the

thought that their shipyards could always rebuild the fleet. It made a major contribution to the Spanish decision to turn against the French. Napoleon was only once to attempt a major naval engagement again – and that with caution. The plans for invading England would never be renewed. He would never consider the project seriously again. Trafalgar was to Britain what the Battle of Britain was in the 1940s – a lifting of the shadows of invasion, fighting in the towns and countryside of Britain and enemy occupation.

The travails of those exhausted, exultant seamen were not over yet. As the dying Nelson had realized, with his last fevered ounce of seamanship, a fate almost as dangerous as an enemy fleet would soon be upon them. As though in heavenly rage at the the appalling suffering inflicted by man that day, a truly devastating gale struck the British fleet. Collingwood had decided to ignore Nelson's orders to anchor, partly because some of the anchors aboard British ships had been lost in the fighting, and partly to move as far as possible from the dangerous lee shore of Spain, with its treacherous shoals at Trafalgar.

Whether he was right or not, he sailed straight into the teeth of the gale on that fateful night of 21 October. Colossal waves battered the ships, many of them already crippled, rolling about helplessly with gaping holes and hundreds of wounded men lying in agony aboard. The *Redoutable*, the French hero of the fight, sank behind the ship towing her. The flagship *Bucentaure* had to be cut adrift and was seen crashing on to the shoals three miles away with the loss of the remainder of its crew. The whole fleet was being driven back towards the rocks. During the gale, as the ships struggled to maintain position and feared that they would all perish ashore, the wind veered abruptly, allowing them to gain a few miles distance. As dawn struck the storm continued unabated, and other French prizes went aground, sank or had to be destroyed.

Blackwood, towing the once mighty *Santissima Trinidad*, the floating colossus that had been the pride of the Spanish fleet, evacuated the crew and burned the ship; the *Santa Anna*, its proud, unwieldy sister, suffered the same fate. 'The French commander-in-chief is at this moment at my elbow', commented Blackwell. Villeneuve gazed out impassively at the wild and fearful scene of these towering infernos

tossing and turning in a raging gale. His emotions can only be imagined at the loss of his greatest ships, wrestling with relief that at least they would not now join the British fleet.

Blackwood wrote to his wife: 'Ever since last evening we have had a most dreadful gale of wind, and it is with difficulty that the ships who tow them [the prizes] keep off the shore. Three, I think, must be lost, and with them, above 800 souls each. What a horrid scourge is war.' It was one of the strangest scenes in history, a glimpse into the Apocalypse. Altogether twelve prizes were destroyed in three days of continuous raging gales. The British limped home with none of their ships lost, but with, only four prizes out of the original sixteen. In the hold of the *Victory*, the body of Nelson had been preserved in a huge cask filled with brandy.

It was Guy Fawkes night, and the same evening an officer aboard the fastest messenger in the English fleet, the schooner *Pickle*, landed and was conveyed at speed up to London to reach the Admiralty at one o'clock in the morning with the news of the victory and of Nelson's death. The secretary of the Admiralty received him and conveyed him to the sleepy, elderly First Lord, Barham. The two men promptly informed Pitt, who unusually could sleep no longer, and the King, who was dumbstruck for five minutes, before settling down to write by urgent despatch to dozens more, including Fanny and Lady Hamilton.

The latter fell into a catatonic trance for ten hours. The wife of George Fremantle, a captain who had survived, remarked accurately that 'regret at [Nelson's] death is more severely felt than joy at the destruction of the combined fleet'. Lady Harriet Cavendish observed: 'Poor Lord Nelson. The universal gloom that I hear of from those who have been in town is the strongest proof of the regret he so justly deserved to occasion as otherwise I suppose such a victory at such a moment is everything, both for our honour and safety, and could have driven us half wild.' The Prince of Wales was unable to compose himself.

The report that the 'combined fleet is defeated but Nelson is no more' ran like wildfire into the streets. Lady Bessborough commented: 'How truly he has accomplished his prediction that when they met it must be to extermination. He could not have picked out a finer close to

such a life. Do you know, it makes me feel almost as much envy as compassion; I think I should like to die so.' The *Morning Chronicle* wrote sadly: 'What is likely to be the inward ejaculation of Buonaparte? – "Perish the twenty ships – the only rival of my greatness is no more!" – He was, as a captain, equal in his own element of the sea, to what Napoleon, with a base degeneracy of motive, has proved himself to be on land.'

A day later the London mob went wild in celebration of Trafalgar. On 9 November Pitt gave a brief and laconic reaction after his carriage was drawn by huge crowds to the Lord Mayor's banquet. 'Europe is not to be saved by any single man. England has saved herself by her exertions and will, I trust, save Europe by her example.'

Modern historiography has understandably tried to demythologize Nelson and rightly has focused upon his weaknesses as well as his strengths. Of the former he had plenty: the early readiness to suck up to his masters, including such unworthy objects of his attentions as Prince William, his colossal vanity, his severity, his involvement in the corruption and brutality of the Neapolitan court, his obsession with Emma Hamilton, who was nothing if not a hard-boiled social climber for all her charms (although she may have genuinely been devoted to him). But these were the defects of a naïve, not a bad man. Even his friends considered him a 'baby' in many respects. Like many sailors he was a simpleton when it came to politics and women, and he should not be faulted for being so. He certainly aspired to heroism and gloried in fame, but saw no need to moderate his private conduct accordingly. He had become a symbol in a country desperate for heroes after years of hardships and unrelenting war, and quite understandably felt that this should not invade his personal life.

He was also the greatest commander of fleets Britain ever possessed, a fearless leader of men with a magnificent understanding of how to lead his ships. Like so many masters of their craft he saw no need to adjust his habits to the expectations of the crowd: it was enough that he delivered the victories they needed. The road to glory was arduous, dogged by ill-health, false starts and setbacks. The string of victories attests to his genius – Cape St Vincent, the Nile, Copenhagen and

Trafalgar. He was peerless, in a country that depended on the naval service for its survival.

His personal conduct was childish rather than malevolent, and comparatively mild for the period: his affairs in ports overseas were standard practice among most naval officers, and the infatuation of a middle-aged man with a lusty girl half his age far from exceptional in an age graced with the likes of the Prince Regent and Napoleon himself. Childlike vanity can be excused in a man who had so much to be vain about.

There was to be the inevitable unseemly bickering around his bier. His grasping and worthless elder brother William was to secure the earldom that Nelson never had, as well as his pension, of which some £100,000 was paid as a lump sum and £5,000 a year was granted to himself and his successors tax-free in perpetuity – colossal sums for the time. Nelson's long-suffering wife Fanny, by contrast, secured only £2,000 a year as a pension, and the £1,000 a year her husband had left her – which however provided for a comfortable middling existence.

Emma received the house at Merton and just £500 – a belated official revenge. She was shunned. Bitterly she wrote: 'Let them refuse me all reward. I will go with this paper fixed to my breast, and beg through the streets of London, and every barrow woman shall say, "Nelson bequeathed her to us."' She soon got through her modest inheritance from Nelson and her more generous one from Sir William Hamilton, dying at the age of fifty in Calais, pursued by her creditors. Horatia was longer lived and married a clergyman.

Chapter 48

DEATH OF A STATESMAN

It was ironical that in death Nelson was to serve his country almost as much as in life. For catastrophe had overtaken Britain's continental allies of such a magnitude that without Nelson's victory the will of the British people to go on fighting might have been destroyed. At the very instant that Nelson was paying for his last and greatest feat with his slow and agonizing death, his equal on land, Napoleon Bonaparte, was on his way to execute the first of the truly devastating strokes in his career that were to establish him as one of the greatest military commanders that ever lived.

In an incredible demonstration of military mobility and discipline, Napoleon marched an army of 350,000 men, many of them all the way from the Channel ports where they had been posted to strike at Britain, in less than two months to surround a huge Austrian army at Ulm on 20 October, the day before Trafalgar. They secured its surrender almost without bloodshed and then went on to win the greatest victory of his career at Austerlitz on 2 December 1805.

Reports of the Austrian debacle at Ulm reached the British on 3 November. It was a Sunday and Pitt was appraised by Lord Malmesbury, translating a Danish newspaper. Grenville wrote with bleak despondency: 'One's mind is lost in astonishment and apprehension. An army of 100,000 men, reckoned the best troops in Europe, totally destroyed in three weeks . . . Yet even this, I am afraid, is only the beginning of our misfortunes. We are plunging into a sea of hitherto unthought of difficulties . . . Time and reflection may suggest topics of confidence which I have hitherto looked for in vain.' Lady Bessbor-

ough wrote: 'You have no idea of the consternation here. I am so terrified, so shocked with the news I scarcely know what to wish. This man moves like a torrent.'

The prime minister, reeling from the threat of the invasion that had hung over Britain like a dagger throughout the summer, the weakness of his government, of which he was the only real force, and bad news from Ulster, was now an ill and weakened man. Years of responsibility on those still young shoulders, unsupported by a wife and family, whose chief companion had been the port bottle, had taken their toll.

With the news of Trafalgar he made one last show of his old determination. The 'secret expedition' had by now nearly reached Italy. The prime minister despatched General Don with 6,000 Hessian troops to the Elbe and a force of guards under General Edward Paget to follow, with every available unit after that – some 21,000 altogether. 'We shall see Bonaparte's army either cut off or driven back to France and Holland by Christmas,' said Pitt. He had little hope of inflicting an immediate defeat, but his aim was to stiffen the Prussians, dithering in indecision, to enter the war and support their Austrian and Russian allies who might otherwise sue for peace.

During the next few weeks there was virtually no news from the continent, only conflicting rumours: fog and ice held up despatches from Germany. It was rumoured that the French had suffered a terrible rout and that Napoleon had been killed. Pitt himself was too much of a realist to believe the gossip. But he preserved his show of optimism: '. . . Great as have been the pecuniary efforts which His Majesty has made for the common cause, he is ready still to extend them to such a farther amount as may enable those Powers to bring an active force of from two hundred to two hundred and fifty thousand men; and His Majesty has no doubt of being enabled himself to augment his own active force . . . to not less than sixty thousand men.' He urged the 'ancient spirit of Austria' to 'remain unshaken and undismayed'. Arthur Wellesley, who spent several days with him at the same country house in November, found him resolute, lunching heartily, riding a great deal and, as always, drinking port copiously in the evening. On the advice of his doctors he went to Bath, where the waters improved his gout.

On 29 December the news first reached him of Napoleon's great

victory at Austerlitz and the possibility that the defeated Austrians were suing for a separate peace. Rosebery memorably described the scene:

> Austerlitz killed him. He was at Bath when he received the news. Tradition says that he was looking at a picture gallery when he heard the furious gallop of a horse. 'That must be a courier,' he exclaimed, 'with news for me.' When he had opened the packet he said, 'Heavy news indeed,' and asked for brandy. He hurriedly swallowed one or two drams; had he not, says an eye-witness, he must have fainted. He then asked for a map, and desired to be left alone. He had gout flying about; the shock of the tidings threw it back on some vital organ. From this day he shrank visibly. His weakness and emaciation were painful to witness. Still, he did not abate his high hopes, or his unconquerable spirit.

Simultaneously eight British transports with 2,000 troops had got lost on their way to Bremen. The British army on the Elbe was also clearly in serious trouble – even though Lord Paget remarked optimistically: 'I long to be at the rascals. You may depend upon it we will play with them.' The young Arthur Wellesely had been despatched in charge of a brigade in Lord Cathcart's division. Although the mob ran riot in dismay at news of Austerlitz, and the troops had to be called in, order and optimism soon returned. The size of the defeat had not been confirmed, nor the Austrian collapse. Pitt remarked cheerfully: 'It is impossible not to disbelieve above nine tenths of the French bulletins and not to doubt a good deal of the armistice as stated.' But on 4 January he was seized with another acute attack of gout.

The last great event of his life was still to be played out. Pitt had personally supervised arrangements for Nelson's funeral with the Garter King of Arms, down to details of the military decorations to be awarded. On 9 January 1806, the funeral was held, attended by 30,000 troops lining the way from Greenwich, where the body had been lying in state, to St Paul's. It was drawn on a wagon shaped like the *Victory* and took three and a half hours to reach the cathedral through the hundreds of thousands lining the route.

The crew of the *Victory* followed the coffin on foot, which arrived in

deathly silence. Inside 7,000 dignitaries sat on a specially built dais seventeen tiers high. The huge flag of the *Victory* had been torn in pieces for each one of the forty-eight surviving crewmen to keep and the body was lowered to the tomb twenty feet below. It was a magnificently choreographed occasion of solemnity by Pitt to sustain the national spirit of defiance at a desperate time. Nelson in death had performed his final duty, and the legend was now to snowball steadily, gathering size, with the dedication of Trafalgar Square to the hero, the erection of Nelson's column and perhaps most humbly and most movingly, the placing of replicas of Nelson's ships along each of the lampstands that line London's stateliest avenue, the Mall, where the admiral can look down upon them for posterity. Thus Nelson's fleet still lives on in the centre of London today.

Now it was Pitt's turn to breathe his last. He arrived at his villa on Putney Heath, Bowling Green House, on 12 January. On entry he told his eccentric niece, Lady Hester Stanhope, who acted as his hostess to 'roll up that map [of Europe hanging on the wall]; it will not be needed these ten years.' This may have reflected an intention to concentrate the war effort in the colonies, now that Europe was apparently lost. He believed he would still see Britain through to victory, but he knew that years of struggle lay ahead after Austerlitz.

After the weekend he felt better and went out for a ride, but on the afternoon of 13 January the news of the Austrian armistice was confirmed, as well as of a pact between the Prussians and the French. The King and the cabinet had agreed that the British expeditionary armies should be recalled. Pitt acquiesced. The following day Wellesley, recently returned, called on him and as they talked at length Pitt fainted. Unlike Nelson he seems to have had no presentiment of death, but was undoubtedly dying. Wellesley went to Grenville, Pitt's closest colleague through so much of the war and now in sad opposition. Grenville broke down in tears at the news of his first cousin's final illness.

Pitt sat blankly staring, neither conversing nor reading. Gout had spread throughout his body. He took to his bed. After a brief rally, he became feverish, then delirious. He talked of his faithful niece: 'Dear soul, I know she loves me.' James Stanhope, his nephew, reported: 'He

spoke a good deal concerning a private letter from Lord Harrowby, and frequently inquired the direction of the wind; then said, answering himself, "East, ah! That will do; that will bring him quick"; at other times he seemed to be in conversation with a messenger, and sometimes cried out, "Hear, hear!" as if in the House of Commons.'

Benjamin Disraeli heard an amusing story about what he claimed were Pitt's last words. An elderly House of Commons waiter and keeper of its secrets told him: 'You hear many lies told as history, sir,' he said; 'do you know what Mr Pitt's last words were?' – 'Of course,' said Mr Disraeli, 'they are well known . . . "O my country! how I love my country!"' for that was then the authorized version. 'Nonsense,' said the old man. 'I'll tell you how it was. Late one night I was called out of bed by a messenger in a postchaise, shouting to me outside the window. "What is it?" I said. "You're to get up and dress and bring some of your meat pies down to Mr Pitt at Putney." So I went; and as we drove along he told me that Mr Pitt had not been able to take any food, but had suddenly said, "I think I could eat one of Bellamy's meat pies." And so I was sent for post-haste. When we arrived Mr Pitt was dead. Them was his last words: "I think I could eat one of Bellamy's meat pies."'

This version, although delightful, is almost certainly apocryphal. Canning believed the true words to be: 'I am sorry to leave the country in such a situation.' He was quoting the clergyman attending Pitt, insisting that theatricals were highly untypical of him. He died at 2.30 in the morning of 23 January, just three months after Nelson.

In the space of three short months Britain had gone from euphoria at the news of Trafalgar, to shock at the news of Ulm, to despair followed by grim determination at the news of Austerlitz. Britain had now lost the two towering figures who had come to embody its thirteen-year-long struggle with the militarized hordes of revolutionary France at almost the same time. The country appeared forlorn, rudderless and directionless, in the hands of confused minor politicians.

The twelve previous months had seen history at its most capricious, showering the world with violent shocks – the defeats of the Austrians at Marengo and Hohenlinden, the crowning of Napoleon as Emperor, the naval chase to the West Indies, the resurrection of the coalition

against Napoleon, the near-invasion of Britain, the death of Nelson, victory at Trafalgar, the news of Ulm and Austerlitz and now this, the loss of the leader who had come to symbolize Britain's undying resistance to the French. Nothing had stayed constant for more than a month or two at a time. Every time Britain's hopes had been raised, they were dashed immediately afterwards. The country was numbed by changes of fortune.

The death of Pitt was much more serious a blow than that of Nelson. It was like the death of a king. A young man who had just come of age when Pitt died would have known of only one prime minister almost all his life. He had not just been a politician, but the personification of the British manner: of British coldness, aloofness, fair play, balanced judgement, efficiency and good sense. It is extraordinary how the qualities that to this day are seen as uniquely British probably had their origin in Pitt.

After the robber barons of the Wars of the Roses, the despotism of the Tudors, the autocracy of the Stuarts and the corrupt jobbery of Walpole and the early politicians, two men, William Pitt, Earl of Chatham, the great parliamentary orator and founder of empire, and George Grenville, the meticulous administrator, had laid the foundations for a detached civil service based on sound finance to run a modern imperial country. William Pitt, a product of both clans, had epitomized the new breed. For all the disappointments and tumult of his ministry, he had presided over a smooth administration of enormous efficiency for the times, which perfectly complemented the radical social and economic changes Britain was going through.

He was still a young man by the time of his death, at forty-six a year younger even than Nelson. He was the effective head of state, more of a rock than the nominal one, George III, whose early attempts to guide the political process had long since mellowed to interventions on those matters he cared most deeply about, and then were marginalized by recurring bouts of illness.

In war ordinary people all that time had been able to look to Pitt's trusted leadership. For all the mistakes he had made, he had never faltered, never been anything less than cool, determined, stubborn towards Britain's enemies, nor projected anything but confidence and

leadership. Few people of any class in Britain liked Pitt, but they all respected him. His whole career had been something of a tragedy, the youthful idealist overtaken by events and forced to take on policies he had initially opposed. The paradox of Pitt's career was described brilliantly by the historian W.H. Fitchett:

> He was, by bent of genius, a peace minister, yet he spent most of his years of office in what to him was the hateful business of war. No other British minister, perhaps, ever so much hungered for peace, or spent so much money in breaking it. He began his administration with the dream of extinguishing the national debt, and betwixt 1793 and 1801 he added nearly £300,000,000 to it. He had a wise and generous zeal for liberal reforms, yet more than half his official life was spent in strangling them. He proposed the abolition of the rotten boroughs fifty years before Lord Grey accomplished it, yet he left the franchise as narrow as he found it. The Habeas Corpus Act was suspended continuously betwixt 1795 and 1801.
>
> The irony of fate pursued Pitt through all his career. By the most eloquent speech of his life he carried a bill against the slave trade; by refusing to interfere with what was supposed to be the 'interests' of the newly-captured slave-holding colonies he doubled that evil traffic. Perhaps his greatest legislative feat was the union of England with Ireland. Yet that feat cost him his office, and is held by multitudes to be a blot on his fame. No living Englishman of that generation was less the enemy of France than Pitt, yet none was so much hated by all good Frenchmen.

The extraordinary thing about a man who dominated his country for so long and presided over such great events was that the quality of greatness somehow eluded him. It was not just a matter of his detached, shy personality or the absence of the rhetoric that attached to, for example, his father or, later, men like Gladstone and Disraeli, Lloyd George and Churchill: it was his inability to shape the tide of events, or at least give the impression of doing so and rouse the nation with a single clarion call.

Yet he was clearly a cut above not just the ordinary people, but almost everyone else, noble or commoner, and perhaps the most

precise and efficient administrative brain ever to have governed Britain. He laid the foundations for eventual victory in the Napoleonic wars and for Victorian imperial greatness.

With the most formidable military leader in Britain and its dominant political leader now scythed from the scene, the country seemed adrift, unable to comprehend its plight or alter its course. Charles James Fox, Pitt's great political rival, expressed it best and for once succinctly: 'It feels as if something is missing in the world.'

Yet appearances were to some extent deceptive. If his cold, calculating pragmatism made him the ideal foil for the emotional, impulsive Napoleon, it also made him surprisingly unimaginative, missing many possible opportunities in the war, often hedging his bets and dispersing his forces, never grasping, for example, the opportunity to support the royalist uprisings in France and the seizure of Toulon when given the chance.

A failure on his own terms, he was certainly a dominant statesman. But he was not indispensable, as so many such figures believe they are. Yet the British people, desperate for reassurance after the enemy's triumphs on the continent, could not know that. Of one thing they were certain: France was no longer a threat by sea, which was what they had been most concerned about. But Napoleon, savouring the scent of great victories and absolute master of much of Europe, had had the satisfaction of seeing off his two greatest British enemies one after another.

Part 8

KING OF KINGS

Chapter 49

THE WAR MACHINE

The hurricane that was about to descend on Europe was the product of years of evolution, preparation and training. A military machine, equipped with revolutionary new tactics, had been prepared to wreak havoc against the traditional armies of Europe. Napoleon had not considered Amiens to be more than a delaying tactic. Sooner or later he intended to fight, and although war was forced upon him more quickly than he expected, he now headed an engine of war of fearsome magnitude, speed, force, manoeuvrability, motivation and innovation.

Its size alone was unlike anything hitherto experienced. The 350,000-strong *Grande Armée* consisted of seven huge corps, more or less independent self-supporting armies, each containing two to five infantry divisions, a brigade or division of cavalry, some forty cannon, a corps of engineers and support troops. Napoleon also established a formidable cavalry reserve of two divisions of cuirassiers (the breast-plated elite), four ordinary dragoon divisions, one of dismounted dragoons and one of light cavalry, amounting to some 22,000 cavalry and an artillery reserve of 24-guns.

The original political purpose of creating the *Grande Armée* was to overcome the feuding between Moreau's old Army of the Rhine and Napoleon's veterans from Italy and Egypt. The *Grande Armée* was set up in 1802 and Napoleon began systematically training the two merged armies, as well as re-equipping them, levying additional conscripts and formulating tactics. At first there were serious shortages of horses, transport and artillery.

Napoleon set up a centralized command under his own small staff,

the Maison, which was highly effective in issuing orders to the commanders of his quasi-separate armies, permitting the flexibility and manoeuvrability that were to give him his early military victories. This was supplemented by the much larger and more cumbersome Imperial Headquarters, which initially had 400 officers and 5,000 men and eventually swelled to some 3,500 and 10,000 respectively, stifling initiative through bureaucracy and elaborate chains of command and holding up the despatch of instructions, as was to occur spectacularly in later campaigns.

The two key men around Napoleon were trusted staff officers. General Alexandre Berthier, minister of war, was a gifted organizer as long as the staff was reasonably self-contained. At fifty he was older than most of his colleagues. Christophe Duroc, Napoleon's grand marshal, was the other key figure. Duroc was the Emperor's favourite. Well born, from Lorraine, three years younger than Napoleon, he was tall and good-looking with dark hair and wide, frank eyes. He was gentle, patient, hard-working and loyal. The master of horse, General Auguste de Caulaincourt (brother of the man who was to become Napoleon's finest civilian aide Armand), and the map officer Bacler d'Albe were also indispensable.

The individual corps were each commanded by one of the marshals. The officers numbered around 5,000, most of them already combat veterans, and an increasing number of them trained at the elite École Spéciale Militaire at St Cyr. The ranks were conscripted under the Jourdan law of 1798, predating Napoleon. Surprisingly few received any further training except in 1802–5, but they were encouraged to have a strong *esprit de corps*.

The army was equipped by a steadily growing munitions industry in France which already assembled some 125,000 weapons a year, mostly by hand. The level of production increased: by 1815 some 4 million weapons had been manufactured. Gaspard Monge, the chief of artillery production in 1793, had created an advanced casting method, had turned churches seized in the Revolution into foundries, and pillaged copper from their bells for barrels. Seven new factories were set up by Napoleon. Demand always outstripped supply.

The Imperial Guard was the most under-used part of his army.

Formed as an elite, and better paid and housed, it was originally no more than a personal bodyguard of some 5,000 infantry, 2,000 troopers and twenty-four guns. It mushroomed into a force of 56,000 by 1812 and an army in its own right of 112,000 by 1814. Napoleon's real motive was to guarantee his safety and dominance against the over-mighty marshals of the rest of the army, which was the main reason he so often kept it out of battle. He was as paranoid as any dictator about the possibility of a military coup. It consisted of veteran Old Guards, Middle Guards, who were mostly trained sharpshooters, and Young Guards, the pick of the light infantry. But it was so special to the Emperor that it was not sent into battle at all until 1813.

Napoleon's tactics were far from original. Just as Nelson's tactics had originally been inspired by Howe, the revolution in French tactics derived from the middle of the eighteenth century. The introduction of the flintlock musket in place of the matchlock, and the bayonet replacing the lengthy and unwieldy pike at around the same time, had been responsible for the introduction of lines of battle just three or four foot deep in place of the huge amorphous forces of earlier times. These had been made necessary by the long and dangerous fuses of the matchlock which meant men had to be at a safe distance from one another.

The usual practice through the early part of the eighteenth century was for each army to deploy from its marching column in lines two or three deep protected by cavalry on their flanks, several yards before engaging an enemy. Brent Nosworthy in his classic work on the subject, *Battle Tactics of Napoleon and his Enemies*, has explained the procedure:

> Forced to maintain a lengthy line of battalions, the army formed a 'single, unified body' in the sense that it functioned as a single entity acting along a single axis of operations. Once the troops were to advance they would have to do so along the length of the line, or at the very least a major portion of it. Without taking special precautions, it was difficult in open terrain to order part of a line forward while holding another part back. The very nature of a line made this impractical. If, for example, two brigades along a line had advanced

beyond supporting range of a portion of the line which remained
stationary, their flanks which had previously run into the remainder
of the line would now be exposed, while the line which remained
behind now had a large gap in it. Under the worst conditions, the
entire two brigades which had advanced could be rolled up in an
instant by enemy cavalry, if the latter made an unexpected appearance.

Talented commanders such as Marlborough and Frederick cir-
cumvented these difficulties and devised ways of fragmenting the
line into manageable parts, so that each could be assigned a different
grand tactical objective. However, this was only achieved by over-
coming the intrinsic limitations of the linear system. The most usual
method was to fragment a line so that individual groups of battalions
in line were separated by natural terrain, such as woods or villages, or
when in a large open area deploying the groups so that significant
gaps were left between each.

However, in the middle of the century Frederick the Great's Prussians
had evolved a new way of manoeuvring columns swiftly into line,
traditionally a risky moment of maximum vulnerability. This permitted
a much speedier deployment of troops into battle order. But Frederick
was a hierarchical ruler who still insisted on absolute obedience from
his lines acting as a single army, which counteracted this improvement
in speed. What he had not realized was that he had stumbled on a way
of giving soldiers much greater flexibility in action.

Frederick then inadvertently discovered that if his flanks were
attacked by cavalry it was a relatively speedy process for the third line
to run up alongside the other two from behind and face outwards to
protect them: this latter became known as a closed square. This meant
that lines would no longer need to have their flanks protected by
cavalry, which freed the cavalry to attack the enemy and also gave the
infantry room for greater manoeuvre and redeployment around the
battlefield.

This in turn permitted 'columns in waiting' – reserve infantry – and
'mixed order columns' – a mixture of lines and columns – to evolve,
which then led to the discovery that the line-of-battle was an

appallingly cumbersome formation: it was much easier to manoeuvre compact bodies of troops which could change shape from columns into squares and manoeuvre all over the battlefield. Just as significant, cavalry could now rush into the battlefield, supporting an infantry unit here or there, or be ordered into attacking the enemy where it was most vulnerable.

Thus the impact of Frederick's discoveries in the eighteenth century, although the Prussian army was slow to implement them, was to turn the old rigid duelling between lines of infantry supported by flanking cavalry into a much more complex and intricate battle of squares and columns with cavalry attacking in between. This made fighting much more elaborate and skilled on the part of individual commanders, although far untidier in appearance.

At about the same time as Frederick was evolving these revolutionary new tactics without taking full advantage of them, the French decided to organize their army into divisions, each more or less autonomous under the control of a lieutenant-general, who took only broad orders from the commander-in-chief. As Nosworthy explains:

> At the same time, the division became a much more organic entity than a lieutenant-general's command of comparable size during the linear era. Subject to conforming to the overall grand tactical dictates imposed by the army's commander, the corps or divisional commander was usually free to employ his forces as he saw fit. The divisional commander decided where the artillery was placed, the extent of the skirmishers to mask the front, and how the infantry was deployed and when its individual elements would come into play.
>
> A similar increase in flexibility was also encountered at the army level. No longer forced to deploy along lengthy extended lines, the army ceased to function as an indivisible unit. It thus became easier to split up available forces so that each of the corps- or divisional-size forces could temporarily function independently while still working towards a common overall goal or plan. The battle ceased to be a single expansive action raging from one side of the battlefield to the other. Instead, at least during the initial phases, it became a number of separate actions fought by individual corps or even divisional-

level forces. Each division, if ordered, could operate along a unique axis of operations. One part of the army, for example, could fight an action along the army's front while another either held off a threat to its flank or even its rear or, if on the offensive, worked its way around the enemy's position. Not only could each division or corps now orient itself independently of the remainder of the army, it no longer had to be physically connected to its neighbours. It became possible, at least occasionally, to allow significant intervals to appear between these forces, even during the heat of an engagement. When circumstances demanded, a division, now deployed in depth along several tiers, could easily defend itself on an exposed flank.

Although the great leap forward in thinking had thus taken place under the *ancien régime*, it was only properly implemented with the French Revolution. In the early stages of this there was a vigorous debate between proponents of the traditional line system, the *ordre mince* (thin line) school, and the new school, the *ordre profond* (deep line), which believed in converting fast from columns into squares to break through enemy lines. General Charles Dumouriez, the great general of the early part of the Revolution, practised a mixture of these tactics. At Jemappes, Dumouriez used the new thinking to considerable effect, even though at the end of the battle he brought his men back into traditional lines. Others were more radical still, preferring to order their men straight into battle in columns simply because the raw recruits that increasingly made up the new conscript army found it difficult to carry out complex manoeuvres.

France's aggressive use of massed artillery bombardment was also an innovation, and it helped win the Battle of Valmy in 1792. The French were not alone in employing the new tactics. The Prussian general Gebhart von Blücher used concealed forces split into several units and twice spectacularly surprised and routed much larger French forces at the Battle of Kirrweiler the same year.

Instead General Moreau, Napoleon's great rival, made use of the traditional line tactics in fighting against the Austrians. At the Battle of Biberach the French under Moreau and Jourdan inflicted a major defeat on the Austrians, taking some 5,000 prisoners, by using a

mixture of the new and old tactics long in advance of Napoleon. The latter adopted these tactics in Italy and also in Egypt, where at the Battle of the Pyramids employed the principle of independent infantry squares to devastating effect against the Mameluke cavalry. This, of course, was very different to fighting in Europe where armies were much better equipped. But the French learned from the experience of Moreau, Jourdan and Napoleon three things: how to deploy different divisions to act independently of each other, how to co-ordinate infantry, cavalry and artillery along these independent axes of the battle, and how to concentrate overwhelming force at the enemy's weakest point at the crucial stage in the battle.

The last was Napoleon's greatest strength. In his Italian campaigns he pioneered the idea of marching with two or three independent smaller armies to liaise at a single weak point in the enemy line, providing a concentration of overwhelming force where the latter least expected it. With three armies approaching independently, the enemy had no way of telling where they would converge until it was too late to concentrate their own strung-out line. Not surprisingly, this gave the advantage to the attacker, which Napoleon almost invariably was.

Napoleon also made great use of skirmishers, of which the stuffier commanders disapproved, preferring well-ordered ranks to the appearance of indiscipline which might encourage their men to attack or retreat in confusion – although their impact has perhaps been exaggerated. The French also developed excellent mobile field guns, such as 4-pounders, 8-pounders and 12-pounders (the famed Gribeauval cannon) under Napoleon, whose specialty was artillery, while their adversaries tended to use general fixed artillery behind the lines.

The *Grande Armée* was also enormously assisted by its meritocratic regime, which differed from the traditional armies in which aristocrats were officers and poor men were infantry. The army was no longer packed with terrified conscripts but considered itself an elite, lavishly rewarded from the spoils of the countries it plundered. To be a soldier in Napoleonic France was to be part of an upper echelon and was even a good career for the lower classes, accustomed to a life that was nasty, brutish and short.

This was the great military engine of the war to be unleashed on

Europe. It was a colossal force of soldiers who swarmed and plundered the land, living off, murdering and despoiling those outside their ranks. Apparently unstoppable, it was to set the example for more than a century. It has been argued that Napoleon committed his first great error in marching this huge force from west to east across Europe, leaving the British undefeated and a danger behind him. This is absurd. The British, bottled up in their island fortress, presented no immediate continental threat and Napoleon was entirely realistic in reckoning that with their control of the sea, he had no early prospect of defeating them.

Chapter 50

AUSTERLITZ

The march across Europe was to be one of Napoleon's most formidable military achievements. In some ways his innovative, impetuous and dramatic tactics were a mirror image of Nelson's at sea – 'always up and at 'em', as the latter had put it, concentrating overwhelming force against a particular weak spot in an old-fashioned defensive line. Napoleon calculated correctly that his enemies would expect his great armies to be slow to cross the continent and to liaise, and would thus walk into a trap sprung by the union of their equally slow-moving armies. So he deployed speed and overwhelming force in one of the greatest marches in history.

Facing him was a huge continent-wide extension of the 'line' principle – a series of smaller armies, each under different commanders and some under different national control, drawn up into a large, vastly over-extended, arc across hundreds of miles of central Europe. In the north there was a 40,000 strong Russian army under General Benigsen seeking to support the Prussian army threatening Hanover and Holland. In the centre was Mack's 90,000-strong Austrian army (originally commanded by Archduke Ferdinand), which was to liaise with the 55,000-strong Russian force under General Kutuzov coming from the east, as well as General Buxhovden's army in Bohemia.

To the south Archduke John commanded 22,000 men in the Tyrol and south of that Archduke Charles, around 100,000 to reinforce northern Italy. Against these Napoleon would field around 350,000 men. The coming clash was to be on a scale never before seen in Europe.

The most powerful of his adversaries were, of course, the Austrians. It is easy to underestimate just how formidable a force they were under the Habsburgs. These were second only to the Bourbons in longevity, the inheritors of the Holy Roman Empire, occupiers of a still great swathe of eastern Europe, Italy and the Balkans, locked by marriage into a gridlock of subordinate relationships, and long balancing their power with the French Bourbons. This was no decadent or fraying empire like the Spanish or the Ottoman, but a powerful well administered structure, possessed of one of Europe's two most formidable armies and a vast subject population.

The last was in fact a great weakness: most of these subjects deeply resented such domination. Both Italians and Germans were not particularly hostile initially to French takeover as a counterweight to the heavy-handed rule of the Austrians. This was a key factor throughout the Napoleonic conflict in Europe; for the French were initially seen as liberators from Austrian oppression – until the predatory actions of the Napoleonic *Grande Armée* dispelled this illusion, as did Napoleon's own brand of clannish imperialism. In a sense, the Austrians were burdened with their huge empire of subject peoples, while the French at this stage were not.

Only later, when the French had established themselves as imperialists and the Austrians had lost most of their vassals, were the roles reversed, with the result that the French were rolled back. But at this stage, as Napoleon's vast force approached, the general hostility of Austria's subject peoples to their colonial masters was a huge advantage for the Emperor, with his high-flowing rhetoric of liberation and modernisation, which appealed to chafing, subject elites.

The Austrian Emperor Francis was cautious, well-meaning and uninspiring. He was a gentle if narrow-minded family man who could chair committees but provide no real leadership: Austrian policy was consequently decided by a collection of senior advisers who fell in and out of favour according to results – as indeed befitted a well-established empire. The Emperor's inner council consisted of Baron Johann Thugut, his foreign minister, who was committed to war against France, and his former tutor, Count von Colloredo, a hard-headed, highly intelligent man who was deeply religious, somewhat affected in

manner and effectively prime minister. A third member of the inner core was Ludwig Coblenzl. The army chiefs were divided up between the Emperor's three brothers, the amiable Ferdinand, the able Charles and the young and inexperienced John. Charles was the only good soldier among them and had opposed an early Austrian re-entry into the war: instead he had undertaken a major programme of modernization of the Austrian army to meet the French challenge, having learnt the lessons of the previous fighting. That involved field training rather than interminable parade-ground drilling.

His first priority was to try and reform the gigantic central bureaucracy that ran the army. This made him enemies. Charles created a permanent staff organization, the Quartermaster General Staff, subordinate to the Hoffriegsrat, the military-minded supreme body controlling the army; he also reintroduced conscription. The Austrian army was nominally huge, with around 430,000 men divided into fifty-seven infantry regiments, thirty-two cavalry regiments, seventeen grenadier peasant regiments and three artillery regiments. It was run by the aristocracy subordinate to the court at Vienna. Unlike the French army, the Austrian army had no divisions or corps and was wedded to traditional linear tactics. The Austrian cavalry was second to none, but also a stickler for the old rules, as was the formidable artillery.

Charles's attempts at reform soon ran into opposition, and his wise advice to stay out of the war until the army was fully reformed irritated his brother Francis, who gave effective charge to General Karl Mack von Lieberich, a mediocrity, wedded to entirely conventional tactics. There can have been few such disastrous appointments in the history of any army.

Mack believed in going on to the offensive. He confidently predicted that Napoleon would take sixty-nine days to march the 500 miles across Europe to the Upper Danube and that the Russian army of Kutuzov would arrive to join the Austrians in sixty-four days. Therefore he decided upon an invasion of Bavaria before the two allied armies met up. On 8 September 1805, Mack and Archduke Ferdinand crossed the Inn river at Brautman and marched on Munich. The Bavarians, who were secretly in league with Napoleon against their Austrian oppressors, put up no resistance. Mack rode into Munich

triumphantly five days later. Mack's refusal to wait for his Russian reinforcements was incredibly ill-advised. He simply did not believe Napoleon could move in such numbers so fast.

To the north, however, the French armies based in Hanover and Utrecht marched to meet up at Wurtemberg, while the centre and the southern armies marched on Mannheim and Strasbourg. The French army of 200,000 men had been divided into seven autonomous corps. Napoleon himself was still deceptively in Paris on 23 September, lulling Mack into a sense of false security. The Emperor left to join his units by fast carriage the following day. This colossal force crossed the Rhine in good formation between 27 September and 3 October.

Meanwhile six cavalry divisions under Joachim Murat and Lannes' corps marched against the Austrian centre, taking the traditional invasion route through the Black Forest. The French marched at around twenty miles a day, starting out at around four in the morning and retiring to bed early. It was a technique perfected by the French in the American War of Independence, when Rochambeau's speed astonished and exhausted his American allies under George Washington and resulted in trapping General Cornwallis's army at Yorktown, which decided the fate of the war.

The pace was punishing: there were soon some 8,000 on the sick list. Even Napoleon was exhausted. A staff officer wrote:

I had dined with the Emperor and on leaving the table he had gone alone to see the Empress Josephine. A few minutes later he came back hurriedly to the salon and taking me by the arm led me into his room. M. de Rémusat . . . came in at the same time. We were hardly there before the Emperor fell to the ground; he had only time to tell me to shut the door. I tore off his cravat because he appeared to be stifling; he was not sick, but groaned and foamed at the mouth. M. de Rémusat gave him water and I poured eau-de-Cologne over him. He had a kind of convulsion which lasted a quarter of an hour; we put him in an arm-chair; he began to speak, dressed himself again, and swore us to secrecy. Half an hour later he was on the road to Carlsruhe.

The speed of the advance caught Mack entirely by surprise. Still overconfident, he had proceeded with his army of 24,000 men to occupy the fortress at Ulm in an exposed position on the Danube in western Bavaria on 6 October. The same day the French curved around the Danube to the north and now threatened Mack's lines of communications. Napoleon's aim was to divide the Austrian and Russian armies and fall upon each in turn. He could hardly have expected Mack to drop so willingly into the trap by marching blindly on.

A horrified Mack learnt that the French army was now moving down from the north behind him to cut off his rear. Desperately he tried to break out, sending one part of his army east towards Bohemia, then another north, then another south. Each was blocked and destroyed by superior French forces. Archduke Ferdinand and twelve squadrons escaped on 14 October, and then Mack's army was completely surrounded. The Russians were nowhere near, with Kutuzov still approaching the Bavarian border some 150 miles to the east.

On 20 October, like a fly who had flown directly into the centre of the spider's web, completely surrounded, hopelessly outmanoeuvred and massively outnumbered, Mack surrendered, along with 24,000 men and eighty guns. Only Frederick had escaped. The victory of Ulm had been a brilliant feat of encirclement achieved by the speed, better intelligence and perfectly executed strategy of the French. The wretched Mack was despatched by Napoleon to the Austrian Emperor to urge peace. It was the day before Trafalgar.

To the south the sensible and cautious Archduke Charles, in his humiliatingly lesser command, decided to avoid action if at all possible. The French army under Masséna attacked across the Adige on 18 October, but Charles had already withdrawn to defensive positions at Caldiero. After three days of bloody and indecisive fighting, Charles withdrew farther into the mountains. Meanwhile Kutuzov's Russians, anxious not to suffer the same fate as Mack, ignored Emperor Francis's pleas to defend Vienna and withdrew west along the Danube, which they crossed, inflicting a minor defeat on the French advance force.

The way was now open to Vienna. Arthur Paget, the British ambassador in the capital, wrote: 'I don't know which is most feared,

the arrival of the Russians, or their retreat, or that of the French.
Everybody who possesses or can have a horse is moving off.'

The Austrian Emperor decided to evacuate the city and abandon it
to the French. The combined forces of Lannes and Murat approached
the outskirts of Vienna. There they pretended to local commanders
that an armistice had been reached and secured the main bridge across
the Danube, which had been mined. Within days Napoleon was
sleeping in that most delightful of all Habsburg palaces, the Schön-
brunn outside Vienna. His army helped itself to 100,000 muskets and
2,000 cannon from the Austrian arsenal. Beethoven nevertheless went
ahead and conducted the orchestra at the premiere of *Fidelio* in the
Theater an de Wien. It was ill-attended, hardly surprising under the
circumstances.

Napoleon meanwhile had learnt of the defeat at Trafalgar, just as he
was accomplishing great things in central Europe. In a rage he ordered
the news to be suppressed in France for fear it would stir up his enemies
behind him. *Le Petit Journal* published an imaginary list of British ships
sunk at Trafalgar, while *Le Moniteur* wrote of Nelson's death and how
his ship had been captured by the French fleet:

> They boarded the ship at the same moment – Villeneuve flew to the
> quarter-deck – with the usual generosity of the French, he carried a
> brace of pistols in his hands, for he knew the admiral had lost his
> arm, and could not use his sword – he offered one to Nelson: they
> fought, and at the second fire Nelson fell; he was immediately
> carried below – Oliva, Gravina, and Villeneuve attended him, with
> the accustomed French humanity. Meanwhile fifteen ships of the
> line had struck – four more were obliged to follow their example –
> another blew up – our victory was now complete.

Napoleon remarked furiously: 'I cannot be everywhere,' and then
dismissed the defeat as 'the loss of a few ships after a battle imprudently
fought'. It was at this moment that the British spy, Wright, who had
been implicated in the plot against Napoleon, was found with his
throat cut with a razor, supposedly in despair at the news from Ulm.
Admiral Villeneuve, who was returned to France by the British some

months later, was found stabbed six times in a country inn on the way to Paris in another supposed suicide. The Emperor's wrath against those who failed him was pitiless.

Nor could he rest on the laurels of Ulm – he had little time to waste. The Tsar himself was on his way to Austria to command his army. Snow delayed his journey, as did a few pleasant days at Weimar, where he met Goethe. In Berlin he had persuaded Frederick William III, ever hesitant, to commit Prussia to join the allied cause with an attack on the Rhineland. There the Tsar and the Kaiser had sworn an oath of friendship across the coffin of Frederick the Great. Kutuzov meanwhile had been reinforced by the Russian Second Army and then the Russian Imperial Guard, as well as Archduke Ferdinand's Austrian army: there were now some 50,000 Russians and 35,000 Austrians altogether. To the south, just ten days away, the Archdukes Charles and John had joined forces to make up an army of 80,000 men. Napoleon was believed to have no more than 40,000 men. To the overconfident young Tsar, aged just twenty-nine, it seemed that Napoleon had overreached himself.

The Tsar was an extraordinary personality. Blessed with remarkable good looks of an almost feminine kind, blond curly hair, blue eyes, soft features, tall and elegant, he also possessed great charm which alternated with increasingly violent mood swings of depression and anger that bordered on mania. He was also fanatically religious. Kutuzov urged Alexander to withdraw to the Carpathians which would finally break French lines of communication. Emperor Francis of Austria also urged caution. But Alexander and Prince Bagration, his preferred general, were eager for battle and scoffed at 'General Dawdler', as he called Kutuzov.

Napoleon by this time, after the elation of Ulm had worn off, was growing increasingly alarmed: if the joint Russian-Austrian army escaped to the east, he would become overstretched and unable to follow. There was also a danger that they would link up with the Austrian army approaching rapidly from the south, or that the latter by itself would cut French lines of communication; and then there was the further fear that the Prussians would at last throw in their lot with the coalition. Moreover Napoleon had had to send part of his army to cover his flanks, and his strength was now down to 70,000 men.

The Emperor decided on a characteristically bold strategy: to lure the enemy into battle before it had moved out of reach or the strength of the southern army could be brought to bear. He carefully selected his planned field of battle some eighteen miles east of the small town of Brunn alongside the road from Vienna to the north. The town was bordered by that road in the west and another road to the north. To the south were two large bodies of water, Satschan Pond and Meinitz Pond, as well as a large natural barrier of marshes. Bordering the marshes in the centre was a low hill, the Pratzen Heights: to the east was the small village of Austerlitz.

The position was a natural defensive one, with woods and small valleys in which his troops could hide. All he had to do was entice his enemies to battle.

He took an extraordinary risk. He withdrew from both Austerlitz and his strong position on the commanding Pratzen Heights, apparently in some disorder at the nearby presence of the coalition armies, and sued for an armistice. On 29 November, at a meeting with a Russian envoy, Count Dolgorovki, he appeared timid and indecisive. Meanwhile he secretly ordered Bernadotte's First Corps and Davout's Third Corps to reinforce him by forced marches. The two armies covered the sixty miles from Vienna in some seventy hours. He concentrated his main forces to the north and centre, with Lannes and Murat in the front line. To the south he placed most of Soult's Fourth Corps, strung out thinly. Concealed to the north were Bernadotte's First Corps and, to the south, Davout's Third Corps.

On 1 December the combined Russia and Austrian armies marched forward to occupy the abandoned Pratzen Heights, seemingly the key to the battle, from which they could gaze down contemptuously on the French forces below. There they held a council of war, during which Kutuzov slept ostentatiously, saying that his advice had been ignored. They decided to attack through the weakened French southern flank and attempt to cut Napoleon off from his supply line along the road to Vienna, thus encircling his army. They had taken the bait.

Napoleon was unusually animated at dinner that evening. An eyewitness described the scene at 9 p.m.

[The Emperor] decided to go the round of the bivouacs on foot and incognito; he was nearly at once recognized. It would be impossible to describe the enthusiasm of the soldiers when they saw him. In an instant blazing torches of straw were raised on a thousand poles, and 80,000 men were standing and acclaiming their Emperor, some for the anniversary of his coronation, others saying that the army would present the Emperor with a bouquet on the following day. An old grenadier came up to him and said: 'Sire, keep out of the firing, I promise you in the name of the grenadiers, that you need not fight otherwise than as a spectator, for we will bring you the standards.' When the Emperor returned to his own bivouac, a straw shanty without a roof that the grenadiers had built for him, he said: 'This is the most glorious night of my life; but I regret that so many of these brave fellows will be lost. They really are my children.'

He also had luck on his side: a thick fog enveloped the lakeside in the early hours of the morning, which helped further to conceal Davout's and Bernadotte's arrival, as well as Soult's cavalry behind the main lines: the shallow valleys of the terrain helped further to hide the French. To the allies it seemed the French were heavily outnumbered, in inferior positions and demoralized, almost on the verge of retreat.

The allies decided on a two-pronged attack: Bagration was to strike in the north against Lannes's Fifth Corps; and Buxhovden, commanding a second Russian army, was to lead the main attack with 45,000 men against Soult's apparently weakened forces in the south; the Russians and Austrians, thus lulled by a sense of false security, took the immense risk of moving off the Pratzen Heights in a southerly direction.

At around 4 a.m., the attack began, with the Russians and Austrians being checked in the north, but making steady progress against the French in the south across difficult terrain which was also bounded by the marsh and the shallow lakes, potential death traps in the freezing conditions. After some four hours of fighting, the coalition troops in the south suddenly came up against 7,000 fresh soldiers commanded by Davout and were blocked.

At this moment Napoleon ordered Murat's cavalry to attack the Russian cavalry which had been left occupying the Pratzen Heights: a

colossal cavalry engagement involving some 10,000 men ensued. Napoleon waited until just after nine, when the sun had more or less cleared the mists, to order Soult's two divisions in waiting to move. In a disciplined and steady march the infantry ascended the gentle incline of the heights against the by now much reduced allied army at its weakest point – the centre.

Kutuzov, seeing what was happening, ordered reinforcements to the weakened centre, but it was too late: the allies were being pushed back. Bernadotte's concealed corps was also now ordered into the fray. The Russians turned desperately to counter-attack. The Russian Imperial Guard, headed by the Tsar's brother, Grand Duke Constantine, bravely dashed into the centre, but the Austrians, retiring in confusion, got in their way and they were forced back at around one o'clock.

By now the French commanded the heights and were in a position to turn the tables, threatening to cut off the bulk of the Russian army to the south, which was caught between the heights and the ponds. French artillery was brought to bear on the trapped army, blowing holes in the shallow ice below. Both Napoleon and Alexander later suggested that thousands of Russians fell through the ice to a freezing death in the waters of the ponds – the one to rub in the extent of his triumph, the other seeking to blame natural causes for his defeat. Yet when the ponds were drained a few days later only two or three bodies were found, along with 150 dead horses and thirty cannon. Most of the Russian soldiers fled across the narrow strip of land between the ponds: the ice was too thin to bear them.

As the retreat turned into a rout, only Bagration's forces in the north retired in good order. By the end of the day, however, the French were too exhausted to give chase. It was nevertheless an overwhelming victory. Some 11,000 Russians and 4,000 Austrians had been killed and 12,000 taken prisoner along with 180 guns. Only 1,300 French soldiers had been killed and some 7,000 wounded, along with the loss of around 600 prisoners.

It had been a textbook victory, secured by Napoleon's skill in deceiving the enemy, in positioning his troops, in making perfect use of the features of the battlefield and in ordering the various corps into battle with split-second timing. Essentially, through concealing most of

his troops and feinting a retreat from the strategic centre ground on the obverse side of a hill, he had lured the enemy into a trap – a trick which was later to be used time and again by his most dangerous enemy, the Duke of Wellington.

The remarkable mobility of his troops had also overcome the static and predictable linear attack of his opponents. And once again he had shown his ability to mass overwhelming force where it could be used to devastating effect: he had cut the enemy line in two by the simple device of slicing straight through their weakened centre. Finally the battle was a rare masterpiece of precision, command and control – his orders were executed rapidly and faultlessly, his generals operating with just the right degree of co-ordination and independence as in some flawlessly executed field manoeuvre rather than in battle.

Never were Napoleon's military skills more in evidence than at Austerlitz. Of all his battles, it was the most flawless, the most perfect, the most inspired – as Napoleon probably himself thought, although he had a habit of trying to inflate his achievements on much less impressive occasions. The Russians retreated at speed to Poland while the Austrian Emperor sued immediately for peace. In the Battle of the Three Emperors, the greatest engagement that had ever yet been fought in Europe, two had been comprehensively routed.

Napoleon spent the cold night out in the open among his dead, and then the following one in comfort. In his words: 'The battle of Austerlitz is the most splendid of all I have fought. I have fought thirty battles of the same sort, but none in which the victory was so decisive, and so little in doubt. The infantry of the guard was not sent into action – the men were weeping with rage. Tonight I am lying in a bed, in the beautiful castle of Count Kaunitz, and I have changed my shirt, which I hadn't done for a week past. I shall get two or three hours' sleep.'

Archduke Charles arrived at the head of his Italian armies to insist on the need for peace and to dismiss his enemies at court as 'obscure quacks gathered round the monarchy's deathbed'. Both Colloredo and Coblenz were dismissed. Napoleon spent Christmas at the Schonbrunn and also met the Archduke, his most formidable Austrian adversary.

At the Treaty of Pressburg, signed on 26 December, Francis and the

Austrians were utterly humiliated. Venice, as well as Dalmatia and Istria, was ceded to the Kingdom of Italy. Sweden and the Tyrol were granted to Napoleon's allies, the electors of Wurttemberg and Bavaria. Austria was forced to pay 40 million francs to the French.

Napoleon had also secured a buffer zone of German states. Murat was given charge of the Grand Duchy of Berg and Berthier that of Neuchâtel. The King of Prussia hastened to make peace and broke off relations with Britain, being rewarded with the electorate of Hanover.

The French Emperor now engaged in dynastic policies on a mega-lomaniacal scale, aping royal lines that had taken centuries to build, awarding whole countries as baubles to his singularly untalented and ill-equipped family. For this former Jacobin, supporter of Robespierre and 'meritocrat', it was grotesque.

To his stepson Eugène de Beauharnais, admittedly the only talented member of the clan, he awarded Bavaria by marrying him off to the beautiful Augusta, daughter of the King. To his dim, timorous, head-in-the clouds elder brother Joseph he gave the Kingdom of Naples. There was a small detail to fill in: first it had to be captured. Joseph and Masséna marched on the kingdom with 40,000 men, forcing the crass King Ferdinand IV and Maria Carolina to flee to Sicily once again. The 'Batavian Republic' was abolished and the new Kingdom of Holland was awarded to his younger brother Louis, a nervous, but essentially well-meaning man without an ounce of administrative ability but who was sensitive to the needs of his subjects – as Napoleon discovered to his cost.

Thus the extraordinary vulgarity of Napoleon's nature fused in a kind of mania: the distribution of the spoils of Corsican brigandage on a pan-European scale to members of his own family.

If Napoleon had followed his triumph at Austerlitz with an attempt to put in place a lasting settlement in Europe based on French domination, and had also shown moderation in his treatments of his defeated foes, the Austrians and their allies, he might have laid the foundations for lasting peace and indeed his own survival, for Britain had no wish to prolong a war in which it was isolated. Instead he trampled on his defeated foes in an unprecedented display of

triumphalism, which was guaranteed to nourish hatred and feelings of revenge at the earliest opportunity. Admittedly Napoleon's recently acquired subject peoples were uncertain what to make of their new masters at first: they preached freedom and equality and might be an improvement upon their stiff-backed Austrian predecessors. But such hopes were soon dashed.

Napoleon's triumphalism was soon apparent in his own country. He ordered the patchwork of mediaeval Paris to be slashed across with great avenues to celebrate his triumph – admittedly by a great city planner, Haussmann. The Arc de Triomphe was built, 150 feet high and nearly as wide, at the head of the Champs Élysées, sweeping down to the Tuileries, where the Arc d'Austerlitz (now known as the Arc de Carrouse) was also built, with a column nearby in the Place Vendôme surmounted by Napoleon dressed as Caesar.

For the moment Napoleon's more dangerous rivals in the army were entirely subdued. The opposition, faced by the ferocious surveillance of Fouché's spy system, went to ground. Napoleon seemed unchallenged – master both of France and the continent. Yet the French power elites, although subdued, still existed. Talleyrand, in particular, so often depicted as a scheming opportunist at this moment of Napoleon's apotheosis, showed strength and firmness by telling his master what he did not want to hear. He urged the Emperor to reach a generous peace with Austria so as to secure it as an ally, not a sullen and resentful defeated enemy:

> The Austrian monarchy is a combination of ill-assorted states, differing from one another in language, manners, religion, and constitution, and having only one thing in common – the identity of their ruler. Such a power is necessarily weak, but she is an adequate bulwark against the barbarians – and a necessary one. Today, crushed and humiliated, she needs that her conqueror should extend a generous hand to her and should, by making her an ally, restore to her that confidence in herself, of which so many defeats and disasters might deprive her for ever. I implore Your Majesty to read again the memorandum which I had the honour to submit to you from Strasburg. Today more than ever I dare to consider it as the best and wisest policy.

The wily foreign minister, who had been given the Principality of Benevento in the Kingdom of Naples as his share in the spoils, was right; for Archduke Charles, the most intelligent and resolute Austrian leader, favoured a strategy of eastern expansion for his country at the expense of Turkey, leaving Europe as Napoleon's domain. This would have been a not unreasonable compromise, but the Emperor Francis was disposed to oppose Napoleon and feared that the French Emperor was scheming to have him replaced on the throne by one of his more pliable brothers.

In the summer of 1806 Napoleon set up his Confederation of the Rhine, which effectively turned the states of Germany into French satellites, whose security and foreign policy he now ran. Francis formally dissolved the Holy Roman Empire for fear that Napoleon would adopt that title too. In fact it had been merely an expression of Austria's continuing influence in the region, which was already under challenge from the Prussians; with France's victories, it had become obsolete.

Napoleon now enjoyed a unique position. Like Julius Caesar he did 'bestride this world like a colossus'. France ruled the Low Countries, virtually all of Italy and effectively dominated most of Germany. To the south Spain was in sullen alliance with France, while only tiny Portugal was hostile, thanks to its old alliance with Britain; to the east Austria had been stripped of many of its possessions and neutralized, although not entirely subdued; Prussia was timorous and fearful under a weak and vacillating king, and the arrogant young Alexander's Russia had been badly burnt in its first sally towards western Europe.

Napoleon's conquests were not quite Roman in scale – they did not extend round the shores of the Mediterranean to Spain or Britain – but they exceeded Charlemagne's and were the largest European empire in some 1,300 years. If the thirty-six-year-old Emperor sincerely wanted peace – and the French nation, exhausted by years of revolution, upheaval, war, economic crisis and conscription seemed to thirst for it – it was his for the asking. Moreover Napoleon himself had for the first time proved himself as a general of the first rank, both at Ulm and at Austerlitz. He could no longer be dismissed by his military peers as merely a winner of small victories in Italy, or as a 'colonial' general in Egypt.

Chapter 51

THE GRENVILLE INTERLUDE

When Pitt died at the end of January 1806, William, Lord Grenville, Pitt's brilliant cousin, formed the Ministry of All Talents, so named for its dazzling array of senior political figures from all parties and its engaging liberalism. It featured such luminaries as Charles James Fox, foreign secretary until his death in September 1806, a dissolute figure in his youth who became a politician of notable calibre and Pitt's perennial opponent; Lord Howick, who later as Earl Grey steered Britain to peaceful political reform in 1832; and, as secretary for war, William Windham, an enthusiast for a British role in South America.

Exhausted by war and with Pitt dead, the British now made a fresh attempt to make peace with France based upon an entirely new concept – not in fact dissimilar to that advocated by the Archduke Charles in Austria. France could dominate the west and centre of the European continent, leaving Austria, Prussia and Russia to contend and expand in the east, while Britain would be left with its maritime empire, possibly carving out a massive new province of this from the crumbling of the Spanish empire in South America. There had been an extensive history to this plan – and it was under Pitt's successor that it seemed ready at last to take flight.

Britain had long played host to an extraordinary figure, Francisco de Miranda, the former French revolutionary general and self-styled Liberator of Latin America. In May 1790, Miranda, a mixture of skilled professional soldier, dreamer, poseur, man of letters, traveller and sexual obsessive, had first met William Pitt. Miranda prepared himself feverishly, drawing up an ambitious and wholly unrealistic plan

for liberation. He gave a careful estimate of the colonies' resources, and of Spanish strength there. There were 21 million people, he claimed, in 'the Spanish Indies', half of them Spaniards, criollos, whites and of mixed blood, the rest Indians and blacks. The colonies produced annually about 55 million pesos in gold, silver, sugar, cacao, hides, tobacco, indigo and cochineal, and imported roughly 22 million pesos' worth of goods from Spain, and a similar amount on contraband. Spain had around 36,000 troops in the colonies, of whom some 20,000 were locally raised militia, the rest regular soldiers; and a navy of 123 ships and 44,000 sailors.

Miranda subtly underlined South America's potential by suggesting – with remarkable foresight – that a canal could be cut through the isthmus of Panamá to facilitate trade to the Far East for Britain and America. He argued that although Spanish America, more populous than Spain, should be able to stage its own revolt, its communities were cut off from one another by distance and poor communications. With control of the seas, the Spanish could send reinforcements wherever they liked – a crucial insight. Britain, he insisted, as a maritime power, could cut the Spanish lines of communication. He argued that Britain was a natural ally for South America, and ended on an elevated and flattering note: 'In view of the similarity that exists in the character of these two nations, and the effects that must naturally flow from liberty and the fact that a good government can instruct the general mass of men, progressively doing away with the religious prejudices that cloud its people's minds . . . these being otherwise honest, hospitable, and generous – we must expect soon to see a respectable and illustrious nation emerging worthy of being the ally of the wisest and most famed power on earth.'

His grandiose blueprint was for a kind of united states of Spanish America, stretching from the Pacific to the Atlantic, excluding Brazil and Guiana, but including the land east of the Mississippi and south of the source of the river, below Parallel 45. The constitution of this great new state would be a hybrid of the monarchical and republican systems: a descendant of the Incas would sit on the throne – this to give the monarchy an authentically pre-Columbus flavour – but he would be accountable, British-style, to a two-chamber congress, with

an upper house elected for life and a lower one by regular popular (if restricted) vote. A two-thirds majority would be needed to amend the constitution, as well as a three-quarters majority of a council composed of the Inca Emperor sitting with the highest judges of the land. The clergy would retain many of their privileges, but the Inquisition would be done away with. The Spanish monopoly of trade would be ended and the new state would be open to commercial treaties with Britain and other countries. (On seeing this blueprint later, President Adams of the United States is said to have remarked that he didn't know whether to laugh or cry. The son of the Bostonian James Lloyd, however, wrote to Adams describing Miranda as 'the most extraordinary and marvellously energetic man I have ever met'.)

In May 1790, equipped with his fantastic plan, Miranda had met the cold, analytical Pitt. He asserted to Pitt that the South American people would rise up in revolt as soon as a British fleet appeared, although he was in no position to give this assurance, having not set foot in South America for twenty years and being in contact only with a handful of wealthy criollo dissidents. He had not the slightest idea of the real opinion of the educated classes there, much less that of the populace. Pitt made it clear that he would help only in the event of a war between Britain and Spain. This, at that time, looked to be imminent, which was why Pitt's officials had set up the encounter in the first place: Spain was claiming as its own the Nootka Sound, high up on the Pacific coast of North America, then in Britain's possession. Miranda no doubt left the meeting with a spring in his step.

Five months later, however, the Nootka Sound dispute was settled, and the project was off. Miranda, given financial support by the British government so long as his potential nuisance value to the Spaniards was useful, now found this source of funds drying up, and was upset that he had revealed his plan to Pitt. Miranda them moved on to France. After a series of breathtaking exploits in the French Revolution (see pages 36–46), during which he narrowly escaped the guillotine, Miranda set off to try and launch an invasion of Venezuela on his own. This duly proved a fiasco.

Miranda had however, convinced the British that the Spanish colonies were indeed ripe for the picking, and that Britain could soon

help itself. With Spain effectively under the control of the decadent Manuel Godoy and Queen Maria Luisa of Parma (her amiable but vacant husband Charles IV was virtually powerless), the opportunity seemed to present itself. After a brief conflict between Spain and revolutionary France, Godoy, fearful of French incursions across the frontier and heartened by the re-emergence of moderate elements after the fall of Robespierre, sued for peace in 1795 – a catastrophically inept move which undermined every diplomatic gain of the first four years of his ascendancy. As well as ceding to France Santo Domingo (the western half of the island of Hispaniola, of which Haiti was the eastern half), Godoy sought to appease the French further by introducing some of their reforms into Spain; these included an attack on the Inquisition and on clerical privileges, the threat of land redistribution, and permitting the circulation of revolutionary texts. At a stroke, he alienated Spanish sympathisers and the still dominant Spanish colonial classes, who viewed France's ambitions in the Caribbean with deep suspicion, facilitated the spread of revolutionary ideas and, not least, reinvigorated the old enmity between Spain and a Britain dismayed by this pro-French tilt.

The British moved to disrupt Spanish trade with the Americas, and the colonists made up their shortfall by trading illicitly with Britain and the United States. British landings were staged in Puerto Rico and Central America, and Trinidad was occupied. Then the Spanish fleet was mauled off Cape St Vincent in 1797. In the space of just three years, Spanish Americans acquired a withering contempt for the weakness of the mother country. This was added to the sense of grievance and injustice they had long borne against Spain for her commercial monopoly and the dismal quality of the administrators and traders sent to lord it over them. Meanwhile Godoy, supposedly dismissed in 1800, continued to act as the court's chief adviser, pursuing his policy of appeasement towards France.

A dramatic new turn ensued with the accession to power in France of Napoleon Bonaparte. His policy towards Spain was to bully her. She and Portugal must close their ports to the British; this the Spanish did promptly, while the Portuguese put up only a show of resistance. The criollo upper class was horrified afresh by these signs of Spanish

cowardice, and by the arrival on their doorstep in 1802 of the French force of 20,000 under the command of Napoleon's brother-in-law, General Leclerc. Leclerc's attempt to reintroduce slavery into Haiti was met by a fresh black revolt, ending with the expulsion of the French into Santo Domingo and in 1804 the assertion of Haitian self-government – the first declaration of independence in Latin America.

Spain was now involved in an unpopular alliance with France; and the British were again bent on subverting her empire, desperate for commercial outlets now that Napoleon had closed the continent to them, and very aware of tempting opportunities. The seriousness of Britain's long-term desire to add the supposedly suppurating Spanish empire to her dominions – thereby making good the losses in North America – should not be underestimated.

On 27 June 1806 the Spanish Viceroy of La Plata, Rafael, Marques de Sobremonte, was at the theatre in Buenos Aires when he was informed that a British army of 1,600 men had landed outside the city. The first-ever overthrow of a Spanish colonial administration in South America had begun. British soldiers commanded by General William Carr Beresford and naval forces under Commodore Sir Home Popham had sailed from Cape Town, having retaken it in the name of the British Crown following the breakdown of the Peace of Amiens and Nelson's victory at Trafalgar.

Although the British government claimed to have no hand in the Popham–Beresford expedition – Popham sailed without orders – the roots of it ran deep. William Pitt had long coveted South America as a potential market for the products of Britain's growing industrialization, and other eminent men of the time also interested in its possibilities included Lord Melville, First Lord of the Admiralty between 1802–6, Nicholas Vansittart, a young Tory politician who later became chancellor of the exchequer, and the prominent trading house of Turnbull & Sons. Popham later recorded that in 1805:

> I had a long conversation with [Pitt] on the original project of the expedition to South America, in the course of which Mr Pitt informed me, that from the then state of Europe, and the confederation in part formed, and forming against France, there was a

great anxiety to endeavour, by friendly negotiation, to detach Spain from her connection with that power, and, until the result of such an attempt should be known, it was desirable to suspend all hostile operations in South America; but, in case of failure in this object, it was his intention to enter on the original project.

The British forces occupied Buenos Aires with the loss of only a single man and twelve wounded, while Viceroy Sobremonte fled inland to Córdoba with the treasury. Beresford proclaimed himself governor on behalf of King George III, but promised that private property and the Catholic faith would be respected by the British Crown, and announced the establishment of free trade – a display of breath-taking arrogance. Popham later noted: 'The object of this expedition was considered by the natives to apply principally to their independence.'

A French-born officer, Santiago de Liniers, assembled a force of irregular soldiers outside Buenos Aires, while inside the city Juan Martin de Pueyrredón, an able criollo aristocrat, organized opposition in the form of passive resistance and a general strike. Six weeks later the two forces joined up; the British were surrounded, Popham was taken prisoner, and with impressive magnanimity the whole expedition was placed aboard ship and despatched ignominiously to London. Liniers was treated as a hero while Sobremonte, now regarded as a coward, was informed he would be shot if he returned to Buenos Aires. It was unprecedented for a Spanish viceroy to be so humiliated; he took refuge in Montevideo, capital of the Banda Oriental across the Plate estuary, and Buenos Aires' traditional rival.

When news of Beresford's and Popham's success in Buenos Aires reached London, the City went wild – crowds thronged the streets, singing 'God Save the King' and 'Rule, Britannia!' Britain's trade with South America was already running at £1 million a year, and it seemed as though her next great colonial adventure was beckoning. Windham bristled with ideas: Cape Horn would be navigated and the port of Valparaiso in Chile seized, then an expedition eastwards across the Andes would establish a chain of forts before conquering the whole Audiencia of Buenos Aires and thus securing the southern half of the continent. Sir Arthur Wellesley, recently returned from his successes in

India, would be appointed to replace Beresford. Grenville himself favoured the seizure of Montevideo, and the despatch of troops from India to take Manila from the Spanish and then sail on across the Pacific to land on the west coast of New Spain (Mexico).

The news of Beresford's subsequent surrender of Buenos Aires in August 1806 did not reach London until 25 January 1807; when it did, all these dreams crashed to earth with the implication that here were no ill-used children grateful to exchange the harsh paternalism of the Spanish Crown for the comparative benevolence of the British, but a mature and sophisticated people. However, the affront to British arms could not be tolerated; all other plans were to be shelved until Buenos Aires was regained, and an expedition under General Samuel Auchmuty and Lieutenant-General John Whitelocke was despatched to this end. The unfortunate Sobremonte was still in Montevideo when news reached him that 12,000 British had landed on the east bank of the Plate estuary. The inhabitants of Buenos Aires, across the water, unilaterally deposed him as viceroy, proclaiming Liniers their chief.

Auchmuty announced that the royal court of the Audiencia had been abolished and the Spanish King's authority set aside, and that the Spanish flag should no longer be hoisted. He wrote later:

These reports were circulated with avidity, and I soon found that they were acceptable to the principal part of the inhabitants. The persons who before appeared hostile and inveterate, now pressed me to advance a corps to Buenos Aires; and assured me, if I would acknowledge their independence, and promise them the protection of the English government, the police would submit to me . . . The party now in power are mostly natives of Spain . . . It has been their policy to inflame the minds of the lower orders against the English, by every species of exaggeration and falsehood, and to lead them to such acts of atrocity as may preclude the possibility of any communication with us. The second party consists of natives of the country, with some Spaniards that are settled in it . . . they aim at following the steps of the North Americans and erecting an independent state.

If we would promise them independence, they would instantly revolt against the government, and join us with the great mass of the

inhabitants. But though nothing less than independence will perfectly satisfy them, they would prefer our government, either to their present anarchy or to the Spanish yoke, provided we would promise not to give up the country to Spain at a peace. But until such a promise is made, we must expect to find them open or secret enemies.

Whitelocke made the same point: 'It has been repeatedly told to me . . . that had General Beresford and the Admiral, on their first arrival, and before any blood was shed or property confiscated, declared South America an independent state, we should now have her as an ally without her witnessing any of the horrors attendant on revolutions.'

The British government favoured establishing their own foothold on the Plate, and in the summer Whitelocke's forces were ferried across the huge estuary to march on Buenos Aires. After crossing the swamps of Quilmes, Whitelocke drove back a force of 6,000 under Liniers. But as they entered Buenos Aires, calamity ensued: 'The British troops,' as General Mitre wrote later, 'worthy of a better general, marched resolutely to their sacrifice, advancing as fearlessly as on parade along those avenues of death, enfiladed at right angles every 150 yards: Whitelocke remaining with the reserve at the Miserere, entirely cut off from the rest of his army. The result of such tactics could not but prove disastrous.' By nightfall 2,200 Britons had been killed, wounded, or taken prisoner, and Whitelocke had promised to evacuate the Plate region within two months.

Complimented on their good behaviour in defeat, the British sailed away from Montevideo after this latest debacle. A former protégé of Liniers, Francisco Xavier de Elio, was installed as governor of the city, as Liniers was a Bonapartist stooge, and the Spanish took advantage of this to send out their own viceroy, Baltasar Hidalgo de Cisneros. Neither Montevideo nor Buenos Aires was happy with this imposition. In 1808, in the wake of an incendiary pamphlet on the subject of free trade written by Mariano Moreno, a brilliant local economist, Cisneros was obliged to offer to open Buenos Aires as a free port. Twice now the city had cocked a snook at the Spanish government – first in appointing

Liniers, now in breaking the Spanish trade monopoly. The British intervention had, unwittingly, sparked off local defiance.

The expedition to South America represented a British distaste for continuing entanglement in continental politics. With Pitt's passing, the British government, under Lord Grenville, was now prepared to offer Napoleon peace in Europe in exchange for a free hand elsewhere around the globe.

Of Grenville, a contemporary, Henry Lord Brougham, gave this description:

> The endowments of this eminent statesman's mind were all of a useful and commanding sort – sound sense, steady memory, vast industry. His acquirements were in the same proportion valuable and lasting – a thorough acquaintance with business in its principles and in its details; a complete mastery of the science of politics, as well theoretical as practical; of late years a perfect familiarity with political economy, and a just appreciation of its importance; an early and most extensive knowledge of classical literature, which he improved instead of abandoning, down to the close of his life; a taste formed upon those chaste models, and of which his lighter compositions, his Greek and Latin verses, bore testimony to the very last. His eloquence was of a plain, masculine, authoritative cast, which neglected if it did not despise ornament, and partook in the least possible degree of fancy, while its declamation was often equally powerful with its reasoning and its statement. The faults of his character were akin to some of the excellencies which so greatly distinguished it; his firmness was apt to degenerate into obstinacy; his confidence in the principles he held was not un-mixed with contempt for those who differed from him. His unbending honesty and straightforward course of dealing with all men and all subjects not unfrequently led him to neglect those courtesies which facilitate political and personal intercourse, and that spirit of conciliation which, especially in a mixed government chiefly conducted by party, sometimes enables men to win a way which they cannot force towards the attainment of important objects.

The one characteristic that this stern, hardworking, highly intelligent man possessed in abundance was principle. He was soon to leave office forever on the grounds that he could not secure Catholic emancipation; and throughout his career he fought for peaceful parliamentary reform. The finest action of his ministry, in which he must share the credit with Fox and, of course, the great William Wilberforce, was the abolition of the slave trade.

The second goal of Grenville and Fox was not so easily obtained: peace with France. When a French dissident approached Fox with a further plot to assassinate Napoleon, the British foreign minister immediately communicated the news to Talleyrand as evidence of Britain's goodwill. Talleyrand responded by freeing a British aristocrat with royal connections, Lord Yarmouth, from prison, to act as an emissary. This proved a mixed blessing: Yarmouth was much fonder of wine and women than diplomacy, and his conduct was later to cause a national scandal.

Napoleon offered to respect Britain's colonial possessions in exchange for peace. But he soon began to make further demands, insisting on the return of Britain's only Mediterranean foothold, Sicily, and that Britain make a separate peace, abandoning Russia, which was still nominally an enemy of France. This would have been dishonourable for the British and would have poisoned Anglo-Russian relations for years. In order to secure Sicily, to complete Napoleon's royal flush of possessions in the central Mediterranean, he offered Britain an extraordinary inducement: the Electorate of Hanover, so dear to the ageing George III. This however infuriated Prussia, which had just been given Hanover as a reward for staying out of the allied offensive before Austerlitz, to apoplexy.

Even Fox was by now deeply disillusioned with the Emperor. He had good reason to be. Napoleon declared in March 1806, '48 hours after peace with England is signed, I will shut out foreign produce and manufacturers, and pass a navigation act that will exclude all but French ships from our ports.' But on 13 September 1806, Fox, Pitt's great rival and friend, himself died, and with him any further prospect of peace.

The Ministry of All Talents itself fell the following March when, almost like Pitt, Grenville pressed upon the King the need to allow

Catholics to become officers in the army. The half mad, prejudiced old man promptly dismissed him, with the bill to abolish the slave trade fortunately having passed parliament. Grenville was succeeded by a Tory administration under the Duke of Portland – 'all Mr Pitt's friends without Pitt' – as a contemporary remarked, which was wholly committed to pursuing the war. Napoleon's last chance of peace with England had passed, not because of any reluctance on Britain's part but again because of Napoleon's bullying tendencies. He, the master of Europe, saw no need to make peace under any terms except his own.

Napoleon's outlook, as he surveyed a Europe prostrate at his feet was a curious mixture of bombastic self-confidence and insecurity. Angry as he was at his failure to destroy the British threat, he could not really believe that that foppish offshore nation posed much danger except at sea and in trade. He seems genuinely to have considered that the British had no further stomach for fighting, even though they might continue subsidizing his enemies and stirring up trouble.

His only other real opponents were the negligible Sweden, a windswept and impoverished land under another mad king, and the far more dangerous Russia. The latter was a huge and unknowable quantity. It possessed an enormous army of tough peasants, in some respects similar to the French conscript army rather than the old-fashioned ones of other European powers, and was continuously probing southwards and westwards. Now it had joined Napoleon's enemies.

Talleyrand, as profound and far-seeing a foreign minister as he was duplicitous and corrupt, believed that the best barriers to Russia in eastern Europe were a humbled Austrian empire; a relatively strong but neutral Prussia; and an independent Poland. Behind these three France would be insulated from Russian attack and if war threatened France could go to the rescue in the interests of defending western Europe, not as an aggressor.

Napoleon had a different perspective. He was ruler of an economically exhausted France and feared that if peace broke out in Europe for any length of time, Frenchmen would begin to question their warlord's right to rule over them; worse, any prolonged peace would inevitably lead to demands for a reduction in the expensive army, which would

anger Napoleon's fellow generals, powerful princes in their own right
and possessed of huge, loyal military corps. In order to retain their
support, to provide further spoils for France and to keep his empire, he
convinced himself that he had no alternative but to keep his eastern
enemies cowed.

The defeated Austrians were indeed cowed and presented no
danger. As for the Prussians, for whom he had no great regard,
Napoleon's tactic was to seek to subdue them through bullying,
believing them to be incapable of starting a war, and certainly not
alone. He therefore insisted that the Prussians join his economic
blockade of Britain, which resulted in the impounding of virtually
the entire Prussian merchant fleet – some 700 ships – in British ports.
He flagrantly disregarded the supposed neutrality of Saxony by ordering that an anti-French bookseller there, named Palm, be seized by his
special forces from across the border and executed. Palm's crime was to
have distributed early German nationalist pamphlets – which was to
give the lie to those who later believed that Napoleon favoured the
building of nationalist entities upon the ashes of the old order in
Europe.

Looking at Napoleon's pronouncements at the time, it is hard not to
conclude that Austerlitz and Ulm – his greatest major military victories
to date – had turned the Emperor's head. On 28 February he boasted to
Berthier: 'I have 510,000 men with the colours; I have ordered heavy
expenditures for the ports and the increase of the navy; I am going to
increase the army by 100,000 men, and I am going to impose
additional taxation on France.' He added later, crazily: 'In the report
on burials I see that in the average year there are 14,000 deaths in Paris;
this is equal to a splendid battle.'

This bizarre militarism was accompanied by lordly proclamations to
the French.

I want to create in France a lay state. Up till now the world has only
known two forms of government, the ecclesiastic and the military.
Constantine was the first to establish, by means of the priests, a sort
of civilian state; Clovis succeeded in founding the French monarchy
only with this same support. Monks are the natural enemies of

soldiers, and have more than once served to check them. The lay order will be strengthened by the creation of a teaching body, and even more strengthened by the creation of a great corporation of magistrates. I think it is unnecessary to take into consideration a system of education for girls, they can get no better teaching than that of their mothers. A public education does not suit them, for the reason that they are not called on to live in public; for them habit is everything, and marriage is the goal.

The education of young people, he felt, should be taken away from the church, which he despised, and made a task of the military.

In the teaching body we must imitate the classifications of military rank. I hold strongly to the idea of a corporation, because a corporation never dies. There need be no fear that I want to bring back the monks; even if I wanted to I couldn't. The vices and scandal that arose among the monks are well known; I had opportunities for forming my own opinion in that matter, having been in part educated by them. I respect what religion holds in respect; but as a statesman I dislike the fanaticism of celibacy; it was one of the means whereby the Court of Rome attempted to rivet the chains of Europe by preventing the cleric from being a citizen. Military fanaticism is the only sort that is of any use to me; a man must have it to get himself killed. My principal object in instituting a teaching body is to have some means of directing political and moral opinion.

He was deeply cynical about religion.

At Cairo, and in the desert, the mosques are inns as well; as many as 6,000 persons may shelter and eat in them; or even use the fountains and water for bathing. Our ceremony of baptism comes from this; it could not have arisen in our climate, in which water is not precious enough – this year we are deluged. When water fails the Egyptians baptize with sand. As for me, it is not the mystery of the Incarnation that I see in religion, but the mystery of social order. Heaven

suggests an idea of equality which saves the rich from being massacred by the poor. To look at it another way, religion is a sort of inoculation or vaccine which, while satisfying our sense of the supernatural, guarantees us from the charlatans and the magicians.

He was quite willing to pick a quarrel with the Pope who, to his intense irritation, showed few signs of being overawed by his new, mighty temporal responsibilities: 'On the 13th of November the Pope wrote me a letter of the most ridiculous, most insane, character: those people think I am dead! I am a religious man, but I am not a bigoted idiot. For the Pope I am Charlemagne, because like Charlemagne I unite the Crowns of France and of the Lombards, and my Empire touches the East. I will reduce the Pope to be the mere bishop of Rome.'

Napoleon believed that the Pope had inspired a rising in Parma in 1806 and was behind continuing Italian resistance to French rule; he considered Rome a hotbed of British spies. Napoleon introduced a new Catechism which called upon Catholics to state their allegiance to the Empire:

> We in particular owe to Napoleon I, our Emperor, love, respect, obedience, loyalty, military service, the dues laid down for the conservation and defence of the empire and of its throne; we also owe him fervent prayers for his safety and for the temporal and spiritual prosperity of the state. . . .
>
> Are there not particular reasons which should attach us more closely to Napoleon I, our Emperor?
>
> Yes, because it is he whom God has sustained, in difficult circumstances, so that he might re-establish public worship and the holy faith of our fathers, and that he might be their protector. He has restored and maintained public order by his profound and active wisdom; he defends the state with his powerful arm; he has become the anointed of the Lord by the consecration he has received from the sovereign pontiff, head of the universal Church.
>
> What must one think of those who should fail in their duty to our Emperor?

According to the apostle Paul, they would resist the established order of God himself, and would render themselves worthy of eternal damnation.

Napoleon's underlying ruthlessness was if anything sharpened. When a small revolt broke out in Hesse, Napoleon ordered the village where it occurred to be razed to the ground and 200 people to be shot, in a foretaste of Nazi occupation tactics the next century. To his brother Joseph, whom he considered too soft-hearted, he issued instructions that make the brutality of the old Bourbon court of Naples pale. 'Shoot without pity any lazzaroni who indulge in dagger play. You can keep an Italian population down only by holy fear. Impose a war contribution of 30 millions on the kingdom. Your policy is too hesitating.'

Paranoia, although probably in this case justified, was never far below the surface:

You trust the Neapolitans too much, especially in the matter of your kitchen and your personal guards, which means that you are taking chances of being poisoned or assassinated. You have not known enough of my domestic arrangements to realize that, even in France, I have always been guarded by my most faithful and my oldest soldiers. No one should enter your room at night except your aide-de-camp, who should sleep in the room next to your bedroom; your door should be locked on the inside, and you should not let your aide-de-camp in before having recognized his voice, and he should not knock at your door until after closing the door of his room, so as to be sure no one can follow him. These precautions are important; they are not troublesome, and they inspire confidence, quite apart from the fact that actually they may save your life. You should regulate your way of living this way once and for all. Don't be obliged to adopt it in an emergency, which would be humiliating both for you and for those about you. Trust my experience.

Joseph had, in fact, been uncharacteristically active. He forged an alliance with the local anti-Bourbons in Naples, and abolished feudal rights in his kingdom in April 1806; he also introduced land reform,

breaking up the large estates and handing out small parcels to the peasants. He set up a ruling council in a small bow to democracy, and introduced the Code Napoleon. He seized the monasteries and their estates and used the proceeds to pay the national debt of some 130 million ducats, a familiar French revolutionary method. He stripped most of the clergy of their rights (there were some 82,000 clerics and 31,000 nobility owning two-thirds of the land in this kingdom of 5 million people). He also introduced an income tax. Most of the measures were taken in order to raise revenues to maintain the 50,000-strong army of French occupation. He lived with a Neapolitan mistress, Maria Giulia Colana, and regarded himself as the 'people's King' – or 'philosopher king', but was genuinely shocked when an uprising broke out against him in the summer which was quickly suppressed.

Louis, now King of Holland, was almost ludicrously ill-equipped to become a king, being physically crippled, unable to talk properly, mentally unstable and prone to acute jealousy. Yet Louis was ultimately to gain popularity in Holland by seeking to defy Napoleon's ban on trade with Britain and through his gentle treatment of anti-French partisans, as well as his decision to end conscription. Napoleon wrote angrily to him: 'A prince who gets a reputation for good nature in the first year of his reign is laughed at in the second. The love that kings inspire should be virile – partly an apprehensive respect, and partly a thirst for reputation. When a King is said to be a good fellow, his reign is a failure. How can a good fellow – or a good father if you prefer it so – bear the burdens of royalty, keep malcontents in order, and either silence political passions or enlist them under his own banner?' The Emperor described Louis as 'a Dutchman, a dealer in cheese', but he eventually became known as 'Good King Louis' among his subjects before Napoleon finally relieved him from command in 1810.

The family spoils system soon extended to the youngest brother, Jérôme, who was given the new kingdom of Westphalia. After Napoleon had pensioned off his first wife, the American Elizabeth Patterson from Baltimore, Jérôme had married Catherine, the good-natured daughter of the former king. Jérôme was of generous disposition, encouraging the arts, and vaccinating his people. But he too was

singularly ill-fitted for kingship. Napoleon had issued precise instructions: 'What is above all desired in Germany is that you will grant to those who do not belong to the nobility, but possess talents, an equal claim to offices, and that all vestiges of serfdom and of barriers between the sovereign and the lowest class of people shall be completely done away with. The benefits of the Code Napoleon, legal procedure in open courts, the jury, these are points by which your monarchy should be distinguished . . . your people must enjoy a liberty, an equality, a prosperity unknown in the rest of Germany.'

Jérôme, however, ran up colossal debts which were paid for by exacting punitive taxes. He kept ninety-two carriages and 200 horses. He had fourteen chamberlains dressed in scarlet and gold to administer extravagant parties and private theatricals. He also was sexually incontinent, conducting an open affair with Josephine's cousin, Stephanie de Beauharnais (whom Napoleon himself admired); and in Westphalia he was said to sleep with any girl who was willing to say yes. He became known as the 'merry monarch'.

Lucien Bonaparte alone had eschewed becoming a viceroy of Napoleon's empire – he was offered Italy – having quarrelled with Napoleon over his choice of wife, whom he refused to give up on the orders of his older brother. However, when she died after an agonizing mysterious 24-hour illness, some alleged she had been poisoned. The only one of the brothers who stood up to Napoleon and with real political talent, he had left-wing, Jacobin convictions. He decided to leave France to start a new life in America; en route he was captured by the British who kept him in comfortable confinement in Ludlow and Worcestershire.

Of all Napoleon's siblings, his somewhat masculine sister Elisa was the one who showed greatest talent as a ruler, and she was, needless to say, given the smallest kingdom. She was appointed Princess of Lucca, where she ruled quite well, and had responsibility for the marble quarries at Carrara, from which she had innumerable busts of her brother made. She was then appointed Grand Duchess of Tuscany, where she renovated the Pitti Palace in Florence.

Napoleon's second sister, Caroline, married Joachim Murat, who was later to succeed Joseph as King of Naples with distinctly mixed

results; Caroline was intelligent and had earned a reputation as a schemer, not least against her brother, while Murat was one of Napoleon's greatest generals but also far from overwhelmed by the talents of his leader.

The sole real success story as a King of Napoleon's family circle was not one of his own blood line, but his stepson Eugène de Beauharnais, who was appointed regent of Italy, a job he performed with detachment and efficiency, the qualities he also brought to the battlefield.

The Emperor's appointment of his inadequate and unqualified family to thrones across Europe demolished any pretence that he was an idealist: he was in fact a throwback, strutting and posing as a dynastic monarch and appointing his Corsican clan as its princes. One reason he did so was because he felt he could trust his mediocre family better than more talented proconsuls. In this he was mistaken.

Chapter 52

THE PRUSSIAN CAMPAIGN

The issue remained whether Napoleon could mutate into a pacific and wise ruler creating a new Europe under French hegemony but at least at peace. However his bullying had at last galvanized feeble and opaque Prussia into action. A senior British diplomat in Dresden, Henry Williams Wynn, commented that 'the king is well disposed. But unfortunately he is a coward and is surrounded by a set who know how to attack the weak side.' Yet faced with the possibility of losing Hanover – its bribe for not entering the last war against France – Prussia, although alone and isolated in Europe, was affronted into declaring war. Napoleon viewed this spectacle with contempt, and even amusement.

He was offered the double chance to emasculate Prussia and to deal a knock-out blow to the enemy he really feared, Russia, which was in alliance with Prussia. On 10 September he wrote witheringly:

the attitude of Prussia is still provocative. They need to be taught a good lesson . . . Prussia is arming in ridiculous fashion: she will, however, soon disarm, or pay dear for it. Nothing could be more foolish and more hesitating than the conduct of the [Prussian] cabinet. The Court of Vienna makes great protestations of friend-ship, which its extreme weakness makes me believe in. Whatever happens I can and will face it out. The conscription which I have just levied is coming in on all sides; I shall call-up the reserves; I am thoroughly supplied, and lack nothing. I may possibly take com-mand of the Grand Army in a few days. It numbers about 150,000 men, enough to put down Vienna, Berlin, and St Petersburg.

On 6 October he proclaimed boldly to his soldiers: 'Fools! the lessons of experience fade away, and with some men hatred and jealousy never die. Soldiers! Not one of you would wish to regain France by any other path than that of honour; we must return only under triumphal arches. Forward, then! Let the Prussian army meet with the same fate as it did fourteen years ago.' A few days later he remarked incredulously: 'Their generals are perfect idiots. It is inconceivable how the Duke of Brunswick, who has a reputation, can direct the operations of his army in so ridiculous a fashion.' Yet he was in for a shock: it was not to be so easy.

The dim Prussian Kaiser, Frederick William III, had despatched his beautiful, strong-willed young wife Queen Louise and the young and dashing Prince Louis to reach a secret agreement with Tsar Alexander. But the Russian army was still a long way away and Prussia, which in the last conflict would have joined two formidable allies, Austria and Russia, was now alone.

Undeterred, on 12 September the Kaiser ordered his troops into Saxony to seek new recruits. Although the Prussian army's natural strength was 245,000, it had a field strength of only around 140,000. The army was largely unchanged in tactics and weaponry from Frederick the Great's day. Even its leadership was obsolescent; its chief commander, Field Marshal Von Mollondorff, was eighty-two; three other generals were over the age of eighty, thirteen over the age of seventy and sixty over the age of sixty, as were a quarter of regimental and battalion commanders lower down the hierarchy. The seventy-one-year-old Duke of Brunswick, the defeated commander at Valmy, was still the principal commander in the field.

The army leadership was also entirely aristocratic and the soldier conscripts accustomed to blind brutalized obedience and immaculate parade ground routine. The army was wedded to three-line formations and to volleys; the cavalry was still trained for the mass charge designed to panic and rout the enemy. The field artillery was too heavy for quick manoeuvres, and the army clung to muskets dating from the 1754 model. The sole innovation had been the introduction of a few independent light battalions. It was small wonder that Napoleon regarded the Prussians as easy prey.

The bulk of his army was in southern Germany along the Rhine, so Napoleon's plan was simple: to outflank the Prussians, who were drawn up in a crescent in Saxony, and cut them off from Berlin before the Russians could reinforce them. Napoleon's army of 130,000 marched in three huge columns of two corps each along parallel roads over the Pass of Thuringia.

The Prussians divided their forces in two, one of around 60,000 under the Duke of Brunswick and the Kaiser, and another of 80,000 under Prince Hohenlohe-Ingelfingen – a cardinal mistake, as Napoleon's superior army could pick each off at leisure. Napoleon learnt that the main Prussian army was at Erfurt, to the west.

On 10 October the French advance guard under Lannes intercepted the Prussian advance guard under Hohenlohe and routed it, taking 1,200 prisoners. Napoleon went after the main Prussian force, which was believed to be at Jena, and despatched Davout with some 26,000 men and forty-four guns northwards to cut off the Prussian retreat to the Elbe. The Prussians had already been ordered to retreat.

Napoleon ordered up his main corps, under Soult, Augereau and Ney to reinforce Lannes. In the early morning of 14 October they joined battle, with Lannes and Ney valiantly leading their men. They were unprepared for the ferocity of the Prussian resistance and Ney was soon cut off. Napoleon had to organize a major artillery attack to rescue his beleaguered lieutenant.

The Prussians held off an army twice their size for six hours, and then staged an orderly retreat, until Murat's cavalry finally broke Hohenlohe's army, which was also under fierce artillery fire. Losing some 5,000 men themselves, the French inflicted losses of 10,000 on the Prussians and took 15,000 prisoners and 200 guns.

Napoleon was then astounded to discover he had been fighting the Prussian rearguard: the main army was some ten miles to the north at Auerstadt, facing the force that had been despatched under Davout and Bernadotte. However the latter had inexplicably disobeyed orders and marched to Camburg, between the two Prussian forces, missing both fights. Davout was on his own with just 26,000 men and forty-four guns facing Brunswick's 64,000 and 230 guns. At first it seemed the battle was going the Prussian way: Davout organized his men into

squares to resist the cavalry attacks and was pounded by heavy fire from the Prussian artillery, but by lunchtime the French centre was weakening.

At that moment Brunswick was mortally wounded and the fastidious Frederick William was no substitute as a commander. Davout skilfully organized a flanking movement – or 'envelopment' – to take advantage of the Prussians' plodding linear tactics. After four hours of hard fighting, with Frederick William barely leading at all, the Prussians began to give way. The Kaiser ordered a general retreat in the direction of Jena, while Davout ordered an immediate further attack. The retreat turned to chaos as the two Prussian armies, both retreating in opposite directions, ran into each other. Davout had inflicted some 12,000 casualties and taken 3,000 prisoners, but had suffered losses of some 8,000 himself.

The French gave chase to the retreating Prussians, and Murat's cavalry relentlessly harassed the rearguard as they crossed some 600 kilometres in twenty-three days. The valiant Queen Louise, who had watched the battle, escaped from a squad of hussars who arrived just three hours after she had left her post. Napoleon rode to Weimar and took up residence in the magnificent Sans Souci Palace of Frederick the Great, where he rhapsodized about the enemy Queen, dubbing her 'an Amazon' and 'the lovely Queen, a being as fatal to the Prussians as Helen to the Trojans'.

The Prussians who had earlier fought bravely and well, although hampered by outdated tactics and equipment, now collapsed, with fortresses surrendering and the population panicking before the French advance. Bernadotte, smarting from a furious official reprimand for disobeying orders and missing the battle, led the rapid French advance along with Murat and Lannes.

Only General Blücher's forces salvaged Prussia's honour, putting up a spirited stand at Lübeck on the Baltic, where his 20,000 men hoped to be evacuated by a British fleet which never came. He was hopelessly outnumbered by Bernadotte's forces. 'The slaughter is awful,' wrote Napoleon himself. On 6 November Blücher surrendered. There were now only some 20,000 Prussian soldiers left in east Prussia.

From Berlin Napoleon dictated a victor's peace: all territory be-

tween the Rhine and the Elbe was to be ceded and a colossal 160 million francs levied in reparations. Saxony was to be incorporated in the puppet Confederation of the Rhine. The state of Prussia had in effect ceased to exist, with three-quarters of it under French domination. 'Sir, the war is over owing to the lack of combatants,' declared Murat delightedly.

Jena-Auerstadt was very different to Austerlitz. Napoleon won through superior numbers at Jena but was saved by Davout's brilliant stand at Auerstadt. He had been overconfident, his tactics had been unimaginative, and he had shown dismally inadequate knowledge of the enemy's movements. It was a victory, but not an impressive one. By contrast the Prussians had fought well, if unimaginatively – an achievement marred by their subsequent rout and the collapse of resistance.

Talleyrand caught up with his master in Berlin. Count Haugwitz, seeking to preserve a vestige of Prussian self-respect, wrote to his representative in Paris: 'Provided that Monsieur de Talleyrand arrives, I do not despair of your being able to arouse some sounder political ideas than this terrible principle of the destruction of Prussia as a guarantee for the future peace of France. That enlightened minister will easily understand that when Prussia is rendered powerless to restrain Russia or to threaten Austria . . . those two powers will be in a stronger position to disturb the peace of France.' He was to prove prophetic. But Napoleon was implacable in his revenge and determination to dismember Prussia: only a rump of some 5 million people remained. Queen Louise announced that she would fight on at the head of what remained of Prussia's patriots.

Napoleon chose that moment to inform Talleyrand of his determination to bring the Bourbons of Spain to heel. The minister was horrified, realizing for the first time that there were no limits to his master's ambition: 'I then swore to myself that I would cease to be his minister as soon as we returned to France.'

Napoleon also issued his fateful decree of 21 November at Berlin prohibiting all trade, commerce and correspondence with Britain. This was the formal recognition of the blockade already in place and is regarded as the day of the imposition of what was called 'The

Continental System'. It was to have fateful consequences: it was a declaration of economic war on Britain, and from then on the balance of opinion in London tilted in favour of all-out war. All real hope of peace – which had burned quite brightly in Britain during the previous decade – was extinguished.

The economic war also ravaged Europe, causing, in the end, more suffering to the French and their subject peoples than to the British, and sparking arguably all the successive wars, from that with Denmark to those with Portugal and Spain and ultimately Russia. The names of the great battles of the Napoleonic wars still resonate today; but the Berlin decree of 1806 and the economic war are perhaps more significant still.

The Emperor's immediate gaze was still fixed on the east: he had successfully isolated and defeated the Prussians: now he sought to lure the troublesome Russians into battle and inflict a defeat which would discourage them from ever dabbling in European politics again. The strategy made sense. He informed the chiefs of the Polish independence movement that he was sympathetic to their cause and demanded that they put 40,000 men into the field to fight the Russians. Kosciusko, their leader, a hero of the American War of Independence, declared angrily, 'He will not reconstruct Poland; he thinks only of himself and he is a despot.'

The distrust was mutual. Napoleon wrote: 'The Poles who show so much prudence, who ask for so many conditions before declaring themselves, are egotists who cannot be kindled to enthusiasm for love of their country. I am old in my knowledge of men. My greatness does not depend on the help of a few thousand Poles. It is for them to take advantage of the present circumstances with enthusiasm; it is not for me to take the first step.' Napoleon had, however, a loyal supporter in the gallant Prince Poniatowski, one of the leaders of Polish irregular forces. Napoleon also tried to stir up trouble for the Russians by inveigling the Ottoman empire to attack in the south. The Russians were forced to divert some 20,000 men there. Napoleon ordered his armies into Poland, and himself arrived in Warsaw on 19 December.

The winter enveloped his troops, while the port of Danzig – which received supplies from the sea – was still held by the Prussians, who also

controlled the east. Large Russian armies were circling. The Russians had reorganized their armies into mixed divisions, roughly similar to the French corps, having learnt the lessons of Austerlitz. Each of these had six front-line infantry regiments, twenty horse squadrons and eighty-two guns. The Russians had two armies on the northern front led by Buxhovden and by Count Bennigsen, a Hanoverian cavalry commander who loathed Napoleon and was passionately pro-British. Between them these armies were 90,000 strong and had some 450 guns.

In November, as the French approached, Bennigsen was in central Poland but he prudently withdrew across the Vistula to the town of Pultuski from which he threatened the over-extended French lines. Napoleon responded by trying to cut the Russian lines of communication. He despatched a force to Pultuski where bitter fighting took place along the Narew river over Christmas. The French captured the town, but the Russians withdrew intact to Rozan.

The French did not give chase: they were exhausted, demoralized and winter had closed in. The roads were a sea of mud and snow. Nearly half of the *Grande Armée* had simply disintegrated. Napoleon desperately called for reinforcements of 35,000 men from Switzerland and Holland and for a conscription drive in France. He ordered more than 700 million francs to be raised for his campaign, including 160 million from beaten Prussia.

Napoleon now indulged in magnificent parties in Warsaw in his most extravagant *nouveau riche* mode to shut out the miseries of winter. When Josephine wrote to him from Paris of a dream in which she saw him dancing with a beautiful woman, he wrote: 'You say that your dream does not make you jealous . . . I think therefore that you *are* jealous and I am delighted. In any case you are wrong. In these frozen Polish wastes one is not likely to think of beautiful women . . . There is only one woman for me. Do you know her? I could paint her portrait for you but it would make you conceited . . . The winter nights are long, all alone.'

On 31 December he wrote again: 'I laughed heartily at your last letter. You exaggerate the attractions of the beauties of Poland.' Undoubtedly she had heard rumours. On that very day Duroc had

introduced Napoleon to a shy, stunning blonde, Countess Marie Walewska, the eighteen-year-old wife of a seventy-seven-year-old count. The Emperor was immediately smitten, and rained letters upon her. On 2 January he wrote:

> I saw only you, I admired only you, I desire only you. A quick answer will calm the impatient ardour of N. . . . Was I mistaken? You have deprived me of sleep! Oh, grant a little joy, a little happiness, to a poor heart that is ready to adore you. Is it so difficult to obtain an answer? You owe me two. N. . . . Oh come! come! All your wishes shall be complied with. Your country will become more dear to me if you take compassion on my poor heart. N. . . . Marie, my sweet Marie, my first thought is for you; my first wish is to see you again. You will come again, will you not? You have promised that you would. If not, the eagle would wing its way to you!

To Josephine, who wanted to join him, he wrote: 'It is out of the question that I should allow women to undertake such a journey: bad roads, unsafe, and quagmires. Go back to Paris; be gay and happy; perhaps I shall soon be back myself. I laughed over your saying that you had taken a husband to live with; in my ignorance I supposed that the wife was made for the husband, the husband for his country, his family, and fame.' At a ball he chided Marie for her severe appearance, and secured the support of Polish activists, eager to enlist the French on their side, in his seduction of her, in a typically cynical act of power rape. Even her aged husband connived.

Surprisingly, this simple, strong-willed girl gradually began to fall for her middle-aged suitor, who showered her with charm and affection. Napoleon had had a string of lovers by that time, not least on the road to Poland. But this time it was different: Napoleon had not been so besotted since he first fell for Josephine; and Marie was soon madly in love with him.

More serious matters required his attention. Towards the end of the month Ney was foraging for fuel close to the winter quarters of the

Russians. Bennigsen decided to strike across the Vistula in an attempt to sever his lines of communication. Napoleon was delighted. He decided to withdraw from the Russian border and spring a trap. However his orders fell into Bennigsen's hands and the latter withdrew towards Konigsberg, stopping at the village of Eylau, which he defended by placing several regiments in the church and cemetery, while occupying the strategic plateau behind.

Napoleon sent forward his advance guard under Soult and Murat, intending to rally his men for a decisive attack on the Russians. It was bitterly cold. The French succeeded in driving the Russians out of the village on 7 February and prepared to assemble their forces for a decisive push. But Bennigsen himself decided not to wait. For once it was the French who were sluggish and ill-organized, and the enemy who seized the initiative. At daybreak the Russians, who had considerable superiority in artillery, some 400 cannon to 200 French guns, opened up on the French positions; as the guns blazed, some 4,000 men were killed on both sides in a cannonade which continued after night fell on the short winter day, with temperatures falling to minus 20 degrees. It was an unprecedented slaughter by artillery alone. The French hesitated to attack, because they were outnumbered by some 70,000 to 45,000 while Napoleon waited for reinforcements from Davout and Ney. At last, though, the supporting armies arrived and Napoleon ordered his men into an attack on the classic pattern. Davout and Ney were to manoeuvre around the flanks, while Soult would wait to launch a frontal attack: behind him Murat's cavalry would be held in reserve for a decisive push, with the Imperial Guard behind that.

Napoleon confidently ordered Soult to advance on the centre – only to discover the Russian main force moving towards them. Soult was driven rapidly back and the Russians attacked the French left under Ney, which had not even begun to march. Davout's division had not yet attacked on the right. Taken by surprise, and fearing that he would lose the field, Napoleon rashly ordered Augereau forward. But a blinding blizzard descended, obstructing the view of both armies, and Augereau's corps stumbled directly under the Russian guns, which inflicted massive damage. The French line was now broken, and some 6,000 Russians forced their way into Eylau, where Napoleon, who had

taken up his position in the church, narrowly avoided capture. With Augereau's corps all but destroyed and Soult's thrown back, it seemed that the French were on the verge of losing the battle.

Desperately, Napoleon ordered Murat's cavalry forward. Murat then led perhaps the most famous cavalry charge in history, his 11,000 men thundering right into the enemy front line and their guns. This saved the battle for the French. Napoleon's laconic comment was that this attack was 'as daring as war had ever seen and covered our cavalry in glory'. Murat lost 1,500 men, but captured the seventy guns that had ravaged Augereau's forces.

More important still, the ferocity of the attack unnerved Bennigsen, who feared that the French centre was much stronger than it actually was and fatally hesitated to pursue the advantage he had won at midday. This gave time for Davout to encircle the Russians on the right. With his usual skill and ferocity, Davout drove the Russians back and forced them off the higher ground.

The French believed they had victory in their grasp, barely hours after defeat had stared them in the face. But a force of Prussians under General Lestocq, which had managed to evade a corps of 15,000 men under Ney who had been sent to intercept them, fell upon Davout's unguarded flank and started fighting the French back off the commanding heights at around four o'clock. The French, fighting furiously, fell back, and it seemed the Russians were carrying the day once again.

As darkness fell, at around 7 p.m. Ney's men, who had blundered about in the blizzards, finally arrived to reinforce Davout and halted the Russian advance. With darkness, snow and plummeting temperatures enveloping the battlefield, Bennigsen held a council of war and overruled his generals, who wanted to fight to the death: he decided to withdraw while he had the advantage.

It is impossible to conclude who would have prevailed if the fighting had gone into a third day. The French had clearly lost – some 20,000 men to the Russian tally of around 10,000 and 2,500 prisoners taken. Yet the Russian tactics of withdrawing in good order allowed Napoleon to claim victory, lying that he had lost only around 2,000 dead and 5,000 wounded. But even he admitted: 'We had a great battle

yesterday; victory is mine, but my losses are very heavy; the enemy's losses, which were heavier, do not console me. The great distance at which I find myself makes my losses even more acutely felt.'

Ney remarked as he toured the battlefield: 'What a massacre. And without result.' The surgeon-general of the *Grande Armée*, Percy, described the scene:

> Never was so small a space covered with so many corpses. Everywhere the snow was stained with blood. The snow which had fallen and which was still falling began to hide the bodies from the grieving glances of passers-by. The bodies were heaped up wherever there were small groups of firs behind which the Russians had fought. Thousands of guns, helmets and breastplates were scattered on the road or in the fields. On the slope of a hill, which the enemy had obviously chosen to protect themselves, there were groups of a hundred bloody bodies; horses, maimed but still alive, waited to fall in their turn from hunger, on the heaps of bodies. We had hardly crossed one battlefield when we found another, all of them strewn with bodies.

In spite of Napoleon's gloss, it was his first significant tactical defeat. Of the first three great pitched battles under his command he had won the first, Austerlitz, devastatingly; the second, Jena-Aurstadt more by good fortune than by skill, and he had lost the third at Eylau however much he tried to persuade himself it was a victory.

He and his troops returned to winter quarters – the Russians reoccupying the field of Eylau, which by now was full of frozen bodies. Gloomily he wrote to Joseph in Naples:

> The staff, colonels, officers, have not undressed in two months, some not in four; I, myself have gone two weeks without getting out of my boots; we are in the midst of snow and mud, without wine, without brandy, without bread, eating potatoes and meat, making long marches and countermarches, without any kind of luxury, and fighting with bayonets and grapeshot; the wounded are often compelled to go fifty leagues in open sleighs. Therefore it is a

pretty poor joke to compare us with the army of Naples, making
war in a lovely country, where one can get wine, oil, bread, cloth,
sheets, social life, and even women. After having destroyed the
Prussian monarchy, we are fighting against what is left of the
Prussians, against the Russians, the Kalmucks, the Cossacks, the
northern tribes that long ago invaded the Roman Empire. We are
making war in the strictest sense of that term. In the midst of these
great fatigues we have all been more or less sick. As for myself I have
never been stronger, and have become fatter.

It had been a major setback and exaggerated accounts of the disaster
started to circulate in the salons of Paris. The myth of Napoleon's
invincibility had been badly dented. The invincible *Grande Armée* had
been outfought, outmanoeuvred, outgunned, slaughtered in their
thousands and very nearly routed by a plodding Russian army
equipped with obsolescent conventional tactics. Worse, Napoleon
had tried to fight on ground of his own choosing, had been ambushed
and forced to fight on the enemy's terms – even though by the end of
the battle he enjoyed considerable superiority in numbers.

He was now plunged into the bitter realization that Russia was one
of his most dangerous enemies, the power that threatened his hold on
Europe: in a sense he was right, for Russia, unlike Austria and Prussia
which were essentially defeated, was an aggressive nation with as many
ambitions as France. From the defeat at Eylau dawned the realization
that he could not hope to beat Russia and must instead seek peace. But
he could hardly now abandon his position without risking a Russian
counter-attack, the possible loss of Prussia and even his own throne, as
all of Europe would fall upon him after barely one and a half years of
unbroken triumph.

Paradoxically, defeat had the effect of making him even more
determined than victory. He immediately sought to avoid further
disaster by strengthening his depleted army. Through colossal conscription drives that drained and disrupted the French people as well as
subject nations, Napoleon increased his total manpower to 600,000
men altogether; the *Grande Armée* in Poland and its supporters in
Germany comprised two-thirds of this. Six new divisions had been

enlisted – two in Poland, two in Germany, and two in Italy, as well as 100,000 men in Saxony and Baden.

Napoleon himself dallied in great comfort with Marie Walewska in the castle of Finkenstein – 'a splendid castle with chimneys in all the rooms, which was a very pleasant thing'. To the unhappy Josephine who was deeply suspicious and trying to rally support for him as the rumour of his defeat reached Paris, he wrote:

> Dear friend: Your letter has caused me pain. There is no occasion for you to die; you are well, and have no reasonable cause for worry. You must give up all idea of a journey this summer; it is not possible. I am as anxious to see you as you are to see me, and even to lead a quiet life. I know how to do other things than wage war, but duty must come first. All my life I have sacrificed everything, my repose, my interests, my happiness, to my destiny . . . I have your letter. I don't know what you mean by ladies who correspond with me. I love only my little Josephine, good, sulky, capricious, who can quarrel gracefully, as she does everything else, for she is always fascinating except when she is jealous, and then she becomes a little devil.

While he reassembled his forces, renewed his strength and made love to Marie Walewska, he ordered his troops to Danzig, which surrendered after an old-fashioned siege on the classic style, lasting three months on 27 May, furnishing Napoleon with badly needed supplies. The 20,000 or so French besiegers marched to reinforce the Emperor, who was showing signs of the old cockiness, writing to the despairing Talleyrand:

> General Gardanne wishes to proceed to Persia. Maret will draw up his credentials and instructions. They turn on [the following] points: Investigate the resources of Persia from the military point of view, studying particularly the obstacles that would have to be overcome by a French army of 40,000 men marching to India with the help of the Persian and Turkish governments. Deal with Persia in regard to England by urging her to prevent the passage of English despatches

and messages, and to hamper the trade of the East India Company in every way possible.

In summer 1807, Napoleon decided to resume the offensive. He pushed forward in a renewed effort to cut the Russian army off from its base at Konigsberg, entering Russian forward positions at Heilsberg on 10 June in a frontal attack of the crudest kind which cost him some 11,000 men to the Russian's 8,000, although he did force Bennigsen to withdraw.

This was now the third battle against the Russians in which the French had been bloodied. Bennigsen decided to march down the east side of the Alle river. Napoleon tried to forestall this by sending lancers down with a vanguard on the opposite bank to the village of Friedland. On 13 June Bennigsen ordered four pontoon bridges to be built over the river and sent 10,000 men across to trap the French, who by now had been reinforced by some 9,000 infantry and 8,000 cavalry. As the Russians continued reinforcing their position to some 60,000 men, attacking the French but not in force, Napoleon decided to move swiftly.

He had not planned the battle: as late as 13 June he had written to Lannes. 'My staff officer . . . does not give me sufficient information to judge if it is the enemy's army that is debouching at Friedland or only a detachment.' But the Emperor recalled that the next day was the anniversary of the Battle of Marengo, and declared exultantly: 'I am going to drub the Russians, just as I drubbed the Austrians.' He brought massive reinforcements forward to trap the unsuspecting Russians with their backs to the river and just four pontoon bridges behind them. Lannes held out valiantly during the night under a massive artillery barrage before dawn on 14 June. By 9.30 a.m. the French had been reinforced to some 40,000 troops against the Russians' 60,000.

By 4 p.m. Napoleon himself had arrived with the main French army, and some 80,000 French soldiers were attacking the Russians. Napoleon ordered an advance from the south, where the Russians were at their weakest. Bennigsen's cavalry counter-attacked. Marshal Victor, an old comrade-in-arms of Napoleon from Toulon days, moved up his

corps and thirty cannon, and decimated the Russian cavalry and the retreating infantry. Bennigsen charged against the French centre, but was repulsed, and then against the south once again, before retiring to the north, abandoning Friedland and losing three out of his four pontoon bridges.

The French had adopted a new tactic: massive artillery attack followed by a huge infantry assault. The Russians succeeded in escaping with part of their army intact, across the fourth pontoon bridge in the north. But the defeat was decisive: some 30,000 Russian casualties compared with the French 10,000. The Russians had simply been trapped with their backs to the river by a superior force and although they had fought bravely, had no chance of prevailing.

Chapter 53

THE TREATY OF TILSIT

For Napoleon, Friedland had been a victory of opportunity. With his usual quick reactions he had immediately taken advantage of a huge mistake by his enemy and pressed forward. It was also a desperately needed victory: military success was Napoleon's entire *raison d'etre*. He was as aware as anyone that the price of military failure would be his overthrow in Paris. His country and empire were being drained of resources, facing perpetual economic crises and being badly mismanaged by his family and cronies. He must either deliver military triumphs or lose power.

To his great relief he learnt that the Tsar was not prepared to fight on. Alexander had decided that the Prussian cause was lost, and preferred to make peace with Napoleon with his armies more or less intact, diverting his designs southwards again. The two most aggressive and expansionist powers in Europe had fought each other to a bloody standstill.

On 18 June Napoleon marched forward to the village of Tilsit to engage the enemy, should they have the impudence to stand their ground. But the following day he wrote: 'A curious incident which made the soldiers laugh, occurred for the first time near Tilsit; we met a horde of Kalmucks, who fought with bows and arrows. I control the Niemen. I shall probably conclude an armistice this evening.'

The ensuing 'summit' – a meeting between two unbalanced and aggressive autocrats – was staged amidst incredible theatre. Alexander would not recognize that he had been defeated, quite justifiably, as his six-month-old duel had ended with honours about even, and refused

to come to French-held territory. Napoleon refused to cross over into Russia. So they met on a huge raft in the middle of the river Niemen near Tilsit. The raft consisted of a sophisticated tent which contained a large and comfortable room and two waiting-rooms, one for each potentate, which opened into it. At midday on 25 June two boats set off from opposite banks, Napoleon with his childish vanity insisting that his oarsmen get there first, which they did, permitting him to stride through the raft to the door where the Tsar was expected and greet him patronizingly.

The Tsar met him with the remark, 'Sire, I hate the English as much as you do.' There was, in fact, some justice in this observation: for months, as Napoleon re-equipped his defeated army after Eylau, the Tsar had begged the British to open a second front against the French by sending an expeditionary force into the Baltic. This Grenville, desperate for peace and seeking to disengage Britain from the continent, had refused to do. Now the Tsar was deeply disillusioned with his old ally.

Instead, he sought to divide up Europe with the other continental predator. There was no reason why this should not work: Napoleon had no territorial designs on Russia: in Poland, the German states and Austria he had a buffer against possible Russian expansionism. An arrangement with Russia would allow him to dismember the already cowed Prussia, and would enable him to dispense with any threat from Austria, which was already beaten and would be deprived of the two allies which could make her dangerous – Russia and Prussia.

A favourable agreement with Russia would, in short, secure the eastern boundaries of Europe for a dominant French empire. Once it was concluded, France would be free to do anything she chose, expand in the Middle East or, as Napoleon had told Talleyrand, invade Spain, and strangle economically his most hated enemy, enfeebled Britain. He regarded Portugal and Sweden, Britain's two remaining allies, as ineffectual.

Napoleon's reply to Alexander's opening sally was 'in that case, peace is established'. The two men eyed each other in the comfort of the barge's well appointed central room. Small and now growing tubby, Napoleon was much less prepossessing than the lean, and

bright-eyed young man he had been during his twenties and early thirties. Yet he combined extraordinary mental and physical energy with a delight in the pleasures of life. By contrast the manic-depressive young Tsar had an inscrutable human dimension which the Frenchman could not fathom. He described him initially as 'handsome and excellent', with 'more intelligence than is generally supposed'. It has often been said that the sexually ambivalent Napoleon was physically attracted to the handsome young Tsar: 'Were Alexander a woman, I think I should fall passionately in love with him,' Napoleon said. But he would hardly have meant that remark to be interpreted literally: it reflected their common interests at that stage. There were compelling political reasons for their closeness.

Altogether they spent twenty days in each other's company, exchanging reviews, dinners and presents on the raft and on their respective opposite banks, while the real business was conducted by their underlings on shore. The feeble King of Prussia watched as his country was gobbled up. The only figure to emerge with credit was his tough-minded, beautiful young wife, to whom Napoleon took a shine even while refusing her entreaties. (According to a respected British envoy in Germany, Henry Williams Wynn, she had already had an affair with the Tsar). He wrote later:

> The Queen of Prussia had decided ability, a good education and fine manners; it was she, really, who had reigned for more than fifteen years; and, in spite of all my efforts and skill, she retained command of our conversation, and always got back to her subject, perhaps even too much so, and yet with perfect propriety and in a manner that aroused no antagonism. In truth, the matter was an important one for her, and time was short and precious . . .
>
> She was tormenting me for Magdeburg; she wanted to obtain a promise from me. I kept refusing politely. There was a rose on the chimney; I took it, and offered it to her. She drew her hand back, saying: If it is with Magdeburg! – I answered at once: – But Madam, it is I who am offering the rose! – After this conversation I conducted her to her carriage; she asked for Duroc [Napoleon's closest friend], whom she liked, and began to cry, saying: – I have been deceived!

She found an unlikely ally in Talleyrand who wrote:

> I was indignant at all that I saw and heard, but I was obliged to hide
> my indignation. Therefore I shall all my life be grateful to the
> Queen of Prussia – a Queen of another age – for having appreciated
> it. If when I look back upon my life much that I find there is
> necessarily painful, I can at least remember as a great consolation
> what she was then good enough to say and almost to confide to me.
> 'Monsieur the Prince of Benevento,' she said, the last time that I had
> the honour to conduct her to her carriage, 'there are only two
> people here who are sorry that I came – you and I. You are not
> angry, are you, that I should go away with this belief?' The tears of
> emotion and pride that came into my eyes were my answer.

The resulting treaty, signed on 7 July, was one of the most cynical in
history. Prussia was reduced to its 1772 frontier and in spite of the
Queen's entreaties the province of Magdeburg, seat of Prussian
power, was to remain in French hands. All of western Prussia as
well as much of Hanover was incorporated into the new kingdom of
Westphalia, to be ruled by Jerome Bonaparte, and would be part of
the French puppet Confederation of the Rhine. Danzig was also to
remain under French occupation. The Prussian army was to be
reduced to 42,000 men. French troops would remain until Prussia
paid colossal reparations, and the latter would also have to embrace
the Continental System.

Russia also agreed to abandon its old ally Britain and join the
Continental System. Napoleon and Alexander agreed to partition
Poland: part of the territory was given to Russia, while the rest was
to become the Grand Duchy of Warsaw, which would be ruled by the
French puppet King of Saxony, and would form part of the Con-
federation of the Rhine. In a secret protocol Russia agreed to help
France capture Gibraltar from Britain and not to oppose French
ambitions in Spain and Portugal.

In exchange for these concessions, Alexander was offered his share of
the spoils. As well as the slice of Poland and suppression of the
independence movement there, he was given a free hand to take

over Finland. Finally, Napoleon abandoned his recently acquired Turkish ally and gave Alexander a free hand to attack Turkey's provinces in the Balkans. In addition Napoleon abandoned another ally, Persia, to which he had promised Russian-occupied Georgia; instead he proposed a 50,000-strong joint Franco-Russian expeditionary force to conquer Persia and British India. Finally, Napoleon sought the hand of Alexander's sister Catherine in a dynastic marriage that would symbolize the carve-up of a continent between its two most aggressive powers, although he reckoned without the snobbery of the Romanovs and the hatred of the Tsar's mother.

The Prussians were not the only ones to feel resentment after Tilsit. In Austria there was revulsion at the treaty. Philippe Stadion, the new Austrian foreign minister, suspected that Napoleon was planning to install the Archduke Frederick, Francis's younger brother, as Emperor. Prince Clement von Metternich, who had been appointed Austrian ambassador in Paris, was a little more optimistic, believing the alliance would not last long.

Napoleon returned in triumph from Tilsit to Paris on 27 July to celebrate his birthday the following month amid scenes of extraordinary splendour. He had to reassert his authority in the capital, which had been seething with resentment against both its economic difficulties and his long absences. The chief intriguer was the duplicitous chief of police, Fouché, who was both a rival and an ally to Talleyrand, with whom he corresponded. The latter was by now thinking of overthrowing Napoleon: on his return to Paris he was 'promoted' to the meaningless post of vice-grand elector, losing his job as foreign minister, and joining the equally powerless former Second and Third Consuls who held the posts of Arch Chancellor and Arch Treasurer respectively. The new foreign minister, Champagny, was merely a tool of Napoleon.

The Emperor himself was not content with having secured his empire's eastern boundaries and with ruling over a population of 70 million people, unparalleled in Europe since the reigns of Charlemagne or Augustus Caesar. His country was crying out for effective administration. But to settle down to an era of peace was entirely foreign to his nature. He was a general, not a man of peace. Besides, he still was

opposed by a yet unvanquished enemy. So it was to Britain that he now turned.

Britain by the middle of 1807 appeared hardly to present much of a challenge. Pitt and Nelson were gone. Politically, the country was in a shambles: the collapse of the Grenville government had left the undistinguished Duke of Portland in power precariously with only the young bloods, George Canning at the foreign office and Lord Castlereagh at the war office, lending it a guiding hand. Even as they took power, the half-hearted nature of British resistance to Napoleon was apparent in a series of extraordinary and mostly failed minor military expeditions.

Only the first proved at all successful: this had been designed by Grenville. In 1806 the commander of British forces in Sicily, Sir John Stuart, set off with 8,000 of the 12,000 garrison for the Italian mainland, reaching the Bay of Santa Euphamia, some fifty miles north of Messina on 1 July. A French force under General Reynier attacked across the Lamato river on 4 July. The British doggedly stood their ground, then volleyed repeatedly and charged with their bayonets, entirely routing the French. Soon the remaining 40,000 or so French were moving to attack them and Stuart and his naval commander Sir Sidney Smith decided hastily to re-embark.

Two more peculiar episodes were to follow. The first was launched in February 1807, when it seemed that Turkey had decided to ally itself to France. Sir John Duckworth, a somewhat unimaginative admiral in charge of eight ships of the line and three frigates, was ordered to go to the Dardanelles and seize the Turkish fleet – twelve warships and nine frigates – to prevent this falling into Napoleon's hands.

On 19 February Duckworth sailed into the narrow Channel of the Dardanelles – twelve miles long and two miles wide in places – under intense fire from the Turkish forts on either side. Sir Sidney Smith, heading the squadron, destroyed eight frigates and some lesser ships in a vigorous exchange of fire before the little fleet proceeded to Constantinople. Duckworth ignored his orders to attack and negotiated with the Turks for ten days before getting nowhere, and deciding to withdraw.

By that time the Turks had reinforced their forts along the Dardanelles bringing 'stone-shot' guns to bear capable of firing giant pieces of
granite some 800 pounds in weight. These inflicted massive damage on
the retreating warships, nearly sinking five ships and killing 167 men.
The expedition had been costly and entirely pointless.

It was followed up by another under Major-General Fraser from
Messina to Egypt, with the aim of expelling the Turks from that
country. At first Fraser's 5,000 landed safely on 21 March and took the
fort of Alexandria, losing just seventeen men and taking two Turkish
frigates. The hapless Duckworth now also arrived and decided to seize
the port of Rosetta. He landed two regiments which marched into the
town with its narrow streets and were ambushed from the surrounding
buildings with the loss of a staggering 400 men, many of whose heads
were chopped off and put on pikes. The remainder struggled back to
Alexandria.

Another, larger, expedition was organized, but by that time the
Turks had rushed up reinforcements from Cairo. For some reason, the
British decided not to use artillery, and their 2,500 men were again
ambushed in the narrow streets and repulsed after appallingly bloody
fighting, leaving an even worse tally of 1,000 dead. Fraser withdrew
from Alexandria in September having accomplished nothing.

These desultory and largely disastrous expeditions were the sole
significant British operations against Napoleonic France in Europe in
some twenty months after the victory at Trafalgar. They reflected the
Grenville government's desire for peace on the continent and its
intention to concentrate on the further-flung British colonies. It
was in fact ridiculous for Napoleon to assert that at this time the
British posed a real threat to peace or even a challenge to him. But the
Emperor, having vanquished continental Europe, still needed an
enemy: and it was his attempt to enforce the Continental System –
the blockade of Britain – that finally once again galvanized Albion into
action.

Canning and Castlereagh, of a more warlike disposition, both learnt
of Napoleon's intention to issue an ultimatum to the Danes to join an
alliance with France and hand over the fleet at Copenhagen through an
extraordinary British intelligence coup at Tilsit.

A great spy of that period was the shadowy A. Mackenzie: nothing is known of his origins or identity. This extraordinary man had wormed his way into the confidence of the Russian commander-in-chief, General Bennigsen, before the historic encounter between Napoleon and the Tsar on the raft at Tilsit. Bennigsen at the time was furious with the way the Tsar had blamed him for the previous debacle at the Battle of Friedland. It has been suggested that Mackenzie actually managed to get aboard the raft, but it seems extraordinarily unlikely that a British agent could have smuggled himself aboard without being detected. He probably instead received his intelligence at second-hand from Bennigsen, who was aboard.

Mackenzie discovered the secret clause in the Tilsit Treaty by which Napoleon and Alexander agreed to 'summon the three courts of Copenhagen, Stockholm, and Lisbon to close their ports to the English, and declare war against England.'

His report reached Canning, then in charge of British policy, who promptly acted upon it by issuing an ultimatum to the Danes:

> Sir – Intelligence reached me yesterday, directly from Tilsit, that at an interview which took place between the Emperor of Russia and Bonaparte on the 24th or 25th of last month the latter brought forward a proposal for a maritime league against Great Britain, to which the accession of Denmark was represented by Bonaparte to be as certain as it was essential. The Emperor of Russia is described as having neither accepted nor refused this proposal . . . But the confidence with which Bonaparte spoke of the accession of Denmark to such a league, coupled with other circumstances and particulars of intelligence which have reached this country, makes it absolutely necessary that His Majesty should receive from the court of Denmark some distinct and satisfactory assurances either that no such proposition has been made to that court by France, or that, having been made, it has been rejected, and some sufficient security that, if made or repeated, it will meet with the same reception. I am therefore commanded by His Majesty to direct you to demand a conference with the Danish minister, and to request, in a firm but amicable manner, a direct and official answer upon these important points.

On 26 July an expeditionary force of 18,000 men under Lord Cathcart set sail for Copenhagen in twenty-nine transports, accompanied by a British fleet under Admiral Lord Gambier. Among the officers was the young Arthur Wellesley. On 16 August Wellesley's force landed at Uedboek and pushed towards Copenhagen, routing the defending militia with their 'long, lank hair and wild rugged features' at Kioge. Meanwhile Gambier's fleet opened up on the beautiful old city of Copenhagen and bombarded it for three successive days, setting the old wooden buildings ablaze from end to end in an act of wanton vandalism.

On 7 September, the Danes surrendered and for the loss of 200 men the British seized fifteen Danish line-of-battle ships, nine frigates, fourteen sloops and many smaller craft, as well as ninety troop transports. It was a triumph against virtually non-existent opposition. The expedition aroused controversy in Britain, where the public had not been told of Bernadotte's intention to seize the Danish fleet. Cathcart and Gambier's bombardment was crude: a more skilled commander might have found another way of cutting out the fleet.

To many it seemed little more than an act of piracy against a neutral. The reputation of Canning, who had ordered it, suffered accordingly. But it had at least been carried out with an efficiency untypical of previous British military operations on the European landmass. It was to have momentous, entirely unexpected consequences. On 23 September, at a diplomatic reception, an incandescent Napoleon, eager for vengeance, buttonholed the Portuguese minister in one of his contrived rages: 'If Portugal does not do what I wish,' he shouted at the Portuguese minister, 'the House of Braganza will not be reigning in Europe in two months! I will no longer tolerate an English ambassador in Europe. I will declare war on any power who receives one after two months from this time! I have 300,000 Russians at my disposal, and with that powerful ally I can do everything. The English declare they will no longer respect neutrals on the sea; I will no longer recognize them on land!'

Chapter 54

ECONOMIC WAR

The Berlin decree of November 1806 had marked the beginning of an intensification of the economic war between France and Britain. The British had replied with a series of orders in council: these declared a blockade on all ports from which the British were banned. Neutral ships were required to report to British ports and pay duty there before they could proceed to enemy ports. The French had banned all trade with Britain; Britain had now banned all trade with France, except through Britain, upon pain of seizure. Just a month later, on 17 December, Napoleon responded: any neutral which did call in at a British port or was seized by a British ship was deemed to be liable for seizure if it was intercepted by the French at sea or entered a French port. This in turn triggered off fury among the neutrals: the United States, for example, banned all trade with western Europe.

The impact both on Britain and on Europe of this trade war was colossal. Britain's exports to northern Europe fell from £10 million to £2 million in the space of two years. With the country in the middle of an industrial revolution, it was massively overproducing and desperately needed markets. The warehouses were overflowing. The Spanish empire, which had seemed such a promising target, looked less inviting after the defeat at Buenos Aires. Mills and factories closed and unemployment soared.

The effect was worse in France. An American traveller passing through the country remarked that most of the major commercial towns were destroyed and that there was little traffic on the streets: beggars were everywhere in evidence. Prices soared on the continent:

sugar rose to 5 shillings a pound, coffee to twice that, cotton to seven shillings a pound. As the economic crisis grew ever deeper, Napoleon added insult to injury by selling all British goods seized on the continent, undercutting French producers. Bourrière, the French resident at Hamburg, wrote melancholically: 'Persons who at this epoch were living in the interior of France can form no idea of the desolation which so savage a measure spread through countries accustomed to live by commerce. What a spectacle offered to peoples impoverished, and lacking everything, to see the burning of articles the distribution of which would have been an alleviation to their sufferings! What a means of attaching conquered peoples, to irritate their privations by the destruction of a number of articles of the first necessity!'

The ferocity with which Napoleon enforced his sanctions further alienated people. In Hamburg itself a German was shot for smuggling in a piece of sugar loaf for his children. Napoleon himself ordered the authorities at St Omer 'to have the crew and gear of the fishing-boat which communicated with the English seized at once. Make the skipper speak . . . If he should seem to hesitate, squeeze his thumbs in the hammer of a musket . . . Send me a general report on all the smugglers. Could we not get eight or ten millions out of them? What means can we take of bringing them to justice?' Napoleon instructed the lethal Fouché to bring smugglers to justice.

He also encouraged French privateers to wage war against English and neutral merchant shipping. Some 200 such privateers were operating in the West Indies alone, while Mauritius acted as a privateer base in the Indian Ocean. Underwriters stopped insuring ships trading between Britain and the continent, while insurance rates for American ships trading with Britain were up by half. Collingwood remarked of the sudden drop in merchant traffic in the Mediterranean that 'it is lamentable to see what a desert the waters are become'. The supply of British luxury goods to continental Europe – spices, coffee, sugar, silks, tobacco, dyes – all dried up.

The inevitable result of the blockade was a huge increase in smuggling. The British showed great ingenuity in continuing to smuggle goods in through the Mediterranean, in particular to southern Italy and along the coast of the Balkans, as Holland did in the Baltic.

Louis Bonaparte infuriated his older brother by openly conniving in illicit trade by his merchant people. He called the Berlin blockade 'atrocious' and 'barbaric', saying that it would 'effect the ruin of France and all commercial nations connected with it before it could ruin England'.

The French themselves were forced to connive in the smuggling in order to obtain essential goods. Bourrière recorded that shortly after the Berlin decree was issued, the French government had issued an order to Hamburg for the supply of 500,000 greatcoats, 200,000 pairs of shoes, 16,000 coats and 37,000 waistcoats for the *Grande Armée*. The bulk had to be bought in England. Napoleon would sell illegal licences for the import of sugar. Bourrière in Hamburg reported that in a single night, he allowed in some 60 million francs worth of smuggled goods from England, a third of the sum being passed to Napoleon on the quiet. In the Hanse, a single consignment of smuggled goods made Napoleon some £80,000.

In the long run, the Continental System also turned the Russians against Napoleon. At a stroke Russian merchants had been deprived of their prime market of timber – the Royal Navy. The Russians connived in the sanctions-breaking. Napoleon in 1810 urged Alexander instead to seize 600 'neutral' ships in Russian ports which in reality he claimed were 'all of them English'. 'If you abandon the alliance and burn the Convention of Tilsit, war must follow a few months sooner or later.'

Napoleon was furious with Count Tolstoy, the Russian ambassador in Paris, writing:

I have no doubt that Tolstoy writes home many foolish things. At a hunting party a few days ago at St Germain, he was in the same carriage as Marshal Ney; a quarrel arose, and they went so far as to challenge one another. Three things that Tolstoy said on this occasion were noted: the first, that we would soon have war; the second, that the Emperor Alexander was too weak; and lastly, that if Europe was to be divided the Russian right must reach Hamburg and the left Venice. You can imagine what might be said in reply by Marshal Ney, who knows nothing of what is going on,

and is as ignorant of my plans as a drummer of the line might! The fact is that Russia is poorly represented. Tell Romanzoff and the Emperor that I am inclined to favour an expedition to India, that nothing could be easier. If the Emperor Alexander can come to Paris, I would be delighted. If he can come only halfway, put the compasses on the map and strike the middle point between St Petersburg and Paris.

Lisbon and Oporto acted as huge entrepots for British smuggling into the continent and for distribution into Spain. And it was to tiny Portugal that the Emperor now turned his baleful attention.

The mutual blockades, the trade war and the licensed piracy on the seas deeply impacted on both adversaries. But its effect was worse on France because Britain retained mastery of the sea. After Trafalgar, there was a huge decline in British ships being captured. This was because so few French warships ventured out of port. Between 1805 and 1812, including at Trafalgar, some sixty-five French ships of the line and seventy-six frigates were taken, for the British loss of not a single ship of the line. On average just eight British ships were captured by the French every year.

Three British-French naval actions captured the spirit of this continuing war at sea. One was the strange episode of the Diamond Rock, as the British navy colourfully described it. This was in fact a basalt needle jutting vertically out of the sea about a mile south of Martinique some 600 feet high and less than a third of a mile wide. On three sides the rock was sheer. But in 1803 Commander Hood decided to land five guns by means of a cable to an encampment on the rock, manned by 120 sailors under the command of a lieutenant. From the lofty pinnacle the guns repeatedly harassed French shipping.

When Villeneuve's fleet arrived in the West Indies, with Nelson in hot pursuit in 1805, he was stationed in the great French base of Port Royal, just six miles away, from which he could hear the little outpost's guns blazing away against passing ships. He sent two ships of the line, two frigates and eleven gunboats to take it. The lieutenant promptly abandoned the two guns at the bottom of the cliff and held out with the other three, a 24-pounder halfway up the rock and two 18-

pounders on the summit. After three days' relentless barrage, two Britons had been killed and one wounded, while three French gunboats and two rowing boats had been sunk, with a loss of seventy men. Only when they finally ran out of ammunition did the British surrender.

In 1804 a French squadron consisting of the 74-gun *Marengo*, two frigates and two cutters under Admiral Linois came across sixteen plump East Indiamen off Pulo Auro. These were loaded with merchandise, were less fast than the French warships, and possessed only the most rudimentary weapons. They were easy prey, and Linois expected them to seek to escape under full sail. Instead Captain Dance, their commander, arrayed his merchant ships in a line-of-battle and made no attempt to escape, which puzzled the French, who feared a trap. (It was not unknown for warships to disguise themselves as merchantmen and roll out their cannon at the last moment.)

Tentatively, the French tried to cut off the rearmost ships, and Dance veered round to attack the French warships – something of a first for a convoy of merchantmen. When Linois opened fire, the East Indiamen with their few guns went straight for his ships and inflicted so much damage that he had to break off the engagement. Dance signalled a 'general advance' and for two hours pursued the French warships. For this extraordinary achievement – a merchant fleet actually driving off a predatory squadron of French warships – Dance was awarded a knighthood.

In November 1806 an even more remarkable engagement occurred: four British frigates, under the command of Captain Brisbane, of the *Arethusa*, were cruising off the island of Curaçao off Venezuela. Brisbane decided to have a go at securing the island, then under the control of the Dutch, who had four warships there and several gun batteries, including Fort Amsterdam at the harbour entrance with sixty guns. The attempt was to be made on New Year's Eve, when it was calculated the Dutch would be drunk and unaware.

At 5 a.m. the British entered the port of St Ann, and one of the ships grounded, but the *Arethusa* reached the quayside and the British gave the garrison five minutes to surrender or be bombarded. When the time was up the British opened fire on the frigates and boarded. Then

Brisbane landed and took the 300-strong garrison of Fort Amsterdam in ten minutes, including the governor in his nightdress. This was followed by the seizure of Fort Republique. Around 300 Dutch soldiers were taken prisoner and 200 killed or wounded, for the loss of three British dead and fourteen wounded.

Chapter 55

THE SEA WOLF

It was the exploits of another British seaman, in particular, which were at last to grasp the public imagination following the death of Nelson. In a country deprived of statesmen and heroes, an extraordinary Don Quixote of the seas now emerged with as much bravery and glamour as Nelson, yet who was even more wayward, eccentric, unconventional and determined to snub his superiors. Although far too individualistic and not senior enough to be a fleet commander, he was if anything a better seaman than Nelson and shared with him a fearlessness that very nearly made him his equal. Unlike the bourgeois Nelson, this young man was born the elder son of impoverished Scottish aristocrats. While Nelson was sickly and frail, the newcomer was tall, sandy-haired and dashing. His name was Thomas, Lord Cochrane, son of the Earl of Dundonald, an eccentric Scottish inventor and lord of Culross Abbey House on the Firth of Forth.

At the age of 17 years – much later than Nelson – Cochrane enlisted aboard ship as a midshipman under the command of his uncle, Sir Alexander Cochrane, a distinguished sailor. He had served without seeing action in the North Sea and the Atlantic before transferring to the Mediterranean under Lord Keith, where he had encountered Nelson, who gave him the never forgotten advice: 'Never mind manoeuvres; always go at 'em.'

Nelson gave Cochrane his first command, putting him in charge of a disabled French prize which he conveyed safely from Italy to Minorca in the teeth of a gale. Then in 1800 Cochrane was given his first ship: the tiny 158-ton *Speedy*, a brig equipped with just 14 tiny 4-pound

guns and manned by six officers and 84 men. His cabin was no more than four feet high, and the gawking six-foot-two youth had to shave by poking his head through the skylight.

Cochrane knew he was either being tested by his superiors, or that they had decided quietly to dispose of him as being too independent-minded – he had every reason to suspect the latter. They little realized that the diminutive craft would soon become as famous as its captain. He was asked to convoy a group of merchantmen off Italy. In the brilliant summer sun off Cagliari in Sardinia, with its picturesque, huddled houses, as the *Speedy* emerged on its first mission, the 25-year-old commander proudly gazed over his ship's company, which included an energetic and able second-in-command, Lieutenant William Parker, and his brother Archibald, still a midshipman. After several hours sailing across the glittering blue sea, one of his lookouts noticed a boat moving in like a shark to pick off one of the stragglers, a Danish vessel, in the now dispersed convoy.

Cochrane promptly ordered the *Speedy* to turn around and caught up with the little French privateer, the 6-gun *Intrepid*. Firing a warning shot, the *Speedy* boarded the prize and hauled her in. It had been a battle of the pygmies, secured without bloodshed, but Cochrane's first day's fighting had yielded a catch – the first in his career – 'my first piece of luck'. The long journey to Leghorn proceeded. Four days later five more 'sharks' moved in on two stragglers in the convoy and boarded them. Once again Cochrane immediately turned the *Speedy* about and caught up with the two stricken vessels. The five gunboats made off, but were forced to abandon their prize crews. Arriving a week after in Leghorn, Cochrane delivered one prize and 50 French prisoners to Admiral Keith.

Cochrane's tactic was simple: always go on the offensive. The following month he captured three prizes, and then three more in July. To the young commander, zigzagging across those dreamy blue seas at the height of summer, capturing craft with a warning shot and a boarding party, the whole dance seemed unreal and idyllic. He was a man in control of his ship, utterly confident of his sea-faring skills and facing little resistance from the small French privateers. He was fishing minnows, although to the captured merchant ships they must have

seemed like predators until they were rescued. The impression of the firefly skimming across the waters was captured in the young commander's log:

> June 16 – Captured a tartan off Elba. Sent her to Leghorn, in the charge of an officer and four men.
>
> 22. – Off Bastia. Chased a French privateer with a prize in tow. The Frenchman abandoned the prize, a Sardinian vessel laden with oil and wool, and we took possession. Made all sail in chase of the privateer; but on our commencing to fire she ran under the fort of Caprea, where we did not think proper to pursue her. Took prize in tow and on the following day left her at Leghorn, where we found Lord Nelson, and several ships at anchor.
>
> 25. – Quitted Leghorn, and on the 26th were again off Bastia, in chase of a ship which ran for that place, and anchored under a fort three miles to the southward. Made at and brought her away. Proved to be the Spanish letter of marque Assuncion, of ten guns and thirty-three men, bound from Tunis to Barcelona. On taking possession, five gunboats left Bastia in chase of us; took the prize in tow, and kept up a running fight with the gunboats till after midnight, when they left us.
>
> 29. – Cast off the prize in chase of a French privateer off Sardinia. On commencing our fire she set all sail and ran off. Returned and took the prize in tow; and the 4th of July anchored with her in Port Mahon.
>
> July 9. – Off Cape Sebastian. Gave chase to two Spanish ships standing along shore. They anchored under the protection of the forts. Saw another vessel lying just within range of the forts; – out boats and cut her out, the forts firing on the boats without inflicting damage.
>
> July 19. – Off Caprea. Several French privateers in sight. Chased, and on the following morning captured one, the Constitution, of one gun and nineteen men. Whilst we were securing the privateer, a prize which she had taken made sail in the direction of Gorgona and escaped.
>
> 27. – Off Planosa, in chase of a privateer. On the following morning saw three others lying in a small creek. On making

preparations to cut them out, a military force made its appearance, and commenced a heavy fire of musketry, to which it would have answered no purpose to reply. Fired several broadsides at one of the privateers, and sunk her.

31. – Off Porto Ferraio in chase of a French privateer, with a prize in tow. The Frenchman abandoned his prize, of which we took possession, and whilst so doing the privateer got away.

August 3. – Anchored with our prizes in Leghorn Roads, where we found Lord Keith in the Minotaur.

For the commander of the *Speedy*, life must never have seemed so intoxicating. Keith ordered Cochrane to the west, to attack enemy ships off the coast of Spain, a more serious commission. For the *Speedy*, if it got into trouble, would have no support within striking distance from the British fleet, and there were more likely to be large enemy warships about. But the young commander jumped at the chance, as it gave him a perfect opportunity to improvise and close with the enemy. Left to his own devices, he adopted an unusual and intelligent tactic – the first real sign that he was not some ordinary if brave young lieutenant, but a commander of real intelligence and ability. He kept well away from the Spanish coast by day, then moved in by night to attack vulnerable and unsuspecting ships. This required total command and respect of his crew, as well as immensely skilful seamanship, for the dangers of running aground were multiplied at night.

He struck again and again, picking off prizes without resistance; and as he did so, his reputation grew not only among the British public but also the enemy. The mighty Spanish fleet was increasingly irritated at this gadfly operating off its coast. It was time to swat the insect. But audacity was not the 25-year-old commander's only virtue: now for the first time he was to deploy another exceptional skill: deception. As Cochrane buzzed about harassing Spanish merchantmen, he fought no real engagement. Instead, showing superb sailing skills, mostly at night, he seized his prizes. But the risks were always present. He had his men repaint the *Speedy* in the colours of a Danish ship, the *Clomer*, which he had observed in the area. He recruited a Dane and dressed him up as an

officer; he was preparing the ground for the inevitable Spanish counterattack.

In the blustery, cold winter of that year, on 21 December, he was intrigued that a group of gunboats twice made out of Barcelona to attack him, and then turned tail, challenging him to give chase. This he did. Soon a huge ship appeared. As he approached, broadside, the ship's portholes suddenly opened to reveal that it was bristling with cannon. The trap was deliberate: the Spaniards had caught the fly. They had reckoned without his indifference to intimidation or brazen resourcefulness. He immediately ran up a Danish flag, as he watched this large Spanish frigate lowering a boatload of men to board him. Cochrane ordered his Danish crewman to parley with them, saying that they were a Danish ship coming from Algeria.

The Spanish boat continued towards them, unbelieving – and then Cochrane raised the yellow flag of quarantine. The Dane explained that the plague was rampant in Algeria (which was true), and that there were cases aboard. The Spanish party was aghast. If this was true, any Spaniard climbing aboard was liable to die. The boat rowed back to the mother ship, preferring to give the Dane the benefit of the doubt. The young lieutenant had bluffed his way through by a whisker. Cochrane wrote afterwards:

> By some of my officers blame was cast on me for not attacking the frigate after she had been put off her guard by our false colours, as her hands – being then employed at their ordinary avocations in the rigging and elsewhere – presented a prominent mark for our shot. There is no doubt but that we might have poured in a murderous fire before the crew could have recovered from their confusion, and perhaps have taken her, but feeling averse to so cruel a destruction of human life, I chose to refrain from an attack, which might not, even with that advantage in our favour, have been successful.

Meanwhile the merry chase continued

He stayed in Malta to see in the New Year on friendly territory. He dressed up, as a jape, in the clothes of an ordinary seaman for a fancy dress ball, but was blocked by a group of status-conscious French

royalist officers. Cochrane may have been drunk, unusually for him, and he lashed out at one of them. Although it was quickly clear that Cochrane was the audacious young British lieutenant making a name for himself off the coast of Spain, the Frenchman demanded satisfaction. The two of them went through the absurdities of a duel, Cochrane wounding the other in the leg and being himself hit in the ribs. But the experience shook him: 'It was a lesson to me in future, never to do anything in frolic which might give even unintentional offence.' It was a narrow escape for the immature young man but it also showed him the dangers of taking life too lightly, and losing his temper.

A couple of months later he pursued a French brig into Tunis harbour, violating its neutrality and plundering its cargo of ammunition but setting its crew free. Taking his prize back to Port Mahon in mid-March 1801, he realized he was being shadowed by a large Spanish frigate. Knowing he was no match for her, he flew before the wind at such speed that a sail fell from the mast. As he raced on through the night, he thought he had lost her. But in the grey of the morning he saw that the pursuer was still on his heels, although out of range. He pressed on through the next day, while the frigate, steadily closed on him. By nightfall it was almost within range and Cochrane's crew was exhausted. In a last attempt to escape, Cochrane instructed the ship's carpenter to secure a lantern to the top of a barrel and lower it from the stern, changing direction the moment the barrel was bobbing in his wake. The Spanish frigate bore down on the barrel, all eyes on the single light glowing in the dark, and found that the *Speedy* had disappeared.

It was inevitable, however, that, sooner or later, the daring 25-year-old would be caught. On 5 May 1801, came the reckoning. Almost insolently close to Barcelona, Cochrane set off in pursuit of a group of small Spanish gunboats, capturing one and then returning for another among the fishing ships clustered near the harbour the following morning. From behind those ships there suddenly emerged one of the most powerful Spanish frigates. The gunboats had been deliberately sent out as a decoy to lure Cochrane in. It was the *Gamo*, four times the size of the *Speedy*, carrying 319 men with 32 guns – 22

12-pounders, eight 8-pounders and two 24-pound carronades (capable of firing a huge amount of grapeshot). The *Speedy*, by contrast, had just 54 men, half of its complement because so many had been sent off to crew prizes. Its pathetic firepower of 14 4-pounders could inflict only minimal damage at 50 yards, and none at all at 100 yards.

Cochrane had three possible courses of action. He could surrender, he could make a break for it and run, although the *Gamo* would overtake him and was already nearly within range; or he could commit apparent suicide and engage the monster. In what was to become one of the classics of naval engagement he chose the latter course. He sailed straight towards the *Gamo*, placing himself within range of the guns, although his own were still out of range. The *Gamo*, astonished, fired a warning shot. Cochrane ran up the American flag to gain time. The Spanish captain, Francisco de Torres, already amazed by the *Speedy*'s decision to approach him, was thrown momentarily into confusion. The decision was made not to open fire, partly because the Spaniards knew that the little ship could not escape.

The *Speedy*, which was to windward of the *Gamo*, made the perfect target, and was within range. Cochrane's objective was to get around to the other side, where the hull was low and the guns would be aiming into the sea. The Spaniard's hesitation permitted him to do just that, and he ran up the British flag. The result was an immediate broadside from the Spaniard which, as he expected, fell short of the *Speedy* and into the sea. The next British move was more startling still: the *Speedy* moved straight towards the side of the *Gamo* as the other ship rolled back with the sea and reloaded its guns, to get so close that the next broadside would fire harmlessly overhead. It was a matter of seamanship, the movement of the sea itself, and split-second timing: a few seconds too late, and the *Speedy* would have faced a devastating broadside. He succeeded, and the spars of the *Speedy* locked with those of the *Gamo*. Another large Spanish broadside belched forth, passing over the smaller ship's decks, which were ten feet below those of the *Gamo*, the shot falling harmlessly into the sea beyond.

The fly seemed merely to have closed with the spider and was easy prey. But Cochrane had made his preparations: like a boxer grappling with his larger opponent at close quarters, preventing him landing a

punch, he had ordered his cannon to be 'treble-shotted' and 'elevated' – aiming upwards as far as possible. With the swell tilting his ship sideways so that it aimed up into the *Gamo*, he was able to fire straight up into the other's gun-deck looming overhead. He was lucky: the captain, de Torres, was killed in this first devastating broadside from below, which did remarkable damage for such small guns at point blank range. The little ship was still too close for the *Gamo*'s broadsides to harm it. As Cochrane put it later: 'From the height of the frigate out of the water the whole of her shot must necessarily go over our heads, while our guns, being elevated, would blow up her main deck.'

The two ships now engaged in a bizarre pas de deux. Cochrane spotted Spanish marines assembling and preparing to board the little ship beneath her; he veered away just far enough to prevent this, but not so far as to bring the ship into a position where the Spanish could bring their guns to bear. Then he returned to inflict a further upwards broadside. This happened three times during the course of an hour. One slip would bring about a collision, or result in boarding, or would have permitted the Spaniards to fire a devastating volley.

Cochrane in the smaller ship had the advantage of much greater manoeuvrability. But he was locked in: if he bolted, he would be picked off easily. Once again, attack seemed the only option available to him, even against a ship with six times as many men. He told his crew that the Spaniards would give them no quarter if they won, and ordered several to blacken their faces in preparation for boarding. The *Speedy* moved forward to the *Gamo*'s bows and, cutlasses in mouth as though in some old pirate story, some 20 of its men, including the young Archibald Cochrane, climbed up onto the Spanish ship.

As his advance party scaled the bows, he and Parker led the rest of his men from the back of the *Speedy* onto the middle section of the *Gamo*. Only the ship's doctor was left to steer the *Speedy*. By that time the Spaniards were confused and demoralized, and were uncertain of what to do about the vicious little ship attacking them in defiance of all naval convention and common sense. Cochrane wrote of the first sortie:

> The greater portion of the Spaniard's crew was prepared to repel
> boarders in that direction, but stood for a few moments as it were

transfixed to the deck by the apparition of so many diabolical-looking figures emerging from the white smoke of the bow guns; whilst our other men, who boarded by the waist, rushed on them from behind, before they could recover from their surprise at the unexpected phenomenon.

Minutes later, more were attacking them from behind. In the confusion they could not know how heavily they outnumbered the British attackers. Cochrane yelled at Dr Guthrie, who had been left in charge of the *Speedy*, to send in the next wave of attackers – although, of course, there was no one left on board. The startled Guthrie yelled back that he would. The Spanish officers heard and believed that another boarding party was on its way. They had been lured into a trap, believing the *Speedy* to be a small ship with a regular crew: instead it seemed crammed with attackers.

Cochrane yelled at one of his men to lower the Spanish colours, which, with remarkable coolness and skill, he did. The leaderless Spaniards, confused and demoralized, took this to be an order to surrender. The battle was over. Fifteen Spaniards, including the captain, had been killed and 41 wounded; just three British seamen had been killed and 18 wounded, one of them the valiant Parker, slashed in his leg and wounded by a musket shot. Cochrane could not yet pause. Before the Spaniards could realize that fewer than a sixth of their number had taken them prisoner, the fighting captain ordered them into the hold and had the two most powerful guns on the ship, the carronades, trained down upon them and manned by British sailors with burning fuses. Cochrane appointed Archibald to command the giant prize, which the little *Speedy* proudly led into Minorca.

The fight between the *Speedy* and the *Gamo* was the first of Cochrane's great naval feats. There had been no luck involved, and no piracy in taking on a much larger and more heavily armed vessel. Cochrane had shown a dazzling array of talents as a commander: the first and most important was that his crew were now so accustomed to his natural leadership that they had no hesitation in obeying him when he ordered

apparently suicidal tactics. Their behaviour was of men acting perfectly in co-ordination as a team.

His choice of tactics bore out his judgment: it would have been more dangerous and suicidal to run away than to engage. He and his crew had displayed faultless skills that had saved them in an almost impossible situation – in particular those precise movements backwards and forwards from the larger ship to avoid being boarded without bringing them out from under the arc of the *Gamo*'s guns. Further, he had displayed his remarkable courage in boarding a vessel when his men were so overwhelmingly outnumbered. His coolness, clear-thinking, and superb tactics under nearly impossible conditions had been extraordinary. Finally he had shown the talent for mischievous deception that was to become his trademark. It was, as has been said, an engagement unique in naval history.

Cochrane's astonishing feat did not capture the imagination of the old men in the Admiralty. The real start of the feud between the dashing young commander and his superiors can be dated from this moment. When he had been appointed to the command of the insignificant little *Speedy*, his superiors had never envisaged such a triumph as this. Their attempt to tame him or relegate him to obscurity, however, had backfired. He had performed as an individual commander operating on his own but that grated on men accustomed to co-ordinated team action. He had been continually contemptuous of such men as Lieutenant Beaver, his immediate superior; and he had too full an opinion of himself. The crusty Lord St Vincent, now elevated to First Sea Lord, was not impressed by Cochrane's reputation for insubordination, and possibly even less so by the popular interest his spectacular action had aroused. The old man had almost certainly come to hear of Cochrane's criticism for the escape of the French fleet in the Mediterranean in 1799.

The system of promotion from lieutenant to post-captain was through political favour, or through coming to the attention of the commander-in-chief, usually by serving aboard his flagship; or, more legitimately, through distinction in action. Cochrane qualified on at least two counts. He was clearly being victimised. Cochrane, although

formally a lieutenant, was effective commander of the *Speedy*, a position equivalent to major in the army. They took rank from the moment of their appointment, and would qualify to become admiral in this order, so it was of immense importance. After three years they became equivalent to an army colonel.

The young hero, who although critical of his superiors, bore no particular grudge against them and was in the full flush of success, suddenly found himself steamrollered by the naval establishment, as though, far from having achieved one of the most spectacular single-ship victories in British naval history, he had committed a major transgression. After a much lesser triumph, it was customary for an officer to be made post-captain (the modern equivalent of captain). Cochrane was denied this accolade for capturing a ship four times bigger than his own.

It was normal, too, for a warship of such enormity as the *Gamo* to be absorbed into the British navy, with a large part of the prize money being paid to those who had captured her. Instead it was announced by the Admiralty, without explanation, that the *Gamo* would be sold off as a merchantman to the ruler of Algiers, so that there would be virtually no prize money. Most offensively of all, the Admiralty resolutely blocked Cochrane's attempts to secure promotion for his able and courageous second-in-command, Parker, badly wounded in the fighting. How is this to be explained? Presumably the old disciplinarian could not bear that so junior and independent an officer should achieve such popular fame so quickly. For all his incorruptibility, St Vincent was a deeply unattractive figure, and he was certainly the prime mover in the Admiralty's unprovoked vendetta against the young lieutenant. But many of Cochrane's own contemporaries disliked him because he did not play by the rules and had thus in a sense 'betrayed his class'. On the other hand, Cochrane arguably had shown that he was not prepared to abide by the rules or take slights lying down, and a show of deference might have restored him to official favour. Treated badly by his superiors immediately after so extraordinary a victory, he showed exactly the same fearlessness towards them that he had in attacking the *Gamo*.

Meanwhile, he was ordered to go on a routine diplomatic mission to the ruler of Algiers who, ironically, had bought the *Gamo*. As he reported:

I was ushered through a series of galleries lined with men, each bearing on his shoulder a formidable-looking axe and eyeing me with an insolent scowl, evidently meant to convey the satisfaction with which they would apply its edge to my vertebrae, should the caprice of their chief so will . . . On reaching the presence of the Dey – a dignified-looking and gorgeously-attired person, seated cross-legged on an elevated couch in one corner of the gallery and surrounded by armed people of most unprepossessing appearance – I was marched up between two janizaries, and ordered to make three salaams to his highness.

This formality being complied with, he rudely demanded, through the medium of an interpreter, 'What brought me there?' The reply was that 'I was the commander of an English vessel of war in the roads, and had been deputed, on behalf of my government, respectfully to remonstrate with his highness concerning a vessel which his cruisers had taken contrary to the laws of nations'. On this being interpreted, the precocious scowls of the bystanders were exchanged for expressions of injured innocence, but the Dey got in a great passion, and told the interpreter to inform me that 'remonstrance came with an ill grace from us, the British vessels being the greatest pirates in the world, and mine one of the worst amongst them', which complimentary statement was acknowledged by me with a formal bow.

'If I did right', continued the Dey, through his interpreter, – 'I should put you and your crew in prison, till' (naming a captured Algerine vessel) 'she was restored; and but for my great respect for the English government, and my impression that her seizure was unauthorized, you should go there. However, you may go, with a demand from me that the vessel unjustly taken from us shall be immediately restored.'

Disappointed in promotion, he was allowed to resume his raiding career in the *Speedy*. He, soon capturing a six gun Spanish privateer which he put under the command of his brother Archibald and embarking on a raid in conjunction with a bigger ship, the *Kangaroo*, on the Spanish convoy at Oropesa. Cochrane was a strong advocate of

raiding along the Spanish coast, but he was one of its few practitioners. It was at this time, as he continued relentlessly capturing prizes, that he began to develop a paranoid hatred of the Admiralty's system for awarding prize money.

Cochrane's obsession with prize money, although driven by a strong mercenary trait in his character, was far from unjustified. The pay of able seamen at the time was a derisory 33/6 a month and for ordinary seamen 25/6, and this was usually awarded only when a ship had returned to port after what might be years of sailing on a long posting, and for a ship in port not until six months in arrears to discourage desertions. Sailors often quickly spent this in binges on shore. Prize money offered the temptation of huge potential rewards, however infrequently realized. One quarter of the prize was awarded to the lower ranks; two eighths went to the captain, and one eighth to the Admiral under whose command he sailed. An eighth was awarded to 'captains of marines, land forces, sea lieutenants and masters', to be divided equally among them. An eighth went to 'lieutenants and quartermasters of marines, lieutenants, ensigns and quartermasters of land forces, boatswain, gunner, purser, carpenter, masters' mates, surgeons and chaplains'. Yet another eighth went to the midshipmen, surgeons' mates, sergeants of marine and various petty officers, while the remaining quarter went to the crew and marines.

Cochrane's success was startling: by July 1801, after just a year in command of the *Speedy*, he had captured more than 50 prizes equipped with 122 guns and taken 534 prisoners. This meant that his own ordinary seamen were better rewarded than the officers in some other ships. But in a great many cases the prize money obtained was derisory, and Cochrane felt he had been cheated. His view was that other British commanders did not bother taking prizes simply because there was no money in doing so.

His evident concern for his men was a particularly attractive feature of life under his command on the *Speedy*. It was observed from the first how extraordinarily easy it seemed to be for the young lieutenant to get the best out of his men. This was no easy task in some ships, where

sullen and resentful men would barely do the bidding of their commanders.

Cochrane secured this respect in part because he was as good a seaman as any on board, in part because of his approachability and unfailing courtesy and above all because of his dazzling success. It was exciting to serve under such a commander, and the men would follow him willingly into danger. He lost remarkably few because he calculated the odds so carefully in undertaking such apparently suicidal actions as the attack on the *Gamo*. In addition, although Cochrane ran his ship efficiently, discipline was not excessive and he never had a man flogged – although he did not express opposition to flogging in principle. It was just that he had no need to resort to this deterrent. He was a natural-born captain.

Another spectacular joint action followed. At noon on 9 June the *Speedy* attacked a 20-gun xebec accompanied by three gunboats escorting a Spanish convoy. For several hours the ships fired broadsides at each other, until a 12-gun felucca and two more gunboats arrived from Valencia to reinforce the Spaniards. But the *Speedy* gained the upper hand, sinking the xebec and, eventually, all four gunboats. By now the *Speedy* had used up 1,200 shot and the *Kingfisher* had also almost run out of ammunition. Extreme measures were required to finish the action, and Captain Pulling ordered his ship to close on the fort, whose defenders promptly fled, while the *Speedy* sailed straight at the felucca and the other gunboats, which also turned tail. Three merchantmen were captured, three sunk, and four driven on shore, where they were protected by Spanish troops.

The legendary career of the plucky little *Speedy* was brought to an end, fittingly, in one of its most glorious actions. To Cochrane's fury, in the summer of 1801 he was assigned to act as convoy to the mail packet that ran between the British naval base of Port Mahon in Minorca and Gibraltar. The packet ship was barely seaworthy and the mail was transferred to the *Speedy* as soon as the two ships were out of port, and then back aboard the packet as they approached Gibraltar, to give the impression the packet had carried the mail all the way. Impatient and frustrated, Cochrane cruised along the coast, keeping an eye out for

possible prizes. He soon spotted some small merchant ships near Alicante, and got close. The Spaniards ran them aground. Cochrane could not disembark to capture them where they lay beached so he fired his cannon at them to set them on fire. One happened to be carrying oil, which blazed fiercely through the night, to Cochrane's satisfaction.

But the flames attracted the attention of three French battleships also heading for the Straits of Gibraltar. Cochrane's lookouts spotted the topsails on the horizon the following morning. Cochrane concluded that they must be Spanish treasure ships. He had made a fatal mistake. As he sailed towards them, it gradually became apparent that they were the pride of the French fleet: the *Indomitable*, the *Dessaix* and the *Formidable* were fast closing on the *Speedy*, which was trapped between them and the shore.

Faced with such odds, any other commander would have surrendered at once. Once they came within range, a single broadside by any one of them would be enough to sink the *Speedy*. But Cochrane was determined to make a break for it, believing, as with the *Gamo*, in the surprise of so bold a policy on his enemies. He put on all possible sail, dumped his little guns overboard, as well as all other surplus weight. He then began to tack as the ships approached so as to ensure that he was never broadside to them. The French guns in bow and stern managed to damage his rigging, but his bobbing and weaving prevented them concentrating their fire. He suddenly made a break for it between the *Dessaix* and the *Formidable*. The astonished French, who had expected the *Speedy* to flee at their approach, managed to let off a single broadside as the little ship sped past, but missed. The *Speedy* made it out into the open sea.

For a moment it seemed Cochrane had succeeded. But as repeated shots from the Frenchman's bows ripped into the *Speedy*'s canvas, the little ship began to slow and the *Dessaix* caught up after an hour, at last overhauling it. As Cochrane reported:

> At this short distance she let fly at us a complete broadside of round and grape, the object evidently being to sink us at a blow, in retaliation for thus attempting to slip past, though almost without

hope of escape. Fortunately for us, in yawing to bring her broadside
to bear, the rapidity with which she answered her helm carried her a
little too far, and her round shot plunged in the water under our
bows, or the discharge must have sunk us; the scattered grape,
however, took effect in the rigging, cutting up a great part of it,
riddling the sails, and doing material damage to the masts and yards,
though not a man was hurt. To have delayed for another broadside
would have been to expose all on board to certain destruction, and
as further effort to escape was impotent, the Speedy's colours were
hauled down.

He was rowed aboard the *Dessaix* and offered his sword to Palliere. 'I
will not accept the sword of an officer who has for so many hours
struggled against impossibility', the Frenchman told him chivalrously,
in exultation at having at last brought to an end the career of the
legendary terror of the Spanish coast and its commander. Cochrane was
treated with full courtesy on the remainder of the trip to anchorage at
Algeciras near Gibraltar.

When they reached Algeciras, Cochrane was informed of the
approach of a squadron of six British warships of 74 guns each
under the command of Admiral Sir John Saumarez. Palliere asked
him whether they would attack. Cochrane replied: 'An attack will
certainly be made, and before night both the French and British ships
will be at Gibraltar, where it will give me great pleasure to make you
and your officers a return for the kindness I have experienced on
board the *Dessaix*.'
     The French commander ordered his ships to move closer to the
protection of the Spanish batteries but, in their haste, the three ships ran
aground. As the two men had breakfast the following day a cannonball
smashed into the cabin, spraying them with glass from a shattered wine
bin nearby. They ran on deck to witness several marines being cut
down by intense British fire. Cochrane, not wishing to be killed by his
own side, discreetly withdrew to a safe place. He recounted what
happened next:

The Hannibal, having with the others forged past the enemy, gallantly filled and tacked with a view to get between the French ships and the shore, being evidently unaware of their having been hauled aground. The consequence was that she ran upon a shoal, and remained fast, nearly bow on to the broadsides of the French line-of-battle ships, which with the shore batteries and several gunboats opened upon her a concentrated fire. This, from her position, she was unable to return. The result was that her guns were speedily dismounted, her rigging shot away, and a third of her crew killed or wounded; Captain Ferris, who commanded her, having now no alternative but to strike his colours – though not before he had displayed an amount of endurance which excited the admiration of the enemy.

A circumstance now occurred which is entitled to rank amongst the curiosities of war. On the French taking possession of the Hannibal, they had neglected to provide themselves with their national ensign, and either from necessity or bravado rehoisted the English flag upside down. This being a well-known signal of distress, was so understood by the authorities at Gibraltar, who, manning all government and other boats with dockyard artificers and seamen, sent them, as it was mistakenly considered, to the assistance of the Hannibal.

On the approach of the launches I was summoned on deck by the captain of the Dessaix, who seemed doubtful what measures to adopt as regarded the boats now approaching to board the Hannibal, and asked my opinion as to whether they would attempt to retake the ship. As there could be no doubt in my mind about the nature of their mission or its result, it was evident that if they were allowed to board, nothing could prevent the seizure of the whole. My advice, therefore, to Captain Palliere was to warn them off by a shot – hoping they would thereby be driven back and saved from capture. Captain Palliere seemed at first inclined to take the advice, but on reflection – either doubting its sincerity, or seeing the real state of the case – he decided to capture the whole by permitting them to board unmolested. Thus boat by boat was captured until all the artificers necessary for the repair of the British squadron, and nearly all the sailors at that time in Gibraltar, were taken prisoners!

The British sent a boat under a flag of truce to suggest an exchange of prisoners. Palliere refused, but he did agree to parole the young British lieutenant. Cochrane returned to a hero's welcome at Gibraltar.

It was still a moment of extreme danger and anxiety for the British garrison on the Rock. A Spanish flotilla of six warships was on its way to rescue the three French craft. Saumarez, with just five ships, sailed into the attack as night fell. In the ensuing confusion two of the biggest Spanish warships of 112 guns started firing and destroyed each other, in two spectacular night explosions as their magazines went up, giving the British victory. Cochrane watched the whole show along with the garrison at Gibraltar.

A few days later Cochrane was formally court-martialled for the loss of the *Speedy*. Such court-martials, with all their ceremony and pomp, automatically took place on the loss of a ship. Cochrane was acquitted with honour. The same day Cochrane was promoted to post-captain, reflecting his achievement at last in capturing the *Gamo* – but the appointment was not backdated, so he was left at the bottom of the seniority list, well below many undistinguished colleagues of his own age and with no chance at all of being given a command in view of the huge surplus of officers to ships.

Cochrane's naval uncle, Alexander, and his father lobbied the crotchety old St Vincent on his behalf. This proved counterproductive. 'The Cochranes are not to be trusted out of sight', he thundered. 'They are all mad, romantic, money-getting and not truth-telling'. When he was told he must give young Cochrane a ship, St Vincent retorted, 'The First Lord of the Admiralty knows no must'. As another remarked, 'It became almost a point of etiquette with the Earl not to make [Cochrane] a captain'. To Cochrane's former commander, Admiral Keith, St Vincent wrote more reasonably 'It is unusual to promote two officers [Cochrane and Parker] for such a service – besides which, the small number of killed on board the *Speedy* does not warrant the application'.

Cochrane, a captain without a command, was made doubly re-dundant by the short outbreak of peace between France and Britain as a result of the Treaty of Amiens, and returned to Britain, where he visited his father whose second marriage to the wealthy Mrs Raymond

had given Culross a few more years' lease of life. Astonishingly, he decided to cross the Firth of Forth to go and study moral philosophy at Edinburgh under a famous pedagogue, Dugald Stewart. Cochrane was nothing if not a man of paradox, and high intelligence and deep thoughtfulness underlay the popular image of a half-crazed warrior.

In March, 1803, war was renewed between Britain and France, and Cochrane promptly and predictably applied for command of a ship. He was promptly and predictably fobbed off. He then compiled a list of all the ships under construction and sent it to the Admiralty. St Vincent replied huffily that they had all already been allocated to other commanders. Cochrane took a coach down to London to see personally the crotchety First Lord. Once again the old disciplinarian, after refusing to see him for several days, stonewalled him. The incensed young officer played his last and only card, threatening to resign the service. The First Lord looked at him with icy thoughtfulness and told him that after all there was a ship available at Plymouth. Cochrane was exultant, and travelled down on the first available coach. When he arrived at the great dockyard and saw her, his first words were, 'she will sail like a haystack!' HMS *Arab* was a converted collier, a sluggish flat-bottomed hulk with neither speed nor manoeuvrability. He had been outwitted by St Vincent once again.

As soon as Cochrane took to sea with her, he discovered that her greatest problem was that she would not sail against the wind. Ordered to Boulogne, he found it impossible to return: 'With a fair wind, it was not difficult to get off Boulogne, but to get back with the same wind was – in such a craft – all but impossible. Our only way of effecting this was by watching the tide, to drift off as well as we could. A gale of wind anywhere from N.E. to N.W. would infallibly have driven us on shore on the French coast: her employment in such a service could only result in our loss by shipwreck on the French coast.'

In a thunderous rage, whether by accident or design, when Cochrane managed to struggle back across the Channel, he intercepted an American merchant ship, the *Chatham*, on its way to Amsterdam, informing its startled and indignant captain that there was a British blockade of the River Texel. This was news as much to the Admiralty as to the Americans. Cochrane was promptly ordered north to protect

the Shetland fishing fleet, which was odd, as the Shetlands had no fishing fleet to protect. He was in effect in exile for nearly 14 months aboard a wallowing and useless tub, far away from any action.

Fate is nothing if not ironic, even capricious. Cochrane had secured his initial advancement largely through the connections of his aristocratic, if impoverished family. He had then made his name through superb seamanship and captaincy, excoriating those of lesser talents who had ascended through favouritism, and been obstructed every step of the way. The man who had most come to hate him, Earl St Vincent, despised Cochrane for his aristocratic hauteur and for his general lack of respect for authority. Now, with the accession of a new Tory government under William Pitt, a political supporter of his, Henry Dundas, First Viscount Melville, was appointed in St Vincent's place. Melville was political jobbery and corruption personified.

As a Scot he took notice of the incestuous lobbying of Scottish families, in particular the Duke of Hamilton, on behalf of young Cochrane, whose fortunes took a remarkable new twist: he was appointed to be commander of the *Pallas*, a brand new 667-ton frigate of 38 guns – 12 of them 24-pounders, 26 of them 12-pounders – with a crew of over 200. Cochrane, bemused by this astonishing change in his fortunes, was forced to resort to the pressgang to recruit his crew (his old one on the *Speedy* had been dispersed) and he was ordered to attack enemy convoys crossing the Atlantic.

The young captain left Plymouth on 21 January, 1805, and after a month's training at sea made his way to the Azores, where he could intercept ships making the Atlantic crossing. On February 6th he reported:

> We fell in with and captured a large ship, the Caroline, bound from the Havannah to Cadiz, and laden with a valuable cargo. After taking out the crew, we despatched her to Plymouth. Having learned from the prisoners that the captured ship was part of a convoy bound from the Havannah to Spain, we proceeded on our course and on the 13th captured a second vessel which was still more valuable, containing in addition to the usual cargo some diamonds

and ingots of gold and silver. This vessel was sent to Plymouth as before. On the 15th we fell in with another, La Fortuna, which proved the richest of all.

When *La Fortuna* was taken, its cargo proved to be worth £132,000. Cochrane generously allowed the Spanish captain and cargo-manager, much of whose fortune this was, to retain 5,000 dubloons each. His crew was consulted and shouted 'Aye aye my lord, with all our hearts.' As well they might because they stood to gain so much. By the end of March, four major prizes had been sent home.

Then disaster struck in an uncanny repetition of the events that had led to the capture of the *Speedy*. As one morning the *Pallas*'s masts poked above a heavy sea mist the lookout called that he could see three masts approaching. Cochrane himself scrambled up the rigging and immediately recognized them as French ships of the line. He had no choice but to run. Even as the chase began, the wind blew up, the sea grew choppier, and the mist dissipated. The water deepened into the troughs of an approaching gale. The three ships had much more sail than the *Pallas*, and were soon gaining upon him. But the gale was an advantage to him too: As Cochrane remembered:

> The Pallas was crank to such a degree, that the lee main-deck guns, though housed, were under water, and even the lee quarter-deck carronades were at times submerged.
>
> As the strange ships were coming up with us hand over hand, the necessity of carrying more sail became indispensible, notwithstanding the immersion of the hull.
>
> To do this with safety was the question. However, I ordered all the hawsers in the ship to be got up to the mast-heads and hove taut. The masts being thus secured, every possible stitch of sail was set, the frigate plunging forecastle under, as was also the case with our pursuers, which could not fire a gun – though as the haze cleared away we saw them repeatedly flashing the priming. After some time the line-of-battle ships came up with us, one keeping on our lee-beam, another to windward, each within half a mile, whilst the third was a little more distant.

This was extremely dangerous in a gale, risking the masts snapping or the ship foundering under its own speed in heavy seas. The ship plunged furiously forward, its bows swamped under water with each breaking wave. Even so the battleships gained upon him, two approaching at half a mile's distance on each side, with one coming up behind. But Cochrane had trained his men perfectly, and he had a plan. Ordering his topmen up into the rigging, as the boat thundered through the spray he gave them the signal to furl every sail at once. The French ships ploughing through the waters alongside could not fire because of the violence of the seas and because they were not yet within range. At exactly the moment the sails of the *Pallas* disappeared from view, Cochrane's helmsman turned hard over.

For the ship it was a moment of supreme danger. Still moving fast, but now broadside to the waves in these ferocious seas, the *Pallas* could easily have capsized – except that with no sails, as Cochrane had calculated, the wind would be unable to assist the sea in turning the ship over. Even so, she 'shook from stern to stern in crossing the trough of the sea'. In effect, she had stopped dead in her tracks, and the French ships of the line, their sails billowing, shot past for several miles downwind, while the *Pallas* tacked off slowly in the opposite direction, against the wind.

> There was no time for consideration on our part, so having rapidly sheeted home, we spread all sail on the opposite tack. The hawsers being still fast to the masts, we went away from our pursuers at the rate of thirteen knots and upwards; so that a considerable distance was soon interposed between us and them; and this was greatly increased 'ere they were in a condition to follow. Before they had fairly renewed the chase night was rapidly setting in, and when quite dark, we lowered a ballasted cask overboard with a lantern, to induce them to believe that we had altered our course, though we held on in the same direction during the whole night. The trick was successful, for, as had been calculated, the next morning, to our great satisfaction, we saw nothing of them, and were all much relieved on finding our dollars and his Majesty's ship once more in safety.

Cochrane's new orders were to join up with the fleet under Admiral Thornburgh to harass enemy shipping off the French coast. By May Cochrane had arrived off the island of Aix again. He embarked on a new kind of warfare – commando raids to destroy French signal positions:

> The French trade having been kept in port of late, in a great measure by their knowledge of the exact position of his Majesty's cruisers, constantly announced at the signal-posts; it appeared to me to be some object, as there was nothing better to do, to endeavour to stop this practice.
>
> Accordingly, the two posts at Point Delaroche were demolished, next that of Caliola. Then two in L'Anse de Repos, one of which Lieutenant Haswell and Mr Hillier, the gunner, took in a neat style from upwards of 100 militia. The marines and boats' crews behaved exceedingly well. All the flags have been brought off, and the houses built by government burnt to the ground.

He spotted a large French frigate, the *Minerve*, with 40 guns, which was twice the size of the *Pallas*, nestling under the battery of Aix. This 'large black frigate' had been plaguing the British for some time. Cochrane nevertheless ordered the *Pallas* to sail straight down the Aix Channel towards it. The French, astounded by this medium-sized ship taking on such odds, in their best protected and most formidable anchorage, their equivalent of Plymouth, 'scrambled'. Tacking backwards and forwards, Cochrane managed to avoid the notoriously dangerous shoals of the Aix Channel and destroyed another brig, while also doing damage to the rigging of the *Minerve*. The French were unnerved by the rashness of this crazy ship in their midst.

Cochrane sailed the *Pallas* between the *Minerve* and the shore battery, both of which were pounding away ineffectually. He ordered his ship to close with the *Minerve*, in preparation for battle but this was done too sharply. The two ships collided, their masts locking with one another, the guns of the *Pallas*, which had just loosed off a broadside, being knocked back momentarily. Under Cochrane's frantic direction, the British crew recovered far more quickly from the impact of the collision than the French, and let off another devastating broadside at

point blank range. No more than three solitary pistol shots came back in retaliation. The *Minerve*'s captain, Joseph Collet, had been the only man not to flee below under the onslaught of fire, and he coolly raised his hat in salute through the smoke. Cochrane, only a few feet away, was deeply impressed by his gallantry: when later he found the same officer as a captive in the stable block of Dartmoor prison, he had him moved to better quarters.

Meanwhile Cochrane was in greater danger than ever. His own ship was almost as crippled as two French frigates which were now bearing down to the *Minerve*'s help. Fortunately a British ship, the *Kingfisher*, under Captain George Seymour, was a little way off. Seymour had orders from Thornburgh not to proceed beyond a lighthouse above Aix. Seeing Cochrane's predicament, however, he decided to ignore these. He sailed south to escort Cochrane out. The two frigates had seen enough of the danger posed by the British and sheered off to go to the rescue of the crippled *Minerve*.

Cochrane returned to Plymouth a week later. His tour in the Bay of Biscay had been a dazzling display of aggression, fearlessness and skill: no other British commander since Nelson had achieved what Cochrane had, with his flying galley he had initiated the first commando raids; he had penetrated the very centre of French naval power at Rochefort, destroying its signals system; and he had crippled a major French ship twice his size and destroyed two brigs. The effect upon French morale was overpowering: nowhere along the coast seemed safe from this marauder. The effect on the British war effort, at a time of despondency, was equally electric. In the highest personal compliment of his career following this attack, Cochrane was dubbed by Napoleon 'le loup de mer' – the sea wolf (actually a sea bass, which is a fast-moving and fast-feeding inshore fish).

Cochrane's performance in the Bay of Biscay, coming after his exploits in the Mediterranean and off the Azores, clearly demonstrated he was the outstanding sea-captain of the time. But he had one colossal defect in the eyes of the Admiralty: he cared not a fig what they thought. So confident was he of his own abilities that he saw no need to ingratiate himself with his superiors or toe the line.

His new ship was the *Imperieuse*, a 1,064-ton frigate, about twice the size of the *Pallas*, and even faster, with 38 guns and 300 men, many of whom Cochrane had arranged to be transferred from the *Pallas*. Among the new recruits was a 14-year-old boy, Frederick Marryat, the son of a rich MP and West Indies merchant. Marryat was later to become the first great novelist of the navy in Napoleonic times, as Captain Marryat. He was vividly to describe his experiences under Cochrane.

When Cochrane arrived at Plymouth to take up his command in November 1806 Admiral Sir William Young ordered the *Imperieuse* to sea before she had been properly prepared. Cochrane was furious:

> She was ordered to put to sea, the moment the rudder – which was being hung – would steer the ship. The order was of necessity obeyed. We were therefore compelled to leave port with a lighter full of provisions on one side, a second with ordnance stores on the other, and a third filled with gunpowder towing astern. We had not even opportunity to secure the guns; the quarter-deck carronades were not shipped on their slides; and all was in the utmost confusion.

Cochrane took to raiding the French coast once again, capturing ship after ship with languid professionalism. Cochrane embarked on another raid inshore, against a French convoy guarded by small warships south of the Gironde. The convoy was protected by the formidable guns and defences of Fort Roquette. The French, hearing of his approach, had ordered the soldiers from the fort down to the beach. As they waited for the expected attack, Cochrane landed a raiding party further up which attacked the almost undefended fort, destroying its guns and blowing up the arsenal. On hearing the explosion the French soldiers on the beach ran in the direction of the attack, abandoning the ships while Cochrane's boats silently pounced, setting fire to seven merchant ships and gunboats. In the space of only 12 weeks, he destroyed or captured 15 ships.

Cochrane was ordered to the Mediterranean to serve under Admiral Lord Collingwood, who sensibly respected his independence and sent him to command the Corfu squadron, patrolling the Ionian Islands.

Collingwood, an exceptional and enlightened commander who had banned the use of flogging aboard his ships, then appointed him to harass the enemy of France and Spain. The vigorous young captain-MP resumed his old activities along the Spanish coast with gusto. He found it almost too easy – and he was now commanding a much bigger and better ship.

On 17 February, the *Imperieuse* spotted a convoy some eight miles west of Cartagena and pursued the ships along the shore. It veered away when it spotted four gunboats, anchoring out of sight of land, and waiting for these to leave their anchorage just after sunset. The predatory *Imperieuse* then moved in among them, firing broadside after broadside, sinking two with all hands and boarding a fourth gun vessel. The fourth escaped to Cartagena, where the Spanish fleet was at anchor.

From the captured prisoners, he learnt that a large French ship filled with munitions was at anchor in the Bay of Almeria, and he decided to 'cut her out' – take her at anchor. The *Imperieuse* hoisted American colours, sailed in close to the French ship and sent out two boats with boarding parties. The French opened fire, but were successfully boarded although the leader of the boarding party, Lieutenant Caulfield, was killed as he jumped aboard. However, the wind suddenly died away, leaving the *Imperieuse* and its prize becalmed under a heavy fire from shore batteries just half a mile away. The battery damaged the hull of the prize, which Cochrane had skilfully placed between the *Imperieuse* and the enemy guns, and at 11a.m. a light breeze took them out of range – not a moment too soon, as a Spanish ship of the line had arrived to help. The *Imperieuse* was, however, the faster ship, and got away.

After securing a number of prizes laden with wine, the *Imperieuse* ran into a gale and was compelled to seek the nearest safe anchorage – under a cliff dominated by an enemy barracks. The troops there opened fire, but broadsides from the *Imperieuse* demolished the barracks. Near Majorca, Cochrane landed a party to blow up the battery of Jacemal. But he was running short of food and water. He landed a force nearby which captured some sheep, bullocks and pigs. He landed a boat to forage water near Blanes. A large body of troops appeared, but

as they fired their muskets, the *Imperieuse*'s cannon, a quarter of a mile off, responded, and they fled back into the woods.

On 20 May a convoy of eight boats was spotted, escorted by four gunboats. These ran close inshore, firing briskly, and three of them grounded. Keeping up a hail of musket fire, Cochrane's men soon compelled the crews of two of them to abandon their vessels, and captured the third whose wounded captain had refused to strike his colours. As the wind got up suddenly, Cochrane decided to set the two grounded ones on fire, while managing to get one off as a prize.

But the *Imperieuse* itself was now in deadly danger, in only four fathoms of water as a gale blew up. Luckily the wind veered away from off the sea and onto the land and the *Imperieuse* was able to sail off by nine o'clock. In the course of the night the Spanish captain died. 'Every attention possible was paid to the poor fellow, from admiration of his gallantry, but anything beyond this was beyond our power. On the following morning we committed his remains to the deep, with the honours of war.'

Chapter 56

THE INTELLIGENCE WAR

Britain's war against France had been pursued on three main fronts: diplomatic and financial, in the form of subsidies to the continental powers of astounding dimensions; naval, in the constant fight to protect trade, disrupt French commerce and attack or blockade French warships; and military, in its continental exploits. But there was a fourth, shadowy front about which much less is known because so much was concealed.

Spies are drawn to wars like wasps to jam. The revolutionary and Napoleonic wars probably attracted the biggest swarm of spies, double agents, infiltrators, secret police, codemakers and codebreakers since the Elizabethan wars with Spain and possibly up to the two World Wars.

Equally, there were a stunning series of intelligence lapses. What the spies failed to find out was as often more important than what they did: for two thirds of the time the main adversaries, Britain and France, behaved like blindfolded men stumbling about trying to find each other in a darkened room. When they did encounter each other, it was sometimes more by accident than design. That didn't stop the two sides trying. Spying has been described as the second oldest profession: it was probably a great deal less satisfying than the oldest in delivering what it promised.

Among the truly spectacular intelligence failures of the Napoleonic wars, nine stand out: Britain's failure to foresee the French Revolution; its blind faith in the unthreatening nature of that rebellion until war was literally thrust upon it; its inability to infiltrate the royalist groups in

France; its failure to support them; the misjudgements surrounding the occupation of Toulon in 1793; the almost incredible failure to detect the immense armada preparing for the invasion of Egypt in 1798 and its destination which, in a brilliant piece of preventive espionage, was concealed from most of the French themselves; Nelson's chase across the Mediterranean in which he missed the French fleet by a few miles, his finding them being based on a hunch, rather than intelligence; and an almost exact repetition of this experience with the chase across to the West Indies in the months preceding Trafalgar.

On the French side there were awesome failures of intelligence as to the power and the nature of the British fleet, which led to the assembling and then dismantling of a giant invasion armada in 1804–5; a failure to anticipate the scale and ferocity of the Spanish resistance to French occupation; and a repetition of this experience in Russia in 1812. Perhaps the worst of all intelligence blunders was the British failure to detect first the movement, and then the direction of Napoleon's thrust into Belgium before the Battle of Waterloo, which so nearly secured him the battle.

Conversely the French attributed many dramatic events to British agents for which they were probably not responsible. One such was the assassination of the pro-French Tsar Paul of Russia; another, the murder of the ablest French general in Egypt, Kléber; a third, the assassination attempt on Napoleon on Christmas Eve 1800. The myth of the virtual invincibility of British intelligence probably dates from these times – at least a century and a half before James Bond.

For all that, intelligence was vital at many key moments. It can be subdivided into seven key areas, some of which persist to this day. These can be summarized as, 'special operations' – strikes at certain key targets by irregular troops or commandos under individuals outside the normal command structures, of whom Sir Sidney Smith was a towering British example; the activities of embassies and the spies around them to discern enemy intentions; counter-intelligence – the prevention of similar activities on domestic territory by the enemy; the infiltration of enemy émigré communities; the passage and interception of communications carried by despatch riders and – an innovation – by systems of interlinked signal stations within sight of each other on land;

the coding and decoding of despatches; and, most mundane but perhaps most important, the continuing watch of lowly agents for enemy ship and troop movements.

The most bizarre aspect of British intelligence during the revolutionary war was its tiny budget compared with the seniority of those that took an interest. From a fairly early stage it was apparent that William Pitt, the prime minister himself, devoted an inordinate amount of attention to intelligence-gathering, some of it of very dubious quality. It is hardly an exaggeration to say that he was for a long time effectively the head of British intelligence.

The chain of command ran down to William Windham, the Norfolk-based squire who became secretary of war. This able but shadowy personality reported directly to Pitt; beneath him was an under-secretary disbursing an almost incredibly small budget.

Shortly before war broke out, annual spending on Britain's 'foreign secret services' was around £25,000 (only about £5 million today). The staff consisted of two under-secretaries in each office, twelve clerks for home and ten for foreign intelligence, a gazette writer, a gazette printer, a keeper of state papers, interpreters in Latin and oriental languages, a collector and transcriber of state papers, an embellisher and two codebreakers. Foreign office spying was done almost directly through embassies abroad, the most important of which, of course, was that in Paris.

It was by and large a pretty rackety operation. A flavour is given by one early French-born British agent, a M. de St Marc, who was motivated entirely by money. Grenville outlined:

> the terms on which M. de St M. proposed to be employed and on which Mr Pitt imagined that it might be worthwhile to try him for a short time. They were that he was in the first instance to receive 100 guineas for the information which he is to give here, and if it appeared satisfactory 100gs more. That he was to be employed at Paris to give intelligence to Mr Hailes at an allowance of 60gs a month for three months and at the end of that time of 250gs if government was satisfied with his services. He states that it will be in his power to give copies of all material despatches sent by the French

Court to India, and also to furnish correct accounts of the number and distribution of the ships at Rochefort.

His masters were quickly disillusioned. One British official wrote:

> I have only seen St Marc once within these three weeks, that is to say, since I gave him the last hundred guineas. He is either afraid, or indolent, or unwilling. He has a very pretty Englishwoman with him that he calls his wife, but I rather suspect from her appearance that she is his concubine, and I think the style in which he lives is hardly warranted by his frequent complaints of distress, and his precarious existence. I cannot help doubting his having been to Rochefort as he pretended. I really do not think he shows any activity, and I find him uninformed upon the most common topics in public affairs.

All of this was small-scale stuff in the buildup to war. What was much more explosive, later, was the widely held belief in many French royalist circles that the French Revolution itself was a dastardly plot hatched by British agents working for Pitt to cripple Britain's traditional enemy. Certainly the French ambassador in London, Le Luzerne, believed this and pointed to the presence of Danton in London before the Revolution. A leading French writer, Camille Desmoulins, alleged that 'our revolution in 1789 was an affair arranged between the British ministry and a minority party of noblemen (in France).'

Pitt was alleged by one French journalist to have been behind the 1788 financial crisis in France, the meeting of the states general and the Revolution itself. An important part of the French court, including by some accounts the Queen, believed Pitt to have been behind the Revolution. The British ambassador in Paris, the Duke of Dorset, was moved to protest: 'It is unnecessary that I should tell Your Grace how entirely destitute of foundation is this as well as all other reports of the same kind . . . The French, I find, suspect, or at least wish to have it supposed that we have done by them what they would have done by us in similar circumstances; they are completely wrong in this idea.'

There had indeed been contacts between the British government through the secret service and members of the dissident community in France criticising the King of France. The purpose was to try to prevent the French joining the Spanish in the dispute between the British and the latter over the Nootka Sound. A British agent, Hugh Elliott, was despatched to deal directly with the leader of the dissident faction in the aristocracy, Mirabeau.

Pitt himself wrote to the King about the purpose of the mission:

> Elliott went lately to Paris, principally from curiosity, but before his departure he mentioned to Mr Pitt, that he had formerly happened to be in habits of intimacy with M. de Mirabeau, and might probably be able to learn something from him respecting the views of the prevailing party in France on the subject of the discussion with Spain. Mr Pitt recommended to him to be very cautious not to commit any body by his conversation but to endeavour to find out whether there was any chance of making any of the leading persons see in a just light the nature of the dispute between this country and Spain, and of thereby preventing or delaying any hostile measures which might be taken by France.

The King was somewhat alarmed and wrote that 'no encouragement must be given to forwarding the interested views of the democratical party'.

Elliott appears to have relished the role of agent: he wrote to Pitt: 'The sentiments expressed in my conversation with the deputation of the diplomatic committee were such as I thought best suited to my audience, and the particular purpose I had in view, but were not to be taken as literally mine. The speech I made was in every sense a French speech, and therefore the terms glorious revolution and others of a similar nature are applicable to their notions and not to my own opinion.' He claimed that the existing government of France was 'bent upon cultivating the most unbounded friendship with Great Britain'. A cryptic sentence says, 'what has taken place in my more intimate conversations with individuals cannot be committed to paper.' He added: 'I must observe that there is no such thing as a private

negotiation to be carried on here. Everything like a secret is avoided as dangerous, and likely to expose.'

This spy, moreover, assured the early French revolutionaries that the British government had no sympathy with Edmund Burke's celebrated attack on the Revolution. He argued:

> Burke and his book [should be treated] with that degree of levity, which I believe the best means of preventing government here, from being harassed with formal applications from the French court, for the prosecution of the author, as a libeller either of the present government of France, or indeed of the persons of the sovereigns themselves. You will also be pleased to observe, that I have fully expressed to Mirabeau, our resolution to take no share in the internal divisions in France, and have, I hope, fulfilled the whole of your idea upon that delicate subject . . . [He added that he] did not humour the erroneous wishes of our court by assuring ministers that a counter-revolution would not be interrupted in its march, that any attempt to stay it would only enrage an immense population.

This astonishing letter supports the view that Pitt, attacked later as the greatest prosecutor of the war against France, was perfectly ready to negotiate with the French revolutionaries at an early stage – many of them then being, of course, aristocrats.

One reason for Pitt's dalliances with the revolutionaries was the influence of the French King's relation, the dubious Duc d'Orleans, who it was believed – certainly by the French – was being heavily subsidized by the British. After his expulsion from France in October 1789 d'Orleans was said by French newspapers to be indulging in 'delicious orgies with the Prince of Wales and all the English lords'. The French ambassador in London did not share these suspicions of treachery, suggesting that d'Orleans was merely enjoying the social round of 'wine, horses, gambling, girls and Madame de Buffon'.

Nevertheless there seem to be grounds for believing that the British government, with the limited resources it had at its disposal for espionage, was secretly delighted by the political crisis affecting its greatest enemy, even if it is probably far-fetched to suggest that the

British instigated or even assisted the French Revolution (but American ideas, originally influenced by British ones, certainly played a major part). Pitt was to realize his grotesque mistake when within a few years the terrifying military machinery of revolutionary France was to turn upon Britain with an effectiveness never displayed by Bourbon France.

The importance of traditional cloak-and-dagger spying was thus limited. On a much larger, if even more dubious, scale, was that of the growing and eventually enormous French exile community in England and, conversely, the possibility that they were infiltrated by French agents, something about which the British authorities could do little. There were continual stories of French royalist groups in Paris betrayed by what would now be called French counter-intelligence moles in London who had penetrated the émigré groups.

The émigré situation was rendered all the more complicated by the intense divisions that existed within it: in particular those between the supporters of the fat, obtuse and indolent Comte de Provence, the pretender, and the ambitious and scheming d'Orleans, who to most seemed a more plausible candidate. The British preferred the first as being more pliable. The details of these émigré intrigues need not concern us, except in two respects: the impact of French agents stirring up dissent in Britain, and the harm done to British backing of royalist resistance groups in France.

The first can be quickly disposed of. As has already been noted, Pitt, an enlightened, tolerant and idealistic young man, was hardened by the impact of war into imposing deeply illiberal restrictions upon his country which violated many traditional British constitutional principles and were besides, largely ineffectual: the authorities of about 1795 behaved as though revolution in Britain was imminent – which was not just untrue but, had it been true, could hardly have been instigated by a handful of French spies. A repressive regime was instigated against traditional British principles of toleration which, on and off, was not to be lifted until the Grey administration in 1830: the only brief moment of light was to be Grenville's Ministry of All Talents, which reactionary circles in Britain quickly undermined.

Revolutionary and Napoleonic propagandists attempted to portray Britain as being on the brink of revolution, French-style, which overlooked the fact that Britain had already been through two such revolutions in the seventeenth century and was not ready for another. As far as 'the mob' was concerned, their power in mainland Britain was always much exaggerated, even throughout the French Revolution being largely manipulated by aristocratic and middle-class intellectual dissidents; it only occasionally emerged in sporadic riots. The French Revolution had a much more potent appeal among agitators and ordinary people in Ireland, but that was to do with the wretched conditions of most of the inhabitants coupled with the sense of colonial domination and the existence of a racial and sectarian overclass in the Protestant Scotch-Irish community.

Ironically, as has been noted, Pitt himself flirted with opponents of French absolutism and Fox openly and unashamedly espoused many of the ideals of the French revolutionaries until the process got out of control. Perhaps the most significant impact of the French Revolution on British politics was its splintering of the old Whig opposition into three distinct groups: the grandees, led by Grenville, who upheld traditional freedoms, and despised the small-minded court party around the King and its allies in the lesser country gentry, the 'Tory' squires: Grenville, although the second most ardent prosecutor of the war against France, was nevertheless much more open to negotiation than Pitt; the parliamentary liberals, surrounding the charismatic Charles James Fox, who were openly attracted to American and French revolutionary ideals; and the extra-parliamentary Radicals, around men like Bright, Cobbett and Cochrane, who occasionally slipped into parliament in those few constituencies where the franchise was a genuinely large one, and seemed to pose the most dangerous threat to the authorities.

The latter found it convenient to paint the Radicals in French revolutionary colours and openly to persecute and imprison such men. Thus the effect of French intelligence agents and revolutionary propagandists in Britain was largely counterproductive: to precipitate a crackdown by the government on opposition groups seeking to address the huge problems of a new industrial age of social change in

which workers and their families were crammed into the unsanitary conditions in the new cities of Britain. There is not the slightest evidence that Britain was on the verge of a French-style revolution at the end of the eighteenth century, or that French agents and their sympathisers could inspire one.

The effect of the British secret services in even comprehending, much less supporting, the counter-revolutionary effort in France was not just inadequate but laughable. Pitt himself veered between attempting to accommodate the revolutionary regime in France and seeking to overthrow it. He seriously botched the opportunity offered by the counter-revolutionary uprising in Toulon in 1793, which had it been backed with speed and efficiency by the British, might have ignited a ferocious anti-Jacobin flame throughout France: instead the insurgents were abandoned by the British and butchered in a frenzy of blood letting.

The failure to support the insurrection in mid-western France was even more culpable. The sad fate of the pro-rightist explosion in Toulon has already been described, as has the ultimate tragedy of the revolt in the Vendée. But there was an earlier, much less well-known failure surrounding the contacts of British intelligence with a legendary royalist leader, known only as Gaston, who in 1793 was said to be commanding an army of 200,000 men in the Vendée. Nepean, the operational head of the British secret service, commissioned a ship, the *Lydia* to come to Gaston's aid: 'For a cover the *Lydia* was cleared out for Lisbon, and to call at Nantes, by way of looking for freight; whatever information she could pick up she was to deliver to the government of Jersey or Guernsey, and all the English men of war had notice of her, that she might not be molested.' The *Lydia* provided money and equipment to the insurgents until captured later by a French warship. It was soon discovered that Gaston, a young peasant leader, had actually been captured and shot in April 1793.

Thus the performance of British intelligence during the Long War was far from impressive. In the case of French intelligence in Britain, it was negligible, except on three counts: the encouragement of Irish insurgents, which was a case of pushing at an open door; the infiltration of royalist émigrés in London; and the infiltration of French agents into

Britain and Brussels before Waterloo which nearly secured a French triumph by lulling the British into a sense of false security.

The work of a number of extraordinary individuals redeemed the general inadequacy of British intelligence. Apart from Mackenzie, who discovered the secret element in the Tilsit treaty, the three giants of British intelligence warfare were Sir Sidney Smith, his close and tragic associate, Captain John Wright and Thomas Cochrane, the master of irregular naval warfare.

Smith in some ways presaged T.E. Lawrence: his exploits at Acre have been outlined, and on his return to England from that expedition he arrived in Turkish dress, turban, robe, shawl and girdle around his waist with a brace of pistols, according to *The Times*. A brilliant linguist, he became a rival of Nelson, who in his extreme vanity resented him. Curly haired, hook-nosed and weatherbeaten, he was to become an instant popular hero celebrated by his own hornpipe and dances.

The son of an impecunious naval captain distantly related to Pitt, Sidney Smith was born in about 1764. He joined his first ship at the age of thirteen in 1777, taking part in the Battle of Chesapeake Bay in 1781 and Rodney's great victory in 1782. He then enlisted as a mercenary under the Swedes in 1788, fighting in two furious actions with the Russians, receiving a knighthood for his bravery.

The outbreak of war in 1793 found him in the pay of the Turkish navy. He chartered a ship, manned it with British sailors and arrived off Toulon, where he found Hood preparing to leave under attack from French revolutionary forces. Smith volunteered to burn the French fleet. The contemporary naval historian John Marshall described the scene:

> Sir W Sidney Smith, and the officers immediately under his orders, surrounded by a tremendous conflagration, had nearly completed the hazardous services assigned to them, when the loud shouts, and the republican songs of the approaching enemy were heard at intervals amid the bursting of shells and firing of musketry. In addition to the horror of such a scene . . . the dreadful explosion of many thousand barrels of gunpowder on board the *Iris* frigate, in the Inner Road, will ever be remembered by those who were witnesses

of the scene. The concussion it produced shook the houses in Toulon like an earthquake, and occasioned the sudden crash of every window in them; whilst the scattered fragments of burning timber which had been blown up, descending with considerable force, threatened the destruction of all the officers and men who were near the spot. Fortunately, however, only three of the party lost their lives on the occasion. This powder-ship had been set on fire by the Spaniards, instead of scuttling and sinking her, as had been previously concerted.

Sir W Sidney Smith having completed the destruction of every thing within his reach, to his astonishment first discovered that our perfidious allies had not set fire to any of the ships in the basin before the town; he therefore hastened thither with the boats under his command, for the purpose of endeavouring to counteract the treachery of the Spaniards; when lo! To his great mortification, he found the boom at the entrance laid across, and was obliged to desist in his attempts to cut it, from the repeated volleys of musketry directed towards his boats from the flagship, and the wall of the Battery Royale. He therefore proceeded to burn the *Héros* and *Thémistocle*, prison-ships, in the Inner Road, which he effected, after disembarking all the captives. This service was scarcely performed, when the explosion of the *Montreal*, another powder-ship, took place, by means equally unsuspected and base, with a shock even greater than the first; but the lives of Sir W Sidney Smith and the gallant men who served under him, were providentially saved from the imminent danger in which they were thus a second time placed.

Smith followed this up with raiding parties against the French in the Atlantic, before being captured in April 1796 and spending two years in the grim Temple prison in Paris before his famous escape; the heroic defence of Acre followed.

Smith was a close friend of the notorious Lord Camelford, cousin of both Grenville and Pitt, and had an affair with Princess Caroline, the abandoned wife of the Prince of Wales. In 1805 he was posted to serve under Nelson. Sir William Hamilton wrote: 'Be assured that Lord Nelson now understands Sir Sidney well and really loves and esteems

him; and . . . will give him every proof of it, if ever they should meet on service together . . . They are certainly the two greatest heroes of the age.'

Smith urged an attack on Boulogne using Robert Fulton's torpedoes and William Congreve's rockets. He reconnoitred the coast with General Sir John Moore, who displayed a soldier's caution. Smith replied: 'General Moore, I am persuaded, would do his utmost to realize any plan laid down for him . . . but he is too wary to undertake such a task voluntarily, though, of course, foremost when ordered to go to work. We go on, as usual, pleasantly and well together.'

On 1 October 1805 Smith set out in eight ships carrying Fulton's primitive torpedoes, as well as catamarans equipped with some 500 rockets each. These craft were thought to be more stable on recoil than ordinary boats, which proved to be the very opposite of the case. They rolled so badly that most of the rockets hit the water. The torpedoes also proved ineffectual. The First Sea Lord, Lord Keith, fulminated: 'We shall get our ships crippled, fail of success and at a great expense . . . To support this kind of warfare . . . will bring our judgment into disrepute and end in nothing but disgrace. The vessels employed upon it might be used to much more advantage in an attempt on the enemy's fleet at Cadiz.'

In spite of his record for crazy antics, Smith was given command of a squadron of Collingwood's Mediterranean fleet in 1806 where he accurately reflected on Napoleon's megalomania: 'Knowing Bonaparte as I know him, I can easily imagine his thirst to realize a speculation manqué on Constantinople and the route to India. He cannot fail to find it increase on being nearer to the capital of the Eastern Empire than he is to his own . . . All this he can do if he is not counteracted . . . it will be a giant's labour to eradicate them from the Hellespont and Bosphorous if they once establish themselves there. I dare say I shall be looked to for the Herculean labour.' The following year he took part in Duckworth's assault on Constantinople.

He also successfully supervised the evacuation of the Portuguese court from Lisbon later in the year. Towards the end of the war he fought off Sicily and besieged Algiers. He lived his later life in Paris, ironically enough, surviving to the ripe age of seventy-five, dying in 1840.

Most poignant of all was the fate of the third great spy, Captain John Wright, Smith's great friend. Wright had been imprisoned along with Smith at the Temple prison in 1798. After acting as a spy and liaison officer with royalists they had been captured while becalmed off Le Havre. Smith had nearly been executed before his spectacular rescue in 1800 by royalists under the direction of William Windham, head of the British secret service.

Soon afterwards Wright turned up in Paris to the disgust of the British ambassador, the able Lord Whitworth:

> I fear he is too well known to be of any material service; and I will confess to your Lordship that I am not without apprehension that, in a moment of irritation like the present, it may be recollected that he was a prisoner here and that he escaped from prison. I cannot but help think a less remarkable person, however intelligent Captain Wright may be, might have been equally useful without the risk of adding another pierre d'achoppement to the many which we may expect to find in our way. I have, however, told him that he might remain here for the present and see his old friends, if they are willing under the present circumstances to renew their acquaintance – which I very much doubt.

Nevertheless Wright behaved with unexpected sensitivity. In August 1803 he performed his most spectacular mission, landing George Cadoudal, the wily planner of the assassination attempt on Napoleon in rue Nicaise, near Dieppe, and General Pichegru, another royalist plotter, ten days later. Wright reported directly back to Pitt at Fort Walmer on the Dover coast, which acted as a base not just for espionage but for shipping goods, supplies and guns to sympathizers in France.

Subsequently Wright was given command of a small squadron of spyships off the French coast, only to be wounded and captured. A week after the Battle of Trafalgar he was found dead, as we have seen, his throat slit, supposedly having committed suicide on learning of the French victory at Ulm.

Mackenzie, Smith, Wright and Cochrane: these were the fathers of British intelligence. Mackenzie's intelligence was responsible for one of

the most controversial episodes of the war; Smith was to perform spectacularly in a single military action, a series of minor naval ones, and supremely as an intelligence officer; Wright missed immortality only because of the failure of the plot against Napoleon. Cochrane became the second greatest sailor of the age. Such was the glamorous, secretive hit-and-miss world of the early cloak-and-dagger men. But the greatest of all perhaps were the legions of lowly men observing troop and fleet movements, at great danger to their lives, in an age when there were no telephone or satellite intercepts to allow them to do so without risk.

Chapter 57

PENINSULAR UPRISING

Napoleon, after his triumphal return to Paris from Prussia in the summer of 1807 and the reassertion of his authority, was getting restless. Bored by the capital, and neglecting the threat still posed by Britain, he looked to new areas of conquest. He conceived a dream of first sewing together a three-pronged alliance, supposedly against England, but in reality to add to his dominions. He would join the Russians and the Austrians and invade the Ottoman empire, thence march through Persia to occupy British India. A second offensive would be mounted to take control of Britain's naval base in Sicily and thus ensure total control of the Mediterranean. (As a start, Reggio Calabria was taken on 2 February 1808 and Scylla, across the Strait of Messina, on 17 February). Thirdly he would occupy the Iberian Peninsula and from there launch an expedition across the Straits of Gibraltar and invade North Africa. Of the three, the last was to be pursued most vigorously. A variety of pretexts was trotted out: it was necessary to enforce the Continental System by taking over Britain's last ally and major trading entrepot, Portugal, and therefore it was necessary to cross Spain. Spain also needed liberating from the Bourbons.

It seems clear that Napoleon simply wanted to add the plump prize of Spain, with its glittering South American empire, to his domains. First though, he needed to take Portugal and its rather poor – in those days – Brazilian colony, close allies of Britain. In September 1807 Marshal Junot and an army corps were sent to the Spanish border, with the demand that Godoy allow them to cross northern Spain to subdue

Portugal. Godoy, cowardly and venal, agreed in exchange for his being given the huge slice of Portugal south of the Tagus as his personal kingdom.

The regent of Portugal, Prince João, was approached. He agreed to close his ports and declare war on Britain, but then prevaricated. Losing patience, Napoleon instructed Junot to invade Portugal on 12 October as João dithered. Junot crossed the rugged and sodden hills of northern Spain to Salamanca, which he reached on 12 November and then drove on towards Lisbon.

The British moved swiftly. Under the rival dual leadership of Canning and Castlereagh – Portland being a figurehead – Lord Strangford, the energetic British ambassador in Lisbon, Sir Sidney Smith in charge of a naval squadron, and the crusty Lord St Vincent himself had decided to make up João's mind for him. St Vincent may have actually threatened to bombard Lisbon to persuade the Portuguese court to depart for Brazil – in those days little more than a tropical backwater – which they were deeply reluctant to do.

There followed a remarkable exodus. On 27 November 1807 the mad Queen Maria made an appalling scene on the quayside, refusing to embark because she believed she was being taken to die on the guillotine, like Louis XVI. She had to be coaxed aboard gently. Almost the entire court and nobility of Portugal were leaving Lisbon. With them the royal family took the crown jewels, the royal library, the royal silver, the royal carriages, a multitude of other belongings, and a huge personal retinue. About 10,000 Portuguese retainers and officials boarded some forty ships to make the long journey across the Atlantic to Brazil, escorted by British warships.

All were aboard, but there was no wind. On the 28th Junot reached Santarém, his progress held up by an incessant downpour and the resultant mud. The following day he had reached Cartaxo, but a slight breeze had by then enabled the ships to slip down the Tagus as far as the mouth of the estuary. The speed with which the Portuguese court moved took Junot by surprise. On the night he heard of it he leapt from his bed at Cartaxo and ordered 1,000 of his grenadiers down the rain-sodden road to Lisbon. The following day they reached the Bay of Bom Suceso at the tip of the Tagus estuary in time to open fire on the

sails disappearing over the horizon. When news of the Portuguese court's escape reached Napoleon he exploded in one of his more spectacular rages. Years later, in exile on St Helena, he described João as 'the only one who ever tricked me'.

Napoleon was now determined to seize Spain itself, although as a vassal state it was much more conveniently governed through the puppet Charles and Godoy than directly by the French. Napoleon's seizure of Italy, and in particular of Naples, as well as the punitive treatment of Prussia, were the moments at which French conquests ceased to be defensible and became merely acquisitive. The invasion of Spain was on another plane altogether. The Prussian annexation could be defended in theory as self-defence against an attacker, Naples as a pre-emptive strike against a British base. There was no such excuse for the invasion of Spain. It was imperial aggrandisement. And it was a terrible misreading of the country. Unlike Italy, so long supine before invading and occupying powers, as well as fragmented, Spain was the hub of a powerful global empire which even then was perhaps the world's most extensive. Spain was in decline, certainly, and had no military ambitions in Europe, but it was a misjudgement to assume that it could simply be colonized and that its people would tamely accept this.

The turn of the tide against Napoleon therefore began in Spain in 1808, not with the invasion of Russia in 1812. He had embarked upon an impossible campaign of conquest against one of the proudest people on earth. Nor was it the British initially who mounted the greatest struggle against the Emperor: it was the Spanish and Portuguese themselves. Napoleon wrote contemptuously: 'If this thing were going to cost me 80,000 men I wouldn't do it; but it won't take 12,000; it's mere child's play. I don't want to hurt anybody, but when my great political chariot is rolling, it's as well to stand from under the wheels.'

Napoleon, the supreme opportunist, as always took advantage of events as they occurred. Some 100,000 French troops crossed the Pyrenees. On 16 February the French, on a pretext, seized Pamplona, San Sebastian, Figueras, and Barcelona. Napoleon then ordered Murat, at the head of the invading army, to march on Madrid.

There is no doubt he had annexation in mind. But an uprising

occurred on 17 March, known as the Tumult of Aranjuez, in which a column of dissident Spanish soldiers and peasants, furious at the corruption of the court and its supine pro-French policy, as well as the country's economic crisis, marched against Godoy, who had to take refuge in a rolled up carpet to preserve his life.

The chief minister's fall was followed by that of the King himself, who was forced by the mob to abdicate in favour of his twenty-four-year-old son, Ferdinand VII, a spiteful and cruel reactionary under the influence of his appalling aunt, the hunchback dwarf Carlota, who had married the regent of Portugal. Ferdinand loathed Godoy, who he believed was plotting to exclude him from the succession. All this provided the pretext for French intervention in Spain and its conversion from a quasi-colony of France into a full-blown one.

Ferdinand had, in fact, been conspiring secretly with Napoleon, and had been arrested by Godoy for treason, but the Spanish people were unaware of this, and believed him to be an anti-French patriot by comparison with his parents and with Godoy. Napoleon moved swiftly: he travelled immediately down to Bayonne, where he arrested Charles IV as well as Godoy and Ferdinand, declaring that he would mediate between the warring factions. Ordinary Spaniards understood what that meant, and crowds attempted to decouple Ferdinand's carriage from its horses in an effort to delay him; but the lantern-jawed prince took no notice, believing that he was Napoleon's trusted ally and that his father and Godoy would be regarded by the French as enemies.

He arrived at Bayonne on 20 April, ten days ahead of his parents. There, to his astonishment, Napoleon took Charles's side against him, insisting that the young King abdicate immediately, and threatening to arrest him if he did not. Napoleon wrote on May 1st:

I have just met the King and Queen, who are very glad to be here. The King received his sons with displeasure. All the Spaniards have kissed hands: but the old King appears to be very angry with them.

The Prince of the Asturias is very stupid, very surly, very hostile to France; with my knowledge of how to handle men, his twenty-four years' experience makes no impression.

King Charles is a good soul. Whether it comes from his position, or from his circumstances, he gives the impression of an honest and kindly patriarch. The Queen's heart and history are revealed in her face; that is saying everything. It surpasses all one could imagine. They are both of them dining with me. The Prince of Peace [Godoy] looks like a bull.

The next stage was to force the old man to hand over his throne to Napoleon. The Emperor had already asked his brother Louis, King of Holland, to take over Spain. When he refused, the almost equally reluctant Joseph was told to abandon his throne in Naples – which he was deeply unhappy about doing – and become King of Spain. This incensed the much more capable Murat, who had not been chosen because of Napoleon's suspicion that he was conniving against him.

Napoleon insouciantly behaved as though he was merely adding a jewel to the imperial crown. The wretched Charles IV, Queen Maria Luisa and Godoy were exiled to an unhappy house arrest in the forest of Compiègne and later Italy, while Ferdinand and his retainers were sent off to Talleyrand's estates in Valençay – a kind of punishment, in fact for the former French foreign minister, who entirely disapproved of the Spanish venture. There they enjoyed hunting, music and dancing as well as girlfriends – including, by all accounts, the delectable Madame Talleyrand. Talleyrand never forgave the Emperor for this personal humiliation, as well as for the contemptuous way in which he had treated one of the foremost monarchs in Europe.

Even before Ferdinand's 'abdication' in favour of his father on 5 May, there had occurred one of the bloodiest yet most potent moments in that country's proud history: 2 May, the Dos de Mayo, was perhaps the greatest assertion of Spanish national spirit there has ever been. The people of Madrid rose in their thousands to cut down every Frenchman they could find. The massacre continued for three hours until Murat regained control and ordered an equally bloody repression. French artillery was brought in to mow down demonstrators in the main streets.

If Murat and Napoleon thought the nation was cowed, they were appallingly mistaken. On 20 May a mob seized the governor of

Badajoz, suspected of French sympathies, and dragged him through the streets to his death. On 3 May it was the turn of the garrison of Cartagena. On 24 August an uprising took place in Valencia, and the following day in Asturias, 500 miles away, in an uncoordinated insurrection. There the local notables called for a declaration of war on France and the restoration of Ferdinand to the throne. On 27 May Seville rose up. Oviedo and Zaragoza also took to the streets, as did Galicia on 30 May and Catalonia on 7 June. At Cadiz the governor was beaten to death.

This spontaneous national resistance movement caught Napoleon entirely by surprise. All over Europe local populations had sullenly acquiesced in his rule once their rulers had made peace, in some cases actually welcoming the French as liberators from colonial oppression, in others believing that they were merely exchanging masters. Paradoxically in Spain, where the peasantry lived in conditions of wretched misery while their court had been one of the most corrupt and decadent in Europe, the people did not acquiesce in their Napoleonic takeover. Moreover, Spain was one of the most fractured countries in Europe, with a strong sense of local identity in each of its regions: Catalonia, the Basque country, Cadiz and Extremadura. That the country should have united against the common foe was even more astonishing.

One explanation is that the Spanish had not actually been defeated in battle by the French, as had happened elsewhere. Their rulers had effectively been kidnapped and national pride was affronted. Another is the power of the provincial gentry and clergy and the strong sense of local identity in the incredibly remote country regions of Spain at that time. In the case of Austria and Russia, moreover, occupied border territories had been taken by the French (although this was not the case with Prussia, which had been dismembered). In Spain the very heartland of an ancient empire had been seized: Napoleon was later on to encounter the same sort of resistance from the brutalized yet nationalist peasants of Russia.

On 30 May the gentry of Oviedo despatched an emissary to seek help from Britain: it took him seven days to arrive. They reached London to be feted by Canning, the foreign minister. A junta was set

up in Seville and Cadiz declaring war against France and proclaiming allegiance to Ferdinand VII.

At Cadiz, Collingwood's ships helped the Spanish seize the remaining French ships trapped after Trafalgar. For once the British had troops available to help their continental allies – 9,500 men under Sir Arthur Wellesley at Cork, who had been preparing to depart with Francisco de Miranda to seize Venezuela, or possibly Mexico, from the Spanish empire; 5,000 men more at Venga; 3,000 at Malta; and 8,000 off Sweden under the country's best soldier, Sir John Moore (who had been stuck at Gothenburg for three months negotiating with the insane King, who ordered him arrested: the British general had escaped his captors from Stockholm at midnight).

For once, too, the British resolved to act with speed and decisiveness. Quite why must remain a matter of conjecture. Under Pitt virtually every opportunity for a major continental entanglement had been rebuffed except in concert with big continental allies: conflicting chains of command usually condemned their expeditions to disaster. The British had singularly failed to help the rebels in the Vendée and at Toulon.

The cautious Pitt and the more interventionist Grenville had now been replaced by entirely new blood: the brilliant and mercurial young Canning, and the highly efficient, if cold and reactionary, Castlereagh, represented both major strands of British opinion, liberal and conservative: both were determined to seize the opportunity provided by the uprising in Spain for continental intervention. They instantly realized the potential in a country that had arisen almost in unison against Napoleon. The Peninsular War was about to begin.

Chapter 58

MOORE'S ARMY

The British army, on the eve of its first great continental commitment since Marlborough (although the forces sent to begin with were, as usual, inadequate) had very little reputation to speak of.

If this sounds harsh, it is accurate. The greatest military achievement of the mid-eighteenth century had been the conquest of India by Robert Clive who, ironically, was not a regular officer at all. Even in the Seven Years War the British had been badly outmanoeuvred by their French and Indian adversaries in North America, although they had won Canada largely through overwhelming strength and a few brilliant tactical coups, like Wolfe's storming of the heights at Quebec.

During the American War of Independence, a rabble of tenacious but ill-armed militiamen had held their own against the disciplined ranks of British soldiers; eventually Britain tired of the struggle in which they usually won the pitched battles without ever eliminating their enemy. The British army relied far too heavily on German mercenaries, and its British recruits were drawn primarily from the lowest ranks in society – Irish, Scottish and Welsh peasants, English criminals and drunks. Its officer class was very largely drawn from the young scions of the aristocracy or the landed gentry, with commissions purchased instead of promotions being made on merit.

Discipline was almost inhumanely stern, except under the more enlightened officers. So savage were the beatings that Americans protested at the treatment inflicted by the British on their own men in the American war. The war office stipulated that a maximum of 300 lashes could be inflicted on any one soldier – which was horrific

enough. However, one soldier received 500 lashes for conduct unbecoming a soldier; another, on an equally vague charge, received 600
lashes.

Responding to a parliamentary report, Mr Bennett the MP who had
raised the matter, is reported as follows:

There was one particular circumstance which had always operated
most powerfully on his mind with respect to these punishments,
namely, the utter and entire failure of their object: they appeared to
have no effect whatever, and he was fully persuaded that crimes
were rather increased than diminished by the severity of those
punishments.

He called on every military man to say whether he had ever
known a regiment or a man reformed by such severe inflictions? On
the contrary, he was perfectly convinced that every evil propensity
was increased, since the miserable victim found himself degraded in
his own eyes, and fallen in the estimation of his officers. The best
and most intelligent men had repeatedly contended that corporal
punishments produced no reform whatever. These punishments,
indeed, were the more odious and intolerable in the eyes of
Englishmen, since every foreign nation had abandoned them; they
formed no portion of a system in any other nation than this. In the
early period of the French Revolution, the Count de St Germain
wished to introduce it into the army, but they would not submit to
it. These punishments were not known in Austria, and scarcely ever
inflicted in Russia, where they had been accustomed to the lash.
Surely, then, no one would venture to say that an English soldier did
not feel the same degree of honour which other nations possessed.

Last year he had made a very extensive tour in France, and he
could assure the house, that while the people spoke of the English
soldiers as their benefactors, they expressed the utmost horror at the
corporal punishments which they were doomed to suffer: 'You have
been kind to us,' they said, 'but your ferocity to your own countrymen is horrible.' These were the sentiments of the inhabitants of
Brussels, who complained that their ears were stunned with the cries
and groans of brave warriors, smarting under the lash. What could

be more disgusting and revolting to the souls of men? What could be more tyrannical and abominable?

One of the peculiar characters of this mode of punishment was – that it was inflicted, not in open places, and under the public eye, but in barrack rooms, and other obscure situations. What could the generous spirit of an Englishman think of this? There was no man at Charing-Cross who would dare to treat an animal as we treated those unfortunate persons who had braved death in the field of battle [*hear hear*]. What, then, must be the feelings of such men?

The limit in the navy at the time was around seven dozen lashes, except in the rare case of a flogging round the fleet. Many of the offences involved no more than drunken or rowdy behaviour, although the system was a little more defensible in seeking to prevent excesses against the civilian population which, to their great credit, British officers unlike French ones, tried manfully to restrain.

Tactics were Prussian – with the emphasis on drill, smart appearance, clean uniforms and powdered hair. The British marched in column and fought in line, just like the Austrians and the Prussians. This had rendered them highly vulnerable to the tactics of the American irregulars, particularly when the Americans had been supported by disciplined French soldiers who, however, had absorbed the lessons of American-style fighting by employing irregular skirmishers and light divisions to fight alongside the main forces. They possessed one great advantage: as a volunteer army, unlike their French counterparts and the many subject nationalities conscripted by the Austrians, they seemed to show much greater bravery and eagerness to fight.

However, they were plagued by the lack of imagination of their commanders. Mediocre generals such as Burgoyne and Clinton were excelled by the merely competent Howe and Cornwallis. Occasional British commanders had shown modest flair: Sir Ralph Abercromby in the West Indies, where, however, he was facing an inferior force and presided over the decimation of his forces through disease; Sir David Baird, a dour and competent lieutenant-general who had served with distinction in India; and Sir John Stuart, who boldly supported the Calabrian insurgency.

These, however, were not Nelsons or Cochranes, nor even Howes or St Vincents. They were not the stuff of skilful victories. Britain was desperately short of army heroes for the first few years of the war. Then it appeared to find a real hero at last, a man of the hour: John Moore. Of Nelson's and Napoleon's generation, Moore had been born in November 1761, of humbler origins even than the former, the son of a doctor from Glasgow. He seemed, in Pitt the Elder's famous phrase about Clive of India, to be a heaven-born general.

He was skilled, fearless and ambitious and rose quickly by merit alone, serving in America, Corsica, the West Indies, Holland and Egypt, where he had performed heroically. He was a brigadier at thirty-four, major-general at thirty-six and lieutenant-general at forty-three. Although of modest means he was generous and made a point of sharing in the privations of his men, for example sleeping on straw during the siege of San Fiorenzo. 'Everyone admires and loves him,' commented the Duke of York's aide. Strong, tall, and handsome, he was every schoolboy's idea of a romantic soldier, every woman's of a dashing young officer. Sir John Moore seemed to be Britain's answer to Napoleon.

Nor was he an empty-headed man of courage. He quickly realized that British army tactics were in radical need of revision to meet the challenge posed by the new French ones. Securing the support of the Duke of York, he started training British units to become light infantry and reconnaissance forces. An experimental Rifle Corps was set up at Horsham, recruiting men from fifteen regiments. They were trained in Windsor Forest to use the new Baker rifle in place of the clumsier smooth-bore musket by two gifted commanders, Colonel Coote Manningham and Lieutenant-Colonel William Stewart, and were then placed under Moore's command at Sharncliffe Camp looking across the Channel at France.

Moore was a brilliantly innovative soldier for the period. His reforms were designed first to motivate the soldiers and improve their morale; secondly to introduce greater mobility – a speciality of his which was the basis of his decision to take soldiers off the parade ground and train his men in the field and bivouac them outside towns and villages; and thirdly to improve tactics. Moore abandoned the rigid discipline

enforced through the hanging and flogging of his predecessors. Instead he believed in the 'thinking fighting man' and he put these ideas into practice with a thoroughly modern approach. Officers, who in the past had been discouraged from fraternizing with their men, were encouraged to get to know them and observe their strengths and weaknesses. Soldiers, who previously had been discouraged from independent action or thought, for fear of encouraging indiscipline or even insubordination, and were often judged as too stupid, were taught to use their initiative and encourage regimental pride, Napoleonic-style. Moore's objective was:

> that each individual soldier knows what he has to do. Discipline is carried on without severity, the officers are attached to the men and the men to the officers . . . The discipline of modern times, which consists of parades, firelock exercise, etc is easy to the officer, as it takes up but an hour or two in the day. The discipline of the ancients consisted in bodily exercise, running, marching, etc terminated by bathing. The military character of sobriety and patience would completely answer in this country; but officers and men in following them would be completely occupied with their profession and could pursue no other object.

Despising parade-ground exercises, Moore instructed his light infantry in the new art of marching – an easy rhythm for general marching without the discomfort of the old Prussian-style stiff marching. He also taught his soldiers to have their wits about them at all times, to be aware of all that went on around them, to reconnoitre and to observe. This was a radical change for soldiers accustomed to marching, wheeling about and manoeuvring with parade-ground stiffness and firing as separate manoeuvres.

Soldiers were instructed to shoot to kill, and fire independently as well as in a volley, which was more possible with rifles that had a 300-yard range (500 for sharpshooters). They were also taught to reload and fire quickly – five rounds per minute. The British tactic of repeated, disciplined volleys was in fact a refinement of Prussian tactics, and could be effective. However, the most effective tactic of all, which was now

introduced, was of withholding fire until the last moment: this of course required discipline and courage among the men.

Modern research suggests that victory was often achieved by a single volley at close range followed by a bayonet charge. 'The British soldiers rejoice in the bayonet,' remarked a contemporary officer. Brent Nosworthy has observed: 'The overall psychological and physical dynamics underlying the British infantry tactic were pre-eminently simple: wait until the distance separating the two forces has been reduced to where, when the fire was finally delivered, it could not help but be effective, if not overpowering. Then, while the enemy is still recoiling from the shock caused by the devastating volley, rush in with lowered bayonets. The enemy staggering from their casualties and totally overawed by a ferocious charge delivered in a moment of vulnerability, almost inevitably turns and flees.'

Their coolness under fire was carefully inculcated under psychological pressure, with officers exhorting their men to be 'steady lads steady' in contrast to the equally deliberate French technique of advancing to drums and shouts, to give the men courage. George Gleig, a British officer, observed:

> They come on, for a while, slowly, and in silence; til, having reached within a hundred yards or two of the point to be assailed, they raised a loud but discordant yell, and rush forward . . . The ardour of the French is, however, admirably opposed by the coolness and undaunted deportment of Britons. On the present occasion, for instance, our people met their assailants exactly as if the whole affair had been a piece of acting, no man quitting his ground, but each deliberately waiting till the word of command was given, and then discharging his piece.

The British did however, frequently resort to three cheers to give them heart when attacking. According to Nosworthy: 'The cheers before the charge in part served as a signal that the attack was to enter the next and final phase. It also helped the men make the transition from struggling to maintain complete control to rushing in on the enemy with unbridled passion. By retaining a reservoir of emotion and unleashing

this in the final moments long after the enemy's emotional outlets had crested, the British had almost guaranteed the success of their attack or defence. The charge, when it finally came, completely transformed the infantrymen from inconsequent cogs in a large formation passively following orders, to a collectivity of furious warriors monomaniacally trying to kill the enemy in front of them.'

A contemporary officer wrote: 'No movement in the field is made with greater confidence of success than that of the charge; it affords little time for thinking, while it creates a fearless excitement, and tends to give a fresh impulse to the blood of the advancing soldier, rouses his courage, strengthens every nerve, and drowns every fear of danger or of death; thus emboldened amidst shouts that anticipate victory, he rushes on and mingles with the fleeing foe.' Fear of this steely British discipline – withholding from attacking until the last moment, then charging an enemy whose own fire had already become disordered and which had lost its initial impetus – meant that traditional British linear tactics worked against the French columns and squares, as they did not for the Austrians and Russians, which relied on a disciplined line firing volleys into the middle distance. Provided the British irregulars and skirmishers could protect the line's flanks, the British saw no reason to counter the French advance in column, as the Austrians did.

The British commanders also considered that their smaller guns were more manoeuvrable and accurate than the French artillery. They were equipped with far more 3- and 6- pound guns than the French, who instead had far more 8- and 12-pound ones which had a longer range and much greater ability to inflict damage.

Moore's revolution in British tactics and morale can hardly be overstated. The British army had grown in strength from around 100,000 regulars in 1803 to double that in 1807. Although Castlereagh failed in his attempt to introduce conscription into this martially averse nation, a huge quantity of recruits were attracted by the need to fight for King and country against the barbarous Napoleon: this army was a professional force, no longer merely a refuge for undesirables.

Part 9

BRITAIN ALONE

Chapter 59

ARTHUR WELLESLEY

The job of leading the expeditionary force to Portugal fell to a very different sort of man who happened to have 9,500 men at Cork ready for the projected invasion of Venezuela – Sir Arthur Wellesley. By an incredible series of accidents, it was Wellesley who was to lead the new military machine crafted by Moore to greatness.

Had Wellesley drowned in a near shipwreck off Egypt, had his brother not been governor-general of India, had Moore not shown an almost reckless aggression towards Napoleon in the first phase of the war and behaved with more of Wellington's natural caution, Sir John would almost certainly have been viewed as Britain's greatest ever soldier instead of the Duke of Wellington. For Arthur Wellesley had that greatest of all military assets: luck.

Arthur Wesley – as he was then called – was born almost as much a child of privilege as Moore had been of merit. His family hailed from the middling aristocracy of Ireland, which counted as the lower aristocracy of England. It originated in England under the name Colley and had travelled to County Kildare in the early sixteenth century. Sir Henry Colley had been prominent in Ireland under Queen Elizabeth. His descendant and Arthur's grandfather, Richard Colley, adopted the name Wesley when he inherited a fortune from his maternal line, which descended from an ancient Somerset line, the de Wellesleighs, who had travelled to Ireland in Henry II's reign. Richard Wesley served in the Irish House of Commons and was appointed to the Irish peerage as Lord Mornington.

His son Garret was an attractive, fun-loving and extremely talented composer who secured promotion to an Irish earldom,

but used up most of his inheritance living beyond his means. The infant Arthur's mother, Anne, was the daughter of Viscount Dungannon. This formidable woman held her family of six children together after her husband's early death. It was to this long-faced, distinguished-looking woman that Arthur owed his looks, rather than to his plump, bleary-faced father. While Garret penned captivating melodies, such as 'Come Fairest Nymph' and 'Gently hear me, charming maid', Anne bore him a succession of children – Richard in 1760, William in 1763, Anne in 1768, Arthur in 1769, Gerald in 1770 and Henry in 1773.

Arthur was born on 1 May at the family's Dublin house. Their country residence was Dangan castle, a day's ride away. This was an elegant Georgian mansion with its own ornamental lake. Much has been made of Arthur's having been born of a large family on an island which was somewhat looked down upon by the English socially – just like Napoleon. Yet Napoleon's highly-strung personality had more in common with Nelson's. The young Arthur appeared anything but highly strung – in fact something of a dolt. He seemed an amiable, sometimes mischievous, slow-witted, dreamy dunce. A year younger than either Napoleon or Nelson, of a higher social background to Bonaparte, and much superior in pedigree to either Nelson or Moore, in an age when this was hugely important, the boy trundled dreamily through his uneventful childhood as his family's fortunes subsided about him.

His elder brother Richard seemed to have everything he lacked: he was strikingly good-looking and highly intelligent. He was nine years older than Arthur, which placed him in a paternal supporting relationship to the young brother rather than one of sibling rivalry. Nevertheless he once pointed his brother out to a friend as 'the biggest ass in Europe'. Arthur was sent to Brown's seminary in the King's Road, London, and then to Eton. He was shy, with few friends, uninterested in either rowing or cricket, then in vogue at the school, and performed poorly academically. If he did later utter the phrase 'the Battle of Waterloo was won on the playing fields of Eton', it was certainly not his own education to which he was referring. He enjoyed going on long solitary walks: he was slow of speech. That extraordinary mixture

of ambition and introversion that made him one of the most peculiar of men in later life were already evolving.

His ambitious, high-minded mother was impatient with him. 'I swear to God,' she remarked cruelly, 'I don't know what I shall do with my awkward son Arthur.' He was 'food for powder and nothing more'. The only outstanding thing about this minor aristocratic family fallen on hard times seemed to be the burning ambition instilled in the boys, perhaps by their mother; although at this stage Arthur evinced no sign of it.

With the family lacking the money to continue his education at Eton, he was sent to a tutorial establishment in Brighton. A friend of his wrote that he was 'extremely fond of music, and played well upon the fiddle, but he never gave any indication of any other species of talent. As far as my memory serves, there was no intention then of sending him into the army; his own wishes, if he had any, were in favour of a civilian's life.'

He went on to study in Brussels, where his mother was living to save money, before attending a riding academy in the stolid middle-French town of Angers, where he showed a surprising ability to pick up the language as well as adequate horsemanship and, unusually for one so solitary when young, enjoyed the social life of the local nobility.

Although he was still happy-go-lucky and idle, his mother detected a 'remarkable change for the better' in him. The celebrated Ladies of Llangollen, who he visited in north Wales, described him as 'charming . . . handsome, fashionable, tall and elegant'. His dazzling older brother, now Lord Mornington and as an Irish peer permitted to sit in the House of Commons, secured for him an appointment to the 73rd Regiment as an ensign in March 1787 at the age of seventeen.

He was then despatched as an aide-de-camp to the Viceroy of Ireland, Lord Buckingham, of the all-powerful Grenville clan, where he played the naughty boy. Dublin girls would not go to a party if 'that mischievous boy' attended, according to Lady Aldbury, who also turned him out of her carriage because she found him such dull company on one occasion. He would tweak the neck-cloths of his friends, and was dumped in mid-dance by a local beauty, possibly on account of a boorish advance.

His brother seemed happy enough at his progress, speaking *in loco parentis* of his 'excellent judgment, amiable manners and admirable temper and firmness' and secured him a seat in the Irish parliament. Arthur now set his sights on marrying a local heiress, Kitty Pakenham, daughter of Lord Longford, with a huge estate in County Westmeath. The two were clearly deeply in love and Arthur's rejection by her brother, Tom, on the grounds that he was impecunious, stung him deeply, although later they were to become the firmest of friends.

He resolved to pursue a more determined career in the army to achieve the necessary social and financial standing. In June 1794, at the age of twenty-five, his days of indolence were over. By the same moment in their careers, Nelson had been at sea for eight years, having travelled all over the world, while Napoleon Bonaparte had staged his first great achievement in storming Fort Mulgrave at Toulon. Wesley was a late developer; a young man in no hurry.

By now the features that were to become so famous had emerged. He was of medium height; his face was long, with a pointed, determined chin, a thin-lipped, haughty, aristocratic mouth, a formidable, aquiline but hawk-ended nose, a languid, still dreamy expression and prominent, contemptuous eyes beneath full brows and a high forehead. He was extremely neat and well turned out, dapper even, and certainly good-looking, although not so much as his older brother.

His detached expression and slow diction did not make him immediately charismatic. He seemed an embodiment of the classic English gentleman, which he ardently desired to be, rejecting his long roots in Ireland. Being a Protestant nobleman in a country largely made up of landless Catholic peasants instilled in him the hauteur of a colonist towards native people, although he came from the most enlightened social class in Ireland and afterwards showed some sensitivity to the claims of the Catholics. While the English aristocracy was more relaxed and had fewer airs, Wesley came across as amiable but reserved and even snooty in the manner of a nouveau riche.

It was now time for Wesley's first baptism of fire in a typical British military catastrophe. With the declaration of war in Europe in 1793, the disappointed suitor asked to be sent as part of the army to

Martinique in the West Indies, but was turned down – which saved him from the disease that decimated the troops that went there. So he borrowed money from his brother to buy a lieutenant-colonel's commission and was despatched to join the Duke of York's force in Flanders. In June 1794 he left Cork, reaching the barren flat shores of Flanders later that month. His commander was Lord Moira. Thus at the age of twenty-five – such was the unpreparedness of the British army – he was placed in command of a brigade without having ever seen a shot fired in anger.

He was not slow to show his mettle. Moira put him in charge of a force ordered to take Ostend, while the main reinforcements went off inland to join the Duke of York's army, which after the rout in Flanders was in headlong retreat along the Scheldt. No sooner had Moira departed than Wesley re-embarked his men and sailed to Antwerp, where he reinforced the Duke of York before Moira arrived by land.

In September Wesley was ordered to the aid of General Sir Ralph Abercromby to reinforce Boxtel behind the river Dommely which had been taken from the French. Abercromby had, however, blundered into the main French army and had to beat a hasty retreat. Wesley was given control of the rearguard where he arrayed his troops in line and coolly stopped the French advance, allowing the main force to retreat safely. He was commended for his courage in the engagement. The army made a stand behind the river Waal and then went into winter quarters for several months under continuing French fire. He was bitter at being thus exposed with no real plan of campaign, spending most nights on the bank of the river under attack.

At last, in January 1795, he and his men were allowed to retreat through the grim winter of snow, ice, slush and mud to Bremen. As a contemporary described it:

Far as the eye could reach over the whitened plain were scattered gun-limbers, wagons full of baggage, of stores, of sick men, sutlers' carts and private carriages. Beside them lay the horses, dead; around them scores and hundreds of soldiers, dead; here a straggler who had staggered onto the bivouac and dropped to sleep in the arms of the

frost; there a group of British and Germans around an empty rumcask; here forty English Guardsmen huddled together around a plundered wagon; there a pack-horse with a woman lying alongside it, and a baby, swathed in rags, peeping out of the pack, with its mother's milk turned to ice upon its lips – one and all stark, frozen, dead.

Wesley and his troops were evacuated in March. The inexperienced young colonel and his raw recruits were safely embarked. He was warmly commended by Lord Cornwallis as 'a sensible man and a good officer'.

Wesley renewed his suit for Kitty's hand, failed again, and departed upon another expedition to the West Indies, which however was driven back by severe gales in a matter of weeks. He was now ordered to a more exotic location – India. He left for India in June 1796 at the age of twenty-seven. He reached Calcutta after a sea journey of eight months, stepping ashore opposite the elegant fortress of Fort St George along the foetid, disease-infested banks of the Hoogley in February 1779.

Wesley had occupied himself on the claustrophobic journey by extensive reading. The governor-general, Sir John Shore, described him as sensible but full of 'boyish playfulness'. He spent his first few months gadding about Calcutta, Madras and Penang, enjoying the luxury of innumerable Indian servants and drinking raucously with his brother officers. But real opportunities for advancement at last beckoned: with Britain and France at war the latter decided on a more forward imperialist policy of expansion in India at the expense of the local princes supported by the French.

He also had a superb stroke of luck: his brother, Lord Mornington, was appointed governor-general of India by his friend William Pitt. Mornington, whom a contemporary maliciously described as living for 'nothing else' but display, accepted this superb opportunity. He decided that the family name was too plebeian and adopted the name of Wellesley, linked back to the female line of his grandfather. He was accompanied by another brother, Henry, as his secretary. The nepo-

tism of this arrangement caused considerable muttering among other officers. Arthur Wellesley, as he now became, was soon to be promoted to full colonel well in advance of longer-serving officers of his rank. Like Nelson he had official favour to thank for his first major promotion.

Mornington's target was the state of Mysore, under the control of the most fearsome and effective of Indian princes, Tippoo Sultan, the 'Tiger', son of Hyder Ali who had been a consistent thorn in the British side but had been kept behind his borders by the competent Cornwallis, Mornington's predecessor as governor-general. Tippoo was a wise and enlightened ruler by contemporary Indian standards, showing considerable religious tolerance for a Moslem towards the Hindu majority and being interested in economic and scientific advances.

The British concluded treaties with Tippoo's neighbours, the Peshwa at the head of the Mahratta confederacy and the Nizam of Hyderabad, the largest state of central India. Mornington set about pressing the reluctant governor of Madras, Lord Clive, to adopt a more aggressive attitude towards Tippoo. When the Indian prince made an alliance with the governor of French Mauritius, Mornington was provided with his pretext for action, namely 'the transactions which have passed between the enemies of my country'. In fact Mornington had already heavily reinforced Madras, despatching his brother Arthur to the town in 1798.

Wellesley was placed under the command of General George Harris, the commander in chief at Madras. As a junior officer reporting directly to his brother, the governor-general, he was immediately detested by his brother officers. His demeanour, by turns bumptious and superior for so young an officer, yet boyish and seeking to win friends, did little to improve matters.

Wellesley was placed in control of a contingent of the Nizam's troops with the rank of brigadier. This was instructed to march 250 miles from Madras to Mysore, where he displayed unusual efficiency in provisioning troops and transporting the necessary artillery – two huge 24-pound cannon, eighteen almost as heavy 18-pounders and eight 9-pounders. The offensive was two-pronged, with a force of

4,000 British and 16,000 Indian troops marching from Madras to join up with a smaller force under General James Stuart from the west coast of India.

Wellesley came across as a brave but blustering officer with little experience. He described Stuart as 'a gallant, hard-headed big-hearted officer, but no talent, no tact'. After a long and slow march, the army advanced into Mysore, into which Tippoo had retreated, pursuing a scorched-earth policy and using his horsemen to harass the British – which Wellesley had thoughtfully anticipated by securing his supplies. Reaching the eastern Ghat range on 10 March, the Indian cavalry attacked Wellesley's troops near Kellamungellum; but Wellesley led a counter-attack which drove them off.

Meanwhile Stuart's column had also beaten back an attack at Sedaseer in the western Ghats, causing Tippoo to disperse his men. At Malavelly, Tippoo established two heavy guns to cover the main road, attacking with about 2,000 infantry, who were dispersed by ordered linear fire from infantry under Wellesley's command.

The British marched on to Seringapatam, Tippoo's stronghold, located on a peninsula between two branches of the Cauvery river which was dry at that time of year. The position was an immensely strong one. Harris's approach was to flank it from the south-west, before ordering his men to attack a grove near the village of Sultan-pettah. It was badly handled, and Tippoo counter-attacked in force, driving Wellesley's men north and then west. Wellesley's first real engagement had ended in failure. The following day he took the outpost with a much larger force; but his cocky self-confidence had been dented.

General Stuart arrived to the north of the Cauvery River and a concerted attack on the fortress was made on 26 April in which Wellesley took part, clearing an area beneath the walls of enemy troops so that assault cannon could be brought forward. But he was placed in reserve for the actual assault which was to be commanded by his immediate superior General Bernard: it took place in classic fashion after breaches had been made in the walls on 4 May.

The attack was highly successful and Tippoo was killed. Wellesley, who arrived afterwards, found his body. The British lost some 400

killed or wounded to 9,000 on Mysore's side – largely the result of a rampage of atrocities committed by British troops on storming the fortress, which showed definitively that the Indians were not the only ones to perpetrate horrific cruelties on their opponents. Wellesley, to his credit, was horrified.

Bernard apparently asked to be relieved of his command, as he was exhausted, although he later denied having said this. He was dismayed to find that he was to be replaced by his junior rival, the pampered governor-general's brother who had played little part in the actual fighting. 'Before the sweat was dry on my brow,' he remarked, 'I was superseded by an inferior officer.' The failure to prevent the murderous rampage of his men, after the brilliant success of the assault, may have been the reason for his being relieved.

Wellesley added to his personal unpopularity by rightly imposing a stern hand on his raping, murdering and looting soldiers, hanging four of them and flogging others. This episode marks another crucial step in his evolution as a personality: his ruthless disciplinarian streak had been born out of justifiable circumstances, and was aggravated by an enduring contempt for his own men, which caused their respect and fear of him as a commander to contain a streak of hatred as well – his attitude was much more typical of an upstart Irish officer than a traditional British patrician with a paternalistic streak towards his inferiors. In this Wellesley was way behind the thinking of enlightened soldiers like Burgoyne and Moore.

For all his snobbery and disdain for the lower classes, however, Wellesley was genuinely moved by casualties among his own men and sought to minimize them – even if he did not hesitate for a moment to risk their lives if he thought it necessary. In this he was like his equally ruthless future adversary, Napoleon.

He was appointed senior military officer in the region, a vast swathe of the subcontinent, while the main armies withdrew leaving a five-year-old Hindu prince nominally on the throne. The impecunious Arthur also secured some £4,000 in prize money. The young officer ruled his new fiefdom from the splendid comforts of Tippoo's palace. He launched a campaign against the countryside bandits, in particular Dhoudiah Wauga, whose huge force was routed by a much smaller

disciplined force commanded by Wellesley with far superior firepower in 1800.

Mornington, after his long-distance success against Tippoo Sultan, had ascended ever higher up the ladder of pomposity. He was appointed an Irish marquess, which however infuriated him as supposedly inadequate to his merits – it was 'a pinchbeck' reward. Pitt wrote a conciliatory but firm letter in response. He concluded to this seeker after titles and rank:

> I have said nothing on the little intrinsic difference under the present circumstances between an English and Irish marquisate, because I conceive you look rather to the public impression than to the thing itself. But as far as in itself it may be an object, it will certainly not escape you that under the circumstances of the Union, the difference to any person already possessed of a British title is little more than nominal; scarcely extending further than to a question of style in the journals and debates of the House of Lords or of relative precedence as to four or five individuals; objects on which I do not believe such a mind as yours can set much serious value.

When the new marquess appointed his younger brother to lead an expedition to Egypt Bernard, furious at being superseded yet again by the governor-general's brother, stormed in to see the marquess and forced him to transfer the command. Arthur Wellesley, learning this, was for the first time furious with his brother. Wellesley flatly refused to act as second-in-command, a convenient excuse being provided by his catching 'Malabar itch', a painful condition which was rendered even more so by its cure – baths in nitric acid which actually dissolved the towels he used to dry himself. He was appallingly rude to his brother and corresponded coldly with his secretary. Only later was he to acknowledge the 'evil consequences of all this to my reputation'.

Indeed he was cordially loathed by most officers as a mediocrity who had achieved his position through his brother and manifested his family's *folie de grandeur*. Fate, at least, was kind to him: the ship in which he was to have departed for Egypt sank with the loss of all hands.

Wellesley's fortunes were, however, about to change. In March 1803 he was assigned to take advantage of the divisions between the five great Maratha princes of central India to extend British rule. He was placed under the command of General Stuart with around 15,000 men and a force of 9,000 from Hyderabad under his personal command. He marched this large army a full 600 miles under his customary iron discipline, carrying its own supplies. The force reached Poona in mid-April to rescue the Peshwa Baji Rao, the ruler to the throne from which he had been deposed by another Peshwa, Jeswant Rao. Baji was to become a puppet of the British. This was the classic pattern of colonial expansionism.

The other Maratha princes combined against the British, raising an army of about 15,000 infantry, 20,000 skirmishers and some 40,000 light cavalry. Wellesley, ordered by Stuart, decided to strike the first blow and seized the highly defended fort of Ahmednuggar in August. After much marching and countermarching, two British-led armies, under Wellesley and Colonel James Stevenson, managed to surprise the main Maratha force, now 200,000-strong, at Assaye near the rivers Kaitna and Juah.

Wellesley decided to attack without waiting for Stevenson's reinforcements in case the Marathas escaped. It was a precarious position. He moved due east along the Kaitna to what he believed was a ford between two villages, had to cross the river with his force in full view of the Marathas and draw it up in lines of battle. If the Marathas had attacked first, he would have been exposed with his small force unready for battle with its back to the river. As it was, the Maratha artillery commanded by German mercenaries, swung their guns around to fire upon the British. Once across, Wellesley placed his cavalry on the right and his infantry on the left in the narrow space between the two rivers. The British came under intense artillery fire.

Infantry detachments under Lieutenant-Colonel William Orrock misread his orders and attacked the strongest Maratha position outside the village of Assaye to the north under intense bombardment. An eyewitness wrote: 'The pickets and the 74th regiment were charged by a wonderful fine body of cavalry and infantry. The pickets lost all their officers except Lt Colonel Orrock and had only about 75 men left out

of 400 men of whom only about 100 are likely to survive. Every officer of this corps except Major Swinton and Mr Grant the quartermaster were either killed or desperately wounded.'

The result was that the Maratha line gave way in the south at its weakest point, under steady infantry attack, while it held in the north. Wellesley, without hesitating, ordered another attack with his sparse forces. This time the whole Maratha line broke and fled. Some 1,500 British and Indian forces had been killed or wounded to 6,000 Marathas.

It had been a hard-fought battle against overwhelming odds decided by the greater discipline and steadiness under fire of the British-led force. Wellesley always considered it his finest battle and proof that old-fashioned linear tactics coupled with disciplined last-minute volleys followed by bayonet attacks could prevail. Wellesley's brigade-major said of him: 'The general was in the thick of the action the whole time, and had a horse killed under him. No man could have shown a better example to his troops than he did. I never saw a man so cool and collected.'

Wellesley had two horses shot from under him. He had shown a lightning readiness to seize opportunities, a cool and decisive grasp of battlefield tactics and great courage. At last he commanded the respect of his brother officers.

In November Wellesley set out again alongside Stevenson to take on two Maratha armies at Argaum. Again he staged a frontal attack, bringing his own artillery to bear. Under his disciplined volleys the enemy ranks gave way. This time it was a walkover – some 350 British casualties to 5,000 Maratha ones.

He now set about bringing order to the area under his command. He himself showed a deep concern for the soldiers' welfare, as well as enforcing discipline, sending bottles of Madeira to the sick and visiting them. He also visited his far-flung dominions. Water was always a problem:

It was painful to see large bodies of men calling out for water and to have no water to give them. There are no springs to be found in that country; but the armies usually encamp near the dry beds of rivers,

and there, by digging a little way into the sand, water of good quality is generally found. But sometimes this resource fails, and then both men and animals suffer greatly, or rush to any neighbouring village – for where there is a village there is water – and obtain the supply of its tank. But sometimes the tank is small and soon exhausted, and then, where scarcely anything remains but thick mud, one sees the men struggling and fighting in it for the last drop of water.

He was yearning to return to England. 'I don't exactly see the necessity that I should stay several years in India in order to settle affairs . . . I look to England, and I conceive that my views in life will be advanced by returning there. I don't conceive that any man has a right to call upon me to remain in a subordinate situation in this country, contrary to my inclination.'

When Mornington was recalled to be replaced by the elderly Cornwallis, Arthur decided to call it a day too, knowing that his victories would not be enough to preserve him from the revenge of his brother officers in India under a new and less sympathetic governor-general. In March 1805, he returned with a knighthood from the British and a fortune of over £40,000. He was worn out bodily – 'sallow and wan' – but recovered his health aboard the enforced idleness of the long voyage home and bracing sea air. His motto had been 'dash at the first fellows that make their appearance and the campaign will be ours' – a strong echo of Nelson.

The campaigns had aged him. The youthful jollity and japes were things of the past. He was a stern and incorruptible disciplinarian, refusing bribes from Indian princes, methodical and careful to a fault in his preparation. He arrived in England in September. The country had just emerged from the threat of French invasion, and was only a month away from the contradictory battles of Trafalgar and Austerlitz.

At thirty-six, he was temporarily unemployed, being sent to command a brigade at sleepy Hastings. He was philosophical: 'I have ate of the King's salt, and therefore I conceive it to be my duty to serve with unhesitating zeal and cheerfulness, when and wherever the King or his government may think proper to employ me.'

Although he had acquired a reputation for womanizing in India, on his return he was thrilled to hear that his old love Kitty Pakenham still longed for him. But she had aged too and had become religious and serious-minded. Wellesley resolved to seek her hand without first meeting her, now that he had established his position in society and earned significant wealth. But when he met her first after twelve years away he remarked to his brother, 'She is grown damned ugly, by jove.' Yet he stuck by his promise and married her in Dublin in April 1806. She was sweet, domesticated and narrow-minded, and despised by most of Wellesley's newly glamorous circle. But she was devoted to him, at least to begin with, and he cannot have been an easy man to get on with – reserved, commanding and with a roving eye for other women. They had two sons.

He secured election to parliament as part of the Grenville faction, his old friend Pitt having died. With the fall of Grenville and the accession of Portland he was offered the job of chief secretary for Ireland, which he dutifully fulfilled in that divided land until the summer of 1807, while pressing for another military command. At last he was given the job of carrying out the land operation on Lord Gambier's expedition to Copenhagen to cut out the Danish fleet, a job he performed with spectacular efficiency. He was now a respected military commander with a string of distinguished engagements behind him. Yet he was far from being a household name.

Wellesley now seemed destined for an extraordinary adventure: to travel with Francisco de Miranda at the head of the expedition to liberate Caracas. With the French invasion of Portugal, however, he was given a new assignment. In July 1808 he spoke to a good friend: 'I am thinking of the French that I am going to fight . . . Tis enough to make one thoughtful; but no matter: my die is cast, they may overwhelm me, but I don't think they will out-manoeuvre me . . . I am not afraid of them, as everybody else seems to be.'

Behind him he left an undistinguished political career which chiefly revolved around defending his brother Richard from the inevitable charges of corruption, lavish expenditure and tyranny that had followed his return from India – just as similar changes had followed the

incontestably more gifted Clive and Warren Hastings, but with better reason. In addition their brother William Wellesley-Pole was charged with covering up corruption in the Admiralty.

Sir Arthur thus came from a clan that was distrusted by the public, and his appointment was greeted by a storm of opprobrium. Once again he was superseding senior generals: he had only just been promoted lieutenant-general. Even the King had serious doubts. His brother's friend Lord Castlereagh had been instrumental in the choice. The expedition was limited in scope and small in size, and seemed as doomed as other previous British military adventures on the continent. It consisted of 9,000 men sailing on 12 July 1808 and arriving a week later at La Coruña (Corunna to the British) on the Peninsula that was to make his reputation.

Arriving there he found to his dismay that the northern Spanish army under General Blake had been defeated by Marshal Bessières at Medina del Rio Seco. Meanwhile General Dupont with 15,000 men had just taken Córdoba in the south and General Masséna had just occupied Valladolid in the centre. The new 'King' of Spain, Joseph Bonaparte, entered Madrid with 4,000 troops to take up his throne just the day after Wellington first set foot on Peninsular soil. The news was all bad. Only the town of Zaragoza, it seemed, had held out. It appeared that everywhere the French were invincible, moving relentlessly forward to occupy the huge, rugged Spanish interior. What possible impression could Wellesley and his puny force make upon them?

Wellesley's force sailed disconsolately further south to Oporto in northern Portugal. He did not know that an astonishing thing was happening even as he sailed: Dupont had advanced beyond Córdoba to inflict a final defeat on the Spaniards, but the sullen people of the countryside had begun to resist the advance while others rose up behind him. After a few days the increasingly anxious general ordered a retreat in those sunbaked, impenetrable mountains. He was harried and ambushed on all sides. On 23 July he surrendered to the ragged Spanish 'army' of General Castaños.

The first triumph in the Peninsular War had thus been achieved by the Spaniards themselves. They were a people oppressively misgov-

erned for centuries, whose social fabric was antiquated, unaffected by the economic and social revolutions that had taken place elsewhere in Europe, still living as peasants on harsh soils that barely afforded a living in many areas, the upper class grown rich on South American gold and silver and refusing to engage in the menial tasks of trade and industry. But the peasants were proud, and could be bitter fighters. Usually steeped in provincialism, with poor communications linking their enormous country, they had no knowledge of or interest in nearby provinces, but their swelling nationalism and resentment at the foreign invaders had reared its head for the first time.

Wellesley knew nothing of this. Further south there was discouraging news: a Russian fleet was in the Tagus, which might be hostile, as well as several French vessels. He decided it would be safest to make a landing from the Atlantic some hundred miles to the north at Mondego Bay, and from there to march on Lisbon. Encouragingly, he learnt that the Portuguese countryside had also risen against the French, and that the latter occupied only the capital and a few strongholds to the west around the Tagus.

When Wellesley's men at last went ashore, they were joined by a force of some 4,000 men from Gibraltar led by General Sir Brent Spencer. But Wellesley also learnt to his chagrin that he was soon to be reinforced by an army of some 16,000 under three senior officers. Sir John Moore had at last extricated himself and his men from the clutches of the King of Sweden and was preparing to embark from England; before him General Sir Hew Dalrymple, an old buffer who had not seen active service for fourteen years, was to arrive with General Sir Henry Burrard, another amiable officer of limited intelligence. That had been the decision of the King and the Duke of York, who considered Wellesley too junior. Castlereagh wrote to him: 'I shall rejoice if it shall have befallen to your lot to place the Tagus in our hands; if not, I have no fear that you will find many opportunities of doing yourself honour and your country service.' Wellesley promised to respect his seniors but said privately, 'I hope that I shall beat Junot before any of them arrive, and then they may do as they please with me'.

It was brave talk, yet he cannot but have feared that his first great opportunity was to be snatched away from him after his adventure had

barely begun. Wellesley calculated that with the defeat of Dupont confirmed, the French armies in Spain would be too busy to threaten him from the east. He decided to move down along the coastal road to Lisbon with 12,300 British troops and 1,500 Portuguese, so that he could not be attacked from the east without possibility of evacuation and had naval support.

He had little artillery and virtually no cavalry, but his men made good progress in the intense heat of a Portuguese summer through fertile and well-provisioned countryside. Junot had sent General Laborde with 4,000 men up the main road to Lisbon along the Tagus and instructed General Loison with another army across the river to reinforce him. On 15 August there was a first skirmish as the enthusiastic British advanced guard routed a French patrol, only to pursue it straight into the main French army: two officers and twenty-seven men were lost. Two days later Wellesley ordered a general attack on Laborde's small army for fear that he would soon be reinforced by Loison.

One observer described the spectacle of the British army that morning on the Plain of Obidos:

> The arms piled, and the men occupied as they usually are on all occasions of a morning halt – some sitting on their knapsacks, others stretched on the grass, many with a morsel of cold meat on a ration biscuit for a place in one hand, with a clasp-knife in the other, all doing justice to the contents of their haversacks, and not a few with their heads thrown back and canteens at their mouths, eagerly gulping down his Majesty's grog or the wine of the country, while others, whiffing their pipes, were jestingly promising their comrades better billets and softer beds for the next night, or repeating the valorous war-cry of the Portuguese.
>
> But to the person of reflecting mind there was more in this condensed formation than a causal halt required. A close observer would have noticed the silence and anxious looks of the several general officers of brigades, and the repeated departure and arrival of staff-officers and aides-de-camp, and he would have known that the enemy was not far distant, and that an important event was on the eve of taking place.

Wellesley divided his army in two, sending 4,000 towards the French rear, also to intercept Loison if he should arrive. Laborde in response occupied a ridge overlooking the Lisbon road, where he looked down upon the advancing British, inflicting great damage before again withdrawing to avoid being outflanked on both sides. The British lost some 500 men, the French around the same, but they retreated intact. The first little battle of the Peninsular War between two able generals had been a stand off.

Learning that British reinforcements were being landed to the west at Vimeiro, Wellesley lengthened his position to protect them. There were now up to 17,000 infantry and 18 guns, as well as the 1,500 Portuguese. Wellesley decided to march for the defile of Torres Vedras, but Sir Henry Burrard had just arrived and assumed command. He ordered Wellesley to adopt a defensive position until further reinforcements arrived. Wellesley was incensed, believing he had a good opportunity to seize Lisbon, but had no choice but to obey. He took up a defensive position on a ridge to the east and on Vimeiro hill, south of the village of that name.

Junot himself had arrived to take command of his 13,000 troops and twenty-four guns; his 70,000 remaining men were left in and around Lisbon to maintain order there. His aim was to drive the inexperienced British forces to the east. Wellesley sent his skirmishers forward along and down the sides of the ridge while placing his main forces intact behind it. The French came bravely forward under fire from their flanks and in front, unaware that a larger force awaited them on the reverse slope.

British artillery opened up, using shrapnel for the first time – named after the captain who invented it – a shell which blew up in the air raining grapeshot on the men below. Rifleman Harris described the motionless lines in the August sunshine 'glittering with bright arms, the stern features of the men as they stood with their eyes fixed unalterably upon the enemy, the proud colours of England floating over the heads of the different battalions and the dark cannon on the rising ground'. At close range the volleys were fired at fifteen-second intervals by the disciplined British soldiers, drawn up in two lines of 800 men. After the volleys a textbook bayonet attack decisively dispersed the French,

exhausted by the uphill walk under intense fire and surprised by the main British army.

As they broke and ran, Wellesley's few horse were ordered forward where they at first put the French infantry to flight. But they went too far, to Wellesley's irritation, and came up against superior French cavalry before galloping back to the main British lines with a quarter of the men lost. A renewed French attack on the left failed and by midday Junot's force was in full retreat. They had lost some 2,000 men to 700 British casualties as well as fifteen guns.

Wellesley rode up to Burrard who had arrived on the battlefield and urged him to march on Torres Vedras. 'We shall be in Lisbon in three days,' he said. The cautious general flatly refused, and was reinforced in his dithering by Sir Hew Dalrymple who arrived the following day. Moore, who arrived several days later, took Wellesley's view: 'Several of our brigades had not been in action; our troops were in high spirits and the French so crestfallen that probably they would have dispersed. They could never have reached Lisbon.' But it was too late: the French had entrenched themselves at Torres Vedras.

There was then an offer from Junot to withdraw all French forces from Portugal. To Dalrymple and Burrard this seemed a vindication of their caution, although Wellesley fumed at 'Dowager Dalrymple and Betty Burrard'. In fact Junot had shrewdly assessed that it would have been disastrous for him to remain at Lisbon. The British had assembled a fleet under Sir Charles Cotton which could bottle up or attack the Russian and French ships in the Tagus and bombard Lisbon from the sea. They had an army approaching from the north which could trap the French in an enclave surrounded on three sides by water. In addition the people of Lisbon were highly restive and might stage an insurrection.

The two generals reached agreement with the French General Kellerman at the Convention of Cintra, then ordered Wellesley to sign the terms. He read them with astonishment, describing them as 'very extraordinary', but obeying his superiors' orders in an untypical show of humility. The terms were surprising indeed: the French were to be evacuated by the Royal Navy, to a French port no less, and retain

their arms and baggage and all their personal property. French troops were to be allowed to return to the fight from the port in which they were landed. Those Portuguese who had collaborated with the French were not to be punished. The Russian fleet was to be allowed to depart for the Baltic.

Wellesley promptly wrote to Castlereagh to dissociate himself from the agreement, but it was too late. The French interpreted the agreement to mean that they could take everything they could plunder from the capital away with them, including £25,000 from the Portuguese treasury. At first, as news of the French defeat at Vimeiro reached Britain at the end of August, a nation so long accustomed to the failure of British armies on the continent, there was a great outburst of popular emotion. Lady Errol wrote: 'I hear that hero Kellerman, who last November was dictating strict humiliating terms to Emperors and Kings, was obliged to go down upon his knees to Sir Arthur Wellesley – I like it *loads* and quantities.'

In mid-September news of the agreement signed by the three British generals arrived and joy turned to fury. Wellesley had begged Castlereagh to relieve him of his post as he could not continue in a subordinate capacity to these two old gentlemen, and departed after making arrangements for the French withdrawal. After his spectacular victory and his bottling up of the French army in a trap where it faced certain defeat, he was now unfairly blamed for snatching defeat from the jaws of victory: The enemies of the Wellesleys – of which there were many – closed ranks and attacked him as well as Richard and William.

In November an inquiry was set up at the Royal Hospital at Chelsea at which Dalrymple and Wellesley gave conflicting accounts. The army proceeded to exonerate all three officers. Parliament voted to thank Wellesley for the victory at Vimeiro. Dalrymple was dismissed as governor of Gibraltar, while Burrard was retired to domestic duty. It had been a major scandal smoothed over in traditional British fashion so as not to ruffle feathers. Wellesley himself retired to Dublin bitter and angry at what seemed a terminal setback to his career.

Chapter 60

CORUNNA

Command in the Peninsula now devolved upon the capable shoulders of Sir John Moore. Admiral Sir Charles Cotton, in charge of the British squadron off Portugal, insisted that the three generals had no right to decide naval dispositions and ignored the Convention of Cintra; instead he forced the Russian admiral to give up his ships to the British until the end of the war, a minor but significant victory.

Castlereagh determined that Britain should go on the offensive. He had agreed to despatch a fresh army of 30,000 troops to the Peninsula. In the event 14,000 infantry, 4,000 cavalry and 800 artillerymen were sent under Sir David Baird, Wellesley's old *bête noire*, to Corunna in northern Spain. There they were to link up with the 20,000 of the 30,000 troops in Portugal under Moore's command. Quite quickly Britain's commitment in Portugal had escalated to the status of major intervention.

Good news started to flood in across the Peninsula. Imaginations were kindled by the defiance of Zaragoza and the story of the brave girl named Augustina who fought against the invaders in the ruins of her burnt house with a cutlass at her side and dressed in pantaloons. After just eleven days, Joseph had fled Madrid for Burgos, and then for Vitoria in the north. Some 60,000 French troops were now confined to the north-east of Spain behind the Ebro, leaving behind some 40,000 dead or prisoner. It had been a reversal for the French in an area which Napoleon had contemptuously believed would be a walkover.

British opinion came to the conclusion that the war was all but won, that the British and Spaniards united could drive France out of the

Peninsula and march on Paris. The ever-realistic Moore did not share
that illusion. He had a different task ahead: to march to Salamanca
across the mountains and join up with a force that was being shipped to
Corunna, under Sir Henry Barclay, before, as he feared, Napoleon
could reinforce his army in northern Spain and launch a counter-
offensive.

What followed was to become one of the great epics in British military
history. Moore immediately set about organizing his dispersed men
outside Lisbon. The British troops there were openly contemptuous of
the Portuguese. In spite of the incredible beauty of the city, its streets
were littered with dead horses, sewage and refuse piled in the famous
'dunghills'. Some 10,000 pariah dogs, which normally acted as mobile
waste disposal units, had been shot by the fastidious French, merely
adding to the mountains of rotting food in the streets. One soldier
wrote: 'What an ignorant, superstitious, priest-ridden, dirty, lousy set
of devils are the Portuguese. Without seeing them it is impossible to
conceive there exists a people in Europe so debased. The filthiest pig
sty is a palace to the filthy houses in this dirty stinking city, and all the
dirt made in the houses is thrown into the streets, where it remains
baking for months until a storm of rain washes it away.'

Moore instilled a new spirit into his men through his energy. On 16
October 1808 he led 20,000 on a march into Spain which was to cross
some 300 miles across mountains rising to 4,000 feet. He had very few
horses and no heavy artillery because the roads were unable to bear it:
just 6-pounders pulled by 4,000 troops along the main road to Madrid,
where they would be unable to support his main forces in the north.

At first the going was easy across the pleasant Portuguese countryside, through prosperous villages amidst hills and valleys. Then the
troops began to climb into sparsely populated areas, and finally
mountain passes where the men had to carry equipment across rough
tracks, through torrential rain and close to precipices. They bore all
their supplies with them, as there were none available here, and no
shelter either.

After these rigours they descended into the gentler regions of
western Spain. There, according to Rifleman Harris: 'We had fought

and conquered and felt elated. Spain was before us and every man in the Rifles seemed only too anxious to get a rap at the French again. It was a glorious sight to see our colours spread in those fields. The men seemed invincible and nothing, I thought, could beat them.' The goal was Salamanca, where they were to rendezvous with Barclay's army, which had arrived off Corunna on 13 October and had been following behind three weeks later. From there they intended to march to join three Spanish armies and converge on the French in northern Spain.

The British and Spaniards had underestimated the enemy they were dealing with. Napoleon had always regarded Spain as a 'sideshow', on a par with the almost bloodless seizure of Naples. A string of disasters, first at Bailen and then at Gerona, Valencia, Zaragoza and Vimeiro, had brought him down to earth. He feared that failure might be contagious across Europe and was bent on a crushing revenge and re-establishment of French authority in the Peninsula. He poured vitriol on his commanders in Spain whom he blamed for the debacle. Writing to his brother Joseph, he complained:

I don't like the tone of your letter of the 24th. There is no question of dying, but of fighting, and of being victorious. I shall find in Spain the pillars of Hercules, not the bounds of my power. In all my military career I have seen nothing more cowardly than these mobs of Spanish soldiers . . . I can see from the report of the cuirassier officer that Dupont's corps will have to retreat. The whole thing is inconceivable. Brute! Fool! Coward! Dupont has lost Spain to save his baggage! It's a spot on my uniform! . . . The enclosed documents are for you alone; read them with a map, and you will be able to judge whether there was ever anything since the world was created so senseless, so stupid, and so dastardly! Here are the Macks and the Hohenlohes justified! One can see clearly enough, by General Dupont's own report, that all that happened resulted from his inconceivable folly. This loss of 20,000 picked men, with the moral effect which it is bound to have, have made the King take the grave decision of falling back towards France. The influence which it will have on the general situation prevents my going to Spain in person; I am sending Marshal Ney there.

The knowledge that you have been thrown into the midst of events that are beyond your range of experience and of character grieves me, my dear friend. Dupont has covered our standards with infamy. An event like this makes my presence in Paris necessary. I feel the sharpest pang at the thought that at such a moment I cannot be at your side and in the midst of my soldiers. Let me know that you are keeping your spirits up, that you are well, and getting used to soldiering – here is a splendid opportunity for studying the business . . . What is going on in Spain is lamentable. My army is not commanded by generals who have made war, but by postal inspectors.

Napoleon's main worry was that the Austrians, in spite of their formal treaties, were planning to open a new offensive. As early as 25 July 1808, he had written perceptively: 'Austria is arming, but denies it; she is therefore arming against us. She is spreading the report that I demand some of her provinces: she is therefore trying to cloak as a rightful defence an unprovoked and hopeless attack. Since Austria is arming, we too must arm. I am therefore ordering the Grand Army to be reinforced. My troops are concentrating at Strasbourg, Mainz, Wesel.' His first preoccupation was to deter an Austrian attack and to this end he sought to renew his links with Russia.

However, after Tilsit the Tsar had become increasingly dissatisfied: he was also under fire at court for having been too subservient to Napoleon on the raft. Many Russians were furious that the French now occupied the Grand Duchy of Warsaw, traditionally a sphere of Russian influence and that, contrary to their promises, they still occupied three-quarters of Prussia. Moreover, Russia had lost its lucrative export market to Britain, one of its chief customers for wood and corn. Alexander was no longer as naïve as Napoleon believed he was, although he was still possessed of a highly erratic temperament.

Moreover he had secured an extraordinary spy: Napoleon's chief foreign adviser, Talleyrand, an aristocratic traditionalist, who by that time regarded Napoleon as 'a devil' leading France to disaster, and hated him. He believed in a general settlement in Europe which would put France at peace with Austria, Russia and England.

Napoleon decided to hold a summit with the Tsar at Erfurt. He ordered all his vassal princes to attend in an extraordinary attempt to overpower the Tsar into renewing his support for him. The conference was to last for two and a half weeks. Napoleon said he wanted 'the Emperor Alexander to be dazzled by the spectacle of my power'.

A gorgeous array of thirty-six princes was on hand to meet the Tsar. Talleyrand was also there, proposing to the Tsar that they should meet secretly every evening at the house of a sister of the formidable Queen of Prussia. Alexander spent his time there each evening either talking to the wily French diplomat or making love to Princess Stephanie of Baden. Talleyrand told him baldly at the first meeting: 'Sire, it is in your power to save Europe, and you will only do so by refusing to give way to Napoleon. The French people are civilized, their sovereign is not. The sovereign of Russia is civilized and his people are not: the sovereign of Russia should therefore be the ally of the French people.'

Talleyrand argued that the French people were desperate for peace and believed that if Alexander resisted Napoleon's demands it would be possible to secure it for Europe. Alexander was only too happy to oblige. In fact, Talleyrand was not close to Russia: he was an ally of the Austrian Habsburgs who had paid him the colossal sum of a million francs for his services. Metternich, the equally able and devious Austrian ambassador in Paris was his partner. Talleyrand was not just deceiving Napoleon, but also Alexander while posing as his secret friend: he was a triple agent and one being rewarded very handsomely.

He completely outwitted his French master. The final treaty was a gift to the Russians. Alexander was to be given a free hand in Finland, as well as part of modern Romania, in exchange for France abandoning its support for the Ottoman empire. Most important of all, Russia was vague about whether it would support France in the event of renewed hostilities with Austria — which had been Napoleon's main concern. He had no wish to go to Spain leaving weakened eastern boundaries of his empire to be attacked by Austria. The Austrians, indeed, had not been invited to Erfurt.

For all the splendour and lavish entertainment, huge shooting parties and nine performances by the Comédie Française, Napoleon left without the assurances he needed. As in politics, so in diplomacy:

Napoleon could be easily outmanoeuvred: it was only in warfare that he really excelled. In the event Napoleon, having achieved little, also refused to moderate his policies of aggression. He set off personally to put down the rebellion in Spain.

As Napoleon departed on his long journey, some 60,000 French troops were ordered to reinforce the army along the Ebro. Napoleon took a further 100,000 along with his best marshals, Lannes, Soult, Ney, Victor and Lefebvre. It was to be a war of annihilation: crushing Spanish resistance and slaughtering their allies in the civilian population – one of the most brutal campaigns ever mounted.

The Spanish with their ill-disciplined, ill-equipped and ill-clad forces in the army of Galicia under General Blake attacked Ney frontally, bravely but foolishly, and were massacred at Durango. Napoleon himself arrived at Vitoria on 5 November in charge of a force superior to the ones in central Spain. He promptly decided to attack. Two of the Spanish armies got away. Napoleon marched impatiently to Burgos and on to the Somosierra Pass, where he encountered unexpected Spanish resistance, before reaching Madrid itself on 1 December. This he took easily.

He issued imperial decrees reminiscent of his arrival in Cairo, abolishing feudal dues and the customs paid between the various Spanish provinces. It remained for him to march southwards with his huge army and pound the fragmented Spanish resistance there. Meanwhile the French had occupied Valladolid. Sir John Moore's army, first at Ciudad Rodrigo and then at Salamanca, heard the news from the defeated Spanish commander. Barclay was still a hundred miles away in Lugo; and Moore realized that he was only sixty miles' distance from the overwhelming French force.

The foolhardy Spanish armies under Generals Castaños and Palafax that had escaped being massacred by the *Grande Armée* set off to attack the French from the east in an effort to cut their lines: the French in Burgos decided to march to face this threat. That gave Moore a breathing space. He knew now that he was in great danger, cut off from retreat by the mountains behind as winter approached and facing an overwhelming French army in front. He wrote to his closest friend,

Pitt's niece, Lady Hester Stanhope: 'Farewell, my dear Lady Hester. If I extricate myself and those with me from our present difficulties, I shall return to you with satisfaction; but if not it will be better I shall never quit Spain.'

He asked Baird to move forward to join him: 'I see my situation in as unfavourable a light as you or any one can do. But it is our business to make every effort to unite here and to obey our orders and the wishes of our country. It would never do to retreat without making the attempt. If the enemy prevent us, there is no help for it, but if he does not, I am determined to unite the army. When that is done we shall act according to circumstances. There is still a chance that the presence of so large a British force may give spirits to the Spaniards.'

Lord Paget, one of Baird's ablest commanders, was astonished: 'The game is considered as completely up. The Government must have been grossly deceived . . . We do not discover any enthusiasm anywhere. The country appears to be in a state of complete apathy. A junction of Moore's corps and of Baird's corps is impossible . . . Even if we were now to form the junction, we have no ulterior object. There is no Spanish army and there is no salvation for the Spanish nation, take my word for it.'

Then Moore heard the appalling news that Castaños and Palafax had been crushed at Tudela: the Spanish armies in northern Spain had been annihilated. There was clearly no alternative but a desperate escape back across the barren Portuguese northern border mountains.

On 5 December Moore made the astounding decision not to turn and run, but to attempt what the northern Spaniards had tried and failed – to strike north-east and cut off Napoleon's lines of communication. It was the first time that a British army – and a tiny one at that – actually sought to confront the Emperor: it was like a mouse attacking a cat. It seemed an utterly suicidal move, calling into question not just Moore's judgement but his sanity. He appeared to be heading directly into a trap against a far superior French army with another one just to the south, with which it could join in a pincer movement.

Yet there was a logic. Napoleon's huge army would be forced to provide for itself in desolate central Spain if it was cut off from its

supplies. Moore believed that Napoleon would have to come after him instead of moving on to wipe out what remained of the Spanish armies to the south and conquer the whole country. Moore's men had by now rested in Salamanca. He discovered that Valladolid had been abandoned by the French, who had been unaware of the British presence nearby. The Peninsular conflict was already taking on the shape that would define it for several more years: of armies chasing each other in complex patterns around the vast empty interior of Spain until superiority of force or shortage of supplies forced one to withdraw.

On 11 December he ordered his army forwards across the frozen territory of northern Spain towards Valladolid. Then Stuart intercepted French despatches which revealed that Marshal Soult was racing with an army westwards towards the river Carrion, while Junot, with his army, was moving upon Burgos nearby. Moore conceived another fantastic plan: to join up with Baird and attack Soult before Junot arrived.

On 20 December, again moving further westwards, they joined up with Baird's fresh-faced reinforcements. The next day they skirmished with the French and Moore prepared to attack Soult's army across the Carrion river at Saldana. It was to be a great victory. Moore wrote: 'The movement I am making is of the most dangerous kind; I not only risk to be surrounded at any moment by superior forces, but to have my communications intercepted with the Galicias. I wish it to be apparent to the whole world that we have done everything in our power in support of the Spanish cause.' He was nothing if not aggressive, after the cautious incompetence of the elderly commanders (Wellesley excepted) in Portugal.

Unknown to Moore, however, he was being paid the greatest compliment of all. Napoleon had learned of the cheeky little British army operating behind his lines and instead of carrying on his campaign of attempting to subdue all of southern Spain, as he should have, the lure of inflicting his first decisive defeat on a British army proved irresistible. He wrote in astonishment: 'I am starting immediately to operate against the English, who appear to have received reinforcements and to be making a show of boldness. The English move is extraordinary. It is clear that they have left Salamanca. It is probable

Napoleon and Alexander
of Russia: imaginative
depiction of the raft at
Tilsit, 1807

Archduke Charles at
Aspern: Austria's
greatest general, 1809

The French take Oporto, start of the Peninsular War, 1809

Death of Sir John Moore at La Coruña, 1809: a magnificent career nipped in the bud

Salamanca: Wellington's finest battle, 1812

The horrors of the Peninsular Wars as depicted by Goya

Moscow burning: awesome Russian self-immolation, 1812

Suffering beyond endurance: the retreat from Moscow, 1812

Caged beast: caricature of Napoleon in Elba, 1814

Blucher: bluff but great
Prussian general

Iron Duke with British Hussars:
painted to celebrate the bestowal
of the title Duke of Wellington
on Wellesley in 1814

The Battle of Waterloo, 1815

that they have sent their transports to Ferrol, with the idea that a retreat on Lisbon would be dangerous.'

He abandoned the conquest of southern Spain and Portugal. Ney was recalled from Saragoza, now undergoing its second siege, to support Soult and the Emperor's own army was to cross the Guadarrama Sierra, this time by the pass of the same name, to attack and trap the British.

The French made the crossing of the mountains in mid-winter through a raging blizzard. Napoleon, who had earlier told an officer that 'impossible is a word I don't know', was stranded through the snowstorm astride a gun and overheard a soldier saying angrily, 'Convicts suffer less than we do. Shoot him down, damn him.' It was 22 December. The following day he hoped to swoop down upon the British at Valladolid, but Moore had already left for Sahagun forty miles to the east to avoid Soult.

At midnight on 23 December, as the British advanced on the unsuspecting French at Sahagun, Moore learnt that Napoleon was at his heels. If the British army was to survive at all, it had to escape at speed to the north via Astorga and the main road to Corunna down which Baird's army had just descended, avoiding the fast-moving Emperor who could move at remarkable speed when it was required of him. 'I am in a hornets' nest and God knows how I shall get out of it,' remarked Moore.

He reversed direction just as quickly as Napoleon had. He abandoned his luggage and made straight for the gap between Napoleon's large army and Soult's, now reinforced by Junot. The snows had begun to thaw over Christmas and had turned to sleet and mud underfoot, although it remained cold. His men had to move fast: they were deeply dispirited at having to retreat after so much effort without the fight they expected. They crossed the river Esla, which now threatened to become impassable, just before Napoleon realized they had left Sahagun.

The British resorted to looting as they went, for they were short of supplies, demoralized and facing a barren and empty land on their hazardous journey. One soldier wrote: 'I blush for our men. I would blame them, too; alas! How can I, when I think upon their dreadful

situation, fatigued and wet, shivering, perishing with cold? – no fuel to be got, not even straw to lie upon. Can men in such a situation admire the beauties of art?'

Their rearguard was protected by cavalry which fought furiously against the crack imperial cavalry which had just crossed the Esla. Some 600 chasseurs were captured or killed, along with their general, in this first significant clash. Moore had only narrowly escaped what would have been Britain's biggest ever military defeat in the war: his army was already down to 25,000 men as they raced across the plain from Astorga for the barren mountains of the north-west.

The defeated Spanish army of General La Romana now hampered their progress. At last reaching the safety of the mountains, they struggled up through increasingly deep snow, reaching the village of Bembibre on New Year's Eve, which they celebrated by raiding the wine cellars and raping the local women. 'Bembibre,' wrote an officer, 'exhibited all the appearance of a place lately stormed and pillaged. Every door and window was broken, every lock and fastening forced. Rivers of wine ran through the houses and into the streets, where soldiers, women, children, runaway Spaniards and muleteers lay in fantastic groups with wine oozing from their lips and nostrils.'

The following day they groggily resumed their flight. Napoleon wrote furiously: 'The English are running away as fast as they can. They have abandoned the Spaniards in a shameful and cowardly manner. Have all this shown up in the newspapers. Have caricatures made and songs and popular ditties written. Have them translated into German and Italian and circulated in Italy and Germany.'

The same New Year's Eve he decided to return to Valladolid to consider news from afar: Austria was arming, there was unrest in Paris and revolution had occurred in Turkey. Mercurial as ever, Napoleon decided to return to Paris, despatching part of his army south to Madrid to reinforce Joseph and sending Soult and Ney with 50,000 men in pursuit of Moore's fleeing army. It was the first and only time as Emperor he came close to fighting a British army in person before Waterloo. Napoleon rode on a fast horse from Valladolid to Burgos – seventy-five miles – in just four hours. He was still in peak physical condition, although the plumpness

that characterized his later years was beginning to set in. It took him six further days to reach Paris.

Moore's army continued its retreat through the frozen mountains to Villafranca, which the desperate British soldiery pillaged again: 'Every soldier took what he liked, everything was plundered, carried away and trampled under foot; the casks of wine were broken open so that half their contents were spilt over the floor, and the general fury and unruliness of these hordes of men was such that those officers who attempted to maintain order had to make haste to fight their way out of the crowds, if only to save their lives.'

General Paget tried to restore order through the time-honoured methods of flogging and hanging. As he was about to hang two men he declared: 'My God! is it not lamentable that, instead of preparing the troops confided to my command to receive the enemies of their country, I am preparing to hang two robbers. If I spare the lives of these two men, will you promise to reform?' There was a great shout and the prisoners were taken down.

They struggled on up precipitate mountain passes at Los Royales and Constantino: 'The misery of the whole thing was appalling. Huge mountains, intense cold, no houses, no shelter or cover of any kind, no inhabitants, no bread. The howling wind, as it whistled past the ledges of rock and through the bare trees, sounded to the ear like the groaning of the damned.' They reached the coastal plain on 10 January and at last found the food they craved. The following day they arrived at last at Corunna: there were only 15,000 left, some 5,000 having died or been captured in the last ten days alone.

However the necessary troop transports to lift them off had been delayed and did not arrive for another four days. There were 110 of them, escorted by twelve ships of the line, and they came not a moment too soon. As Moore ordered a hurried embarkation, Soult's forces arrived the following day and took up position along the range of hills that surrounded the port. They brought up eleven 12-pound cannon, eight 6-pounders and twenty heavy-calibre guns, as well as 20,000 men.

On the afternoon of 16 January, as the British were being embarked,

the French guns opened up and the surrounding troops marched down the hillsides. The twenty-six-year-old Captain Charles Napier observed Moore as he ordered the rearguard to its posts to fend off the attack:

> He came at speed and pulled up so sharp and close he seemed to have alighted from the air; man and horse looking at the approaching foe with an intentness that seemed to concentrate all feeling in their eyes. The sudden stop of the animal, a cream-coloured one with black tail and mane, had cast the latter streaming forward; its ears were pushed out like horns, while its eyes flashed fire, and it snorted loudly with expanded nostrils, expressing terror, astonishment and muscular exertion.
>
> My first thought was, it will be away like the wind! But then I looked at the rider, and the horse was forgotten. Thrown on its haunches the animal came, sliding and dashing the dirt up with its fore feet, thus bending the general forward almost to its neck. But his head was thrown back and his look more keenly piercing than I ever saw it. He glanced to the right and left, and then fixed his eyes intently on the enemy's advancing column, at the same time grasping the reins with both his hands, and pressing the horse firmly with his knees: his body thus seemed to deal with the animal while his mind was intent on the enemy, and his aspect was one of searching intentness beyond the power of words to describe. For a while he looked, and then galloped to the left without uttering a word.

Moore coolly ordered two divisions to remain in reserve behind his lines while his infantry fell behind the main line to guard against the French attack. Other Frenchmen veered to the eastern flank of the British, failing to spot the reserves. Moore coolly ordered them out at the last minute, routing the advancing French infantry and counterattacking to take several guns. The British rearguard advanced against a vastly superior force uphill.

As Moore rode among his men, a roundshot knocked him from his horse smashing his left shoulder and collarbone and leaving a gap wide

open to his lungs. His arm dangled uselessly. It was clearly a mortal wound. He was carried by six Highlanders through the streets of Corunna. He said, 'I have always wanted to die this way.' Once in shelter he added: 'I hope the people of England will be satisfied. I hope my country will do me justice.' The embarkation was carried out with complete success.

On the morning of the 17th Moore's body, wrapped in his cloak, was borne along the ramparts of the citadel and buried. Baird had his own arm shattered but survived. A few days after the evacuation, Corunna and Ferrol surrendered to the French. Even Zaragoza, after the loss of 50,000 inhabitants and three heroic stands, surrendered with its remaining 16,000 starving people. When the ships bearing the defeated army of Sir John Moore reached England, it seemed that once again the country was on the defensive. Yet another continental expedition had failed, just after the fiasco at Cintra had allowed the entire French army to escape from Lisbon intact.

Yet it was not so; for Moore's extraordinary march had diverted Napoleon from subduing all of Spain. And the British army's escape from the jaws of death had a legendary quality: the flight across the mountains had been followed by an evacuation of the kind that at Dunkirk a century and a quarter later established a legend of indomitability. In spite of the looting and indiscipline, the British had gained a year's respite for Spain, had tweaked the nose of the greatest army hitherto known – the 300,000-strong *Grande Armée* – with a far inferior force, and had escaped to fight another day.

Moore's heroic death added to the legendary quality and was immortalized in the famous poem by Charles Wolfe: 'Not a drum was heard nor a funeral note/As his corse to the rampart we hurried' There are few things the British like so much as a fallen hero of the calibre of Wolfe at Quebec, Nelson at Trafalgar and now Moore. He had won his last battle, even as he himself expired.

For the first time too in this long war, which had already lasted fifteen years with only a brief interlude, the British land army had distinguished itself for being brave, well-led, disciplined. Wellesley's men had made a start at Vimeiro; Moore had shown what they were capable of, after their disasters in Belgium and Holland. Moore's tactics

and humane methods survived him; for he had fundamentally reformed the British army and the way men were treated by their
commanders. His campaign of 1808 was the turning point for the
British army on land.

There were many now in Britain who argued in favour of abandoning
the Peninsula, like the Low Countries. With Moore dead and Baird
wounded that left only Wellesley as a promising field commander –
and he was still unfairly tainted by the Convention of Cintra, Wellesley, however, had no doubts. From Ireland he pestered Castlereagh
with his advocacy of a further expedition to Portugal. He argued that it
would require only 20,000 to 30,000 troops to hold Lisbon, which he
believed he could protect indefinitely. The Spaniards had made clear
that any further expeditionary force landing on their territory would be
unwelcome: yet Cadiz, Seville, Castile, Granada and southern Spain
remained free.

Moreover the whole country remained mired in a guerrilla war of
unbelievable ferocity on both sides. After the surrender at Bailen the
Spaniards had landed 10,000 Frenchmen to die of starvation on a
remote island. Other Frenchmen who were captured were often
crucified, boiled or buried alive. Goya's gruesome etchings of the
disasters of war give an idea of the methods employed, with people
being impaled on stakes or on trees. The French responded with mass
executions by firing squad or hanging, and by raping as a matter of
course to sustain the carnal appetites of the troops stuck in this hostile,
barren land. The cruelty and suffering in Spain awoke the indignation
not just of the British but of people across Europe, whether Napoleon's
subjects or not. It also tied down some 300,000 French troops. It
seemed that a barbarous but brave people had at last found the courage
to resist the Napoleonic steamroller.

The British could not just act the part of spectators. Castlereagh and
Canning were determined to stand up to Napoleon. The guerrilla
struggle in the Peninsula also kindled sparks of resistance elsewhere in
Europe. Everywhere Napoleon began to be denounced as a tyrant
rather than a liberator. The German philosopher Fichte issued an
'Address to the German People' in late 1807 which stoked feelings of

latent nationalism. In Prussia, Stein, a liberal nationalist who had been appointed by the Kaiser to run his truncated state, was hunted down by the French and forced to flee to Austria.

The Spanish resistance also encouraged the sputtering anti-French insurrection in Calabria, which had continued from 1806, although this was finally more or less crushed by the new King of Naples, Joachim Murat (far more ruthless and effective militarily than Joseph Bonaparte) by the end of 1811. In the Tyrol, with Austrian backing, anti-Bavarian anti-French guerrillas rose up in May 1809 seizing control of the capital of Innsbruck and forcing its garrison of 6,000 to surrender. They were led by a huge innkeeper called Hofer. But after terrible atrocities had been committed by both sides, the insurrection dwindled away by 1810. There was a smaller uprising in Westphalia.

In Britain at last Wellesley won the argument and on 6 April 1809 he was authorized to lead a new expeditionary force on the Peninsula; General Beresford had already been sent to Portugal to organize Portuguese resistance. On 14 April Wellesley embarked, and his old ill-fortune with sea travel returned. Sailing into a gale, the captain told him the ship was sure to founder. 'In that case', replied Sir Arthur in one of the curt soundbites that were increasingly becoming his trademark, 'I shall not take off my boots.' He had been given a second chance to resume his controversial career.

Chapter 61

AIX ROADS

As Sir Arthur sailed off to Spain, Thomas Cochrane, that even more peppery, fiery and bizarre commander, was about to reach the climax of his own career. Since the stinging defeat at Trafalgar in 1805, Napoleon had not been idle at sea: he had thrown himself into a programme of naval building and in 1809 for the first time in four years, appeared seriously to be threatening Britain with invasion once again. He had constructed fourteen new ships of the line at the superb new dockyard in the Scheldt estuary, while ten more were being built at Antwerp and Flushing. Others were being made in French dockyards.

The French fleet was now located at Aix Roads. Although not doing mischief at sea, this was a seemingly impregnable anchorage, close to the French frontier with Spain. From there it could threaten the British sea lines of communication with the expeditionary army in Portugal. It was also liable to emerge to attack merchant shipping with the West Indies, if not the West Indies themselves, where the British had just captured Martinique once again. West Indian trade was a lifeline to Britain while the Continental System was in force. The Aix anchorage, with its long and treacherous approaches, was much more difficult to blockade closely than Brest, and rough weather in the Bay of Biscay always threatened to force British flotillas to stand well out to sea.

It appeared that Napoleon was regaining his confidence at sea. The Admiralty would have none of it and ordered Admiral Lord Gambier, the commander who had so brutally bombarded Copenhagen, to attack the French with fireships: 'The enemy's ships lie much exposed to the operation of fireships, it is a horrible mode of warfare, and the

attempt hazardous, if not desperate; but we should have plenty of volunteers in the service. If you mean to do anything of the kind, it should be done with secrecy and quickly, and the ships used should be not less than those built for the purpose – at least a dozen, and some smaller ones.'

Gambier, however, was simply too cautious a man for this kind of warfare, although he had been commander of the seventeen-strong fleet when the British had bombarded Copenhagen in 1807 with appalling results for that beautiful city. Gambier was a dedicated tractarian Christian who distributed fundamentalist pamphlets to his crew, fiercely opposed alcohol, and refused the common practice of allowing women on board in port. He was known as 'dismal Jimmie' by his men. He was fully in the tradition of St Vincent, a new type of Admiralty bureaucrat, determined to bring greater morality on board ship, espousing middle-class values and despising old-style aristocratic pretensions of the kind Cochrane personified.

Gambier's religious concerns seemed doomed from the start. As one contemporary chaplain wrote: 'Nothing can possibly be more unsuitably or more awkwardly situated than a clergyman in a ship of war; every object around him is at variance with the sensibilities of a rational and enlightened mind . . . The entrance of a clergyman is, to a poor seaman, often a fatal signal . . . To convert a man of war's crew into Christians would be a task to which the courage of Loyola, the philanthropy of Howard, and the eloquence of St Paul united would prove inadequate.'

The poet Thomas Hood mocked the Admiral:

> Oh! Admiral Gam – I dare not mention bier,
> In such a temperate ear;
> Oh! Admiral Gam – an Admiral of the Blue,
> Of course, to read the Navy List aright,
> For strictly shunning wine of either hue,
> You can't be Admiral of the Red or White.

Gambier's intense religious beliefs did not prevent him being a good commander, but as he so patently was not – he was cautious and

indecisive – they merely grated on the officers beneath him, none more so than Admiral Eliab Harvey, the celebrated captain of the *Temeraire* at Trafalgar. Harvey detested his superior. The bad blood between these two senior commanders of the fleet further demoralized it.

With Gambier in a mire of uncertainty off Aix Roads, the Admiralty conceived of an extraordinary idea. The one officer with close knowledge of Aix Roads from his tour of duty three years before was Thomas Cochrane, who had long suggested invading the anchorage with fireships. Here at last was a use for this tiresome but fearless seaman.

Cochrane was ordered immediately to report to Whitehall. Where once Cochrane had striven desperately to gain an audience with Lord St Vincent, he was now received warmly, even effusively, by the new First Sea Lord, Lord Mulgrave, a red-faced Tory just appointed to office, who was a connoisseur of the arts and displayed an enviable unflappability towards all events, good and bad. Mulgrave was to the point, welcoming him and informing him that in spite of Gambier's reservations, twelve transports were being converted for use as fireships. 'You were some years ago employed on the Rochefort station and must to a great extent be acquainted with the difficulties to be surmounted. Besides which, I am told that you then pointed out to Admiral Thornburgh some plan of attack, which would in your estimation be successful. Will you be good enough to detail that or any other plan which your further experience may suggest?'

Cochrane was immediately interested, and launched into his own pet project for building 'explosion ships' to add to the fireships. Even Cochrane was taken aback by how seriously, he, a mere captain, was being taken by the First Sea Lord. Now came the shock: Mulgrave told Cochrane that he was to command the expedition.

At this Cochrane was aghast: he knew the fury that giving command of so major a venture to so junior a captain would arouse not just in Gambier, but all the senior captains serving with him. He was deeply sceptical of the Admiralty's motives.

> It was now clear to me why I had been sent for to the Admiralty, where not a word of approbation of my previous services was uttered. The Channel fleet had been doing worse than nothing. The nation was

dissatisfied, and even the existence of the ministry was at stake. They wanted a victory, and the admiral commanding plainly told them he would not willingly risk a defeat. Other naval officers had been consulted, who had disapproved of the use of fireships, and, as a last resource, I had been sent for, in the hope that I would undertake the enterprise. If this were successful, the fleet would get the credit, which would be thus reflected on the ministry; and if it failed, the consequence would be the loss of my individual reputation, as both ministry and commander-in-chief would lay the blame on me.

Mulgrave brushed aside his objections: 'The present is no time for professional etiquette. All the officers who have been consulted deem an attack with fireships impracticable, and after such an expression of opinion, it is not likely they would be offended by the conduct of fireships being given to another officer who approved of their use.'

Cochrane argued that any senior officer could command the expedition as effectively as he: 'The plan submitted to your Lordship was not an attack with fireships alone, and when the details become known to the service, it will be seen that there is no risk of failure whatever, if made with a fair wind and flowing tide. On the contrary, its success on inspection must be evident to any experienced officer, who would see that as the enemy's squadron could not escape up the Charente, their destruction would not only be certain but in fact easy.'

Mulgrave promised to think the matter over. The following day he summoned Cochrane: 'My Lord, you must go. The Board cannot listen to further refusal or delay. Rejoin your frigate at once. I will make you all right with Lord Gambier. Your confidence in the result has, I must confess, taken me by surprise, but it has increased my belief that all you anticipate will be accomplished. Make yourself easy about the jealous feeling of senior officers. I will so manage it with Lord Gambier that the amour propre of the fleet shall be satisfied.' To Gambier and the officers of the fleet, a single instruction was sent selecting Lord Cochrane 'under your Lordship's direction to conduct the fireships to be employed in the projected attack'. For once, military considerations had overridden political ones in the Admiralty.

★ ★ ★

Cochrane's head was swimming with the opportunity offered as his
carriage galloped back with all speed to Plymouth to join the twelve
transports and to meet up with William Congreve, the inventor of a
new type of explosive rocket, who was to take part in the attack. They
set off to join the Channel Fleet where Cochrane went aboard
Gambier's flagship to witness an extraordinary scene.

Harvey, incensed by news of Cochrane's appointment, was giving
vent to his spite. As the embarrassed young Cochrane stood by, the
veteran seaman hurled a stream of invective upon the self-righteous
Admiral. Cochrane recalled that Harvey's 'abuse of Lord Gambier to
his face was such as I had never before witnessed from a subordinate. I
should even now hesitate to record it as incredible, were it not officially
known by the minutes of the court-martial in which it sometime
afterwards resulted.'

The young captain stood by in embarrassment and afterwards sought
out Harvey to apologize to him:

> Harvey broke out into invectives of a most extraordinary kind,
> openly avowing that he never saw a man so unfit for the command
> of the fleet as Lord Gambier, who instead of sending boats to sound
> the Channels, which he (Admiral Harvey) considered the best
> preparation for an attack on the enemy, he had been employing,
> or rather amusing himself, with mustering the ships' companies, and
> had not even taken the pain to ascertain whether the enemy had
> placed any mortars in front of their lines; concluding by saying, that
> had Lord Nelson been there, he would not have anchored in Basque
> Roads at all, but would have dashed at the enemy at once. Admiral
> Harvey then came into Sir Harry Neale's cabin, and shook hands
> with me, assuring me that he should have been very happy to see me
> on any other occasion than the present. He begged me to consider
> that nothing personal to myself was intended, for he had a high
> opinion of me; but that my having been ordered to execute such a
> service, could only be regarded as an insult to the fleet, and that on
> this account he would strike his flag so soon as the service was
> executed. Admiral Harvey further assured me that he had volun-
> teered his services, which had been refused.

That provoked this exchange.

> Cochrane began: 'The service on which the Admiralty has sent me
> was none of my seeking. I went to Whitehall in obedience to a
> summons from Lord Mulgrave, and at his Lordship's request gave
> the board a plan of attack, the execution of which has been thrust
> upon me contrary to my inclination, as well knowing the invidious
> position in which I should be placed.'
>
> Harvey replied: 'Well, this is not the first time I have been lightly
> treated, and that my services have not been attended to in the way
> they deserved; because I am no canting Methodist, no hypocrite,
> nor a psalm singer. I do not cheat old women out of their estates by
> hypocrisy and canting. I have volunteered to perform the service
> you came on, and should have been happy to see you on any other
> occasion, but am very sorry to have a junior officer placed over my
> head.'
>
> Cochrane responded: 'You must not blame me for that. Permit
> me to remark, that you are using very strong expressions relative to
> the Commander-in-Chief.'
>
> 'I can assure you, Lord Cochrane, that I have spoken to Lord
> Gambier with the same degree of prudence as I have now done to
> you in the presence of Captain Sir H Neal.'
>
> 'Well, Admiral, considering that I have been an unwilling listener
> to what you really did say to his Lordship, I can only remark that you
> have a strange notion of prudence.'

Harvey was soon afterwards removed from command for using
'grossly insubordinate language' towards Gambier. He was court-
martialled and dismissed from the service. But he was an immensely
popular figure, one of Nelson's most famous commanders and was
reinstated the following year, although he was never given a
command again.

Cochrane, assured by Harvey that he had no personal grudge against
him, went off to his own ship, the frigate *Imperieuse*, to make preparations. He wrote directly to Mulgrave in response to his request to
detail his original plan of attack, dating from Thornburgh's time:

My Lord – Having been very close the Isle d'Aix, I find that the western wall has been pulled down to build a better. At present the fort is quite open, and may be taken as soon as the French fleet is driven on shore or burned, which will be as soon as the fireships arrive. The wind continues favourable for the attack. If your Lordship can prevail on the ministry to send a military force here, you will do great and lasting good to our country. Could ministers see things with their own eyes, how differently would they act; but they cannot be everywhere present, and on their opinion of the judgement of others must depend the success of war – possibly the fate of England and all Europe. No diversion which the whole force of Great Britain is capable of making in Portugal or Spain would so much shake the French government as the capture of the islands on this coast. A few men would take Oléron; but to render the capture effective, send twenty-thousand men who, without risk, would find occupation for the French army of a hundred thousand.

The Admiralty took no notice.

Cochrane supervised the conversion of the transports into fireships as they arrived from England. The construction of fireships was an old technique. Five large trails of gunpowder were laid criss-cross on the deck. Wood and canvas were stretched between them. Up above, tarred ropes dangled down from sails also covered in tar. Chains were fixed to the sides with grappling hooks – *a chevaux de frise* – so that it would be difficult for a ship which a fireship drifted against to detach itself. Resin and turpentine were poured all over the fireship to help it to burn. Finally huge holes were made in the hull so as to help suck in air and feed the flames after the ship began to burn.

With the arrival of a further nine fireships from England, Cochrane now had twenty-one under his command. But he was busier still on his own invention, explosion ships. The French would be prepared for fireships, but they would have no understanding of his new secret weapon, just approved by the Admiralty. The preparations for these were more elaborate still: 'The floor was rendered as firm as possible by means of logs placed in close contact, into every crevice of which other

substances were firmly wedged so as to afford the greatest amount of resistance to the explosion. On this foundation were placed a large number of spirit and water casks, into which 1,500 barrels of powder casks were placed, several hundred shells, and over these again nearly three thousand hand grenades; the whole, by means of wedges and sand, being compressed as nearly as possible into a solid mass.'

Vice-Admiral Allemand had anchored the French fleet in an apparently impregnable position. They were drawn up in two lines, between two small islands, the Île d'Aix and the Île Madame, which dominated the approaches to the Charente river. There were gun batteries on the Île d'Aix and the Île d'Oleron, a large spur of land to the west, as well as on the mainland. Cochrane had, however, already personally observed that the battery on Aix was in a poor state of repair, and its firepower grossly exaggerated. Moreover his earlier reconnaissance had led him to discover a remarkable thing. The only clear line of attack upon the French would have to be between a large reef, around three miles wide, called the Boyart Shoal, which was uncovered at low tide, and the Île d'Aix. 'From previous employment on the spot on several occasions I well knew there was room in the Channel to keep out of the way of red-hot shot from the Aix batteries even if, by means of blue lights [flares] or other devices, they had discovered us. The officers and crews of the line-of-battle ships would be impressed with the idea that every fireship was an explosion vessel, and that in place of offering opposition they would, in all probability, be driven ashore in their attempt to escape from such diabolical engines of warfare, and thus become an easy prey.' In other words, the fort providing protection for the French fleet was no use at all. The 'lethal' fire of their guns could not reach the British ships if the latter stuck to the right-hand side of the Channel. There was no threat from this quarter, which Gambier persisted in regarding as extremely dangerous.

'Dismal Jimmie' had written to the Admiralty just a few days before:

The enemy's ships are anchored in two lines, very near each other, in a direction due south from the Isle d'Aix, and the ships in each line not father apart than their own length; by which it appears, as I imagined, that the space for their anchorage is so confined by the

shoaliness of the water, as not to admit of ships to run in and anchor clear of each other. The most distant ships of their two lines are within point-blank shot of the works on the Isle d'Aix; such ships, therefore, as might attack the enemy would be exposed to be raked by red-hot shot, etc, from the island, and should the ships be disabled in their masts, they must remain within range of the enemy's fire until they are destroyed – there not being sufficient depth of water to allow them to move to the southward out of distance.

Having thus set out the dangers of an attack in alarmist tones, Gambier then typically reached an ingratiatingly ambiguous conclusion: 'I beg leave to add that, if their Lordships are of opinion that an attack on the enemy's ships by those of the fleet under my command is practicable, I am ready to obey any orders they may be pleased to honour me with, however great the risk may be of the loss of men and ships.'

What neither Gambier nor Cochrane knew was that the French had their own secret defence – a 900-foot long boom made of wooden trunks held together by chains and anchored to the sea floor. Allemand had also taken other precautions: he had stationed four frigates along the boom, as well as some seventy smaller boats whose purpose was to tow any fireships away from the main fleet should they succeed – which seemed unlikely – in breaking through the boom. The ten French battleships in the front line had lowered their sails in order to lessen their chances of catching fire.

On the morning of 10 April Cochrane went to Gambier to seek formal authorization to put his plan into action. To his astonishment, Gambier refused, citing the danger to the crews of the fireships: 'If you choose to rush on to self-destruction that is your own affair, but it is my duty to take care of the lives of others, and I will not place the crews of the fireships in palpable danger.' Depressed and frustrated, Cochrane returned to the *Impérieuse*. The following day the wind got up from the west and a heavy sea began to run. Far from being deterred by this, Cochrane saw that it presented an opportunity: the sea would favour the British, especially as the tide came in, and, although the swell would make

navigation much trickier in the treacherous Channel, the French would be less on their guard, thinking the conditions too dangerous for an attack.

Gambier, meanwhile, had had time to reflect. His explicit orders were to allow Cochrane to make the attack; and he could not continue to refuse him authority without risking injury to his own reputation. Cochrane returned on board the flagship to ask for permission; and this time it was grudgingly given.

His ships would attack in three waves. The first would be his three explosion ships, the foremost of which he, never reluctant to place himself in intense danger at the front of the fighting, would command. The second wave would consist of the twenty fireships. Behind them were three frigates, the *Pallas*, the *Aigle* and the *Unicorn*, accompanied by HMS *Caesar* to pick up the returning crews of the explosion vessels and fireships; but they would not come close to the action at this stage.

There were two sobering thoughts. First, the French understandably regarded fireships as a barbaric instrument of war, and would execute anyone they caught that could be identified as crewing them; the sailors were instructed to say, if caught, that they belonged to victualling ships nearby. Second, although the flood-tide to shore in this heavy swell favoured the fireships' approach, it would make it very difficult for their crews, now in small boats, to go out against the flow and regain the safety of the rescue ships.

Gambier, astonishingly, anchored his fleet nine miles away. It was such a distance that it could only be supposed he wanted to be able to make a break for it and escape if the French fleet came out after him – the reverse of virtually all British naval tactics for a century or more, which were based on carrying the fight to the French. The fleet would be too far to exercise the slightest influence on the initial action and, worse, it was impossible for him to see what was really going on; even signals were liable to be misinterpreted at that distance.

Cochrane floated in on the flood tide aboard the foremost explosion vessel – itself a desperately dangerous venture, as he and his men were sitting on top of tons of explosive; one lucky shot from the French and they would be annihilated. Besides Cochrane and Lieutenant Bissel of

the *Impérieuse* there were just four seamen. Behind him a second explosion ship followed with Midshipman Marryat – later to make a name as a great story teller – on board, commanded by a lieutenant. Cochrane had no idea there was a boom but his ship navigated successfully down the Channel at dead of night, in spite of the heavy swell, approaching as close to the distant huddle of the French fleet as he dared. Then he lit the fifteen-minute fuse of the explosives aboard. He was certainly very close to the boom when he did so; his men were already aboard the getaway gig.

As soon as he jumped aboard, they rowed for all they were worth away from the explosion ship in the pitch darkness. According to press accounts Cochrane, hearing barking, saw a dog aboard – the ship's mascot – and rowed back to fetch it. Certainly something delayed his departure, and the fuse, for some reason, went off after only nine minutes. Cochrane's boat had barely managed to get clear of the ship again when it went up. He was saved by his failure to get further. If he had not gone back he would have been on the receiving end of the shower of debris that soared overhead and landed in an arc in the sea just beyond.

The explosion was awesome. Cochrane vividly described the scene:

For a moment, the sky was red with the lurid glare arising from the simultaneous ignition of 1,500 barrels of powder. On this gigantic flash subsiding, the air seemed alive with shells, grenades, rockets, and masses of timber, the wreck of the shattered vessel; whilst the water was strewn with spars shaken out of the enormous boom, on which, on the subsequent testimony of Captain Proteau, whose frigate lay just within the boom, the vessel had brought up before she exploded. The sea was convulsed as by an earthquake, rising in a huge wave on whose crest our boat was lifted like a cork and as suddenly dropped into a vast trough, out of which, as it closed on us with a rush of a whirlpool, none expected to emerge. The skill of the boat's crew however overcame the threatened danger, which passed away as suddenly as it had arisen, and in a few minutes nothing but a heavy rolling sea had to be encountered, all having become silence and darkness.

The boom lay in pieces. The second ship passed through its broken fragments some ten minutes later, and the decision was taken to detonate it and abandon ship in the same way. Another tremendous explosion shattered the peace of the night sky. The third explosion ship had, however, been pushed away from the scene by the *Impérieuse* because a fireship had come too close, and there was a risk of all three blowing up together. Marryat was ordered to go aboard the fireship and steer it away, a heroic action, after which Cochrane asked him laconically whether he had felt warm.

To Cochrane's disappointment the fireships were badly handled. As he rowed back to the *Impérieuse*, three or four passed him, being towed by small rowing boats towards their destination. But the towing boats of some seventeen others had abandoned them about four miles out to sea, judging the risk too great, and most drifted harmlessly ashore. The whole spectacle, however, had been enough to cause havoc among the French fleet. Their first experience of the attack had been the ear-shattering explosion and conflagration aboard Cochrane's ship, followed by another even closer to hand. Then the night sky had been lit up by the spectacle of twenty blazing vessels, some close, others out to sea, in a massive attack to destroy the French fleet.

Their first assumption was that the fireships coming towards them were also explosion vessels, and in the small space of water of the Aix anchorage, the French ships of the line manoeuvred desperately to avoid them, while both wind and tide drove them relentlessly towards the shore. The flagship *Océan* was the first to run aground. According to one of its officers:

At 10.00 we grounded, and immediately after a fireship in the height of her combustion grappled us athwart our stern; for ten minutes she remained in this situation while we employed every means in our power to prevent the fire from catching the ship; our fire engines and pumps played upon the poop enough to prevent it from catching fire; with spars we hove off the fireship, with axes we cut the chains of the grapplings lashed to her yards, but a *chevaux de frise* on her sides held her firmly to us. In this deplorable situation we thought we must have been burned, as the flames of the fireship

covered all our poop. Two of our line-of-battle ships, the *Tonnerre* and *Patriote*, at this time fell on board of us; the first broke our bowsprit and destroyed our main chains. Providence afforded us assistance on this occasion. At the moment the fireship was athwart our stern, and began to draw forward along the starboard side, the *Tonnerre* separated herself from us, and unless this had happened the fireship would have fallen into the angle formed by two ships and would infallibly have burnt them. The fireship having got so far forward as to be under our bowsprit, we left it there some time to afford the two ships above mentioned time to get far enough away to avoid being boarded by this fireship. While this fireship was on board of us we let the cocks run in order to wet the powder, but they were so feeble that we could not do that.

Some fifty of the *Océan*'s men fell into the water and drowned. In the confusion the French ships made towards the coastal mud-flats and the Palles Shoal off the Île Madame; they got too close. The tide was on the turn and now ebbing fast: the *Océan* was joined aground by the *Aquilon*, *Tonnerre*, *Ville de Varsovie* and *Calcutta*, with their hulls stranded like ducks' bottoms out of the water.

As the first streaks of light illuminated the morning sky, Cochrane looked on the scene with deep satisfaction. His victory had been far from perfect: he had been forced to blow up the explosion ships before they could reach the fleet but they had destroyed the boom that protected the French fleet. The fireship attack had almost been a disaster: but the confusion sown by the first two explosion ships and the four fireships that had reached the enemy had been enough effectively to disperse the French fleet, run most of it aground, and place it at the mercy of the British. Complete victory lay in the offing, thanks to his imagination, and the bravery of his crews.

At 5.48 a.m., at first light, he signalled triumphantly to the flagship, the *Caledonia*, some nine miles away: 'Half the fleet to destroy the enemy. Seven on shore.' Gambier signalled back with the answering pennant – a bare acknowledgement. Cochrane, just outside the Aix Channel, watching the floundering French fleet, waited for Gambier's

ships to approach and give him the signal to attack with his small flotilla of frigates. He wondered why there was no movement by Gambier's ships, but watched delightedly through his telescope as four more French ships were beached.

At 6.40 he reported this to the *Caledonia*. The answering pennant was hoisted and Gambier made no move. Cochrane's notoriously short fuse was now burning to explosion point. He had just taken in a ship laden with explosives at enormous personal risk to himself and narrowly escaped with his life. He had seen his attack effectively incapacitate the entire French fleet. It was impossible for beached ships to fire broadside, indeed any guns at all. Now that they could be picked off at will, Gambier and his huge fleet were still hesitant to come in and finish them off.

An hour later, at 7.40, Cochrane sent off another signal: 'Only two afloat.' The reply was the answering pennant again and the fleet made no move. Whatever the explanation he gave at the subsequent court-martial, Gambier's motives in refusing to attack the beached French fleet were probably mixed. He had been witness to the amazing fireworks of the night before. He heartily disapproved of the whole tactic of sending in explosion ships and fireships, and disliked the impulsive and reckless Cochrane. His captains had been almost mutinous about Cochrane's appointment.

How could the commander-in-chief even be sure that Cochrane was telling the truth and not seeking to entice the fleet into a dangerous engagement from which it might emerge badly damaged? His duty was the protection of the fleet, and he could not put it at risk on the word of an impertinent young captain. He decided, first, not to risk his ships in the confined waters of the Aix–Boyart Channel under the guns of enemy batteries; and, second, to teach Cochrane a lesson and show who was in command. The Admiralty had ordered him to support Cochrane's fireship attack; it had not insisted that he risk any of his own ships.

This was to be one of the most contemptible acts of any commander-in-chief in British naval history, far eclipsing Admiral Byng's realistic decision to surrender Minorca only half a century before – for which he had been shot. The ideal chance to move in and destroy

the beached French fleet would be short-lived. The British ships would have the perfect chance to come in on the flood before the French ships floated once again. It was a small window of opportunity.

Cochrane fumed in an agony of frustration and impotence. He signalled at 9.30: 'Enemy preparing to move.' Gambier was later to claim that 'as the enemy was on shore, [I] did not think it necessary to run any unnecessary risk of the fleet, when the object of their destruction seemed to be already obtained.' There is a small possibility that he was telling the truth − in other words that he believed the French ships to have been incapacitated by their grounding − although any sailor with more experience than Gambier would have realized that a ship beached by a tide was perfectly capable of floating off with little damage done. It is true that there was a slight element of ambiguity in the first three signals − but only to the most obtuse commander. Cochrane claimed later that he then sent another signal 'the frigates alone can destroy the enemy' − which allowed of no ambiguity, but was clearly impertinent. It was not, however, logged aboard the flagship. But after his 9.30 signal even Gambier could have harboured no illusions that the enemy was anything but destroyed.

At 11.00 a.m. the Admiral at last ordered his ships inshore − and then, to Cochrane's astonishment, the fleet stopped some four miles out. Cochrane watched in utter disbelief: victory was ebbing away with the incoming tide. As he wrote: 'There was no mistaking the admiral's intention in again bringing the fleet to an anchor. Notwithstanding that the enemy had been four hours at our mercy, and to a considerable extent was still so, it was now evident that no attack was intended, and that every enemy's ship would be permitted to float away unmolested and unassailed! I frankly admit that this was too much to be endured. The words of Lord Mulgrave rang in my ears, "The Admiralty is bent on destroying that fleet before it can get out to the West Indies."'

Having displayed so much courage the previous night, he now took what is said to have been the bravest decision of his entire career, because it involved both defying his commander-in-chief and taking on alone the might of the French navy − although to him the risk may have seemed small as the ships were at his mercy. But they were

floating off, and Gambier's prevarications had left it almost too late even for him to attack successfully.

In an action that compared with Nelson's raising the telescope to his blind eye at Copenhagen, Cochrane decided to raise anchor aboard the *Impérieuse* and drift, stern foremost, down the perilous Aix Channel – that is, with his vulnerable rear exposed to enemy fire – straight into the midst of a dozen warships. This required superb seamanship. The idea was not to let Gambier see what he was doing until the last moment, and to be able to claim that he had floated accidentally with the tide. The shore batteries on the Île d'Oleron opened up, but the shells fell reassuringly far from the ship – as Cochrane had always predicted they would. The ones on the Île d'Aix were so ineffectual that, according to a British gunner: 'we could not find above thirteen guns that could be directed against us in passing; and these we thought so little of that we did not return their fire.'

However, the huge flagship *Océan* was now afloat again, as were four other ships, which immediately turned tail and made for the safety of the Charente estuary upon the *Impérieuse*'s backwards approach. The French were now so demoralized they were not prepared to take on even Cochrane's single ship. Cochrane wrote later: 'Better to risk the frigates or even my commission than to suffer such a disgraceful termination [of the engagement].' At last, when he had safely emerged from the Channel, he unfurled his sails, signalling at the same time to Gambier:

1.30 p.m. The enemy's ships are getting under sail.

1.40 p.m. The enemy is superior to the chasing ship.

1.45 p.m. The ship is in distress, and required to be assisted immediately. Thus he had cleverly outwitted his admiral: he could claim that he had not been responsible for the *Impérieuse*'s approach to the French fleet; and it was unheard of for a commander not to come to the help of one of his ships in distress, thus forcing Gambier's hand.

By two o'clock the *Impérieuse* was close enough to deliver a broadside into the 50-gun French magazine ship, the *Calcutta*, while her forecastle (forward) guns fired upon the *Aquilon* and her bow guns fired on the *Ville de Varsovie* – three ships at the same time. Captain Lafon of the *Calcutta*, fearing that his explosive-laden ship would blow

up, climbed understandably but ignominiously out of his stern cabin window and ran away across the mud – for which he was later shot by the French.

The *Impérieuse* itself came under fire. Marryat recalled graphically how a seaman in the fo'c's'le was decapitated by a cannonball, and how another was blown in two while the spine still attached the two parts: the corpse, its reflexes still working, jumped to its feet, stared at him 'horribly in the face', and fell down. In fact only three members of the crew were killed and eleven wounded throughout the whole engagement – another example of the 'reckless' Cochrane's meticulous care for the safety of his men. The *Calcutta* surrendered at 3.20 and Cochrane's men took possession.

Behind him, Gambier had at last been goaded into action. He sent in two battleships, the *Valiant* and *Revenge*, along with the 44-gun *Indefatigable*, described by Marryat: 'She was a beautiful ship, in what we call "high kelter"; she seemed a living body, conscious of her own superior power over her opponents, whose shot she despised as they fell thick and fast about her, while she deliberately took up an admirable position for battle. And having furled her sails, and squared her yards, as if she had been at Spithead, her men came down from aloft, went to their guns, and opened such a fire on the enemy's ships as would have delighted the great Nelson himself.'

The *Revenge* fired at the *Calcutta* before she realized it had already been occupied by Cochrane's sailors. The *Aquilon* and the *Ville de Varsovie* surrendered at 5.30. The *Caesar*, under Rear-Admiral Stopford, had also joined the battle by then. At 6 p.m. the crew of the *Tonnerre* abandoned ship and set fire to her; she blew up an hour later, as did the *Calcutta*, which had been set alight by Cochrane's men, at about 9 p.m. Six of the French ships had however escaped up the Charente. Stopford sent in hastily converted fireships after them, but these were unable to prevail against the wind, and he used them instead against other ships.

The fighting raged on through the following night. At 4 a.m., however, Gambier hoisted three lights aboard his flagship as a signal for the recall of the British ships. The two ships Cochrane had captured, the *Aquilon* and the *Ville de Varsovie*, were set alight by Stopford –

although Cochrane had hoped to bring them back as prizes. As the *Indefatigable* sailed past, Cochrane tried to persuade her captain to join him in a final attack on the French flagship, the *Océan*, but he refused. So Cochrane set off in pursuit, accompanied by a flotilla of small boats.

Gambier thereupon sent him an astonishing letter, which had to be rowed all the way to his ship:

> You have done your part so admirably that I will not suffer you to tarnish it by attempting impossibilities, which I think, as well as those captains who have come from you, any further effort to destroy those ships would be. You must, therefore, join as soon as you can, with the bombs, etc, as I wish for some information, which you allude to, before I close my despatches. PS: I have ordered three brigs and two rocket vessels to join you, with which, and the bomb, you may make an attempt on the ship that is aground on the Palles, or towards Île Madame, but I do not think you will succeed; and I am anxious that you should come to me, as I wish to send you to England as soon as possible. You must, therefore, come as soon as the tide turns.

Cochrane replied curtly: 'I have just had the honour to receive your Lordship's letter. We can destroy the ships that are on shore, which I hope your Lordship will approve of.' For four hours now Cochrane and his little boats had engaged the mighty *Océan*, convinced that further successes could be obtained.

But at 5 a.m. a further letter arrived from Gambier unambiguously relieving Cochrane of his command: 'It is necessary I should have some communication with you before I close my despatches to the Admiralty. I have, therefore, ordered Captain Wolfe to relieve you in the services you are engaged in. I wish you to join me as soon as possible, that you may convey Sir Harry Neale to England, who will be charged with my despatches, or you may return to carry on the service where you are. I expect two bombs to arrive every moment, they will be useful in it.'

At last, after nearly thirty-six hours of exhausting battle, Cochrane obeyed orders and returned to the flagship. The battle-stained and

exhausted young captain confronted the impeccably dressed and pompous non-combatant admiral who had done so little to help him, and had turned what should have been an overwhelming victory into half of one. Cochrane:

> begged his lordship, by way of preventing the ill-feeling of the fleet from becoming detrimental to the honour of the service, to set me aside altogether and send in Admiral Stopford, with the frigates or other vessels, as with regard to him there could be no ill-feeling: further declaring my confidence that from Admiral Stopford's zeal for the service, he would, being backed by his officers, accomplish results more creditable than anything that had yet been done. I apologised for the freedom I used, stating that I took the liberty as a friend, for it would be impossible, as matters stood, to prevent a noise being made in England.

Gambier replied huffily: 'If you throw blame upon what has been done, it will appear like arrogantly claiming all the merit to yourself.' Cochrane retorted: 'I have no wish to carry the despatches, or to go to London with Sir Harry Neale on the occasion. My object is alone that which has been entrusted to me by the Admiralty − to destroy the vessels of the enemy.'

Cochrane was peremptorily ordered to depart for England the following morning, and arrived at Spithead six days later. Even the French acknowledged the magnitude of the victory: 'This day of the 12th was a very disastrous one: four of our ships were destroyed, many brave people lost their lives by the disgraceful means the enemy made use of to destroy our lines of defence.' The planned French expedition to Martinique had been completely destroyed.

It had been the last great naval battle of the Napoleonic wars, a victory won largely by a single captain in a single ship, on a par with the Glorious First of June, St Vincent, Copenhagen, the Nile and Trafalgar. Although fewer ships were destroyed, thanks to Gambier's ineptitude, Aix had momentous effects; for the French never stirred out of port in force again, nor threatened Britain seriously with invasion. There were to be no more great sea battles.

Cochrane however was far too junior and controversial to enjoy the thanks of the Admiralty or the government. On the return of the British fleet to Britain, it was Gambier who was granted the honours of victory. When Cochrane protested publicly, a court-martial was held which was a travesty of justice. When Gambier was commended, Cochrane was considered disgraced. He furiously turned down an offer to command a flotilla in the Mediterranean.

Britain's greatest living seaman was eventually offered in 1814 command of a ship of the line. Before he could sail, however, he was implicated, almost certainly falsely, in a spectacular stock exchange fraud and was sent to prison for a year. The career of the *loup de mer*, as Napoleon had admiringly dubbed him, was later rescued when he was given command of the fleets that helped to liberate Chile and Peru from Spanish rule and Brazil from Portugal, as well as, less successfully, of the fleet in the Greek war of liberation. It was a fitting end to a career even more eccentric, topsy-turvy and in some ways brave and dashing than those of Nelson and Wellington.

Chapter 62

THE AUSTRIANS STRIKE BACK

The destruction of the French fleet at Aix Roads reaffirmed Britain's complete naval superiority. It occurred just as Wellesley was making his stormy way across the Bay of Biscay with his new expeditionary force. The victory could hardly have been better timed. Napoleon now had a great deal more on his plate than the 'side-show' in the Peninsula. The fragile peace on his eastern borders had collapsed, and something approaching a conspiracy to overthrow him was taking place in the salons of Paris.

When he had turned back to Paris from Valladolid, he had done so because he had learned of an extraordinary reception given by Talleyrand to which Joseph Fouché, the all-powerful minister of police had been invited. The two men had long detested each other. When they were seen in earnest conversation while their master was away in Spain, it seemed a direct challenge.

There were also rumours of a plot to put Joachim Murat in power. Talleyrand was certainly aware of this. Further, Talleyrand appeared to be conspiring with Metternich, the brilliant young Austrian ambassador in Paris, who was openly pressing his masters in Vienna to renew war against France. Metternich reported back home that Murat and Talleyrand were working for a general peace in Europe, although not the overthrow of Napoleon. Instead they sought to tie his hands with a dynastic marriage – and Talleyrand, as much as Metternich, favoured an Austrian royal wife. First, though, in Metternich's view, it was necessary for Austria to administer a severe military drubbing to Napoleon.

This episode is highly revealing. It shows the extent to which the boastful, all-powerful Emperor in fact survived on the sufferance of two powerful constituencies; the marshals around him, whom he could berate and order in battle and the powerful political constituencies represented by men like Talleyrand and Fouché who could conspire with senior officers if they believed Napoleon was damaging France. The generals as a whole had the power to depose Napoleon because they collectively could muster greater military force than he could (which explains his continuing inability to dismiss these senior soldiers except in cases of military failure). This showed how weak the Emperor immediately became if he was exposed to unexpected military setbacks of the kind occurring in Spain. He had miscalculated disastrously over Spain, and there were mutterings against him in dark corners. He could rant and rage at these conspirators but he was powerless even to arrest them, much as he would have liked to. All he could do was travel posthaste to Paris to reassert his authority.

The mystery remains why Talleyrand chose so publicly to signal his discontent with the Emperor by openly fraternizing with Fouché. It may be that he wanted to signal that he was not engaged in any underhand plotting, but was quite open and candid about his opposition. It may simply have been because Talleyrand believed Fouché had learnt of the plot and thought it best to implicate the powerful police chief before he was able to report to the Emperor. Perhaps he merely thought so public a display would force the Emperor to undercut him by following the exact course he recommended – the Austrian marriage, which was in fact what occurred. In the case of a mind as devious as Talleyrand's, there was certainly a motive.

Napoleon's reaction on learning of this cabal was instantaneous. Arriving in Paris, he summoned a meeting of the privy council after first scolding Fouché in private. Then, in front of the senior members of his government, he told them that to doubt the Emperor was the beginning of treason, to criticize him treason itself. He turned on Talleyrand and shouted himself hoarse with personal abuse, including references to his lameness and the infidelity of his wife. 'You are a thief, a coward, a man without honour, you disbelieve in God, you have betrayed everyone, to you nothing is sacred, you would sell your own

father! You suppose, without rhyme or reason, that my Spanish affairs are going wrong. You deserve that I should smash you like a glass, but I despise you too profoundly to put myself to that trouble!'

He finished by describing him as excrement in a silk stocking. Then he stormed off. Talleyrand merely remarked, 'What a pity that so great a man should be so ill-bred.' But Napoleon did not arrest him. He finally condescended to speak to Talleyrand three days later. The biggest source of his fury was probably the awareness that Talleyrand had urged the Austrians to wage war against France – which was by any standards high treason. On the following day Napoleon buttonholed the scheming Metternich. 'Well! This is something new at Vienna! What does it mean? Has a spider stung you? Who is threatening you? Whom are you aiming at? Do you want to set the world aflame again?'

He remarked to a companion: 'Metternich has almost become a statesman, he lies very well. [Austria] wants to get slapped; she shall have it, on both cheeks. If the Emperor Francis attempts any hostile move, he will soon have ceased to reign. That is clear. Before another ten years mine will be the most ancient dynasty of Europe.'

This time, for once, Napoleon could not be blamed for starting the war. It was declared upon him unilaterally by Austria. It marked a huge turnabout in his fortunes. For until that moment the Emperor had held the initiative in Europe. He was the man who had threatened Britain with invasion in 1805, who had declared himself Emperor and then behaved so provocatively in Italy and Germany that the reluctant Austrians had no choice but to declare war upon him in the year that culminated at Austerlitz. It was he who had goaded the Prussians the following year, leading to their declaration of war and the hammer-blows struck against them and the Russians by the French. He had set the agenda, the others had merely reacted.

When his juggernaut rolled into Spain, supposedly to punish Godoy's disloyalty but, in practice to acquire another huge province for his empire, once again he was the aggressor, but also unquestionably the moving spirit in Europe. With the setbacks in Spain, however, with his army for the first time bogged down in a war of uncertain duration, and even occasionally being defeated, he had lost the initiative for the first time.

The Austrians, still his most formidable land enemy, were quick to seize it from his grasp. In this they could be labelled the aggressors. But it was primarily Napoleon's fault. Talleyrand had been right in remarking that all his victories would count for nothing unless they were used as the foundation for a new settlement of Europe – French-led no doubt, but broadly acceptable to the others. It had been useless to force a punitive peace on Austria and then to dismember Prussia because sooner or later those formidable states would fight to recover their lost territory.

If Napoleon had been generous in victory, established his succession and a dynastic alliance with Austria as Talleyrand had long urged, with Austrian self-respect guaranteed and a compromise on the Italian territories, and if he had treated Prussia with generosity, then perhaps a peaceful and lasting settlement in the east could have been achieved. France might then have controlled all of the territory west of the Rhine, with a group of German buffer states and Austria and Prussia acting as a shield against unpredictable Russia with its barbarian and expansionist tendencies. Neither Austria nor Prussia harboured any expansionist designs towards France. But Napoleon had humiliated both, as well as the German states which now watched like hawks for the chance to restore their fortunes.

Worse, he had ill-advisedly sought out Russia as his ally. Not only were the Russians unreliable and sought a deal with France solely to carve up smaller countries like Poland and Finland between them: the alliance was between Europe's two most aggressive and predatory countries. The Austrians and Prussians feared, with justice, that it would be at the expense of more settled countries like their own. A strong party at the Russian court also favoured an alliance with Russia's traditional ally, Britain, France's mortal enemy.

Instead of being seduced by the roguish Alexander, whose charms were subject to snake-like transformations into enmity, Napoleon would have been much wiser to make friends with the muddle-headed Frederick William of Prussia and the worthy, pedantic Emperor Francis of Austria. By failing to resolve his eastern frontier Napoleon made himself susceptible to further attack at any time.

By suddenly choosing to overthrow the decadent Bourbons of

Spain, he did something even worse. He reminded his royal antagonists that he was at heart an upstart and a revolutionary, a lower-born commander accustomed to overthrowing the established order and replacing them with his puppets in alliance with the anti-feudal minor nobility and urban bourgeoisie of Europe. He could hardly pose as the creator of a new, stable royal dynasty equal to the great dynasties of Europe (and look to marry into them) as he sought to overthrow one of the most ancient of their number in the name of liberty.

Even for the slow-reacting Emperor Francis, there was a danger that the same fate might befall him one day, that Napoleon would seek to replace him with a puppet from the Habsburg royal family or, worse still, one of Napoleon's own extended family. If Napoleon had merely intimidated the feeble Godoy, or sought his replacement by a tamer Spanish minister, he would have amply secured Spain's continued subordination. Instead he had sought to overthrow the other most hallowed royal family in Europe as though he was still some rabid Jacobin: he had shown that France's appetite for conquest was insatiable and that it remained revolutionary at heart, bent on upsetting the natural order of things. Metternich in particular, with his deeply reactionary instincts found this upsetting and was to spend much of his later career seeking to re-entrench absolutism all over Europe.

Napoleon's invasion of Spain established one thing for Francis: that there could be no peace in Europe while Napoleon ruled. So Francis decided to strike while much of the *Grande Armée* was tied down in Spain. The invasion of Spain and the check to his ambitions there had provided a golden opportunity.

Napoleon's career as military dictator can now be said to have gone through four phases: as First Consul in 1801–2 he needed military victories to preserve France and his own authority; in 1803–4 when European peace was at last possible, and was briefly achieved; in 1805–7 when his thirst for expansionism prodded the Austrians, Russians and Prussians onto the offensive, although it had ended with his extraordinary triumphs – and which also sowed the seeds for his own downfall when he missed the opportunity to establish a just peace; and now a fourth phase in which a further act of unprovoked aggression provided the opportunity for his continental enemies to attack. The last

real opportunity for a peaceful settlement in Europe was missed between 1805–7, and the point of no return had been reached with the 1808 invasion of Spain. From now on Napoleon's enemies believed that he must be overthrown for them to survive.

Austria, even after Pressburg, was still a great empire. It had been defeated three times by Napoleon in the field but it had not been conquered or altogether cowed. Austria's armies had been mauled but they remained large. Austrian possessions had been hacked away in the west, but the empire retained huge possessions, colonies and reserves of men.

Nor, for all his mediocrity was the Emperor Francis either a coward or unintelligent. He, his court and his officers had concluded after Austerlitz that they could not fight on, or go to war again, without profound military reforms to meet the revolutionary new type of warfare pioneered by the *Grande Armée*. And it was to this admirable long-term objective that Austria's greatest military commander, Archduke Charles, had been turning his attention for four years after the disastrous failure of his commoner rival, General Mack. It was Austria's great misfortune that Charles could be no more than lieutenant to the dim, uninspiring Francis, or the empire would have had the leadership it required. The final great passage of arms between Napoleon and Charles was now approaching.

Following the defeat at Austerlitz Charles had been made commander-in-chief and had co-authored a new army manual, the *Fundamentals of the High Art of War*, for the generals of the Austrian army. This retained much the same formations, manoeuvres and practices as before. But skirmishers were now to be permitted, drawn from 'the brightest, most cunning and most reliable' in the third rank of the traditional three-line formation of the Austrian army. Charles also introduced closed columns of waiting troops to supplement the traditional lines, an idea borrowed from the French which was unpopular with traditional-minded Austrian generals.

Charles's new plan of battle was for skirmishers to advance with the regular infantry in line behind them, to quicken the pace at 150 yards, to deliver a volley at sixty paces, and then to charge with fixed bayonets. The Austrians were unusual in starting their charges at

such distances, which meant that the soldiers would have more ground to cover, would be exposed to enemy fire longer, might get out of breath and would become vulnerable to a counter-charge. The British, in particular, would wait until the enemy was much closer. The Austrian motive may have been fear that their conscripted ranks of eastern Europeans would break if they got too close to enemy fire.

Charles also introduced nine corps in imitation of the French flexible and decentralized model. But the commanders-in-chief still tended to centralize overall control – as indeed did the more skilful Napoleon, increasingly so to his detriment in later years – and the Austrian corps commanders, accustomed by training to obey their orders, were lacking in initiative, so the corps were not used with the same flair and flexibility as the French.

Charles refused initially to abandon the Austrian practice of attacking in line. Wellesley was already showing in the Peninsula that traditional line formations against French attack could be effective in defence, and the Austrians remained to be convinced by the imaginative French models of attacking in columns, or mixed line and columns, or massed attack. But Austrian line attacks against Napoleon had failed in the past and were to do so again. However Charles did experiment at Essling with keeping his rearguard in columns, where they very effectively repelled French cavalry attacks. The same thing happened at Wagram, so Charles became committed to the use of columns behind the front lines.

The Austrians also began, at last, to realize the value of artillery packed together in strength. Napoleon, as a former artillery officer, seemed to have an obsession with the concept. 'It is with artillery alone that battles are won,' he declared with hyperbole, a view only partially born out by his own victories.

Charles pedantically argued that 'war is governed by immutable laws . . . based on irrefutable mathematical truths'. He retained the aristocratic British-style system of promoting generals by birth and status rather than on merit. This further inhibited the independence of the corps as dull-witted staff officers refused to take the initiative. However under attack the corps system proved its worth, permitting large

Austrian forces to extricate themselves without the complexity of a movement of the whole army or authorization by the centre.

Charles also tentatively introduced a militia, the *Landwehr*, an idea he had previously opposed, drawn from all males between the ages of eighteen and forty-five in Austria and Bohemia. In theory this provided him with an additional 180,000 men to resist the French hordes. However the militia were kept to the rear, and were no match at all for the enforced conscript drives of the Napoleonic army. Napoleon had raised huge conscript armies from his subject peoples – Belgium, the west Bank of the Rhine, Savoy, Nice and Piedmont, Italy, Germany, Holland, Carolina, Westphalia and Poland. Westphalia provided 70,000 soldiers out of a total population of 2 million. Bavaria provided 110,000. The Kingdom of Italy provided 120,000 and the Grand Duchy of Warsaw some 90,000. Altogether a total of more than 700,000 subject peoples were to serve under the French at any one time or other. In addition to these subject troops, Napoleon raised some 270,000 French men by levies over fourteen years. Including the force he withdrew from Spain, and those gathered by conscription drives, Napoleon was able to put some 275,000 men in the field against Austria in 1809, a staggering total by previous standards.

While the Austrians had begun to improve their tactics in their traditionally cautious and stuffy fashion, the impact of French tactics had now begun to deteriorate from its peak. First, no longer faced by simple line formations but ones backed up by the columns now introduced by Archduke Charles, the old French tactic of manoeuvring quickly and massing at a weak spot was no longer so effective: the Austrians were able to bring up reinforcements in depth to hold off such attacks. Secondly, as the quality of the French and allied troops declined with the huge recruitment drives for raw conscripts, it became necessary to take measures to improve their morale. This was first done by dispersing artillery pieces around the units to help build up French offensives, giving the men the feeling that they were being supported. In fact concentrated artillery fire, as Napoleon well knew, was militarily much more effective.

In addition 'cuirassier' regiments, equipped with heavy breast plates and body armour were introduced. Highly popular with the men, as providing at least the illusion of greater protection, this armour slowed up the horses. Lancer regiments were also introduced which had the benefit of making cavalrymen feel they could strike the enemy before the enemy had a chance to strike them with their swords, but in practice the lances were unwieldy and sabres were more effective, particularly after rival cavalry formations had converged for close fighting.

Most significant of all, the French army began to lose the flexibility of operating in a mass of quasi-independent units with the objective of eventually concentrating to defeat the enemy at one particular point. Instead, again in order to improve the confidence of the soldiers, the French became wedded to attacking in might from the first to over-whelm the weak points. A soldier in a large body of troops would have much greater confidence. But these were much less manoeuvrable than the old smaller formations, and if those at the front were stopped or repulsed by the enemy, panic was liable to set in throughout the whole huge column (as was to happen at Waterloo). Massed battalions, even multiple-regiment columns were deployed.

Thus the battlefield was now to return to the bloody formality of earlier years. When great linear armies clashed, huge numbers of casualties had been inflicted along the line. When Napoleon developed his methods of movement and manoeuvre on the battlefield, punching through and staging flank attacks, these often yielded localized blood-baths, with morale collapsing all along the line, followed by great victories and smaller casualties. With the Austrians now deploying in depth, with columns behind the lines, and the French less flexible in their tactics and attacking en masse, battles tended to revert to sanguinary slugging matches.

On 8 February Austria took the plunge and declared war. The decision to go to war was dictated by a variety of factors. In particular, a large part of the French army was bogged down in Spain and the Russian Tsar had indicated that he would not come to the help of his ally, Napoleon, although he refused to intervene on the Austrian side

either. The Austrians also believed that the Prussians were ready to join them, and that the smaller German states were ripe for insurrection against France. The British too were desperately keen for an Austrian second front, although they balked at the cost of £2.5 million outright and a further £1 million in subsidies every year demanded by Vienna.

Archduke Charles hesitated, and made no move until 9 April. He first planned to strike in a central thrust through Germany, then he decided to revert to a traditional Austrian strategic mistake – a three-pronged offensive with Archduke Frederick attacking the Grand Duchy of Warsaw in the north, Charles himself leading the main thrust through the centre and Archduke John looping down through Italy. Charles first planned to take the main route into Bohemia, then switched at the last moment to a route further south so as to protect the capital, Vienna, from a French counter-thrust; the change in route tired his men.

If Charles had struck as early as March he would have taken the French by surprise. Davout's main Third Corps was then still travelling towards the French centre at Ratisbon in Bavaria, and Masséna's Fourth Corps had not yet caught up with him. Napoleon was still back in Paris. But he had secured a breathing space of three vital weeks to get organized.

Charles issued a ringing declaration of war: 'Comrades in arms . . . the eyes of all who maintain their sense of national honour focus on you . . . Europe seeks freedom beneath your banners. Your victories will loose her bonds . . . Your German brethren wait for salvation at your hands.'

The following day he crossed the river Inn with his main army, while John marched to Piave in Italy and Ferdinand went north. Some 12,000 troops were despatched to help the Tyrolese revolt. However the main Austrian army made slow progress and only reached Landshut after six days. From there Charles tried to cut off Davout's smaller corps at Ratisbon – which he certainly could have done if he had been quick enough. But Napoleon, who had acted with his usual astonishing speed, taking over command from his worthy but slow-moving chief of staff Berthier, realized the danger and ordered Davout to join up with Lefebvre east of Ingolstadt to the west of Ratisbon.

He berated his approaching corps commanders, Masséna, Lannes and Oudinot, to hurry. He ordered Lannes and Masséna to attack in the south; they pushed back the Austrian left wing. Realizing that the bulk of Charles's army was pressing up against Oudinot in the north, Napoleon ordered Masséna and Lannes's 40,000 men to attack his southern flank. A succession of small engagements left Charles's army reeling at Thann, Abensberg, Landshut and Eckmehl. When the French pushed forward to Ratisbon, they found their path blocked by Charles's rearguard.

In that action Napoleon was for the first time lightly wounded by a cannonball in the foot. This was highly symbolic for Europeans as well as himself: it suggested that the Emperor was, after all, a mere mortal. To Josephine he wrote: 'Dear friend: I have received your letter. The bullet that struck me did not wound me; it just grazed the tendon of Achilles. My health is excellent and there is no cause for worry. My affairs are going well.' Charles was able to escape with his armies intact across the Danube, burning all the bridges for several miles. Napoleon had shown uncharacteristic slowness in dealing a quick knockout blow, although he managed to seize the main road to Vienna.

In northern Italy the competent French commander, Napoleon's stepson and Viceroy of Italy, Eugène de Beauharnais, had suffered an unexpected defeat, although commanding a superior force. Napoleon scolded him:

war is a serious business in which one risks one's own reputation and that of one's country; a reasonable man should examine himself and decide whether or no he is fitted for it. I know that in Italy you affect a great contempt of Masséna. Yet he has military talents to which we may well doff our hats; we must forget his foibles; every man has some. I made a mistake in giving you the command of the army; I should have placed you under Masséna in command of the cavalry. Kings of France, even reigning Emperors, have often enough commanded a regiment, or a division under the orders of an old Marshal.

However, news of the setback to Charles in the north compelled John to withdraw from the Adige to the Piave and then up to Austria, while Archduke Ferdinand had also had to fall back from Warsaw. Charles meanwhile had withdrawn north-east to Bohemia, while Napoleon pressed on towards Vienna on the south side of the Danube.

Chapter 63

DUEL OF THE TITANS

Napoleon entered Vienna for the second time on 10 May, returning to his bedroom in the Schönbrunn Palace: the Austrian garrison had evacuated the city once again. But this time there was real resistance to the French: the citadel held out for four days and the French had to fire warning cannon into it, threatening to raze it in a total bombardment. One cannonball fell next to the home of the elderly composer Joseph Haydn, the shock of which helped to hasten his death three weeks later.

All four bridges across the Danube had been destroyed by the retreating Austrians. They had amassed some 115,000 troops on the opposite bank. Napoleon's forces were down to 82,000 men. However he was determined to crush the Austrians this time. As they had no intention of exposing themselves by recrossing the Danube to liberate Vienna, he ordered the flooded river to be crossed through the erection of pontoons a few miles downstream to Lobau Island. From there he wrote: 'The nearest villages are Aspern, Essling, and Enzersdorf. To cross a river like the Danube in the presence of an enemy knowing the ground thoroughly, and having the sympathies of the inhabitants, is one of the most difficult military operations conceivable.' Nine rafts and sixty-eight pontoons were floated, the final link being some seventy-five feet long. Masséna and his corps crossed rapidly and took the villages of Aspern and Essling. Soon some 25,000 men had crossed.

But the floodwaters rose, while the Austrians floated heavy timbers downstream which broke the pontoon in two places, preventing further reinforcement. Masséna's men were cut off. On 21 May

Charles arrived in force with 100,000 men and 250 guns and in fierce fighting succeeded in driving the French out of the two villages. The French across the river were now in desperate straits thanks to Napoleon's rashness: with both retreat and reinforcements potentially cut off and their backs to the river against a vastly superior army, it seemed that Lannes and Masséna risked annihilation or capture.

As they worked feverishly to repair the pontoon bridges on the night of the 21st, reinforcements were at last able to arrive and the French strength rose to some 50,000 infantry, 12,000 cavalry and 144 guns; Charles had missed his chance to attack in devastating force. The French regained control of part of Essling and then of Aspern in desperate hand-to-hand streetfighting.

Napoleon now ordered one of his classic concentrated attacks on the Austrian centre, and Lannes threw them on to the defensive until the Archduke Charles arrived in person to rally his troops. The bridge had been wrecked again, and Napoleon realistically ordered a retreat to the two villages to draw up defensive positions. The Austrians attacked and retook Essling before the Imperial Guard managed to take it. With the fighting having seesawed and the villages changed hands so often, and the bridge once again damaged, Napoleon had had enough. He ordered an evacuation from the two villages to the island of Lobau in the Danube's midstream. Charles called off his men and ordered a bombardment of Napoleon's forces marooned on the island in the middle of the river. As they rested, a cannonball took Lannes's legs off. It was the agonizing end of one of Napoleon's most skilled and principled marshals.

Charles had won an extraordinary victory through sheer hard fighting against an enemy that had gambled and lost. It was Napoleon's first ever defeat in the field, although he had come close at Friedland and Marengo. The Emperor's sense of invincibility had been shattered as much through his own foolhardiness as anything else. The thrice beaten Austrian foe had proved his equal at last, at least in one battle. Casualties on both sides were enormous – some 5,000 dead and 20,000 wounded on each.

Princess Louise, daughter of the Emperor Francis, caught the mood of Austrian exultation from the palace at Buda to which she had been

evacuated: 'My first reaction was to thank God profoundly for granting us such a victory. I wish I could convey to you the delight of Often [Buda] yesterday . . . everybody was laughing! Wherever we went, we were welcomed with cheers and vivas. We saw people get together in little groups, congratulate each other and give thanks for the victory.'

As for Napoleon, he was for the first time plunged into shock, not emerging for thirty-six hours from a nearly catatonic state. Whether this was the vanity of a man who had believed his own propaganda and had simply been astonished to find it untrue, or one who suddenly feared that his empire might unravel, or merely self-anger for the succession of mistakes he had made in battle, is impossible to guess. More important was the question whether it would affect his future behaviour and temper his ambition and self-belief. (The evidence suggests that it did, and indeed marked a turning point.) But he hardly had the luxury of introspection at this moment: the situation was desperate, and he had to rise to the immediate challenge first.

He lamented Lannes's death, after acute suffering.

> There are some wounds to which death itself is preferable. It is at the moment of leaving life that a man clings to it with all his might. Lannes, the bravest of men, Lannes, deprived of his two legs, did not want to die, and said to me that the two surgeons who had treated a Marshal so brutally and with such scant respect ought to be hanged. With his remnant of life he clung to me; he wanted only me, thought only of me. A sort of instinct! For surely he loved his young wife and his children more than he did me; yet he never spoke of them, which was because he expected no help from them. But I was his protector; for him I was some vague and superior power; I was his Providence, and he was imploring . . .

The stakes were now extraordinarily high: the future of Europe was in the balance. If Archduke Charles could make good his advantage and bombard the French out of their forward position on the island of Lobau, he would inflict a decisive defeat. Conversely if Napoleon withdrew, or attempted another attack which failed again, the blow to his prestige would be irreparable: subject peoples in Germany and

elsewhere would rise against him. His enemies at home would close in for the kill. Even if he merely failed to press his offensive, he would be seen as having been checked at last in the east, while his armies were challenged in the west in Spain.

The sullen, occupied people of Vienna had witnessed the terrible battle that had raged by day and night from just a few miles upstream, the lightning of gunfire and the thunder of cannon providing an eerie backdrop to their misery; all of Europe would witness his humiliation. In the event, with that extraordinary courage and indomitability that were his greatest traits, Napoleon snapped out of his self-pity and chose to strike again, this time making sure that the ground was better prepared.

Archduke Charles, meanwhile, did nothing, possibly because he believed the battle had already been won. In spite of his formidable artillery, he halted his artillery assault on the island. Suddenly, he had become cautious, preparing to redeploy his troops to stave off another attack across the Danube, uncertain whether to place them at the water's edge or further back on the Marchfeld Plain. He was almost certainly right in holding back his infantry: he would have faced the same perils as Napoleon had just faced in reverse, with his men exposed as they crossed and then with their backs to the water.

Napoleon set about reinforcing Lobau and the neighbouring island into an armed camp protected by 130 heavy guns. He built new bridges to Lobau and across from the island to the north bank. Small bridge-heads were established protected by redoubts and gunboats. Upstream, boats were scuttled to prevent the Austrians floating debris down the river to demolish the bridges. Meanwhile Eugène de Beauharnais and General MacDonald had at last beaten Archduke John's retreating army at Raab. Napoleon summoned their 23,000 men to join him. With further reinforcements under Davout and Bernadotte also arriving, Napoleon by the beginning of July had nearly 180,000 men and 500 guns. Archduke Charles's caution had proved lethal.

On 4 July Napoleon moved. With his usual skill at deception he erected three bridges across from Lobau to Aspern-Essling, as he had on his previous attack, as a decoy, while simultaneously throwing seven

bridges to the east towards the village of Gross Enzerdorf lower down the river. In Napoleon's favour, there was a thunderstorm and torrential rains which masked the movement of the troops. The Austrians, utterly deceived, prepared to meet them at Aspern-Essling only to discover that at that very moment a massive French army of 150,000 men and 500 guns had crossed to the north bank of the Danube to the east: a bolder commander might have attempted to attack the French as they crossed; but Archduke Charles held back. Napoleon's forces now outnumbered the Austrians.

At midday the French advanced against the 136,000 Austrian troops and their forty guns. The Austrians were spread out in a giant semi-circle centred on the village of Wagram, at the edge of the Marchfeld Plain. The French mustered their main force on the right (the north) with the object of breaking through the Austrian centre: they had ample space for manoeuvre on the extensive plain. At 5 p.m., as light was fading, Napoleon launched his attack for fear that reinforcements expected from Archduke John's army would soon reach the Austrians. (In fact John's force had been whittled down to just 12,000 men.)

The French attack went badly: de Beauharnais's forces were driven in disarray from directly opposite Wagram, while Oudinot's forces were also forced to withdraw. Davout and Bernadotte, behind these two, found their way blocked, and Bernadotte withdrew from the village of Aberklaa, just west of Wagram, to Napoleon's spitting fury. He dismissed Bernadotte on the spot (although to general bemusement he never carried out his threats against this vainglorious, often disobedient and mostly incompetent general, perhaps because he feared making an enemy of the still powerful radical Jacobin faction in the army). The much criticized defences of the Archduke Charles had in fact held well against a superior force commanded by Napoleon himself. The fighting died down at 10 p.m., its lurid glow visible to the tens of thousands of inhabitants of Vienna.

Battle was resumed the following morning, not by a French offensive but an Austrian one on two fronts – the main thrust directed at the weakest French southern flank towards Aspern and the Danube, which was commanded by Masséna, and a centre-north offensive aimed at driving the French back to the Danube. Charles's attacks were

superb, perfectly crafted pincer movements by a general who had chosen his ground carefully from the defensive heights half encircling the wide plain.

When these attacks seemed to be succeeding Napoleon desperately ordered Masséna further south and ordered Davout forward to hold the French centre, supported by the reserve cavalry under General Mac-Donald, and also by a huge 112-gun battery firing straight into the Austrian centre. Meanwhile Davout began to push back the Austrian left in the north and to encircle Wagram from that direction. However, in the south the French left along the Danube was buckling under Austrian pressure. The battle hung in the balance.

At that moment, Napoleon showed his old inspiration and flair: he ordered MacDonald with one of the earliest 'giant squares', some 30,000 men, eight men across and six ranks deep, with the Young Guard behind and some 6,000 cavalry in support, to strike at the Austrian centre. This huge sledgehammer moved upon the Austrian centre. Even so the Austrian line held. But it had been weakened by Davout's attacks in the north, and Napoleon saw that an opportunity existed to push through between the Austrian centre and left, to which forces had been rushed to resist Davout.

Davout now started to try and break through at this weak point, while Napoleon committed the entire French reserve except a couple of regiments. At this moment, Charles gave the sensible command to withdraw in good order while he still controlled a line of escape to the north, and broke off the engagement. The French were so over-stretched that, had Archduke John arrived in time with his depleted forces, the Austrians might have won. As it was, the Austrians withdrew with all their artillery intact and an army of some 80,000 men to fight another day. The French were too exhausted to pursue and would probably have anyway been beaten back.

With more than 300,000 troops in the field, it had been the biggest battle ever fought in Europe, with casualties in proportion – some 35,000 on each side. It was a French victory on points – they had gained the battlefield – but had been anything but overwhelming, partly because the French army was in fact the superior force: the

Austrians' much derided linear approach had held and even MacDonald's battering ram had caused it only to buckle, not break.

Charles has been criticized as too cautious a commander: yet it was his boldness in seeking to outflank the French on both sides that had perhaps been fatal: if he had remained on the defensive in the north while in the south he had cut the French off from their means of escape across the Danube, Napoleon might have been finished. As it was the Emperor only just prevailed.

After a few minor further engagements between the two large armies, Charles, instead of rallying his troops, decided to seek an armistice. That was the Austrian way, to compromise after calculating the results of a battle, not to fight to the bitter end. Yet again he had failed to take advantage of a formidable performance in battle for which he had no reason to feel ashamed; the Austrians had fought as well as the French. The myth of Napoleon's invincibility had been challenged: he had nearly lost against a smaller Austrian force; he had shown himself to be only narrowly more skilled as a general than Charles, talented but no genius. Even the Emperor Francis, who was usually more pacific than Charles, wanted his army to go on fighting, which led to a rift with his brother and the latter's premature retirement.

The Austrians' peace overtures were rebuffed, however, by Napoleon's vengeful demands for Francis to abdicate, to dismiss his ministers and to emasculate his regular army. Francis initially stalled the negotiations in the hope that the British would open a more substantial second front than that in Portugal, or that the Russians would enter the war on Austria's side. Once again it seemed that Napoleon, although now in possession of Vienna, had overplayed his hand.

Francis had good reason for stalling, as Britain was just about to open up a second front, with an attack on the Scheldt. Unfortunately through, it was an embarrassing disaster. It was called the Walcheren expedition. This was no mere sideshow, like Wellesley's expedition to the Peninsula: it was supposed to send the French reeling and bring the rest of Europe into renewed combination against her. The leader of the expedition was, in classic politico-dynastic style, the Earl of Chatham, Pitt's elder brother, a capable politician and administrator. But it did

not help that his sole military experience was to have commanded a brigade in Holland a decade before and to have served as a subaltern in Gibraltar; the real business of war was left to subordinates like General Sir Eyre Coote, a tetchy veteran from India with a decidedly mixed record.

Chatham was a man of great integrity and intelligence, but he was also comparatively old at fifty-two to be a general of the time. Canning, the brilliant but far too clever mainstay of the government, had put him in charge of the expedition to elevate him to a position from which he might be expected to succeed the decrepit Duke of Portland as prime minister. Canning knew he was himself too controversial for the job: but Chatham would be an ideal figurehead and would block Canning's great rival Castlereagh.

On the naval side, Admiral Sir Richard Strachan had won his spurs by defeating the last squadron that had tried to escape Trafalgar and was energetic, straightforward and short-tempered. He held Chatham in contempt as a political appointee. Both men assumed the attack on the Scheldt would be as much of a walkover as the taking out of the Danish fleet had been years before.

The expedition consisted of some 40,000 men along with 400 transports and 200 escorts, thirty-seven of them ships of the line. It was possibly the greatest expeditionary force Britain had ever assembled, a kind of Napoleonic invasion in reverse: with his puny forces in Portugal, Wellesley could only have looked on in frustrated envy. The objective was: 'The capture or destruction of the enemy's ships either building at Antwerp and Flushing or afloat in the Scheldt, the destruction of the arsenals and dockyards at Antwerp, Terneuse and Flushing, the reduction of the island of Walcheren and the rendering, if possible, the Scheldt no longer navigable for ships of war.'

The expedition was an absurdity from the start. It would have achieved little other than a morale-boosting naval victory. It could certainly not have opened up a second front, because there was no real sign of disaffection against Napoleon in the Low Countries, which the highly strung King Louis, through his moderate policies, had effectively won over. The whole thing was in fact designed to be a magnificent showpiece with the objective of destroying more of

Napoleon's naval capability, which had anyway been effectively emasculated after Aix Roads. It was also intended to impress the Austrians that the British were serious in their desire to open up a second front, but it came too late. In fact, the Battle of Wagram took place ten days before the British embarkation began.

On 28 July the armada left Kent and had reached Holland by the evening. The Scheldt estuary was divided in two by three big islands: the most navigable entrance was the West Scheldt, which would open the way up to the city of Antwerp. To enter this it was necessary to take the Dutch forts on Kadzand on the south side of the Wielengen Channel leading to the West Scheldt and then strike north at Flushing. The first goal was to land 5,000 troops to take the Kadzand.

Unfortunately, a gale drove the British into the entrance to the East Scheldt to the north. Even so, some 12,000 troops under Coote were disembarked at Veere to march across the island of Flushing at the entrance of the estuary and take the town of Flushing. They had to take two towns in the middle of the island before they got there. By now Flushing had been reinforced.

Meanwhile a force of British troops, supposed to take Kadzand on the other side of the Channel, had not yet done so. These almost incredibly leisurely proceedings took place as the French, caught entirely by surprise with only 1,500 men to defend the main river entrance to Antwerp, dug in and sent frantic messages to Paris. There, in Napoleon's absence in Austria, the devious police chief Fouché was effectively in charge and brushed aside the minister of war to put Bernadotte, who was in disgrace after his performance at Wagram, in charge of proceedings. Both Fouché and Bernadotte to some extent represented the old revolutionary Jacobin faction, and hated Napoleon. This was clearly an attempt to show that France could defend itself and survive without the Emperor.

Bernadotte arrived in time to reinforce Louis Napoleon, who had around 12,000 troops in Antwerp. The momentum was being lost by the British; by the end of August there were 26,000 French troops in Antwerp. Chatham meanwhile had settled down in agreeable quarters at Middelbourg on the island of Walcheren. One officer observed:

'God knows! Everything goes on at headquarters as if they were at the Horse Guards; you must signify what you want, you must call between certain hours, send up your name and wait your turn.'

At last on 13 August the British opened fire on Flushing. It was a devastating broadside, in which virtually the whole town was set alight and 600 civilians were killed. As soon as the British entered on 18 August, the 6,000-strong French garrison surrendered. It was a repeat, without even the dash, of the attack on Copenhagen.

The British had suffered some 700 casualties. They proceeded, with great deliberation, to Batz, just off the point where the estuary narrowed to give access to Antwerp. While they waited for the order to advance, malaria, in that low-lying marsh, exacerbated by the French opening the sluices so that it would flood, attacked the troops, along with dysentery caused by salt meat and fat.

While the leisurely Chatham and the more impatient Strachan tried to decide which was the most suitable route for attack, they observed the reinforcement of Antwerp. Chatham, realistically, decided that an attack was out of the question and at the end of August ordered an evacuation to England. Some 3,000 had died and the rest, 11,000 of them seriously ill, were shipped to hospitals in Kent. Chatham had at least shown the good sense to cut his losses. But thousands had died and nothing had been gained. A doggerel of that time ran:

> Lord Chatham, with his sword half-drawn,
> Stood waiting for Sir Richard Strachan.
> Sir Richard, longing to be at 'em,
> Stood waiting for the Earl of Chatham.

As a result of the fiasco, Portland's sickly government at last fell, to be replaced by a mediocrity, Spencer Perceval, and Francis was eventually forced to accede to most of Napoleon's terms. Francis was allowed to stay on as Emperor. But Napoleon, after his near-miss, was in an angry mood: the Austrian empire was shorn of its share of Poland and all of its remaining lands down the Dalmatian coast, as well as Croatia and most of Slovenia. Bavaria's pro-French puppet regime was given Salzburg, Berchtesgaden and a slice of Upper Austria. Part of eastern Galicia was

given to the Russians as a prize for staying out of the war. The Austrian army was to be reduced to 150,000 men, the militia disbanded, reparations of some 85 millions francs were to be paid, and Austria was ordered to join the Continental System.

Chapter 64

RULER OF ALL HE SURVEYED

Napoleon seemed to recover all his bounce and self-confidence after Wagram. In spite of the narrowness of victory, and his first ever defeat at Aspern-Eylau, he behaved as though the Austrian campaign had been one of his greatest achievements. Once again he had not understood that by treating the Austrians vengefully he had made another war inevitable. Much less had he realized that the Austrians had regained their self-respect during the Wagram campaign. Like a man who has suddenly peered over the edge – as he had at Aspern-Essling – and then saved himself, he behaved with an exuberance that had suddenly found its release. This expressed itself in a number of ways: an extraordinary attack on the Pope; a new bossiness towards his proconsular brothers; and the final decision to divorce Josephine.

Napoleon's hubris was never more on public display than in the autumn of 1809 when he believed he had finally confounded all his enemies. Napoleon's relations with the saintly but clever Pope Pius VII had long been deteriorating. He wrote to his stepson, Eugène de Beauharnais:

> My son, I perceive by his Holiness' letter, which he certainly never wrote himself, that I am threatened. I would not tolerate this from any other Pope. What does Pius VII wish to do when he denounces me to Christendom? Put an interdict on my throne? Excommunicate me? Does he imagine that their muskets will drop from my soldiers' fingers? Or is it to place a dagger in my people's hands to assassinate me? . . . I shall doubtless hear that the Holy Father

intends to apply the scissors to my head and to lock me up in a monastery! . . . The present Pope has too much power; priests are not made to rule; let them follow the example of St Peter, St Paul, and the holy Apostles.

The Pope had been chafing at certain aspects of his Concordat with France and had taken the provocative step of refusing to apply the Continental System to his territories. Privately the Vatican was urging Austria to reignite its war with France. In response Napoleon had ordered a French occupation of the Papal States in 1808, which took place without resistance. Now the States were formally annexed. The Pope issued a bull of excommunication against whoever attacked the Holy See 'whatever their honours or dignities' – a transparent reference to Napoleon. The Emperor's reaction was that 'the bull of excommunication is so ridiculous a document that one may as well take no notice of it'. Napoleon was not prepared to put up with insolence, as he saw it, from the Pope who was his subject as a temporal ruler – indeed had no business to be a ruler himself or to meddle in temporal affairs.

Yet he did not want to offend the church, for which he had a healthy respect because of its hold over the spiritual loyalties of half the citizens of his empire. As he had once written:

Never throw oil, but throw water, on the passions of men; scatter prejudices, and firmly strive against the false priests who have degraded religion by making it the tool of the ambition of the powerful and of kings. The morality of the Gospel is that of equality, and hence it is most favourable to the republican government which is now to be that of your country. Experience has undeceived the French, and has convinced them that the Catholic religion is better adapted than any other to diverse forms of government, and is particularly favourable to republican institutions. I myself am a philosopher, and I know that, in every society whatsoever, no man is considered just and virtuous who does not know whence he came and whither he is going. Simple reason cannot guide you in this matter; without religion one walks continually in darkness; and

the Catholic religion alone gives to man certain and infallible information concerning his origin and his latter end.

He once told his minister in Rome, 'Treat with the Pope as if he had 200,000 men.' But now in 1809 after his excommunication he railed: 'What can the Pope do? I have 300,000 men under my orders.'

Napoleon professed disdain for atheism on the grounds that 'it takes from man all his consolations and hopes' – which was hardly a ringing endorsement of religion. He also insisted:

How can morality exist? There is only one means – that of re-establishing religion . . . Society cannot exist without inequality of fortunes, and inequality of fortunes cannot exist without religion. When one man is dying of hunger near another who suffers from surfeit, he cannot resign himself to this difference unless there is an authority that can say to him, 'God wills it so; there must be rich and poor in this world; but hereafter, and for ever, their lot will be different.'

But he never appeared to be a believer himself: he expressed doubt as to whether Jesus ever existed on two occasions, and on several others compared Him as an equal to Mohammed or Plato. Sometimes he expressed the view that Islam was a simpler and more effective religion than Christianity.

Following the papal bull of excommunication, Napoleon retaliated by having the Pope arrested and moved to Florence, in case Rome rose up in revolt against his arbitrary action; then he brought him to Nice, before holding him in Savona. The Pontiff was held in miserable and humiliating conditions, but the dignified sixty-seven-year-old scholar did not yield: on the contrary he refused to consecrate Napoleon's bishops and instructed his followers not to co-operate with the Emperor.

Napoleon eventually sought a compromise, but the pontiff refused. He was brought to Fontainebleau by an angry Napoleon, where the new French court feared that Napoleon would get so angry that he would reverse the Revolution's opposition to atheism. Cardinal Fesch,

his uncle, who remonstrated with him, was told to look up at the sky: 'Do you see anything?' Napoleon asked.

'No,' said Fesch.

'In that case, learn when to shut up. I myself see my star; it is that which guides me. Don't pit your feeble and incomplete faculties against my superior organism.'

The row with the Vatican had a final chapter to go; but Napoleon had no reason to prosecute it except his own desire to squash a lingering pocket of resistance against him: if the church was as powerful as he believed, it was not worth making an enemy of its leader; if it was powerless, he had no reason to proceed against it. But after Wagram he believed he could do anything with immunity, even overawe the Vicar of Christ on earth.

Napoleon's attitude towards the lesser rulers of Europe was far more insulting. Of the Emperor Francis he wrote contemptuously: 'The Emperor of Austria is always of the opinion of the last speaker . . . in five or six years he [will] begin the war again and become once more the tool of England.'

He scolded his younger brother, the playboy-ruler Jerome:

I have seen an order of the day signed by you that makes you the laughing stock of Germany, Austria and France. Have you no friend who will tell you the truth? You are a King and a brother of the Emperor – ridiculous title in warfare! You must be a soldier, and again a soldier, and always a soldier! You must bivouac with your outposts, spend night and day in the saddle, march with your advance guard so as to get information, or else remain in your seraglio. You wage war like a satrap. By Heaven! Is it from me you have learned that – from me, who with an army of 200,000 men live with my skirmishers? You have much ambition, some intelligence, a few good qualities – but spoiled by silliness, by great presumption – and have no real knowledge. In God's name keep enough wits about you to write and speak with propriety.

He even delivered pompous lectures to Joachim Murat, his brother-in-law and one of the princes of his army as its greatest cavalry com-

mander, who he believed had tried to supplant him. 'As a rule give nothing to people who have not worked 10 years for you . . . base yourself on the principle that the less the diplomatic corps see you the better.'

Napoleon's motive in ruling his dominions through members of his family was not dynastic nepotism pure and simple – it was that these men were pliant and owed everything to him, so that he believed they would do as he ordered, whereas self-made men from outside the clan might not do so, particularly if they were talented. This was a partial misjudgement: independent they might not be, but that did not stop them bitterly resenting their overbearing relation – particularly in the case of Murat, who was merely married to his sister and who loathed him and considered his military talents inferior to his own.

Napoleon's vainglory seemed to know no bounds. He wrote:

The Institute proposes conferring on the Emperor the title of Augustus and of Germanicus. Augustus gained one battle, at Actium. Germanicus won the sympathy of Rome by his misfortunes, but his life shows a decidedly moderate record. There is nothing to provoke emulation in the memory of the Roman Emperors. The only man, and he was not an Emperor, who was distinguished by his character and by his many illustrious achievements was Caesar. If the Emperor could wish a new title it would be that of Caesar. But so many puny princes have dishonoured that title – if such a thing were possible – that it no longer evokes the memory of the great Caesar, but that of a mass of German sovereigns, as feeble as they were ignorant, of whom not one has left a reputation behind him.

On a more sensible note he observed:

In a battle even the most skilful soldiers find it difficult to estimate the enemy's numbers, and as a rule, one is apt instinctively to exaggerate the number. But if one is foolish enough to accept an inflated estimate of the enemy's forces, then every cavalry colonel on reconnaissance espies an army, and every captain of light infantry

battalions. Again I repeat that in war morale and opinion are half the battle. The art of the great captain has always been to make his troops appear very numerous to the enemy, and the enemy very few to his own. So that today, in spite of the long time we have spent in Germany, the enemy do not know my real strength. We are constantly striving to magnify our numbers. Far from confessing that I had only 100,000 men at Wagram, I am constantly suggesting that I had 220,000. In my Italian campaigns, in which I had only a handful of troops, I always exaggerated my numbers. It served my purpose, and has not lessened my glory. My generals and practised soldiers could always perceive, after the event, all the skilfulness of my operations, even that of having exaggerated the numbers of my troops.

His vanity and conviction of his own omniscience were childlike. Although he possessed the directness of a supremely important political leader and military commander, as well as his own acute intelligence, his absolute lack of modesty was abhorrent and even highly comical to the more subtle, if sometimes crass and stupid, dynastic monarchs he sought to ape.

Whether it was Napoleon's splendid surroundings in the Schön-brunn Palace that had gone to his head that summer – he delighted in the cool spring water in the garden – is uncertain: he was certainly playing the part of conqueror and imperial proconsul denied him in Paris, where he was always nervous of plots against him and the derision of his peers and the barbs of polite society. His bombast often reflected insecurity and paranoia, especially towards his fellow marshals. Some twenty plays and operas were performed for him as well as ballets by the great impresario Filippo Taglioni.

Meanwhile the Countess Marie Walewska had been summoned from Warsaw as his mistress and dallied with him every evening until August, becoming pregnant. He also pursued an affair with a nineteen-year-old Austrian girl who also became pregnant. He was delighted, not because he intended to marry either – although he entertained the idea that his son by Marie Walewska would become King of Poland one day – but because it was proof that he could father an heir. This

was much on his mind: he had been wounded at Ratisbon, and was anxious for the future of his dynasty.

More recently, a young man from Saxony had succeeded in getting close to him at a military parade and attempted to stab him, being deflected at the last moment by one of Napoleon's aides. The Emperor was highly disturbed and personally interrogated the boy, the seventeen-year-old Fredrick Staps.

'What did you want of me?'

'To kill you.'

'What have I done to you? Who made you my judge?'

'I wanted to bring the war to an end.'

'Why didn't you go to the Emperor Francis?'

'He? What for? He doesn't count. And if he died another would succeed him; but after you the French would disappear from Germany.'

'Do you repent?'

'No!'

'Would you do it again?'

'Yes!'

'What, even if I spared you?'

Napoleon wrote to Fouché:

The wretched boy, who seems to be fairly well educated, told me that he wanted to assassinate me to rid Austria of the presence of the French. I could find in him no traces of religious or political fanaticism. He seemed to have no clear idea of who Brutus was. His excitement prevented my finding out more. He will be questioned after he has cooled down and fasted. Possibly it all amounts to nothing. I have sent you the news of this incident to prevent its importance being exaggerated. I hope nothing will be said about it; if there should be talk, make out that the fellow is insane. If there is none, keep the matter a close secret. There was no scene at the parade; I myself had no notion that anything had happened.

The young man was executed shouting 'Long live Germany! Death to the tyrant!'

Perhaps the saddest chapter in Napoleon's personal life now occurred, again fuelled by the humiliation and megalomania after Wagram. The extraordinary thing was that his near-miss at Wagram did at least seem to dispel – albeit temporarily – his massive complex of personal insecurity. He really did believe he had confounded his foes both at home and abroad, with the exception of the running sore or ulcer of the Iberian Peninsula. At the age of forty, when he publicly considered himself too old to dance, he could afford to relax, to think of becoming *primus inter pares* among the great families of Europe, of a peaceful, respectable existence presiding wisely over the greatest European empire ever forged. It was time to think of a son and the succession to a French imperial dynasty that would preside over Europe for generations.

The sacrifice had to be made – and Napoleon was convinced it was his sacrifice primarily – of the woman he truly loved, in the interests of France: Josephine. The marriage between Napoleon and Josephine has often been portrayed as a loveless one of convenience marked by cynicism and infidelity on both sides. Yet it is hard to read Napoleon's early letters to Josephine without concluding that there was great passion, indeed profound love on his side at first harshly matched by her own indifference. As the relationship progressed his own attitude grew more realistic and bitter, while this hardened woman softened towards him. As two tough survivors, their relationship was extraordinarily complex, but it would be wrong to view their hatreds and quarrels and passions as reflecting an absence of love; quite the reverse.

Precisely because of an essential similarity in their makeup, their relationship went deeper than the idealized romantic love the Emperor believed he felt for Marie Walewska. Napoleon married Josephine when he was inexperienced sexually, and was certainly passionately in love with her brand of worldly wise, older sensuality, clinging to her in the teeth of fierce opposition from his own family and others, and despite his intense jealousy when bruised by her infidelities. Certainly she married him initially for convenience: she was a widow with her

most beautiful years behind her, marrying a somewhat unprepossessing but already highly successful young man.

It was only on Napoleon's Egyptian campaign that he appeared to fall out of love with her, when the evidence of her infidelity became overwhelming and his cuckoldry public knowledge. But he must have known before, and his angry reaction then seems as much a show staged for the benefit of his public image as a true reflection of his feelings: he was angry because he had been humiliated by her before others. Although by no means always faithful to her before then – which was typical of most men of his class at that time – his own sexual incontinence now became chronic and public, presumably in an act of revenge.

His Egyptian dalliances were succeeded by a string of girlfriends (he and his wife now slept in separate apartments) including the beautiful young Louise Rolandeau, the more mature Marguerite George, Josephine Raffin and Mlle Bourgoin, all of them actresses. By the time of his coronation he even had a 'love nest' on the rue de Vennes. A more serious liaison was with the twenty-year-old Adele Duchâtel, which Josephine tried to stop, arousing Napoleon's fury. Another passion was the twenty-year-old Auna Roche de la Coste, followed by the eighteen-year-old Eleonore Denuelle, who was also Murat's mistress. Napoleon also lusted after Josephine's famously beautiful niece Stephanie de Beauharnais, whom however he never bedded.

When he fell in love with Marie Walewska in December 1806 and Josephine learnt of their passion the following April, Napoleon went overboard to assure his wife that he still loved her.

Maybe this was because he feared her continuing political influence, sometimes with the Jacobins, sometimes with Murat's supporters; but it is more probably the action of a man genuinely devoted to his oldest love, although wise to her faults and incapable of fidelity himself. She also possessed a psychological power over him, however all-powerful he was politically, and was adept at bending his often childlike emotional nature to her will. By this time Josephine's infidelities had calmed down a good deal and she would throw jealous rages at her husband, which he occasionally reinforced by violent acts such as breaking the chairs or the furniture.

In the second part of the relationship it seemed that Napoleon behaved to her with enormous affection, treating her as a sister, never ceasing to write to her, and that she reciprocated by forgiving him for his sexual excesses, even overlooking his mistresses, while behaving with surprising dignity as Empress. She was a tolerant and worldly wise woman who treated the younger and more emotionally immature Napoleon as a naughty boy, putting up with his tantrums, girlfriends and his extraordinarily brutal initial treatment of her (indeed he treated most of his women as sexual playthings).

Josephine was not a particularly attractive woman in many ways: hard, calculating, manipulative, cynical and often conspiring; but she fuelled a need in this strange man. By the end it is possible to believe that deep in the thickets of her own self-interest there lay a genuine affection for a man who in many ways was another hardbitten conspirator. In 1807 Josephine had a brief liaison with the thirty-year-old Duke Frederick Louis of Mecklenburg, a man half her age, which roused Napoleon to fury. But he adored her nevertheless. 'I truly loved her, although I didn't respect her. She was a liar, and an utter spendthrift, but she had a certain something which was irresistible. She was a woman to her very fingertips.' On learning of her death in 1814 Napoleon's *cri de coeur* was too agonized to be dismissed: 'I have not passed a day without loving you. I have not passed a night without clasping you in my arms . . . No woman was ever loved with more devotion, ardour and tenderness . . . only death could break a union formed by sympathy, love and true feeling.'

Truly there was an element of the Macbeths in this strange relationship. But at this moment Josephine was about to fall victim to Napoleon's *folie de grandeur*. For years Fouché and Talleyrand had been pressing him to divorce Josephine on the grounds that she could not provide him with an heir to the throne. Both had previously considered her politically dangerous, but now a largely spent force.

His fathering of a child with Marie Walewska proved to him that he was capable of siring an heir and that Josephine, having produced two children by her previous husband, was now barren. Fouché, whose hands were stained with Bourbon blood, wanted an heir to prevent the dynasty's return. Talleyrand wanted to regularize the line of succession;

both agreed that any of Napoleon's brothers would be a disaster. Napoleon himself longed for the respectability that marriage into one of the old European dynastic royal families would give him, which was not surprising for one of his background. First, he sought the hand of one of the Tsar's sisters; Alexander replied that the decision was his mother's. A fortnight later the sister was engaged to another. It could hardly have been a more blatant snub, but it did not deter Napoleon. Snubbed by the Russians, he began to consider other possible links – in particular a marriage to one of the daughters of his oldest enemy in Europe, the Emperor Francis of Austria.

On his return to Paris from one of his amorous dalliances with Marie Walewska, he treated Josephine with coldness, walling up the connecting door between their apartments at Fontainebleau and passing his time with his favourite sister Pauline. He asked Josephine's daughter Hortense and her son, the loyal and able Eugène, to inform their mother that the marriage was at an end, and then did so himself, for political necessity and for 'the welfare of the nation'. She screamed and fell to the floor 'weeping and moaning'.

On 14 December he announced the dissolution of the marriage at a ceremony in the throne room of the Tuileries. He presented her with honours, presents and an income of 3 million francs a year. He wrote with stomach-churning self-pity:

The ceremony took place in the state apartments of the Tuileries and was very touching; all those present wept.

The policy of my Empire, the interests, the needs of my people, which have guided all my actions, demand that I should leave after me, to my children – the heirs of my affection for my people – the throne on which Providence has placed me. I have, however, for some years past, lost hope of having children from my marriage with my beloved wife the Empress Josephine: and it is this that has brought me to sacrifice my dearest affections, to consider only the good of the state, and to wish the dissolution of our marriage. At the age of forty I may yet hold the hope of living long enough to bring up in my own way of thinking the children which it may please Providence to grant me. God knows how much my present resolve

has cost me, but no sacrifice goes beyond my courage when it can be shown to be for the interests of France . . .

I think, dear friend, [Josephine] that you were weaker than you should have been today. You have shown courage; you must keep it up; you must not give way to a dangerous melancholy; you must be happy, and look after your health, which is so precious to me. If you are attached to me, if you love me, you must show strength. You cannot doubt my constant and loving friendship, and you would only show how little you know me if you thought that I could be happy unless you are. Goodbye, dear friend, sleep well – remember that I want you to.

Napoleon was no less crude and insensitive in the foolish way he now determined to 'marry a womb'. First he persuaded his ambassador to Russia, Caulaincourt, to seek the hand of the Tsar's youngest sister Grand Duchess Anna Pavlovna, who was only fourteen, following the botched marriage pass at the older Catherine. The Tsar claimed that she was too young yet for such a match. Impatiently, Napoleon sent Eugène de Beauharnais – of all people, Josephine's son, in another demonstration of the Emperor's quasi-sadistic insensitivity – to ask for the hand of the nineteen-year-old Marie Louise of Austria. The Austrians were told they had to agree within days. He treated the humiliated Francis contemptuously as a vassal over whom he could exercise droit de seigneur.

As repellent as was Napoleon's behaviour, Francis's cold-bloodedness was perhaps even worse. Marie Louise was by that time a tall blonde with a strikingly pink and pretty complexion, full-cheeked and with beautiful eyes, a sensuous, vulnerable mouth and a touch of the long Habsburg nose and chin, enough to lend distinction but not to spoil her looks. She carried herself in the haughty Austrian manner that befitted the daughter of an Emperor: her bosom was well developed and her figure slim and attractive. In short, she was a thoroughly desirable match – quite apart from being the daughter of the Emperor of Austria.

This girl had twice been evacuated from Vienna as Napoleon's armies had approached: to her he was the anti-Christ, the devil

incarnate, the bogeyman who had haunted her life ever since she was aware of the world outside her palace. Almost as bad, he was an upstart, a commoner whom no aristocratic woman, let alone a royal or Habsburg, could consider with anything but contempt. As a child she once wrote of swatting an enormous bug in her bedroom which she called Napoleon. When it was suggested that he might meet the Habsburgs she wrote, 'I assure you that to meet this creature will be for me a worse torture than all the martyrdoms.'

In January 1810 a terrible presentiment came upon her, possibly promoted by gossip at court. She wrote to her father:

Today I read in the newspaper of the act of separation between Napoleon and his wife. I must admit, dear Papa, that I am very disturbed by this news. The thought that it is not impossible that I may be counted among those from whom he will choose his future wife impels me to let you know something I would lay in your fatherly heart. . . . Since I have been in Often [Buda] I have met Archduke Francis. I am certain he has all the qualities which would make me happy. I have confided in Mama [Maria Ludovica] and she shares my unbounded confidence and has had the kindness to suggest that I write to you about my sentiments.

She remarked to a friend: 'I pity the unfortunate woman on whom his choice falls; that will certainly put an end to her fine days.'

Gradually the terrible truth dawned on her that she was to be the sacrificial lamb. The match was hugely favoured by Metternich, now the rising star of the imperial court; it would restore Austria to Napoleon's favour and would make him moderate the punitive terms of the peace treaty; it would lull the French into a sense of false security and buy Austria time to recover from the war and even prepare for the next one.

Overriding the views of a nineteen-year-old girl, even the highest ranking princess in the land, was a small price to pay for such a colossal political advantage. Marriages at that time, particularly dynastic ones, usually took little account of the views of those being paired off. But rarely can such an awful sacrifice have been demanded of a girl in the

first flush of adulthood than to marry the ogre that had terrorized her
countrymen and women in four wars, the monster of Europe, two and
a half times her age. It was a kind of official rape, connived in by her
own family. Her stiff, unimaginative father belatedly approved this
terrible fate for the daughter he loved most.

On 23 February there arrived a letter from the beast she had never
met, who was now to share her bed, concocted in suitably treacly
terms.

> The brilliant qualities which make you an outstanding person have
> inspired us with the desire to serve and honour you. While
> addressing ourselves to the Emperor, your father, and begging
> him to entrust us with the happiness of Your Imperial Highness,
> may we hope that Y.I.H. will share the sentiments that prompt us to
> make this step? May we flatter ourselves that Y.I.H. will not be
> driven solely by the duty of parental obedience? Should Y.I.H. have
> even the least amicable feelings for us, we wish to cherish them; and
> we set ourselves the constant task of pleasing you in every way so
> that we presume that one day we shall succeed in winning Y.I.H.'s
> affection. That is the goal we hope to attain; and we pray that Y.I.H.
> will look upon it with favour.

They were married by proxy on 11 March. Then she travelled to the
French border, where Caroline Murat, Napoleon's sister, was on hand
to dress her in the French style. The wretched Marie Louise wrote:
'She took two hours re-dressing me. I can assure you that by now I am
scented like the French ladies.' It was lamb being prepared for the
slaughter.

Napoleon, awaiting her at the village of Courcelles, exclaimed
angrily: 'Not one of these confounded young fellows will say she is
pretty. But it doesn't matter. So long as she is kind and gives me healthy
sons, I will love her as though she was the most beautiful woman in the
world.'

On the evening of 27 March Napoleon himself stopped her carriage
to meet his bride. They were almost as soon in bed, Napoleon never
being one to waste time. Years later he boasted that, 'She liked it so

much that she asked me to do it again.' It never occurred to the imperial boor that this terrified, proud girl who had been asked to make such a sacrifice for her country was simply ingratiating herself to her new master. Soon she was pregnant and apparently seduced by the many kindnesses Napoleon showered upon her, as well as indulging in her own favourite pastimes of painting and playing the piano and harp.

Yet the marriage was not universally popular in France: the old revolutionaries saw the return of an Austrian Habsburg Queen as a reincarnation of Marie Antoinette – the new Queen's aunt. The Revolution had truly turned full circle. However, on 20 March 1811, when a baby boy was born after a difficult delivery, the crowds of Paris went wild: '*C'est bon, bon, bon, c'est un garçon, vive Vive Napoleon!*' The Emperor was deliriously happy. Beauty too, it seemed, had been won over by the beast; for Marie Louise wrote: 'Never would I believe I could be so happy. My love for my husband grows all the time, and when I remember his tenderness I can scarcely prevent myself from crying. Even had I not loved him previously, nothing can stop me from loving him now.' The boy was christened Napoleon Francis Joseph Charles and given the title King of Rome.

This was the happiest and most settled period in Napoleon's almost unceasingly turbulent life. Apart from the Iberian Peninsula, from which he averted his gaze while he experienced the joys of a new bride and fatherhood, his empire was at peace. It seemed that years of prosperity beckoned, leading to the foundation of Europe's greatest dynasty. Even the restless reshaper of the continent seemed to have mellowed into a doting husband and would-be father. In the event the calm was to be deceptive, merely another eye of the storm: the next four years were to bring his empire to its terrifying and tumultuous denouement. But few would have guessed it then, least of all the British, who feared that the Austrian marriage had robbed them of their most reliable ally in Europe.

The first great challenge to Napoleon was to open up unexpectedly with the long and bloody Peninsular War, which will be recounted in the next section. The end of this overlapped with Napoleon's apocalyptic invasion of Russia, whose story will be told in the following section.

Part 10

THE PENINSULAR WAR

Chapter 65

OPORTO

Sir Arthur Wellesley was a distinctly odd man; fastidious, snooty and intelligent all at once. He was also deeply ambitious and powered by intolerance towards others. He could hardly have been more different temperamentally in his buttoned-up style, to the mercurial, emotional Nelson or to the excitable, angry Napoleon. Undemonstrative, except in private to his officers and girlfriends, he was clipped and economical with words, but cultivated soundbites with the care of a modern politician. They resonate to this day.

There were three features of genius to his personality: a brilliant eye for a battlefield and the disposition of forces to give him maximum advantage, particularly in defence, which was on a par with Napoleon's skill in strong offensive deployments; strategic caution allied to an ability to strike lethally at the enemy's weakest point at exactly the right time that surpassed even Napoleon; and an awesome dedication to the minutiae of military life — supplies, feeding his soldiers, preparing the ground and reconnaissance. Finally there was his remarkable ability to co-operate with the insurgent forces on the Peninsula, both Spanish and Portuguese. In addition, his cool and detached demeanour under fire was awe-inspiring, and inspirational to his men. Like the best generals, he seemed to think better and more calmly the hotter the action around him.

In spite of his semi-privileged background Wellesley was one of Britain's first truly professional soldiers. The military commander he most resembled was not Napoleon, with his instinct for aggression in all circumstances, but the American George Washington. His skill in

being patient in the face of intense provocation was of the same order. Like Washington he would retire to secure winter quarters, bide his time, and then suddenly strike a decisive blow. Like Washington he could provision and march his men for weeks at a time to preserve his forces. Like Washington he had an eye for the jugular, after years of inertia – suddenly spotting the enemy's weaknesses and inflicting a decisive defeat.

Wellington was also unflappable and almost inhumanly courageous, a born leader of men in battle. It is from him that the tradition of the cold, aloof British military commander descends. While Britain's foremost naval commanders were often primadonnas, no one could ever accuse Wellesley of being hysterical. But his contempt for the lower classes, his sharp tongue towards his less gifted subordinates, his insensitivity even towards his own veterans, and his addiction to discipline make him a deeply unattractive personality, as did his private behaviour. While the childishly infatuated Nelson was unintentionally cruel to his wife, Wellington was coldly, calculatingly so. Yet as a military professional, he had the forensic mind of a Sherlock Holmes – a fictional character whose personality might have been modelled on him.

On 27 April 1809 he landed at Lisbon with 23,000 men – including 3,000 Hanoverians. Some 6,000 men had already arrived under Sir Rowland Hill, an amiable, outgoing personality who was beloved of his men. These liaised with General William Beresford who had been placed in command of a considerable force of 16,000 Portuguese troops, with Captain Robert Harvey as his chief aide. Wellesley did not waste time: the plight of his army was precarious. In the north Marshal Soult had occupied Oporto, Portugal's second city, with 23,000 men, while Marshal Victor, to the east was approaching the frontier with Spain with 25,000 men; between these two was a small army under General Lapisse. There were a staggering 250,000 French troops altogether in the Iberian Peninsula.

The British had just one advantage. The incredible brutality of the French, combined with their unpopularity as invaders, meant that the Spanish and Portuguese were united in their hatred of them. But they were almost equally suspicious of the British, whose motives they

suspected and whom they regarded as mere allies of convenience. This led in turn to considerable British distrust, mingled with contempt, for their Iberian allies.

The Peninsular War was to become a three-way conflict in which the bitter and continuing resistance of the Spanish and Portuguese against the invaders, usually involving small-scale attacks, was supplemented by a disciplined regular British force. The British would not have prevailed without the local resistance, which was widespread and which tied down enormous number of French troops. Equally the partisans would eventually have been crushed without the British, who posed the greater military threat. The British regarded the Spanish and Portuguese with distaste and the latter responded with deep suspicion and sometimes non-co-operation. The Spanish armies in particular were poorly commanded and ill-disciplined. Spaniards often showed a small-minded parochialism that led them to fight in their own immediate neighbourhoods, not co-ordinate with the wider national effort, but their fighters could also be incredibly daring and brave – and cruel.

Wellesley moved with the speed he had learnt in India. The country in Portugal was somewhat different – a rugged one of hills, woods and ravines, all of which grew more impassable the further north he travelled. That did not delay him: he was no Chatham. He assembled nearly 18,000 men at Coimbra on the way to Oporto, reasoning that if he immediately defeated Soult, he would prevent a junction of French armies that would otherwise be larger than his own. It was his fortieth birthday.

Beresford led some 6,000 Portuguese militia on the army's right flank to try to check the enemy's expansion eastwards into Spain. Some 12,000 troops were left to guard Lisbon and central Portugal. Wellesley marched northwards, routing a small French force of around 4,500 men above Grija, reaching the town of Vila Nova along the upper bends of that wide and beautiful river, the Douro. He was now overlooking Oporto, an ancient and picturesque city crammed down the opposite slope, the trading entrepot of the area with its access along the river to the sea. It was also the great wine-producing centre of the region, traditionally supplying the British with enormous quantities,

particularly now that trade with the rest of the continent had been blocked off. To make the shipping of this wine on the long journey back to Britain possible, the wine was fortified with brandy, which created that unique beverage, port, named after Oporto itself.

Soult had little warning of Wellesley's arrival. He promptly destroyed the single bridge across the Douro and ensured that all river craft were on his side. If an attack came, he thought it would be from the west, using fishing boats brought up by the British from the sea. Wellesley instead turned his attention eastwards, upstream along the river, where he found several unguarded boats, mostly for carrying wine. Wellesley is usually considered a defensive general, but he was capable of offensive boldness when necessary.

He sent across a small force to seize a large enemy-held seminary on the opposite bank. General Paget, leading the raid, was badly wounded; but Hill, along with an infantry brigade, held the seminary against repeated attack. By that time Portuguese boats were ferrying the British across in increasing numbers. The French, fearful of being attacked by the vengeful Portuguese in the steep, narrow streets of the riverside town, ordered a retreat to the east. The British captured nearly 1,300 prisoners and some sixty guns. Some 500 Frenchmen were killed, for a loss of just twenty-three Britons.

To the east Beresford had repulsed another French force and occupied the town of Amarante on the old road from northern Portugal into Spain, thus cutting off Soult's retreat. Blocked off to the east, the French army swung north into the hilly and wooded country towards Galicia abandoning their guns and provisions in a desperate attempt to get away. They had several thousand troops in their way, many of them Portuguese insurgents who responded to the routine raping of their womenfolk by castrating French soldiers and stuffing their genitals into their mouths or nailing them alive to trees and doorways.

Soult's retreating army had circled toward the Tagus valley. The twenty-four-year-old Captain Harvey had linguistic skills which made him a natural scout and spy, travelling undercover, stirring up the Portuguese resistance and liaising with anti-French clerics and Portuguese irregulars. On reconnaissance, he saw Soult's movement and

reported it to the Duque del Parque, the Spanish general with whom he was liaising, enabling his army to draw up into defensive lines at Tamames in the north and there block a junction between Soult's and Victor's forces.

The British were unable to follow. Wellesley remarked: 'If an army throws away all its cannon, equipment and baggage and everything which can strengthen it and enable it to act together as a body, and abandons all those who are entitled to its protection but add to its weight and impede its progress, it must be able to march by roads through which it cannot be followed by any army that has not made the same sacrifices.'

The British instead proceeded to march from Abrantes into Spain to take the battle to the enemy. Their intention was to liaise with the 30,000-strong Spanish army of General Don Gregorio de la Cuesta, a sixty-nine-year-old Spanish *caudillo* – top general – bedecked with medals, who trundled about in a huge coach drawn by mules. De la Cuesta, who treated Wellesley as a subordinate and the British as junior partners, proposed encircling Marshal Victor's 23,000-strong army across the border. As Wellesley descended from Portugal with his 21,000 men, leaving Beresford and 4,000 to defend Portugal, they found that Victor had withdrawn towards Talavera to the south-east.

Wellesley followed Victor to Plasencia, the local capital, early in July, where he was now just a hundred miles from Madrid. While Soult's forces held back for the moment, it was planned that the Spanish army should cross the Tagus to the northern bank and march eastwards to join up with the British at Talavera. To the south another 23,000-strong Spanish army under General Venegas was to engage the French forces in Madrid and stop them reinforcing Victor.

Chapter 66

TALAVERA

Wellesley's chief problem was a shortage of supplies, for he insisted that his men should not plunder the countryside so as not to antagonize the local population. He continued his march and on 16 July moved forward from Plasencia, reaching Talavera six days later. It was the height of a Spanish summer, and the heat on the baking plains was intense, the dust kicked up by the marching army choking. Even so, there was snow on the sierra to the north, which extended nearly as far as the river at Talavera. The French were surprised by the British advance but quickly retreated east towards Madrid.

Cuesta, that 'desperate-looking lump of pride, ignorance and treachery' as one British soldier called him, or a 'perverse stupid old blockhead' as an officer described him, ordered his army forward in pursuit, with Wellesley wisely refusing to follow. As Arthur Bryant picturesquely described it: 'All that day the astonished British watched it pour past – a bewildering kaleidoscope of turbulent half-armed brigands emerging from clouds of dust, regular regiments in blue and scarlet marching in perfect order, of cavalry staff officers, priests, musicians, women, carts, guns and artillery wagons, and herds of sheep, pigs and cattle. It looked like the last army of the Middle Ages pouring out to do battle with the French Revolution.'

The Spaniards soon ran up against a force of 46,000 Frenchmen, a combination of Victor's army and Joseph's reinforcements from Madrid. Of Venegas there was nothing to be seen. He had stopped at Aranjuez to the south. Cuesta was forced immediately to retreat to the British position behind him.

There Wellesley, with his extraordinary eye for a good defence, had drawn up the British between the mountains and the river. He allowed the Spaniards to occupy the most protected front beside Talavera itself, while the British were in the exposed gap and the steep foothills of the mountains, the Cerro de Medellin, overlooking the valley.

There were only 20,000 British and German troops and just thirty light cannon against the 40,000 French troops and their eighty cannon. Wellesley himself narrowly evaded capture as he tried to escort the Spanish into their defensive positions. On the same evening of 27 July Victor ordered his men to attack and they succeeded in taking the top of the Cerro de Medellin before Hill led a counter-attack and drove them back down.

The following morning the battle began in earnest. The French opened up with their guns. Wellesley ordered his men back over the brow of the hill and told them to lie down. The French infantry marched up the hill but as they reached the top the British rose in good formation and fired volleys before Wellesley ordered them down the slope, routing the French with their superior forces.

There was a lull in the fighting before a general advance was ordered. On the British right, near Talavera, General Campbell repelled the French so successfully that he had to restrain his men from advancing too fast and breaking the already overstretched British line. To the north a British pursuit was counter-attacked by the French, who killed half of them as well as their commander, opening up a huge gap in the British line which 15,000 French infantry moved quickly to occupy. The British reserves were hurried up.

Wellesley also ordered infantry down from the Cerro de Medellin to plug the hole. But there was a further danger: the French had scrambled up the rocky ravine to the north of the Cerro de Medellin to outflank the British where they were weakest. Cavalry were ordered forward to stop them, but many plunged to their deaths into a hidden gully, although enough survived to halt the advancing French.

At this stage the French commanders decided to cut their losses and withdraw on learning that Venegas was at last advancing from the south to threaten the capital. A particular horror of the battle now ensued when the long grass on the slopes of the Cerro de Medellin

caught fire, leading to the burning alive of hundreds of wounded lying there. Yet it had been a victory of sorts, with 7,000 French dead and captured, compared to some 5,000 British, Spanish and Germans, who had also taken the battlefield. Wellesley had shown that he was not just a capable and lucky commander, as at Vimeiro and Oporto, but a first-rate one, who made careful preparations and maintained absolute coolness in the heat of the fighting. Talavera was also a triumph for Sir John Moore's reforms – although modified by Wellesley's much stricter enforcement of old-fashioned discipline.

Victor withdrew towards Madrid with just 18,000 men to defend the capital from the attack believed to be imminent under Venegas from the south. The British and the Spanish armies also prepared to march on Madrid from the east. However on 1 August Wellesley learnt that Soult had been reinforced from the north by Ney and Masséna to 50,000 men. Spain's northern commander, the Duque del Parque, had been forced to stand aside to escape annihilation and the French were marching on Plasencia having driven off the 3,000-strong Spanish force guarding the crucial Pass of Banos.

Wellesley learnt of the French concentration of forces in the nick of time and escaped to the south-west across the only available bridge across the Tagus. General Cuesta followed reluctantly and his rearguard was badly mauled by the French who captured most of the Spanish guns. Meanwhile Venegas's army was also badly beaten at Almonacid de Toledo. Wellesley's force huddled in the barren hills south of the Tagus, quarrelling with Cuesta's troops and in danger of starving as the Spaniards took what little was available from the peasantry. After a few weeks Wellington, disgusted with the Spaniards whom he blamed for failing to fight effectively at Talavera, decided to bolt back into the fertile land of southern Portugal. He had overreached himself and been forced back to his heartland.

The Spaniards were furious with what they saw as British desertion. They staged a quixotic attack which was crushed at Ocaña in November by 50,000 against their 34,000. The Spaniards fought bravely but lost 18,000 men and were routed. The Spanish governing junta were driven south by a French attack in January and fled to the safety of Cadiz where it was overthrown by its fellow countrymen. But the

French were stopped outside the city as Spanish troops under Sir Thomas Graham held the isthmus to the great port. Some 70,000 French troops now found themselves tied down in the south besieging Cadiz.

Chapter 67

THE LINES OF TORRES VEDRAS

Wellesley led his men back to the temperate valleys of Beira and Mondego in southern Portugal. After their gruelling marches the mood of relief and lightheadedness in this cheerful winter quarters is caught by the episode when Wellesley, visiting a convent, was astonished to see a nun perform a somersault – until from her petticoats there emerged the boots of a British officer, the practical joker being Captain Dan Mackinnon (who also dressed up on another occasion as the Duke of York, fooling his Spanish hosts, until he dunked his head into the punchbowl in front of him).

Wellesley had now been awarded a peerage as Viscount Wellington, after the town in Somerset. The new milord knew that his position in Portugal was virtually impregnable because Lisbon, from which British forces could be evacuated by sea in a crisis, was at the tip of a peninsula twenty miles wide with the Tagus encircling it to the south and east and the Atlantic to the west. If he built fortifications across the neck of the isthmus on the hills to the north – which rose to 2,000 feet in some places – he had a defensible enclave.

At the end of October he ordered his chief engineer, Colonel Fletcher, to start building these lines of defence – one at the bottom of the Peninsula to cover an embarkation, another across the Cabeca de Monchique, a mountain area which formed an outer perimeter six miles to the north. The extent of the work was astounding: forests were cut down, walls erected and towers strung out along the lines. Much of this work, called the Lines of Torres Vedras, survives to this day, more than fifty miles in extent – a miniature version of the Great Wall of China.

While the Lines were being constructed, Wellington had to fight calls from England for the withdrawal of his army. He was accused of causing his men needless suffering after Talavera, which was partly true. With the fall of the Duke of Portland's government, the new secretary for war was Lord Liverpool, a pleasant, deeply unimaginative mediocrity but a staunch admirer of Wellington. The latter defended himself with uncharacteristic modesty and urged a continuing presence in the Peninsula: 'During the continuance of this contest, which must necessarily be defensive on our part, in which there may be no brilliant events, and in which, after all, I may fail, I shall be most confoundedly abused, and in the end I may lose the little character I have gained; but I should not act fairly by the government if I did not tell them my real opinion which is, that they will betray the honour and interests of the country if they do not continue their efforts in the Peninsula, which, in my opinion, are by no means hopeless.'

Liverpool was persuaded: 'We must make our opinion between a steady and continued exertion upon a moderate scale and a great and extraordinary effort for a limited time which neither our military nor financial means will enable us to maintain permanently. If it could be hoped that the latter would bring the contest to a speedy and successful conclusion, it would certainly be the wisest course; but unfortunately the experience of the last fifteen years is not encouraging in this respect.'

Not since Addington had so mediocre a man as Spencer Perceval led Britain against France. Brougham sums up his personality:

Of views upon all things the most narrow, upon religious and even political questions the most bigoted and intolerant, his range of mental vision was confined in proportion to his ignorance on all general subjects. Within that sphere he saw with extreme acuteness – as the mole is supposed to be more sharp-sighted than the eagle for half a quarter of an inch before it; but as beyond the limits of his little horizon he saw no better than the mole, so like her, he firmly believed, and always acted on the belief, that beyond what he could descry nothing whatever existed; and he mistrusted, dreaded, and even hated all who had an ampler visual range than himself. But

here, unhappily, all likeness ceases between the puny animal and the powerful statesman. Beside the manifest sincerity of his convictions, attested, perhaps, by his violence and rancour, he possessed many qualities, both of the head and the heart, which strongly recommended him to the confidence of the English people. He never scared them with refinements, nor alarmed their fears by any sympathy with improvements out of the old and beaten track; and he shared largely in all their favourite national prejudices.

Perceval's absurd attempts to secure a monopoly of neutral trade for Britain led to the needless War of 1812 with America. In the absence of both Canning and Castlereagh, the most powerful players in his government were the Wellesley brothers – the marquess promoted from ambassador to Lisbon to Foreign Secretary – with Liverpool another mediocrity whom they dominated. Perceval was a narrow-minded conservative, whose response to the threat posed by Napoleon was of straightforward obduracy, as it was to any manifestation of popular discontent prompted by Britain's economic difficulties under the Continental System and the rapid social and economic transformation the country was undergoing.

The sole benefit of such leadership was that it gave the domineering Wellington a free hand in Portugal. In addition to establishing the Lines of Torres Vedras, Wellington proved a genius in irregular warfare. He sought to integrate his Portuguese troops under General Beresford. In this Major Harvey, the assistant quartermaster-general with the Portuguese army, was the key. He was sent to organize a force of Portuguese guerrillas in Beira province. These became highly effective guerrillas, usually under the command of priests. On one occasion Harvey's irregulars captured a heavy convoy near Penamacor, fighting off the 150 French irregulars accompanying it just four miles away from a full French division: no fewer than fifty-three cartloads of ammunition and tobacco were taken.

Another leader of irregulars was the ferociously disciplinarian Brigadier Robin Crauford, 'Black Bob', who flogged any man who broke ranks crossing a stream and who could get his men under arms from sleeping quarters at night in just seven minutes. Crauford's guerrillas

guarded the Portuguese frontier, bringing reports of suspect French troop concentrations. 'The whole web of communication quivered at the slightest touch,' wrote one observer admiringly. Both Harvey and Crauford reported back enemy movements in the valley of the Mondego from the vantage points of the Serra d'Estrella.

Wellington and his small army remained in their hill fastnesses in central Portugal, as Washington's armies had done in the interior of America, while the imperial armies of their opponents blundered about the plains and plateaux, under constant and relentless harassment from the local population. Every day on average more than a hundred French soldiers were killed. While bungling and ill-equipped Spanish armies were always at the mercy of the French on the field of battle, in guerrilla fighting it was the other way around.

One fearsome guerrilla boasted that he had killed 600 Frenchmen himself. El Empecinado – Inky Face – roamed Castile with his guerrilla band, seizing and holding the sizeable town of Guadalajara for a day. Camilo, a guerrilla chief whose wife and daughter had been raped, formed a small army which killed thousands. Don Julian Sanchez sent the severed heads of French commanders to Wellington as trophies and massacred 160 prisoners in a single sitting, promising to slice Soult into strips. One of his commanders boiled a French general alive and sawed another in half.

The fortress of Gerona held out under its governor, Mariano Alvarez de Castro. He told his men when they ran out of food to eat the cowards, and instructed his officers that their only place of retreat should be the cemetery. Half of Gerona's townspeople and 6,000 of its 9,000 defenders were killed before it surrendered.

Napoleon, relaxing with his pretty young bride after Wagram, had long promised to go to Spain to take personal charge of the campaign but perhaps sensing that the war there was unwinnable against resistance on this scale, he had already despatched his two best generals, André Masséna and Michel Ney. These two supported the forces under the incompetent King Joseph (known as Pepe Botellas by the Spaniards for his alleged fondness for the bottle), and other marshals: Soult in Andalucia, Suchet in Aragón (who alone controlled his

fiefdom through enlightened policies designed to win over the local population) and Augereau in Catalonia. These men reported directly to the Emperor in order to prevent Masséna acquiring too much power, but the result was that they competed with one another, rarely combining their armies. They each ran their own areas of Spain as personal fiefdoms.

Wellington wrote with detachment in July:

> This is not the way in which they have conquered Europe. There is something discordant in all the French arrangements for Spain. Joseph divides his Kingdom into *préfetures*, while Napoleon parcels it out into governments; Joseph makes a great military expedition into the south of Spain and undertakes the siege of Cadiz while Napoleon places all the troops and half the kingdom under the command of Masséna and calls it the Army of Portugal . . . I suspect that the impatience of Napoleon's temper will not bear the delay of the completion of the conquest of Spain.

But Masséna with his 30,000 vanguard was already approaching the frontier town of Ciudad Rodrigo. Although the fortress was almost indefensible, its heroic Spanish commander General Herrasti held out for nearly two months with 5,000 men, until more than 1,200 had been killed. Some 30,000 shells and roundshot had to be fired before the French managed to take the garrison. Wellington refused to come to the rescue, for once out in the open plain he was easy prey for French cavalry. Masséna's army now moved on to the more impressive fortress of Almeida. However, here a shell blew up the main ammunition dump, leaving the garrison almost out of ammunition, and it surrendered unexpectedly quickly.

Chapter 68

COIMBRA

As Masséna approached, Wellington withdrew behind the Lines of Torres Vedras, but British public opinion clamoured for him to make a stand. He decided to do so at a place of his own choosing, near the fortress town of Coimbra. Masséna's army approached down the rain-sodden road, to Ordenanza, his supply train attacked by Portuguese guerrillas. One group of 2,000 under a notoriously daring Irish officer, Colonel Trant, nearly succeeded in cutting off the entire French artillery. Then the French army came up against a great nine-mile long ridge running from the banks of the Mondego to the central spine of Portuguese hills at Bussaco.

Here Wellington took up his position. He had 27,000 British troops and 25,000 Portuguese. In front of them, in the valley below, were 60,000 French soldiers. Wellington, clad in his simple frock coat, cocked hat and cloak without decorations, watched from above. 'If Masséna attacks me here, I shall defeat him,' he observed simply.

On the morning of 27 September the French drums beat for the attack. They were drawn up in two huge columns, each composed of several divisions: one in the south under Reynier was ordered to break through the British right along a track, and wheel about to envelop it; the other under Ney was to come straight along the main road and strike through the centre in overwhelming force. Behind it a further corps, and Ney's and Junot's own divisions, were held in reserve. Masséna seemed unaware there were two further British divisions under Hill to the right. The French had every confidence their overwhelming force of hardened veterans would prevail.

They attacked at dawn in a mist, the steepness of the climb to the ridge soon causing them to pause. One French division made it to the top at a point that was lightly defended, but British and Portuguese troops hurried down the road that ran along the ridge to reinforce it. After a fierce firefight that left 2,000 dead and wounded, the assailants were forced down the slope. A second French attempt to break through at the same spot was also repulsed. To the left the main French thrust reached the crest of the hill, only to be blocked by 1,800 men of the 43rd and 52nd Regiments, concealed behind the brow. 'Now 52nd, avenge the death of Sir John Moore!' yelled Crauford. After a few minutes the 6,000-strong French column was in full retreat down the steep bank.

Masséna decided to call the attack off with the loss of more than 4,000 men to some 1,200 on the Anglo-Portuguese side. He had found a trail over to the coastal plain which would bypass the British position, but Wellington had no intention of being outflanked. He ordered a retreat to the first Line of Torres Vedras seventy miles away, to the consternation of Portuguese civilians, who had to abandon their belongings and join in a chaotic refugee column. Trant and his Portuguese forces briefly recaptured Coimbra behind French lines and took 4,500 French wounded and the small garrison there prisoner.

The characteristic rains of October burst upon the two armies. Masséna, closing in for the kill, ordered a general surge forward. At last the British army reached the awesome fortified lines – earthworks interrupted by forts with the ground cleared in front of them, interspersed by cliffs blown by the British out of solid rock. On the coastal side there was a huge artificial marsh created by diverting streams. The British and the Portuguese armies were safe: most of these troops had no idea of the extent or even existence of these fortifications. 'The devil cannot surely have built these mountains,' was Masséna's dismayed reaction as he came up against them. He staged one botched attack near Sobral, then realized his men would be massacred if he proceeded.

For five weeks his troops were camped miserably in front of the Lines as their supplies dwindled and Portuguese partisans attacked in the rear.

The British soldiers tossed them biscuits out of sympathy. Finally the French erected straw dummies at night and pulled back to some thirty miles further north. There they camped and starved through that wretched winter. The British held off attacking, Wellington remarking with his usual detachment that there was no need to sacrifice his men: Masséna's men would sooner or later have to retreat in full winter over the mountain passes to Spain.

Masséna was well entrenched in the hills around Santarém and there he waited for a diversionary attack to be mounted by Soult with his army from Seville. In October, as Soult's forces approached, Major Harvey was despatched to take command of the Ordeneza, the Portuguese guerrilla Army of the South, to prevent the French crossing the Tagus. These Portuguese brigands traditionally would not obey British orders and he had no supporting British troops. Nevertheless he succeeded in patrolling the west bank of the river. When the French tried to seize sixty boats to carry their forces over the river at Chumusca, they were supported by six cannon, but intense fire from the Portuguese partisans under Harvey's command drove them back and he succeeded in scuttling the boats.

On 30 December Soult set out with 20,000 men north-west into Estremadura, taking two weeks to reach Olivenza, where he captured or killed the 4,000 Spanish soldiers defending the garrison. At the end of January 1812 it was the turn of the massive castle of Badajoz, which lay on the road to Portugal: outside its walls a Spanish army was again trounced. Wellington could spare no men himself to relieve it.

However General Thomas Graham, commanding the British forces in Cadiz, decided to stage a diversionary attack by landing from the sea behind the lines besieging that city. In late February some 10,000 Spaniards and 5,000 British soldiers sailed from Cadiz to Algeciras to attack the French army from the rear. Their commander, however, was the notoriously highly strung General Manuel (Dona Manuela to his soldiers) La Peña.

On arrival opposite the French besieging army under General Victor, La Peña attempted to bypass this and link up with the forces inside Cadiz. This exposed him to being cut down by the French cavalry on his flank: Graham led a force of just 470 men up the hill

against vastly superior French forces: some 200 were killed in the first French volley alone. But this onslaught gave time for reinforcements to be brought up, and the French were routed, losing 2,000 of their 7,000 men. Some 600 British soldiers were lost altogether, along with twenty-five officers, around a third of the total.

The Spanish army was thus saved; but, exhausted by La Peña's forced marching, it did nothing. Wellington remarked:

> They march the troops night and day without provisions or rest, abusing everybody who proposes a moment's delay to afford either to the famished and fatigued soldiers. They reach the enemy in such a state as to be unable to make any exertion or to execute any plan, even if any plan had been formed; and, when the moment of action arrives, they are totally incapable of movement, and they stand by to see their allies destroyed, and afterwards abuse them because they do not continue, unsupported, exertions to which human nature is not equal.

The two forces were compelled to return to the safety of Cadiz more or less intact, but having accomplished little. However they had dealt a psychological blow. Soult to the north, learning of Graham's diversionary attack, felt his rear to be threatened. Although he had captured Badajoz, he hastily returned southwards.

Masséna now was on his own again in Portugal. At long last his starving army began to retreat: it had been reduced by around 30,000 men to just 44,000. Behind them they left a wasteland strewn with the corpses of their own starved men, the Portuguese they had massacred and raped and a countryside stripped of all sustenance.

Wellington moved into close pursuit across this desolate countryside to prevent Masséna turning north to establish a new base in Portugal. He marched to the valley of the Ceira where he attacked Ney's forces as they tried to cross the river, killing some 400. After chasing the French a hundred miles across valleys and mountains in torrential rains, Wellington called a halt to resupply. Masséna promptly attempted to turn south and march across the 4,000-foot-high central massif of

Portugal to stage a new thrust against Lisbon from the Tagus valley. In the wake of the French myriad horrors occurred. As a British soldier wrote: 'This retreat brought to my mind the Corunna race. We could not advance a hundred yards without seeing dead soldiers of the enemy . . . The retreat resembled more that of famished wolves than men. Murder and devastation marked their way; every house was a sepulchre, a cabin of horrors!'

It was as though a plague of locusts had ravished the land. Arthur Bryant vividly described the devastation:

The road was covered with dead soldiers and abandoned carriages; the houses filled with sick and dying in the last loathsome stages of disease. Many lay on the floor in full uniform, their arms still grasped in their hands as if asleep, or sat in chairs, stiff and upright, with shakos on and pinched features frozen in death. The route their comrades had taken was marked by straggling wretches with pallid, swollen faces which they turned with inexpressible pathos on their pursuers. The Rifles in the British van threw them their biscuits in pity as they passed. But their pity turned to anger as they saw what they had done. For everywhere were burning and ravaged houses, mutilated peasants with slit throats and gouged-out eyes, polluted churches and rifled graves. The whole countryside had been transformed into a waste fit only for wolves and vultures. The few surviving inhabitants looked like skeletons risen from the tomb. Gaunt and ghastly figures fed off the grass in the fields or scoured the woods for acorns and rotten olives. Violated women lay bleeding in charred and unroofed houses, the streets were strewn with putrid carcasses, children with bones sticking through their skin clung to the bodies of dead parents. Searching for a stream on the first night of the British advance, Rifleman Costello stumbled on a fountain into whose waters the brains of three peasants were oozing, while all that had possessed life in the village 'lay quivering in the last agony of slaughter and awful vengeance'.

The atrocities had been a deliberate policy to crush the resistance of the local population. Wellington relayed the horrors to London, to force

the British government to continue its support of the Peninsular War.

Masséna's counterattack fizzled out. First Ney, then Reynier and Junot refused to obey the suicidal orders from the grim old general. On 5 April the exhausted, demoralized and defeated French army recrossed the Spanish border. The chase had lasted 300 miles. The French had been ignominiously ejected from Portugal. It had been the greatest setback for Napoleon's invincible armies yet.

Chapter 69

INTO SPAIN

Wellington, camped along the Spanish frontier, was himself in a dilemma. He could not risk striking deep into Spain without dangerously over-extending his lines, especially as the French controlled the key fortresses of Almeida, Ciudad Rodrigo and Badajoz on both his flanks. He set out to win back control. He rode down furiously to Badajoz to give orders to Beresford for taking the fortress, which the French had enormously reinforced; he was nearly captured on the way. He rode equally swiftly back north on learning that in three weeks Masséna had regrouped to stage an offensive to relieve the British siege of Almeida with an army of nearly 50,000.

Wellington, with only 21,000 British soldiers and some 10,000 Portuguese, needed to take Almeida to hold his position along the Spanish frontier, and so had no choice but to fight to prevent Masséna's army relieving the fortress. He deployed his exhausted army in woods and hills five miles from Almeida. The French army marched from the south from Ciudad Rodrigo to channel their forces into a hammer-blow of three forces against Wellington's weakest point, his right flank at the village of Fuentes de Onoro. The French succeeded in gaining control of most of the streets in the village before Wellington ordered a counter-attack. This drove them out of most of the village in brutal hand-to-hand fighting

Thus blocked, Masséna went probing to the north-west in search of a way around the British position, while Wellington sought to counter this by sending 1,000 British and nearly 4,000 Portuguese in the same direction, at the cost of weakening his centre. On the morning of 3

May Masséna sent some 17,000 infantry and 4,000 cavalry to attack the British right, while simultaneously ordering a fresh attack against the weakened British centre at Fuentes de Onoro again. It was a desperate moment for the heavily outnumbered British. Wellington decided to risk the centre and throw more of his sparse forces in to counter the threat on his right. However there was a danger that a division would be cut off by the reinforced French attack in the centre. The division withdrew in good order under repeated attack from heavily superior French forces. The British soldiers fought in squares in a beautifully executed and difficult movement across three miles of open plain, where they were at their most exposed, to the safety of rocky hillocks.

The French with 50,000 men launched their main attack against the British centre at Fuentes de Onoro. They drove back the 71st and 79th Highlanders, who fought with desperate bravery down the bloodied streets of the village again against hugely superior odds as far as the church and graveyard. But the British were able to bring forward new reserves to relieve the Highlanders and drive the French out. Both attacks had failed, at a cost of more than 2,000 French casualties to the British total of 1,400. The French withdrew southwards to Salamanca, claiming they had won a victory by driving the British back some three miles. But the siege of Almeida was resumed, and the town fell to the British, although most of the garrison escaped at night. It had been Wellington's narrowest victory in the whole campaign, and his costliest one yet. Still, he could now concentrate his forces on Badajoz.

Unknown to him, though, events had changed rapidly. Soult's army had marched northwards to relieve the besieged garrison against which Beresford, with his antiquated guns opposing the formidable fortifications, had made little impression. On learning that Soult was approaching with an army of 25,000, Beresford decided to move forward to meet him with his 10,000 British and 12,000 Portuguese soldiers. His aim was to rendezvous with three Spanish armies amounting to 15,000 men fighting in Extremadura under the overall command of General Castaños. This would give him numerical superiority; but it would also involve fighting in open flat country where the French had the advantage and the Spanish were traditionally bad at manoeuvre. Moreover Soult had cavalry and artillery superiority – some 8,000

horse compared with 5,000 under Beresford, only a quarter of them British, and some fifty guns compared with fewer than forty. The British were also at a tactical disadvantage: they had their backs to the Guadiana river, with only one crossing available to them.

On 15 May Beresford's army took up position at Albuera along a low ridge across which the main road to Badajoz passed. It was expected that the French, coming along the road, would attack frontally. Instead, on the following morning, while minor attacks were staged in the centre, the great bulk of the French marched off the highway through olive groves to attack the lightly defended allied right with the intention of encircling Beresford's men and forcing them off the ridge to fight on the exposed plain below or lose their line of communications with Portugal. It was a brilliant French manoeuvre, carried out largely in darkness.

They fell upon the Spanish forces defending the flank, catching them by surprise and throwing them into confusion, although most fought bravely. Beresford, equally surprised, ordered 500 British troops from the centre under General William Stewart to rush to the rescue. They moved with speed but with little order. At the same time, the Second Division also marched crack troops which had fought at Oporto and Talavera from its position in the centre. Portuguese cavalry were also deployed.

At that moment a hailstorm obscured all visibility for more than a few yards. There was complete confusion and great carnage. The allies were reinforced by another two brigades which threw themselves into the mêlée. The British were outnumbered by some 8,000 to 3,000, exchanging fire across a shallow valley. The fighting caused appalling bloodshed on both sides with neither side yielding. After what seemed an eternity, British reinforcements arrived late to the battle under the command of General Lowry Cole, consisting of 2,000 British and 3,000 well-trained Portuguese under Harvey, now Beresford's chief of staff and chief liaison between him and Wellington.

Soult promptly threw in his reserves of some 10,000 men, which he had withheld, believing the battle to be his, but the Portuguese were as

resolute as the British and faced down the French cavalry. Major Napier provided the finest description of that celebrated advance:

> Such a gallant line, issuing from the midst of the smoke, and rapidly separating itself from the confused and broken multitude, startled the enemy's heavy masses, which were increasing and pressing onwards as to an assured victory; they wavered, hesitated, and then vomiting forth a storm of fire, hastily endeavoured to enlarge their front, while a fearful discharge of grape from all their artillery whistled through the British ranks. Myers was killed, Cole, the three colonels, Ellis, Blakeney, and Hawkshawe, fell wounded, and the Fusilier battalions, struck by the iron tempest, reeled, and staggered like sinking ships.
>
> But suddenly and sternly recovering, they closed on their terrible enemies, and then was seen with what a strength and majesty the British soldier fights. In vain did Soult, by voice and gesture, animate his Frenchmen; in vain did the hardiest veterans, extricating themselves from the crowded columns, sacrifice their lives to gain time for the mass to open out on such a fair field; in vain did the mass itself bear up, and fiercely striving, fire indiscriminately upon friends and foes while the horsemen hovering on the flank threatened to charge the advancing line.
>
> Nothing could stop that astonishing infantry. No sudden burst of undisciplined valour, no nervous enthusiasm, weakened the stability of their order; their flashing eyes were bent on the dark columns in their front, their measured tread shook the ground, their dreadful volleys swept away the head of every formation, their deafening shouts overpowered the dissonant cries that broke from all parts of the tumultuous crowd, as slowly and with a horrid carnage, it was pushed by the incessant vigour of the attack to the farthest edge of the height. There, the French reserve, mixing with the struggling multitude, endeavoured to sustain the fight, but the effort only increased the irremediable confusion, the mighty mass gave way and like a loosened cliff went headlong down the steep. The rain flowed after in streams discoloured with blood, and fifteen hundred unwounded men, the remnant of six thousand unconquerable British soldiers, stood triumphant on the fatal hill.

Soult withdrew at last to Seville, licking his wounds, declaring furiously: 'They were completely beaten, the day was mine and they did not know it and would not run.' Beresford's mistaken deployment of his troops had very nearly caused a major British defeat: he had been saved by the extraordinary resolution of his riflemen and that brave single-line attack by Cole and Harvey's men. But it had been an appallingly costly victory – some 7,000 allied casualties of the total 35,000 involved in the fighting and no fewer than 4,400 of the actual 6,500 infantry in the thick of the fighting. The French also lost 7,000, nearly a third of their total force.

Wellington arrived soon afterwards with reinforcements from the north, and renewed the siege of Badajoz with quixotic fury, but his guns were all but useless and two assaults resulted in half those taking part being killed. In the north Masséna had been replaced by the dashing thirty-six-year-old Marshal Marmont, one of Napoleon's personal protégés, and he was hurrying to join up with the weakened Soult. At Merida the two armies joined up in the middle of June 1811, forming a force of some 60,000 men. This huge army promptly marched to relieve Badajoz.

Learning of Marmont's approach, General Sir Brent Spencer, whom Wellington had left in charge in the north, moved with equal speed to reinforce him, swelling his own army to some 54,000 men. Wellington withdrew to the Portuguese frontier across the Guadiana and then to one of his carefully chosen defensive positions along a twelve-mile line of hills stretching north from Elvas. The French wheeled about in front of this but warily refused to do battle.

Back in Seville and Andalucia to the south, two Spanish armies had started to challenge Soult's control of the region. Soult decided to shift the bulk of his army back to protect it, infuriating Marmont: he was left with 50,000 troops, reversing the odds against the British who were now the superior force; yet Wellington had no more intention of descending from his carefully chosen positions to fight the French on the plain than the French had of attacking him uphill. The two armies remained in stalemate opposite each other for a fortnight in the intense heat of the Spanish summer.

Eventually the growing scarcity of provisions to plunder and a series of guerrilla offensives by the Spaniards in the regions stripped of their French troops by Marmont forced the French general to blink first and withdraw in mid-July. With Portugal no longer under threat of French invasion, Wellington did likewise, withdrawing further north to more temperate and well-stocked land around Portalegre and Castelo Branco. There the army recovered from 'Guadiana fever', ate well, and was reinforced from England. There was a pause; the old standoff continued: Wellington had driven the French out of Portugal but could not yet invade Spain for fear of leaving the French-controlled fortresses on his flanks and over-extending himself: the French had been driven out of Portugal but had succeeded in keeping the British bottled up.

The Peninsular War is traditionally viewed as one between these two nations and their armies. But of course it was much more than that. For all the shambolic incompetence of ill-equipped, ill-commanded Spanish armies in the field, with their absence of tactics and manoeuvrability, their medieval notions of discipline and their persistent refusal – unlike the Portuguese – to learn anything or be trained or commanded by the British, the countryside was up in arms against the French. Brave and ruthless guerrilla bands continued to encircle and isolate French armies of occupation whose colossal total of 370,000 was incapable of controlling any part where they were not represented in force.

In Figueras, practically on the Catalan border with France in the far north-east of Spain, guerrillas broke in and massacred the French garrison. The Spanish commander, Martinez, and just 4,000 men then held out the entire summer against a huge French force. Another Catalan force actually crossed into France and laid waste a remote French canton – to Napoleon's humiliation and intense anger. Further south, although the French at last captured Tortosa, the garrisons of Tarragona and Vanecia still held out.

South in Andalucia the enterprising guerrilla leader Ballesteros was helped by British ships to land at various points along the coast to attack French outposts, forcing the French to march and counter-march to try and intercept this raiding brigand. In north-western Spain two cele-

brated guerrilla leaders, Porlier and Longa, raided remorselessly from the Asturias mountains and were joined by the warlord of Navarra, Mina. The shambolic Army of Galicia descended from its mountain fastnesses to threaten León. Julian Sanchez, the greatest and most murderous brigand leader, terrorized Ciudad Rodrigo with his attacks.

The effectiveness of the guerrillas was hardly in doubt. Comte Miot de Melito, King Joseph's closest adviser, wrote:

> By that time the Junta had . . . adopted the formidable system of guerrillas. Spread out in parties in every part of the territory . . . that the French occupied, they did us more damage than the [Spanish] regular armies by intercepting all our communications and forcing us never to send out a courier without an escort or leave isolated soldiers on the roads . . . Large parties of guerrillas . . . often advanced to the gates of the capital. General Franceschi . . . one of the most distinguished officers of the army, was taken prisoner by them, along with young Antoine, a nephew of the King who was then an aide-de-camp of Marshal Soult. The hatred and fury of the Spaniards was carried to the last excess: they breathed vengeance and exercised it on any Frenchman who fell into their hands. This small-scale warfare quietly undermined us. We only possessed the ground actually occupied by our armies, and our power did not extend beyond it. The business of administration ceased, and there was neither order, nor justice, nor taxation.

A French hussar commented:

> In these mountainous provinces of the north of the Peninsula, the French, although always conquerors where the . . . Spaniards showed themselves in battle, were not . . . the [latter] assailed by clouds of armed mountaineers, who, never coming near to fight in close ranks, or body to body, retreated from position to position, from rock to rock, on heights, without ceasing to fire even in flying. It sometimes required entire battalions to carry an order of a battalion to another distant one. The soldiers, wounded, sick or fatigued, who remained behind the French columns, were imme-

diately murdered. Every victory produced only a new conflict. Victories had become useless by the persevering and invincible character of the Spaniards, and the French armies were consuming themselves . . . in continual fatigues, nightly watchings and anxieties.

Most of these guerrillas were mere brigands and much of the local population, as well as the French, hated them because of the atrocities they committed and because they prompted local French reprisals. But they kept up the pressure on the French occupiers in a manner that had occurred nowhere else in Europe. Many were motivated by simple hatred of civil society and by poverty, vendetta and resistance. King Joseph sought desperately to abdicate, complaining that he was penniless, his palace plundered and his soldiers unpaid. 'I live here in the ruins of a great monarchy,' he wrote. Madrid, a once fine city, was now in a wretched state.

Chapter 70

CIUDAD RODRIGO AND BADAJOZ

In August 1811 Wellington was on the move once again with 45,000 men back in the mountains behind the Agueda river and Ciudad Rodrigo. The French reacted with alarm and alacrity, mustering an army of 60,000 men at Tamames to the east under Marmont. Wellington responded by retreating again into one of his strategic fastnesses some fifteen miles south of Ciudad Rodrigo. When the French failed to follow he emerged from this safe position on to the plain only to be very nearly surprised by a huge French force. He immediately returned to the hills.

While this game of cat and mouse continued, General Hill marched some 8,000 men across the highest point of the Portuguese mountains – 6,000 feet – through rain and gales in October and surprised a force of some 5,000 French soldiers near Merida, killing 800 and taking 1,500 prisoner for the loss of just seven men killed.

Wellington stayed on the alert in his defensive position waiting for the opportunity to cross over into Spain. He seemed certain that the days of fighting to defend Portugal were over. He scented the kill, awaiting the opportunity to push into Spain.

In Paris Napoleon continued to affect indifference to the situation in the Iberian Peninsula. He refused to appoint an overall commander over his feuding generals. Joseph was no general, and exercised no real control over them. Only Napoleon could have done so, but he was hopelessly out of touch and ill-informed about the state on the ground, issuing long-distance directives to which most of his commanders paid no attention. He ordered Soult to renew the attempt to suppress

Andalucia, and then told Marmont to send nearly half of his army from the Portuguese border to help General Suchet besieging Valencia and on the east coast of Spain against the Spanish General Blake with 30,000 men supplied by the British from the sea. Marmont was left with just 30,000 men opposing the predatory Wellington.

Wellington prepared to move from Ciudad Rodrigo to Badajoz, which was almost impregnable, because the French armies in the south were mired in Andalucia. The march also offered the opportunity for a daring strike across the French lines of communications from Badajoz to Madrid, and even possibly into France itself. His army had refreshed itself in the bracing upland villages where they were quartered, indulging in sports such as wild boar and fox hunting as well as partying with the local girls. Meanwhile a siege train had at last landed from Britain and been dragged across the mountains.

It was January 1812 before a meticulously prepared Wellington was ready to attack Ciudad Rodrigo, which was now much less strongly defended: the very season caught the French unarmed. The same night he reached the fortress, the British began a classic siege, digging parallel trenches in a zigzag to close in on the fortress, a process which lasted five days and nights under heavy mortar attack which killed some 500 men.

After just a week Wellington decided to storm the fortress to forestall Marmont, who was about to hurry to the rescue. He made two breaches in the walls with his light guns – his heavy ones had not yet arrived – and then prepared three simultaneous attacks, two of them feints. It was to be a difficult operation.

A young officer, Grattan gave his impression of the men as they prepared for the assault:

They were in the highest spirits, but without the slightest appearance of levity in their demeanour – on the contrary, there was a cast of determined severity thrown over their countenances that expressed in legible characters that they knew the sort of service they were about to perform, and had made up their minds to the issue. They had no knapsacks – their firelocks were slung over their shoulders – their shirt-collars were open, and there was an inde-

scribable *something* about them. In passing us each officer and soldier stepped out of the ranks for an instant as he recognized a friend to press his hand – many for the last time. Yet, notwithstanding this animating scene, there was no shouting or huzzaing, no boisterous bravadoing, no unbecoming language; in short, every one seemed to be impressed with the seriousness of the affair entrusted to his charge, and any interchange of words was to this effect: 'Well, lads, mind what you're about tonight'; or, 'We'll meet in the town by and by'; and other little familiar phrases, all expressive of confidence. The regiment at length passed us, and we stood gazing after it as long as the rear platoon continued in sight; the music grew fainter every moment, until at last it died away altogether. They had no drums, and there was a melting sweetness in the sounds that touched the heart.

The unit which entered the breach first was called the Forlorn Hope – so-called because so few would survive of the vagabonds of which they consisted, although the survivors were promised fine rewards. It was to be followed by a 500-strong force under General Crauford, the army's leading disciplinarian, who declared: 'Soldiers! the eyes of your country are upon you. Be steady – be cool – be firm in the assault. The town must be yours this night. Once masters of the wall, let your first duty be to clear the ramparts, and in doing this keep together.'

Crauford himself was one of the first to be killed. After fierce fighting the British at last reached the top of the breach and within half an hour were rampaging through the streets of the citadel. The citadel had been seized at a cost of around 1,000 British casualties. The entire French garrison were captured or killed. The British went on a wild plundering spree.

Wellington considered next attacking the French headquarters at Salamanca but decided against it, as Marmont could quickly summon reinforcements on the open plains. Methodical and cautious as always, except when an unmissable opportunity presented itself, Wellington decided to repeat his feat of taking the fortress at Badajoz, a seemingly impregnable garrison to crack.

Before this, however, he had to cope with a British political crisis. The government had elevated him from viscount to earl after the capture of Ciudad Rodrigo. But his grandstanding older brother, Lord Mornington, chose this moment for an attempt to bring down the government of the insignificant Spencer Perceval by resigning the post of foreign secretary, in which he had been a key supporter of his brother's Peninsular campaigns. Mornington believed he would now attain the highest office himself, but his reckless love life – Wellington once declared he should have been castrated for his own good – and his grand manner counted against him.

Perceval survived, but not for long, as he was killed in the lobby of the House of Commons by a half-insane bankrupt merchant, who had in fact no quarrel with him. Perceval was the first and only British prime minister ever to be assassinated. His successor was a man of almost equal mediocrity, Lord Liverpool, who was to become the third longest serving prime minister in British history, after only Walpole and Pitt.

In Brougham's damning description, he was also one of its least talented:

> The abilities of Lord Liverpool were far more solid than shining. Men are apt to be jealous, perhaps envious, certainly distrustful, of great and brilliant genius in statesmen. Respectable mediocrity offends nobody. Nay, as the great bulk of mankind feel it to be their own case, they perhaps have some satisfaction in being correctly represented by those who administer their affairs. Add to this, that the subject of these remarks was gifted with extraordinary prudence, displaying, from his earliest years, a rare discretion in all the parts of his conduct. Not only was there nothing of imagination, or extravagance, or any matter above the most ordinary comprehension, in whatever he spoke (excepting only his unhappy flight about marching to Paris, and which for many years seemingly sunk him in the public estimation) – but he spoke so seldom as to show that he never did so unless the necessity of the case required it; while his life was spent in the business of office, a thing eminently agreeable to the taste, because closely resembling the habits, of a nation composed of men of business.

Wellington was anxious lest the change might diminish government backing for his Peninsular campaign, but he need not have worried. Castlereagh was an inveterate ally and Wellington stood out as the victor of so many battles against Napoleon's forces as to make him invulnerable in the eyes of public opinion at home. He was also a master of 'spin', forcing the disconsolate Beresford, for example, to rewrite his gloomy despatch after the carnage at Albuera in order to portray it as a magnificent triumph.

Indeed Wellington was almost the only jewel in the government's crown. Its difficulties were quite otherwise. Under Liverpool's and Castlereagh's tutelage it was so reactionary and suppressive of political change at a time of seething social discontent that it seemed to be risking outright revolution on occasion. As far back as 1810 revolution seemed to beckon.

The spark of revolt was, as always, an unlikely one. Typically the House of Commons decided to hold its inquiry into the fiasco of the Walcheren expedition in February 1810 in secret. John Gale Jones, a veteran and professional radical who was probably slightly off his head, put up a poster denouncing this 'outrage'. Charles Yorke, former First Lord of the Admiralty and a veteran of the cabal of die hards in the cabinet, promptly inflated the whole affair into a breach of the House of Commons' privileges. Jones was thrown into Newgate gaol without a trial.

The radical leader Burdett wrote a stinging denunciation of parliament, accusing it of indulging in arbitrary practices of the kind which the Tudors and Stuarts had practised, and witheringly labelling his parliamentary colleagues 'as part of our fellow subjects collected together by means which it is not necessary for me to describe', an allusion to the bribery and purchase of rotten boroughs and the unrepresentative nature of most MPs.

Indignantly, the government held a vote, which, by 189 to 152 votes, narrowly found Burdett guilty of breach of privilege and in medieval fashion ordered his committal to the Tower of London. The size of the minority was in fact a triumph for Burdett, but the vote had to be acted upon. The sergeant-at-arms, Francis Colman, was despatched to Burdett's sumptuous house at 78 Piccadilly, but found that

the radical leader was not there. Burdett, from hiding, proclaimed the warrant illegal and said he would submit only to overwhelming force. Popular agitation spread in Burdett's defence. Soon tens of thousands had taken to the streets, spreading across London in what seemed the prelude to a general insurrection.

On the night of 7 April the mob was occupying the main approaches to the Tower. Small boats were also blocking the river approach. The crowds outside 78 Piccadilly, where Burdett had now taken refuge, continued to grow, spreading into Albemarle Street, Berkeley Square and St James's Square. Violence erupted and windows were smashed in the houses of leading political figures, some of the houses being broken into and furniture carried off. Anyone who passed Burdett's house and refused to raise his hat and shout 'Burdett for ever' was pelted with mud.

The authorities responded by sending in the troops: the Horse Guards were ordered out to charge the demonstrators, while the Foot Guards and Light Dragoons attacked demonstrators by hitting them with the flats of their swords. Batteries of artillery were erected in St James's Park, Berkeley Square and Soho Square – and fortified. The moat of the Tower was flooded, the guns there were prepared for action, and all troops within a hundred miles of London were recalled to the capital. It was suggested that Wellington himself should be recalled from the Peninsular War to take charge. To the nervous minor politicians running Britain, there were echoes of the tumbrils, the Bastille and the guillotine.

The Life Guards charged the demonstrators, who fled into the side streets down Piccadilly. As the cavalry regrouped, enterprising rioters seized ladders which they pulled suddenly across as barricades when the cavalry charged again, forcing their horses to shy away under a hail of stones and mud. The demonstrators kept up a torchlight vigil outside Burdett's house long into the night. The authorities could not approach through the crowds.

The following day, 8 April, the tall, distinguished figure of Thomas Cochrane, the hero of Aix Roads and now a radical MP, arrived by coach. To the crowd's delight he rolled out a barrel of gunpowder, which he took into the house, busily knocking holes in the wall to

accommodate charges, so that he could threaten a massive explosion if the house was raided.

Even by Cochrane's standards this was extreme. He was crossing the line dividing legitimate protest and revolution. Nothing in his previous or subsequent career suggested that he was wedded to the cause of violent revolution as the solution for the country's many abuses. Was this simply the act of someone whose mind had been unhinged by the Gambier affair? The answer is probably less dramatic. Cochrane was first and foremost a man of action and a fighter. The first course that would come into his mind when the threat of force was proposed against his fellow radical MP was to set up defences which could not be crossed, and defy the authorities to do their worst. Mining the house was not, in itself, an offence. It is unlikely that he thought through the consequences of his actions. If violence did break out and half the façades of Piccadilly were blown up, along with countless soldiers and demonstrators, it could be classed as open insurrection and terrorism. He would then have had no alternative but to lead the Revolution or be brought to the gallows.

Inside, Burdett and the radical tailor, Francis Place, a pioneering advocate of universal suffrage, education and contraception, were aghast at Cochrane's plans. Cochrane was overruled. Francis Place wrote: 'The gallant Tar then retired, apparently much disconcerted, and he was particularly required to take away with him the cask of gunpowder.'

It all came to nothing. On the morning of 9 April, an enterprising constable climbed through an open back window of the house, followed by several colleagues. They found Burdett teaching the Magna Carta to his son at breakfast. He was seized, smuggled out and put in a coach, which was escorted by cavalry on a roundabout route to the Tower.

The authorities hesitated to inflame popular passion by taking action against Cochrane, who had come so close to an act of revolutionary violence but not actually broken the law, but the popular naval hero became the focus of agitation for Burdett's release, frequently being carried shoulder-high to the House of Commons to present petitions while MPs debated whether to expel him or not. After two months

Burdett was released upon the prorogation of parliament, the government hesitating to turn him into a martyr. Although Place had organized a triumphal progression for him, he slipped away from the Tower by boat and the half-idiot 'Citizen' Jones took his place on a coach ranting at the waiting crowds. It had all ended in farce, but to many, as the war in Europe showed no signs of abating, it seemed that Britain was teetering on the very brink of revolution under the unimaginative, hardline conservatives that governed the nation. Of those Wellington himself was the dazzling star.

The able young Marshal Marmont was not slow to hear of Wellington's march to Badajoz, leaving Ciudad Rodrigo in the hands of a poorly trained Spanish force. Marmont sought to shadow him, but Napoleon from his lofty court in the Tuileries refused to give him authority, instructing him to attack Ciudad Rodrigo instead. In fact, this was not a bad idea because of the poor quality of the Spanish defences. However Napoleon had denuded his best commander in Spain of the troops he needed. Moreover, he also suggested another march on Lisbon, which was of course wildly impractical in hostile territory with the Lines of Torres Vedras in place, as Masséna's fate had shown.

The Emperor seemed utterly detached from the realities of the Iberian Peninsula. He appointed the ineffectual Joseph military commander-in-chief in Spain, an appointment on a level with that of Caligula's horse as consul, as Joseph's martial skills were if anything less obvious than his administrative abilities. Most of his principal generals simply ignored him. Joseph ordered troops to support Soult in an attempt to prevent the capture of Badajoz, while Marmont attempted to blockade Ciudad Rodrigo under direct orders from Napoleon. Marmont, judging its recapture impossible, ordered the few troops at his disposal to move south into the vast empty area around Beira in an attempt to distract Wellington. Napoleon's meddling had served unnecessarily only to disperse his forces.

On his arrival at Badajoz in mid-March Wellington found the fortress very nearly impregnable. The approaches had been mined, the walls reinforced, the two outlying forts, San Cristobal and Parda-

leras, strengthened and an impassable moat created on the east side of the fortress. The siege works were dug on the south-east side of the fortress and as the British approached the walls in torrential rain, the French opened up a ceaseless artillery barrage. Once again, news arrived that a large French army under Soult was approaching to relieve the fortress. The usually cautious Wellington was driven into speedy action, ordering an assault on 6 April, long before the customary softening-up artillery attack had been completed.

One of the bloodiest assaults in history followed, seemingly untempered by Wellington's usual concern for losses among his men. He had acquired an almost psychopathic ability to switch off his feelings when required, arguably a necessary trait for a great commander and a characteristic shared by Napoleon. The attack very nearly failed against the formidably murderous French defences which included mines, *chevaux-de-frises*, hand grenades and the moat.

The British attacks, staged over the bodies of their dead and wounded comrades, were repulsed time and again – some forty times in all, the 'butcher' Wellington constantly urging them forward. Some 2,000 men were killed in these repeated assaults against murderous fire and defences. All appeared to be lost. Wellington's medical aide, Dr James McGrigor, saw his commander as defeat stared him in the face. 'At this moment, I cast my eyes on the countenance of Lord Wellington lit up by the glare of the torch . . . I shall never forget it to the last moment of my existence . . . The jaw had fallen, the face was of unusual length, while the torchlight gave to his countenance a lurid aspect; but still the expression of the face was firm.'

Wellington ordered one final assault on the castle. One participant told what happened:

When we first entered the [ditch] we considered ourselves comparatively safe, thinking that we were out of range of their shot, but . . . they opened several guns . . . and poured in grape shot upon us from each side . . . Our situation at this time was truly appalling . . . When the ladders were placed, each eager to mount, [the soldiers] crowded them in such a way that many of them broke, and the poor fellows who had nearly reached the top were precipitated a height of

thirty to forty feet and impaled on the bayonets of their comrades below. Other ladders were pushed aside by the enemy on the walls, and fell with a crash on those in the ditch, while [men] who got to the top without accident were shot on reaching the parapet, and, tumbling headlong, brought down those beneath them. This continued for some time, until at length, a few having made a landing . . . [they] enabled others to follow.

At last this terrible final assault succeeded. While the 4,000-strong French garrison retreated, another assault on the San Vicente fortress along the town walls followed. Terrible scenes ensued as the British soldiery exacted their revenge in a wild orgy of pillage almost without precedent in British military history. Robert Blakeney, a British officer, observed:

There was no safety for women even in the churches, and any who interfered or offered resistance were sure to get shot. Every house presented a scene of plunder, debauchery and bloodshed committed with wanton cruelty . . . by our soldiery, and in many instances I saw the savages tear the rings from the ears of beautiful women . . . When the savages came to a door which had been locked or barricaded, they applied . . . the muzzles of a dozen firelocks . . . against that part of the door where the lock was fastened and . . . fired [them] off together into the house and rooms, regardless of those inside . . . Men, women and children were shot . . . for no other . . . reason than pastime; every species of outrage was publicly committed . . . and in a manner so brutal that a faithful recital would be . . . shocking to humanity. Not the slightest shadow of discipline was maintained . . . The infuriated soldiery resembled rather a pack of hell-hounds vomited up from the infernal regions for the extirpation of mankind than . . . a well-organized, brave, disciplined and obedient British army.

Only repeated floggings restored order. It had been a terrible victory: the British lost more than 4,500 men at Badajoz.

The siege shows Wellington in a new light; The careful husbander

of resources and his own men's lives had been willing to risk all in a brutal act of bloodletting he believed to be militarily necessary. Wellington had shown himself to be more than just a supremely skilled and cautious defensive general: he could be a ruthless gambler with his men's lives when the stakes were high enough.

Had the siege really been necessary? Wellington judged so: as long as so major a fortress lay in enemy hands along the Portuguese border, any British thrust into Spain was in danger of being outflanked, having its supply lines cut or becoming a staging post for a French attack into undefended Portugal. Yet with the British possessing the other frontier fortresses, a decisive French move of this kind would have been difficult; the French could have attempted such a movement even without possession of Badajoz. A less old-fashioned and meticulous commander might perhaps have taken the risk of leaving Badajoz as a stranded outpost rather than inflict such suffering on his own men.

Learning that Ciudad Rodrigo was now under siege from Marmont, Wellington lost no time trekking north to relieve the citadel. He then set about ordering a complex set of manoeuvres involving Spanish forces in various parts of the country – supporting Ballesteros in Andalucia, occupying Málaga, leading a French force on a wild-goose chase through mountainous Granada and finally escaping to the coast. Admiral Sir Home Popham led a series of raids along the northern coast, while Rowland Hill tied down French troops in the west in Extremadura. All of this helped to prevent the French forces in Spain concentrating to defeat Wellington. In truth the French were far too widely spread across the Peninsula under the control of jealous rival commanders to inflict a decisive defeat upon the British, however enormous their paper superiority in numbers.

Wellington himself remained passive outside Ciudad Rodrigo, despatching Hill, his best raiding commander, in mid-May to take the bridge at Almaraz which commanded the route from Madrid to the Portuguese frontier and the main commercial links between the northern and southern Spanish armies. This he did brilliantly, destroying Fort Napoleon at one end of the bridge, causing its defenders at the end of the other to flee, and blowing up the bridge and its fortifications.

Chapter 71

SALAMANCA

Wellington waited on the frontier for his next opportunity. Not until 13 June did he make his move, with his army now nearly 50,000 strong, first to León, then advancing on Salamanca. Here Marmont had left a small force behind its fortifications which held out bravely until 27 June. Wellington was given a superb Spanish welcome into the beautiful, liberal university town on the edge of the great plain of Salamanca, the warmth embarrassing the soldiers and even the unflappable British commander himself. He was pulled from his horse, losing his dignity for a moment – to his chagrin. He attended a *Te Deum* in the cathedral and a glittering ball given in his honour that evening.

He moved his cavalry out into the great plain to entice Marmont into battle. Such ground was traditionally favourable to the French, but he believed that for once he could use it better. He waited for his foe to come to him. Marmont was equally cautious: the two great armies of 50,000 manoeuvred in parallel across the plain in the heat of the day as though on a giant parade ground, then rested in the freezing nights like wary prizefighters watching for their opponents to lower their guard. Wellington at this anxious time was described by one observer as 'in the prime of life, a well made man five foot ten inches in height, with broad shoulders and well-developed chest. Of the cruiser, rather than the battleship build, the greyhound, rather than the mastiff breed, he seemed all made for speed and action, yet as strong as steel, and capable of great endurance.'

A revealing incident was also described: 'While Lord Wellington was riding along the line, under a fire of artillery, and accompanied by a

numerous staff, a brace of greyhounds in pursuit of a hare passed close to him. He was at the moment in earnest conversation with General Castaños; but the instant he observed them he gave the view-halloo and went after them at full speed, to the utter astonishment of his foreign accompaniments. Nor did he stop until he saw the hare killed.'

The historian Oliver Brett has come closest to capturing the complexity that was the Duke of Wellington, a man who dressed himself modestly on the battlefield and never asked for honours, yet gloried in his prominence and titles and the glitter of high society.

If he lacked personal charm, he had the far rarer gift – personality. He was always in all circumstances, in every word he spoke, in every step he took – himself; one of those men in whom everything they do and say at once strikes onlookers as characteristic. Frankness, honesty and integrity were combined with the large dignity of unquestioned greatness. He could throw off his seriousness in his leisure hours and be cordial in hospitality, and open in comment; he delighted in jokes and a rude sense of fun.

His bare frugal life was combined with an amusing vanity in dress. There was no nonsense or mystery about him; he looked straight at things as they were. He stands as the complete opposite of his great opponent; he was as English as the latter was Latin. Wellington's qualities were indeed so essentially English that he could hardly appreciate the greatness of Napoleon. 'The fellow wasn't a gentleman,' was his comment at the end of the great war. It implied that he could not respect Bonaparte enough to be much interested in him. He had beaten him and could not be bothered to determine what exactly he had been up against.

From the military point of view good fortune had almost invariably been his. He never had lost a gun and hardly ever had he lost a battle, and the chances of battle, which he never shirked, had spared him. But his good fortune had been the reward of his hard work. 'The French planned their campaigns just as you might make a splendid set of harness,' he said afterwards. 'It looks very well; and answers very well until it gets broken; and then you are done for. Now I made my campaigns of ropes. If anything went

wrong I tied a knot and went on.' He had never had Napoleon's desire to fight a great battle; his constant numerical inferiority, indeed, had made such a desire impracticable. He only fought a battle when he had to, endeavouring always to be 'a quarter-of-an-hour earlier than he was expected'. But he was just as ready to retreat as to fight. The war of attrition, demanding infinite patience in officers and men, had been a constant test of the morale of his army; the test of his own morale had been aggravated by the political difficulties that converged upon him from England, Portugal and Spain.

His temper was not always proof against these things. His code was a simple one: duty, discipline and hard work. He had been resolute against the oppression of non-combatants, against loot, robbery, seduction, drunkenness and devastation. It is not surprising that his determined attitude against the common crimes of war made him popular with the people of Spain and France, but unpopular with his own officers and men. He was no doubt difficult to deal with in business. His quick and positive mind, unhesitating in its judgments, found expression in peremptory and often hasty speech.

To inspire a wholesome fear and to keep subordinates at a distance is part of the military technique. Wellington in his relations with his officers seldom went further than curt approval, and he was not at much pains to reprimand considerately. Every word, for instance, of his famous circular to his officers after the Retreat from Burgos was true. But he omitted to draw the distinction between those who had done well and those who had not, and so produced in the former an indelible sense of injustice. He seemed a thankless master to serve, since he blamed so often and praised so rarely. He could not see why men should be praised for doing their duty, and indeed there is no reason except the vital one that they like it . . .

He was not an easy man to please; no man whose standard of behaviour was so rigid as his could be so. On one occasion Colonel Waters, whose exploits in disguise among the enemy were one of the romances of the war, was captured and imprisoned. He made a miraculous escape and suddenly appeared at Wellington's dinner table. Wellington imagined that he had broken his parole, and

onlookers said that the expression of anger on his face was terrible to behold. As a matter of fact, Waters had refused to give his parole; Wellington's code of honour had not been infringed.

A man of great mental capacity, he was fully conscious of his superiority, and perpetually engrossed as he was in the number and intricacy of the matters which required attention, his impatience readily expressed itself in the form of contempt. He found it difficult to listen with patience to advice and criticism, and he was too preoccupied to give adequate consideration to the sentimental and personal side of a situation. The result of his aloofness was that men credited him with an entire lack of sympathy; he excited admiration but not affection. He never tried to stimulate devotion; he could not feign regret for the absent or dead when he did not feel it. Display of emotion was antipathetic to him and theatricality loathsome. 'The advantage which Bonaparte possessed,' he said characteristically, 'was his full latitude of lying; *that* I could not do.' But he was not wholly lacking in heart. His affections were not ardent but absolutely stable and genuine. He grew to be very fond of some of his staff.

Marmont manoeuvred skilfully, crossing the Duero river and forcing Wellington's forces back towards Salamanca, threatening his communications with Portugal. The plain was not in fact flat, being crisscrossed by a line of low hills that helped to conceal the movements of one army from another.

By 22 July Wellington's forces were drawn up just south east of the city along one of the ridges, whose southern end was marked by a little hill called the Arapil Chico. Marmont moved forward to occupy a large hill due south of the allies, the Arapil Grande, from which he could observe the British position. Marmont, anticipating Wellington's response, was determined not to repeat the mistakes of previous French commanders by attacking frontally on a well entrenched British position, and instead decided to march his army westwards around the British southern flank – their right – to catch them at their weakest point and sever their communications with Portugal.

Wellington, his acute mind immediately realizing what was going

on, promptly responded by shifting his divisions from their previous line to one running eastwards along another spur of hills, thus creating a new line facing the marching French. He had wheeled about. Marmont, believing Wellington to be a defensive general who would never attack, assumed he was preparing his army for a westward march in parallel to the French to protect his communications, and spurred his men to march still faster westwards to outflank him.

While his officers ate their lunch in a farmyard, Wellington observed the French through his telescope marching across his new front, in contravention of the most basic rules of warfare. He could see that the French, hurrying forward, were strung out along a vast extended line, widely dispersed, and would not be able to concentrate in time to repel a concentrated British attack at a single point. Famously, he threw the chicken leg he had been eating over his shoulder, exclaiming, 'By God, that will do!' 'Marmont,' he added, 'is lost.'

He ordered Ned Pakenham, his brother-in-law, to attack the French left, the vanguard of their moving line. Pakenham led his men in column against the vulnerable and exposed French line in a frontal charge across the plain where the startled French vanguard was advancing. A British officer described the scene:

> We were going up an ascent on whose crest masses of the enemy were stationed. Their fire seemed capable of sweeping all before it . . . Truth compels me to say . . . that we retired before this overwhelming fire, but . . . General Pakenham approached and very good natured said, 'Reform,' and in . . . a moment, 'Advance . . . There they are, my lads; just let them feel the temper of your bayonets.' We advanced, everyone making up his mind for mischief. At last . . . the bugles along the line sounded the charge. Forward we rushed . . . and awful was the retribution we exacted for our former repulse.

Having destroyed this division, Pakenham raced westwards down the line to attack the next part of the dispersed French column. They were already under attack from another column of British infantry and

cavalry combined and were caught in the act of forming squares: they were soon overwhelmed. The units immediately behind simply broke and fled with the rest of the routed French. In just an hour the French advance had been smashed and 2,500 prisoners and twelve guns taken.

'By God, Cotton,' Wellington said to his cavalry commander General Sir Stephen Cotton, who was beside him with Harvey, as his cavalry charged. 'I never saw anything more beautiful in my life. The day is yours.' However Wellington's depleted forces on the left fared less well attacking the French right, its rearguard, and were forced back. Seeking to follow up this advantage, the French commander General Clausel – Marmont having been wounded – launched an attack with two fresh divisions against the British centre. Wellington immediately ordered his skilfully hidden reserves behind the ridge forward to reinforce his centre; these included the Portuguese brigade. Beresford, commanding it, was wounded in the chest. Wellington himself was grazed by a bullet in the thigh.

The British attacked again, reversing the French charge and the French centre crumbled. As night began to fall the entire French army fled in headlong and disorganized retreat: some 13,000 French soldiers had been killed or taken prisoner, along with fifteen guns. In the darkness the British were unable to pursue, and the following morning the German auxiliary dragoons supporting the British inflicted another huge blow by breaking up a massed infantry square at the village of Garcia Hernandez. But the British decided not to over-extend themselves by pressing forward, and the French rallied at Valladolid and then Burgos.

It had been a superb triumph, the greatest of Wellington's career so far, an offensive action of brilliant improvisation and skilled manoeuvre that exceeded even those of Napoleon. Though on a smaller scale, it was comparable to Austerlitz as a perfectly executed victory. The French General Foy remarked of his adversary: 'Hitherto we have been aware of his prudence, his eye for choosing a position, and his skill in utilising it. At Salamanca he has shown himself a great and able master of manoeuvres. He kept his dispositions concealed for almost the whole day: he waited till we were committed to our movements before he developed his own: he

played a safe game: he fought in the oblique order – it was a battle in the style of Frederick the Great.'

Wellington was now faced with the difficult choice of pursuing and attempting to destroy the retreating Army of the North which could be quickly reinforced by other French armies, or staging a largely symbolic blow by liberating Madrid, which was poorly defended. He chose the latter course, which many believe to have been a mistake, for he could probably have destroyed the fleeing army. A part of his calculation was that after his great victory at Salamanca, the Spanish might at last have united their vast shambolic armies in a great drive to liberate Spain from the French. Occupying Madrid would provide a favourable position for this.

The triumph of Salamanca reverberated around the Peninsula. On 12 April Soult's besieging forces outside Cadiz learnt of Wellington's great victory. He immediately raised the siege and also abandoned Seville, marching to the safety of the more defensible Valencia in the east. A Spanish eyewitness described the scenes of joy in the long-besieged port:

> The day this happened was one of unequalled joy. The people rushed to embark in boats to visit the abandoned French encampment . . . There was a great desire to walk on the earth of the continent, to breath in fresh air . . . I went with the officials of the Ministry [of State] . . . Accompanied by a numerous crowd we went round . . . the batteries which had contained the mortars whose effects we had been experiencing for such a long time. On the way back . . . all the boats carried a bunch of grass at their mastheads as a way of showing that they had completed a return trip that had been denied to the inhabitants . . . for more than thirty consecutive months.

Meanwhile King Joseph and his chief general, Junot, with only 22,000 troops, mostly ill-equipped and untried, set off in early April from Madrid with 15,000 refugees and 2,000 wagons on the long trek through the heat of the Spanish summer to Valencia. Most of southern,

eastern and western Spain – Extremadura, Andalucia and now Castile – had been liberated, well over half the country. It was a heady moment of glory for the unflappable British commander. It seemed only a matter of time before the French were chased from their remaining strongholds across the Pyrenees.

Wellington arrived in the capital to a rapturous reception on 12 August. A Spanish officer wrote:

> When the bells began to announce the entrance of our troops at about ten o'clock, it was wonderful to see the people rushing to . . . the Portillo de San Vicente, which was the one through which they were said to be coming. A new town council was formed, and this immediately set forth to greet . . . the immortal Wellington . . . To the accompaniment of a crescendo of bells, the people massed in ever greater numbers round the Plaza de la Villa. When a portrait of our Don Fernando [Fernando VIII] was placed in the window of the town hall, they simply went mad. The cheering was incessant; hats and caps were thrown in the air; on all sides people were giving thanks to God; and everyone was filled with the greatest joy and happiness. Another of the incidents that made the day shine out was the behaviour of the women and children of the poorer quarters. Joseph . . . had made a new avenue from the palace to the Casa de Campo [the royal hunting park] . . . This had been lined with fruit trees . . . but the crowd . . . fell upon them . . . and ripped them up . . . When Lord Wellington arrived, many of the people who greeted him were therefore carrying branches and sprigs of greenery which they waved in time with their cheers and happy shouts of greeting. In this manner he was accompanied to the town hall. When he got there the cheering redoubled . . . Amidst thunderous applause, everyone flung their arms around one another, and gave themselves over to congratulating their neighbours in the most unreserved fashion.

As so often, however, triumph was to be followed by disappointment and a reversal of fortune.

Chapter 72

NEMESIS IN MADRID

In taking Madrid, Wellington had secured a huge propaganda victory. But by advancing into the Spanish heartland he had dangerously lengthened his own lines of communication with Portugal; moreover the French had been boxed up into a region from which they could stage a united counter-offensive, while the expected junction of the Spanish armies and general uprising did not take place.

As that glorious August of 1812 mellowed into autumn Wellington showed signs of becoming almost deranged with impatience and frustration with his allies. Always a man who considered himself indispensable, reluctant to delegate to his subordinates and obsessed with detail, his celebrated laconic sang-froid and carefully chosen phrases now gave way to outbursts of blind anger. His portrait painted by Goya at this time gives him a hunted, harassed look, unlike the cool self-confidence he preferred to project.

To his chief medical officer, James McGrigor, who had the temerity to differ with him on an issue he snapped: 'I shall be glad to know who is to command the army, you or I?' However, he asked the good doctor to sit next to him that evening by way of atonement. Meanwhile he railed against the Spanish for their incompetence, and McGrigor kept a record of his outbursts. 'I do not expect much from the exertions of the Spaniards . . . They cry "viva" and are very fond of us . . . but they are in general the most incapable of all the nations that I have known, the most vain, and at the same time the most ignorant . . . I am afraid that the utmost we can hope for is to teach them how to avoid being beat.'

On another occasion: 'Lord Wellington declares that he has not yet met with any Spanish officer who can be made to comprehend the nature of a military operation. If the Spanish officers had knowledge and vanity like the French, or ignorance without vanity as our allies in India, something might be done with them. But they unite the greatest ignorance with the most insolent and intractable vanity. They can therefore be neither persuaded, nor instructed, nor forced to do their duty.'

Wellington was acutely aware that he was over-exposed to a major French offensive against Madrid once their armies united. He abandoned his usual prudence in an attempt to regain the initiative. He decided to do what he should have done while his enemy was on the run after Salamanca and go in pursuit of the Army of Portugal which had regrouped and launched a minor counter-offensive in the north. It was a disastrous miscalculation. As he approached the French retreated, leaving a garrison of veterans in the formidable castle of Burgos, capital of Castile.

Wellington, never one to leave a castle behind his lines if he could help it, felt he had no alternative but to besiege it. But he had only three cannon, picturesquely dubbed Thunder, Lightning and Nelson. It was a hopeless task. Burgos was to be no Badajoz. Displaying again that ruthless disregard for his own men's lives that now characterized his sieges, he stormed the outer redoubt. A British officer present wrote:

The Forty-Second, as the strongest regiment in the division, was selected for the purpose, supported by the light companies of the Highland brigade and General Pack's Portuguese brigade. At eight o'clock they advanced . . . but the Portuguese, who thought to raise their spirits by it, began to shout . . . and thereby drew the enemy's fire upon them. The Forty-Second advanced gallantly and planted their ladders which proved to be too short, and after persisting for some time they were beat back. They returned again, and with Major Cocks and his light . . . companies got in . . . scrambling over without ladders.

Then they attacked the main defences:

> During the whole of this time [the French] kept up a constant fire
> from the top of the wall and threw down bags of gunpowder and
> large stones. At last, having been twenty-five minutes in the ditch
> and not seeing anything of the other parties, [our men] retired,
> having lost half their numbers in killed and wounded . . . Thus
> ended the attack, which was almost madness to attempt.

The British attempted to mine the walls, with mixed results, although a
breach of sorts was made at last. Meanwhile the French staged repeated
sorties from the fortress, which took dozens of lives. A further attempt
to storm the walls was made on 18 October:

> Our party was to escalade the wall in front. Burgess ran forward with
> thirty men, [and] Walpole and myself followed with fifty each . . . A
> most tremendous fire opened upon us from every part which took
> us in front and rear. They poured down fresh men, and ours kept
> falling down into the ditch, dragging and knocking down others.
> We were so close that they fairly put their muskets into our faces,
> and we pulled one of their men through an embrasure. Burgess was
> killed and Walpole severely wounded. We had hardly any men left
> on the top, and at last we gave way. How we got over the palisades I
> know not . . . the fire was tremendous: shot, shell, grape, musketry,
> large stones, hand grenades and every missile weapon were used
> against us.

In the attack Wellington's closest military protégé, Major Edward
Somers Cocks, was killed. Wellington was rendered speechless by the
news and was bent over with grief at his burial. Some 2,000 British
soldiers had been lost to 600 Frenchmen.

Wellington had placed himself in serious danger. In the north the
French general Clausel had been reinforced by the French army in the
Basque region to some 80,000 in total, compared to Wellington's
25,000; the rest of his army had remained behind in Madrid. To the

south, Joseph and Soult had joined up and were moving on Madrid with 60,000 men. Wellington believed that the autumn rains he was experiencing in Burgos would prevent such an advance: but near Madrid the rains had been light.

The downpour in the north had rendered the roads there virtually impassable. If he stayed where he was he risked being crushed by his far more numerous opponents, trapped by the rains and mud, his garrison in Madrid overwhelmed and annihilated by the approaching pincers of two colossal French armies.

He had blundered into a trap. His decision to divide his army as a superior force approached and threatened his lines of communication had been utterly out of character for this meticulous military planner. It can only be explained by his misplaced confidence that the French were virtually beaten in Spain after Salamanca – and the need to go on notching up victories, not to be seen in England to falter. In this, his behaviour was uncharacteristically similar to that of Napoleon.

He was ready to accept responsibility: 'I see that a disposition already exists to blame the government for the failure of the siege. The government had nothing to say in the siege. It was entirely my own act.' One of his officers was less kind: 'I have not been in the habit much of questioning the conduct of our chief, even when it differed from what I expected, but . . . it appears in this instance to be extremely impolitic, not to say most wantonly reprehensible.'

After three days' further futile siege he ordered his angry men to retreat to save his endangered army. Even so, Wellington would have been overwhelmed by the advancing French forces but for the reconquest of the Basque capital of Bilbao by a Spanish force, which compelled the French to pause and detach part of their army to the city. The Spaniards Wellington so often railed against had saved him.

Wellington ordered his army in Madrid similarly to save itself and abandon the city. They blew up the powder depots and the fortifications of the capital as they withdrew. A British officer recalled: 'I never recollect on any occasion . . . being more melancholy and depressed than in passing by the Puente de Toledo, and giving up Madrid to the plunder and wanton cruelty of the enemy. I would willingly have lost a limb in battle to have saved it, and I know every man felt the same

sentiments.' Napoleon was to undergo a similar experience in Moscow soon afterwards: the allure of capital cities was often deceptive.

Hill led the army out of Madrid and they marched at some speed to catch up with Wellington's army before reaching Salamanca, in mid-November. The retreat was marked by atrocities comparable to those of the French, carried out by sullen and disappointed men. One officer remarked that 'many peasants lay dead by the roadside, murdered. The old trade was going on, killing and slaughtering while capturing our daily bread.'

They consoled themselves with the abundant wines of the region. An officer observed: 'I remember seeing a soldier fully accoutred with his knapsack on in a large tank; he had either fell in or been pushed in by his comrades, there he lay dead. I saw a dragoon fire his pistol into a large vat containing several thousands of gallons, in a few minutes we were up to our knees in wine fighting like tigers for it.'

Reaching Salamanca again a witness remarked that Wellington reviewed his troops in clothes 'unaccompanied by any mark of distinction or splendour. His long brown cloak concealed his under-garments; his cocked hat, soaked and disfigured under the rain.' Another commented that 'he looked extremely ill'. He was also bad-tempered and issued a general censure of his men for their looting and ill-behaviour which caused resentment.

The largest French army was approaching Salamanca from the south, and Wellington had no option but to resume the retreat knee-deep in mud to the safety of Ciudad Rodrigo. Corpses and dead horses lined the route as disease took its toll. The nightmare of eating beef was captured by one officer:

> Each man received his portion of the quivering flesh, but, before any fires could be relighted, the order for march arrived, and the . . . soldiers were obliged either to throw away the meat or put it with their biscuit into their haversacks . . . In a short time the wet meat completely destroyed the bread, which became perfect paste, and the blood which oozed from the undressed beef . . . gave so bad a taste to the bread that many could not eat it. Those who did were in general attacked with violent pains in their bowels, and the want of salt brought on dysentery.

By the time they reached Ciudad Rodrigo, after the French had given up the chase, some 6,000 had been lost.

Wellington was back at last on the Portuguese border, his old fastness. Now at least his men could rest. They were desperately disappointed. Two large British armies had previously penetrated deep into Spain – the army of Sir John Moore and Wellington's own at Talavera – and twice they had been driven out. This seemed a third re-run. It had been demonstrated yet again that the French could not advance into Portugal without endangering themselves, and that the British could not do so into Spain and hold their ground. It appeared to be stalemate.

In fact, the British had made significant progress. The French had been driven from Andalucia, Extremadura and Asturias and the British remained in possession of the frontier fortresses at Almeida, Ciudad Rodrigo and Badajoz. Wellington assuaged his wounded vanity by riding down to liberated Cadiz, where the provisional Spanish government was sitting. There the provisional government had given him titular control of all Spanish forces, as well as British ones. But to his fury he discovered that in practice this amounted to little: the Spanish generals simply ignored his directives, Spanish armies remained as disorganized as before and some commanders were deeply offended by the decree. One, General Ballesteros, came out in open revolt against the British 'oppressors'.

Back at his headquarters on the northern frontier at Freneida, he indulged in the long idle months of winter and spring in more agreeable pursuits than quarrelling with the Spaniards. Captain Thomas Browne, a British officer observed: 'He had at headquarters a pack of hounds from England and hunted two or three times a week with such officers of headquarters as chose to join in the chase. There were not many, as few could afford to have English horses, and our Spanish and Portuguese steeds were not equal to the work. There was no want of foxes, but it was a difficult and rocky country to ride over. He went out shooting every now and then, but did not appear fond of it, as he was a very indifferent shot.'

He wrote to General Stuart: 'The hunting season is coming on apace. The hounds are on the road, and I shall want Waters for the

earth-stopping business, if not for that of Adjutant-General. He has been very near dying, poor fellow, and what is worse, I hear he has lost all his dogs.' He was accustomed to rising at six and doing paperwork for three hours before breakfast. Then he would hold meetings with his officers until three in the afternoon. After a light meal he would go riding for three hours.

He was curt and brusque in the morning, but extremely good company in the evening. The subaltern George Gleig (later Wellington's biographer) wrote that in company he was 'most interesting and lively. The Duke himself spoke out on all subjects with an absence of reserve which sometimes surprised his guests . . . He was rich in anecdote, most of them taking a ludicrous turn, and without any apparent effort he put the company very much at their ease . . .'

He was fastidious in appearance, wearing his celebrated 'Wellington boots' frequently; Francis Larpent, Wellington's advocate general, observed: 'like every great man, present or past, almost without exception, he is vain . . . He is remarkably neat and most particular in his dress . . . He cuts the skirts of his coat shorter to make them look smarter: only a short time since, going to him on business, I found him discussing the cut of his half-boots and suggesting alterations to his servant.'

During that long period of rest and recreation, Wellington became increasingly convinced that 1813 would be the decisive year of the war. He had at last recovered his old bounce and self-confidence after the awful setbacks of the previous autumn.

Chapter 73

THE KILL: VITORIA

It was not until 22 May, however, that he at last recrossed the frontier with his rested and reinforced army. The men were told not to bring their great coats. It was the equivalent of Wellington burning his boats: he did not believe they would have to return in winter. As they crossed the border, Wellington stagily took off his hat and shouted: 'Farewell, Portugal. I shall never see you again.' He had already remarked that there was 'scarcely any French army left, except that in our front'.

His own army now consisted of 80,000 men, including the Portuguese, and 20,000 Spaniards. The French in Spain meanwhile had been depleted of 20,000 of their best troops to reinforce Napoleon's beleaguered northern armies: worse still, Napoleon had ordered Wellington's old adversary, the Army of Portugal, to hold down the mounting insurgencies in the Basque country, Navarra and Aragón. General Clausel, the new northern commander, was a fine and energetic soldier, but even he proved unable to control the rebellions in the north.

Wellington's offensive had been brilliantly and meticulously planned through the winter and spring, in contrast to the improvised and disastrous one of the previous autumn. He would use as a forward base the Spanish port of Santander in the north, controlled by the Spaniards, where he assembled voluminous supplies and a siege train. He would no longer need to depend on the long supply line to Lisbon. Santander would also provide a point of evacuation if necessary. His army moved forward in two giant columns, one under Hill heading for Salamanca,

the other much larger under Wellington himself and Sir Thomas Graham.

The second crossed the river Douro with great skill, Wellington himself supervising the operation from a basket slung over the cliffs, and then marched on to Valladolid. Joseph and Marshal Jourdan had had to evacuate the city, as well as Madrid. The two British columns joined up at Toro and, instead of attacking the French stronghold at Burgos, bypassed it and did what they should have done the previous year – moving into the sparsely populated hills to the north, threatening to surround Burgos and cut off the forces there from possible retreat to France. The French abandoned the fortress without a fight and retreated further across the Ebro to Vitoria.

There at last Joseph decided to make a stand. The town was approached from the west by a valley bounded on one side by the Zaderra river and on the other by virtually impassable mountains, although the French feared that an attack might be mounted from the north as well. On 21 June there was skirmishing from the south-east, to which the French immediately rushed troops, imagining this to be the main thrust of the British attack. In fact the bulk of the British forces were concentrated to the south-west, on the other side of the river valley, under the nominal command of Lord Dalhousie but under the actual command of Sir Thomas Picton and behind him Wellington.

From the north there appeared out of the supposedly impassable mountains another body of troops under Graham. Wellington's artillery pounded away. The French fought bravely under this three-pronged attack, battling continuously as all three advanced. Harvey, Wellington's aide, had two horses shot under him in the thick of the fighting. If the northern force had advanced with speed, the French would have been completely trapped: instead they hesitated and the French troops, in full retreat, were able to make their escape across the Pass of Salvatierra, leaving most of King Joseph's baggage train in its wake. This was promptly plundered by the British troops, who swarmed into Vitoria in an undisciplined mass.

Some 8,000 French soldiers were killed or taken prisoner, and 150 guns were captured. Five million francs were left behind, along with

golden dubloons and Napoleons. Some 500 prostitutes of the French army were also taken. One British soldier wrote:

> I had not proceeded far when I met one of the Sixty-Eighth Regiment with a handkerchief full of dollars. He was followed by about a dozen Portuguese soldiers. One of these fellows . . . cut the handkerchief and down went the dollars. A general scramble followed. As the Portuguese were down on their hands and knees picking up the money, we paid them off in style with the sockets of our bayonets. After this fracas was over . . . I started off in the direction I heard most noise [and] soon came to the place where the money was. After much difficulty I secured a small box of dollars, and was fortunate enough to get back safe to camp.

Wellington, as usual, was incandescent at the indiscipline of his troops. Yet the battle had been one of his finest victories, because, rather than in spite of, the fact that it had been over relatively quickly. His strategic skill had ensured that the French had never stood a chance, were wholly overwhelmed and were so assaulted from every direction that they had little idea how to regroup and react.

The French were now in total disarray. Clausel fell back to Zaragoza and then to France, another French army withdrew from Aragón, and only Catalonia now remained under French control. The escaping and defeated French army from Vitoria headed straight for the French border, leaving a few garrisons behind at Pamplona, San Sebastian and Santona – which did little to slow the British advance. Vitoria had broken the back of French control of the Peninsula. But the Peninsular War was not over yet. Wellington was acutely aware that the tide could turn again, particularly if developments on the eastern front allowed Napoleon to send fresh troops back into the Peninsula. He was offered the command in Germany, but refused: 'Many might be found to conduct matters as well as I can, both here and in Germany; but nobody would enjoy the same advantage here, and I should be no better than another in Germany. If a British army should be left in the Peninsula, therefore, it is best that I should remain with it.'

His next objective was to take San Sebastian, a well-fortified fortress protected on one side by the sea and on the other by the river Urumea. The unreliable if courageous Graham was put in charge of the siege. Once again Wellington's caution was evident in his inability to bypass a fortress which he feared could threaten his flank. The siege proved a disaster, with attacks being made at low tide between the sea and the fortress under intense fire. A sergeant present wrote:

> Waiting for the tide to be sufficiently low to admit men to reach the breach, it was daylight ere we moved out of the trenches, and, having to keep close to the wall to be as clear of the sea as possible, beams of timber, shells, hand grenades and every missile that could annoy or destroy life were hurled from the ramparts on the heads of the men . . . Those who scrambled onto the breach found it was wide and sufficient enough at the bottom, but at the top . . . from thence to the street was at least twenty feet . . . Some little idea may be formed of the destructive fire of the enemy when [I say that] on the breach were left by the tide more [men] than would have loaded a wagon of fish, killed in the water by the shot of the garrison . . . And it not being sufficiently low at the time of the attack those who fell wounded and might have recovered were swept away by the current which runs here very rapid. Nor was it an easy matter for any man to keep his feet as the stones were so slippery.

While this was being botched, Napoleon ordered a counter-offensive into Spain under Soult. A huge army of 85,000 poured through two passes in the Pyrenees to fulfil Napoleon's desperate need to secure a victory in the Peninsula. This in turn would display his power in the European theatre and in particular prevent the Austrians declaring war upon him again in the east.

Wellington was caught with his army spread out between San Sebastian and inland Pamplona. One of the two immense French columns ran up against Wellington himself on a ridge with a much smaller but substantial force in a typically well-chosen defensive position on high ground. Wellington actually saw his adversary, Soult,

when a spy told him to look. 'I levelled my glass exactly as he pointed, and there, sure enough, I distinctly discerned Soult with his staff around him, several of them with their hats off and in animated conversation . . . I saw his features so distinctly that when I met him in a drawing-room in Paris for the first time I knew him at once.'

Wellington slept on rough ground for the next two days, and would fall asleep whenever he got the chance, anxiously awaiting the attack. He was very nearly captured, but when Soult attempted a break-through to San Sebastian, the British were ready. They attacked down the hill: the French were routed and made their escape back to the passes of the Pyrenees where they took up strong positions and impeded any further British advance. Some 13,000 French casualties and prisoners had been taken.

Chapter 74

INTO FRANCE

With Soult's army departed, the siege of San Sebastian intensified and two breaches were made in the walls. The suffering of the besiegers was intense, however, as one eyewitness recalled:

I was coming away making use of my firelock as a crutch, having received a grapeshot in the right leg. . . The scene before me was truly awful. Here you might observe . . . legs and arms sticking up, some their clothes in flames, [and] numbers not dead, but so jammed as not to be able to extricate themselves. I never expected to reach my trench with my life, for, not content with depriving me of my limb, the fire shot away my crutch also . . . Contrary to my expectations, I gained the trench which was a dreadful sight. It was literally filled . . . with the dead and dying. 'Twas lamentable to see the poor fellows here. One was making the best of his way minus an arm, another so disfigured . . . as to leave no trace of the features of a human being; others creeping along with the leg dangling to a piece of skin; and, worse than all, some endeavouring to keep in the bowels.

The citadel was carried, and then the towers. The usual horrors ensued, the British soldiery showing again that they were little different from the French when motivated by revenge and plunder and unrestrained by their officers. An officer wrote:

As soon as the fighting began to wax faint, the horrors of plunder and rapine succeeded. Fortunately there were few females in the

place, but of the fate of the few which were there I cannot even now think without a shudder. The houses were everywhere ransacked, the furniture wantonly broken, the churches profaned, the images dashed to pieces; wine and spirit cellars were broken open, and the troops, heated already with angry passions, became absolutely mad by intoxication. All good order and discipline were abandoned. The officers no longer had the slightest control over their men, who, on the contrary, controlled the officers, nor is it by any means certain that several of the latter did not fall by the hands of the former, when they vainly attempted to bring them back to a state of subordination.

On 7 October Wellington crossed the Bidassoa, the Rubicon of France. It was but lightly defended. As a young ensign wrote:

We commenced the passage of the Bidassoa about five in the morning and in a short time infantry, cavalry and artillery found themselves upon French ground. The stream at the point we forded was nearly four feet deep, and had Soult been aware of what we were about, we should have found the passage of the river a very arduous undertaking. Three miles above we discovered the French army and ere long found ourselves under fire. The French army, not long after we began to return their fire, was in full retreat, and after a little . . . fighting, in which our division met with some loss, we took possession of the camp . . . of Soult's army. We found the soldiers' huts very comfortable: they were built of branches of trees and furze and formed . . . streets which had names placarded up, such as Rue de Paris, Rue de Versailles, etc.

It was an historic moment, a turning point in the entire revolutionary and Napoleonic wars. For the first time the British were on French soil in force, not as at the beginning of the revolutionary war in alliance with continental countries or counter-revolutionaries, not as a raiding party, but through their own military success. Instead of Napoleon invading British territory, as he had so often threatened, Wellington was invading the territorial mainland of France.

Wellington's emotions at this juncture can only be imagined: in particular his army had been the first to penetrate France, which was still uninvaded from the east after so many bitter campaigns there by the far larger forces of Austria, Prussia and Russia. He was under no illusions that the war was over, but held out the hope that the terror, strife and suffering which had dominated all of Europe for nearly two decades might at last be approaching the beginning of the end. Yet there could be no certainty: Napoleon and France were far from beaten. Wellington had learned to his chagrin the dangers of over-confidence the previous year and had been appallingly humiliated on the retreat from Burgos.

On 31 October Pamplona surrendered at last, finally ending the threat of a fresh strike across Wellington's rear and permitting him to advance tentatively to the French Pyrenees. His 55,000-strong army moved forward up the mountain passes against the heavily fortified but lightly manned French positions above. The British and Portuguese displayed extraordinary determination and bravery. In spite of considerable casualties – more than 3,000 – they prevailed and drove the French from the passes. The latter lost over 4,000 men and sixty guns in the murderous fighting. This was the Battle of the Nivelle, the first fought by Wellington on French soil.

The British commander rudely but wisely decided to dispense with the services of his Spanish allies for fear that they might antagonize the French population needlessly through acts of brutality – which of course infuriated the Spaniards: 'I despair of the Spaniards. They are in so miserable a state that it is really hardly fair to expect that they will refrain from plundering a beautiful country into which they enter as conquerors, particularly adverting to the miseries which their own country has suffered from its invaders. I cannot, therefore, venture to bring them into France . . . Without pay and food, they must plunder, and if they plunder they will ruin us all.'

He was in a small spearhead between the coast and the Pyrenees, liable to be attacked at any time. He advanced across the Nivelle towards Bayonne. Soult launched a desperate counteroffensive on 10 December against the British-Portuguese vanguard. This failed, and

Soult staged a further one, this time against the extremely able Sir Rowland Hill who struck back with force and drove the French back to Bayonne, giving them, in Wellington's phrase, 'a hell of a licking'. Altogether in both battles the French suffered some 6,500 casualties to 4,500 Anglo-Portuguese ones – an illustration of the intensity of the fighting. Now some 4,500 German troops fighting for the French deserted. Behind Wellington Spain had been liberated and in 1814 the final French stronghold in Catalonia fell almost without a fight.

In an act of supreme cynicism, the struggling Napoleon sought to do a deal with Ferdinand VII, the young and cruel Bourbon heir to the throne of Spain and one of the most reactionary figures in contemporary Europe, to place him back on the throne; he offered him the hand of Joseph's daughter. The Spanish Cortes (Parliament) rebelled against this and told Ferdinand that any agreement he reached with Napoleon would not be respected. Napoleon himself wrote: 'The system that I pursued in Spain . . . would have eventually been for the good of that country, yet it was contrary to the opinion of the people, and therefore I failed.'

Wellington remained stuck at St Jean de Luz for a while because of the weather and established comfortable quarters. Astonishingly, he asserted that peace could yet be made with Napoleon. 'If Bonaparte becomes moderate, he is probably as good a sovereign as we can desire in France,' he wrote to London. He spent his time hunting or promenading along the sea wall. Not until the end of February 1814 did he decide to advance across the river Adour below Bayonne which was bridged with a magnificent pontoon.

Hill staged a major diversionary attack against Soult at Bayonne itself. Completely surprised, Soult abandoned the town and retreated to Orthez. There occurred Wellington's closest brush with death. He had been tactlessly laughing at General Miguel Alava, who had sustained a blow to his bottom, when he was hit by a musket shot in his thigh, deflected by his sword. He fell, exclaiming, 'By God, I am *ofendida* [wounded] this time.' He limped for days thereafter.

The battle at Orthez was largely fought by the Portuguese forces on the left, under the command of Beresford and his quartermaster-general, Harvey. The French lost some 4,000 casualties to 2,000 British

and Portuguese ones. On 27 March the British attacked at Toulouse where Wellington's sure military touch seemed to desert him. The pontoon bridge across the river Garonne was swept away by a flood, which left part of his army stranded on the wrong side. 'I used to cross over every morning to the other side and return at night. I thought the troops might be out of spirits at seeing themselves in a position so exposed; but not a bit – they didn't mind it at all.'

On 10 April he attacked at three points, and his forces were routed at two of them. 'Well damn me if I ever saw 10,000 men run a race before,' Wellington commented caustically. Even so, Soult was forced to abandon the city. The great campaign of so many battles, setbacks and so much bloodshed and savagery was over at last.

What had been the significance of the Peninsular War? Many historians consider it a mere sideshow to more significant events in eastern Europe, as Napoleon himself often offhandedly remarked. Contrary to conventional wisdom, however, the significance of the war in Napoleon's overall defeat was colossal. First, it provided a huge boost in Britain's continuous and often lonely campaign against Napoleon: given that the string of naval victories had ended – largely because the French had chosen no longer to fight at sea – it completely reversed the common concept in Britain as well as in Europe of the British army as incompetents officered by aristocratic dunderheads. Wellington won battle after battle against the most formidable fighting force in Europe, which had defeated such professional armies as those of Prussia and Austria, as well the nearly suicidal Russian conscript armies. If he had sometimes made serious misjudgements, he had also displayed superb professionalism and his soldiers had shown discipline, courage and ability.

Secondly, the Peninsular War had been a colossal drain on French resources, with anything up to a third of a million soldiers engaged, many of them crack troops that Napoleon could ill afford to spare from his other fronts, particularly in 1812–14. The drain on France's financial resources was equally acute. It was a deeply unpopular war in France, which had never felt itself threatened by Spain, as it had been by Austria and its eastern enemies. Enforced recruiting drives had been

raised every year for nearly six years, most of them falling upon the peasantry, which had been one of Napoleon's main bulwarks of support. Undoubtedly this contributed to the Emperor's growing unpopularity within France itself.

As for Austria, Prussia and Russia, here was further evidence that Napoleon could be beaten by a dogged and skilled commander and that although a fine general, Napoleon possessed no magic touch: both his strategic vision and his political vision could be seriously flawed, as proven by the whole invasion of Spain and Portugal.

It is of course absurd to argue that Napoleon's eventual defeat became inevitable as a result of the Peninsular War. The Russian campaign was the crucial factor and, even after that, he could conceivably have survived but, taken jointly with the Russian defeat, it was a turning point: neither was fatal on its own. The Peninsular War had a colossal psychological impact in Britain, France, Austria, Germany and Russia and helped to trigger the events that followed with extraordinary rapidity. It was the start: the unravelling of the Napoleonic myth on land – as Nelson had demolished it on sea.

The most extraordinary fact of the Peninsular War is that Napoleon himself took no further part in such a key campaign after his initial four-month intervention in 1808–9. There has never been a satisfactory explanation for this. During the critical year of 1810 he was at war with no other country. This most energetic of generals, who could hardly be drawn away from the front line if there was another battle to be won, stayed aloof from the Peninsular War, only issuing instructions from a distance – at crucial times sending armies to the wrong side of the Peninsula and actually contributing to France's defeat.

This has been ascribed to his infatuation with his new wife and then infant son. Yet bourgeois tenderness towards his loved ones was not remotely typical of the man; Napoleon was capable of ardour and passion, but not of sentimentality, especially when his interests were at stake. It seems far more likely that Napoleon astutely realized that he had committed the initial blunder of invading, and wanted to steer clear of being personally associated with defeat. This way, he could blame his generals. The invasion of Spain had been hubris in an attempt to add another satrapy to his empire, supposedly a stepping stone to

Africa but in reality just another jewel for the imperial crown. He believed it would be a walkover as the decadent Bourbons and Godoy were in no shape to resist.

Nothing prepared him for the ferocious internal resistance from a people he considered a mere mongrel race, nor for the remarkable success of an initially little-known British general commanding a small force. Wellington made mistakes, certainly, but the bulk of his campaign was one of scientific, forensic brilliance, conducted with an almost Napoleonic ruthlessness.

Part 11

THE INVASION
OF RUSSIA

Chapter 75

THE GRANDE ARMÉE

The great irony of Napoleon's invasion of Russia is that it was one of the few of Napoleon's apparent acts of aggression that could in fact be justified – although history has long heaped scorn upon the apparent insanity of the venture he undertook. The blame for the war lay squarely with the Russians and the vain, shallow, unstable, youthful Tsar Alexander. The confrontation had long been brewing, with Alexander increasingly impatient of the French Continental System which he decided to flout by resuming importation of British goods. He was being pressed to do this both by his mother, who loathed Bonaparte, and by his equally anti-French army commanders. In December 1810 Alexander issued tariffs on French luxury goods and permitted the importation of British goods via neutral shipping. These included vital supplies, such as corn, wood, iron, tallow and wattle.

By 2 April Napoleon was warning Alexander ominously: 'The Emperor Alexander is already far from the ideas of Tilsit; every suggestion of war has its origin in Russia. Unless the Emperor turns the current back very promptly, it will certainly carry him away next year in spite of himself, in spite of the interests of France, and of those of Russia; I have so often watched the process that my experience of the past unfolds the future to me. It is all an opera setting with the English pulling the wires.'

Yet Napoleon had offered a little provocation: he gave Bernadotte the post of crown prince of Sweden in succession to Charles XIII, to get the troublesome leader of the Jacobin faction as well as one of his

most useless generals out of the army. The Russians took this as an attempt to encircle them. Napoleon also annexed the Duchy of Oldenburg, although its ruler was married to the Tsar's sister, Countess Pavlovina, and the Russians had always regarded the territory as part of their own sphere of influence. It was the old story of Napoleon acting as a bully – but this time against a power which had never reconciled itself to his dominance, and whose territory he had never occupied.

When his ambassador, Armand de Caulaincourt, surely one of the greatest and most honest envoys in history, returned from Russia in June 1811, he bluntly attempted to dissuade Napoleon from ever contemplating war with Russia. Alexander had followed events in Spain with fascination, in particular the guerrilla war and the scorched-earth policy. In addition, Caulaincourt attempted to alert Napoleon to the ferocity of the Russian winter. Alexander had said: 'I shall not be the first to draw my sword, but I shall be the last to sheathe it.' Napoleon contemptuously called Alexander, whom he had once almost loved, 'fickle and feeble'.

Napoleon followed this up in August with a furious and preme-ditated dressing down for the Russian ambassador in Paris, Count Kurakin, in front of witnesses, raging against Alexander's proposal for a share in the Grand Duchy of Warsaw: 'Don't you know that I have 800,000 troops? If you are counting on allies, where are they?' He threatened to bring 2,000 cannon to besiege Moscow. Revealingly in November he wrote, 'If Russia will disarm, I am perfectly willing to do the same . . . but she must not show us displeasure on a thing which, as between great powers, always implies war.' Even at this stage he was far from resigned to the inevitability of war: but he was certainly not going to be seen to yield to Alexander in any way.

Yet the latter was behaving with growing boldness and contempt in a manner that seemed to suggest he was intent on provoking war. The last month of 1811 and the first of 1812 were spent in diplomatic manoeuvring between the two increasingly hostile powers: war became inevitable because Napoleon believed that he would inevitably win, and because the inexperienced Alexander had a quasi-religious faith about the Russian motherland's ability to repel him. In February Napoleon forced his Prussian subjects to provide

20,000 troops and persuaded his reluctant ally Austria to provide some 30,000.

Meanwhile, however, he invaded Swedish Pomerania early in July, which infuriated his unreliable old comrade-in-arms Bernadotte. Napoleon apparently believed that no Frenchman would wage war on him. Instead Bernadotte reached a secret agreement with Russia to assist Alexander, provided Sweden was permitted to conquer Norway. In May Alexander reached an agreement with his country's oldest enemy, Turkey, which permitted him to redeploy his southern armies to meet the Napoleonic threat in the north. This took the Emperor entirely by surprise and provoked a fresh outbreak of anger.

Alexander further prodded Napoleon by issuing a set of conditions for rejoining the Continental System at the end of April: he would do so if France evacuated Prussia, provided compensation for the seizure of Oldenburg and created a buffer zone between the two empires. Napoleon regarded these terms an insult, which they were almost certainly intended to be.

Napoleon clumsily sought to make peace overtures to his oldest enemy, Britain, offering to restore both the Portuguese and Spanish sovereigns to their thrones. After Britain consulted both countries, the offer was rejected. Instead British diplomats subsidized the Russians and sought to reinforce Alexander's determination for war.

Napoleon was furiously preparing the greatest army the world had ever seen for a Russian campaign that he now regarded as virtually inevitable. It was to consist of the First Corps commanded by Davout, the Second commanded by Oudinot, the Third commanded by Ney; the Imperial Guard commanded by Napoleon himself; and the cavalry commanded by Murat: all of them would add up to 250,000 men. Along with this would go the corps commanded by Eugène de Beauharnais; the Fifth Corps, consisting largely of Poles under Ponia-towski; the Sixth Corps commanded by St Cyr; the Seventh Corps of Saxons commanded by Reynier; and the Eighth Corps of Westphalians and Hessians commanded by Vandamme. Two other massive armies, the Second (150,000 men) and the Third (165,000), were to act as a reserve and protect lines of communication. There was to be another

supporting army commanded by Jérôme Bonaparte. Altogether these amounted to some 675,000 men, of whom 400,000 were actually to enter Russia.

The colossal size of this army was intended to intimidate the Russians out of war, even at this late stage, and to steamroller all before it if hostilities were declared. The army would need 20 million rations of bread, 20 million tons of rice, 2 million bushels of oats to feed its 150,000 horses and 30,000 wagons to carry supplies. There were 1,200 cannon. Napoleon's headquarters alone would require fifty wagons and 650 horses to transport them, while his senior officers travelled with their wives, servants and ample possessions. Murat brought a group of the best cooks in Paris and Naples and requested sixty horses for his baggage.

Napoleon had most of the supplies landed at the port of Danzig, while he travelled across in great style to the Saxon capital of Dresden. His army resembled a travelling township, or one of those huge caravans of military might and camp-followers that typified the great Moghul armies of India more than a sleek efficient European military machine.

At Dresden he indulged in an orgy of pomp and circumstance that suggested he preferred display to military skill. His entire court travelled in 300 carriages while he occupied the baroque royal palace and filled it with French furniture and luxuries, commanding his puppet rulers from across Europe to come to do him homage. Quite what he sought to achieve with this display is not clear: it certainly did not intimidate Alexander, who had assembled his own court at Vilnius, just seventy-five miles away.

General Philippe-Paul de Ségur, one of Napoleon's generals whose account remains the most gripping of the whole campaign, wrote:

> We were about to reach the extremity of Europe, where never European army had been before! We were about to erect new columns of Hercules. The grandeur of the enterprise, the agitation of co-operating Europe, the imposing spectacle of an army of 400,000 foot and 80,000 horse, so many warlike reports and martial clamours, kindled the minds of veterans themselves. It was im-

possible for the coldest to remain unmoved amid the general impulse, to escape from the universal attraction. In conclusion: the composition of the army was good and every good army is desirous of war . . .

Napoleon addressed his troops before the invasion with a ringing declaration:

> Soldiers, the second Polish war is commenced. The first was concluded at Friedland and at Tilsit. At Tilsit, Russia swore eternal friendship with France and war with England. She now violates her oaths. She will give no explanation of her capricious conduct until the French eagles have repassed the Rhine, by that means leaving our allies at her mercy. Russia is hurried away by fatality; her destiny must be accomplished. Does she then believe us to be degenerated? Are we not still the soldiers of Austerlitz? She places us between war and dishonour: the choice cannot be in doubt. Let us advance then, let us cross the Niemen and carry the war into her territory! The second Polish war will be as glorious for French arms as the first; but this time, the peace we shall conclude will carry with it its own guarantee; it will put an end to the fatal influence which Russia for the last fifty years has exercised over the affairs of Europe.

His plan was simplicity itself: to draw the Russians into a battle he believed they would fight to defend their borders and inflict a crushing and punishing defeat. He believed the campaign would be over in three weeks – a short sharp shock – which explains why he had taken so long to make his way to the border, wasting the valuable spring and summer months.

The Grande Armée was to march to take Niemen on the frontier with Russia in two main columns: the biggest of 220,000 men under the Emperor himself towards Kouno; and another under Jérôme and de Beauharnais to the south moving towards Grodno and Pilony. Napoleon himself abandoned his comfortable carriage to ride on horseback at dusk and scout the Niemen – until he was suddenly thrown

from his horse, at which he is said to have exclaimed, 'That is a bad omen. A Roman would recoil.' (Napoleon was highly superstitious for a man who professed such rationalist scepticism towards traditional religions.)

At night they crossed the river on pontoon bridges to find the opposite bank almost entirely undefended except for a single Cossack officer who appeared completely taken by surprise by their appearance. The crossing was effected on 23 June. Ségur captured the mood of the moment:

> Three hundred yards from the river, on the most elevated height, the tent of the Emperor was visible. Around it the hills and valleys were covered with men and horses. As soon as the earth presented to the sun those moving masses, clothed with glittering arms, the signal was given and instantly the multitudes began to file off in three columns towards the bridges. They were seen to take a winding direction as they descended the narrow plain which separated them from the Niemen; to approach it, to reach the three bridges, to compress and prolong their columns in order to cross them; and at last reach that foreign soil which they were about to devastate (and which they were destined to cover with their own dreadful wreckage). So great was their enthusiasm that two divisions of the advanced guard disputed for the honour of being the first to pass and were near coming to blows, some exertions being necessary to quiet them. Napoleon hastened to plant his foot on Russian territory. He took this first step towards his ruin without hesitation. At first, he stationed himself near the bridge, encouraging the soldiers with his looks. The latter all saluted him with their accustomed cries. They appeared, indeed, more animated than he was: whether it was that he felt oppressed by the weight of so great an invasion, or that his enfeebled frame could not support the effect of the excessive heat, or that he was already intimidated by finding nothing to conquer.

Then another omen occurred – a first small display of the power of the Russian weather:

The Emperor had scarcely passed the river when a rumbling sound began to agitate the air. In a short time the day became overcast; the wind rose and brought with it the inauspicious murmurings of a thunderstorm. That menacing sky and unsheltered country filled us with gloomy impressions. There were even some among us who, enthusiastic as they had lately been, were terrified at what they conceived to be a fatal omen. To them it appeared that the tempest would descend upon the country we approached, in order to prevent us from entering it! It is quite certain that the storm in question was as great as the enterprise in which we were engaged. During several hours its black and heavy clouds accumulated and hung over the whole army: from right to left, over a space of fifty leagues, it was completely threatened by its lightnings and overwhelmed by its torrents. The roads and fields were flooded, the insupportable heat of the atmosphere was suddenly changed into a disagreeable chill. Ten thousand horses perished on the march and more especially in the bivouacs which followed. A large quantity of carriages remained abandoned on the sands and great numbers of men subsequently died.

On the few days' march to Vilnius, there was a further foretaste of things to come: the troops were soon overusing their supplies and consuming excessive rations.

They had been entirely unprepared for the intense summer heat and the appalling road which held up their wagons. They were also soon plagued by diarrhoea and dysentery. Soon they were falling by the wayside through exhaustion, disease, desertion and suicide at the rate of thousands a day. Arriving on the river Vilia, a typically tragic and futile Napoleonic sacrifice of his men was ordered. Ségur sets the scene:

At Kovno, Napoleon was exasperated because the bridge over the river Vilia had been thrown down by the Cossacks and opposed the passage of Marshal Oudinot. He affected to despise the obstacle – like everything else that opposed him – and ordered a squadron of his Polish Guard to swim the river. These fine fellows threw themselves into it without hesitation. At first they proceeded in

good order and when out of their depth redoubled their exertions. They soon reached the middle of the river but the increased rapidity of the current broke their formation. Their horses then became frightened and were carried away by the violence of the torrent: they no longer swam but floated about in scattered groups; their riders struggled and made vain efforts; their strength gave way and they at last resigned themselves to their fate. Their destruction was certain: but it was for their country, it was in her presence and for the sake of their deliverer that they had devoted themselves; and even when on the point of being engulfed forever, they stopped their futile struggles, turned their faces towards Napoleon and exclaimed, '*Vive l'Empereur!*' Three of them were witnessed who, with their heads still above the billows, repeated this cry and perished instantly. The army was struck with mingled horror and admiration. As to Napoleon, he supervised with anxiety and precision the measures necessary to save the greater number but without appearing affected: either from the habit of subduing his feelings; from considering the ordinary emotion of the heart as weaknesses in times of war (of which it was not for him to set the example and therefore necessary to suppress); or, finally, that he anticipated much greater misfortunes, compared with which the present was a mere trifle.

Napoleon had crossed the border with a vast and unwieldy army containing a huge proportion of subject foreign troops with far less motivation than the French and the Poles: there were, for example, 30,000 Italians, 30,000 Austrians, 28,000 Westphalians, 27,000 Saxons, 26,000 Bavarians, 20,000 Prussians and 30,000 other Germans.

He had also seriously underestimated his enemy. In 1808 Alexei Arakchev, the Russian minister of war, a hardline reactionary but a fine artillery officer and administrator, had begun the process of modernization that would be completed by his successor, General Barclay de Tolly. Arakchev introduced smaller 6- and 12-pound cannon and modern howitzers, bringing the Russian army's complement up to 1,700 guns, to enable it to pursue a strategy of massed artillery attack. Barclay, who was of Scottish descent and was also unusual in that he

had served fourteen years in the ranks of this aristocrat-dominated army, actually tried to improve conditions for the brutalized Russian peasant conscripts as well as seeking to train them in marksmanship and the use of bayonets.

At a time when the French were increasingly reliant upon huge massed divisions, which were much less wieldy than the smaller units of before, Barclay cut the big Russian divisions down into small mixed ones, each consisting of infantry, artillery and cavalry. He also introduced French-style corps into which the divisions would be integrated yet retain freedom of manoeuvre. Barclay encountered stiff resistance from the sixty-seven-year-old General Kutuzov, a fierce traditionalist.

The Russians had around 220,000 men available for the western front out of a total army of 600,000 men. This was divided between Barclay's First Army of about 130,000 men, based to the north of Napoleon's positions at Orissa on the Duna, and Bagration's Second Army of 60,000 men, to the south of Napoleon's army, based near the vast Pripet Marshes. Napoleon's strategy was to divide the armies – which in fact he had already done – and with his enormous forces take on first one and then the other.

The Russians had intended to attack him on both flanks until they realized that the size of his army made this impossible. Ironically, a battle was what Napoleon most wanted, but his overwhelming force deterred the Russians from attacking. Under the Tsar's plan, it was intended to make a stand at Orissa. But the fortress there, which had only just been built, was too small and only half completed. Caution set in: the Russians wisely decided to avoid a fight for the time being.

Napoleon remained for two weeks at Vilnius, setting up an administration for his new fiefdom of Lithuania. Meanwhile he sent off Murat, Ney and Oudinot in pursuit of Barclay de Tolly, and Davout and Jérôme in pursuit of Bagration. The French troops, already exhausted, failed to catch the latter's smaller army in a giant pincer near Minsk. Jérôme, however, ordered his army to halt to deal with an issue of discipline involving embezzlement by General Vandamme, and Bagration consequently escaped the trap.

Napoleon furiously gave overall command to Davout, whereupon Jérôme flew into a rage and quit, returning to his Kingdom of

Westphalia. Davout marched speedily forward to capture Minsk on 8 July, but Bagration had already escaped by marching sixty miles further on. To the north Barclay abandoned the useless fort at Orissa and made for Vitebsk, 200 miles from Vilnius, where he proposed to join his army to that of his aristocratic rival, Bagration, and make a stand against the French.

Chapter 76

VITEBSK

The French, plagued by shortages of staples, supplies, heat and disease, were facing the old problem of plundering. Ségur stated the position:

> A situation of so much excess engendered fresh excesses. These rough men, when assailed by so many monstrous sufferings, could not remain reasonable. When they arrived near any dwellings they were famished. At first they asked: but either for want of being understood or from the refusal (or impossibility) of the inhabitants to satisfy their demands, quarrels generally arose. Then, as they became more and more exasperated with hunger, they became furious; and after tumbling either cottage or palace upside-down without finding the food they were in search of, they, in the violence of their despair, accused the inhabitants of being their enemies and revenged themselves upon them by destroying their property. There were some who actually destroyed themselves rather than proceed to such extremities: others, after having done so. These were the youngest. They placed their foreheads on their muskets and blew out their brains in the middle of the highroad. But many became hardened: one excess led them on to another, as people often get angry with the blows they inflict. Among the latter, some vagabonds took vengeance for their distress upon civilians. In the midst of so unfavourable an aspect of nature, they became denaturalised. Left to themselves at so great a distance from home, they imagined that everything was allowed them and that their own sufferings author-ized them to make others suffer.

However, with Napoleon encamped outside Vitebsk, he was at last elated: the decisive battle he had long sought was about to happen. The Russians later claimed that their scorched earth policy was premeditated, as was their strategy of retreat. But they were not acting with any such forethought: they intended to fight at the first available opportunity. Although poisoning the wells at the approach of the French, they had not burnt the few villages in their path: there were simply too few to provision the huge invading force.

Murat's cavalry had at last caught up with the Russian rearguard. With his usual fearlessness he charged into this. Ségur continued: 'Murat's cavalry, first into action, bore the brunt of the fighting and he himself led more than one charge. Once, to rescue a hard-pressed regiment, he dashed at the Russian horsemen with his staff and personal escort, some sixty sabres at most. It was one of the few occasions when he drew his diamond-hilted sword at the head of a charge. His life was saved by one of his equerries killing a Russian who was on the point of cutting him down.'

On 27 July Napoleon at last viewed the Russian army drawn up on the plain before Vitebsk. 'Tomorrow at five o'clock, the sun of Austerlitz,' he declared. Murat begged him in vain to attack at once, fearing that Barclay's army would disappear overnight: in fact the latter intended to fight, only to be told the same evening that Bagration had withdrawn towards Smolensk.

Barclay decamped during the night, to Murat's chagrin. When the French arrived the following morning, they found the countryside deserted and a single Russian soldier asleep under a bush. The same day Napoleon entered Vitebsk and threw his sword down on the table at his imperial headquarters. 'Here I stop! Here I must look round me; rally, refresh my army and organize Poland. The campaign of 1812 is finished; that of 1813 will do the rest.'

He had sensibly decided to stop with the Dnieper and the Düna as his front line. Vitebsk was eminently defensible, with wooded hills which could be fortified. In the north his artillery would protect him; in the south the marshes provided a neutral boundary. He had conquered Lithuania and penetrated Russia; that was sufficient for

one campaign. He would winter in Vitebsk and summon actors and courtesans from Paris, Warsaw and Vilnius to amuse his troops. Thirty-six bread ovens were ordered. Unsightly houses in front of the palace which was to be his winter quarters, were ordered to be pulled down.

When the impatient Murat urged him forward, Napoleon exhibited the caution of a Wellington or Washington: 'Murat, the first campaign in Russia is finished: let us here plant our eagles. Two great rivers mark out our position; let us raise block-houses on that line; let our fires cross each other on all sides; let us form a battalion square, cannon at the angles and the exterior, and let the interior contain our quarters and our magazines. 1813 will see us at Moscow, 1814 at Petersburg. The Russian war is a war of three years.'

In this he showed wisdom and restraint: he had advanced nearly 400 miles against his foes and could claim a great achievement: his position was virtually impregnable. His supply lines were secure; and he could threaten Alexander with a new offensive the following year or impose a humiliating peace. It seemed that the middle-aged Napoleon was indeed a more mature and mellow man than the young hothead.

But as the days passed, the worm began to turn. The second greatest miscalculation in Napoleon's career – the first was the invasion of Spain – was in the making: he became tempted, then seduced, then obsessed with the idea of conquering Moscow, an idea he had always flirted with. Ségur captured beautifully the process of temptation:

> In the first instance he appeared hardly bold enough to confess to himself a project of such great audacity. But by degrees he assumed courage to look it in the face. He then began to deliberate and the state of great irresolution which tormented his mind affected his whole frame. He was seen to pace his apartments as if pursued by some dangerous temptation. Nothing could fix his attention. Every moment he began, quitted, and resumed his occupation. He walked about without any purpose, enquired the hour and remarked the weather. Completely absorbed, he stopped, then hummed a tune with an absent air and again began pacing.
>
> In the midst of his perplexity he occasionally addressed the people he met with such half-sentences as, 'Well! What shall we do? Shall

we stay where we are, or advance? How is it possible to stop short in the midst of so glorious a career?' He did not wait for their reply but still kept wandering about, as if he was looking for something or someone to end his indecision.

At length, quite sinking under the weight of such important considerations and in a way overwhelmed with this great uncertainty, he would throw himself on one of the beds which he had caused to be laid on the floor of his apartments. His body, exhausted by the heat and the struggles of his mind, could only bear a light garment. In this manner did he pass a portion of his days at Vitebsk.

But when his body was at rest, his spirit was only the more active. How many motives urged him towards Moscow! How to support at Vitebsk the weariness of seven winter months? He, who till then had always been the aggressor, was about to be reduced to a defensive role, a part unworthy of him, of which he had no experience and undeserving of his genius.

Moreover, at Vitebsk, nothing had been decided and yet, at what a distance was he already from France! Europe, then, would at length see him stopped: him, whom nothing had been able to stop! Would not the duration of the enterprise increase its danger? Ought he allow Russia time to arm herself completely? How long could he protract this uncertain condition without breaking the spell of his infallibility (which the resistance in Spain had already weakened) and without engendering dangerous hopes in Europe? What would be thought if it were known that a third of his army, dispersed or sick, were no longer in the ranks? It was indispensable, therefore, to dazzle the world quickly with the brilliance of a great victory and hide so many sacrifices under a heap of laurels.

If he remained at Vitebsk, he considered that he should have the displeasure, the whole expense and all the inconveniences and anxieties of a defensive position to bear; while at Moscow there would be peace, abundance, a reimbursement of the expenses of the war and immortal glory. He persuaded himself that boldness was the only prudential course; that it is the same with all hazardous undertakings, in which there is always risk at the beginning but frequently gain at the finish; that it was indispensable, therefore, to

terminate this operation; to push it to the utmost, astonish the universe, beat down Alexander by daring and carry off a prize which might compensate so many losses.

Thus it was, that the same danger which perhaps ought to have recalled him to the Niemen or kept him stationary on the Düna urged him towards Moscow! Such is the nature of false positions: everything in them is perilous. There is only a choice of errors.

He had still to convince his generals. Although it was Moscow that tempted him, he did so by pretending that his real object was Smolensk, only fifty miles away. It nevertheless proved a difficult task. Caulaincourt argued against him stubbornly. Duroc presciently told him that the Russians were no more likely to make peace at Smolensk or at Moscow than at Vitebsk. Daru argued with faultless logic: 'It is not a national war. The introduction of some English merchandise into Russia and even the restoration of the Kingdom of Poland are not sufficient reasons for engaging in so distant a war; neither your troops nor ourselves understand its necessity or its objects and, to say the least, all things recommend the policy of stopping where we now are.'

Napoleon overruled them all: he ordered his army on to Smolensk, with a characteristically brilliant flourish: he crossed the Dnieper to the south, crossing the bridge at Orsha and erecting four pontoons as a feint that suggested he would bypass the city.

The Russians were not suffering the problem of a single domineering leader, as the French were, but were plagued instead by a bitterly squabbling collective. The humble Barclay de Tolly and the aristocratic Bagration were at daggers drawn over strategy for their now united army. Bagration accused Barclay of cowardice in so many words, and appealed over his head to the Tsar. Barclay, whose strategy was in fact the correct one, was ordered to launch a cautious advance towards the French: as soon as he encountered French forces on 8 August, the cautious Barclay decided to withdraw to Smolensk, in the nick of time to reinforce the city from the main French threat now approaching from the south east.

Chapter 77

SMOLENSK AND BORODINO

On 14 August Ney attacked and repulsed Barclay's rearguard at Krasnoi, some thirty miles west of Smolensk. There, inexplicably, the French paused to celebrate Napoleon's forty-third birthday with due pomp and ceremony, which included a 100-gun salute. Two days later Murat reached Smolensk, Russia's third biggest city. This picturesque city, straddling the Dnieper, consisted of the medieval old town in the south, protected by a huge rampart, a wall ten feet thick and twenty feet high, boasting no fewer than thirty-two towers, well equipped with artillery. Around the walls were a huddle of wooden huts. To the north was the St Petersburg suburb consisting of more recent buildings. As Murat's advance cavalry and Ney's infantry reached the city, they did not hesitate to attack the well-manned defences, losing some 10,000 men in the process. Murat, who had bitterly opposed his brother-in-law's decision to advance, seemed to be courting his own death in battle. The French attacks failed to make any impression on the thick walls of the city.

Napoleon's decision to stage a frontal assault had been a fatal miscalculation: if he had advanced eastwards and then northwards he could have cut the road between Smolensk and Moscow and trapped the 125,000-strong Russian army. But Barclay, anticipating this, decided that discretion was the better part of valour and withdrew during the night of 17–18 August after a blazing row with Bagration who wanted to stay and fight.

Junot, remarkably, had managed to enter the city, but failed to press the attack, to Napoleon's fury. (Junot, one of France's finest marshals,

was so abashed that he turned suicidal and finally succeeded in throwing himself from a window less than a year later.) During the same night the French observed fires starting in different parts of the city, eventually erupting into a single vast conflagration which Napoleon likened to the eruption of Vesuvius: the Russians were burning down the city as they withdrew: it was an awesome display of grim, ruthless determination.

Napoleon's army entered into the desolation of a city levelled by fire, with mounds of charred and slaughtered corpses alongside the still smoking shells of wooden buildings. 'You should remember the saying of one of the Roman Emperors, the corpse of an enemy always smells good,' he remarked grimly. He rode across the city to gaze across the Dnieper at the St Petersburg suburb, only to see that the Russians had already evacuated that too. The French made a half-hearted attempt to pursue them. But Napoleon was content to remain a week in the smouldering ruins of Smolensk, a city which now could offer no shelter or sustenance and only a handful of intact buildings for use as hospitals.

Napoleon was again faced with a fateful choice: to call a halt to his advance or to press on; once more the Russians had escaped more or less intact and a decisive victory had eluded the Emperor. It seems that Napoleon was more determined at Smolensk than at Vitebsk, although he was later to say that the decision to press on from Smolensk was the greatest mistake in his life. Moscow was some 200 miles away and offered an irresistible target: the Russians, Napoleon believed, were sure to fight to save their capital. Napoleon was also afraid that the Russians would be able to recruit new forces if he delayed, and that even the Austrians and the Prussians might join in on the Russian side if he failed to inflict a decisive defeat upon them.

Virtually all of Napoleon's top commanders disagreed: while the *Grande Armée* had been reduced to 125,000 infantry, 32,000 cavalry and under 600 guns, the French risked further extending their supply lines in order to fight a difficult battle before Moscow. Napoleon brushed aside their fears: 'We have gone too far to turn back. Peace is in front of us; we are but ten days' march from it; so near the goal, there is

nothing more to consider. Let us march on Moscow!' In fact there was logic to Napoleon's position, given the distance he had already travelled into the Russian heartland: what were a couple of hundred miles more?

Yet it was the same logic that had precipitated the whole disastrous Russian adventure: the need to maintain the myth of French invincibility, of Napoleon's ability to vanquish any foe on which Europe's subjugation depended. Napoleon had become the prisoner of his own mythology. If he had wintered in Smolensk – although he might have had trouble securing the necessary supplies to do so safely and would have had to build proper shelters – he might have avoided the terrible debacle that was to follow. If he had stayed in Vitebsk, he would certainly have done so. But he now believed the only chance of success was to inflict a decisive defeat on Moscow.

On 25 August 1812, under a burning sun in searing heat and choking dust, with supplies already so scarce that the men were forced to drink their horses' urine, the *Grande Armée* marched forward to its doom. They reached the small town of Viasma a hundred miles further on: its 15,000 men had been driven out and the town burnt down by the retreating Russians: there was nothing to be had there.

They marched on forty miles to find the same desolate scene of flames and ruin at Gzhatsk. From there the French plodded onwards, haemorrhaging men at the appalling rate of 6,000 a day to disease, desertion and suicide in the torrid summer heat: indeed the *Grande Armée* lost more men on the advance to Moscow than it was to lose on the much more famous retreat: Napoleon himself, in a luxury carriage jolting along in the stifling heat, was suffering from a host of minor ailments and had lost his usual vigour.

On the Russian side, the constant sniping against the defensive and cautious policies of Barclay de Tolly finally made their mark. Alexander was forced to bow to the pressure of his senior officers to replace the dour, solitary general. But his rival Bagration was not the beneficiary: instead the job went to the failed Russian commander at Austerlitz. General Mikhail Kutuzov, now sixty-seven, was fat, pleasure-seeking, a noted philanderer with an idle streak, impatient with bureaucracy and

prone to fall asleep at staff meetings. Kutuzov had enjoyed a remarkable rollercoaster career. He was nevertheless enormously shrewd. His greatest asset was that, being Russian and a disciple of the famous Suvorov, [who had rolled back Napoleon's conquests in Italy after the latter's departure for Egypt in 1797,] he was acceptable both to the Russian people and to senior officers.

He shared Barclay de Tolly's sensible reluctance to do open battle. However, he had been given clear instructions to stand and fight – which would give Napoleon his chance at last. Kutuzov decided to make the stand which might determine the fate of Mother Russia at the small village of Borodino on the banks of the river Moskva just seventy-five miles west of Moscow. Inexplicably, he sent a force across the river to secure the Shevardino Redoubt in the face of the advancing French, believing it could be defended. This was promptly taken by the French at a cost of some 4,000 casualties and some 6,000 Russian losses.

The remaining army of Kutuzov was drawn up in a strong defensive position along hills straddling the Moscow–Smolensk road. The most heavily entrenched Russian force followed the line of the river Kalatsha, a tributary of the Moskva; the centre was based on Borodino; and the more weakly defended left was around the village of Semi-ovskaya. In the centre the Great Redoubt, a hill bristling with several hundred of the 640 Russian guns at the battle made a formidable defensive position. Further south were three entrenched defensive earthworks – the Bagration Flèches (arrows). Perhaps because of the strength of these, and also because Kutuzov believed Napoleon would attack in the centre along the road, he kept the bulk of his forces on the right and centre.

Napoleon, always contrary, chose to march his forces to his right flank and attack the centre and the south, forcing Kutuzov hastily to transfer troops from the north. After this, however, Napoleon's strategy was an unimaginative frontal assault. He refused Davout's request to stage a flanking movement further around the Russian left with 40,000 men. Napoleon was fearful this would take time and permit the Russians to escape as they had so often done before; and the terrain Devout's forces would have to cross was broken and uneven.

Napoleon's choice of a frontal attack seems to have been dictated by his near certainty that the Russians had inferior forces compared to his own: again he was a prisoner of his own propaganda. The armies were, in fact, evenly matched, with some 120,000 Russian men against 130,000 French and about 600 guns on the French side to the Russians' 640. Napoleon badly underestimated the fighting spirit of the Russians, believing that a direct assault would quickly break them. Throughout the night preceding the battle – that of 6 September – he repeatedly awoke to check that the Russians had not slipped away as they had on so many previous occasions. Here at last was his chance to inflict a decisive defeat, which would threaten Moscow and bring the recalcitrant Tsar to the negotiating table.

The following morning Napoleon issued his proclamation as he at last joined battle with his elusive foe:

> Soldiers, here at last is the battle that you have so long expected! Victory now depends on your efforts, and is essential. It will give us abundance, good winter quarters, and a speedy return to our country. Do what you did at Austerlitz, at Friedland, at Vitebsk, at Smolensk, and let posterity point with pride to your conduct on this day: let people say of you: 'He was at that great battle fought under the walls of Moscow!' The battle of Borodino is the most glorious, most difficult, and most creditable operation of war carried out by the Gauls, of which either ancient or modern history makes mention. Dauntless heroes, – Murat, Ney, Poniatowski, – it is to you the glory is due! What great, what splendid deeds History might place on record! How our intrepid cuirassiers charged and sabred the gunners on their guns; the heroic devotion of Montbrun, who found death in the midst of their glory; our gunners, in the open and without cover, firing against a heavier artillery protected by earthworks; and our brave infantry, at the most critical moment, not in need of their general's steadying voice, but calling out to him: 'It's all right! Your soldiers have sworn they will conquer, and they will!'

Borodino has, in fact, entered history as an unimaginative slugfest of two almost evenly matched armies confronting each other frontally

and inflicting huge casualties upon one another. Both Kutuzov, and more surprisingly Napoleon, remained a mile behind their respective lines at the village of Gorky and in the captured Shevardino Redoubt respectively. Certainly Napoleon's old spark appeared to be missing. Yet it was much more decisive than it appeared: although the Russians are said to have lost, in fact they won. Napoleon's objective was to inflict a colossal and shattering defeat on the Russians of the kind he had craved ever since he had entered that forbidding country; the stakes were thus much higher for him. The Russian objective was simply to deny him that victory.

At dawn on 7 September a hundred French guns initiated the battle with a tremendous barrage against the Russian centre. After this softening up, Ney's infantry were ordered into action against the Bagration Flèches and Eugène de Beauharnais against the Russian centre. At first the ferocity of the French assault carried all before it: De Beauharnais took Borodino after fierce fighting, while Ney, supported by Murat and Davout, captured the Flèches but then was pushed back. At around 10 a.m., Poniatoski's Polish cavalry attacked the centre, threatening a breakthrough that would cut the Russian line in two. The Great Redoubt was also captured in a brave and unsupported attack by General Morand; the Russians counter-attacked and retook it, but only after major casualties. Bagration himself was mortally wounded, and it seemed that the French were about to secure the decisive victory they had craved.

Napoleon from his comfortable and far-off vantage point could be well satisfied. But the Russians now staged a superb cavalry attack, outflanking the French left, which for a time diverted them into easing the pressure on the Great Redoubt. Ney, Davout and Murat sent an urgent emissary to Napoleon, who could not see the battle, demanding that he send in the Imperial Guard. But Napoleon refused to give the order. The emissary found him seated, his features sunken and dull-looking, giving orders weakly 'in the midst of these dreadful warlike noises, to which he seemed a complete stranger!' At this account, which was communicated to Ney, the latter – furious and carried away by his passionate and impetuous nature – exclaimed,

What business has the Emperor in the rear of the army? There, he is only within reach of reverses and not of victory. Since he will no longer make war himself, since he is no longer the general, as he wishes to be Emperor everywhere, let him return to the Tuileries and leave us to be generals for him!

Murat was more calm. He recalled having seen the Emperor the day before, as he was riding along observing part of the enemy's line, halt several times, dismount and with his head resting upon a cannon, remain there some time in an attitude of suffering. He knew what a restless night he had passed and that a violent and incessant cough cut short his breathing. Murat guessed that fatigue had shaken his weakened frame and that at that critical moment, the action of his genius was in a sense chained down by his body; which had sunk under the triple load of fatigue, fever and a malady which, probably more than any other, drains the moral and physical strength of its victims.

Napoleon remarked lamely. 'And if there should be another battle tomorrow, with what is my army to fight?' This was a changed man from the bold risk-taker of the past.

It was not until 3 p.m. that de Beauharnais sent Caulaincourt in with his cuirassiers in a final attempt to carry the Great Redoubt and its eighty murderous cannon 'bristling with iron and flames'. Caulaincourt rode in declaring: 'You shall see me there presently alive or dead.' He was as good as his word. His charge was successful and at last spiked the guns, but he was killed by a musket bullet.

After a further cavalry and infantry attack to retake the redoubt, the Russian line was broken at last. But to the astonishment of the French the Russians simply withdrew to another line of hills overlooking the former position and their guns renewed their ceaseless barrage against the French, who were forced to take shelter in the Russian defences they had captured. Napoleon at last deigned to come forward and inspect the battlefield, and to tell Ney and Murat, both impatient to renew the attack, that it was too late to continue the battle. He remained, according to Ségur, in a state of 'great mental anguish added to his previous physical dejection'.

During the night, Kutuzov's army stole away from its new positions,

unhindered by the exhausted French. The following day Napoleon rode over the field of battle. Ségur described what met his gaze:

> Never did one present so horrible an appearance. Everything concurred to make it so: a gloomy sky, a cold rain, a violent wind; houses burnt to ashes, a plain turned topsy-turvy, covered with ruins and rubbish, and in the distance the sad, sombre trees of the north; soldiers roaming about in all directions, hunting for provisions, even in the haversacks of their dead comrades; horrible wounds (for the Russian musket balls are larger than ours), silent bivouacs, no singing or storytelling. Around the eagles were seen the remaining officers, subalterns and a few soldiers: scarcely enough to protect the colours. Their clothes had been torn in the fury of the combat, blackened with powder and spotted with blood; and yet, in the midst of their rags, their misery and disasters, they had a proud look; and at the sight of the Emperor uttered some shouts of triumph: but they were rare and forced. For in this army, capable at once of reason and enthusiasm, everyone was sensible of the position of all.

As he passed, some suffering men begged to be put to death, but Napoleon's entourage did not answer their pleas. A man with just his torso and a single arm remaining was rescued, such was his state of animation, hope and even gaiety, although complaining of feeling pain in limbs no longer possessed.

The battle had been the bloodiest so far in all the sanguinary history of Napoleon's wars some 60,000 killed on the Russian side, some 40,000 on the French. The French had fired some 2 million cartridges and 90,000 artillery rounds. It was slaughter on a mass scale never before experienced in military history, a presage of the terrible fighting of the First World War just over a century later. Kutuzov declared he had won a victory. Napoleon, ailing and anguished, did likewise. Yet, although he had been driven from the field, Kutuzov was the real victor: Napoleon had been denied the decisive victory he sought because the Russians had been prepared to die in their thousands for their homeland, although they were inferior fighters to the French.

Some 60,000 Russians had escaped to provide the nucleus of a new

army. Already battered in the Iberian Peninsula – where Wellington had just won the spectacular battle of Salamanca – the mystique of French invincibility was fast disappearing: and at Borodino the French had been commanded by the Emperor himself – if that is the right description for his listless issuing of orders from well behind the front line. That Russia's infamous 'army of barbarians' had been able to resist an army which had scored such great victories against the formidable armies of Austria and Prussia was another humiliation.

Chapter 78

MOSCOW BURNS

On 13 September 1812 the battered but still formidable Russian army reached Moscow. At a desperate council of war Kutuzov took the unimaginable step – with Barclay de Tolly's support – of ordering that Moscow be abandoned: another battle could not be fought, the city could not be defended, the army must be preserved to fight for the Russian heartland. The Russians were far from satisfied with their performance at Borodino: they considered themselves defeated, but must fight on.

After a tearful intervention, the old soldier got his way. The Tsar declared: 'We would rather perish under the ruins than make peace with the modern Attila.' Early the following morning the Russian troops, many openly weeping, marched out of Moscow, their banners furled, along with much of the civilian population.

The same afternoon the *Grande Armée*, which had just crossed the sandy desert wastes near Mojaisk, a further geographical obstacle which took Napoleon and his entourage by surprise so close to 'one of the great capitals of the world', arrived outside that capital. It was an incredible spectacle, a dream come true; it was, like arriving before one of the fabled cities of the east in some oriental epic: at long last the sufferings of the troops in that interminable summer march through rain, heat and misery across desert, mud and grass steppe seemed vindicated.

The Napoleonic army had captured one of the greatest cities of the east, with a population of 250,000, and its onion domes, turrets, minarets, fabulous palaces and medieval winding streets between

picturesque wooden houses. Ségur wrote vividly: 'It was two o'clock. The sun caused this great city to glisten with a thousand colours. Struck with astonishment at the sight, they paused, exclaiming "Moscow! Moscow!" Everyone quickened his pace; the troops hurried on in disorder and the whole army, clapping their hands, repeated with joy, "Moscow! Moscow!" just as sailors shout "Land! Land!" at the end of a long and wearisome voyage.' The Emperor rode down to the Dorogomilov Gate to accept the city's surrender. But instead of a deputation of dignitaries, there was only an old man who offered to show him the sights.

Impatiently he sent Murat into the city. The latter, strong, dashing and fearless, was wearing a magnificent hat surmounted by ostrich feathers and a blue tunic with a scarlet pelisse made of velvet and fur, as well as red breeches and yellow boots. He galloped past lines of Russian Cossacks who cheered him, and struck a deal with the commander of the departing Russian troops to grant the latter safe conduct in exchange for a peaceful surrender of the city.

Napoleon, disappointed to find the city largely deserted, did not make his formal entrance until next day, when he entered the Kremlin, the great, medieval and renaissance palace of Ivan the Terrible. 'At last I am in Moscow in the ancient palace of the Tsars, in the Kremlin.' He issued peace proposals to the Tsar. He appointed Marshal Mortier governor of the city with the stern injunction: 'No pillage.' A wonderfully beautiful medieval city of wooden houses and fabulous churches had fallen into his hands. He was the conqueror, the man who could subdue the world, an almost godlike figure. Yet there was an eerie emptiness about the deserted city, a feeling that something was not quite right, that the victory was a hollow one.

There followed surely the most apocalyptically symbolic event in the whole of Napoleon's terrible and awesome career of bloodshed, destruction, plunder and inflicted suffering, a window opened into hell itself, the sudden snatching of his great prize and its reduction to ashes before him. Not until the fall of Berlin a century later and of the bombing of Tokyo was such damage to be wrought to a great capital, such vandalism upon a thousand years of history.

Even as Napoleon occupied the Kremlin, fires had been discovered in a number of houses. The French authorities tried to put them out but discovered that all fire-fighting equipment had been deliberately withdrawn by the departing Russians. What they did not know was that the departing governor of Moscow, Count Feodor Rostopchin, almost certainly acting on the Tsar's direct orders, had left instructions to Russian police officers remaining in the capital, as well as professional incendiaries, many of them recently released from gaol, systematically to start fires throughout the Russian capital.

Initially, the French feared that their own drunken soldiers might be responsible for the arson. Then there were eyewitness reports of these professional fire-raisers, of the police stirring the flames with tarred lances, of howitzer shells being used to start conflagrations. The night after Napoleon arrived in the Kremlin, a string of elegant palaces caught fire, with the north wind driving the flames and sparks towards the Kremlin, which contained a huge cache of gunpowder. As dawn broke it was over a city bathed in flames and covered in dense columns of smoke.

Napoleon, now awake, was in a state of manic agitation. He exclaimed feverishly: 'What a tremendous spectacle! It is their own work! So many palaces! What extraordinary resolution! What men! These are indeed Scythians!' As he watched, the fires spread and crept even closer. Thousands of French soldiers began to stream out of the city while others were trapped and perished in the flames. Murat and de Beauharnais went to the Kremlin to urge the Emperor to leave. He refused to abandon the symbol of his conquest, the bejewelled and dazzling city that had been his hard-won prize and which was now being devoured by the flames before his eyes.

Soon it was reported that the Kremlin itself was on fire: it had been set alight in the tower which contained the arsenal by a policeman who was brought before Napoleon. He was promptly hauled off to be bayoneted: the order went out to shoot all incendiaries on sight. Napoleon at last decided to leave – too late, it seemed.

Ségur took up the story of how the Emperor himself nearly suffered the terrible fate of being consumed by the flames in the doomed capital.

We were encircled by a sea of fire which blocked up all the gates of the citadel and frustrated the first attempts that were made to depart. After some searching, we discovered a postern gate leading between the rocks to the Moskva. It was by this narrow passage that Napoleon, his officers and Guard, escaped from the Kremlin. But what had they gained by this movement? They had approached nearer to the fire and could neither retreat nor remain where they were; and how were they to advance? How force a passage through the waves of this ocean of flame? Those who had crossed the city, stunned by the tempest and blinded by the ashes, could not find their way, since the streets themselves were no longer distinguishable amidst smoke and ruins.

There was no time to be lost. The roaring of the flames around us became every moment more violent. A single narrow street, completely on fire, appeared to be rather the entrance than the exit to this hell. The Emperor rushed on foot without hesitation into this winding passage. He advanced amid the crackling of the flames, the crash of floors and the fall of burning timbers which tumbled around him. These ruins impeded his progress. The flames, which with a wild bellow consumed the buildings between which we were proceeding, spreading beyond the walls, were blown about by the wind and formed an arch over our heads.

We walked on a ground of fire, beneath a fiery sky and between two walls of fire. The intense heat burned our eyes, which we were nevertheless obliged to keep open and fixed on the danger. A consuming atmosphere parched our throats and rendered our breathing short and dry; and we were already almost suffocated by the smoke. Our hands were burned, either in attempting to protect our faces from the heat, or in brushing off the sparks which every moment covered and penetrated our clothes.

In this inexpressible distress and when a rapid advance seemed to be our only means of safety, our guide stopped in uncertainty and agitation. Here would probably have ended our adventurous career, had not some pillagers of I Corps recognized the Emperor amidst the whirling flames: they ran up and guided him towards the smoking ruins of a quarter which had been reduced to ashes in the morning.

Reaching safety at last, Napoleon gazed out over the Sodom destroyed not by act of God but by the deliberate act of one man – the very Russian Emperor whose capital it had been. 'The whole city appeared like a vast spume of fire rising in whistling eddies to the sky which it deeply coloured . . . This forebodes great misfortune to us,' he proclaimed, observing this biblical scene. He declared with a typically grandiose flourish that he would now march on St Petersburg – which was utterly impractical for his reduced, exhausted army, now denied the comforts and shelter of Moscow.

Napoleon desperately wrote a conciliatory letter to Alexander.

Monsieur Mon Frère:

The beautiful and splendid city of Moscow no longer exists. Rostopchin has burnt it down. Four hundred incendiaries have been caught in the act; all declared they were starting fires by order of the governor and of the chief of police: they were shot. The fire seems to have died out at last; three quarters of the houses have gone, a quarter remains. Such conduct is atrocious and aimless. Was the object to deprive us of a few resources? Well, those resources were in cellars that the fire did not reach. Even then the destruction of one of the most beautiful cities in the world, the work of centuries, for so slight an object, is inconceivable. If I supposed that such things were being done under the orders of Your Majesty, I should not write this letter; but I hold it impossible that any one with the high principles of Your Majesty, such heart, such right feelings, could have authorized these excesses, unworthy as they are of a great nation. I have conducted the war against Your Majesty with no animosity. A line written to me before or after the last battle would have stopped my march, and I would gladly have foregone the advantage of entering Moscow. If anything of our old friendship remains, Your Majesty will take this letter in good part. In any case I shall deserve thanks for rendering this account of what is happening in Moscow.

In that terrible act of self-immolation, the destruction of his own capital and the nation's heritage, the Tsar had turned the tables. Contemp-

tuously he declined to answer. The cold young man with the psychopathic personality would offer Napoleon no hope of peace: the self-destruction of Moscow had been his answer. Truly, the Frenchman was helpless against such an enemy as this.

Napoleon was left facing an appalling dilemma. He could hardly move on into the vast interior of Russia without endangering his army – and what anyway would be the objective – another city, another pile of ashes, another retreating Russian army? But with much of Moscow in ruins and deserted, there was soon likely to be a severe shortage of horses and such supplies as winter clothing for his men, although there was some food. Daru advised that he should stay in Moscow. Napoleon replied:

> Remain here, make one vast entrenched camp of Moscow and pass the winter in it. Here we might stay till the return of spring, when our reinforcements and all Lithuania in arms should come to relieve us and complete the conquest. This is a lion's counsel! But what would Paris say? What would they do there? What have they been doing for the last three weeks that they have not heard from me? Who knows what would be the effect of a suspension of communications for six months? No: France would not accustom itself to my absence and Prussia and Austria would take advantage of it.

It was in fact his main concern that his absence from Paris would encourage his enemies there to move against him, both within and without France. Daru's counsel was hopelessly unrealistic.

The man of decision, Napoleon, did nothing: he was thrown into a miasma of indecision. With every passing day the predicament of Napoleon's shrunken army amid the ruins of Moscow grew more precarious. To do nothing was not a neutral option: it was further to endanger his men.

His scant lines of communication, back to Smolensk were threatened by the emergence of peasant guerrillas who visited Peninsular-style atrocities upon the French soldiers they caught along the road: eventually Napoleon ordered that the French could only move in

force – a minimum of some 1,500 men – along that highway of death. Napoleon sought a guarantee from Kutuzov to desist from this barbaric method of warfare; he was rebuffed: 'It is difficult to control a people who for three hundred years have never known war within their frontiers, who are ready to immolate themselves for their country, and who are not susceptible to the distinction between what is and what is not the usage of civilized warfare.' Meanwhile Napoleon sent foraging expeditions southwards to provide for the army camped miserably in blackened Moscow, which was still burning. When the men set out in small groups, they were attacked by peasants. The Russians set fire to whole villages to deny them provisions.

Worst of all, Kutuzov was busily reinforcing his army. His 70,000-strong force was swollen to some 215,000 men by the soldiers of General Wittgenstein, recently reinforced from Finland, and by other troops from the south. Moscow was turning into a gigantic trap while Napoleon dithered. If Napoleon's army stayed much longer, it would be faced with slow starvation, complete encirclement and isolation from outside, dwindling as his men were picked off and eventually facing a far larger force than his own. Daru's counsel had indeed been madness.

Napoleon's best option after the burning of the city would have been to declare he had won a great victory by capturing the capital and to retire to winter quarters at Vitebsk, or perhaps across the Prussian border, declaring his honour satisfied, his troops undefeated and continuing to threaten Russia with a renewed offensive by a much strengthened French army the following spring. But having come so far and been deprived of the object of his dreams, Napoleon was now prey to delusions and indecision – the latter entirely untypical of him. He could not bear to abandon his charred and ruined prize, the pile of ashes that were all that remained of his triumph.

The surreal atmosphere of burned-out Moscow seemed to turn his mind. Ségur wrote:

> Scarcely a third of his army – and of that capital – now existed. But himself and the Kremlin were still standing. His renown was still

intact and he persuaded himself that those two great names, Napoleon and Moscow combined, would be sufficient to accomplish everything. He determined, therefore, to return to the Kremlin, which a battalion of his Guard had unfortunately preserved. The camps which he crossed on his way there presented an extraordinary sight. In the fields, amidst thick and cold mud, large fires were kept up with mahogany furniture, windows and gilded doors. Around these fires, on a damp straw, imperfectly sheltered by a few boards, were seen the soldiers and their officers, splashed all over with mud and blackened with smoke, seated in armchairs or reclined on silken couches. At their feet were spread or heaped cashmere shawls, the rarest furs of Siberia, the gold stuffs of Persia and silver dishes, off which they had nothing to eat but a black dough baked in the ashes and half-broiled and bloody horseflesh. A singular assemblage of abundance and want, of riches and filth, of luxury and wretchedness!

Amid this wreckage, Napoleon wrapped himself in false hopes. The destruction of Moscow, he said 'is no doubt a misfortune . . . But this misfortune is not without advantage. They have left us nothing but ruins, but at least we are quiet among them. Millions have no doubt slipped through our hands but how many thousand millions is Russia losing! Her commerce is ruined for a century to come. The nation is thrown back fifty years: this, of itself, is an important result. When the first moment of enthusiasm is passed, this reflection will fill them with consternation.' He alternated between ferocious and undignified outbursts of temper in front of his troops, sleepless nights in which he unburdened himself to his faithful Davout, huge meals, reading novels in a reclining position, and playing cards with the reliable de Beauharnais.

He despatched an envoy, Jacques-Alexandre Lauriston, to Alexander, with a litany of despair in his instructions: 'I want peace, I must have peace, I absolutely will have peace – only save my honour.' Kutuzov met Lauriston but refused to permit him to travel to St Petersburg to deliver the message to the Tsar. A Russian emissary took the message instead.

Alexander's contemptuous response was: 'Peace? My campaign is just beginning.' He did not trouble to reply. Alexander explained his

view: 'Let us vow redoubled courage and perseverance! The enemy is in deserted Moscow as in a tomb, without means of domination or even of existence. He entered Russia with 300,000 men of all countries, without union or any national or religious bond; he has lost half of them by the sword, famine and desertion: he has but the wreck of his army at Moscow. He is in the heart of Russia and not a single Russian is at his feet!'

The same hand that had burnt down his own capital city showed no inclination to display the slightest weakness towards his opponent. Napoleon lingered in Moscow for five fateful weeks, in a miasma of indecision, depression and wishful thinking, waiting for Alexander's reply which never came, while his enemies reinforced themselves around Moscow and the Russian winter inexorably approached.

In the event, this long and needless delay was to decide the fate of his men. The master of instant decisions and lightning manoeuvres was behaving like a befuddled old woman in the grip of hubris, unreality, uncertainty and fear. At times listless and inert, Napoleon seemed a spent force, the victim not the master of events. This was to change. But for the moment, the illusions of this conqueror of a city of ashes, this lord of the flies, were shattered.

Chapter 79

GENERAL WINTER

On 18 October, Murat, in command of the French forces probing south of Moscow for food under an armistice agreement, was shot at by a Cossack. Murat promptly abrogated the armistice, then realized that his men were dangerously exposed with the Cossacks to the left moving around them to cut them off. Attacking frontally and then engaging in a forced march to his rear, Murat nearly lost his force and 4,000 of his men were killed or wounded. Murat himself was wounded, Two generals perished and twelve cannon were taken. Murat rallied his forces and, with Poniatowski's cavalry coming to the rescue, the remainder of his men were saved. Hostilities had broken out again.

At last the inert Emperor realized that his position in Moscow was no longer tenable. He departed from the city the following day, ordering the rest of his army to follow and leaving behind Mortier with 200,000 pounds of gunpowder and orders to blow up the Kremlin. Following him there were 140,000 men and 50,000 horses, some 220 cannon and 2,000 wagons. It was, in Ségur's words, 'a caravan, a wandering nation or rather one of the armies of antiquity returning loaded with slaves and spoil after a great devastation'. The army was equipped with vast quantities of useless booty, dressed in splendid furs and fabrics, and already extremely ill-disciplined; yet it was a massive body of men and still a formidable fighting force. It boasted of having taken the enemy's capital and won a major battle. It was far from demoralized. It had no idea of the terrible fate that awaited, the horrors to come.

The retreat from Moscow had started. Deciding neither to stay in Moscow nor to march on St Petersburg, Napoleon had in fact belatedly decided on the right course of action – to march down to Kaluga a hundred miles further south in the rich heartland of Russia, which would allow him to circle westwards, plundering across prosperous territory towards Poland. It was to be a retreat, but one in which the army could sensibly reprovision itself and prepare for another campaign in the spring. This was also a strategy of some boldness, even representing an advance into Russia rather than a retreat.

Kutuzov's army, having marched eastwards on its withdrawal from Moscow had circled south and to the west, presumably to block a French march into these fertile areas. Napoleon was moving to confront him head on, thus recovering some of the *Grande Armée*'s tarnished glory. Napoleon's real intention was to bypass Kutuzov's base at Tarutino and enter the fertile region. If this move had succeeded the *Grande Armée* might have been reinvigorated and moved more or less intact back to the west to fight another day against the Russians. It was the right policy, the only possible exit from the colossal debacle of the burning of Moscow.

Heavy rains soon began to bog the French down. Much worse, Napoleon had failed to take the elementary precaution of sending forward a force to seize the one key bridge on his route south – that at the small, nondescript town of Maloyaroslavets, which commanded the vital river crossing over the Luzha. Although few have ever heard that mouthful of a name, it was to prove a far more decisive turning point than the huge and indecisive Battle of Borodino or the burning of Moscow itself: for it marked the point of no return for the French, the moment when the invasion of Russia turned from being a victory on points or at least a draw, to the most terrible, protracted defeat ever suffered by a great army. After Maloyaroslavets, a French victory was no longer possible, defeat inevitable.

Napoleon's army was discovered by General Docturev, one of Kutuzov's aides, by accident. He marched through the night to seize the little timber-framed town with a view to destroying the bridge, and there found a tiny French advance detachment on 23 October. The

fighting between the two small forces was vicious, with the town being burnt to the ground and exchanging hands no fewer than seven times that day. The heroes of the day were undoubtedly the Italians under Colonel Perladi, loyal to de Beauharnais, who with around 18,000 men stormed a Russian position overlooking the town manned by 50,000. Some 4,000 Italians were killed or wounded, but they were eventually triumphant.

Kutuzov's main army of 120,000 had by now had time to position itself further south to block the road to Kaluga. Napoleon, in blissful ignorance of what had transpired at that bloody river crossing, continued southwards himself – until he had his narrowest escape ever from either capture or death. For on the misty morning of 25 October, as he crossed the plain leading to the devastated town escorted by a few officers and his hospital and baggage wagons, he heard cries which he took to be the customary '*Vive l'Empereur!*' They were in fact the war cries of a force of 6,000 Cossacks.

Ségur described the outcome:

> When they had once started, they approached with such speed that Rapp had but just time to say to the Emperor, 'It is the Cossacks! Turn back!' The Emperor, whose eyes deceived him or who disliked running away, stood firm and was on the point of being surrounded, when Rapp seized the bridle of his horse and turned him round, crying, 'Indeed you must!' And really it was high time to fly, although Napoleon's pride would not allow him to do so. He drew his sword, Berthier and Rapp did the same; then placing themselves on the left side of the road, they waited the approach of the horde, from which they were scarcely forty paces distant. Rapp had barely time to turn himself round to face these barbarians, when the foremost of them thrust his lance into the chest of his horse with such force as to throw him down. The other aides-de-camp and a few troopers belonging to the Guard saved the General. This action, the bravery of Le Coulteux, the efforts of a score of officers and chasseurs and, above all, the thirst of these barbarians for plunder, saved the Emperor. And yet they needed only to have stretched out their hands and seized him, for at the same moment the horde, in

crossing the highroad, overthrew everything before them: horses, men and carriages, wounding and killing some and dragging them into the woods for the purpose of plundering them; then, loosing the horses harnessed to the guns, they took them along with them across country. But they only had a momentary victory, a triumph of surprise. The cavalry of the guard galloped up; at this sight they let go their prey and fled and this torrent subsided: leaving indeed melancholy traces but abandoning all that it was hurrying away in its course.

This attack seemed totally to demoralize Napoleon, already a shadow of his former self after the burning of Moscow and the decision to withdraw. The Emperor had never been accused of lack of courage in the past. Now he summoned his generals to a peasant's hut and there Murat, sometimes hotheaded, often treacherous, but always bold and far-sighted, passionately urged upon Napoleon the need to march forward to Kaluga.

Napoleon, his fighting spirit seemingly spent, argued that the time for confrontation was past: the purpose of the march was to save the army. In fact Murat was doubly right, although he did not know it, for at that precise moment, Kutuzov, reeling from the defeat at Maloyaroslavets, had decided to retire southwards to draw his forces up for another Borodino. Napoleon, fatefully, remained timid and decided to retreat from Kutuzov's main force northwards back towards the main road from Moscow to Smolensk down which his army had passed just months before on its approach to Moscow.

It was the single most catastrophic decision of that whole misguided campaign: for it signalled to the world that Napoleon's army was indeed retreating, returning the way it had come, avoiding any further clash with the Russian army of which, it appeared, it was afraid. It handed the initiative to Kutuzov: all he now needed to do was to prevent the French army veering off into the fertile south while harassing its flanks and rearguard; and Napoleon's route would lead the French across territory that had already been stripped bare by two armies – the Russians and the French – only weeks before, and was now not only barren of supplies and food, its villages and towns

sacked, but inhabited by a bitter and intensely resentful predatory peasantry.

The return to the Smolensk road could hardly have been grimmer for the French: they reached it just above the desolate battlefield of Borodino. Ségur described the terrible scene that awaited them:

> After passing the river Kologa we marched on, absorbed in thought, when some of us, raising our eyes, uttered an exclamation of horror. Each instantly looked around him and beheld a plain bare and devastated, all the trees cut down within a few feet from the surface; and farther off craggy hills, the highest of which appeared to be the most misshapen. It had all the appearance of an extinguished volcano. The ground was covered all round with fragments of helmets and cuirasses, broken drums, gunstocks, tatters of uniforms and standards stained with blood. On this desolate spot lay 30,000 half-devoured corpses. A number of skeletons, left on the summit of one of the hills, overlooked the whole. It seemed as if here Death had fixed his empire. It was that terrible redoubt, the conquest and the grave of Caulaincourt. Presently the cry, 'It is the field of the great battle!' formed a long and doleful murmur. The Emperor passed quickly. Nobody stopped. Cold, hunger and the enemy urged us on. We merely turned our faces as we proceeded to take a last melancholy look at the vast grave of so many companions-in-arms, uselessly sacrificed and whom we were obliged to leave behind.

A French soldier was found alive who had been living for fifty days inside the carcass of a horse, which had provided him with food and shelter. The hospital in the abbey at Kolotskoi nearby was hardly more cheerful. Napoleon ordered the wounded to be placed on his wagons, filled with the plunder from Moscow. However the unscrupulous wagoneers threw out many of the wounded at the first opportunity rather than lose their plunder.

The French retreat became drawn out and straggled along the road, offering a tempting target for attack by forces under the vigorous Russian General Miloradovich, who inflicted some 4,000 casualties in a

series of attacks. He might have broken the column had Kutuzov ordered a general attack; but the commander-in-chief was content with harassing the French.

On 6 November the deadliest enemy yet made its appearance – one that might have been avoided altogether had Napoleon made his mind up to leave Moscow earlier. After several days of unseasonably fine weather, Ségur described a sinister fog which descended:

These fogs became thicker and presently an immense cloud descended upon it in large flakes of snow. It seemed as if the very sky was falling and joining the earth and our enemies to complete our destruction. All objects changed their appearance and became confused, not to be recognized again. We proceeded without knowing where we were, without perceiving the point to which we were bound. Everything was transformed into an obstacle. While the soldiers were struggling with the tempest of wind and snow, the flakes, driven by the storm, lodged and accumulated in every hollow: their surfaces concealed unknown abysses, which treacherously opened beneath our feet. There men were engulfed and the weakest, resigning themselves to their fate, found a grave in these snow-pits.

Those who followed turned aside but the storm drove into their faces both the snow that was falling from the sky and that which it raised from the ground. It seemed bent on opposing their progress. The Russian winter, under this new form, attacked them on all sides: it penetrated their light garments and their torn shoes and boots; their wet clothes froze upon their bodies; an icy envelope encased them and stiffened their limbs; a keen and violent wind broke their breathing

The unfortunate creatures still crawled on, shivering, till the snow, gathering like balls under their feet or the fragment of some broken article – a branch of a tree or the bodies of one of their comrades – caused them to stumble and fall. There they groaned in vain. The snow soon covered them. Small heaps marked the spot where they lay: such was their only grave! The road was studded

with these mounds, like a cemetery. The most intrepid and the most indifferent were unaffected: they passed on quickly with averted looks. But before them, around them, there was nothing but snow. This immense and dreary uniformity extended farther than the eye could reach. The imagination was astounded! It was like a vast winding-sheet which Nature had thrown over the army. The only objects not enveloped by it were some gloomy pines – trees of the tomb with their funereal colours and dismal look – which completed the doleful appearance of a general mourning and of an army dying, amidst a nature already dead.

Three days after the first snows had fallen, the bedraggled army arrived at Smolensk: some 6,000 horses had died. Many had been so numbed by cold that they did not flee as slices were taken off their haunches for food by the starving men behind them.

Much of the booty from Moscow had been dumped as men sought desperately to survive and could carry nothing. Many freezing in their light summer apparel ripped clothes off the bodies of dead comrades or wrapped themselves in the furs they had plundered. Napoleon himself decided to walk so as not to succumb to frostbite in his carriage. At Smolensk, however, they found another desolate and ruined city whose stores had largely been exhausted by previous army detachments.

After just four days in the freezing and stricken city, Napoleon ordered its evacuation. He had only 40,000 ill-disciplined men left out of the 100,000 that had left Moscow twenty-five days before. Some 350 wagons – more than half the remaining total – had had to be abandoned. Behind the army were some 60,000 stragglers and hangers-on, a wretched torrent of humanity moving at the speed of a glacier. Napoleon ordered his men to leave in batches – Junot and Poniatowski between 12 and 13 November, the Emperor himself with the Imperial Guard the following day, de Beauharnais on the 15th, and Davout and Ney on the 16th. Ney was ordered to spike the abandoned guns, blow up the remaining ammunition, as well as what was left of the town and city walls, and drive the stragglers before him.

By this means Napoleon sought to impose some order on the retreat.

Instead he merely extended this immense column of misery, making it still more vulnerable to attack. The next milestone along this awesome calvary of human suffering was Krasnoi, where a Russian force under Miloradovich was waiting in ambush along the road to the town. The Russian general permitted the main force under Napoleon to pass, then straddled the road, blocking de Beauharnais. The latter briefly attempted to break through, then marched at night around the Russian force, reaching Krasnoi with just 4,000 survivors.

There Napoleon's troops had repulsed Kutuzov's main force. Napoleon sent a force back to rescue Davout, who had similarly run into Miloradovich's ambush. Of Ney's rearguard there was nothing to be seen, and Napoleon took the agonizing decision to press ahead and abandon his old comrade. With Vitebsk along the old road ahead having fallen into Russian hands, Napoleon was forced to take a more southerly route via Orsha towards Minsk, only to learn that that city too had fallen to the Russians. Napoleon reached Orsha on 19 November with just 6,000 of his original 35,000 Imperial Guard, Eugène de Beauharnais with 2,000 men out of his 42,000 and Davout with 4,000 out of his 70,000-strong army. The mighty *Grande Armée* had been eaten away by attack and by the cold to a mere skeleton.

At last Napoleon, after crossing the Dnieper, found some provisions and rest. The appalling atrocities that had been meted out on those captured by the Russians or seized by bands of marauding Cossacks and peasants exceeded the danger posed by the weather to the French army. Prisoners had been stripped and beaten, stakes rammed down their throats, their arms and their legs were cut off.

Sir Robert Wilson, a British military adviser to the Russian army, reported such atrocities as the burial of some fifty French soldiers alive, the burning of some fifty others, and the brains being beaten out of others as peasants danced about them singing folkloric songs. Wilson wrote: 'The naked masses of dead and dying men; the mangled carcasses of 10,000 horses which had in some cases been cut for food before life had ceased; the craving of famine at other points forming groups of cannibals; the air enveloped in flame and smoke; the prayers of hundreds of naked wretches flying from the peasantry, whose shouts of vengeance echoed incessantly through the woods; the wrecks of

cannon, powder-wagons, all stores of every description: it formed such a scene as probably was never witnessed in the history of the world.'

The temperature had now fallen to −30°C. With only eight hours of daylight left, Napoleon made his men march at night for six further hours each evening. The supply of horse meat was now virtually consumed. Men took to eating their dead comrades to survive. Napoleon wrote to his foreign minister Hugues-Bernard Maret laconically of the conditions, abandoning his previous unbridled optimism: 'Since my last letter to you our situation has become worse. Ice and frost of near zero have killed off nearly all our horses, say 30,000. We have been compelled to burn nearly 300 pieces of artillery, and an immense quantity of transport wagons. The cold has greatly increased the number of stragglers. The Cossacks have turned to account our absolute want of cavalry and of artillery to harass us and cut our communications, so that I am most anxious about Marshal Ney, who stayed behind with 3,000 men to blow up Smolensk.'

There followed the two truly heroic episodes of the expedition, which allowed the French to salvage a modicum of national pride amid this ever deepening disaster.

Chapter 80

NEY'S ESCAPE

Michel Ney was a man of striking appearance with fiery red hair, possessed of utter fearlessness, if limited intelligence. He obeyed Napoleon's order almost too long, staying on in Smolensk with his 6,000-strong rearguard and twelve guns to delay the Russian advance and protect the main French force with its moving township of stragglers. He found himself cut off by Kutuzov's main army of 80,000 men.

An officer was sent by the Russians to negotiate the seemingly inevitable surrender but even as this happened the ill-disciplined Russian troops opened fire on the French. Ney declared furiously to the officer: 'A marshal never surrenders. There is no parleying under fire. You are my prisoner.' Ney ordered his vanguard to attack down a ravine and up the other side against the tens of thousands of astonished Russians: and was repulsed.

Ney took charge himself, personally leading three thousand men into a frontal assault. This time they reached the Russian front line but were blocked by a second massed rank of Russian troops and forced back across the ravine, which the Russians did not dare cross to attack them. His remaining men now faced the Russian army along the road which similarly held back from attacking, believing the French to be stronger than they were. Instead a huge artillery barrage opened up on the French position, to which Ney's six remaining guns bravely if feebly responded.

To the consternation of his men, Ney ordered a return to Smolensk: the last thing they wanted was to withdraw back further into Russia.

On the way Ney saw a ravine with a stream at the bottom: concluding that this must lead to the Dnieper, he decided to follow it, with the help of a peasant guide, reasoning that his men would be safe if they could cross the great river. Ségur described the subsequent appalling, heroic story:

> At last, about eight o'clock, after passing through a village, the ravine ended and the peasant, who walked first, halted and pointed to the river. They imagined that this must have been between Syrokorenia and Gusinoë. Ney and those immediately behind him ran up to it. They found the river sufficiently frozen to bear their weight; the course of the ice which it bore along being thwarted by a sudden turn in its banks, the winter had completely frozen it over at that spot: both above and below, its surface was still moving.
>
> This observation was enough to make their first sensation of joy give way to uneasiness. This hostile river might only offer a deceitful appearance. One officer committed himself for the rest: he crossed to the other side with great difficulty, returned, and reported that the men and perhaps some of the horses might pass over; but that the rest must be abandoned; and there was no time to lose, as the ice was beginning to give way because of the thaw.
>
> But in this nocturnal and silent march across fields, of a column composed of weakened and wounded men and women with their children, they had been unable to keep close enough to prevent their separating in the darkness. Ney realized that only a part of his people had come up. Nevertheless, he might have surmounted the obstacle, thereby securing his own safety, and waited on the other side. The idea never entered his mind. Someone proposed it to him but he rejected it instantly. He allowed three hours for the rallying, and without suffering himself to be disturbed by impatience or the danger of waiting so long, he wrapped himself up in his cloak and passed the time in a deep sleep on the bank of the river.
>
> At last, about midnight, the passage began. But the first persons who ventured on the ice called out that it was bending under them; that it was sinking; that they were up to their knees in water:

immediately after which that frail support was heard splitting with frightful cracks, as in the breaking up of a frost. All halted in alarm.

Ney ordered them to pass one at a time. They advanced with caution, not knowing in the darkness if they were putting their feet on the ice or into a chasm: for there were places where they were obliged to clear large cracks and jump from one piece of ice to another, at the risk of falling between them and disappearing for ever. The first hesitated but those who were behind kept calling to them to make haste.

When at last, after several of these dreadful panics, they reached the opposite bank and fancied themselves saved, a vertical slope, entirely covered with rime, again opposed their landing. Many were thrown back upon the ice, which they broke in their fall or which bruised them. By their account, this Russian river appeared only to have contributed with regret to their escape.

But what seemed to affect them with the greatest horror was the distraction of the females and the sick, when it became necessary to abandon, along with all the baggage, the remains of their fortune, their provisions, and, in short, their whole resources against the present and the future. They saw them stripping themselves, selecting, throwing away, taking up again and falling with exhaustion and grief upon the frozen bank of the river. They seemed to shudder again at the recollection of the horrible sight of so many men scattered over that abyss, the continual noise of persons falling, the cries of such as sank in, and, above all, the wailing and despair of the wounded who, from their carts, stretched out their hands to their companions and begged not to be left behind.

Their leader then determined to attempt the passage of several wagons loaded with these poor creatures; but in the middle of the river the ice sank down and separated. Then were heard, proceeding from the abyss, cries of anguish long and piercing; then stifled, feeble groans and at last an awful silence. All had disappeared!

Only 3,000 soldiers and some 3,000 stragglers made it across: as many again had been lost on the march and in the crossing.

The survivors trooped through the night to a village called Gusinoë which, astonishingly, was well-provisioned and whose wooden houses

provided a desperately needed respite. But even as they rested, a force of some 6,000 Cossacks under General Platov appeared from the woods, threatening them. Ney ordered his men to pull out of their shelters and ruthlessly placed the stragglers between his soldiers and the enemy, which now opened up with light artillery.

For two days the two forces marched in parallel along the banks of the Dnieper, the 1,500 remaining Frenchmen being shadowed by the 6,000 Cossacks. Suddenly a blaze of musketry and artillery opened up on the French from a wood; but Ney ordered his men to charge directly into the fire and the Cossacks withdrew. The French crossed another smaller river in single file under Cossack fire: but Ney again attacked the enemy. They moved further south the following day. De Beauharnais at last came out of Orsha to give them a safe escort for the last few miles. Napoleon jumped for joy when he heard Ney had been saved. 'I have then saved my eyes. I would have given 300 million from my treasury sooner than have lost such a man.'

In spite of this good news and the rest being obtained by the French at Orsha, a deadly trap was now being set. Admiral Chichagov, who had taken Minsk, was now determined finally to annihilate the French: he intended to seize and destroy the single bridge across the Berezina at Borisov ahead of the French forces. The French had already burnt the bridges across the Dnieper behind them. Napoleon's vanguard from Minsk had travelled to Borisov in an attempt to secure the bridge, meeting up with other French, Polish and German troops.

On 21 November these forces faced an overwhelming Russian army. Although fighting furiously, they were finally forced to retreat back down towards the remnants of the *Grande Armée* at Orsha. From there Napoleon had set out through blinding snow which had turned the roads into a quagmire. When he learnt of the capture of Borisov, Napoleon exclaimed loudly, looking upward: 'Is it then written above that he would now commit nothing but faults?' He ordered his remaining cavalry forward on the few horses that had not been eaten or died, in a 'sacred squadron' which was to act as a personal body-guard. It seems clear that he believed the end was near, both for his army and for himself, and he intended to die fighting.

Oudinot, without Napoleon's knowledge, was out with a foraging party and surprised the Russians at Borisov, driving them over the bridge across the Berezina; but Oudinot was powerless to prevent the town being burnt down. The French were trapped. Then came a glimmer of hope: a ford had been discovered across the huge river, which was normally at this time of year frozen over but was now a vast flowing stream bearing huge blocks of ice. This was at Studzianka, where the river was only six feet deep; the ford was some 100 yards across.

Both Oudinot's men and Marshal Victor, who had been driven back by the Russian General Wittgenstein in the north, arrived to reinforce Napoleon: these relatively fresh troops were appalled to witness the pitiable state of Napoleon's *Grande Armée*. Ségur wrote

> When instead of that grand column which had conquered Moscow, its soldiers saw behind Napoleon only a train of spectres covered with rags, female pelisses, pieces of carpet or dirty cloaks – half burnt and riddled by fire – and with nothing on their feet but rags of all sorts, their consternation was extreme. They looked terrified at the sight of those unfortunate soldiers, as they filed before them with lean carcasses, faces black with dirt and hideous bristly beards, unarmed, shameless, marching confusedly with their heads bent, their eyes fixed on the ground and silent, like a troop of captives. But what astonished them more than all was to see the number of colonels and generals scattered about and isolated, who seemed only occupied about themselves, thinking of nothing but saving the wrecks of their property or their persons. They were marching pell-mell with the soldiers, who did not notice them, to whom they no longer had any commands to give, and of whom they had nothing to expect: all ties between them being broken and all distinction of ranks obliterated by the common misery.

Napoleon was grateful to be reinforced by the two small flanking armies: his own had been reduced from 100,000 to 7,000 men, perhaps one of the most terrible rates of attrition in history, without suffering a single defeat. Victor had 15,000 men and Oudinot 5,000. But there

were still 40,000 stragglers, refugees, women, children and wounded following behind.

Oudinot embarked upon a brilliant piece of deception, sending stragglers to other fords down the river to give the illusion that the French would attempt to cross there. Fortunately, General Eble had refused to carry out Napoleon's order to destroy all heavy equipment, and he had saved six wagons' worth of bridging equipment. On the night of 25 November, Napoleon ordered him to build two 300-foot bridges across the Berezina to connect with the causeway across the extensive marshes on the other side.

It was a fantastically risky and arduous operation, made possible only because the bulk of the Russian forces had left the west bank to face what they believed would be the main crossing place further south. The bridges were erected some 200 yards apart, supported by twenty-three trestles. They were connected by sappers doing fifteen-minute shifts during the freezing night in the icy waters, which was all they could sustain; many were swept away and drowned or died of exposure. Only forty of the 400 'pontonniers' who built the bridge survived. Sergeant Bourgogne described the scene: 'We saw the brave pontonniers working hard at the bridges for us to cross. They had worked all night, standing up to their shoulders in ice-cold waters, encouraged by their general. These brave men sacrificed their lives to save the army. One of my friends told me as a fact that he had seen the Emperor himself handing wine to them.'

In spite of these valiant efforts, Napoleon believed the end was imminent. With the Russian artillery across the river, it would take only a few lucky artillery shots to destroy the bridges: the causeway across the marshes was equally vulnerable. The big Russian armies were anyway closing in from all sides – the east, the north and the south. Kutuzov to the east had 80,000 men, Wittgenstein to the north 30,000 and across the river Tchaplitz had 35,000. To the south Chichagov had 27,000. Even reinforced by Oudinot and Victor, the French had just 40,000 and 40,000 stragglers. Yet Kutuzov was still some thirty kilometres away, involved in the hunt for Ney's small force, while both Wittgenstein and Chichagov hesitated, the latter deflected by

reports that the French would cross to the south. Astonishingly, on 26 November, Tchaplitz's division withdrew to the south, making possible a crossing of the river.

Napoleon seized his chance. Using rafts, he had 400 men transported across the river to seize the opposite bank as a bridgehead and clear it of the few remaining Cossacks. At 1 p.m. the infantry bridge was completed and at 4 p.m. the artillery and wagon bridge was finished. The following day Napoleon crossed over with the Guard. The stragglers were told to cross at night, but many instead preferred to take shelter in the village of Studzianka on the east bank. It proved a fatal mistake. That same night a French division blundered in a blizzard into the Russian lines and 4,000 men were killed or captured.

By the night of the 28th the three Russian armies had converged on the east bank in force, launching a ferocious artillery barrage against the French rearguard commanded by Victor, Ney and Oudinot. Ney, fearless as ever, led a charge and inflicted some 2,000 casualties on the Russians. But there were far too many even for him – a total of 60,000 men already, being supported by Kutuzov's 80,000-strong army, compared with the remaining 18,000 French soldiers and the 40,000 stragglers and civilians.

While this desperate rearguard action was taking place, pandemonium broke out on the bridges: the artillery bridge broke and those in front were pushed into the freezing river, while those behind fought to get back against the press of refugees and on to the other bridge. Many of the civilians scrambled down the banks of the river and tried to swim across, grasping at the sides of the pontoons before being swept away. Ségur wrote:

> There was also, at the exit of the bridge, on the other side, a bog into which many horses and carriages had sunk, a circumstances which again embarrassed and slowed the clearance. Then it was, that in that column of desperadoes, crowded together on that single plank of safety, there arose a wicked struggle, in which those in weakest and worst situation were thrown in to the river by the strongest. The latter, without turning their heads and hurried away by the instinct of self-preservation, pushed on towards the goal with fury, regardless

of the cries of rage and despair uttered by their companions or their officers, whom they had thus sacrificed . . . Above the first passage, while the young Lauriston threw himself into the river in order to execute the orders of his sovereign more promptly, a little boat, carrying a mother and her two children, was upset and sank under the ice. An artilleryman, who was struggling like the others on the bridge to open a passage for himself, saw the accident. All at once, forgetting himself, he threw himself into the river and, by great exertion, succeeded in saving one of the three victims: it was the youngest of the two children. The poor little thing kept calling for his mother with cries of despair and the brave artilleryman was heard telling him not to cry, that he had not saved him from the water merely to desert him on the bank; that he should want for nothing; that he would be his father and his family.

At half past eight in the morning the French set fire to the bridge to prevent the Russians crossing:

> The disaster had reached its utmost bounds. A multitude of carriages and of cannon, several thousand men, women and children, were abandoned on the hostile bank. They were seen wandering in desolate groups on the bank of the river. Some threw themselves into it in order to swim across; others ventured themselves on the pieces of ice which were floating along; some there were also who threw themselves headlong into the flames of the burning bridge, which sank under them: burnt and frozen at one and the same time, they perished under two opposite punishments. Shortly after, the bodies of all sorts were seen collecting together against the trestles of the bridge. The rest awaited the Russians.

Some 20,000 French soldiers had perished along with around 35,000 civilians. Some 10,000 Russians had also been killed.

In what had been one of the most terrible scenes in history, the French army escaped a seemingly complete destruction and survived with around half its previous strength. French pride had been saved by those heroic bridgebuilders, nine-tenths of whom had perished, just as

the skippers of small boats would rescue British pride at Dunkirk more than a century later.

Oudinot, one of the heroes of the battle, who had been wounded, was evacuated to a village at Plechenitzi; there he and his small force were surprised by some 500 Cossacks: the marshal, his wound dressed, ran out of the house brandishing two pistols to join the Italian General Pino. With seven or eight men they fought off their Russian attackers, including cannonfire, before being rescued.

The following week's march by the rump of the *Grande Armée* was eased by far fewer Russian attacks: Kutuzov seemed to draw back on the eastern side of the Berezina, preferring not to pursue. But the cold weather now returned in all its ferocity. Thousands more died in the cold, falling in the snow or simply not rising in the morning. By 2 December, as Napoleon limped into Moldechno, there were only 13,000 men remaining – around a thirteenth of the original army.

Chapter 81

NAPOLEON'S FLIGHT TO PARIS

Napoleon now had to make a fateful decision, for which he was forever to be criticized, and even lampooned as a coward. Unlike most others in this disastrous, ill-conceived campaign, it was probably the correct one. He decided to abandon his army. His reason was simple: he had to get back to France, protect his position there, and rally his empire. He had done all he could to bring his men to safety out of the disastrous Russian expedition: now there were more pressing matters.

He had lost a campaign, but not a war, still less his mighty empire, which required his attention. He appeared to be a captain leaving a sinking ship; but he was the Emperor of two-thirds of Europe. No one could accuse him of being a coward; he had accompanied the *Grande Armée* through all its rigours. Now that he believed this depleted force was safe from the Russians, he could no longer remain with it. He turned out to be wrong – his army was not yet out of danger; but he can be forgiven for not foreseeing that. He wrestled with the problem of whom to leave in charge, settling eventually for the authoritarian Murat rather than the loyal and able de Beauharnais and leaving behind, against his protests, his chief of staff Berthier to co-ordinate the army. He took with him the loyal Duroc, and his wisest councillor, Louis de Caulaincourt, brother of Auguste who had perished at the Great Redoubt. Napoleon and his entourage left in three carriages into hostile territory, travelling incognito, on 5 December.

As the Emperor departed, the valiant Ney fought a furious action at Moldechno alongside Victor, driving the Russians out of the village. The same day as Napoleon departed, temperatures plunged to

−37.5°C. Ségur described it: 'The very day after Napoleon's departure the sky showed a still more dreadful appearance. You might see icy particles floating in the air; birds fell from it quite stiff and frozen. The atmosphere was motionless and silent: it seemed as if everything which possessed life and movement in nature – the wind itself – had been seized, chained and, as it were, frozen by a universal death.'

Heinrich Rossier wrote: 'Lack of sound and suitable footwear cost thousands of lives. In many cases extremities simply broke off, in others fingers and toes, and often whole arms and legs had to be amputated. Thousands more dropped by the wayside.' Marbot wrote: 'One of the stoutest and bravest officers in my regiment was so distracted by what he had seen in the last few days that he laid himself down on the snow and no persuasions being able to make him rise, died there. Many soldiers of all ranks blew out their brains to put an end to their misery.'

The very horses were vivisected. Auguste Thirion wrote: 'It was too cold to kill and cut up those we destined for our rations; our hands, exposed for so long to the cold air, would have refused to perform this service . . . So we cut a slice from the quarters of the horses still on their feet and walking, and the wretched animals gave not the least sign of pain, proving beyond doubt the degree of numbness . . . caused by the extreme cold.' When they found a village they simply pulled down the houses and burnt the wood to heat themselves. Soldiers contracted gangrene by standing too close to the fires. To feed themselves the soldiers did not just indulge in cannibalism but cut off their fingers to drink their own blood.

At last the remnants of the *Grande Armée* commanded by Murat covered the miles to Vilnius, reaching it on 9 December. Of the 60,000 altogether that crossed the Berezina, soldier and civilian and the 20,000 that had since joined the march, some 40,000 died in those days of intense cold. Arriving at Vilnius Murat allowed his men to shelter and help themselves to provisions. But he quietly departed, leaving Ney as usual to command the rearguard.

Further atrocities followed. According to Ségur:

> It is true that the Lithuanians, although we had compromised them
> so much and were now abandoning them, received into their houses

and assisted several; but the Jews, whom we had protected, repelled the others. They did even more: the sight of so many sufferers excited their avarice. Had their greed been content with speculating upon our miseries and selling us some meagre supplies for their weight in gold, history would scorn to sully her pages with the disgusting detail; but they enticed our wounded men into their houses, stripped them, and on seeing the Russians, threw the naked bodies of these dying victims from the doors and windows of their houses into the streets and left them to perish of cold.

On 10 December Ney left Vilnius with his rearguard of 2,000 which soon shrank to just 500 men, and then to none at all – Ney having to ride for his life to escape. On 13 December Ney finally reached the borders of the Russian empire to join with the disorganized rabble of what was left of the *Grande Armée* at Kovno. The French had been almost annihilated: the Russians had not fared all that much better during the winter, with Kutuzov's army reduced from its original 120,000 men to around 35,000 and Wittgenstein's from 50,000 to 15,000.

Ney was left at this last outpost with just 700 men to face the Russians and on 14 December defended the last parcel of Russian territory before entering Poland. With thirty men he fought his way across the town to the crossing of the Niemen: he was one of the very last to cross. Ségur captured the pathos of the end of the great expedition to Russia:

> Some there were, however, who, on their arrival on the Allied bank of the Niemen, turned round: there, when they cast a look on that land of suffering from which they were escaping, when they found themselves on the same spot where, five months previously, their countless eagles had taken their victorious flight, it is said that tears flowed from their eyes and that they uttered cries of grief. This then was the bank which they had studded with their bayonets! This the country which had disappeared only five months before under the steps of an immense united army and seemed to them to be metamorphosed into moving hills and valleys of men and horses! These

were the same valleys from which, under the rays of a burning sun, poured forth the three long columns of dragoons and cuirassiers, resembling three rivers of glittering iron and brass. And now men, arms, horses – the sun itself and even this frontier river, which they had crossed filled with enthusiasm and hope – all have disappeared. The Niemen is now only a long mass of ice, caught and chained by the increasing severity of the winter. Instead of the three French bridges, a Russian bridge is alone standing. Finally, in the place of these innumerable warriors, of their 400,000 comrades who had been so often their partners in victory and who had dashed forward with such joy and pride into the territory of Russia, they saw issuing from these pale and frozen deserts only 1,000 infantry and horsemen still under arms, nine cannon and 20,000 miserable wretches covered with rags. This was the whole of the *Grande Armée!*

Murat continued his retreat with around 15,000 men to Gumbinnen, sixty miles to the west of Kovno. Here he summoned a council of war and advocated withdrawal to Königsberg: he was now openly mutinous towards Napoleon, whom he called a madman whom no nation in Europe could rely upon or conclude treaties with.

Murat soon learnt that the army of Marshal MacDonald in the north which had been holding Riga had returned to Tilsit; and that General von Yorck, the Prussian commander, had negotiated a peace agreement with the Russians to extricate his 18,000 men without further difficulty: this excited the Prussian people, chafing under years of French domination. Murat, horrified by Yorck's defection, continued his withdrawal towards the river Oder, still pursued by some 40,000 troops under Kutuzov. On 17 January he decided to abandon his command, taking fast horses to his capital of Naples, which he reached on 13 January.

Eugène de Beauharnais was left to command the remaining troops on their retreat to the river Elbe, even as Kaiser Frederick William of Prussia chose this moment to join Alexander of Russia in the crusade against Napoleon at the Convention of Kalisch on 28 February. With the crossing of the Elbe the war was over: all but some 10,000 of a total army of more than 400,000 which had crossed into Russia had perished

there, 100,000 of them as Russian prisoners of war. The Russians for their part had lost some 450,000 casualties. It was the highest casualty rate and most horrific loss recorded in human history so far; in a campaign that had lasted only nine months. (Casualties in the Peninsular War extended over a six-year period.) To all intents and purposes, Napoleon's army had been annihilated.

Napoleon's Russian war had been the most ironic of all his military adventures. It was the only one which he had entered reluctantly, provoked by the other side. He had been prodded almost beyond measure by Alexander. During its course he had committed a staggering succession of errors entirely atypical of the once great, if far from infallible, general. At every stage he could have extricated himself with fewer losses than he was to suffer as a result of plunging deeper into the mire.

He could have stopped at Vitebsk or Smolensk. He could have saved himself by withdrawing immediately from Moscow after its immolation and returned before the winter set in. Finally and most disastrously, he could have followed up the taking of Maloyaroslavets and moved to Kaluga. He was to display overweening boldness and swagger before the Battle of Borodino – then only caution and timidity. It is fair to say that he exuded none of his old flair for leadership or genius in war either on the way into Russia or on the way out; virtually every decision was a mistake, usually taken against the angry advice of his own marshals. The campaign had been a terrible self-inflicted wound; the heroes of the Russian campaign had been Ney, Caulaincourt, Oudinot, Davout, de Beauharnais and last but not least the bridgebuilders across the Berezina – but not Napoleon. The campaign had been founded on a single mistake: that the Russians would negotiate. He complete underestimated the implacability of the Russian character and the callow Tsar he had flattered and thought he had befriended at Tilsit.

Most historians of the Napoleonic War have traced the downfall of Napoleon from the Russian disaster. But this is mistaken on two counts: first, the Peninsular War, extending over several years, had been possibly an even greater defeat for French arms, although the

personal prestige of the Emperor was not so involved as he wisely kept away. Second, the superman more than forty years old who had apparently gone to seed, become plump and inert and preferred to surround himself with sycophants rather than accept criticism, seemed to rejuvenate himself and return to the almost manic vigour of his earlier years after the Russian campaign had ended.

In adversity, Napoleon was suddenly to recover himself; the impossible legend of infallibility had been destroyed forever. Now he had to show he could recover and that, although merely mortal, he was still a commander of energy and skill. Fight back he did, displaying a ferocity none expected and in a manner that could have protected his throne and extended his domination of Europe for years to come. Russia had dealt him a huge blow, but not a mortal one. The sheer speed of his recovery was to take all his enemies by surprise.

The fightback had begun with his decision to abandon the tattered remnants of the *Grande Armée* and travel to Paris at the fastest possible speed. The journey of 1,400 miles was itself an epic. His three carriages were accompanied at first by an escort of 600 Poles and Neapolitans, almost all of whom perished from cold on the first leg of the journey. He narrowly avoided capture at Osmania, when a Russian force took the town an hour after he had left. Reaching Vilna in temperatures of 37°C, pretending to be the diplomat Louis de Caulaincourt's secretary, the latter had to bang on the windows of storekeepers to obtain supplies.

The Emperor now had to travel on a sledge alone with Caulaincourt and a few outriders – a far cry from the extravagant splendour of his last visit. Caulaincourt took advantage to lecture the Emperor about his oppressive policies and high taxes: the night before, Napoleon, half frozen, had reminisced erratically and contemplated the possibility that they might be captured by the Prussians and exhibited in an iron cage.

At Dresden on 14 December, where just eight months before this King of Kings had presided over the most glittering convocation of courts ever assembled in homage to him, Caulaincourt had to bang on the door for directions from a local doctor, and was rebuffed. Napoleon remarked: 'Between the sublime and the ridiculous there is but one step.' He told Caulaincourt: 'I am a reasonable being, who does no

more than he thinks will profit him. As for the catastrophic outcome of the campaign, we are victims of the climate. The fine weather tricked me. If I had set out a fortnight sooner, my army would be at Vitebsk and I should be laughing at the Russians and your prophet Alexander . . . Everything turned out badly because I stayed too long at Moscow . . . all will be retrieved within three months.' They were at last in friendly territory: the King of Saxony let him have a good coach, and it took only five more days to reach Paris at nearly midnight on 18 December.

The wretched-looking Caulaincourt found it impossible to get the guards to admit him into the Tuileries. 'The porter, who had gone to bed, came out with a lamp in his hand and dressed only in his shirt, to see who was knocking. Our faces looked so strange to him that he called his wife. I had to repeat my name three or four times over before I could persuade them to open the door. Meanwhile, a crowd of footmen and ladies-in-waiting had gathered and proceeded to gape at Napoleon from head to foot, until eventually the penny dropped: "It's the Emperor!" one of them shouted . . . They could scarcely contain themselves.'

Napoleon's reaction to disaster was entirely in character: he staged parties to celebrate the Russian expedition as though it had been a triumph; had not the French captured Moscow itself? This was a mistake, for the disaster could not be concealed from the French people.

He was also fully appraised of a comic-opera plot that had taken place in his absence staged by the half-insane General Malet who on the night of 22 October had announced that Napoleon was dead and proclaimed himself ruler. When the commander of the crucial Paris garrison failed to support him, the half-cocked conspiracy quickly collapsed and Malet was executed bravely by firing squad, himself giving the order for his own execution. Napoleon's two most dangerous civilian rivals, Fouché and Talleyrand, were to his relief not involved nor were any senior generals – most of whom were with him in Russia or in Spain. Napoleon was bitterly disappointed that no one had rallied to his infant son, the King of Rome during that fateful night.

Chapter 82

THE FIGHTBACK

The Emperor now embarked on a frenzy of propaganda and activity that showed he was anything but the spent force his enemies assumed. He despatched a letter of typical vainglory to the Emperor Francis of Austria.

> Every time I met the Russian army I defeated it. My Guard was not once engaged, never fired a shot, nor did it lose a man in the presence of the enemy. It is true that between the 7th and the 16th of November 30,000 of my cavalry and artillery horses died; I abandoned several thousand wagons for lack of horses. In that frightful storm of frost, our men could not stand bivouacking; many wandered off to seek houses for shelter; there was no cavalry left to protect them. Cossacks picked up several thousands. As for France, I could not be more satisfied with her: men, horses, money, everything is offered me. My finances are in good order. I shall therefore make no advances looking to peace.

He volleyed orders at his generals, notably Berthier:

> On hearing of the treachery of General Yorck I immediately decided to issue an address to the nation, which will be out tomorrow, and to raise an extraordinary levy. I have formed a corps of observation of the Elbe which is concentrating at Hamburg, and will have a strength of 60 battalions; I have given the command to General Lauriston. I have formed a corps of observation in Italy,

which is concentrating at Verona, and that will have a strength of 40 battalions; I have given the command to General Bertrand. I have formed a first corps of observation of the Army of the Rhine, of 60 battalions, commanded by the Duke of Ragusa, whose headquarters will be at Mainz. I shall form a second corps of observation of the Rhine, which will also have 60 battalions. I am calling to the colours 100,000 conscripts left over from 1810, so that we shall have men of over 21 years of age. The conscription of 1814 will give us 150,000 men, and will be levied some time in February.

He attacked his sister Caroline for Murat's abandonment of the French army in Russia. 'The King left the army on the 16th. Your husband is very brave on the battlefield, but weaker than a woman or a monk when out of sight of the enemy. He has no moral courage. He has been frightened; he has never for one moment been in danger of losing what he can only hold from me and with me. Show him the absurdity of his conduct. I can still forgive him the harm he has done me.'

He also decided to seek support from the Pope, whom he had previously treated so badly, and offered a new Concordat. He wrote ingratiatingly to Pius VII:

> Holy Father:
> I hasten to send one of the officers of my household to express all my gratification at what the bishop of Nantes has told me of the satisfactory condition of Your Holiness' health; for I had been for a moment alarmed this summer on hearing that Your Holiness had been seriously indisposed. The new residence of Your Holiness will give us an opportunity for meeting, and I have it much at heart to declare that, notwithstanding all that has passed, I have always maintained the same sentiments of friendship for Your Holiness. Perhaps we can now reach a settlement of all those questions that divide State and Church. I, on my side, am altogether disposed that way, so that it will depend entirely on Your Holiness.

The Pope, however, quickly repudiated the new Concordat, driving Napoleon to fresh fury, arresting and expropriating priests.

Napoleon's main concern was the re-creation of his power base, a fresh French army to replace the one all but destroyed during the Russian campaign. He set himself a target of recruiting 650,000 new soldiers in 1813. He would raise only 140,000 of them in France: soldiers, gendarmes, national guardsmen were conscripted into the new army, along with peasant sons, many of whom now sought desperately to evade conscription by giving themselves injuries or entering into false marriages, as it had become apparent that soldiery, far from entry into an elite as of old, was a probable death sentence.

By early 1813 he had raised an army of some 350,000, many of whom were just youths in their upper teens. But he had stirred up huge personal resentment among the French peasantry, from which most of the conscripts were drawn; and the taxes needed to maintain his army had fallen on the shoulders of his chief supporters, the propertied classes: in addition the richer families were also expected to raise troops. Discontent with Napoleon within France reached new heights.

Napoleon's new army thus consisted largely of raw recruits officered by men with no experience of war. He also had very few horses, most of them having perished in Russia. Nevertheless the sheer frenzy of his activity in the first few months of 1813, as he sought to recover from the Russian disaster, must excite admiration.

Napoleon soon believed he had managed to turn the tide in his favour, and there was little reason to think yet that he was mistaken. Less admirable were the wider implications: for Napoleonic France had become a kind of perpetual war machine, capable of keeping its balance only in a state of national emergency, mobilizing, plundering other nations, fighting war after war. If war should cease, the whole edifice of repression, colossal military expenditures and subject peoples would come crashing down. A defeat like the Russian one called for a redoubled effort, in case the logic of perpetual warfare and Napoleon's own military skills were called into judgement by the French.

The most alarming international development was that the Prussians began to follow the lead given by the rogue General Yorck. After Frederick William had escaped from Berlin he called for his people to raise an army and on 28 February he signed a convention with Russia.

The Kaiser had learnt some lessons from his terrible defeat at Napoleon's hands and the years of servitude. He abolished serfdom.

An astonishing revolution had also taken place in the Prussian army
as the legacy of Frederick the Great, once so innovatory, now a dead
hand holding back its modernization, was buried. It had been reduced
to just 42,000 men at the time of Tilsit, with only twenty-two of its
most able generals remaining out of the old total of 142. Mixed
brigades were introduced to make the army more flexible. A school
was set up for elite staff officers. The chief of staff was now to be as
powerful a figure as the commanding general. In addition, the Prussians
were suddenly able to mobilize an army of 80,000. Ingeniously, they
had maintained secret regiments on the quiet and recruited new
soldiers for the day when they would return to the field.

The genius behind the Prussian resurgence was August von Gneisenau, a man of humble origins who had adopted his name from a local
castle and had fought with the British during the American War of
Independence. He had fought at Jena, then in 1807 joined the Military
Reorganization Commission. He was something of a political radical in
his own country advocating political and social change wedded to a
new sense of nationalism: he even urged an insurrection to set up a
constitutional government. He masterminded the new Prussian military doctrine of flexibility.

He joined in a remarkable partnership with the greatest Prussian field
general of the age, Gebhart von Blücher, a veteran seventy-two-year-
old springing from gentry stock in eastern Germany. The latter had
distinguished himself in the earliest campaigns against the French
revolutionary government. At the Battle of Auerstadt, Blücher had
performed magnificently, having his horse shot from under him several
times. One of the last defenders of beaten Prussia in 1807, he was
captured, then exchanged for the distinguished French General Victor,
who had been captured by the Prussians. He urged continuing
resistance to Napoleon, but plunged into depression when Frederick
William refused to do so. Nevertheless he secretly trained Prussian
troops in defiance of the agreement with Napoleon.

Thus within three months of Napoleon's retreat, as he had anticipated, his enemies were beginning to mass. The 80,000 Prussians were

supported by the Swedish army of some 25,000 men, under the renegade Bernadotte. In addition more than 100,000 Russians had entered Prussia. Thus a formidable force of more than 200,000 men had suddenly arisen to face de Beauharnais's defeated and demoralized remnants from Russia, who were steadily beaten back all the way first from the border, then to Dresden.

De Beauharnais put up a fine fight, as was to be expected. He lamented: 'The Italians are dying like flies . . . How happy should we be to see our homes one day! It is my sole ambition now. I search no more for glory. It costs too dear.' He had withdrawn first to the Oder and then to the Elbe, abandoning Berlin. At Magdeburg he stopped and fought around Mockern in early April, before withdrawing behind the Saale river. At last, however, French luck was beginning to improve. The supreme Russian commander, Kutuzov, died on 28 April in Silesia. This left command of the Russo-Prussian forces to Wittgenstein and Blücher, although Alexander was constantly attempting to interfere with the operations of the former.

Part 12

FIGHT TO THE DEATH

Chapter 83

ON THE OFFENSIVE

Napoleon had regained his old self-confidence. In April he led a huge counter-offensive with an army of 250,000 men altogether, many of them new recruits. He displayed a renewed aggressive spirit. He lunged forward into the Prussian heartland towards Dresden. His strategy was to retake Berlin and relieve Danzig, thus rescuing the 150,000 French troops bottled up along the Vistula. The German minor princes still supported him.

On 1 May the now united armies of Napoleon and de Beauharnais delivered a first blow at Weissenfeld and then at Grossgorchen. The following day they won the bigger battle of Lutzen where the French artillery, seventy-strong, pinned the enemy down, permitting the infantry to attack in force; a crushing victory was secured which, however, Napoleon was unable to follow up because of a shortage of cavalry: some 20,000 casualties were inflicted on either side. De Beauharnais was able to pursue the Russians to Colditz, where he routed the forces under General Mikhail Miloradovich.

Napoleon integrated the two armies under his command and sent his valiant stepson down to prepare Italy's defences. The Russians and the Prussians withdrew across the Elbe to Bautzen where they were reinforced by 13,000 men under Barclay de Tolly. Napoleon planned a frontal attack with steady reinforcements, while Ney headed a flanking movement from the south. On 20 May the battle started and the French soon gained control of the centre, taking Bautzen; but Ney, incredibly brave though he was, was no tactician. He had veered away from the main battlefield, disobeying orders, failing to trap the allied

army and instead got bogged down in fighting around the village of Preititz.

Napoleon nevertheless drove the enemy from the main positions, again with the loss of some 30,000 men on each side, and the Russians and Prussians withdrew again. In the pursuit Napoleon's closest friend Duroc was killed. The allies were now in hopeless disarray: Wittgenstein, who was blamed for the defeat at Bautzen, had been replaced by Barclay de Tolly; the Russians and the Prussians were squabbling bitterly. But Napoleon's army was also in difficulties: nearly 100,000 of its raw recruits had fallen sick or deserted, in addition to those that had been lost in battle.

On 2 June the two sides agreed to an armistice, which the neutral Austrians were to referee. But Napoleon was not deceived:

> This armistice arrests the tide of my victories. I decided to accept it for two reasons: my lack of cavalry, which prevents my dealing heavy blows, and the hostile attitude of Austria. That court, in the most friendly, tender, I might almost say sentimental terms, actually presumes to force me, for fear of the army it has concentrated at Prague, to give up Dalmatia and Istria, and even what lies beyond the Isonzo. It demands, further, the left bank of the Inn, and Salzburg, and even one half of the Grand Duchy of Warsaw, leaving the other half to Prussia and Russia. And these benefits are to be secured by the mere display of 100,000 men and without actual hostilities. If possible I shall delay till September, and then strike hard. We must gain time. To gain time without making Austria hostile we must stick to our text of the last six months, that we can do anything provided Austria is our ally.

With two albeit partial victories under his belt, Napoleon had regained his self-confidence. He had been confronted before in Europe by the combination of Britain, Austria and Russia; and then by Britain, Prussia and Russia; but he had never been faced by four enemies at once. He was desperately anxious that Austria should not join his enemies at this moment. His marriage to Marie Louise, who was now besotted with him, was the cornerstone of his alliance with Austria. But that empire's

foreign policy was now in the hands of a supremely able cynic, Prince Metternich, who, wedded to the old order of Europe and despising Bonaparte, had already made up his mind. Napoleon could perhaps have saved the situation if he had displayed true humility – '*reculer pour mieux sauter*'. But pride got the better of him as usual: a fine general, he was always an appalling politician.

At the Mercolini Palace in Dresden he met Metternich in a famous encounter which lasted nearly nine hours on 26 June. According to Metternich Napoleon insisted: 'My reign will not outlast the day when I have ceased to be strong and therefore to be feared . . . I know how to die . . . But I shall never cede one inch of territory. Your sovereigns, who were born on the throne, can allow themselves to be beaten twenty times and will always return to their capitals. But I cannot do that – I am a self-made soldier.'

Napoleon's version was scarcely less provoking:

'Ah! There you are, Metternich! Welcome! But if you wanted peace why didn't you come to see me sooner? We have already lost a month, and your mediation is so tardy that it looks hostile. So it's war you want! You shall have it; I give you rendezvous in Vienna! I win two victories, my defeated enemies are just realising their situation, and all of a sudden you slip into our midst, offering me an armistice, mediation, offering them your alliance, complicating everything. Without your pernicious intervention peace would have been signed by now between me and the allies. You must admit that from the moment Austria assumed the position of mediator you were no longer on my side, no longer impartial, but my enemy. Today your 200,000 men are ready, over there, behind the screen of the Bohemian mountains. And because you think you are in a position to dictate terms, you now approach me. Very well, let us negotiate, I consent. What is it you want?'

'It rests with Your Majesty to give the world peace.'

'My honour first, and then peace. You cannot know what passes through a soldier's mind. A man like me does not count the lives of a

million of men. I have offered you Illyria for your neutrality, does
that suit you? Your neutrality is all I ask for.'

'Ah, sire, we cannot remain neutral any longer; we must be for
you, or against you.'

'If it costs me my throne, I will bury the world under its ruins!'

Metternich remarked that he wished the doors and windows of his
palace could be thrown open so that Europe could hear Napoleon's
words.

Raising the subject of Russia, Napoleon, according to Metternich,
reflected that 300,000 men already had been lost in Russia of which
only a tenth were French. Napoleon then taunted him with having
being bought like Judas. In fact Austria had recently been subsidized by
the British to the tune of £3.6 million, while Prussia had been paid £2
million. 'Sir, you are a lost man,' was Metternich's angry parting shot.

Napoleon's display of braggadocio might have proved fatal but for
the fact that Metternich before the meeting had already resolved to join
his enemies. Napoleon probably understood this from his demeanour,
which may have accounted for his own aggressiveness. The terms
Metternich offered Napoleon at Dresden were little short of humiliating: the return of all former Austrian possessions in Italy, the dissolution
of the Confederacy of the Rhine, the restoration of the Prussian
dominions and the handover of Poland to the Russians. These terms
were designed to be unacceptable, and it was no surprise that Napoleon, with two recent victories under his belt, refused to accept them.

Napoleon's hand was weakened by news of Wellington's great
victory at Vitoria. New talks were arranged with Austria at which
Caulaincourt represented Napoleon. He begged Napoleon to author-
ize him to make significant concessions; in particular to give up the
Confederation of the Rhine, which might have appeased both Austria
and Prussia. Napoleon heatedly argued that this was France's buffer
state on the Rhine. Metternich even seemed disposed to abandon his
Italian demands. Napoleon remained obdurate.

On 11 April Austria declared war. This was the final turning point: if
Napoleon had made concessions, sought to divide his enemies, shown
flexibility, he might yet have survived. He was now faced not just with

a war in Spain which was approaching his own frontiers but the combined might of the three great military powers of mainland Europe, Russia, Austria and Prussia, and a minor one, Sweden, as well as the unremitting hostility of Britain. His ruthlessly conscripted raw army of 680,000 men would face nearly 200,000 Russians, 120,000 Austrians, 160,000 Prussians and 40,000 Swedes; along with other allies, this amounted to 800,000 men. On the face of it this still seemed acceptable odds. Napoleon had overcome larger odds before.

In addition, Napoleon's army was concentrated while others were dispersed into four great forces: the Army of the North, consisting of Swedes and Russians garrisoned in Berlin was under Bernadotte, a deeply flawed commander; the Army of Prussia, which was in fact commanded by the Russians, under General Bennigsen; the Army of Silesia under Blücher; and the biggest force, the 250,000-strong Army of Bohemia under the supreme commander, the Austrian Prince Schwarzenberg, an indifferent general, nominated for his aristocratic connections and loyalty to Metternich. Of the four allied commandeers, only Blücher was outstanding.

Napoleon had every reason to be confident of victory through employing his usual tactic of divide and rule, rapid marches and manoeuvres, and encircling and defeating his enemies one by one. The campaign that followed has been portrayed as an inevitable defeat for a ruler mortally wounded by both the Peninsular and Russian campaigns. It was nothing of the kind: a series of convincing French victories followed by a policy of magnanimity towards his enemies would have saved the campaign and restored Europe to what it had been in 1811. It was not to be.

Chapter 84

THE BATTLE OF THE NATIONS

Napoleon's first mistake was to disperse his forces in the face of the various opposing armies: his biggest army of some 250,000 men in seven corps was based at Dresden, while Oudinot was despatched with 100,000 men to Hamburg to threaten Bohemia and Bernadotte. Davout was given control of 35,000 to defend the lower Elbe. Ney was given command of 85,000 men – a third of the biggest army – but was directly responsible to Napoleon. By a common consent Oudinot was an inferior general to the experienced Davout: and Ney, in spite of his heroic generalship of a small force during the Russian campaign, lacked the intelligence and tactical ability to command a large army. Napoleon believed he could orchestrate all three men himself. His army thus suffered from the presence of two inadequate operational commanders combined with over-centralization, although it was deployed over a wide geographic area.

War was declared on 11 April 1813. Napoleon's strategy was to attack boldly, trying to envelop each allied army in turn; the allies' counter-strategy, elaborated by Schwarzenberg was defensive but in the event inspired – the Trachenburg Plan. When an allied army was attacked, it must withdraw and liaise with the other armies to fight the French: it was like a more defensive and cumbersome version of Napoleon's own earlier tactics of bringing armies together in force at the last minute. Yet because the allied armies were comprised of different nations under rival commanders, and were also interfered with by three militarily inexperienced sovereigns, it seemed impossible that they should succeed. What turned the tables was a combination of

Napoleon's own blunders and overconfidence, and a commander of genius, that fierce old man, Gebhard von Blücher.

Blücher was already seventy, a huge age in those days. Having fought in a minor capacity in the Seven Years War, he was by far the oldest veteran of the major allied commanders who took the field against Napoleon. He had been born of a minor noble family, not unlike Napoleon's, in 1742 in a small town on the Baltic adjacent to the Russian border. He was so poor a student that he could barely read or write. He served in the Prussian army as a typical officer of the time, with little to do in small garrisons except drink and frequent local prostitutes. In his early thirties he offended Frederick the Great and was effectively dismissed, not being readmitted to the army until the monarch died, only becoming a colonel at the late age of forty-eight. He seemed destined for obscurity. Serving in the Netherlands when war broke out with revolutionary France, he soon distinguished himself with extraordinarily bold engagements. In 1795, however, Prussia made peace with France and Blücher was plunged back into provincial obscurity as governor of the small Rhine town of Münster.

After the outbreak of war again eleven years later Blücher served with distinction at Auerstadt at the already advanced age of sixty-three. He was captured by the French and actually exchanged pleasantries with Napoleon, who failed to see any serious threat from the gruff, pipe-smoking old man with his walrus moustaches and appearance of an old rogue. A British officer described him as 'an uncouth old man who was spitting over a bridge when I saw him'.

From 1806 until war was renewed again in 1813, Blücher was out of action. He suffered serious alcoholic symptoms, including delirium tremens and paranoid delusions; he raved about his head being made of stone and feared that he was pregnant with an elephant. However he helped to train the Prussian troops in secret. He was recalled by the King of Prussia to command the Russo-Prussian Army of Silesia largely because of his reputation for bravery.

His surgeon noted that he never entertained any idea of being shot dead: 'If he had not felt certain of it, he would have lost his head as many others, for every man in a greater or less degree, previous to a

battle and when going into it, has an instinctive dread in his bosom; and he who knows how [best to] overcome it is the bravest after all. He always knew at the proper moment how to work upon the soldiers' feelings, and only a few comforting words were necessary, and at once toil, hunger and thirst, and all the hardships of war were forgotten.' He was beloved by his troops who called him 'Marshal Vorwarts' for the most frequent command he gave.

He depended on the intellectual skills of his chief of staff Gneisenau who had been responsible for most of the innovations in Prussian tactics, including giving greater initiative to subordinates and setting up a general staff to formulate decisions collectively, in marked contrast to Napoleon's methods. The combination of dashing commander and calculating support officer was to become the model for the Prussian army of William I and William II, as also initially with Hitler. Gneisenau, of modest social origins, was a brilliant student and at fifty-two was eighteen years younger than Blücher. He was a prickly, difficult man who treated those of lesser intelligence badly. This combination of brain and brawn was to prove remarkably effective.

Blücher started the war by breaking the armistice with Napoleon in south-eastern Germany. What followed was an extraordinary game of chess in which Napoleon (the 'queen') buttressed by two lesser castles, limited in movement, thrust forward where the Confederation of the Rhine juts into southern Prussia and northern Austria. Facing him were the other 'queen', Schwarzenburg's Army of Bohemia, the main allied army in the south, and his two castles and a bishop, the Army of Silesia facing Napoleon's front, and the Armies of Poland and the North further north. Another comparison was that of a great bull charging into a ring with assorted bullfighters around him waving their capes to tire him and seeking to avoid a full charge which would inevitably prove fatal.

Napoleon's predicament was not all that dissimilar to the one that he had just faced in Russia. He sought to take the offensive and secure a decisive victory; but his divided enemies were committed to retreating when he tried to engage them and then to blocking his line of communication. The first to charge forward had been Blücher; and Napoleon moved to meet him on 21 August. Blucher immediately

withdrew, remarking about his seemingly cowardly tactic that he was 'very happy to have played a trick on the great man. He ought to be furious at not having been able to make me accept battle.' Meanwhile the Russians had sent 40,000 troops to Blücher's aid.

Napoleon charged aside to intercept them, and Blücher attacked the French left under General MacDonald at Katsbach on 26 August, which he comprehensively destroyed, taking 18,000 prisoners and a hundred guns. Napoleon reversed direction to attack Blücher, only to find his adversary retreating for the second time. From the south Schwarzenberg's huge Army of Bohemia was marching on Dresden to cut off his supply lines. Napoleon veered away from Blücher again to strike at Schwarzenberg's supply lines, only to learn that Dresden, with its vital artillery and supplies, was in no position to hold out against the approaching army from the south.

At this stage Napoleon seems to have lost his nerve. Instead of circling Schwarzenberg's army in a great flanking attack, which he would surely have won, he left a small force to harass it and spectacularly counter-marched back to Dresden nearly a hundred miles away in just seventy-two hours. He arrived in time to save the city. Nevertheless Schwarzenberg decided to press on with his advance, which could have proved fatal to the allied cause.

The exhausted 120,000 French troops and the equally exhausted Emperor, now suffering from fever, drove the 150,000-strong allied force out of the city, inflicting some 40,000 casualties to 12,000 French ones on 26 and 27 August. The allied army was forced to retreat south, where it was vulnerable to attack from the smaller French flanking corps. But it had narrowly escaped – arousing the contempt of the Tsar, who urged it to fight on.

To the north Oudinot had been defeated and forced back along the road to Berlin. Napoleon nominated Ney to take over his command. The fiery general plunged forward towards Berlin, but was attacked by a superior Prussian force under General von Bülow at Dennewitz some sixty miles south of the capital on 6 September. Ney displayed his usual bravery, leading his men from the front, married to his usual tactical ineptitude, decisively losing the battle and being forced to retreat before Bernadotte's large army arrived towards the end of the battle.

After these French setbacks, the southern German states were one by one defecting to the allies. Bavaria joined at the beginning of October, leaving only Saxony as a French supporter. Blücher's army surged forward across the Elbe at Wittenberge, while Bernadotte followed reluctantly behind: to the south the Army of Poland joined up with Schwarzenberg's main force. Napoleon tried to intercept Blücher, but the wily old Prussian general slipped away to the south-west. By that time the Emperor had marched his army back to the city of Leipzig from Dresden, which was too exposed.

To all appearances Leipzig presented a superb defensive position: to the south there was excellent defensive hilly terrain; to the north lay open country, but Napoleon did not expect an attack from that quarter – a fatal mistake. In an effort to strengthen further the defences of the city, Napoleon blew up all but one bridge westward across the Elster; he never expected to have to use it.

Napoleon had never been a defensive general, and his inadequacies in this field were all too apparent: for his strong position was in fact a trap. Four allied armies were closing in on him simultaneously – Blücher through his relentless marching swerving around the top of the city to the north-west, Bernadotte from the north, Bennigsen to the east and the biggest army, that of Schwarzenberg, to the south.

Facing this encirclement on three sides, Napoleon had drawn up his forces in an inner circle – Marmont, his best remaining commander and Ney in the north facing Blücher, the Imperial Guard and MacDonald in the east and Victor, Murat, Poniatowski, Augereau and Lauriston in the south. Altogether there were 190,000 French troops facing 335,000 allied troops. Napoleon had been hoist by his own petard: his enemies had coalesced against him in much superior force, just as he had done against them so often in the past.

Even so, the battle was far from lost: he had the stronger position, and his allies were continually squabbling over tactics and fighting on a far wider front, always vulnerable to a dividing French thrust. Thus began the greatest battle up till then in the history of the world, which was to decide the fate of a continent.

On 16 October the 'Battle of the Nations' began, which was to last

three days. Unlike previous battles, it was not one of dash and heroism, but one of great attrition and carnage, ultimately decided by sheer force of numbers and firepower, as well as an appalling military mistake which was to foreshadow the terrible slaughter of the First World War.

The battle began in the early morning with an attack by Schwarzenberg's army in the south, under murderous fire from a hundred French guns. The French reacted effectively after initial setbacks. Napoleon planned to send Augereau in with a flanking force on the allied left. However to his surprise a well co-ordinated attack was launched by Blücher from the north, and he delayed a counter-attack in the south until he could be sure his northern defences were holding.

There Murat was fighting valiantly and even contemplated a counter-attack, but reinforcements were too late arriving and a party of the German cavalry refused to move. Just after midday Napoleon ordered his men to the south, followed by Murat's cavalry. They pushed back the Austrians, but Russian reinforcements prevented this retreat turning into a rout. The fighting had resulted in a stalemate on both fronts, with allied losses at around 30,000 to the French 20,000.

By the following day Bernadotte and Bennigsen were in place with their armies and the French were outnumbered two to one, 160,000 to 320,000. Napoleon waited for his own reinforcements, staging no decisive push through allies lines. The following day the huge encircling allied army attacked at ten o'clock. Six major attacks were launched, pushing the French back in the north in spite of an intense defence. At around five o'clock, after remorseless fighting, the Army of Saxony and Würtemberg defected to the allies, handing over its forty guns and opening up a huge gap in the French lines. This permitted an enemy advance to half a mile from Leipzig.

Napoleon was now given the news that there were only 16,000 rounds of ammunition left, which made resistance the next day impossible. He decided to retreat to the ammunition depot at Erfurt at 2 a.m. on the morning of the 19th. This proved a textbook operation at first, with the bulk of his army crossing the sole remaining bridge across the river while the rearguard under Oudinot kept up a stubborn resistance in hand-to-hand street fighting.

These efforts were not to be rewarded: a corporal, misunderstanding

his orders, blew up the bridge while thousands of French soldiers were still in the town. A military catastrophe of the first order followed. Napoleon said bitterly:

> The Emperor had ordered the engineers to mine the great bridge between Leipzig and Lindenau so as to blow it up at the last moment; part of the army was still on the further side with 80 guns and a train of several hundred wagons. The head of column of this part of the army, on seeing the bridge blow up, supposed it had fallen into the power of the enemy. A cry of dismay went up from the ranks: 'The enemy are in our rear; the bridge is cut!' The unfortunate men broke their ranks and sought all means of escape. The Duke of Taranto swam across; Count Lauriston, less lucky, was drowned; Prince Poniatowski, on a spirited horse, plunged in and was never seen again. It is impossible as yet to estimate the loss involved by this unfortunate accident, but the disorder it has caused in the army has completely altered the appearance of things. The victorious French army will reach Erfurt with all the appearance of a defeated army. The enemy, shaken by the battles of the 16th and 18th, have taken heart owing to the disaster of the 19th and have assumed a victorious attitude. I could see clearly enough the fatal hour coming! My star was growing paler; I felt the reins slipping from my fingers; and I could do nothing. Only a thunderstroke could save us. I had, therefore, to fight it out; and day by day, by this or that fatality, our chances were becoming more slender!

The magnitude of the disaster was immediately apparent to him: he displayed a rare lack of his usual ability to rebound in a declaration a few days later. 'I went too far. I have made mistakes. Fortune has turned her back on me these last two years; but she's a woman, and will change . . . I only hope the Allies will burn down two or three of my good cities of France; it would give me a million soldiers. I would offer them battle, I would beat them, and I would drive them at a tap of a drum all the way back to the Vistula.'

Oudinot fought on but had to surrender and swam to safety across the Vistula. It was a catastrophe on an unprecedented scale. The French

lost some 40,000 killed and wounded and 30,000 prisoners taken in Leipzig, as well as more than 390 guns. Other French garrisons, such as Dresden and Danzig, soon fell, with the loss of a further 90,000 men.

The news soon arrived that on 6 October Wellington's army had crossed the French border – the first of his enemies to invade the country. Blücher and Schwarzenberg led a two-pronged advance across Germany to the Rhine. A force of Germans and Austrians tried to intercept Napoleon near Frankfurt but were mauled. Even so, only 70,000 French soldiers crossed the river, with 40,000 stragglers disconsolately behind them.

Chapter 85

THE INVASION OF FRANCE

Napoleon's domination of Europe was shattered beyond repair. He had lost Prussia and the German states; revolts were flaring in Italy and the Low Countries. The Iberian Peninsula was already lost. He had been the victim again of overconfidence, of his belief that attack was the best form of defence. It had been a close-run thing. Leipzig might well have gone the other way. Even so, such was the strength of combined British, Austrian, Russian and Prussian forces that it seems inconceivable he could have re-established his old empire, even if the French had won the battle.

Yet, extraordinarily, there remained still two slender chances of survival: first, the allies were divided about the wisdom of invading France; second, the French might fight to defend their native soil. There was some ground for each of these hopes. Meeting in Frankfurt in November, the Prussians and the Russians favoured an immediate invasion of France; the Austrians instead wanted to restore France's 'natural boundaries' along the Rhine; the British too initially favoured this position, among them the Duke of Wellington even as his army inched up into France.

Blücher argued belligerently: 'We must go to Paris. Napoleon has paid his visits to all the capitals of Europe. Shall we be less polite?' The contrary argument was made by Austria, which feared that Russia would seek to dominate all of Europe; the British too were uneasy about Russian intentions and believed the French would act as a counterweight, properly boxed in, provided that they could be prised out of the Low Countries.

Metternich was able to offer these terms to Napoleon in November. At first he prevaricated, then accepted the offer. But by then Castlereagh had come to the conclusion that France would never cede the Low Countries; in addition both he and Metternich decided that France must be given no time to regroup its forces, in spite of the winter conditions. The invasion of France must proceed at once.

Napoleon was thus thrown on to his last hope: that of rallying the French people against the foreign invaders. But even the French, at last, had had enough of their Emperor. On his return to Paris he found a new spirit of independence among the very institutions he had set up to rubberstamp his rule. The senate still supported him, but the chamber dared to criticize him for continuing the war by an overwhelming vote of 229 votes to 31.

He responded in typically dictatorial manner by sweeping away the legislature: 'You are not the representatives of the nation. The true representative of the nation is myself. France has more need of me than I have need of France.' However it reflected the growing anger not just of the bourgeoisie but of the wealthy and the peasantry, Napoleon's other traditional power base, who had lost sons and husbands in his wars. They had suffered years of economic disruption and trade embargoes, and now faced the prospect of outright invasion, as well as the lawlessness of brigands and bands of desperate penniless soldiers roaming the countryside. After years of sacrifice and suffering, their only reward was defeat.

This resentment through all ranks of French society did not trouble the Emperor unduly: he ruled through force and repression and maintained a formidable police apparatus. But it hampered his efforts to rally the French people against his external enemies; and if he could not protect France, his sole remaining claim to legitimacy as the embodiment of France's greatness and national independence was lost. As long as he had been successful, he had retained the loyalty of the army. Should he fail, his only remaining props – nationalism and brute force – would be gone.

He declared in November:

The alarms and apprehension at Paris amuse me; I thought you capable of facing the truth. I shall defeat the enemy quicker than you

think. My presence is too much needed with the army at this moment for me to leave it. When it is necessary I shall come to Paris . . . One year ago all Europe was marching with us; now all Europe is marching against us. The reason is that the opinion of the world is governed either by France or by England. We should therefore have everything to fear were it not for the courage and power of the nation. Posterity will declare that the great and critical events that face us were not superior to France or to me.

He embarked on a furious conscription drive, calling up pensioners, gendarmes, foresters, customs officers and young teenagers to build up an army of 110,000 men, far short of the 960,000 he demanded. He printed money to finance this, destroying French national solvency.

By now, though, even some of his most loyal supporters were convinced that the end was in sight. Victor abandoned Strasbourg and Nancy. Then, in January, came the unkindest cut of all: Murat, one of his greatest commanders and hero of countless cavalry charges, although a relentless schemer and persistent critic of Napoleon, signed a treaty with Metternich under which, in return for being allowed to keep the throne of Naples, he would wage war upon the most loyal of all Napoleon's proconsuls, Eugène de Beauharnais, in northern Italy. The latter was himself offered the crown of Italy by Metternich, but honourably, and perhaps stupidly, declined.

Murat has been much denounced for his perfidy; yet he was a competent administrator and may have even believed his decision to be in the best interests of Napoleon. Napoleon's fury towards him is well documented. He commented icily, 'The conduct of the King of Naples and that of the Queen is quite unspeakable. I hope to live long enough to avenge for myself and for France such an outrage and such horrible ingratitude.'

Meanwhile he still entertained hopes of victory or a diplomatic settlement, instructing the faithful yet frank Caulaincourt to go to Austria in January:

I doubt whether the Allies are acting in good faith, and whether England wants peace; I do, but only solid and honourable. You must

listen, observe. It is not certain that they will let you reach head-quarters; the Russians and English will want to prevent our coming to an explanation and understanding with the Emperor of Austria. You must try to get the views of the Allies, and to let me know what you find out daily, so that I may be able to draw up instructions for you, instructions for which I have no data at present. Do they want to reduce France to her old frontiers? Italy is untouched, and the Viceroy has a good army. In another week I shall have collected enough men to fight several battles, even before the arrival of my troops from Spain. The pillaging of the Cossacks will drive the inhabitants to arms and double our numbers. If the nation supports me the enemy are on the road to ruin. If Fortune betrays me my resolve is taken, I am not wedded to the throne. I shall abase neither the nation nor myself by accepting shameful terms. The thing is to know what Metternich wants. It is not the interest of Austria to push things to extremes; one step more and the leading role will escape her.

Even the weak-willed, incompetent and lecturing Joseph threatened to leave him. Napoleon, desperate to avoid this further blow to his prestige, tried to conciliate him:

My Brother:

I have received your letter. It is too full of subtleties to fit my present situation. Here is the question in two words. France is invaded; Europe is all in arms against France, but especially against me. You are no longer King of Spain. What will you do? Will you, as a French prince, support my throne? If so you must say so, write me a straightforward letter that I can publish, receive the officials, and display zeal for my cause and for that of the King of Rome, good-will towards the Regency of the Empress. Can you not bring yourself to this? Haven't you enough good sense to do this? Otherwise you must retire quietly to a château forty leagues from Paris. If I survive, you can live there quietly. If I die, you will be assassinated or arrested. You will be useless to me, to the family, to your daughters, to France, but you will be doing no harm and will not embarrass me. Decide at once, choose your path.

To appease Joseph he offered him the post of governor of Paris, a truly disastrous position for the man who had already done so much to lose Spain. Napoleon declared defiantly: 'No preparations are to be made for abandoning Paris; if necessary we must be buried under its ruins.' He ordered the Pope to be bundled out of France, to propitiate him. He was 'to be dropped like a shell' in Rome.

It is impossible not to admire Napoleon in this, the grimmest hour of his career, with his back to the wall. The once ferociously energetic, unstoppably dominant and brilliant young man who had taken power had by 1810 become plump, indolent, indecisive, domesticated and surrounded by an adoring and fawning host of sycophants in a classic example of the corruption induced by power, had gone on to make the disastrous mistake of not intervening personally in Spain, had waged the Russian campaign with a mixture of incompetence and pride and then committed the cardinal folly of allowing his army to be trapped at Leipzig. But he was now a man transformed and rejuvenated.

Not just his energy returned but seemingly his skill. For he was now fighting to defend his own terrain of France, in the manner he was best equipped to do: in nearly absolute command of a small army capable of manoeuvring quickly and unpredictably to strike in front, from the flanks, behind and all around his enemies. It was his first Italian campaign all over again: the great military streetfighter was himself again. He was much less proficient as a commander in the great set-piece battles, which his legion of admirers proclaimed was his real genius – with the notable exception of Austerlitz. But he was the master of military manoeuvre with a small compact army weaving circles around its opponents. He was superb in adversity, when all seemed hopeless.

It was his singular bad luck that the principal opposing general was no parade-ground preener but a tough, wily old warrior addicted to war, seizing with both hands his last chance to bring his career and his life to a glorious close. It resembled the famous Wild West confrontation between the veteran Pat Garrett and Billy the Kid. Blücher's reflexes were not so fast nor his capacity for surprise and deception so great as his adversary's. But the old rogue looked to his own shrewdness

and his ability to muster superior forces while avoiding Napoleon's sudden thrusts. It was the penultimate confrontation of Napoleon's life, a duel of wits that testified to the superb military skills of both men.

Napoleon once summed up his own military philosophy simply: 'The art of war does not require complicated manoeuvres; the simplest are the best, and common sense is fundamental. From which one might wonder how it is that generals make blunders; it is because they try to be clever. The most difficult thing is to guess the enemy's plan, to sift the truth from all the reports that come in. The rest merely requires common sense; it's like a boxing-match, the more you punch, the better it is. It is also necessary to read the map well.' Blücher's philosophy was even more rudimentary – 'vorwarts', but also back-wards when necessary, as his campaign now showed. It was the duel between a bloodied leader of a pack of hounds and an alert fox fighting for its life on its own territory.

The rest of the pack consisted of no fewer than five major components. The northern army was under Bennigsen and Bernadotte with their target the Low Countries, approaching to besiege Hamburg, defended by the superb Davout, and Magdeburg: both Holland and Belgium were almost in revolt, with Amsterdam having risen. The next force further south was to support this: under the Prussian General von Bülow, it was intended to link up with a force sent from Britain under Sir Thomas Graham with the intention of sweeping the Low Countries free of the French.

Further south would come the two main allied thrusts from the east: Blücher would lead the central one of 100,000 men across the Rhine; while Schwarzenberg with the main army would come up from the south-east with around 200,000 men on Napoleon's flank as he engaged Blücher. These would be supported by the Austrian troops now fighting in Italy. Finally, Wellington with his immaculate com-mand of military tactics was now steadily advancing in southern France. Altogether there would be 400,000 allied troops to engage Napoleon's army.

The Austrian aim was so to overwhelm the French with sheer numbers that Napoleon would be forced to come to terms without further bloodshed; they believed the British could be persuaded

privately to support this view, which was not shared by the Prussians and Russians who wanted to inflict total defeat in revenge for the conquest of their capitals. Against these forces, Napoleon deployed 70,000 men to protect Paris and 40,000 more as his fighting forces against the approaching combination of allies.

The flaw in the allied strategy was to overlook the fact that Napoleon was essentially a fighting machine: he had lost all grand stratagems or statesmanlike vision – if indeed he ever possessed any – and believed that with his small army he could still outwit his far larger pursuing forces and drive them to the negotiating table on his terms. He was too realistic to believe he could actually defeat the allies. At first the progress of this lightning war of incredibly quick manoeuvres, marches, battles and defences seemed to justify him: he retained the initiative as long as he could keep the much larger allied forces apart.

Chapter 86

THE GREAT CHASE

The two main southern and eastern prongs advanced at the end of January, Schwarzenberg slowly to the Languedoc plateau, where he halted on Metternich's instructions, Blücher crossing the Meuse, penetrating seventy miles into French territory. On 24 January Blücher fought a first battle with the French vanguard, which ended in a stalemate with high casualties. Napoleon returned to the area the following day, supported by Ney and Marmont. He tried to work his way around the Prussians' rear. But Blücher had retreated to Brienne. He and Gneisenau were nearly captured and had to leave hastily when Napoleon's small army surprised them and dealt them a bloody nose, leaving 4,000 Prussian casualties. In fierce winter blizzards, Napoleon pushed the bulk of Blücher's army down the road to La Rothière.

However Schwarzenberg, who was only fifty miles away, was able to detach some 50,000 men of his large army to reinforce Blücher, and Napoleon blundered into this much larger force in blinding snow, losing some 5,000 casualties as well as a hundred guns. On the road back to Troyes, which he reached on 3 February, he lost a further 4,000 through desertion. The allies had lost some 6,000 men as well, but could much better afford them.

Intoxicated by the victory, Blücher and Schwarzenberg, who could not keep so large an army supplied in winter, separated again, Blücher moving along the Marne and Schwarzenberg up the Seine. Blücher was supremely confident that French resistance was all but over. 'The road to Paris is free,' he declared. 'I do not believe that Napoleon will engage in another battle.' The Prussians made a forced march along the

road to Paris, but Napoleon suddenly veered north and in four days won four separate engagements which cost Blücher some 16,000 men and nearly resulted in his being captured or trampled to death at Vauchamps. Napoleon was satisfied: he had skilfully avoided and then damaged a much larger army.

He could now switch his attention to Schwarzenberg's army, which was threatening Paris from the south. He marched his men fifty miles in thirty-five hours and inflicted serious losses on the enemy in engagements at Mormant, Valjouan and Montereau; at these clashes he inflicted a further 6,000 casualties for the loss of 2,000 of his own men. On 21 February he won a further victory. He sought to trap his retreating enemy at Troyes, but learnt that Schwarzenberg's army had linked up with Blücher to provide a force of some 100,000, compared to Napoleon's 70,000 or so.

The allies withdrew at Napoleon's approach, Blücher moving to join up with Bulow in the north, Schwarzenberg moving south to Langres. Napoleon had thus won seven battles in eight days and forced two much larger armies to retreat. As usual, success went to his head. When he was offered a return to the 1792 boundaries by the allies, he delayed and the moment for peace was soon past.

Blücher, perhaps encouraged by the news that Britain would pay £5 million to subsidize the war, resumed the move towards Paris. Napoleon promptly marched towards him, but Blücher was too quick, crossing to the north bank of the Marne and liaising with the smaller army of General von Bülow to swell his force to 100,000 men. Troyes had fallen to the south. On 7 March Napoleon caught up with Blücher at Craonne, where Ney perhaps foolishly staged an impetuous frontal attack, which resulted in 5,000 casualties on both sides before the combined Prussian-Russian army withdrew. Napoleon scented victory: Blücher's army repeatedly got away, but the latter was under intense pressure, with indiscipline spreading among his men.

Napoleon's renewed cockiness caused him contemptuously to dismiss further allied peace proposals. The Emperor's judgement was being warped by his domination of the field, even though he could still not secure decisive victories. He wrote to Caulaincourt: 'I am so moved at

the sight of the infamous proposal that you send me, that I feel dishonoured at merely being in such a position that such a proposal can be made. I will send you my instructions from Troyes or Châtillon; but I think I had almost sooner lose Paris than see such propositions made to the French people. You are always talking about the Bourbons – I had sooner see the Bourbons back in France, with reasonable conditions, than such infamous proposals as you have transmitted!'

Meanwhile he cherished hopes that the hitherto inanimate French peasantry would rise up in a Spanish-style insurrection against the allied troops as they helped themselves to food and laid waste to the land in the depths of the French winter: 'The enemy's soldiers are behaving horribly everywhere. All the inhabitants are fleeing to the woods. There are no peasants left in the villages. The enemy consume everything, take all the horses, all the cattle, all the clothing and rags of the peasants; they strike everybody, men and women, and commit a great number of rapes. I hope soon to draw my people from this miserable state and from this truly horrible suffering. The enemy should think of this twice, for Frenchmen are not patient; they are courageous by nature, and I expect to see them forming themselves into free companies.' He was in the throes of self-delusion.

Chasing after Blücher, he considered his adversary all but defeated. But the old man suddenly decided to make a stand at Laon, where a steep hill 330 feet high rose abruptly out of the surrounding countryside. It was protected by two villages at its foot, and by marshes and woods to the south, while it commanded flat countryside to the north. Blücher had tired of fleeing and he was reinforced by Dulow's troops in defence of the town itself, covered the hill with snipers and put two battalions each into the villages below. His main corps was stationed on either side and a reserve of two Prussian corps was hidden behind the hill.

On 9 March Napoleon's 37,000-strong army arrived in thick fog from the south-west and the south-east. Blücher, who was exhausted and ill, took up a position on the side of the hill, believing Napoleon's army to be 100,000 strong and expecting the main attack to come from the east, where it was in fact only 10,000 strong. When the fog cleared in the late morning, as one Prussian observer commented from the same vantage point as Blücher:

It was not one continued battle, but different corps of the enemy as they came in sight were attacked, and engagements were taking place at several points distinct from each other at the same time. . . . A mass of cavalry tried to hew a road into the middle of them; but they were not to be broken; they waved every way, and curved and bent, but always drew closer again into a dense mass as if they had been one single living body. It was a grand, a wonderful sight! . . . The generals themselves viewed the spectacle with amazement; Gneisenau was loud in his delight.

A cannonball nearly injured Blücher in his exposed position.

At around four Napoleon, unusually hesitant, ordered a major attack but discovered that the boggy ground behind the woods prevented the cavalry and artillery from softening up the Austrian position. As dusk approached, Blücher realized the weakness of the French column in the east and ordered Yorck forward in a major assault. The column's commander, the usually talented General Marmont, had left for a sleep in a nearby building, and his men panicked and, in the face of the allied attack, fled back along the road by which they had come. Marmont lost 3,500 men and nearly all his officers.

Blücher, delighted, ordered Yorck on a flanking march to the east to cut off the rest of Napoleon's main force. The following morning, however, the Prussian commander was nearly paralysed by an inflammation of the eyes and command passed to his chief of staff, General Gneisenau. However brilliant a planner and military reformer, Gneisenau was indifferent and cautious as a field commander and he feared Napoleon's reputation. He cancelled the flanking move, preferring to stay on the defensive, fearing that Napoleon's army was far stronger than it indeed was.

Napoleon staged a dawn attack against the heavily fortified hill which was easily repulsed before finally deciding to withdraw that evening, having suffered losses of around 7,000 men compared to the Prussian-Russian ones of 2,000. It had been a defeat on points for the French, who had failed to take the hill or destroy Blücher's army, but Napoleon had still escaped being completely overwhelmed by a force nearly three times the size of his own – as would probably have occurred if Blücher had continued with his flanking movement.

The Emperor swiftly got in his retaliation, striking at an unprotected enemy force near Rheims and inflicting 6,000 casualties to 700 French ones. Napoleon veered south to attack Schwarzenberg's bigger but more dispersed army, which appeared to retreat and then suddenly stopped to face him at Arcis-sur-Aube. The French initially drove the Austrians out of the village, but were massively attacked and Napoleon was nearly killed when a shell exploded under his horse: he lamented that he had not been killed on the battlefield. 'During the fight at Arcis-sur-Aube I did all I could to meet with a glorious end defending the soil of our country inch by inch. I exposed myself continuously. Bullets rained all around me; my clothes were full of them; but not one touched me. I am condemned to live!'

The following day the French found that the entire army of Bohemia had arrived, and they had to retreat under fire; they had lost 3,000 men to the allies' 4,000, but had also given up possession of the battlefield. Seemingly irrepressible, Napoleon suddenly surged forward eastward to St Didier behind the allied armies, threatening their supply lines. But the allies, believing that Paris was on the brink of rising up against Napoleon, took no notice and marched straight to the city, three marches ahead. He raced desperately to intercept them.

The 120,000-strong allied army overwhelmed Marmont's forces just outside the capital, and then again in a skirmish at the gates of the city overlooked by Montmartre, where Napoleon's dismayed brothers Jérôme and Lucien watched before they made their getaway. With the third sibling, Joseph, having done nothing to defend the city, Marmont signed the capitulation of Paris on 30 March. The Empress Marie Louise and the infant King of Rome had already left the city. Napoleon marched furiously to Fontainebleau only to learn of the surrender. 'It is the first time I have heard of a population of 300,000 that cannot survive for three months,' he fumed. He believed that after only a few days scarcity of supplies would have driven the allies back from outside the city, although this seems unlikely.

Talleyrand emerged from the shadows to lead a provisional government on 1 April and to welcome the Tsar Alexander and the King of Prussia, Frederick William, into the city. For both monarchs it was a

moment to savour: the former had burned his beautiful city of Moscow in a grim attempt to drive the French back just over six months before, while nearly all of the latter's country had been occupied by the French for some six years.

Talleyrand entertained them at the Opera, where they were received rapturously by the same population that had once cheered the guillotining of monarchs and then welcomed Napoleon's triumphs: their concern now was to prevent a massive bloodletting in revenge. In Fontainebleau an incredulous Napoleon, still at the head of 60,000 men, declared he would attack the enemy in Paris, to cries of 'To Paris, To Paris!' from his men. 'We will go and prove to them that the French nation is mistress of her own soil; that if we have long been masters among others, we will always be so here, and that we are able to defend our colours, our independence, and the integrity of our country.'

Some ninety miles away in Orléans his faithful, sweet Austrian Empress, whom he had named as Regent of France, issued a proclamation to the French people: 'Frenchmen, fortunes of war having put the capital in foreign hands, the Emperor, hastening to succour it, is at the head of his armies, so often victorious . . . Remain faithful to your vows, listen to the voice of a princess entrusted to your loyal support who glories in being a Frenchwoman and sharing the destinies of the sovereign you have yourselves chosen . . . The right and person of my son are under your protection.' It was touching and pathetic.

Ney, his most fearless commander and Berthier, his faithful chief of staff, now had the disagreeable task of telling Napoleon that his army would not march. 'The army will obey me,' insisted Napoleon. 'The army will obey its chief,' replied Ney.

Napoleon realized that the great adventure that had started with the shabby coup d'état at Brumaire eleven years before – or perhaps with his first military action in helping to recapture Toulon in 1795 – was over. He issued a proclamation on 4 April: 'The Allied powers having announced that the Emperor Napoleon is the sole obstacle to the re-establishment of peace in Europe, the Emperor Napoleon, mindful of his engagements, declares that he is ready to descend from the throne, to give up France and even life itself for the good of the country,

inseparable from the rights of his son, those of the regency of the Empress, and the maintenance of the laws of the Empire.'

Marie Louise desperately wanted to join him at Fontainebleau, so close to Orléans, but was partly dissuaded and partly kidnapped by a squadron of her father's troops and forced to join the Austrian Emperor at Rambouillet. Defiantly she wrote to her beloved Napoleon: 'By now you will know that they made me leave Orléans and that orders have been given to stop me from joining you and even by resort to force if necessary. Be on your guard, my dearest, they are out to fool us. I am worried to death for you, but I shall take a firm line with my father. I shall say that I am absolutely set on joining you, and nobody is going to prevent me from doing that.'

Napoleon penned a note to Marie Louise, saying he loved her 'more than anything in the world' and during the night of 13 April he attempted to take poison. Caulaincourt was summoned to find him convulsed in agony. After four hours he began to recover: he had apparently taken a dose he had been given two years before in case of capture by Russian partisans: it had failed to work.

On 16 April an English officer, Colonel Sir Neil Campbell, perhaps the first to meet him since 1803, gave this description of the deposed Emperor at Fontainebleau. 'I saw before me a short, active-looking man, who was rapidly pacing the length of his apartment, like some wild animal in his cell. He was dressed in an old green uniform with gold epaulets, blue pantaloons, and red top boots, unshaven, un-combed, with the fallen particles of snuff scattered profusely upon his upper lip and breast.' The fight was not quite yet over: for Eugène de Beauharnais still held out in Italy, a stepson as faithful to his master as his second wife had been.

De Beauharnais had prepared a spirited rearguard that confirmed the abilities he had shown on the Russian retreat. He had refused allied calls to make him King of Italy, pulling back to the Adige river with 50,000 men as his line of defence against the Austrians, who numbered some 70,000. When Murat, with 50,000 men, declared war on him from the south, he pulled back to a line of defence along the Mincio and the Po rivers. There he fought and won three battles. During the most remarkable, both sides simultaneously attacked in fog, crossing the

Mincio at different points to engage the enemy, and finding themselves in trouble on the reverse side. De Beauharnais had the best of the battle of the Mincio, taking 2,500 prisoners.

Napoleon ordered his stepson to bring his troops to his defence in France. But de Beauharnais refused, pointing out that they were mainly Italians who would desert if asked to fight in France. The British now joined the fight in Italy under Lord William Bentinck who early in March landed with 6,000 British and Sicilian troops at Leghorn. They became the forerunners of Italian independence and unity by calling upon the people to rise up against Eugène and form a free nation.

Bentinck immediately quarrelled with Murat and threatened to march on Naples and overthrow him. Castlereagh ordered him to desist and Bentinck settled for occupying the port of Genoa, while Murat moved north to attack his wife's step-nephew. De Beauharnais, who had already gone into action against Murat, with mixed results, prepared to do so again, but news arrived of the Treaty of Fontainebleau. This had been signed on 11 April. The allies, at the Tsar's urging, had decided to send Napoleon to exile on the island of Elba: Corsica and Sardinia were considered too large, Corfu too remote. The other members of the Bonaparte claim were to be given pensions. De Beauharnais's hopes of becoming Italy's new King were dashed by the Austrians, who had stirred up riots against him in Italy. He agreed to step down and departed for Munich in Bavaria, then to Paris, to be at his mother Josephine's bedside when she died in May. Two years later he was given the small Dutchy of Leuchtenberg by the King of Bavaria but presided over it only another seven years, dying peacefully at forty-three after the strain of so much campaigning.

Napoleon meanwhile left for Elba on 20 April in fourteen carriages escorted by sixty Polish cavalry, travelling to Lyons and the Rhone valley, a hotbed of royalist sentiment. At Avignon a mob stopped his coach and tried to lynch him. Napoleon uncharacteristically showed his fear and went on his way disguised as a servant, insisting on travelling aboard a British ship for greater safety. Once on the island he continued obsessively to rule its 12,000 inhabitants as though they were an empire, issuing decrees and reforming the administration. Unfortunately, he had little money and after a few months' 'activity

and restless perseverance', in the words of Campbell, the British commissioner who guaranteed his safety, he began to keep to his small house, where his faithful mother Letizia and sister Pauline joined him to while away the time playing cards. He snubbed Maria Walewska, however, who sought to join him.

Napoleon soon ran out of money – he had taken four million francs to Elba and had been promised two million more by the new French government, which never came. He feared he would soon not be able to afford his bodyguards and might be assassinated or transferred to the Azores. (Fouché said that Napoleon in Elba was to France what Vesuvius was to Naples.) Above all, he learnt with satisfaction of the rapid disillusion that followed the arrival of France's desperately uncharismatic new King.

Chapter 87

LOUIS XVIII

There can hardly have been a more complete contrast in history than that between the now deposed, hyperactive, quick-witted Corsican upstart and the Bourbon Louis XVIII, the new King imposed largely by the British. It was truly, in Napoleon's phrase, a change from the sublime to the ridiculous. The Comte de Provence was a hugely fat, waddling, prematurely aged man with a fish-like mouth and penetrating gaze surmounted by his sole distinguishing feature, prominent black eyebrows. Pompous, cold and courteous, endowed with little physical courage, considerable indolence, a prodigious love of food and books, and deeply self-centred, he had just two dominant virtues. While of middling intellect, he was politically moderate, pragmatic and shrewd; he was also reasonably humane in an age known for vindictiveness and cruelty. He was in fact a thoroughly civilized, mediocre, egotistical, eighteenth-century-style monarch, like many others of the same period.

Yet the course of this most ordinary man's life had been anything but ordinary. As a younger son he lived in the shadow of his good-looking, blond, blue-eyed, intelligent and prickly autocratic elder brother who became Louis XVI, as well as his own energetic scheming, reactionary and ambitious younger brother, the Comte d'Artois. A scion of the Bourbons, the greatest ruling family in Europe, which had run France since the tenth century, with brother branches on the thrones of Spain, Naples and Parma, he spent the first decades of his life virtually powerless.

He married a hideous Italian princess, Marie-Josephine, with a horse face, a large nose, and thick beetle eyebrows. They enjoyed the

peaceful splendour of life in Versailles. Philip Mansel, in his superb and definitive biography, wrote:

> His increasing size emphasised and helped ensure that he was one of the few Bourbons who did not spend half his life on a horse. At first, however, he had quite enjoyed hunting and shooting: he would be accompanied by sixty-three horses, twenty grooms, two *Ecuyers*, a *Gentilhomme d'Honneur*, a *Capitaine des Gardes* and his *Premier Ecuyer* when he went hunting, and by thirty-two horses and eighteen household officials and servants when he went shooting – impressive testimony to the degree to which his daily life was sheltered and surrounded by his household. And in the 1780s he was still going shooting once or twice a month in the summer.

Like most royal siblings, he cordially detested his older brother. When the events of 1789 occurred, he had been merely a passive spectator. In June 1791 he slipped away into exile with a friend, pretending to be a British merchant, using phrases like 'Come with me' and 'I am ready', and speaking to the coachman in French with an English accent. After drifting aimlessly around Europe as an exile, Louis supported the aborted royalist invasion of France in the autumn of 1792.

With the guillotining of Louis XVI and the death in appalling circumstances of his infant son soon afterwards, this portly indolent, easygoing man became the Pretender to the French throne. However most royalists preferred his scheming, hardline younger brother, the Comte d'Artois. On Napoleon's ascent to power, Louis wrote amicably to the new leader suggesting that he support a royal restoration, only to be brutally fobbed off: 'You would have to walk over a hundred thousand corpses. Sacrifice your interests to the peace and happiness of France' – words which ring a little ironically in view of later events. In 1807 Louis took refuge in England, to the dismay of its government which wanted an accommodation with the French republican regime and refused to allow him to reside in London.

Instead he was patronized by the recently deposed Whig grandee, the outgoing prime minister, William, Lord Grenville, and lavishly entertained at Stowe, ducal seat of the marquess of Buckingham,

Grenville's brother. Louis's son and heir almost fell in love with his lovely twenty-one-year-old daughter, Lady Mary Grenville. In England Louis became still fatter, moving 'like the heavings of a ship', as Charles Grenville commented, and contracted gout, so that he had to be wheeled about his country house. Not until 1811 was he officially received by the court, in the shape of the almost as fat, but quicker-witted and more unscrupulous Prince Regent.

On 12 March 1814 news arrived to a tearfully joyful Louis that Bordeaux had risen against Napoleon and had been liberated by Wellington. On 7 April the French senate proclaimed him King of France. On 24 April Louis set foot in France for the first time after two decades in exile, arriving to a tumultuous welcome in Calais. Five days later at Compiègne the surviving coterie of Napoleon's senior marshals Ney, Berthier, Marmont, Jourdan, Mortier, Oudinot and Victor – arrived to pay him homage and put the army at his disposal. The effective leader of France, Talleyrand, was there too, along with the Vicomte de Chateaubriand. They pledged to 'provide the pillars of your throne'. Louis greeted them generously: 'It is on you, Messieurs les Maréchaux, that I want always to rely; come near and surround me. You have always been good Frenchmen; I hope that France will have no more need of your swords. If ever, which God forbid, we were forced to draw them, I would march with you, if that was necessary.'

All this was an astonishing turnaround. The restoration of the guillotined King of France's corpulent younger brother seemed to wipe out the entire French national experience from 1789 to 1814 and return the country to the *status quo ante*. All the turbulence, murderousness and disruption of the Revolution, all the sacrifice, glory and imperial power had, it seemed, been in vain: the clock had been turned back to what it was before, as if France had awoken from a nightmare to rediscover its former Versailles-type splendour.

In a sense it was Napoleon himself who had paved the way, for his own attempts to create a dynasty had resulted in a France that was if anything more royal, centralized and absolutist than ever before. As Lafayette, in retirement, wrote to his friend Thomas Jefferson in August: 'Bonaparte or the Bourbons, such have been, and such still

are, the only possible alternatives, in a land where the idea of a republican executive is regarded as synonymous with the excesses committed under that name.'

Older revolutionaries like the regicide Fouché were now dukes. The Abbé Sieyès, whose incendiary pamphlets had triggered off the Revolution and who had brought Napoleon to power, was a count. Carnot, creator of the republican military machine taken over by Napoleon, was also a count.

Nor had the Revolution or Napoleon wrought so great a transformation in the French social fabric as they liked to believe. With a population of nearly 30 million, France was still an overwhelmingly agricultural land. Of the 670 richest people in France around that time only a fifth did not derive their fortunes from the land. (Around 75 per cent were nobility either from before, or ennobled by, Napoleon.) France may actually have deindustrialized during the period when industrialization was transforming Britain, thanks to the chaos caused by the Revolution and the Napoleonic wars.

Marseilles and Bordeaux were in decline, and Paris's population had fallen by 50,000 to some 600,000. Fewer than 20 per cent lived in towns of more than 2,000 people. The Revolution had redistributed land to a much lesser extent than is believed. Between 1789 and 1804 it is estimated that the nobility's share of the land had fallen from 21 to 15 per cent, while church lands had been entirely expropriated. The middle classes' share rose from 16 to 28 per cent, and the peasantry's from 30 to 42 per cent. As Mansel observed:

> Land-ownership and government office or military position were indeed perhaps even more important after than before the Revolution, since they had become the most reliable sources of wealth. The great seaports of eighteenth-century France were now declining for lack of trade, for France was almost permanently at war. After his release from prison in 1794, the great eighteenth-century painter Hubert Robert had no need to go to Rome to paint ruins. There were enough in and round Paris. A report addressed to Louis's agent in Vienna in 1804 noted that commerce was languishing, bankruptcies were frequent and only agriculture was flourishing. The

Revolution, far from being 'capitalist' or 'bourgeois', had delayed France's industrial development by fifty years.

The monarchy had been restored to the throne, not by the French people, but by occupying powers; and they were themselves divided.

The main concern of both the British and the Austrians had been to prevent the other predatory power that they considered most dangerous in Europe, Russia, from taking France into its orbit for traditional dynastic reasons. The Tsar detested the French Bourbons, but had been forced to acquiesce in Louis's accession. During the last days of Napoleon's regime, Alexander had continually toyed with the idea of setting up Napoleon's son, the infant King of Rome, as regent. Talleyrand remarked: 'The Emperor Alexander is capable of the unexpected; one is not the son of Paul for nothing.' The Prussians sided with their allies, the Russians. A continent of two separate blocks seemed indeed possible.

Talleyrand wanted to dissuade the Tsar with all the diplomatic dexterity at his fingertips. One contemporary remarked:

> There was this advantage with him, that no question surprised him, and that the most unexpected ones pleased him the best . . . The whole policy of the Provisional Government was the *laisser-aller* and the *laisser-faire* of Monsieur de Talleyrand; his genius hovered above all the intrigues and lurked behind all the business . . . I overcame my awe of this famous statesman; his reputation was more imposing than his personality – he was easy to get on with; phantoms disappear when one is close to them. It was in the simplest conversation that Monsieur de Talleyrand let fall the remarks to which he attached the greatest importance, they always had an object; he sowed them carelessly, like the seed that nature scatters, and, as in nature, the majority perished without produce.

Talleyrand persuaded Alexander that any such regency would be but a figleaf for continuing Napoleonic rule and would swiftly result in the Emperor's restoration. But fortune had indeed proved capricious; for

Alexander, Napoleon's bitterest enemy of 1812, was now a covert sympathizer of the exiled Emperor, with Austria and Britain, who had questioned the wisdom of invading France, the main supporters of the Bourbon restoration, largely because they favoured a weak government in France; Britain was confident that it could control Louis.

Louis from the first disliked having been recalled by the old senate, composed of revolutionaries and Napoleonic sycophants, who had issued a liberal constitution similar to that of 1791 with a two-chamber parliament, a ministry responsible to it and a King who derived his authority from 'the people'. He lost no time in insisting that, on the contrary, the new constitutional regime derived its authority from the monarchy, not the other way around.

Yet he was a paternalist, not an absolutist, unlike the vicious Ferdinand VII of Spain, who on his restoration after the Peninsular War promptly abolished parliament. Louis granted equality of religion, including that of the Jews, whom Napoleon had persecuted in 1808. Political prisoners were released and censorship eased, although not abolished. Louis's governments consisted of moderates like Talleyrand.

However, he revived the unpopular splendours of Versailles. And within months discontent was spreading across France like wildfire. The government from the first showed itself to be disunited and venal, with the bureaucracy expanding rapidly. Worse, it was treated with contempt by the hardline royalists, known as the ultras, who sought to revenge themselves against the revolutionaries, and to return to the old pattern of landholdings and absolutist rule. Many people in France, especially the new landowners, were terrified at the prospect of the ultras coming to power.

Louis also became unpopular for his friendship with his country's traditional enemy, Britain, whose tourists swarmed to Paris. The Prince Regent himself was invited over and Wellington, France's most hated enemy general, became British ambassador, who many suspected gave Louis his orders. The Duke's nomination, was, in truth, one of Castlereagh's most disastrous mistakes, a direct provocation that suggested to the French that they were under British military occupation.

The Duke was far from unenlightened. He charmed many French noblemen with his observation of their customs and his courtly

manner, and played a role in getting the French to abolish the slave trade. He was also thoroughly French, embarking on a string of love affairs with a score of pretty women, two at least of whom had been lovers of Napoleon – Guiseppina Grassini, the opera singer, and Marguerite Josephine Weimar, the actress, who remarked: '*Le Duc était de beaucoup le plus fort.*' He also may have bedded Marshal Ney's pretty young wife. Harriet Wilson, the famous British courtesan, was also seen in passionate embrace with the Duke in the Bois de Boulogne. The Duke had long become bored sexually by the decent, fussy, short-sighted Kitty with her plain dress, who remained in Britain for several months.

At the sumptuous new British embassy in the Faubourg St Honoré, Wellington entertained lavishly, marvelling at the King's ability to eat an entire serving dish of strawberries. He met old adversaries, including Ney and Soult. Masséna remarked: 'My Lord, you owe me dinner for you positively made me starve.' 'You should give it to me, Marshal, for you prevented me from sleeping,' was Wellington's dry retort. He was devastated by news of the death of Ned Pakenham, his adoring young brother-in-law, during the brief war with America.

He sent another young protégé, Colonel Harvey, with urgent despatches to Beresford, now running the British army in Lisbon. Harvey made the ride across immensely dangerous territory in record time, drawing the admiration of the British press.

He performed the journey of nearly 1,400 miles, from Paris to Lisbon on horseback in fourteen days, a feat rarely accomplished by an equestrian, and one which may be truly considered of an extraordinary character, considering the season of the year, the nature of the country to be passed, and the dangers to which he was exposed. That those dangers were of no ordinary character may be gathered from the fact that in passing through Spain, Colonel Harvey was stopped by banditti (who after the war infested every portion of the country), who robbed him of everything but his despatches, and a few pieces of silver which he managed to save from them by pleading that he 'had fought for their country'. His knowledge of the language, and of the people of the various

countries through which he passed on this journey, must have stood Colonel Harvey in good stead. A single anecdote may be narrated as an illustration of the mode in which he turned such knowledge to account. On arriving at Salamanca very late at night, the colonel and his guide found the gates of the city closed to travellers. The guide called, as usual, on the Virgin. The colonel, knowing the Spaniards, as he was accustomed to observe, enquired for the breach that was made last year in the Town Walls. 'I can take you to it,' said the guide. 'Then there will be no difficulty in getting into the town,' said the colonel, 'for I am quite certain they have not thought of repairing it, or of placing any one to guard it, so let us go in.' And go in they did, for on arriving at the breach they found it precisely in the condition the colonel had predicted, unrepaired and entirely unprotected.

Nearly a century and a half later Harvey's great grandson Oliver was to return as British ambassador in the splendid establishment of Rue de Fauborg St Honoré after the Second World War.

Wellington also visited London, where he was rapturously received in society as well as by the crowds. 'It is a fine thing to be a great man, is it not?' he remarked grandly to Lady Shelley, who became a close companion of his, as the crowds parted respectfully to let them through after an opera. Wellington was not a modest man.

A large part of the destroyed Napoleonic army grew increasingly sullen: many were demobbed and unemployed, roaming the country. Most believed they had not been defeated but betrayed by Talleyrand and other civilian intriguers. Nationalism, always a hugely potent force in France, reared its head again: the country was seething under foreign occupation.

Talleyrand was denounced for selling his country's interests at the Congress of Vienna when the exact opposite was true: with scarcely any cards at his disposal he actually secured a peace which expanded France's territorial size from what it had been in 1789 and required it to pay no reparations to the allies for devastating a continent for two generations. He explained his task:

The role of France was singularly difficult. It was very tempting and very easy for the Governments which had so long been hostile to keep her excluded from the major questions affecting Europe. By the Treaty of Paris France had escaped destruction, but she had not regained the position that she ought to occupy in the general political system. Trained eyes could easily detect in several of the principal plenipotentiaries the secret desire to reduce France to a secondary role. It was necessary above all that the French representative should understand, and should make it understood, that France wanted nothing more than she possessed, that she had sincerely repudiated the heritage of conquest, that she considered herself strong enough within her ancient frontiers, that she had no thought of extending them, and, finally, that she now took pride in her moderation.

Talleyrand sought the friendship of Austria and Britain to impede the ambitions of Russia and Prussia. He had the effrontery to chide the Tsar: 'Liberal principles are in accordance with the spirit of the age, they cannot be avoided; and, if Your Majesty will take my word for it, I can promise you that we shall have monarchy combined with liberty; that you will see men of real merit welcomed and given office . . . I admit, Sir, that you have met many discontented people in Paris, but what is Paris after all? The provinces, they are the real France – and it is there that the return of the House of Bourbon is blessed and that your happy victory is proclaimed.'

To Metternich he said: 'There are people here who ought to be allies in the sense that they ought to think in the same way and desire the same things. How have you the courage to put Russia like a belt around your principal and most important possessions, Hungary and Bohemia? How can you allow all the patrimony of an old and good neighbour [the King of Saxony] to be given to your natural enemy [Prussia]?'

In fact, as Castlereagh also saw, Russia's ambition to swallow Poland whole and Prussia's to devour Saxony were as potentially dangerous as an act of Napoleonic aggression. With extraordinary foresight Talleyrand declared that if Prussia succeeded, 'she would in a few years form a

militarist monarchy that would be very dangerous to her neighbours'. He pointed out that the Russians and Prussians were so closely allied precisely because the former would be able to pursue its old goal of dismantling the enfeebled Ottoman empire in the south, outflanking Austria, while the latter could expand steadily to absorb all of Germany.

A second treaty was at last signed at Vienna between Britain, France and Austria to provide a force of 150,000 in case any of them should be attacked by either Russia or Prussia. Triumphantly Talleyrand wrote to Louis: 'The coalition is dissolved . . . France is no longer isolated in Europe . . . Your Majesty possesses a federal system which fifty years of negotiations might not have constructed. You are acting in concert with two of the greatest powers and three states of the second rank, and will soon be joined by all the states whose principles and politics are not revolutionary.'

Castlereagh wrote to his government 'The alarm of war is over', as a result of the deterrent effect upon Russia and Prussia of the treaty. The actual deal, however, was an unsatisfactory compromise over Poland and Saxony. But Talleyrand's success was reviled in nationalist circles who denounced him for conducting an alliance with hated enemies – Britain and Austria.

Thus in the space of under a year the restored Bourbon regime had succeeded in creating a powerful coalition of domestic enemies: nationalists, discontented Bonapartists, army veterans, those seeking repossession of their lands, those fearing dispossession from their newly acquired properties, those disappointed in the hope of a quick economic revival, the old revolutionaries, those who had hated Bonaparte and even welcomed the restoration of the monarchy but feared vengeance if the ultras came to power, and constitutional reformers who suspected Louis would reinstate absolutist rule. Well-meaning as he was, Louis paid the price of indecision. By wavering between his hardliners and his moderates, he made enemies of both.

Chapter 88

RETURN OF THE BOGEYMAN

It was to the new government's mistakes that that extraordinary whirlwind, the rising from the political grave of Napoleon Bonaparte, 'the Hundred Days', must be attributed. Chafing and resentful in Elba, he had watched like a vulture as the new French government stumbled and as discontent on the mainland increased. He soon believed he had enough support to move. He may also have been secretly encouraged in that belief by the falling out of his enemies at Vienna – Britain and Austria versus Russia and Prussia. He may have imagined this would rebound to his advantage, and that he had the tacit support of the Tsar or, absurdly, that Britain and Austria would need his help against the two northern powers.

He chose his moment carefully on 26 February 1815, embarking some 1,000 men aboard the brig *Inconstant* for the hazardous two-day sail to land near Antibes. Napoleon had earlier ordered the same brig to rescue his beloved Marie Louise from Aix, where she was holidaying; but by then she was already under the spell of a dashing general, Count von Neipperg, cunningly sent to chaperone her by her father, the Emperor Francis; so, she refused. Soon after it was clear that the two of them had become lovers. Napoleon had lost both his wives in the space of six months; and he was so offhand towards the adoring Marie Walewska, who visited him on Elba, that she too was put off. Napoleon wrote bitterly: 'My wife no longer writes to me. My son is snatched away from me. No such barbarous act is recorded in modern times.' Napoleon declared that he would reach Paris 'without firing a shot'.

Landing on 1 March, he issued one of his famous rallying cries to his troops:

> Soldiers! In my exile I have heard your voice. I have come to you through every obstacle, every danger. Your general, called to the throne by the voice of the people and raised on your bucklers, is back among you; come to him! Pluck off the colours that the nation has proscribed, and that, for twenty-five years, were the rallying point of all the enemies of France. Put on the Tricolor cockade; you wore it in our great days. Here are the eagles you had at Ulm, at Austerlitz, at Jena, at Eylau, at Friedland, at Tudela, at Eckmühl, at Essling, at Wagram, at Smolensk, at the Moskowa, at Lützen, at Wurschen, at Montmirail! Do you believe that the little handful of Frenchmen who are so arrogant today can support their sight? They will return whence they came; there let them reign as they pretend that they did reign these last nineteen years. Soldiers, rally around the standard of your chief! Victory will advance at the double! The Eagle, with the national colours, will fly from steeple to steeple to the towers of Notre Dame. Then will you be able to display your honourable scars. Then will you be able to claim the credit of your deeds, as the liberators of your country. In your old age, surrounded and honoured by your fellow citizens, all will respectfully listen while you narrate your great deeds; you will be able to say with pride: 'And I also was one of that Grand Army that twice entered the walls of Vienna, of Rome, of Berlin, of Madrid, of Moscow, and that cleansed Paris from the stain left on it by treason and the presence of the enemy!'

He also pledged 'equality among all classes', in an opportunistic attempt to rally France's remaining revolutionaries against the reactionary government of Louis XVIII. Receiving a hostile reception on landing, he chose not to march through Provence, a royalist hotbed, but across the lower Alps to Grenoble, a perilous single track across precipices and made slippery by ice and snow. It was an heroic progress by Napoleon's thousand that lasted six days and covered 240 miles.

The column was blocked at Laffrey, twenty-five miles south of

Grenoble, by a body of troops. Napoleon, ever the actor, walked forward in front of his men, with 'The Marseillaise' being played behind him, and opened his greatcoat to show the white uniform beneath. 'Here I am. Kill your Emperor if you wish.' A resounding cheer was the response: '*Vive l'Empereur!*'

He reached Grenoble where the garrison refused to fire upon him and a crowd welcomed him into the city with flaming torches. A day later he reached Lyons and marched north to Auxerre after sending a note to his old comrade Ney. 'I shall receive you as I did on the morrow of the Battle of the Moskva.' This simple soldier came over to him at Auxerre, which precipitated dozens of other defections by officers and army units.

Louis had received news of Napoleon's landing philosophically: 'I beg you, Messieurs, to inform your Courts that, but for a little gout, I am in good health, and that I am not in the least bit worried by this event. I hope that it will trouble neither the peace of Europe nor my own.' But already crowds were chanting 'The Bourbons to the scaffold! Down with princes! Behead the royalists!'

On 16 March Louis addressed the two chambers, pledging to die in defence of the constitution. The leader of the ultras, the Crown Prince, the Comte d'Artois, for the first time pledged loyalty to the constitution. But with army units defecting in droves, the King was left with only his household troops and a few thousand volunteers.

Louis decided not to die after all, but to fly. At midnight on 19 March, as Napoleon's growing army approached Paris, the corpulent King bade farewell to his tearful supporters. 'Struck by his venerable appearance, we fell weeping to our knees,' said one. Louis set off in his carriage with a military escort to Lille in pouring rain. At 9 p.m. the following evening Napoleon arrived and a delirious crowd carried him up the steps of the Tuileries. Not a drop of blood had been spilled.

Louis's party, bogged down in mud, travelled slowly to Lille. It was met with sympathy by the people of the villages and towns it passed through. He crossed into Belgium, where people were 'on their knees in the mud, raising their hands to heaven and begging the King not to abandon them'. Louis contemplated fleeing to England but instead

went on to a lovely castle. Here he downed a hundred oysters at a single sitting – an extraordinary feat even for this gourmand king. He justified his cowardice to Talleyrand: 'So Bonaparte has force on his side; all hearts are for me. I have seen unequivocal proof of this all along my route. So the powers cannot doubt France's desires this year. That is your text, I leave the commentary to you.'

Napoleon had made a serious mistake in his timing, for the Congress of Vienna was still sitting. There the main sovereigns of Europe and their foreign ministers continued to wrangle, enjoying magnificent hospitality at the Austrian Emperor's expense, and gossiped maliciously about one another with Francis's spies watching their every move. On 7 March a messenger reached Metternich's palace with the news of Napoleon's landing. But he was asleep and refused to read the paper for a while before opening the envelope and dashing off to inform Francis.

By one o'clock he had summoned Francis, the Prussian King and the Tsar. An hour later the Congress was resumed with urgency. Riders were despatched from Vienna to every country in Europe. Within six days each major power had agreed to provide 150,000 men – 600,000 in total to 'crush the ogre once and for all'. The differences between the nations were hastily shelved: with Talleyrand leaving his post as Louis fled Paris, the Russians and the Prussians secured a better deal than they might have expected: two-fifths of Saxony went to Prussia, and even more of the Grand Duchy of Poland was set up as a Russian satellite, the Kingdom of Poland. Napoleon was declared an outlaw, a capital offence. He had gone too far.

Desperately Napoleon sent an emissary to Alexander and Francis accepting the new boundaries of France; desperately he tried to act constitutionally: Carnot was appointed minister of the interior and even Lafayette became official opposition leader in an attempt to woo the old revolutionaries. However the sinister Fouché stayed on as chief of police. The constitution was to be reformed along moderate lines and Benjamin Constant, a widely respected moderate, appointed to perform the task. Constant agreed to set up a liberal constitution and hold a plebiscite on 6 May, although he previously had described Napoleon as 'dyed with our blood . . . He is another Attila, another

Genghiz Khan, but more terrible and more hateful because he has at his disposal the resources of civilisation.'

In this plebiscite only 1.5 million approved the constitution, compared with Napoleon's old turnout of 3.5 million. In Dijon he won less than a quarter of the vote, in Lyons 15 per cent, in Paris just 12 per cent, in Strasbourg 11 per cent, in Toulon 5 per cent, in Bordeaux 3 per cent, in Nantes 2 per cent and in Marseilles 1 per cent. Altogether only 21 per cent voted in favour. He could hardly claim popular legitimacy and certainly no general enthusiasm: his restoration had been the work of a minority, mostly disgruntled servicemen.

Napoleon also promised: 'No more war, no conquests.' 'Can one be as fat as I am and have ambition?' he asked disarmingly. But when the new Assembly defied him, he quickly flared up in his old imperious manner: 'Let us not imitate the example of the later Roman Empire which, invaded on all sides by the barbarians, made itself the laughing-stock of posterity by discussing abstract questions when the battering-rams were breaking down the city gates.'

He was soon bitterly disappointed to find that his peace overtures had been rejected by the allies, and called for mobilization: he raised nearly 300,000 men, but many were untrained and ill-equipped. He now had to decide on a suitable strategy – whether to stay and defend Paris or to strike at one of the great allied armies being hastily assembled to fight him. Already at the Rhine Schwarzenberg had assembled some 200,000 Austrians, while Barclay de Tolly was bringing up 150,000 Russians more slowly behind him. A force of 75,000 Austrians was assembling in Italy to enter France from the south-east. In the north a British-dominated army of 110,000, including Belgians and Saxons, was to be assembled to link up with 117,000 Prussians under Blücher.

Further bad news soon reached Napoleon: Murat had raised his flag against the Austrians, anticipating a victory by Napoleon – but had been badly defeated at the Battle of Tolentino on the eastern shores of the Apennines, south-west of Ancona, on 3 May. Within three weeks the dashing Neipperg, Marie Louise's lover, led a body of Austrian troops to take Naples and the Bourbon Ferdinand IV was placed on the throne for the following decade.

*   *   *

Napoleon decided against a defensive strategy, which would have allowed him to build up his forces: he already had a much larger force to defend Paris in place than in the previous year. But he feared his unpopularity would grow in the capital if the campaign was drawn out. It was a characteristically bold gamble: to strike with his 140,000 strong northern army into Belgium only a few days' march away and divide the British and Prussian armies strung out along a 145-kilometre front, the former with 100,000 men to the west, the latter with 150,000 men to the east and thus seek to counter their joint superiority as they sought separately to protect their communications.

Down in Vienna Wellington had been representing the British for a few weeks in place of Castlereagh, who had been recalled. (The British government had become desperately anxious to remove the Duke from Paris since an assassination attempt had been made on his life, and they knew that he would not budge unless the pretext were important enough.) Wellington sprang into action to face his great adversary as commander of the British army in Belgium. As in a Wild West film the two most formidable commanders in Europe were to meet for the final shoot-out in the last reel.

Wellington, whom Talleyrand described as the most complicated man he had ever met, had always been an indifferent diplomat, just as in later life he was to prove an even less impressive politician. His steely, martinet style was worlds apart from the finesses and evasions of diplomacy, or the compromises and backslapping of politicians. It must be asked what drove this extraordinary man on and on: having become Europe's most famous soldier, he had striven for new successes in diplomacy and politics as though he could not rest.

He always attributed his drive to his sense of duty and noblesse oblige. But duty did not require him to climb the summit of three different careers. Beneath the carefully cultivated air of languor and detachment that were supposed to mark him out as the English gentleman he was not there lay a man of intense ambition, determined to succeed in everything that he did and never to rest on his laurels, perhaps the product of slights he had suffered in his youth, the ugly duckling brother of the glamorous Richard.

In this he again closely resembled George Washington, so apparently

obtuse, with the manner of a Virginian country gentleman which concealed a determination not just to win but to lead his own country. Wellington was no polymath: he was a great soldier, but not a very good diplomat or politician. This was the strange personality who now travelled to Belgium for his appointment with his adversary, the most powerful and famous ruler the world had ever yet seen, to 'get his man'.

They were pretty evenly matched: the meticulous, calculating, defiant British general against the brilliant, bold French soldier, a clash of two military titans rarely experienced in history. It is unsurprising that the Waterloo campaign was to become the most written about in military history.

Yet the reality was somewhat different. Napoleon, like the proverbial outlaw he now was, was making his last throw of the dice. He calculated on inflicting a great defeat so that the government of Lord Liverpool in Britain would fall, to be replaced by the more conciliatory Whigs, while the Prussians and the Russians might peel off and make peace. In reality the chances that this would have happened were slender: in all probability the huge armies of Europe would probably still have continued to march if he had won Waterloo and he would have been crushed. Again like the proverbial outlaw, he preferred to go out and meet his enemies rather than be caught and surrounded and at last vanquished.

At midnight on 11 June Napoleon left Paris to join his 140,000-strong army. He had slept one last time with the loyal Marie Walewska. He spurned the capable but disloyal Murat's offer of help, a mistake as he was so short of good generals, and left the highly capable Davout as military governor of Paris, no doubt to keep order while he was absent and to deter attack from the east and south. His faithful chief of staff, Berthier, had tragically thrown himself from a window of a palace in Bavaria for reasons which are still unknown. His chief lieutenants in the campaign were to be the fearless but strategically inept Ney, the competent but scarcely brilliant Soult, and Grouchy, a cavalry commander without imagination. Napoleon himself was clearly ailing: his face was puffy and he had grown much fatter recently. He appeared

tired and lethargic and required an unusual amount of sleep. On 14 June he issued his last great proclamation to an army.

> Soldiers! This is the anniversary of Marengo and of Friedland, that twice decided the fate of Europe. Then, as after Wagram, as after Austerlitz, we were too generous; we believed in . . . the oaths of the princes whom we left on their thrones! And now, coalesced against us, they are aiming at the independence and the most sacred rights of France. They have begun an unjust aggression. Forward! Let us march against them; are not they and we the same men?
>
> Soldiers! You were one against three at Jena against these same arrogant Prussians; at Montmirail, you were one against six. Madmen! A moment's prosperity has blinded them. If they enter France they will find their graves. Soldiers, we have forced marches to make, battles to fight, dangers to encounter, but with constancy the victory will be ours; the rights, the honour, of our country will be reconquered. For every Frenchman who has courage the moment has come to conquer or to die!

He ordered his men forward with his customary speed and secrecy towards Charleroi, straight for the gap between the British and Prussian armies. It was a typically all-or-nothing strategy, and he caught the allies entirely by surprise.

Chapter 89

WHILE THE DUKE DANCED

Wellington had been in command in Brussels ever since early April, and had made a poor job of it. There he had to integrate Britain, Hanoverian and Dutch units. He complained of his 'infamous army, very weak and ill-equipped, and a very inexperienced staff'. He divided the army into three corps, one under the youthful Prince of Orange, the second under the sturdy Rowland Hill, with himself in charge of the reserve. He had a total of just 92,000 men and 192 guns. Under entirely separate control was Blücher's Prussian army of 120,000 men and more than 300 guns.

Wellington had met Blücher in Paris and, unusually for the acidulous Irishman, got on well with a brother general. But his first duty was to his own men. This in his opinion meant protecting his line of retreat to the ports of Antwerp and Ostend so that he could evacuate his army in the event of a defeat. He was concerned that Napoleon might come up around his west flank towards Tournai and threaten the coastal area, cutting him off. In spite of this worry, he privately believed that Napoleon, if he did come, would move towards Mons in the centre and keep his options open. He disposed his forces with an eye to protecting the coast, which meant they were kept a considerable distance from Blücher's army.

But Wellington did not really believe Napoleon would attack at all. In fact he wanted to invade France to surprise Napoleon. The British commander basked in complacency in the almost carnival atmosphere of Brussels, to which British society had flocked in early summer. He wrote to Lord Stewart on 8 May: 'I say nothing about our defensive

operations because I am inclined to believe we are so well united and so strong that the enemy cannot do us much mischief.' On the very day that Napoleon's army crossed into Belgium, Wellington wrote to the Tsar discussing the best routes for the allies to invade France.

Napoleon crossed the border with his army on 15 June and appointed Ney to command his left flank, the First and Second Corps, while Grouchy commanded the right, the Third and Fourth Corps. Ney was ordered to seize the hamlet of Quatre Bras just beyond the intersection of the main east-west Roman road with the north-south road to Brussels. Wellington was blissfully unaware of his approach, a major failure in allied intelligence. Lieutenant-Colonel Colquhoun Grant, one of his intelligence officers, had tried to warn him on 14 June; but another officer failed to pass the message on. Wellington did not receive news of the first French attacks that day until 6 p.m.

He had been enjoying himself with parties and amorous dalliances in Brussels, including one with Lady Frances Wedderburn-Webster in a leafy glade. Wellington's caddish character in seducing married women, while himself being married, on an unusually large scale for an Englishman, even an officer, has not been given the attention it deserves. In this, if in so little else, he resembled Napoleon; but this behaviour was thoroughly at odds with the image of the dutiful English gentleman he liked to project.

As late as 13 June he had written: 'There is nothing new here. We have reports of Buonaparte's joining the army and attacking us; but I have accounts from Paris of the 10th, on which day he was still there; and I judge from his speech to the Legislature that his departure was not likely to be imminent. I think we are now too strong for him here.'

On 15 June at just before six he first heard the news that the French were attacking Prussian forward posts. He chose not to react, but to wait for further evidence of the size and whereabouts of the French force: the attack was much further to the east than he expected and could prove a feint.

Some German historians have alleged that he learnt much earlier of the attacks, but chose not to come to the help of the Prussians. There is no documentary evidence for this. Blücher sent a message calling for help; but Wellington had already left for a ball given by the Duchess of

Richmond improvised in a large workshop. There he 'affected great gaiety and cheerfulness' but an observer remarked: 'I had never seen him with such an expression of care and anxiety on his countenance.' He was not neglecting his duties: he simply did not yet know how to react to an attack whose direction and intensity he could not guess.

That same night Ney had disobeyed the admittedly ambiguous order from Napoleon to take Quatre Bras and bedded down for the night. There a small Dutch force commanded by Prince Bernhard of Saye-Weimar, and sent there by the Prince of Orange's chief of staff in defiance of orders, had entrenched itself. At nearly nine o'clock in the evening, Wellington, who had escorted Lady Charlotte Greville to the ball, was told by the Prince of Orange of the French concentration outside Quatre Bras. He affected calm, but summoned the Duke of Richmond and said tersely: 'Napoleon has humbugged me, by God, he has gained 24 hours' march on me.'

It was too late to send reinforcements to Quatre Bras. He decided to make a stand farther back towards the village of Waterloo. After snatching three hours' sleep, he breakfasted leisurely, then rode forward towards Quatre Bras, which he found to be peaceful. He ordered troops down to support the Dutch in their outpost. Then he sent a letter to Blücher at 10.30 declaring 'I do not see much of the enemy in front of us, and I await news of your Highness and the arrival of troops in order to determine my operations for the day. Nothing has appeared on the side of Binche, or on our right.'

He rode to meet the Prussian commanders at the village of Brye. Blücher reported to him that he had concentrated three corps around the village of Ligny nearby to the south east. The accounts of the meeting are contradictory: General von Muffling, Prussia's liaison officer, claimed that Wellington, on being asked to lend support to the Prussian stand at Ligny, said: 'Well, I will come, provided that I myself am not attacked [at Quatre Bras].' Another German officer claims that Wellington agreed simply to block the French at Quatre Bras and send the bulk of his forces to Prussia's aid. This seems highly unlikely, as he was hurrying most of his troops forward to the exposed position at Quatre Bras and could not spare many for Ligny; he still could not be sure where the main thrust of Napoleon's attack would

come – whether at Quatre Bras or Ligny – and his army was weaker than Blücher's; he did not know that Napoleon intended to attack both at once.

Privately he considered Blücher had blundered in his choice of ground to meet the French, which was only a mile away from Brye. 'If they fight here they will be damnably mauled.' This was open ground in front of a hill. Meanwhile, in the west, Ney still hesitated to attack Quatre Bras because he was not sure of the enemy strength; owing to the incompetence of Napoleon's chief of staff, Soult, clear orders did not reach him until the mid-afternoon to take the village and then wheel about and fall upon Blücher's exposed eastern flank and rear while Napoleon attacked from the front. The Prussians would thus be annihilated between two fires.

Chapter 90

LIGNY AND QUATRE BRAS

On the morning of 16 June Napoleon ordered his men forward against the exposed Prussian front for the first of three battles over three days of fighting that collectively became known as the Battle of Waterloo. Napoleon declared: 'the intention of His Majesty is that you attack whatever is before you and after vigorously throwing them back, join us to envelop this corps.' However, he believed the Prussians to have only 40,000 men when in fact they had double that and General von Bülow's corps of 32,000 stationed at Liège was on its way, although in the event it arrived too late for the battle.

He ordered a devastating artillery barrage to open up on the exposed Prussian positions, followed by a cavalry attack by Grouchy on the right, as well as by the infantry. Soon the French had captured the villages of St Amand and Sombrette. The gallant Blücher, who had put himself at the head of a cavalry charge, had his horse shot under him and narrowly escaped being trampled to death; but he was rescued, command temporarily devolving to Gneisenau, who anxiously awaited for reinforcements from Wellington that did not come. He later wrote; 'on the 16th of June in the morning the Duke of Wellington promised to be at Quatre Bras at 10am with 20,000 men . . . on the strength of these promises and arrangements we decided to fight the battle . . . ' As we have seen the Prussians had no reason to believe they would be reinforced unless Wellington felt himself secure at Quatre Bras.

At 2 p.m., out of sight three miles to the west, Ney's army had at last launched a major attack and Wellington was desperately trying to bring up the men being hurried down the Brussels road to hold the village of

Quatre Bras. Ney had delayed attacking, believing the Dutch defending force to be greater than it actually was, and that Wellington's army
was largely concealed behind the brow of a low hill. When Ney finally
did attack, reinforcements were hurriedly arriving, already exhausted
by the march in the intense heat.

As the Dutch front line gave ground under the French assault, Picton
and 8,000 troops arrived and pushed them back for a short while,
before more French troops were committed and the Anglo-Dutch
forces were pushed back again. A force of cavalry under the Duke of
Brunswick arrived and charged, but he was mortally wounded. Wellington, mounted on Copenhagen, was nearly captured by a French
counter-charge. He galloped into a British square yelling, 'Lie down,
92nd,' and the men let him pass over and jumped up again discharging
volleys at the pursuing French horsemen, who veered away. Further
French charges followed – in one case right into an incomplete square
of the 42nd Highlanders, who closed it and trapped and killed the
cavalrymen inside.

But Ney's 40,000-strong army just kept on coming, counter-char-
ging the reinforcements as quickly as they could be brought forward.
Meanwhile Napoleon, realizing that Ney had not broken through
Quatre Bras, instructed General d'Erlon, commanding Ney's 22,000-
strong reserve, to stage the flank attack he had planned against the
Prussian right which he believed would deliver a decisive victory. Ney
had been right to press his attack on Quatre Bras: for we now know
that if he had veered off to the right to help Napoleon, the British
would have felt free to reinforce Blücher.

But Napoleon's last-minute change of orders proved very nearly
disastrous, for it deprived Ney of the reserve support he needed to
overwhelm the British position. D'Erlon, misunderstanding his orders,
moved to reinforce the French right rather than attack behind Prussian
lines: this panicked the French right, which mistook his men for enemy
troops. This in turn delayed Napoleon's own advance which had been
going well; but he coolly ordered d'Erlon to march back upon the
Prussian west flank and attack it.

Ney, preoccupied with his intense firefight at Quatre Bras, was
incensed when he learnt that Napoleon had detached his own reserves,

and issued a counter-order to the confused d'Erlon to come back to his support at Quatre Bras: he threatened to have the unfortunate officer court-martialled. D'Erlon was about to attack from the west at Ligny and rout the Prussians when he received the new order: he felt he had no choice but to march back to Quatre Bras, arriving after fighting there had died down. The 22,000 troops which could have decided either battle were thus marching backwards and forwards all afternoon.

Back at Quatre Bras the French had charged again, almost breaking one infantry square, that of the 69th, then attacking the 33rd and forcing the 69th to take refuge in a wood. But another infantry division was brought up in the nick of time. As dusk had started to fall, it became apparent that Wellington had narrowly held the allied position, with casualties on each side about evens, at 4,000 each. It had been a standoff, to the relief of the British, who had been taken by surprise.

Not so at Ligny. Realizing that no help would be forthcoming from Ney or d'Erlon, Napoleon ordered a bayonet attack against the Prussian centre, which had backed up the incline known as the Heights of Bussy, calling in the Old Guard. The Prussians counter-attacked, but by then the French were in control and had beaten them off. With darkness falling, the Prussians were able to withdraw in good order, but they had suffered a major defeat: some 16,000 men and twenty-one guns had been lost, compared to the 12,000 French losses with no guns. A further 10,000 Prussians deserted in the demoralized aftermath. Only nightfall had prevented a complete Prussian route.

Gneisenau decided to withdraw the Prussians to safety in the east, which would have left Wellington's army stranded and heavily outnumbered facing the French. But the battered old Blücher dragged himself from his sickbed just in time to prevent this and the decision was made to retire to Wavre, eighteen miles to the north, giving the defeated Prussians the option of either supporting Wellington, should the fight be renewed, or of retreating down their lines of communication eastward.

Napoleon had thus won the bloody battle of Ligny, although not to the point of destroying the Prussian army, while his forces had been fought to a standstill at Quatre Bras. But he was deeply frustrated: he

had caught the Prussians virtually unsupported by the British and should have inflicted a decisive defeat. Ney's failure to take Quatre Bras, plus the mix-up over d'Erlon's army, had cost him a spectacular victory. He blamed Ney; but he might have been cheated of the victory at Ligny if the British had been able to drive Ney back and reinforce the Prussians; so he owed a great deal to Ney for keeping the British engaged.

Napoleon consoled himself with the thought that complete victory could be achieved the following day, now that the Prussians were badly mauled and licking their wounds. Wellington, caught by surprise by the rapid French advance, now faced the terrifying prospect that the French would move forward on the territory abandoned by the Prussians and outflank him. This seemed to leave him no alternative but to call a full-scale retreat to the Channel ports. But he had one cause for consolation: he had held the position at Quatre Bras and Napoleon had lost the element of surprise.

He considered withdrawing to the defensive position forward from Waterloo he so favoured, and which he had long carefully mapped out. This seemed his last chance, but he was a deeply worried man. Leaving Quatre Bras at 10 p.m., he had supped at an inn in Gemappe and adjourned for three hours' sleep, returning to Quatre Bras at 3 a.m. There he paced about 'at the rate of three and a half to four miles an hour'. With the Prussian retreat to Wavre he considered the game about up: 'As he [Blücher] has gone back, we must go too. I suppose in England they will say we have been licked.' It was 7 a.m.: it seemed that the battle had been won by Napoleon by default.

Two hours later the dispirited Wellington received a Prussian emissary from Blücher, to whom he said he would make a stand at Mont St Jean, his reserve position, if the Prussians promised to send 'even one corps only' in support. His great fear now was that Napoleon would use the early morning to march forward and occupy the position on his left flank vacated by the Prussians and attack before he could withdraw his forces from the exposed position at Quatre Bras, although he was partly protected to that side by boggy ground.

Inexplicably no attack was made by the French and around 11 a.m.

Wellington's forces, which by now had pulled back from the village, were retreating cautiously north, completing the task an hour and a half later, with his second-in-command, Lord Uxbridge, and his cavalry bringing up the rear. What had happened to the French? It seems that Napoleon had an acute attack of piles during the day, and possibly of cystitis, which would have given him a severe fever and pain, redoubled when urinating. Grouchy, one of his key commanders, was refused access to him throughout that night.

At around nine in the morning he rode to the battlefield at Ligny in leisurely, even self-confident, fashion, perhaps so as to diminish the pain, talking to his commanders and men. Grouchy rode up and asked for orders. Napoleon snapped back: 'I will give them to you when I think fit.' The Emperor's problem, quite apart from his embarrassing and painful ailments, was that he had no certain knowledge of the disposition of the allied troops: he believed Blücher and the Prussians to be in full retreat.

He now made another near-fatal mistake. Abandoning his old tactic of attempting to divide the two armies and falling upon one with a superior force, he summoned a meeting of his generals at around ten o'clock and informed them he intended to split his own army into two, sending Grouchy in pursuit of the Prussians with 33,000 men and launching his own force of 70,000 men in a frontal attack against the retreating British and Dutch army. Both Ney, who had patiently awaited orders all morning from his position in front of Quatre Bras, and Soult remonstrated. Napoleon told the latter angrily: 'Because you have been beaten by Wellington, you think him a great general! I tell you Wellington is a bad general, the English are bad troops, and this affair is nothing more than a picnic.' While Soult believed that a frontal attack on the British was suicidal, Napoleon appeared to believe that the Prussians were much further away than they actually were. 'A junction between them is impossible for at least two days.'

Then he mixed overconfidence about his ability to defeat British troops – which he had never personally fought before in a major battle – with a mistaken belief that they were finished if the Prussians did not come to their rescue. Still he did nothing, accepting the advice of his artillery commanders that the ground was too wet to move his guns

forward: possibly he felt he was in no shape personally to command the attack that day, but did not want to delegate the responsibility. At last at 1 p.m. he ordered his forces to Quatre Bras, riding at their head, to find that Ney, lacking specific instructions, had ordered his men to have lunch. Only after a further delay did the two forces combine and move forward, both Ney and Napoleon seeking to engage the British rearguard, but getting bogged down in mud.

By 6.30 Wellington had completely escaped, drawing up his forces into their new positions on Mont St Jean, twenty kilometres to the north. Napoleon had wasted an entire day: a quick follow up that morning could almost certainly have overwhelmed the exposed British forces at Quatre Bras and secured him victory. Now Wellington was entrenched in one of his classic defensive positions, skilfully chosen, along a low ridge, some seven kilometres wide, overlooking a broad and shallow valley. The bulk of his army was sheltered behind the brow of the hill on its reverse slope, which protected them from enemy artillery and concealed their true size and dispositions: it was one of Wellington's favourite tactics.

From the ridge a road ran forward past the heavily built farmhouse of Mont St Jean, which formed a natural defensive bastion, down a cutting in a single lane into the wide valley rising on the other side to an inn called La Belle Alliance, half a mile away. To the right the land was broken up and planted with tall rye, which served to conceal the movements of men from one another. Ahead of his position there was a farmhouse, just as the road began its descent into the valley, called La Haye Sainte; to the right and farther on down the valley was a small château with a walled garden. Wellington ordered these positions to be heavily reinforced to slow the French attack.

He placed his men in a double line behind the ridge, with instructions to form squares if attacked by cavalry. These were supported by British artillery in clusters along the right. The cavalry were in the centre behind the infantry. However, still intent on securing his line of retreat, Wellington sent some 13,000 men to Hale, thirteen kilometres away. They were never to fight at all. It never occurred to Wellington to take the offensive against Napoleon: he had been surprised, was in his element in defence, and had 67,000 men to the French 74,000. A

British attack would have been suicidal. This was almost certainly the right tactic, even if it was far from heroic.

Having made his dispositions he returned to his headquarters at an inn in Waterloo just to the north, where he was spared the rain that drenched his soldiers that historic night. He was desperately anxious, having heard nothing from Blücher and preparing to retreat on Brussels if no aid from the Prussians was forthcoming. Not until 3 a.m. that night did he receive a message from Blücher's headquarters in Wavre:

> I hereby inform you that, in consequence of the communication made to me to the effect that the Duke of Wellington will tomorrow accept battle in the position from Braine l'Alleud to La Haye, my troops will be put in motion in the following way: Bülow's corps will start very early at dawn from Dion-le-Mont and advance through Wavre by way of St Lambert, in order to attack the enemy's right wing. The second corps will immediately follow the fourth [Bülow's] corps; and the first and third corps hold themselves ready likewise to follow thither. The exhaustion of the troops, which in part have not arrived (namely, the tail of the fourth corps), makes it impossible to advance earlier. In return, I beg you to inform me betimes when and how the Duke is attacked, so that I may be able to take measures accordingly.

The order had come after a tense meeting of the Prussian high command at which Blücher had favoured a march to Wellington's aid, and Gneisenau had opposed it as being too risky. In fact Blücher had already been reinforced by Bülow, which more than made up for his losses at Ligny, and the Prussians believed that the French had sent a force of only 15,000 men to attack them at Wavre, so they could easily afford to spare the troops. Still the cautious Gneisenau resisted his master, distrusting the British and instructing General Muffling to 'find out accurately whether the Duke has the fixed intention to fight in his present position, or whether possibly nothing but "demonstrations" are intended, as these can only be in the highest degree compromising to our army'. This delayed the despatch of the First, Second and Third Prussian corps until midday the following day.

Napoleon spent the night in a farmhouse a few miles south, then rode up to La Belle Alliance. There he learnt that Grouchy had progressed only six miles towards Wavre and had bedded his army down at Gembloux. Nervously he went for a walk at 1 a.m. The night made an eerie spectacle, with countless small fires in the rain marking the positions of the two huge armies as the fateful dawn approached.

Still suffering from indecision, Napoleon woke at around 10 a.m. before issuing orders to Grouchy to abandon his march on Wavre and instead outflank Blücher by interposing himself between the British and Prussian armies and preventing reinforcements from the latter reaching Wellington. Grouchy misinterpreted the badly drafted orders and continued to move forward to Wavre, even when he began to hear cannon fire in the direction of Waterloo to his left. Napoleon was incensed when he heard. He took a rest in an armchair, lost in his own thoughts, enjoying the summer sunshine, as did both armies after the rainstorm of the previous night.

He decided to observe the battle from behind La Belle Alliance, delegating operational command to Ney, which scarcely suggested he had lost his confidence in him. But first he reviewed his troops. As the French historian Henri Houssaye wrote lyrically, somewhat over-looking the muddy, grimy state of the men:

> It was a kaleidoscope of vivid hues and metallic flashes. After the chasseurs, wearing bright green jackets, with facings of purple, yellow or scarlet, came the hussars, with dolmans, pelisses, breeches à la hongroise, plumes upon their shakos, all varying in colour with each regiment . . . Then passed the dragoons with brass casques over turban-helmets of tiger skin, white shoulder belts crossed over a green coat with facings of red or yellow, long guns at their saddle bows and bumping against their stiff boots; the cuirassiers wearing short coats with Imperial blue collars, white breeches, top boots, steel cuirasses and helmets, with crests of copper and floating horse-hair manes; the carabiniers, giants of six feet and clad in white, with breastplates of gold and tall helmets with red cords – like those worn by the heroes of antiquity. And now the entire body of the horse guards deployed on the third line; the dragoons in green coats faced

with white and with scarlet plumes on their helmets; the grenadiers in blue coats faced with scarlet, leather breeches and high caps of bearskin, with a plume and hanging cords; the lancers with red kurkas and blue plastrons, with light yellow aiguillettes and epaulettes, red trousers with a blue stripe, and the red shapka cap bearing a brass plate inscribed with an N and a crown, and surmounted with white plume half a yard long; and last the chasseurs, with green dolmans embroidered with orange braid, red pelisses edged with fur and kilbachs [or caps] of brilliant scarlet, with great plumes of green and red upon their heads. The epaulettes, the braids, the stripes, the gimps of the officers glittered with a profuse display of gold and silver.

Across the valley the British troops watched dispassionately, unimpressed by the performance. Wellington had ridden up with his staff officers from Waterloo, jovially as though about to attend a meeting of hounds. His attitude masked a desperate anxiety as to the course of the battle, which he believed hinged on whether the Prussians would fulfil their promise to arrive. He expressed contempt for Napoleon: 'That fellow little thinks what a confounded licking he'll get before the day is over.'

Meanwhile, back in Brussels the entire British community was panicking. Eerily the low cloud had funnelled the sound of cannon fire that night as far as Brussels and Antwerp; and the sight of stragglers and refugees streaming into Brussels had created a shock. Lord Uxbridge's sister wrote: 'The horrors of that night are not to be forgot. The very elements conspired to make it gloomy; for the rain and darkness and wind were frightful and our courtyard was filled during the night with poor wounded drenched soldiers and horses . . .'

Chapter 91

WATERLOO: THE BRITISH BUCKLE

After resting for a while, Napoleon at last gave the order to advance with a concentrated burst of artillery fire against the most advanced British position, the château at Hougoumont, at around 11.30. The British soon replied. The Battle of Waterloo had begun. Napoleon's brother Jérôme was delegated to launch the first attack on the British position, which was defended by a few hundred men under the heroic James Macdonnell; it covered a small valley which would shelter a French column from British artillery: if it was captured the French would be able to pour troops on to the ridge above.

Soon Jêrôme's men were surging forward from the French side of the valley of death, where a total of 140,000 men faced each other, surrounding the walls of the garden around Hougoumont. Fierce fighting between attackers and defenders lasted an hour and a half, while both the main armies watched without moving. The attackers at last succeeded in breaking down the main gate, but Macdonnell counter-attacked and drove them out, killing all of those remaining within the compound. The buildings caught fire.

Wellington coolly wrote instructions to Macdonnell: 'I see that the fire has communicated itself from the hay stack to the roof of the chateau. You must however still keep your men in those parts to which the fire does not reach. Take care that no men are lost by the falling in the roof or floors. After they will have fallen in, occupy the ruined walls inside of the garden, particularly if it should be possible for the enemy to pass through the embers to the inside of the house.' The battle around the château raged all day, the gallant defenders holding out in

their outpost against far superior forces. Hougoumont was never captured: a colossal total of 10,000 men died in the struggle, most of them French.

At around 12.30 Napoleon's main battery on a hill just in front of La Belle Alliance opened up, with its seventy-five guns, followed by a major infantry attack of 16,000 men under d'Erlon. The British counter-attacked with infantry volleys and a cavalry charge which, however, was badly mauled. Both sides disengaged with some 10,000 losses between them after just half an hour. General Picton was killed and Sir William Ponsonby cut up with lances. Uxbridge admitted that mistakes had been made in the charge.

Napoleon could now observe Prussian troops approaching from the east, although he misinformed his troops that these were French reinforcements so as not to discourage them. Of Grouchy there was nothing to be seen. He ordered another full-scale attack on La Haye Sainte to break the British centre before the Prussians arrived. Ney, receiving the order, inexplicably commanded his cavalry forward in a massed attack on the narrow ground between Hougoumont and La Haye Sainte. It seems that Ney had mistaken a redeployment of the British line by Wellington as the beginning of a retreat.

The British were incredulous: an attack by massed cavalry without infantry support against British lines, particularly uphill, was unheard of. Ney admittedly had little sight of the main British lines over the brow of the hill. As the cavalry charged up, packed tightly together, the British formed impregnable squares and the horses shied away while the soldiers' volleys simply mowed them down.

Uxbridge's cavalry counter-charged from their own position behind the infantry, driving the broken lines of French cavalry back. But the latter reformed and charged again and again – a total of twelve times in all, each time breaking ranks as they swarmed around the impregnable squares, each time being driven back by British gunfire and cavalry counter-charges: it was magnificently brave, but utterly foolhardy. Still the British were hard pressed. A British lieutenant wrote that the charges of cavalry were 'in appearance very formidable, but in reality a great relief, as the artillery could no longer fire on us: the very earth shook with the enormous mass of men and horses. I shall never forget

the strange noise our bullets made against the breastplates of Keller-mann's and Milhaud's cuirassiers . . . who attacked us with great fury. I can only compare it, with a somewhat homely simile, to the noise of a violent hail-storm beating on panes of glass.'

Wellington looked 'perfectly composed but . . . very thoughtful and pale,' taking refuge in a square whenever attacked. The Duke was wondering what was holding up Blücher's Prussians, for without them he might still lose the battle and he was desperately hard-pressed. He did not know the difficulty of the terrain they were crossing, nor that Napoleon had sent 16,000 men to intercept them.

What indeed had happened to the Prussians? The first corps, that of Bülow, was the freshest, but also the farthest from the battlefield and it was delayed by marching through, instead of around the town of Wavre, where there was a narrow bridge, and a fire broke out nearby, causing them to pause. A second corps under General Pirch followed him and a third under General von Ziethen set out to the north to join Wellington's left wing which he had deliberately left lightly defended because he was expecting the Prussians there, and it had a steep slope running down to three small villages. The distance to be covered was some ten miles.

Astonishingly the two first corps were assigned to attack Plancenoit, a heavily entrenched village behind French lines: it took the Prussians no less than five hours to dislodge the French from the village. Ziethen's was the weakest Prussian corps, having lost nearly half of its whole strength at Ligny, some 225 officers and 12,500 men, and it did not start on its march until 2 p.m.

Bülow's attack was intercepted by Lobau, whose force was driven back after an hour and a half to Plancenoit. However the Young Guard reinforced him and drove Bülow back. Thus some 14,000 key troops on Napoleon's right flank were diverted from the main battle. However, the Prussians then renewed the attack, and Napoleon was forced to divert two battalions of his Old and Middle Guard to regain the village.

On the main battlefield, the intensity of French artillery fire was making inroads into the British. At around 5 p.m. Ney ordered seven infantry

columns forward to seize the key British position of La Haye Sainte, which was in fact largely defended by Hanoverians. There the defenders held out valiantly but, owing to a serious British oversight, had not been re-supplied with ammunition and now had no choice but to give up before an overwhelming French assault, only some forty members of the 360 strong garrison escaping the carnage on the farm. This threatened to blast a path right through the centre of the allied lines.

At that moment the twenty-year-old Prince of Orange gave orders for the body of Hanoverians still holding the line to attack the French infantry: as these were overwhelmingly superior and supported by cavalry, this was madness; but the order was insistently repeated, and gallantly Christian von Ompteda led the attack: his men were wiped out, and a gaping hole opened in the allied line.

Wellington ordered a few Brunswickers to plug the gap left by von Ompteda, but the battle seemed all but over. Against the massed French infantry attacks the British line was barely holding. He desperately sent an emissary to the nearest Prussian commander, General von Ziethen: but he refused to come to Wellington's aid and instead marched to reinforce the Prussians at Plancenoit. Wellington had made the mistake of dispersing his forces along too broad a front, and had insufficient men to redeploy towards the disintegrating centre.

What he did not know was that Ney, fighting furiously with his usual courage at the head of his men at La Haye Sainte, also had no more reinforcements. Napoleon angrily informed his couriers that he could spare no more. In fact he had fourteen regiments of the crack Imperial Guard, which he was anxious to keep in reserve at all costs. Napoleon now roused himself from his vantage point on a hill at Rossome like some tired old general and moved forward a few hundred yards to the inn at La Belle Alliance itself.

There he could see little of the fighting through the dense columns of black smoke clouding the valley. Instead he could see to Plancenoit, where he feared the Prussians were outflanking the French right and threatening to cut his communications and getaway route to Paris. He was furious with Ney for having attacked frontally without specific orders and thus endangering the battle. He had little idea that Ney was on the verge of victory.

He decided to send two further battalions of the precious Imperial Guard in reserve towards Plancenoit and retain three on the plateau where he was standing. Thus the Prussian diversion in fact kept seven of Napoleon's most elite forces from reinforcing Ney at exactly the moment when he could have broken through; a further seven were in reserve below him.

An extraordinary altercation was taking place to the east where General von Reiche, chief of staff to General von Ziethen, was suddenly intercepted by a staff officer from Blücher, ordering Ziethen to go to the aid of Bülow at Plancenoit as 'things were beginning to go badly there'. Muffling, the Prussian liaison officer with Wellington, rode up and desperately urged him to send the corps to Wellington's aid instead or the day would be lost. Reiche was undecided until Ziethen himself rode up and decided to disobey Blücher's order and go to Wellington's assistance.

The Prussians moved forward and supported Wellington's weak left flank, but were only minimally involved in the battle, just one brigade being engaged and only one of their officers being killed and eight wounded. Napoleon spotted Ziethen's corps and told his men that they were in fact General Grouchy's army, come to the battle at last: it was a bare-faced lie, but understandable in the circumstances. Cries of '*Vive l'Empereur!*' broke out. Ney shouted, 'Courage, France is victorious.'

Napoleon decided at last to send the Imperial Guard into the battle: it was half past seven and the sun was beginning to descend through the thick smoke. A French victory seemed all but inevitable. To the intense joy of the French, it was observed that Napoleon himself was leading the Imperial Guard into battle. This turned to dismay when, supported by some of his generals but not by others, he veered aside and sought the shelter of a small quarry on the side of the road. His brother Jérôme exclaimed, 'Can it be possible that he will not seek death here? He will never find a more glorious grave!'

The exhausted and valiant Ney took command again – but instead of moving the Imperial Guard up the narrow road towards Ziethen's approaching Prussians, preferred the more open ground to the left, the scene of so many cavalry charges, but deep in mud and exposed to

enemy artillery fire. Ney's horse was shot from under him for the fifth time that day: still he picked himself up and urged his men on.

Wellington, exposed on his horse on the ridge, observed the move and ordered reinforcements from his infantry behind the ridge under General Maitland in his five-deep squares, supported by artillery. The British waited behind the brow of the hill, holding their fire until the French reached it, before Wellington screamed in his high-pitched voice: 'Now, Maitland, now is your turn. Up guards, make ready, fire!'

The French front line recoiled in astonishment. A second British line commanded by Sir John Colborne marched in perfect order around the flank of the French: under two fires, the 'immortals' – the Imperial Guard fresh to the battle and jealously husbanded by Napoleon – wavered. The Prussians later claimed, as Muffling wrote, that the presence of Ziethen's corps was the critical factor: yet, as noted, only one brigade of this actually took part in the fighting, and the sixteen guns of the Prussians were only employed for half an hour, half of them being small 8-pounders, while one battery quickly ceased firing when it threatened British forces. Moreover, the Prussian guns and brigades were too far to the right of the French to have much impact.

Chapter 92

THE BRITISH ATTACK

The French cavalry below now counter-charged against the British who for a moment were held in check. The French retreat stopped, and they reformed momentarily with fresh regiments coming up from behind. Wellington (who had just seen his second-in-command Uxbridge shot in the knee, prompting the famous exchange 'By God, Sir, I've lost my leg.' 'By God, Sir, you have.') yelled at Colborne: 'Don't give them time to rally.' Colborne's 53rd charged. But the Imperial Guard was probably also influenced by the sight of the disciplined Prussians to their right, through the smoke of battle in the dying rays of the sun.

The Guard retreated once more. This caused panic through the French infantry behind them. 'The cry " 'the Guard retreats' " reverberated like the collapse of the Grande Armée. Everyone felt that everything was finished. The soldiers on la Haye Sainte . . . saw the Guard give way. They also abandoned the conquered terrain and descended to the foot of the hill. The movement of retreat spread to the whole line-of-battle from left to right. At the same time [the extreme French right] was attacked . . . by the heads of Prussian columns coming down the d'Ohain path. The cry went up, "sauve qui peut. We are betrayed." ' They were betrayed in that the approaching troops were now seen not to be Grouchy's, as Napoleon had claimed, but Prussians. It was hopeless to fight on. The Prussian arrival had much more of a psychological than a military effect upon the French.

As the French line wavered Wellington raised his hat and waved in a prearranged signal and his reserve army charged forward in the centre,

with the few Prussians advancing on the right down that bloody, muddy slope with its tangle of men and limbs. Wellington himself charged forward as the British cheered but he upbraided them: 'No cheering, my lads, but forward and complete your victory.' The wounded Uxbridge shouted: 'Don't expose yourself so,' but Wellington took no notice, in marked contrast to Napoleon's earlier behaviour.

To the south-east, Bülow's troops were still fighting to take Plancenoit. As the British surged forward into the valley, at long last Pirch's corps arrived to reinforce Bülow, and the village was captured. Muffling wrote: 'The enemy was dislodged from Plancenoit; cannon and prisoners were taken, and the remainder got into the same confusion with the same mass, which, near La Maison du Roi, was just rolling along the high road. Had it been possible to take the village an hour sooner, the enemy could not have retreated on the high road to Gemappe.' Napoleon had been right to be concerned at this flanking movement: he and his army would have been surrounded had it worked. The British cavalry officers Vivian and Vandeleur led the British charge, and attacked the French as they retreated from Plancenoit, also routing the remainder of the French cavalry and capturing their guns.

As the main body of French soldiers streamed before the British attack across the valley of death, a squad of fresh Imperial Guards formed around their Emperor to protect him – their prime purpose – and retired in good order fighting bravely. With Blücher's forces on the left joining in the general British charge on the right, the French retreat turned into a rout and Wellington called off his exhausted men.

Although the Prussians have frequently tried to claim all the credit for the rout, it is clear that this was caused almost entirely by the British, joined by Ziethen's limited force – and then by the main Prussian force only after the capture of Plancenoit. The battle was won. After it Wellington rode to meet Blücher at La Belle Alliance, where the gruff old Prussian soldier told him in his halting French, '*Belle affaire*', and Wellington greeted him with exhausted and relieved cordiality.

Wellington rode back in the moonlight across the killing ground accompanied by the screams and moans of the wounded and the

looting and stripping of bodies and slaughter of the wounded by the inevitable ghouls and vultures of war. It was an eerie, spectral and dreadful scene. Wellington was utterly drained and depressed. Reaching the inn at Waterloo, he remarked: 'Well, thank God, I don't know what it is to lose a battle; but certainly nothing can be more painful than to gain one with the loss of so many of one's friends.' He made his most celebrated observation: 'Next to a battle lost, there is nothing so dreadful as a battle won.'

At a lonely dinner he said that 'the hand of God almighty has been upon me this day'. He fell asleep on the floor until 3 a.m., when he composed a victory despatch of great professionalism and cool detachment. He summarized the role of the Prussians generously and fairly. 'I should not do justice to my feelings or to Marshal Blücher and the Prussian army, if I did not attribute the successful result of this arduous day, to the cordial and timely assistance I received from them. The operation of General Bülow, upon the enemy's flank, was a most decisive one; and even if I had not found myself in a situation to make the attack, which produced the final result, it would have forced the enemy to retire, if his attacks should have failed, and would have prevented him from taking advantage of them, if they should unfortunately have succeeded.' He told Thomas Creevey, a Whig observer: 'It has been a damned serious business. Blücher and I have lost 30,000 [actually nearer 23,000] men. It has been a damned nice thing – the nearest run thing you ever saw in your life.'

The horrors of the day were not over yet. Four miles behind La Belle Alliance, the tens of thousands of French soldiers streaming into the village of Gemappe were funnelled onto a single bridge across the river some eight feet wide. It was the crossing of the Berezina in Russia all over again: men trampled each other underfoot and slashed at each other with their sabres to get across. The Prussians caught up, slashing at the French rearguard. Several hundred perished – although the river was only three feet deep and could have been forded.

Napoleon and a small protective guard forced their way through, although his lavishly equipped carriage with its gold dinner service and lavatory, its folding bed and writing desk and his diamond-studded

uniform worth some 200,000 francs had to be abandoned. He escaped across the bridge on his horse. As he reached Quatre Bras on that spectral ride, he saw 4,000 bodies stripped of their clothes by looters, a grotesquely macabre sight in the moonlight, apparently moving with the movement of the clouds. 'We thought we saw ghosts calling from their graves,' remembered one French soldier. Then it was on to Charleroi, where the bridge gave way and still more French soldiers were drowned. Behind him the retreating Emperor had left some 40,000 dead and wounded along with 10,000 horses and 160 guns.

David Howarth in his vivid study of the battle based on eyewitness descriptions, told a story of the horrors on the night of Waterloo:

Among the wounded, somewhere on the slopes below La Belle Alliance, was Colonel Ponsonby of the Scots Greys, the man who had last been seen that morning leading the cavalry charge against Napoleon's guns with both his arms hanging useless and the reins in his teeth.

His horse had carried him into the thick of the enemy cavalry, and he was cut down by a sabre and fell on the ground unconscious. When he came to his senses he raised his head to see if there was any escape – and a French lancer passing by saw the movement, shouted 'You're not dead yet', and ran his sabre through his back. Blood gushed into his mouth, his head fell again, he could hardly breathe and he thought he was dying. A French skirmisher stopped to plunder him, and threatened to finish him off. The colonel told him there were three dollars in his side pocket – it was all he had – and the man took them, but also tore open his waistcoat to look for more and left him lying in a painful position, unable to move at all.

Later in the day, while the battle still raged all round him, a kindly French officer gave him some brandy, turned him on his side and put his head on a knapsack – and told him he had heard that Wellington was dead and six British battalions had deserted. And some time in the afternoon, a cheerful French skirmisher used his body as cover, firing over him and chatting gaily while he loaded. 'You will be pleased to hear we are retreating,' he said at last. 'Good-bye, my friend.' And then, as the French receded, the Prussian

cavalry rode over him at a full trot, kicking and lifting him off the ground and rolling him about most cruelly.

During the night, he found a man was lying on his legs, a man wounded like himself in the lungs: he could hear the breath wheezing through the wound. Prussians wandering about in search of plunder looked at him greedily, and one began to search him. He told the man he was a British officer and had been plundered already, but he would not stop and pulled him about roughly.

About midnight, an English soldier came by. Probably he was looking for plunder too, but when he found a wounded English colonel, he either took pity or saw a chance of reward. He heaved the dying soldier off Ponsonby's legs, picked up a sword and stood sentinel over him until dawn to protect him from other marauders. At six in the morning a cart came long, and Ponsonby was bundled into it and taken to Waterloo. He had lain on the field for eighteen hours with a punctured lung and six other wounds. The surgeons set to work to bleed him.

Wellington had been right: it had been a close run thing.

In fact perhaps the most celebrated battle in history was something of a fraud. It had not been fought at Waterloo, but at Mont St Jean. Wellington chose the name because it had a British ring. Napoleon had been the French commander in little more than name: Ney had a much greater claim to the role; the dim-witted General Grouchy had all but ignored the Emperor's orders.

Although Wellington's biggest battle, it was far from being his finest and he only narrowly avoided a defeat caused by his errors and excessive caution – although the final charge was certainly perfectly executed and a masterstroke. The battle dealt the coup de grâce to Napoleon; but the Emperor was already a defeated man, with scant hope of survival in spite of his reckless adventurism in returning to take power in France: inexorably, large allied armies were advancing on him from all sides.

The battle had been lost by Napoleon, not won by Wellington. Wellington had made a series of mistakes: in exuding complacency

before the battle in the face of so dangerous an opponent as Napoleon, in believing that the main French attack would come to the west, in despatching part of his forces to counter that imaginary thrust, in failing to support the Prussians adequately at Ligny (although his forces were hard-pressed at Quatre Bras), in stretching his forces along too extended a line at Mont St Jean, in showing little urgency in redeploying his troops along the line to where the danger was greatest (a road ran along the ridge) or keeping adequate reserves to resist the main French thrusts which, true to Napoleon's recent tactics, were in massed columns, not lines.

Wellington later made light of this last failing: 'We pummelled them, they pummelled us and I suppose we pummelled the hardest since we gained the day.' And again: 'Bonaparte did not manoeuvre at all. He just moved forward in the old style, in columns and was driven off in the old style.' Yet the British commander should have foreseen these attacks in massed columns: his own 'old style' of a long line simply dispersed his forces: in the past he had expertly brought forces forward to reinforce his weaker points.

Yet, unlike Napoleon, he had also displayed true leadership in battle, remaining in the thick of the fighting throughout, like Ney, never losing his cool judgement and detachment and knowing exactly when to strike as the tide of battle turned. His tactics had been defensive and unimaginative, although his choice of terrain displayed his old meticulous brilliance: a more imaginative general might have taken advantage of the French weakness and his own reserves to seek to turn the tide sooner – although that would have been risky. But his conduct was ultimately vindicated by victory – by the narrowest of margins, and particularly through the luck of the Prussians arriving at the last minute, which helped to panic the French. Wellington's most famous and most significant battle was far from being his best.

Equally, the Prussian record was decidedly mixed. Having blundered in his dispositions at Ligny and been soundly thrashed, Blücher had at least prevented the general retreat favoured by his most senior officers and then prevailed in insisting on marching to Wellington's aid – no mean feat for a defeated and demoralized army. But the contribution the Prussians made to the actual fighting at Waterloo

was hardly decisive – *pace* some modern historians. Their last-minute appearance had been hugely important psychologically – although the French spirit appeared to have been broken before then and the retreat of the Imperial Guard under British pressure was the deciding factor.

But an earlier appearance would have been much more pivotal, and the Prussians' main physical contribution to the actual fighting at Waterloo was the merciless slaughter of fleeing men afterwards, which dispirited even Wellington. The battle at Plancenoit off the battlefield was of course fierce and important, in diverting troops from the main battlefield; a breakthrough there earlier would have wiped out a large part of the French army; but this did not happen until the main battle was already won, so it can hardly be called decisive.

The key factor at Waterloo was Napoleon's own incompetence. It was not just that he made mistakes: it was that he failed in virtually every respect to exercise either the courage or the competence of even a mediocre military commander. His fever and piles do not explain this: he had frequently been ill in battle, yet excelled. The only explanation is that his overthrow the year before – which had driven him to attempt suicide – and his months of exile at Elba had changed him as a man.

At Waterloo he showed himself to be cowardly, indecisive, poor at man-management, remote, haughty, unyielding, unwilling to listen, inept and, as Wellington had observed, extraordinarily lacking in his old flexibility and ingenuity in tactics. Being so far from the front line and delegating to Ney, he inevitably failed to take the right decisions. By leading his men into battle and then shying away at the last moment, he came across as woefully lacking in his old courage. By being so inert, unapproachable and lacking in energy, he behaved like a conventional general well past his prime, not the extraordinary man-machine of manic energy that had prostrated a whole continent before him.

Perhaps seduced by the ease with which he had regained power in Paris, he was lazy, overconfident and detached, seemingly believing that the sheer magic of his name and a single forced march would confound and instil terror into his enemies. At Ligny he had won a straightforward victory but his contrary orders had prevented this from routing the Prussian army. His inertia the following day prevented a

crushing defeat of the Anglo-Dutch forces, which were tamely allowed to escape. At Waterloo itself, far from the battle, he was little more than a spectator, and the few decisions he made himself were almost always damaging.

One of Napoleon's most unattractive traits was his tendency immediately to unburden blame on to the shoulders of his subordinates. Soult and Grouchy were much criticized for the Waterloo debacle, and in many respects rightly so, but none more so than Ney, in spite of his superhuman courage and persistence. Ney made mistakes – he had been uncharacteristically slow and cautious in attacking the small force initially based at Quatre Bras, which may have contributed to his failure to dislodge it; yet Ney's loss of his backup army under d'Erlon at the crucial moment, thanks to Napoleon's blundering order, was just as significant a factor.

Ney's uphill cavalry charge at Waterloo, unsupported by infantry, was also a huge error – although he had little idea of the size of the British army on the reverse side of the ridge and believed that a single act of boldness would finally rout the wavering British line. But, if effectively supported by d'Erlon, he would have won at Quatre Bras. Had he been sole commander at Waterloo he would have had the decisive support from the Imperial Guard at the right moment to overwhelm the British.

Was Napoleon right to keep the Guard in reserve for a Prussian attack from Plancenoit? In the event clearly not; he underestimated the extent of British resistance in the centre, and overestimated the strength of the Prussian attack, perhaps because he feared capture by the later. (Both Blücher and Gneisenau had sworn to kill him on the spot as an outlaw if they caught him.) The Prussians on the Plancenoit front broke through too late to influence the main battle: he should have thrown his Imperial Guard in earlier and in much greater force. By contrast Ney's leadership of men in battle if anything exceeded Wellington's a kilometre away. At Waterloo Napoleon was largely an armchair general. By the standards of his previous battles his tactics were crude, even nonexistent.

Nearly as many fought at Austerlitz, Jena, Eylau and Friedland, and the casualties were much lower. At Aspern-Essling, the armies were

bigger than at Waterloo and the casualties the same. But then the position changed at the much bigger battles of Wagram, Borodino and Leipzig. Waterloo was significantly smaller than each of these: in its frontal assault tactics, Waterloo in fact in many ways resembles Borodino as an example of sheer attrition and relentless 'pounding' – winning the field – although casualties were far smaller than at Borodino. In some ways those two battles were precursors to First World War-style frontal massed assaults.

Napoleon had a slender hope during the Waterloo campaign of inflicting a significant defeat on the allies which would then force them to negotiate and accept his return. It was a forlorn hope in the first place – even if he had won in Belgium he would almost certainly have been defeated by much larger armies elsewhere – and now after defeat he retreated into a world of fantasy. All was not lost – indeed not only nothing had been lost – he could reassemble a huge army to defend Paris at the drop of a hat, as he wrote to 'King' Joseph, his brother, the day after Waterloo. The fantasy was soon cruelly at an end.

Chapter 93

AFTERMATH

Napoleon rode back, still caught up in his dreams of raising new armies. He reached Paris by a circuitous route to avoid being intercepted by the murder-bent Prussians. He arrived on the morning of 21 June. There he found parliament opposed to him, spearheaded by the rascally old Fouché who believed his time had come, while some loyalists urged him to impose martial law and establish a dictatorship. They included the faithful Davout and Carnot, as well as his brother Lucien. Napoleon, who had endured three days without eating or washing on the road, headed straight for a bath and a meal. He hesitated. Fouché promptly seized power, establishing a provisional government.

Napoleon, realizing he had too little support, abdicated in favour of the infant King of Rome and left for Josephine's old palace at Malmaison, which had been lived in by Hortense, her daughter. Marie Walewska was faithfully waiting for him there, as was his mother, the aged Letizia. There he decided to flee to the United States. He disguised himself as a secretary and set off for Rochefort on 29 June.

With the Prussians approaching Paris bent on revenge, his escape was a matter of urgency. He had been led to believe there would be two American frigates ready to carry him away, but the British were closely guarding French shores, with as many as thirty ships in the Bay of Biscay under Lord Keith. The *Bellerophon*, a 74-gun line-of-battle ship under Captain Maitland, was waiting off Rochefort, supported by four corvettes. Two more ships of the line were despatched to prevent Napoleon escaping. After considering no fewer than four means of escape from France, Napoleon decided to throw himself upon the

mercy of his oldest enemy, the British, writing to the Prince Regent: 'Your Royal Highness, exposed to the factions which distract my country and to the enmity of the greatest powers of Europe, I have ended my political career, and I come, like Themistocles, to throw myself on the hospitality of the English people; I put myself under the protection of their laws, which I claim from Your Royal Highness as the most powerful, the most constant, and the most generous of my enemies. Napoleon.'

Maitland, however, had been corresponding with the prime minister, Lord Liverpool, who had declared: 'We wish that the King of France would hang or shoot Bonaparte, as the best termination of the business . . . if the King of France does not feel himself sufficiently strong to treat him as a rebel, we are ready to take upon ourselves the custody of his person.'

The British offered Napoleon no guarantees: Admiral Hotham, who had arrived on board the *Superb* on 15 July, wrote to a British envoy in Paris:

> You may, if you please, assure Lord Castlereagh that no terms, nor promises, nor expectations of any kind were made, or held out, to Bonaparte either by Captain Maitland or by me: and he was distinctly told through the Count Lascasse, who was sent with the proposal for his embarking, that all Captain Maitland could do was to carry him and his suite to England, to be received in such a manner as his Royal Highness might deem expedient. He [Napoleon] appeared extremely anxious to learn how I thought he would be disposed of, but equally confident in the generosity and magnanimity of the Prince Regent and the English nation . . .

He was taken with great courtesy by ship to the spectacular Torbay in Devon, eventually reaching Start Point near Plymouth. There Lord Keith was deeply apprehensive.

> It is become necessary that I am most careful; for the general and many of his suite have an idea that if they could but put foot on shore no power could remove them, and they are determined to

make the attempt if at all possible; they are becoming most refractory, and talk of resisting the Emperor being taken out of the ship. I desired Captain Maitland to inform those gentlemen that if such language was continued I should feel obliged to have recourse to a more rigorous mode of confinement.

A thousand small boats circled the ship every day for a glimpse of the Ogre of Europe. On one occasion, reported the *Morning Post*, 'we regret to say a large portion of the spectators not only took off their hats but cheered him.'

Meanwhile Wellington had painfully reassembled and disciplined his army for the march on Paris in two columns, one British, the other Prussian under Blücher. The Duke was in contact with his close political ally Castlereagh, as well as with Talleyrand and Metternich. Wellington officially told Louis XVIII to fall in with the march of his victorious army, something Talleyrand unsuccessfully advised him not to do for fear of being seen as a puppet of foreign powers by the French people. The Prussians went on a rampage against the French. A private of the 11th Light Dragoons wrote of a village that had been visited by the Prussians: 'The work of devastation I have no language to describe. In the chateau there was not one article of furniture, from the costly pier glass down to the common coffee-cup, which they had not smashed to atoms. The flour-mill, likewise, was all gutted . . . And as to living things, there was none – not so much as a half-starved pigeon.'

Paris soon capitulated and the hugely fat King followed Wellington's army of occupation to be greeted by Fouché and Talleyrand. Chateaubriand captured the irony of this scene. 'Suddenly a door opens; silently there enters vice leaning on the arm of crime, M. de Talleyrand walking supported by Fouché; the infernal vision passes slowly in front of me, reaches the King's study and disappears. Fouché had come to swear allegiance to his lord; on bended knee the loyal regicide placed the hands which had caused the death of Louis XVI between the hands of the brother of the royal martyr; the apostate bishop stood surety for the oath.'

There was no doubt about who the real masters of the city were: Wellington was head of an army of occupation of more than 1.2

million troops altogether in France, occupying sixty-one departments. The *Grande Armée* was exiled to the provinces and demobilized. Louis was treated as a powerless figurehead while Wellington issued Talleyrand and Fouché with their instructions. The Duke also set about stripping Paris of the art treasures, including the famous Venetian horses of San Marco, which had been plundered by Napoleon from all over Europe, and restoring them to their former owners.

Louis was utterly humiliated and began to intrigue with the Tsar who resented British control of France. The reactionary royalists, the ultras, intent on a reign of terror against republicans and supporters of Napoleon, flooded Paris and secured control of the new Assembly, causing the downfall of the moderate Talleyrand and the intriguing Fouché. A new cabinet was set up under a royalist, although not an extreme one, the Duc de Richelieu, supported by the King's moderate favourite, Decazes.

The ultras were not slow to bare their fangs: in Marseilles, Avignon and Nice pogroms took place against former Bonapartists. Some 6,000 were imprisoned for sedition and political crimes. Seven senior Bonapartists were condemned to death immediately, including, most tragically, the heroic Ney who was shot on 7 December. The implacable Louis would not pardon him, fearing perhaps that he would become a rallying point for opposition. Wellington, shamefully, did nothing to save him. It was, an indelible stain on the reputations of both men. Some 30,000 civil servants, a third of the total, were purged from their jobs.

Under the Second Treaty of Paris, the army of occupation was to be reduced to 150,000 and remain for five years, while France was required to pay 700 million francs in reparations. The country's frontiers were restored to those of 1790. Napoleon's second defeat had achieved the humiliation France had been spared on the occasion of the first.

Wellington remained as proconsul with his usual indifference to what people thought of him. An attempt was made to blow up his house and then to shoot him in the Champs Elysées in 1816. He dallied with his girlfriends, in particular the devoted Lady Shelley, Lady Webster, Lady Caroline Lamb and the Caton sisters.

A witness gives this portrait of the victor of Waterloo and now proconsul of France.

> Middle height, neither stout nor thin; erect figure, not stiff; not very lively, though more than I expected. Black hair, simply cut, strongly mixed with grey; not a very high forehead, immense hawk's nose, tightly compressed lips, strong, massive under jaw. After he had talked for some time in the ante-room he came straight to the Royal Family, with whom he spoke in a very friendly manner, and then, going round the circle, shook hands with all his acquaintances. He was dressed entirely in black with the star of the Order of the Garter and the Maria Theresa cross. He spoke to all the officers present in an open, friendly way, though but briefly. At table he sat next to the Princess. He ate and drank moderately, and laughed at times most heartily, and whispered many things in the Princess's ear which made her blush and laugh.

He remained attractively outspoken, as befitted a man who needed no favours from anyone else. Of the Prince Regent he declared: 'By God, you never saw such a figure in your life as he is. He speaks and swears so like old Falstaff, that damme, if I was not ashamed to walk into a room with him.' Of Napoleon's exile he remarked: 'Buonaparte is so damned intractable a fellow there is no knowing how to deal with him.'

Only in November 1818 did the only Englishman ever to have ruled France resign his post and return to join a British cabinet, having left behind a weak French administration which ruled until 1820, when the country returned to more reactionary rule.

As for the ex-Emperor, on 31 July he was informed that he was to be exiled to St Helena. It was worse than a death sentence. Napoleon, according to Lord Keith:

> received the paper, laid it on the table, and after a pause he began with declaring his solemn protest against this proceeding of the British government, that they had not the right to dispose of him in

this manner, and that he appealed to the British people and to the laws of this country. He then asked what was the tribunal, or if there was not a tribunal, where he might prefer his appeal against the illegality and injustice of this decision. 'I am come here voluntarily,' said he, 'to place myself on the hearth of your nation, and to claim the rights of hospitality. I am not even a prisoner of war. If I were a prisoner of war, you would be bound to treat me according to the law of nations . . .

'Let me be put in a country house in the centre of [Britain], thirty leagues from any sea. Place a commissioner about me to examine my correspondence and to report my actions, and if the Prince Regent should require my parole, perhaps I would give it. There I could have a certain degree of personal liberty, and I could enjoy the liberty of literature. In St Helena I should not live three months. With my habits and constitution, it would be immediate death. I am used to ride twenty leagues a day. What am I to do on that little rock at the end of the world? The climate is too hot for me. No, I will not go to St Helena. Botany Bay is better than St Helena. If your government wishes to put me to death, they may kill me here. It is not worth while to send me to St Helena. I prefer death to St Helena.'

In fact St Helena had been chosen expressly as a prison island from which there was no escape: as its former governor General Beatson wrote grimly:

There are undoubtedly several local circumstances peculiar to the island of St Helena which seem to render it pre-eminently suitable to the purpose of confining a state prisoner. Its remote situation from all parts of the globe, its compact form and size, the small numbers of its inhabitants, amongst whom no stranger can introduce himself without immediate detection, together with the extraordinary formation of the island, being encompassed on all sides by stupendous and almost perpendicular cliffs rising to the height of from six to more than twelve hundred feet, and through which there are but few inlets to the interior, are collectively such a

variety of natural advantages that perhaps they are not to be equalled . . .

The only accessible landing-places are James Town, Rupert's Bay, and Lemon Valley on the north, and Sandy Bay on the south. All these points are well fortified by fleur d'eau [between wind and water] batteries, furnished (except Sandy Bay) with furnaces for heating shot, and as cannon are also placed upon the cliffs in their vicinity, far above the reach of ships, it may readily be imagined that if a Martello Tower with one gun could beat off a 74-gun ship in the Mediterranean, how much more efficacious would be those preparations for defence in the island of St Helena. In short, it appeared to be the opinion of several experienced naval officers, who have recently visited that island, that no ships could possibly stand the fire of the defences which protect the anchorage and the whole of the northern coast . . . and the southern is equally secure against a naval attack . . . The precipitous pathways should, of course, be attended to and guarded, and they might easily be defended by rolling stones from the heights . . .

A great acquisition has lately resulted from an admirable establishment of telegraphs. These are placed upon the most commanding heights, and are so connected and so spread all over the island that no vessel can approach without being described at the distance of sixty miles. Nothing can pass in any part, or even in sight of the Island, without being instantly known to the governor . . . In short, the whole island can be under arms at a moment's waiting.

The reality of Napoleon's incarceration proved even worse than he feared: 'Accursed island, one cannot see the sun or the moon for the greater part of the year: always rain or fog. One can't ride a mile without being soaked.' It was a truly terrible fate for a man who once bestrode the world like a colossus to be condemned to this bleak, windswept rock in the middle of nowhere under constant guard. His gaoler was a dull pedant, Sir Hudson Lowe, who was meticulous in his restrictions upon the ex-Emperor, although not actually an unkind man. There were a few desultory plots by exiled Bonapartists in the United States to free him, in one of which also implicated the dashing

but now disgraced victor of Aix Roads, Thomas, Lord Cochrane, who wished to set him up on a Latin American throne alongside Simon Bolivar.

On 14 June 1816 a secret flotilla of small boats equipped with artillery set out from Baltimore with around 300 men under the command of an officer called Fournier. T; the plan was to stay out of sight of the island, but to land a man disguised as a British soldier who would give Napoleon notice of the plot, along with a series of rendezvous points on different nights where he would be picked up by a boat after dark. It appeared that certain inhabitants of the island were in on the plot. In the event Lowe posted sentries at dusk, instead of at 9 p.m. as previously, to Napoleon's intense annoyance. No attempt was made.

The ex-Emperor's health began to deteriorate mysteriously with headaches, feverish symptoms, swollen gums and loose teeth. He believed the British were trying to poison him, although it seems more likely that his household had been infiltrated by a hostile French spy. In March 1821 his health abruptly deteriorated and on 5 May he died after serious internal bleeding, officially of a cancerous ulcer but more probably of hepatitis or arsenic poisoning, of which he displayed many symptoms; traces of the poison were found in his hair. His body was surprisingly fat and well preserved and he appears to have suffered from a rare condition slowly transforming his sexuality to that of a woman which may account for some of the hysteria he often displayed.

Napoleon had survived his two greatest British adversaries, Pitt and Nelson. Of the others, Grenville lived on until 1834 but never held high office again, and Wellington, who became prime minister, lived until 1852. Cochrane was rehabilitated after performing spectacular feats in the Chilean, Peruvian and Brazilian wars of independence and lived to the ripe age of eighty-four, dying in 1860. Castlereagh killed himself in 1822 out of despair at the unravelling of his plans for Europe.

Of Napoleon's chief mainland European opponents, Metternich died in 1859, Talleyrand in 1838, Tsar Alexander in 1825, General Barclay de Tolly in 1818, the Prussian King Frederick William in 1840, Marshal Blücher in 1819, General Gneisenau in 1831, the Emperor

Francis of Austria in 1847 and Marshal Schwarzenberg in 1820. General Kutuzov had died in 1813.

Of Napoleon's personal intimates, Marie Louise went on to rule the Grand Duchy of Parma with her second husband, Count Adam von Neipperg, and died in 1847. Josephine had died in 1814. The indomitable Letizia Bonaparte lived on until 1836, Caroline Bonaparte until 1839, Pauline Borghese until 1825, after being remarried to her husband Prince Camillo Borghese, Eliza died in 1820 near Trieste, while Jérôme Bonaparte became president of the French senate and died in 1860. Joseph died in Florence in 1844, Louis in 1846, Lucien in 1840 and Marie Walewska in 1817.

Of his generals and associates, Marshal Augereau died in 1816, Eugène de Beauharnais in 1824, Bernadotte in 1844 after becoming King of Sweden in 1818 (his dynasty still occupies the throne): Berthier had committed suicide in 1815; Bessières had been killed at Rippach in 1813; Bertrand died in 1844; Bruce was lynched by a royalist mob in 1815; Carnot died in 1823, Caulaincourt in 1827, Davout in 1823. Desaix had been killed in 1800, while Druot had died in 1847. Duhesme was killed at Plancenoit in 1815; Dumouriez died in 1823, Fouché in 1820, St Cyr in 1830, Grouchy in 1847. Joubert had died in 1799. Jourdan died in 1833, Junot in 1813 after jumping from a window, Kellerman in 1835, and Langeron in 1831. Lannes had been killed in 1809, Lefebvre died in 1820, MacDonald in 1840, Marmont in 1852, Masséna in 1817. Moreau had been killed in 1813 at the Battle of Dresden. Murat was shot by firing squad in Calabria in 1815 and Ney was executed in 1815. Mortier died in 1825, Oudinot in 1847. Poniatowski had perished at Liepzig in 1813. Villeneuve had committed suicide or been murdered in 1806.

These were the main protagonists of the longest European war of recent history, the first total war in the modern sense embracing whole populations and waged by huge conscript armies.

Chapter 94

NAPOLEON'S LEGACY

Such was the course of the War of Wars. But in the poet's phrase, 'What good came of it at last?' Napoleon, building on the French Revolution, saw himself as the great modernizer of Europe after centuries of absolutism; Britain saw herself as defending Europe from a more monstrous despotism than had ever been experienced before. Who was right? It is time to attempt to assess the significance of Napoleon's achievements and defeat.

The wheel of history had turned full circle: in fact it may even have gone into reverse. The regime of Louis XVIII was more autocratic and reactionary than that of his more intelligent older brother, Louis XVI. It was less reformist and enlightened and was dominated by a seesaw struggle between the ultras and aristocratic moderates like the Duc de Richelieu and Decazes. Worst of all it was propped up by an army of humiliating occupation under the didactic Wellington.

It can safely be said that France after 1815 was more backward economically, probably politically and, intellectually, and certainly socially – with large numbers of former soldiers and bandits marauding around that devastated country – than it had been before the Revolution of 1789. In a quarter of a century, both the Revolution and Napoleon had succeeded in returning the country back to what it was before the whole process had begun, with a poorer economy than the one expanding sharply under Louis XVI.

Yet many subsequent historians claimed that there were much greater underlying changes, that the revolutionary and Napoleonic period precipitated a great leap forward in European history from the

dynastic autocracies that had frozen the region for so long. In particular, the revolutionary period is said to have ushered in a greater thirst of ordinary people for their rights: the Napoleonic period was a middle-class revolution. Marxist historians have long held this view.

There is a truth here; but it may be that the economic changes that preceded the Revolution under Louis XVI were primarily responsible for both the emergence of a 'proletariat' – the Paris mob – and a bourgeoisie. As the historian Alfred Cobban has shown, the main instigators and beneficiaries of the Revolution were not the new middle classes, but minor functionaries and civil servants under the *ancien régime*, a class of intellectuals who felt they had not received their true deserts in life. Certainly by 1815 the Paris mob was utterly cowed and the bourgeoisie was little more politically dominant than before the Revolution, while aristocratic reactionaries were more powerful than before 1789. Equally this return to an aristocratic ice age was accompanied by economic progress and the general evolution of political thought into a continuing struggle between reactionaries and progressives.

Yet it is possible to argue that this exact process was underway in the enlightened and progressive, if politically autocratic, period before the Revolution. Who was the more enlightened – Voltaire, Robespierre or Napoleon? The process might have moved peacefully ahead in an evolutionary way and perhaps faster through gradualist reform, inevitably so if new industrial methods were imported from Britain, than through the violent upheavals of revolution and wars of conquest.

Further, France, a state at least as powerful as Britain before the industrial revolution, was crippled politically and economically for decades after 1815. It remained a largely backward agrarian country: its own industrial revolution was seriously postponed, its bourgeois economic class in its great trading cities had lost money and competitive advantage with Britain, and it had deindustrialized, if it had ever really industrialized. Possibly the same would have occurred if there had been no revolutionary or Napoleonic periods: yet given the pace of economic change in France before the Revolution, and the intellectual ferment of the period, it seems unlikely.

What is undeniable is that France was considerably worse off economically and more backward politically in 1816 than in 1788,

and that the industrial revolution had been limited to military-related manufacturing, which was not particularly efficient. While Britain was undergoing a dramatic industrial revolution during this period, France in many respects fell way behind, and ceased to be a major economic and political rival to Britain until the late twentieth century.

In political terms, the stability of French institutions before 1789 was never to recover – arguably to this day, with nearly two centuries of unsatisfactory constitutional experiments succeeding each other, from an absolute monarchy to bourgeois constitutions, to a Second Empire to a bourgeois struggle with the working class represented by the Paris Commune, to the chaotic Third Republic. This was followed by an era of weak governments under the Fourth Republic and then a renewed 'strong' government with an unsatisfactory coexistence of president and parliament in the Fifth.

Even France's population growth became sluggish after the Napoleonic period. The enduring legacy of the revolutionary-Napoleonic period was quite different to that intended: a massive further centralization of the French state with the elimination of traditional local legal freedoms and autonomies and an independent aristocracy and gentry. If the court of Versailles was too centralized, the court of Napoleon was virtually all-powerful, a military dictatorship. France never recovered from this: right up to modern times, it has veered between a parliamentary and an autocratic centralist system with the latter usually winning, most recently with the imposition of the Gaullist constitution after 1959.

Napoleon sought to impose the same upon the countries he conquered, sweeping away local 'feudal' privileges, many of them arbitrary and unsatisfactory, ancient structures of princedoms, merchant guilds and complex legal demarcations in favour of a unified Code Napoleon. This has been cited as one of his greatest and most lasting achievements. In fact the Code Napoleon was far from ideal, too inflexible to take account of local circumstances and traditions; it was also state-centred, lacking the guarantees and pluralisms that defined and defended the rights of individuals, insisting that the individual prove his lack of guilt rather than the presumption of innocence, and giving central authority through the magistrature virtually absolute

powers over the citizens. Local circumstances over the past two centuries have modified its often harsh and arbitrary, if effective, application. But it is far from certain that the Code Napoleon was an improvement upon existing legal systems, complex, fragmented and sometimes iniquitous as they might be.

The much shorter-lived attempt by revolutionary and Napoleonic France to 'liberate' other countries from archaic and oppressive feudal rulers was, if this interpretation is correct, almost entirely bogus. Napoleon looted and extorted colossal taxation and tributes from France's subject systems on a par with the Aztec empire in Mexico. He imposed his own extended clan as rulers of most of his dominions in a fashion that harked back to the Middle Ages; the clan ruled arbitrarily and without check by either constitutional institutions or local traditions.

He dispensed with revolutionary institutions, substituting an empire and monarchy far more showy, absolute and despotic than those of their traditional rulers and creating a phoney new aristocracy which depended upon his favour. He behaved more like an Emperor of China or oriental despot than any kind of progressive political modernizer rooted in enlightenment thinking or political philosophy.

It has been said that he catalysed a 'bourgeois' revolution in those countries, advancing the middle class and destroying the feudal aristocracy. In fact he and his clan of flashy nepotistic neo-monarchs promoted their own friends and sympathizers, whether from the old aristocracy – some of whom were happy to collaborate – or the merchant bourgeoisie. But there was no attempt to transform the economies of these countries and seed a new capitalist bourgeoisie of the kind being created for example in Britain. Countries like Italy and Spain remained steeped in agrarian poverty until well into the twentieth century.

He has been credited with stimulating a sense of 'modern' 'nationalist' sentiment which never existed before, and has even been described as the father of the modern European nation state. Neither revolutionary France nor Napoleon ever intended anything of the kind: invasion, domination, subjugation and the reduction of these countries to tributary status were France's objectives. Napoleon

stamped vigorously on any spark of Prussian nationalism, for example. The emergence of Prussian nationalism had occurred long before 1789, and France was determined to crush it. The emergence of a Prussian-dominated Germany – for good or ill – took place decades later.

In Italy, the widespread admiration for Napoleon which emerged towards the middle of the nineteenth century was merely an expression of hostility to autocratic Austrian domination reimposed, along with Papal domination of the centre and the Bourbon state in the south, after 1815. Its unification was neither advanced nor held up during the Napoleonic period: it was merely frozen for a quarter of a century.

In Austria, the revolutionary and Napoleonic interregnum had virtually no impact on the hold of the Habsburgs upon their far-flung, mostly peasant empire: nor until the 1914–18 war did this change. In Spain, Napoleon's defeat was followed by the imposition of the most repressive, reactionary monarchy the country had endured for half a century, that of Ferdinand VII. True, his exactions provoked an angry struggle with liberals; but the latter had been emerging before the Napoleonic intervention and might indeed have taken power gradually and constitutionally had the ravages of Napoleonic rule never occurred.

Russia, of course, was not affected at all by revolutionary and Napoleonic 'progress' for more than a century, its Romanov dynasty becoming largely entrenched in resistance to change during the Napoleonic wars. In Britain, it is possible to ascribe the coming to power of a deeply conservative clique under Lord Liverpool, Castle-reagh and the Wellesleys to a reaction against Napoleon (although there were other reasons too). The wars virtually squeezed out the moderate centre represented by Pitt, Grenville and Canning.

In 1816 Europe in fact was far less 'progressive', 'middle-class', 'democratic', 'nationalist', 'anti-feudal' and even democratically evolved than in 1788. The revolutionary Napoleonic period had set the clock back, not forward, except in one crucial respect: the expansion of the role of the central state, fuelled by the military imperative – in Napoleon's case to conquer, in other cases to resist him – a legacy that was to last well into the twentieth century and which in many respects is continuing.

In other important ways, Europe had regressed: its peoples had been decimated by wars which reduced Europe's population by anything up to a tenth, left few regions untouched, conscripted enormous quantities of cannon fodder, wrecked farmland, trade and commerce and left barely a family unaffected by the first modern, total war, scything through not just particular regions, elites and armies but entire populations.

The second issue that must be addressed is that of the 'Napoleonic myth'. To what extent is it believable that Napoleon himself was the instigator of the Napoleonic wars, or was the phenomenon altogether more complex? Most historians have of course taken this myth for granted, supported not just by much – certainly not all – of French historiography and Napoleon's own self-serving account, but by the opprobrium and denigration heaped upon him by his detractors.

Yet if the concept of one-man rule in a small state as far back as the Middle Ages has to be heavily qualified, it seems absurdly far-fetched in the case of a colossal machine such as that over which Napoleon presided. He was certainly one of the greatest autocrats in history, as the undisputed leader of perhaps the most authoritarian military machine presiding over the biggest empire in history, spanning the most prosperous continent in the world.

But he was also a child of his own age and circumstances – in particular French history and the French Revolution – and the nature of his power, and indeed personality, evolved over time. Napoleon emerged from the turmoil of the Revolution to pursue specifically French national objectives, of a kind that had existed for centuries under the Bourbons, with a newly mobilized population and army at his disposal.

It was Dumouriez, the French revolutionary general who ended up becoming a counter-revolutionary, who first won the string of victories that prevented revolutionary France being invaded. It was under Robespierre and the Jacobins that mass mobilization and totalitarian terror were instituted – under penalty of death. This in turn created the first great conscript army of Europe to face the old-style aristocratic volunteer forces or peasant levies and feudal armies of the rest of

Europe. It was Carnot who really created the *levé en masse* and the huge military machine that was to terrorize Europe at a time when Napoleon was just a rising junior officer. Carnot presided over France's revolution in military tactics, including the division of armies into semi-autonomous corps with great flexibility and freedom of action; the idea of striking in columns at the centre of traditional lines; the importance of flanking attacks or attacks on the 'derrière' – always a French obsession. Carnot too was responsible for the promotion of esprit de corps and the army as a privileged, well-paid, self-contained caste separate and above the mass of the people from which they were recruited (as opposed to the downtrodden militia of feudal rulers); and the virtual liberation of those military castes from normal conceptions of law and civilized behaviour to live off the land and plunder and rape as they pleased.

Most of these ideas had been pushed by reformers in the French army in the half-century prior to the Revolution, and some of them had been pinched from the Prussian ruler Frederick the Great's military innovations. Napoleon was not original in these ideas; but he was picked and promoted by his superiors, including Carnot and the Directory's Barras, because he was enormously energetic, pragmatic and skilful in their execution. When he finally staged his coup d'état in 1801, it was because a consensus had developed that a strong leader was necessary to end the corruption and near paralysis of the Directory and to prosecute France's wars.

However, dynamic though he was, Napoleon at that stage was anything but omnipotent: he had been promoted by conservative financial interests to abort further revolutionary agitation and to avoid a Bourbon restoration. He enjoyed support from the peasantry and depended on continuing military success. Above all he was the choice of a group of senior generals, and what the army had proposed, it could also dispose of. After becoming Emperor in 1804, whether as a personal vanity, in resignation to the anxiety of his supporters about a Bourbon restoration or as a simple reminder to its lingering and aspiring followers that the Revolution was over, he still depended on the loyalty of his generals and a coalition of civilian interests to stay in power.

His hand was immensely strengthened by the string of crushing military successes from 1805 to 1807 against Austria and Prussia which also boxed in Russia; and it was at this stage that his hubris really seemed to get the better of him. He no longer felt he had to kowtow to domestic supporters and he believed that he was militarily invincible. But his legitimacy derived not from his ludicrous coronation robes or laurel crowns or Roman emperor-style statues but from the fact that he had restored stability and leadership to France and delivered handsome victories and plentiful spoils – which were now a substitute for non-existent economic development. Realistically and shrewdly he had to call off his projected invasion of Britain, while less realistically he hoped that he could strangle France's oldest and most powerful foe economically.

In examining Napoleon's pronouncements, it is always necessary to disentangle bombastic rhetoric designed to inflame his followers, which fuelled ideas that he was simply a megalomaniac, from the realism underneath, which sometimes evidently became confused in his own mind, particularly in the later years. He then made the colossal and hubristic blunder of invading Spain, which posed no threat to France and which he regarded as a province to be annexed with little resistance. Ostensibly this was part of his anti-British strategy, in fact it was merely to add to the empire. Within a short time he understood the scale of his mistake – as his refusal to command the troops after the first campaigns showed – but he could not admit his errors in public, and the war continued as a vast, futile haemorrhage of French armies and men.

At that point Napoleon seemed to abandon his hubristic phase, and grew into – or in the modern phrase reinvented himself as – a peaceful statesman determined to maintain French domination of Europe, but seeking alliances, as through his marriage with Marie Louise of Austria, and engaging in no further territorial land grabs, other than occasionally bullying small states. The Spanish quagmire had, in a sense, tamed him. If Europe had been prepared to settle down to a period of French domination, Napoleon might perhaps have died peacefully on his throne as the founder of a new, long-lasting French dynasty.

But the resistance in the Iberian Peninsula, abetted by the British

expeditionary force, became increasingly lethal and widespread; and Europe had not been prepared to accept peace on French terms. Napoleon's own penchant for blustering to secure his ends had been more effective when countries were recoiling from his military successes than when he was exposed to be a merely mortal, if outstanding, military commander. At that stage diplomacy was required.

Finally Napoleon's erstwhile but unreliable ally, the Tsar of Russia, himself effectively declared war on France. This initiated the third phase of Napoleon's rule: from peaceful despotism he was forced to resort again to war, this time under pressure from a hostile foreign power. The Russian campaign has been presented as aggressive and madcap and initiated by Napoleon; but it was in fact a hugely mishandled defensive campaign. Only in his wilder moments did he declare he would conquer the whole country or use it as a gateway to the east. He blundered forward in the hope of inflicting a single huge defeat on the Russians and preventing them ever threatening his eastern dominions. After the retreat from Moscow he could still have preserved his empire. But his inept diplomacy and his enemies' sense of his vulnerability ultimately led to the disaster of Leipzig which brought about his downfall.

Thus the revolutionary wars and the career of Napoleon can be divided into four entirely distinct phases – those of revolutionary change and French aggrandisement from 1792 to 1801, those of French imperialism from about 1803 to 1808, those of imperial consolidation from 1808 to 1812, and those of self-defence and eventual collapse from 1812–1814.

Within France he was secure, so long as he continued to deliver military successes, until about 1808. Then he began to lose support among the key elites personified by Talleyrand. He remained in power because thenceforth he modified his image as an aggressor to become a constitutional monarch at peace with his neighbours, although an overwhelmingly preponderant one. When faced by Russian obduracy, he abandoned his new image in favour of a gamble, which cost him much of his domestic constituency and eventually led to his overthrow.

Yet to survive domestically he felt he had to re-establish himself as a military genius. This led to the disastrous Leipzig campaign, which

went well at first and collapsed when he over-extended himself:
Napoleon as a commander, although gifted, never realized his own
limitations. From then on he was doomed, defeated by Wellington in
the south-west and the allied armies in the east. His domestic base
crumbled until he was left only with the support of his military chiefs,
who also finally deserted him. In all this he can be seen not to be a
megalomaniac or a genius, but a leader reflecting domestic imperatives
who only occasionally allowed his manic self-confidence to overcome
his sense of realism. For the most part, it was revolutionary and
expansionary France which guided Napoleon's policies, not he who
guided them.

This judgement, obviously, qualifies any judgement about his greatness or wickedness. If this book's thesis is correct, he emerges as a much
more human and limited figure than the superman painted by his
supporters, or the globe-conquering megalomaniac portrayed by his
detractors. As a national leader, he was a superb protagonist of French
national interests who went too far, retrenched, was attacked and
blundered to his doom: the responsibility for the horrors inflicted upon
Europe during the period belonged to pre-revolutionary and post-
revolutionary France, of which he was but the helmsman, sometimes
inspired in his steering, sometimes disastrously inept.

As for his political skills – on which he prided himself – they were
virtually non-existent: he seized power in a brutal military coup, his
treatment of allies and enemies alike was that of the martinet throughout the ages – gruff patronage towards his supporters and furious anger
towards his enemies. As a diplomat, on which he also prided himself, he
was a figure of fun: he was seduced by Alexander at Tilsit, duped by
Francis II through an imperial marriage, and completely outwitted by
both Talleyrand and Metternich.

As a thinker, his philosophy was that of the highly intelligent man of
action that he was, but bereft of true insight. His musings on St Helena
were typical.

Man loves the supernatural. He meets deception halfway. The fact is
that everything about us is a miracle. Strictly speaking, there are no
phenomena, for in nature everything is a phenomenon: my ex-

istence is a phenomenon; this log that is being put into the chimney is a phenomenon; this light that illuminates me is a phenomenon; my intelligence, my faculties, are phenomena; for they all exist, yet we cannot define them. I leave you here, and I am in Paris, entering the Opera; I bow to the spectators, I hear the acclamations, I see the actors, I hear the music. Now if I can span the space from St Helena, why not that of the centuries? Why should I not see the future like the past? Would the one be more extraordinary, more marvellous than the other? No, but in fact it is not so.

He was an obsessive egotist. He could even be amusing:

When I was at Tilsit with the Emperor Alexander and the King of Prussia, I was the most ignorant of the three in military affairs! These two sovereigns, especially the King of Prussia, were completely au fait as to the number of buttons there ought to be in front of a jacket, how many behind, and the manner in which the skirts ought to be cut. Not a tailor in the army knew better than King Frederick how many measures of cloth it took to make a jacket. In fact, I was nobody in comparison with them. They continually tormented me with questions about matters belonging to tailors, of which I was entirely ignorant, though, in order not to affront them, I answered just as gravely as if the fate of an army depended upon the cut of a jacket. The King of Prussia changed his fashion every day. He was a tall, dry looking fellow, and would give a good idea of Don Quixote. At Jena, his army performed the finest and most showy manoeuvres possible, but I soon put a stop to their coglionerie, and taught them that to fight and to execute dazzling manoeuvres and wear splendid uniforms were very different affairs. If the French army had been commanded by a tailor, the King of Prussia would certainly have gained the day, from his superior knowledge in that art!

As a human being he was kind, perhaps excessively so, towards his family and friends; he was temperamental but not vindictive towards his subordinates and enemies. Yet he showed a professional soldier's utter indifference to the suffering of lesser people – whether his own

soldiers, the enemy or civilians – as to inflict suffering across Europe on a superhuman scale that appeared not to bother him at all.

As a soldier, the criterion by which he really wanted to be judged, he was a superb professional, perhaps the greatest leader of small armies in history, brilliant at outwitting and outflanking his opponents, inspiring his soldiers, and rewarding them amply, making them capable of almost incredible marches, endurance and feats: his early Italian campaigns and his last-ditch campaign in defence of France in 1814 are rightly military classics. His record in larger battles is more mixed, and to a great extent depended on the abilities of his subordinates as well as his capacity for improvisation, surprise, and the flexible management of army corps – his brilliance during the 1805–7 campaigns was not recaptured during 1807–9 and, 1812–15, apart from the defensive French campaign.

As an inspirer of his men he was perhaps without parallel, remembering the lowliest subordinate's name, regaling them with the most ringing before-battle bombast in military history, fearlessly risking his life in his youth and always understanding the importance of esprit de corps, morale boosting and regimental pride. He was a superb opportunist and im-proviser. He was undoubtedly one of the greatest soldiers in history.

He was also a born propagandist and his ability to tell every story so that it resounded to his credit has rarely been exceeded – hence the Napoleonic myth, fashioned ultimately in the forge of St Helena's steely climate: for Napoleon's final victory was not achieved in war, but in exile, where several years' outpouring of self-justification formed the basis for a Napoleonic legend that has survived to this day. Add to this his extraordinary capacity for dreaming, for articulating great visions which has inspired reformers and monsters alike in later years, and he was certainly what he would call a 'phenomenon', although a more limited one than he would have liked to believe.

In essence he was a military dictator, a superb general, and a conqueror utterly unprincipled and ruthless in the pursuit of his own self-promotion, subordinating France to his own glory even though his country and the French people sacrificed themselves in the hundreds of thousands in his cause – and then, after much suffering, destroyed it. He was a military genius, a political and diplomatic third-rater, and a monster.

*   *   *

How then, in retrospect, should Britain have responded to the challenge posed by revolutionary France and, later, Napoleon? As this book has tried to recount, the early period, that of revolutionary war, was met with by much wishful thinking, indecision and appeasement by William Pitt's government, which sincerely did not want to go to war. The military outcome of the early British expeditions were catastrophic, as was too their failure to support the resistance in France. The West Indies' campaign was militarily successful only at a huge cost in life.

As the war progressed, Pitt, his foreign secretary Grenville and William Windham, his war secretary and chief spymaster, became more resolute and pursued a skilful policy of building continental coalitions against Napoleon, supported by colossal amounts of British money, coupled with a dazzling naval campaign which has never been exceeded in history. All the time, however, both Pitt and Grenville preached peace and reconciliation.

When Napoleon came to power both men decided to continue the war, Pitt eventually dying of nervous exhaustion and Grenville acting only briefly as his successor. Foreign policy devolved, after a brief interlude dominated by the mercurial George Canning, to the unlovely triumvirate of the brilliant but cold Lord Castlereagh, the mediocre figurehead Lord Liverpool and Richard Wellesley and his brothers. Ironically, this was one moment when peace might have been possible, albeit with the continent under French domination and Napoleon content to rest upon his laurels. Instead, probably rightly, the British prosecuted the Peninsular War and sought to bribe and persuade their continental allies into re-entering the fight. They succeeded in both. By this time the British army had been transformed from being brave but inefficient under incompetent commanders to being brave, effective and well-officered. When war broke out on the continent again, Britain's confrontational policy was implacably pursued and ended in a total victory, first in 1814 and then in 1815, with the charmless Castlereagh pursuing a carefully structured settlement for Europe.

Pitt and Grenville can be faulted for rising to the French challenge too slowly, then complimented for pursuing it vigorously. Castlereagh and Liverpool can be faulted for ignoring the possibility of peace with France, and instead seeking war regardless. While many mistakes were

made by both administrations, it is hard to fault Britain's implacable commitment to the war in the belief that the war party under Napoleon would learn nothing except from defeat.

With the bumbling Louis XVIII's restoration, France was neutralized for decades as a political or military power: Britain could be said to have attained its objective. For Britain the Napoleonic war was a thrice-just war – Britain had to take arms against the disruption caused to British commerce, the slaughter wrought throughout the continent, and the threat to British interests not just in the Baltic, the Mediterranean and the Low Countries, but around the world.

Who, in the end, defeated Napoleon? All the coalition members at one time or another now claim to have been the principals. Dogged Austria deserves a large share of the credit for rising from defeat again and again. Prussia, after its lamentable initial performance, renewed some of its national pride at the end. Russia can claim credit for the 1812 campaign, in which although there was no great feat of Russian arms, the French were completely routed.

Yet the lion's share must surely go to Britain, with Pitt and Grenville's policies of coalition-building on the continent, the astounding feats of Britain's navy under Nelson and a host of other outstanding commanders, and Wellington's relentless performance during the Peninsular War. It was the failure of France to invade or strangle Britain economically that first frustrated revolutionary and Napoleonic France when continental Europe lay prostrate at its feet: and it was the Peninsular War that first exposed France's weakness and tied down huge French armies, encouraging first Russia and then Austria and Prussia back into the war. Waterloo was, for all its fame, essentially a postscript, the coup de grâce for an indomitable fighter who had failed to accept his own demise the year before. Nor was it a brilliantly fought battle, although Wellington prevailed: Wellington's true greatness lay in the Peninsular campaign and the resistance of his Spanish and Portuguese allies which brought down a continental giant by the feet. It was through men like him, Moore and Hill in the British army and Howe, St Vincent, Duncan, Nelson, Cochrane and Collingwood in the navy that Britain achieved its deliverance and continental Europe its independence.

SELECT BIBLIOGRAPHY

NB publication dates refer to the most recently published editions

Abell, Mrs Betsy, *Recollections of Napoleon at St Helena*, London, 1848
Abrantes, Laure Junot, *Duchesse d'*, Paris
Alcaide, A , *Historia de los Sitios que pusieron a Zaragoza en los anos de 1808 y 1809*, Madrid, 1830
Aldington, R., *Wellington*, London, 1946
Alexander I, Tsar, Correspondence, Paris 1909–10
Alger, J.G., *Napoleon's British Visitors and Captives*, London, 1904
Anderson, Robert and Ibrahim Fawzy, *Egypt in 1800*, London, 1987
Andolenko, S., *Histoire de l'Armee Russe*, Paris, 1967
Angeberg, Leonard Chodze d', *Le Congres de Vienne a les Traites de 1815*, Paris, 1863
Anon, *The Battle of Lodi*, London, 1803
Anon, *The military exploits of Don Juan Martin Diez*, El Empecinado, London, 1825
Ardagh, John, *France in the New Century*, London, 1999
Arriazu, M. (ed.), *Estudios sobre cortes de Madrid*, Pamplona, 1967
Artola, M., *La Espana de Fernando VII*, Madrid, 1999
Atkinson, C. (ed.), *A light dragoon in the Peninsular War, Extracts from the letters of Captain Lovel Badcock*, JSAHR, XXXIV No.138
Atteridge, A.H., *Joachim Murat*, London, 1911
Aubrey, Charles, *Le Ravitaillement des armees de Frederic le Grand et de Napoleon*, Paris, 1894
Ayling, Stanley, *The life of Charles James Fox*, London, 1991
Aymes, J., *La Guerra de Independencia en Espana 1808–1814*, Madrid, 1975
Azcarate, P. de, *Wellington y Espana*, Madrid, 1961

Bainville, Jacques, *Bonaparte en Egypte*, Paris, 1836
Balhomme, Victor, *Histoire de l'Infanterie en France*, Paris, 1893–1902
Bankes, G. (ed.), *The Autobiography of Sergeant William Lawrence*, London, 1886
Barbaroux, Charles, *Adventures of a French Sergeant 1809-23*, London, 1898
Barnett, Corelli, *Bonaparte*, New York, 1978
Barney, John, *The Defence of Norfolk, 1793–1815*, Norwich, 2000
Barras, Paul, *Autobiography*, 1896
Barrow, John, *The Life and Correspondence of Admiral Sir William Sidney Smith*, London, 1848
Bartlett, C., *Castlereagh*, London, 1966
Beauharnais, Prince Eugene de, *Memoires*, Paris, 1858–60
Becke, Archibald, *Napoleon and Waterloo*, London, 1995
Belliard, Comte Augustin, *Histoire Scientifique et militair de l'expedition Francaise en Egypte*, Paris, 1836
Bennigsen, General Lev., *Memoires*, Paris, 1908

Bentley, N. (ed.), *Selections from the reminiscences of Captain Gronow,* London, 1977
Bergeron, Louis, *France under Napoleon,* Princeton, 1981
Bernardy, Francois de, *Eugene de Beauharnais,* Paris, 1973
Bertaud, Jean-Paul, *The Army of the French Revolution,* Princeton, 1988
Berthier, Louis Alexandre, *Relations des Campagnes en Egypte et en Syrie,* Paris, 1800
Bertier de Saivigny, G. de, *Metternich,* Paris, 1986
Bertin, *la Campagne de 1812,* Paris, 1895
Bertolini, Bartolomeo, *La Campagna di Russia 1812–13,* Milan, 1869
Bertrand, H.G., *Napoleon at St Helena,* London, 1953
Blackburn, Julie, *The Emperor's Last Island,* London, 1991
Blanning, T.C.W., *The French Revolutionary Wars, 1787–1802,* London, 1996
Blond, Georges, *La grande armee,* London, 1995
Boselli, Count, *La Prise de Malte,* Rome, 1909
————————*The Hundred Days,* New York, 1964
Bourgeois, Rene, *Tableau de la campagne de Moscou en 1812,* Paris, 1814
Bourgogne, Sergeant, *Memoires 1812–3,* London, 1995
Bourienne, F. de, *Memoirs of Napoleon Bonaparte,* London, 1905
Bourienne, Louis Antoine, *Memoires,* Paris, 1829
Bragin, M., *Field Marshal Kutuzov,* Moscow, 1944
Brandao, *El-Rei Junot,* Lisbon 1977
Brenton, Edward, *Life of and correspondence of John, Earl St Vincent, 1838,* London, 1966
————————*Europe against Napoleon,* London, 1970
————————*Wellington at War 1794–1815,* London
Brett, Oliver, *Wellington,* London, 1928
Brett-James, Anthony, *1812. Eyewitness accounts of Napoleon's defeat in Russia,* London
Broers, Michael, *Europe under Napoleon, 1799–1815,* London, 1996
Brooke, John, *King George III,* London, 1972
Browning, Oscar (ed.), *England and Napoleon: the Despatches of Lord Whitworth,* London, 1887
Bryant, Sir Arthur, *Years of Endurance, 1793–1802,* London, 1942
————————*Years of Victory 1802–15,* London, 1944
Buckly, R. (ed.), *The Napoleonic war journal of Captain Browne,* London, 1987
Bulow, *The spirit of the modern system of war,* London, 1806
Buturlin, Dmitri, *Histoire militaire de la campagne de Russie en 1812,* Paris, 1824

Cairnes, W.E. (ed.), *The Military Maxims of Napoleon,* London, 1901
Cambronero, C., *El Rey Intruso: Jose Bonaparte,* Madrid, 1909
Carlyle, Thomas, *The French Revolution,* Oxford, 1989
Carr, Raymond, *Spain 1808–1975,* Oxford, 1982
Carr-Gomm, F. (ed.), *Letters of Sir William Maynard Gomm from 1799–1815,* London, 1881
Cassinello, Juan Martin, *'El Empecinado',* Madrid, 1995
Castelot, Andre, *Fouche,* Paris, 1990
Castle, Ian, *Aspern and Wagram 1809,* London, 1998
Castlereagh, Viscount, Correspondence, London, 1853
Cathcart, George. *Commentaries on the war in Russia and Germany in 1812–3,* London, 1850
Caulaincourt, Armand de, *With Napoleon in Russia,* New York, 1935
Caulaincourt, Marquis de, *Memoires,* Paris, 1933
Chair, S., *Napoleon on Napoleon,* London, 1991
Chandler, David, *Dictionary of the Napoleonic Wars,* London, 1979
————————*The Campaigns of Napoleon,* 1966
————————*Napoleon's Marshals,* New York, 1987
Chaptal, Jean, *Memoires,* Paris, 1892
Charles-Roux, Francois, *L'Angleterre et l'Expedition Francaise en Egypte,* Cairo, 1925
————————*Bonaparte, Gouverneur d'Egypte,* Paris, 1935
————————*Les Origines de l'Expedition d'Egypte,* Paris, 1901

Chateaubriand, Francois-Rene, *Memoires d'Outre Tombe*, Paris, 1849
Chatterton, Lady Georgiana, *Memorials of Admiral Lord Gambier*, London, 1861
Chauvin, Victor, *La Legende Egyptienne de Bonaparte*, Mons, 1902
Cherfils, Christian, *Bonaparte et l'Islam*, Paris, 1914
Chevalier, E., *Histoire de la Marine francaise sous la Premiere Republique*, Paris, 1886
Chichagov, *Memoires*, Berlin, 1858
————————*The Campaign of 1812 in Russia*, London, 1843
Chuquet, Arthur, *Human Voices from the Russian Campaign*, London, 1914
Clarke and M'Arthur, *Life of Admiral Lord Nelson*, London, 1809
Clausewitz, Carl von, *On war*, Princeton UP, 1976
Clowes, William, *The Royal Navy*, London, 1899
Cobban, Alfred, *Aspects of the French Revolution*, London, 1968
————————*A History of Modern France*, London, 1957–65
Cochrane, *The Autobiography of a Seaman*, London, 1860
Cochrane, Donald, *The Trial of Lord Cochrane*
Coleman, Terry, *Nelson*, 2001
Connelly, *Blundering to Glory: Napoleon's Military Campaigns*, Wilmington, 1987
————————*Napoleon's Satellite Kingdoms*, New York, 1965
Constant, Louis, *Memoires*, 1830
Corbett, Julian, *The Campaign of Trafalgar*, London, 1910
Corona, C., *Revolution y Reaccion en el Reinado de Carlos IV*, Madrid, 1957
Crauford, Alexander, *General Crauford and His Light Division*, London, 1891
Creevey, Thomas, Papers, London, 1903
Croker, John Wilson, Correspondence and diaries, London, 1885
Cronin, Vincent, *Napoleon*, London, 1990
Crouzet, F., *Economie Brittanique et le Blocus Continental, 1806–13*, Paris, 1958
Cuanca, J., *La Iglesia Espanola antes la Revolucion Liberal*, Madrid, 1971

Dallas, Gregor, *1815*, London, 1996
Dalrymple, H., *Memoirs*, London, 1830
Dard, Emile, *Napoleon et Talleyrand*, Paris, 1935
Davidov, Denis, *In the Service of the Tsar against Napoleon*, London, 1999
Davies, D., *Sir John Moore's Peninsular Campaign 1808–9*, The Hague, 1974
Davis, *The Rise of the English Shipping Industry*, Newton Abbott, 1972
Davout, Marshal Louis, Correspondence, Paris, 1885
De Lancey, Lady, *A Week at Waterloo in 1815*, London, 1906
Denon, Vivant, *Voyage dans la Basse et la Haut Egypte*, Paris, 1802
Derry, J., *Castlereagh*, London, 1976
Desaix, General, Journal, 1801
Desgnettes, Baron, *Histoire Medicale de l'Armee d'Orient*
Desvernois, Baron, *Memoires*, Paris, 1898
Deutsch, Harold, *The Genesis of Napoleonic Imperialism*, Harvard, 1938
Dickinson, H.T., *Britain and the French Revolution*, London, 1989
Dixon, Piers, *Pauline Bonaparte*, London, 1964
————————*Canning, Politician and Statesman*, London, 1976
Diz, M, *El Manifiesto de 1814*, Pamplona, 1967
Djabarti, el Abd el-Rahman, *Merveilles Biographiques et Historiques*, 1888–96
Doguereau, Jean-Pierre, *Journal de l'Expedition d'Egypte*, Paris, 1904
Domergue, A., *La Rusie Pendant les Guerres de l'Empire*, Paris, 1835
Douglas Reed, *From Valmy to Waterloo: extracts from the diary of Captain Charles Francois*, London, 1906
Doyle, William, *The Oxford History of the French Revolution*, Oxford, 1989
Drialt, Edouard, *Tilsit. France et Russie sous le Premier Empire*, Paris, 1917
————————*Le Grand Empire (1809–1812)*, Paris, 1924
————————*Mohammed Ali et Napoleon*, Cairo, 1925

Du Casse, A., *General Vandamme*, Paris, 1870
———————————*Russia's Military Way to the West,* London, 1981
——————————*The Military Experience in the Age of Reason,* London, 1987
Duff Cooper, A., *Talleyrand*, London, 1932
Duffy, Christopher, *Borodino and the War of 1812*, London, 1972
———————————*Austerlitz, 1805*, London, 1977
Dufour, G., *La Guerra de Independencia*, Madrid, 1999
Dumas, Mathieu, *Souvenirs*, Paris, 1839
Dumonceau, Francois, *Memoires*, Brussells, 1960
Dundulis, Bronius, *Napoleon et la Lithuanie en 1812*, Paris, 1940
Dupuy, Victor, *Souvenirs Militaires*, Paris, 1892
Durova, Nadezhda, *The Cavalry Maiden*, Bloomington, 1988
Dwyer, Philip (ed.), *Napoleon and Europe*, London, 2001
Dzieanowski, M.K., *Alexander I. Russia's Mysterious Tsar*, New York, 1990

Egremont, Lord, *Wyndham and Children First,* London, 1969
Ehrman, John, *The Younger Pitt*, three volumes, London, 1996
Elgood, Percival, *Bonaparte's Adventure in Egypt*, London, 1931
Ellis, G., *The Napoleonic Empire*, London, 1991
Elting, John, *Swords Around a Throne – Napoleon's Grand Armee*, London, 1988
———————————*British Society and the French Wars 1793–1815*, London, 1979
Elting, John and Knotel, Herbert, *Napoleonic Uniforms*, London, 2000
Emsley, Clive, *The Longman Companion to Napoleonic Europe*, London, 1993
Epstein, Robert, *Napoleon's last victory and the Emergence of Modern War*, Lawrence, 1994
——————————— *Prince Eugene at War*, Arlington, 1984
Esdaile, Charles, *The Peninsular War*, London, 2002
———————————*The Wars of Napoleon*, London, 1995
———————————*The Spanish Army in the Peninsular War*, Manchester, 1988
Esposito, Vincent and Elting, John, *A Military History and Atlas of the Napoleonic Wars*, New York, 1964

Faber de Faur, Christian Wilhelm von, *With Napoleon in Russia*, London, 2001
Fain, Baron, *Memoires*, 1824
Fairon, Emile and Heuse, Henri, *Lettres de Grognards*, Liege, 1936
Fare, Charles, *Lettres d'un Jeune Officier a sa Mere 1803–1814*, Paris, 1889
Fisher, C., *A Picture of Madrid*, London, 1808
Fisher, H.A.L., *Bonapartism*, London, 1908
Fitchett, W., *How England Saved Europe*, London, 1900
Fletcher, I. (ed.), *The Peninsular War*, Staplehurst, 1998
Flores, F., *El Bandolerismo en Extremadura*, Badajoz, 1992
Ford, Edward, *Napoleon's Russian Campaign of 1812*, London, 1914
Forsyth, William, *History of the Captivity of Napoleon at St Helena*, London, 1853
Fortescue, Sir John, *History of the British Army*, London, 1930
Fouche, Joseph, *Memoires*, Paris, 1824
Foy, M.S., *History of the War in the Peninsula under Napoleon*, London, 1827
Francois, Captaine C., *Journal*, Paris, 1903
Fraser, Flora, *Beloved Emma*, London, 1986
Funck, Karl von, *In the Wake of Napoleon: Memoirs 1807–9*, London, 1931
Furet, Francois, *Revolutionary France 1770–1880*, Oxford, 1992
Fusil, Louise, *Souvenirs d'une Femme sur la Retraite de Russie*, Paris, 1910

Gardiner, Robert, *Nelson against Napoleon, from the Nile to Copenhagen 1798–1801*
———————————(ed.), *Fleet, Battle and Blockade, the French Revolutionary War 1793–7*
———————————(ed.), *The Campaign of Trafalgar 1803–5*, London, 1997
Gates, David, *The Spanish Ulcer*, New York, 1986

——————The Napoleonic Wars, 1803–1815, New York, 1997
Geyl, Pieter, Napoleon For and Against, London, 1949
Giles, Frank, Napoleon Bonaparte: England's Prisoner, London, 2001
Girod de l'Ain, Baron, Dix Ans de mes Souvenirs Militares, Paris, 1873
Gleig, G., The Subaltern, London, 1825
Glover, Michael, Wellington's army in the Peninsula 1808–1814, New York, 1977
——————The Napoleonic Wars: an Illustrated History, London, 1979
Glover, Richard, Peninsular Preparation, Cambridge, 1988
Gneisenau, August von, The Life and Campaigns of Field Marshal Blucher, London, 1815
Godenot, Jacques, La Contre-Revolution, Paris, 1961
Godoy, Prince Manuel, Memorias, Madrid, 1838
Gohier, Louis-Jerome, Memoires, Paris, 1824
Gooch, G.P., Germany during the French Revolution, London, 1920
Gould, Robert, Mercenaries of the Napoleonic War, London, 1995
Gourgaud, Gaspard, Napoleon et la Grande Armee en Russie, Paris, 1825
——————St Helene: journale, Paris
Green, The Vicissitudes of a Soldier's Life, London, 1815
Griffiths, Paddy (ed.), Wellington Commander, Chichester, 1985
Grimble, Ian, The Sea Wolf, London, 1978
Gross, Baron, Duties of an Officer in the Field, London, 1801
Grouchy, Emmanuel Marquis de, Memoires, Paris, 1873
Gruber, Carl Johann Ritter von, Souvenirs, Paris, 1909
Grunwald, Constantin de, Alexander Ier, Paris, 1955
Guedalla, P. (ed.), Letters of Napoleon to Marie Louise, London, 1935
Guemard, Gabriel, Aventuriers Mameluks d'Egypte, Cairo
Guerin, Leon, Histoire Maritime de France, Paris, 1851
Guerrini, Domenico, La Spedizione Francese in Egitto, Turin, 1904
Guerrini, Maurice, Napoleon and Paris, London, 1970

Haffner, Sebastian, The Rise and Fall of Prussia, London, 1980
Hales, E.E.Y., Napoleon and the Pope, London, 1962
Hall, C., British Strategy in the Napoleonic Wars 1803–15, Manchester, 1992
Hall, H.F. (ed.), Napoleon's Letters to Josephine, London, 1903
Hall, Sir John, General Pichegru's Treason, London, 1915
Hamilton-Williams, David, The Fall of Napoleon, London, 1994
Hamnett, B., La Politica Espanola en una Epoca Revolucionaria, Mexico City, 1985
Hampson, Norman, A Social History of the French Revolution, London, 1963
Harbron, J., Trafalgar and the Spanish Navy, London, 1988
Harland, John, Seamanship in the Age of Sail, London, 1984
Harrison, James, Life of Nelson, London, 1806
Harvey, Robert, Liberators, London, 2000
——————Cochrane, London, 2001
——————A Few Bloody Noses, London, 2003
Haussman, Franz Joseph, A Soldier for Napoleon, London, 1998
Hayman, P. Soult, Napoleon's Maligned Marshal, London, 1990
——————Who was Who in the Napoleonic Wars, London, 1998
——————The Napoleonic Source Book, London, 1991
Haythornthwaite, P., The Armies of Wellington, London, 1994
——————Die Hard! Dramatic Actions from the Napoleonic Wars, London, 1996
Heffer, Simon, Moral Desperado: A Life of Thomas Carlyle, London, 1995
Henderson, E., Blucher and the Uprising of Prussia against Napoleon, London, 1911
Herold, J.C., The Mind of Napoleon, New York, 1955
——————Bonaparte in Egypt, London, 1962
Herr, R., The 18th Century Revolution in Spain, Princeton, 1958
Hibbert, Christopher, Wellington: A Personal History, London, 1997

——————————*Nelson: A Personal History*, London, 1994
——————————*Corunna*, London, 1961
Holmes, Richard, *Wellington*, London, 2003
Holtman, Robert, *Napoleonic Propaganda*, Baton Rouge, 1950
——————————*The Napoleonic Revolution*, Philadelphia, 1967
Horne, Alistair, *How Far From Austerlitz?*, London, 1996
Hortense de Beauharnais, Queen, *Memoires*, Paris, 1927
Houlding, J.A., *Fit for Service: the Training of the British Army 1715–1795*, Oxford, 1981
Hourtoulle, F.G., *Borodino – the Moscova: the Battle for the Redoubts*, Paris, 2000
——————————*Le General Comte Lasalle*, Paris, 1979
Houssaye, Henry, *La Premiere Restauration*, Paris, 1920
——————————*Napoleon and the Campaign of 1814*, London, 1914
——————————*Waterloo*, Paris, 1924
Howard, Donald D., (Ed)., *Napoleonic Military History, A Bibliography*, New York, 1986
Howard E.G.C., *The Memoirs of Sir Sidney Smith*, London, 1839
Howard, Frank, *Sailing Ships of War 1400–1860*, London
Howard, J.E., *Letters and Documents of Napoleon*, London, 1980
Howarth, David, *A Near Run Thing*, London, 1968
Hughes, B.P., *Open Fire: Artillery Tactics from Marlborough to Wellington*, Chichester, 1983

Iribarren, Espoz y Mina, *El Guerrillero*, Madrid, 1965
Iung, Theodore, *Lucien Bonaparte et ses Memoires*, Paris, 1883
Ivray, Jehan d', *Bonaparte et l'Egypte*, Paris, 1914
Izquierdo, M., *Antecedentes y Comienzos del Reinado de Fernando VII*, Madrid, 1963

James, Lawrence, *The Iron Duke: A Military Biography of Wellington*, London, 1992
James, William, *The Naval History of Great Britain*, London, 1824
Jeffries, George, *Tactics and Grand Tactics of the Napoleonic Wars*, Boston, 1982
Jerome Bonaparte, *Memoires*, Paris, 1864
Joelsson, Michael and Diana, *The Commander (Barclay de Tolly)*, Oxford, 1980
Johnson, David, *Napoleon's Cavalry and its leaders*, New York, 1978
——————————*The French Cavalry 1792–1815*, London, 1989
Johnston, R.M., *The Napoleonic Empire in Southern Italy and the Rise of the Secret Societies*, London, 1904
——————————*In the Words of Napoleon*, London, 2002
Jomini, Baron, *The Art of War*, London, 1992
——————————*Vie Politique et Militaire de Napoleon*, Brussels, 1842
Jonquiere, C. de la, *L'Expedition de Egypte*, Paris
Jourdain, Armand, *Trente-neuf Jours de Reclusion dans les Prisons de Vilna*, Paris, 1858
Junot, L., *Memoires*, Paris, 1835

Keegan, John, *The Face of Battle*, New York, 1976
Keep, John, *Soldiers of the Tsar*, Oxford, 1985
Keith, Viscount, *Papers*, 1955
Kemble, *Napoleon Immortal. The Medical History and Private Life of Napoleon Bonaparte*, London, 1959
Kemp, Peter, *The British Sailor, A Social History of the Lower Deck*, London, 1970
Kennedy, Ludovic, *Nelson's Band of Brothers*, London, 1951
Ketton-Cremer, *Norfolk Portraits*, London, 1944
Kircheisen, Friedrich, *Napoleon I*, Munich, 1914
Kosciusko, General, *Manoeuvres of Horse Artillery*, New York, 1808
Kraehe, Enno, *Metternich's German Policy*, Princeton, 1963
Kralik, Richard, *Histoire de Vienne*, Paris, 1932

Labaume, Eugene, *Relation Complete de la Campagne de Russie en 1812*, Paris
Labourdette, J., *Le Portugal de 1780 a 1802*, Paris, 1985
Lachouque, Henry and Brown, *The Anatomy of Glory: Napoleon and his Guard*, London, 1997

Lacroix, Desire, *Bonaparte en Egypte*, Paris, 1899
Lafoz, H., *Jose Palafox y su tiempo*
Laissus, Yves, *L'Egypte*, Paris, 1998
La Jonquiere, C. de, *L'Expedition en Egypte*, Paris, 1907
Lallemand, H., *A Treatise on Artillery*, New York, 1820
Langeron, *Memoires*, Paris, 1902
Langford, Paul, *A Polite and Commercial People*, Oxford, 1989
Las Cases, Emanuel, *Memorial de St-Helene*, Paris, 1948
Latrille, General, *Reflections on Modern War*, London, 1809
Laughton, J., *The Nelson Memorial*, London, 1896
Laugier, Cesare de, *Gli Italiani in Russia*, Milan, 1980
Lavery, Brian, *Nelson's Navy*, London, 1989
——————The Ship of the Line, London, 1984
Lawford, James, *Napoleon: the Last Campaigns 1813–5*, New York, 1977
Lecestre, L. (ed.), *New Letters of Napoleon I*, London, 1898
——————Napoleon: from Tilsit to Waterloo, New York, 1969
Lecointe de Laveau, G. *Moscou, Lavant et Apres l'Incendie*, Paris, 1814
Lee, Sir John, *Memoirs*, London, 1836
Lefebvre, Georges, *The French Revolution*, Paris, 1964
——————Le Directoire, Paris, 1946
Lieven, Princess de, *Memoires*, Paris
Linck, Tony, *Napoleon's Generals: the Waterloo Campaign*, Chicago
Llorente, J., *Memorias*, Paris, 1814
Lloyd, Christopher, *The British Seaman*, London, 1968
——————Lord Cochrane, London, 1947
Longford, Elizabeth, *Wellington: the Years of the Sword*, London, 1971
Loraine Petre, F., *Napoleon and the Archduke Charles*, London, 1908
——————Napoleon's Campaign in Poland 1806–7, London, 1901
Louis Philippe d'Orleans, *Mon Journal,* Paris, 1849
Lovett, *Napoleon and the Birth of Modern Spain*, New York, 1965
Lucas-Dubreton, J., *Le Culte de Napoleon 1815–48*, Paris, 1960
——————La France de Napoleon, Paris, 1981
Ludovici, A. (ed.), *On the Road with Wellington*, New York, 1925
Lynch, J., *Bourbon Spain 1700–1808*, Oxford, 1989
Lynn, John, *The Bayonets of the Republic*, Chicago, 1984
Lyons, Martyn, *Napoleon Bonaparte and the Legacy of the French Revolution*, New York, 1994

Macdonald, Marshal, *Recollections*, London, 1892
Mackenzie, Norman, *The Escape from Elba*, Oxford, 1982
Madariaga, Isabel de, *Russia in the Age of Catherine the Great*, London, 1981
Madelin, Louis, *Fouche*, Paris, 1910
Madol, H., *Godoy: The First Dictator of Modern Times*, London, 1934
Magraw, Roger, *France 1815–1914: the Bourgeois Century*, London, 1983
Maitland, Captain F.L., *Narrative of the Surrender of Bonaparte*, London, 1826
Manan, A.T., *The Life of Nelson*, London, 1898
Mansel, Philip, *Louis XVIII,* London, 1981
Mansuy, A., *Jerome Napoleon et la Pologne en 1812*, Paris, 1931
——————Paris Between Empires 1814–52
Marbot, Baron, *Memoires*, London, 1900
Markham, Felix, *Napoleon,* London, 1963
Marmont, Marshal Auguste, *The Spirit of Military Institutions*, Philadelphia, 1862
Marmont, Marshal, *Memoires*, Paris, 1856
Marshall-Cornwall, Sir James, *Napoleon as Military Commander*, London, 1967
——————Massena, Oxford, 1965
Marshall, John, *Royal Naval Biography*, London, 1835

Marte, F., *El Motin de Aranjuez*, Pamplona, 1972
Martel, Tancrede, *Un Gallant Chevalier: le General Lasalle*, Paris, 1929
Martineau, Gilbert, *Napoleon Surrenders*, London, 1971
Martinez de Vlesco, *La Formacion de la Junta Central*, Pamplona, 1972
Masson, Frederic, *Napoleon et les femmes*, Paris, 1894
——————————*Napoleon et sa famille*, Paris, 1897
Mathiez, Albert, *Le Directoire*, Paris, 1834
Maude, *Cavalry versus Infantry*, London, 1896
——————————*The Ulm Campaign*, London, 1912
——————————*The Jena Campaign*, London, 1909
Maurice, Sir John (ed.), *The Diary of Sir John Moore*, London, 1904
Maxwell, Sir Herbert, *The Life of Wellington*, London, 1900
Mayne, E.C., *Lady Bessborough and her Friendships*, London, 1939
McClynn, Frank, *Napoleon*, London, 1998
Memes, J.S., *Memoirs of the Empress Josephine*, London, 1831
Meneval, Claude-Francois, *Memoires*, Paris, 1894
Mercader, Jose Bonaparte, *Rey de Espana 1808–13*, Madrid, 1983
Metternich, Klemens von, *Memoires*, Paris, 1880
Meyer, J., *The Battle of Busaco: Victory or defeat*, London, 1989
——————————*The Battle of Vitoria*, London, 1990
Miot de Melito, *Memoires*, Paris, 1858
Mirabeau, Comte de, *Monarchie Prussienne sous Frederic le Grand*, London, 1788
Mitchell, L.G., *Charles James Fox*, London, 1992
Molas, P., *La Espana de Carlos IV*, Madrid, 1991
Monaque, Remi, *Latouche-Treville*, Paris, 2000
Montagu, Violet, *Eugene de Beauharnais: the Adopted Son of Napoleon*, London, 1880
Montholon, C.T., *Memoires*, 1824
Montigny, L., *Souvenirs*, Paris, 1833
Monton, Juan Carlos, *La Revolucion Armada del Dos de Mayo en Madrid*, Madrid, 1893
Moreau, Jean, *Le Soldat Imperial 1800–24*, Paris, 1904
Morrison, Edward (ed.), *The Hamilton and Nelson papers*, London, 1894
Morier, John Philip, *Memoir of a Campaign with the Ottoman Army in Egypt*, London, 1880
Moxo, S., *La Disolucion del Regimen Senorial de Espana*, Madrid, 1965
Muffling, Baron von, *Memoirs*, London, 1997
Muir, Rory, *Britain and the defeat of Napoleon 1807–1815*, London, 1996
——————————*Salamanca, 1812*, New Havey, 2001
Munoz, Maidonado, *Historia Politics y militar de la Guerra de Independencia*, 1833
Murray, Stewart, *Discipline: its Reason and Battle Value*, London, 1893

Nafziger, George, *The Russian Army 1800–15*, Cambridge, Canada, 1983
——————————*Napoleon at Dresden*, London, 1994
——————————*Napoleon at Leipzig*, London, 1996
——————————*Napoleon's Invasion of Russia*, Novato, 1988
Napier, W., *History of the War in the Peninsula*, London, 1840
Napoleon I, Emperor, Correspondence, Various dates and publications
Narbonne, Joseph, *Bonaparte, le Roi Philosophe*, Paris, 1949
Nash, David, *The Prussian Army 1808–15*, London, 1972
Neale, A., *Letters from Portugal and Spain*, London, 1809
Nelson, Viscount Horatio, *Despatches and Letters*, 1895
Nesselrode, Comte de, *Lettres 1760–1850*, Paris
Ney, Marshal Michel, *Memoirs*, London, 1833
——————————*Military Studies*, London, 1833
Nicholas, Grand-Duc, *Correspondence de l'Empereur Alexandre Ier*, St Petersburg, 1910
Nicholas, Turc, *Chronique d'Egypte 1798–1804*, Cairo, 1950
Nicholson, Harold, *The Congress of Vienna*, London, 1946

Nicolay, Fernald, *Napoleon at the Boulogne Camp*, London, 1907
Norfolk News, *Death of Sir Robert John Harvey*, Norwich, 1860
Nosworthy, Brent, *Battle Tactics of Napoleon and his Enemies*, London, 1995

O'Dwyer, Margaret, *The Papacy in the Age of Napoleon and the Restoration*, London, 1987
Oliver, Michael and Partridge, Richard, *Napoleonic Army Handbook*, London, 2002
Ollivier, *Le Dix-huit Brumaire*, Paris, 1959
Oman, Carola, *Sir John Moore*, London, 1953
————————*Nelson*, 1947
————————*Napoleon's Viceroy, Eugene de Beauharnais*, London, 1966
Oman, Sir Charles, *A History of the Peninsular War*, London, 1997
————————*Wellington's Army 1809–1814*, London, 1913
O'Meara, Barry, *Napoleon in Exile*, London, 1822
Ompteda, Baron C., Memoirs, London, 1894
O'Neill, Charles, *Military Adventures*, Worcester, Mass, 1851

Paget, J., *Wellington's Peninsular War: Battles and Battlefields*, London, 1990
Pakenham, T. (ed.) *Alexander 1st: Tsar of War and Peace*, London, 1974
————————*The Pakenham Letters*, London, 1814
Palafox, O. de, *Memorias Zaragoza*, 1994
Palmer, Alan, *Napoleon in Russia*, New York, 1967
————————*An Encyclopaedia of Napoleon's Europe*, London, 1984
————————*Napoleon and Marie Louise*, London, 2001
Paret, Peter, *Yorck and the era of Prussian Reform 1807–15*
Parkinson, C. Northcote, *Britannia Rules*, London, 1994
Parkinson, Roger, *Moore of Corunna*, London, 1975
————————*Hussar General: the Life of Blucher*, London, 1975
————————*The Fox of the North: the Life of Kutuzov*, London, 1976
Parquin, Charles, *Napoleon's Victories*, Chicago, 1893
Pastre, J-L., *Bonaparte en Egypte*, Paris, 1932
Petit, Joseph, *Marengo or the Campaign of Italy*, Philadelphia, 1801
Petrie, Thomas F. Lorraine, *Napoleon and the Archduke Charles*, London, 1976
————————*Napoleon's Conquest of Prussia*, London, 1907
————————*Napoleon's Last Campaign in Germany 1813*, London, 1974
Pettigrew, *Memoirs of the Life of Nelson*, London, 1849
Peyre, Roger, *L'Expedition d'Egypte*, Paris, 1890
Peyrusse, Baron, *Memorial, Carcassone 1869*
————————*Lettres*, Paris, 1894
Pfuel, Ernst von, *Retreat of the French Army from Russia*, London, 1813
Pils, Francois, *Journal de Marche du Grenadier Pils 1804–14*, Paris, 1895
Phipps, Ramsay, *The Armies of the First French Republic*, London, 1939
Picard E. and Tuetey L., (eds.) *Correspondence Inedite de Napoleon*, Paris, 1913
Pignatelli, Prince, *La Rivoluzione Napoletana del 1799*, Naples, 1999
Pocock, Tom, *Horatio Nelson*, London, 1988
————————*The Terror Before Trafalgar 2002*, London, 1996
————————*A Thirst for Glory: the Life of Admiral Sir Sidney Smith*, Oxford, 1981
Pollard, Sidney, *Peaceful Conquest: the Industrialisation of Europe: 1760–1970*, 1981
Pope, Dudley, *Life in Nelson's Navy*, London, 1997
————————*The Great Gamble: Nelson at Copenhagen*, London, 1972
Porter, R., *Letters from Portugal and Spain*, London, 1809
Potocka, Anna, *Memoires*, Paris, 1897
Pradt, Abbe de, *Recit Historique sur la Restauration de la Royaute en France*, Paris, 1822
Priego, Lopez, *Como fue la Guerra de la independencia*, Madrid, 1936
————————*Guerra de la Independencia 1808–1814*, Madrid, 2000
Prieto, P., *El Grande de Espana, Capitan General Castanos*, Madrid, 1958

Queipo de Llano, *Historia del Levantamiento, Guerra y Revolucion de Espana*, Madrid, 1853
Quennevat, Jean-Claude, *Atlas de la Grande Armee*, Paris, 1966
Quimby, Robert, *The Background of Napoleonic Warfare*, New York, 1957

Ragsdale, Hugh, *Détente in the Napoleonic Era*, Lawrence, Kansas, 1980
Rapp, Jean, *Memoires*, London, 1823
Rath, Reuben, *The Fall of the Napoleonic Kingdom of Italy*, New York, 1941
Rawkins, W.J., *The Bavarian Army 1805–14*, London, 1982
——————————*The Armies of Baden and Wurtemburg*, London, 1977
——————————*The Italian Army 1805–14*, Vienna, 1982
——————————*The Army of Saxony, 1805–14*, London, 1979
——————————*The Armies of Naples and Kleve-Berg, 1806–14*, London, 1978
Read, J., *War in the Peninsula*, London, 1977
Reguinot, *Le Sergeant Isole*, Paris, 1831
Remusat, Claire de, *Memoires*, 1818
Reynier, J. le, *De L'Egypte apres la Bataille de Heliopolis*, Paris, 1802
Richardot, *Relation de la Campagne de Syrie*, Paris, 1839
Richardson, Frank, *Napoleon's Death, an Inquest*, London, 1974
Rigault, Georges, *Le General Abdallah Menou*, Paris, 1909
Rigau, Antoine, *Souvenirs*, Paris, 1846
Riley, J.P., *Napoleon and the World War of 1813*, London, 2001
Roberts, Andrew, *Napoleon and Wellington*, London, 2001
Robertson, Ian, *Wellington at War in the Peninsula 1808–1814*, Barnsley, 2000
Rocca, Albert de, *In the Peninsula with a French Hussar*, London, 1990
Rodger, Alexander, *The War of the Second Coalition 1798–1801*, London, 1964
Rodger, N.A.M., *The Wooden World*, London, 1988
——————————*The Admiralty*, Lavenham, 1979
Rodriguez, Solis, *Los Guerrilleros de 1808*, Madrid, 1887
Roeder, Franz, *The Ordeal of Captain Roeder*, London, 1960
Roederer, Comte, *Journal*, Paris, 1909
——————————*The British Army of the Eighteenth Century*, London, 1977
Rogers, H.C.B., *Napoleon's Army*, London, 1974
Roguet, Christopher, *Memoires Militaires*, Paris, 1865
Rose, J.H., *Napoleonic Studies*, London, 1906
Rosebury, Lord, *Pitt*, London, 1891
Rosetti, Marie-Joseph, *Journal d'un Compagnon de Murat*, Paris, 1998
Ross, M., *The Reluctant King: Joseph Bonaparte*, London, 1976
Rostopchin, Count Feodor, *La Verite sur l'Incendie de Moscou*, Paris, 1894
Rothenberg, Gunther, *Napoleon's Great Adversaries: the Archduke Charles and the Austrian Army*, London, 1995
——————————*The Napoleonic Wars*, London
Rousseau, Francois, *Kleber at Menou en Egypte Depuis le Depart de Bonaparte*, Paris, 1900
Rousseau, I. (ed.), *The Peninsular War Journal of Sir Benjamin d'Urban*, London, 1930
Roustam, Raza, *Souvenirs*, Paris, 1911
Rudorff, R., *War to the Death: the Sieges of Saragossa 1808–9*, London, 1974
Russel, Jack, *Nelson and the Hamiltons*, London, 1969
Russell, Lord of Liverpool, *Knight of the Sword*, London, 1964

Sabine, (ed.), *Letters of Sir Simon Fraser*, London, 1859
St-Cyr, *Memoires*, Paris, 1831
Salvemini, Gaetano, *The French Revolution*, London, 1954
Sarrazin, M., *Histoire de la Guerre de Russie*, Paris, 1815
Sauzet, Armand, *Deseaix, Le Sultan Juste*, Paris, 1954
Savant, Jean, *Les Mamelouks de Napoleon*, Paris, 1949
Savary, Duc de Rodrigo, *Memoires*, Paris, 1828
Schama, Simon, *Citizens: A Chronicle of The French Revolution*, London, 1989

Schneid, Frederick, *Soldiers of Napoleon's Kingdom of Italy*, Boulder, 1995
Schom, Alan, *One Hundred Days*, London, 1993
Scott, Franklin, *Bernadotte and the Fall of Napoleon*, Harvard, 1935
Scott, John, *A Visit to Paris in 1814*, London, 1815
Scott, Sir Walter, *Life of Napoleon Bonaparte*
Sebag-Montefiore, Simon, *Prince of Princes. The Life of Potemkin*, London, 2000
Seco, C., *Godoy*, Madrid, 1978
Sedillot, Rene, *La Cout de la Revolution Francaise*, Paris, 1989
Segur, Comte Philipe de, *Napoleon's Expedition to Russia*, 2003
──────────*Memoires*, Paris, 1894–5
Servieres, G., *L'Allemagne Francaise Sous Napoleon*, Paris, 1904
Seward, Desmond, *Napoleon and Hitler*, London, 1988
Shanahan, William, *Prussian Military Reforms 1786–1813*, New York, 1945
Shorter, Clement, *Napoleon and his Followers*, London, 1908
Shroeder, Paul, *The Transformation of European Politics 1763–1848*, Oxford, 1994
Sidney, Edwin, *The Life of Lord Hill*, London, 1845
Silbert, A., *Les Invasions Francaises et les Origines du Liberalisme au Portugal*, Comibra, 1990
Six, Georges, *Dictionnaire Biographique des Generaux et Admiraux*, Paris, 1934
Smith, Digby, *Borodino*, Moreton-in-the-Marsh, 1998
Smith, W.J., *The Grenville Papers*, London, 1852
Sokolov, Oleg, *La Campagne en Russie*, St Cloud, 2001
Soltyk, Count Roman, *Napoleon en 1812*, Paris, 1836
Southey, Robert, *Life of Nelson*, London, 1813
──────────*History of the Peninsular War*, London, 1832
Sparrow, Elizabeth, *Secret Service: British Agents in France 1792–1815*, London, 1999
Stael, Baronne Germaine, *Considerations sur les Principaux Evenements de la Revolution Francaise*, Paris, 1845
Stanhope, Lady Hester, *Memoirs*, London, 1845
Stanhope, Earl of, *Conversations with the Duke of Wellington*, Cassell, 1953
Stutterheim, General, *A detailed Account of the Battle of Austerlitz*, London, 1807
Suchet, Louis Gabriel, *Memoirs of the War in Spain from 1808 to 1814*, London, 1829
Suckow, C.F.E. von, *D'Iena a Moscou*, Paris, 1901
Sutherland, D.M.G., *France 1789–1815: Revolution and Counter-Revolution*, London, 1985

Talleyrand, Charles-Maurice de, *Memoires*, Paris, 1892
Tarle, Eugene, *Napoleon's Invasion of Russia 1812*, London, 1942
Teffeteller, G., *The Surpriser. The Life of Sir Rowland Hill*, Brunswick, NJ, 1983
Thiers, Adolphe, *Histoire du Consulat et de l'Empire*, Brussels, 1864
Thomas, Donald, *Cochrane*, London, 1978
Thomson, David, *Europe Since Napoleon*, London, 1957
Thomson, J.M., *Napoleon's Letters*, London, 1998
──────────*Napoleon Bonaparte: His Rise and Fall*, Oxford, 1963
Thompson, Norman, *Wellington*, Manchester, 1990
Thornton, M.J., *Napoleon After Waterloo*, Stanford, 1968
Thurman, Louis, *Bonaparte en Egypte*, Paris, 1902
Tolstoy, Leo, *War and Peace*, London, 1978
Tone, John Lawrence, *The Fatal Knot: the Guerrilla War in Navarre and the Defeat of Napoleon*, Chapel Hill, NC, 1994
Toqueville, Alexis de, *L'Ancient Regime*, Oxford, 1904
Tucker, Jedediah, *Memoirs of Earl St Vincent*, London, 1844
Tulard, Jean, *The Myth of the Saviour*, London, 1984
──────────*Le Grand Empire*, Paris, 1982
──────────*Napoleon et la Noblesse de l'Empire*, Paris, 1979
──────────*La Vie Quotidienne des Francais sous Napoleon*, Paris, 1978
Tyran, Joseph, *Laon, Ville Militaire*, Cambrai, 1999

Uffindell, Andrew, *The Eagle's Last Triumph*, London, 1994
————————*Great Generals of the Napoleonic Wars and Their Battles*, 2003
Urban, Mark, *The Man Who Broke Napoleon's Codes*, London, 2001

Vandal, Albert, *Napoleon et Alexandre Ier*, Paris, 1891
Vaudoncourt F.G. de, *Memoires*, London, 1815
————————*Relation Impartial du Passage de la Berezina*, Paris, 1814
Vaughan, *Narrative of the Siege of Saragossa*, London, 1809
Verissimo, Serrao, *Historia de Portugal*, Lisbon, 1984
Viennet, *Napoleon et l'Industrie Francaise*, Paris, 1934
Vilar, P., *Hidalgos, Amotinados y Guerrilleros*, Barcelona, 1999
Villeneuve de Janti, *Bonaparte et le Code Civil*, Paris, 1934
Vitorino, P., *As Invasoes Francesas*, Oporto, 1945
Vlijmen, B.R.F. van, *Vers le Beresina*, Paris, 1908
Von Pivka, Otto, *Armies of the Napoleonic Era*, London, 1979
————————*Navies of the Napoleonic Era*, London, 1980
Vossler, H.A., *With Napoleon in Russia*, London, 1998

Waliszewski, K., *Le Regne d'Alexandre Ier*, Paris, 1924
Walsh, Thomas, *Journal of the Late Campaign in Egypt*, London, 1803
Ward, Stephen, *Wellington's Headquarters*, Oxford, 1957
Warner, Oliver, *The Life and Letters of Vice-Admiral Lord Collingwood*, London, 1968
————————*The Battle of the Nile,* London, 1960
————————*A Portrait of Lord Nelson*, London, 1958
Warre, Sir William, *Letters from the Peninsula*, London, 1909
Watson, S.J., *By Command of the Emperor: A Life of Marshal Berthier*, London, 1957
Webster, *The Foreign Policy of Castlereagh 1812–1815*, London, 1931
Weller, Jac, *Wellington at Waterloo*, London, 1992
Wellington, Duke of, Despatches, 1831
Wheeler, H.F.B. and Bradley A.M., *Napoleon and the Invasion of England*, London, 1908
Wheeler, T., *The Mind of Napoleon*, London, 1910
White, Colin (ed.), *The Nelson Companion*, London, 1995
Wilcock, Paul, *An Elegant Sword*, Royal Armoured Yearbook, London, 2002
Wilkinson, Spencer, *The Rise of General Bonaparte*, Oxford, 1915
Williams Wynn, Lady Charlotte, Correspondence, London, 1920
Williams Wynn, Frances, *Diaries of a Lady of Quality*, London, 1864
Wilson, Sir Robert, *Brief Remarks*, London, 1810
————————*History of the British Expedition to Egypt*, London, 1803
Wilson-Smith, Timothy, *Napoleon*, 2002
————————*Napoleon and his Artists*, London, 1996
Windham, William, Papers, London, 1913
Wirtschafter, Elise, *From Serf to Russian Soldier*, Princeton, 1989
Wise, Terrance, *Artillery Equipment of the Napoleonic Wars*, London, 1979
Wolloch, Isser, *The French Veteran from the French Revolution to the Restoration*
Wood, *The Subaltern Officer, A Narrative*, London, 1825
Wood, Sir Evelyn, *General Cavalry in the Waterloo Campaign*, London, 1895
Woolf, S.J., *Napoleon's Integration of Europe*, London, 1991

Ysarn, Chevalier, *Memoires d'un Habitant de Moscou Pendant le Sejour des Francais en 1812*, Brussels, 1871

Zanoli, Alessandro, *Sulla Milizia Cisalpino-Italiana*, Milan, 1845
Zeldin, Theodore, *France*, Oxford, 1973
Ziegler, Philip, *Addington*, London, 1968
Zweig, Stefan, *Fouche*, Paris, 1969

INDEX

Trotter, John 378
Troubridge, Thomas 232, 271, 275, 291, 296, 354, 358, 372–4
Troyes 849, 850, 851
Truguet, Admiral 73
Tudela, Battle of 625
Tuileries 23, 26, 118
Tunis 546
Turcoine 137
Turin 162, 184, 333, 406
Turkey *see* Ottoman empire
Tuscany 145, 165, 168, 296, 349, 350
Tyrol 166, 479, 490, 633, 663

Ulm 461, 483
Ulster 224–5, 462
uniforms, British 420
United States 142, 353, 404, 535
Uxbridge, Lord 884, 890, 895, 896

Valance, General 39
Valencia 587, 724, 740
Valenciennes 127, 129, 138
Valjouan, Battle of 850
Valladolid 613, 624, 626, 627, 628, 739, 750
Valmy, Battle of 33–4, 37, 165, 476
Vandamme, General 765, 771
Vansittart, Nicholas 497
Vauchamps, Battle of 850
Vendée uprising 121–4, 127, 132, 140, 149, 576, 588
Venegas, General 699, 700, 701, 702
Venezuela 588
Venice 172, 177, 179, 184, 441, 490
Verdun 33
Verona 173, 179, 822
Versailles 19–20, 863
Vertray, Lieutenant 281, 283–4
Vial, General 298
Viasma 780
Vicenza 173
Vicogne 135
Victor Amadeus III, Duke of Savoy, King of Sardinia 34, 120, 162
Victor, Marshal Claude-Perrin 524, 624, 838, 844, 860
    Peninsular War 696, 699, 700, 701, 702
    Russian campaign 809, 811, 814, 824
Vienna 178, 183, 346, 347, 350, 360, 483, 663, 664, 665, 669
    Congress of 865–7, 868, 871, 873
    march on 484
    Napoleon in possession of (1809) 666, 672
Villaret-Joyeuse, Admiral 213, 214, 215, 218

Villeneuve, Comte Pierre de 293, 417, 428, 434–5, 436–8, 439, 440, 441–2, 446, 447, 448, 450, 453, 457–8, 484–5, 538, 912
Vilna 819
Vilnius 766, 769, 771, 772, 815–16
Vimeiro, Battle of 616–18
Visconti, Madame 304
Vistula, River 517, 519, 840
Vitebsk 772, 773–7, 803
Vitoria, Battle of 750–1, 832
Voltaire 14, 914

Wagram, Battle of 660, 670–2, 674, 677, 684, 903
Walcheren expedition 672–5
Wales, Prince of *see* George IV
Walewska, Countess Marie 157, 518, 523–4, 682, 684, 685, 687, 857, 868, 874, 904, 912
Walpole, Horace 257
Walpole, Sir Robert 98, 257
Warren, Sir John 210, 218, 219, 225
Warsaw 134, 516, 517, 529, 622, 663, 665, 764, 830
Washington, George 16, 17, 45, 482, 695, 696, 873
water supplies 255, 277, 281, 300, 610–11, 780
Waterloo
    Battle of 569, 662, 880, 889–903, 926
    village of 878, 883, 886, 888
Waters, Colonel 736, 747
Wavre 886–7
weapons
    military 472, 477
    naval 204–6
    torpedoes 422–3, 579
Wedderburn-Webster, Lady Frances 877, 907
Weimar, Marguerite Josephine 864
Weissenburg 121
Weissenfeld, Battle of 829
Wellesley, Anne 600, 601
Wellesley, Henry 604
Wellesley, Richard, 2nd Earl of Mornington 433, 600, 601–2, 604–8, 611, 612, 618, 726, 873, 925
Wellesley-Pole, William 600, 613, 618
Wellington, Arthur Wellesley, Duke of 92, 105, 137, 139, 443, 462, 463, 464, 498–9, 588, 599–618, 660, 926
    appearance 602, 742, 746, 748, 908
    at Congress of Vienna 873
    at Copenhagen 534, 612
    background 599–600
    in Belgium 874, 876–9